In Conversation with God

Meditations for each day of the year

Volume Two
Lent – Holy Week – Eastertide

Francis Fernandez

In Conversation
with God
Meditations for each day of the year

Volume Two
Lent – Holy Week – Eastertide

SCEPTER
London – New York

This edition of *In Conversation with God – Volume 2* is published:
in England by Scepter (U.K.) Ltd., 21 Hinton Avenue, Hounslow
TW4 6AP; e-mail: scepter@pobox.com;
in the United States by Scepter Publishers Inc.; 800-322-8773; e-mail: info@scepterpublishers.org; www.scepterpublishers.org

This is a translation of *Hablar con Dios – Vol II* first published in
1987 by Ediciones Palabra, Madrid, and in 1989 by Scepter.

With ecclesiastical approval

© Original — Fomento de Fundaciones (Fundación Internacional),
Madrid, 1987
© Translation — Scepter, London, 1989
© This edition — Scepter, London, 2019

All rights reserved. No part of this book may be reproduced, stored in
a retrieval system or transmitted, in any form or by any means,
electronic, mechanical, photocopying or otherwise, without the prior
permission of Scepter (U.K.).

British Library Cataloguing in Publication Data

Fernandez-Carvajal, Francis
In Conversation with God — Volume 2
Lent – Holy Week – Eastertide
1. Christian life — Daily Readings
I Title   II Hablar con Dios *English*
242'.2

ISBN Volume 7   978-0-906138-36-6
ISBN Volume 6   978-0-906138-25-0
ISBN Volume 5   978-0-906138-24-3
ISBN Volume 4   978-0-906138-23-6
ISBN Volume 3   978-0-906138-22-9
ISBN Volume 2   978-0-906138-21-2
ISBN Volume 1   978-0-906138-20-5
ISBN Complete set 978-0-906138-19-9

Cover design & typeset in England by KIP Intermedia, and printed in
China.

CONTENTS

LENT – ASH WEDNESDAY
1. Conversion and Penance   31
1.1 Working towards a conversion of heart, especially
    during this time.
1.2 Works of penance. Frequent confession, mortifica-
    tion, alms-giving.
1.3 Lent, a time for coming closer to God.

LENT – THURSDAY AFTER ASH WEDNESDAY
2. The Cross of each day   37
2.1 No true Christianity without the Cross. Our Lord's
    Cross a source of peace and joy.
2.2 The Cross in the little things of each day.
2.3 Offering up disappointments. Little details of morti-
    fication.

LENT – FRIDAY AFTER ASH WEDNESDAY
3. A Time for Penance   43
3.1 Fasting and other signs of penance in Jesus'
    preaching and in the life of the Church.
3.2 Contemplating the most holy humanity of Our Lord
    in the Way of the Cross. Eagerness to redeem.
3.3 Our daily work the source of the little mortifications
    that God asks of us. Examples. Passive
    mortifications.

LENT – SATURDAY AFTER ASH WEDNESDAY
4. Saving what was lost   **49**
4.1 Jesus comes as the Physician to cure the whole of man-
      kind, for we are all sick. Humility in order to be cured.
4.2 Christ cures our sickness. Effectiveness of the
      Sacrament of Penance.
4.3 Hope in God when we feel our own weaknesses.
      *Those who are well have no need of a physician, but
      those who are sick.* Hope in the apostolate.

FIRST SUNDAY OF LENT
5. The Temptations of Jesus   **55**
5.1 God allows us to be tempted so that we may grow in
      virtue.
5.2 The temptations of Jesus. The devil tries us in a
      similar way.
5.3 Our Lord is always at our side. Arms with which to
      conquer.

FIRST WEEK OF LENT – MONDAY
6. The existence of the Devil, and his activity   **61**
6.1 The devil exists and acts in people and society. His
      activity is mysterious, but real and effective.
6.2 Who the devil is. His power is limited. We need
      divine help in order to conquer.
6.3 Jesus Christ vanquishes the devil. Trust in Christ.
      Means that we have to use. Holy Water.

FIRST WEEK OF LENT – TUESDAY
7. The help of the Guardian Angels   **67**
7.1 Existence of the Guardian Angels. The devotion of
      the first Christians.
7.2 Ways in which they can help us.
7.3 Devotion to the Guardian Angels and our friendship
      with them.

FIRST WEEK OF LENT – WEDNESDAY
8. Confessing our sins 73
8.1 Sacramental Confession; a meeting with Christ.
8.2 We go to the sacrament of Penance to ask for forgiveness for our sins. Qualities of a good Confession: *concise, concrete, clear, complete.*
8.3 Lights and graces we receive in this sacrament. Importance of our interior dispositions.

FIRST WEEK OF LENT – THURSDAY
9. Prayer of petition 79
9.1 Petition and thanksgiving, two ways of coming to know God. Two ways of praying which please God. Rectitude of intention when we make our request.
9.2 Humility and perseverance in our petition.
9.3 God always listens to us. Seeking also the intercession of our mother Mary and our guardian angel.

FIRST WEEK OF LENT – FRIDAY
10. Lent – a time for penance 85
10.1 Sin is something personal. Sincerity required in order to recognise our errors and weaknesses. The need for penance.
10.2 Personal sin affects other people. Expiation for the sins of the world. Penance and the Communion of Saints.
10.3 Penance in everyday life, and in serving the people around us.

FIRST WEEK OF LENT – SATURDAY
11. Called to holiness 91
11.1 God calls everyone to holiness, without distinction of profession, age, social standing, etc, in each one's walk of life.
11.2 *Sanctify work. Sanctify oneself through work.*

Sanctify others through work. If we are to transform
society there is a need for people who are holy.
11.3 Sanctity and apostolate in the middle of the world.
The example of the first Christians.

SECOND SUNDAY OF LENT
12. From Tabor to Calvary   97
12.1 The important thing is to be always with Jesus. He
will help us to progress.
12.2 Often foster the Hope of Heaven, especially in
difficult moments.
12.3 The Lord does not distance himself from us. Living
in this presence.

SECOND WEEK OF LENT – MONDAY
13. Conscience – the light of the soul   103
13.1 Conscience throws light on all of one's life. It can
be deformed and hardened.
13.2 A well-formed conscience. Doctrine and life.
Example.
13.3 Being a light for others. Responsibility.

SECOND WEEK OF LENT – TUESDAY
14. Humility and a spirit of Service   109
14.1 Without humility we cannot serve others, and we
can fail those around us and let them down.
14.2 Imitating the service given by Jesus, the supreme
example of humility and dedication to others.
14.3 We have to serve those the Lord has placed us
amongst, and to serve them in a special way, learning
in this matter from Our Lady.

SECOND WEEK OF LENT – WEDNESDAY
15. To drink of the Lord's chalice   115
15.1 Identifying all our will with that of the Lord. Co-

redeeming with him.
15.2 Offering up pain and voluntary mortification. A spirit of penance in ordinary life. Some examples of mortification.
15.3 Mortifications which are born out of service to others.

SECOND WEEK OF LENT – THURSDAY
16. Detachment 122
16.1 Detachment gives us the freedom we need to follow Christ. Goods are only the means.
16.2 Detachment and generosity. Some examples.
16.3 Detachment from the superfluous and the necessary, from preoccupations with health. God's gifts to us, etc.

SECOND WEEK OF LENT – FRIDAY
17. Abhorrence of sin 129
17.1 Our sins and Redemption. The true evil in the world.
17.2 Lent, an opportune occasion afforded us by the Church to help us in the fight against sin. The malice of venial sin.
17.3 The fight against deliberate venial sin. Sincerity. Examination. Contrition.

SECOND WEEK OF LENT – SATURDAY
18. Each of us is the prodigal son 135
18.1 Sin, man's greatest tragedy. Consequences of sin in the soul. Without God, happiness is impossible.
18.2 Returning to God. Sincerity and examination of conscience.
18.3 The encounter with God our Father in a sincere and contrite confession. The joy of being in the Father's household.

THIRD SUNDAY OF LENT
19. The meaning of mortification   **141**
19.1 Truly following Christ implies practising a life of
     mortification and being close to the Cross. He who
     spurns sacrifice distances himself from holiness.
19.2 With mortification we raise ourselves to the Lord.
     On losing the fear of sacrifice.
19.3 Other reasons for mortification.

THIRD WEEK OF LENT – MONDAY
20. Docility and good dispositions for meeting Jesus 148
20.1 Faith and correspondence with grace. Our souls
     need purification for us to see Jesus.
20.2 The cure of Naaman. Docility and humility.
20.3 Docility in spiritual direction.

THIRD WEEK OF LENT – TUESDAY
21. To Pardon and Forgive   **154**
21.1 To forgive and forget the tiny offences committed in
     the course of the ordinary day.
21.2 Our forgiveness of others in comparison with that of
     Our Lord towards us.
21.3 To forgive and to understand. Learning to see the
     good in others.

THIRD WEEK OF LENT – WEDNESDAY
22. The Virtues and Spiritual Growth   **160**
22.1 Virtues and holiness.
22.2 Human and supernatural virtues. Practising them in
     ordinary life.
22.3 Our Lord always gives his grace to live the
     Christian faith in all its fulness.

THIRD WEEK OF LENT – THURSDAY
23. Sincerity and Truthfulness   **166**

23.1 The *dumb devil*. The need for sincerity.
23.2 Love for the truth. Sincerity, first with ourselves. Sincerity with God.
23.3 Sincerity with others. The word of a Christian. Loyalty and faithfulness. Other consequences of love for the truth.

THIRD WEEK OF LENT – FRIDAY
24. Love of God 172
24.1 The infinite love of God for each person.
24.2 The Lord always loves us. His mercy shown even when we offend him.
24.3 Our response. The first Commandment. Love of God in the incidents of each day.

THIRD WEEK OF LENT – SATURDAY
25. The Pharisee and the Publican 178
25.1 The need for humility. Pride perverts all.
25.2 The hyprocisy of the Pharisees. Signs of pride.
25.3 Learning from the publican in the parable.

FOURTH SUNDAY OF LENT
26. Joy in the Cross 184
26.1 Joy is compatible with mortification and pain. It is the opposite of sadness, not of penance.
26.2 Joy has a spiritual origin, arising from a heart that loves and feels itself loved by God.
26.3 *God loves those who find joy in giving.*

FOURTH WEEK OF LENT – MONDAY
27. Personal prayer 190
27.1 The need for prayer. Jesus' example.
27.2 Personal prayer: confident dialogue with God.
27.3 Using the means to pray in a recollected way.

12   Contents

FOURTH WEEK OF LENT – TUESDAY
28. Patient struggle against defects   **197**
28.1 The paralytic at Bethsaida. Constancy in the
     struggle and in the desire to improve.
28.2 Patience in interior life. Return to the Lord as often
     as necessary.
28.3 Patience, too, with others. Taking their defects into
     account. Patience and constancy in the apostolate.

FOURTH WEEK OF LENT – WEDNESDAY
29. Unity of Life   **203**
29.1 Christians as light of the world and salt of the earth.
29.2 Consequences of original sin. The Redemption.
     Redirecting all earthly realities to Christ.
29.3 Life of piety and work. Sanctity in the middle of the
     world.

FOURTH WEEK OF LENT – THURSDAY
30. The Holy Mass and personal self-surrender   **209**
30.1 Christ's sacrifice on Calvary. He offered himself up
     for all men. Our personal self-surrender.
30.2 The Holy Mass a renewal of the sacrifice of the Cross.
30.3 The infinite value of the Holy Mass. Our partici-
     pation in the Sacrifice. The Holy Mass, centre of the
     life of the Church and of every Christian.

FOURTH WEEK OF LENT – FRIDAY
31. Seeing Christ in the sick and in illness   **215**
31.1 Jesus makes himself present in the sick.
31.2 Sanctifying illness. Acceptance. Learning to be
     good patients.
31.3 The Sacrament of the Anointing of the Sick. Fruits
     of this Sacrament. Preparing the sick to receive it is a
     special sign of charity and, sometimes, of justice.

FOURTH WEEK OF LENT – SATURDAY
32. Making the doctrine of Jesus Christ known   221
32.1 The teaching of Jesus. Every Christian should bear
    witness to his doctrine.
32.2 Imitating Our Lord. Giving good example. Making
    use of every opportunity.
32.3 Different ways of making the teachings of Jesus
    known. Not being surprised at difficult situations.

FIFTH SUNDAY OF LENT
33. A cry for justice   227
33.1 Eagerness for justice and greater peace in the world.
    Living up to the demands of justice.
33.2 Fulfilment of our professional and social duties.
33.3 Sanctifying society from within. Virtues which
    broaden and perfect the scope of justice.

FIFTH WEEK OF LENT – MONDAY
34. *Go and sin no more*   233
34.1 In the sacrament of Penance it is Christ who forgives.
34.2 Gratitude for absolution; the apostolate of Confession.
34.3 The need to cary out the penance given by the
    Confessor. Generosity in our reparation.

FIFTH WEEK OF LENT – TUESDAY
35. Contemplating Christ. Life of piety.   239
35.1 The enemies of grace. The remedy: to contemplate
    Christ.
35.2 Keeping presence of God in the midst of the world.
    'Human devices'.
35.3 Life of piety. Ejaculatory prayers.

FIFTH WEEK OF LENT – WEDNESDAY
36. Co-redeemers with Christ   246
36.1 Jesus redeemed us and freed us from sin, the root of

all evil. The co-redemptive value of pain suffered for
the love of Christ.
36.2 Eternal life comes before all else.
36.3 The merits Christ gained on the Cross are applied to
each one of us. Co-redeemers with Christ.

FIFTH WEEK OF LENT – THURSDAY
37. Meditating on the Passion   252
37.1 The custom of meditating on Our Lord's Passion.
Love of and devotion to the crucifix.
37.2 How we should meditate on the Passion.
37.3 The fruits of such meditation.

FIFTH WEEK OF LENT – FRIDAY
38. The Agony in the Garden   258
38.1 Jesus at Gethsemane. The fulfilment of the will of
the Father.
38.2 The need for prayer in order to follow the Lord closely.
38.3 The first sorrowful mystery of the Holy Rosary.
Meditating upon it. This scene will help us to be
strong in carrying out the will of God.

FIFTH WEEK OF LENT – SATURDAY
39. The arrest of Jesus   264
39.1 Judas' betrayal. Perseverance. Faithfulness in small
things.
39.2 Sin in the life of the Christian. Returning to the Lord
by means of contrition and with hope.
39.3 The flight of the disciples. The need for prayer.

PALM SUNDAY
40. Triumphal entry into Jerusalem   270
40.1 The solemn, yet simple entry into Jerusalem.
40.2 Correspondence to grace.
40.3 The joy and sorrow of this day.

Contents

HOLY WEEK – MONDAY
41. Peter's denials 276
41.1 Peter denies all knowledge of Our Lord. Our own denials.
41.2 The look of Jesus and Peter's contrition.
41.3 True repentance. Acts of contrition.

HOLY WEEK – TUESDAY
42. Before Pilate: Jesus Christ, the King. 282
42.1 Jesus is condemned to death
42.2 The King of the Jews. A kingdom of holiness and grace.
42.3 Our Lord wants to reign in our souls.

HOLY WEEK – WEDNESDAY
43. The Way to Calvary 289
43.1 Jesus with the Cross on his shoulders passes through the streets of Jerusalem. Simon of Cyrene.
43.2 Jesus accompanied by two thieves on his route to Calvary. Ways of carrying the cross.
43.3 Meeting his Mother.

HOLY WEEK – HOLY THURSDAY
44. The Lord's Last Supper 295
44.1 Jesus celebrated the Last Supper with his Apostles.
44.2 Institution of the Holy Eucharist and of the ministerial priesthood.
44.3 The *New Commandment* of Our Lord.

HOLY WEEK – GOOD FRIDAY
45. Jesus dies on the Cross 301
45.1 On Calvary. Jesus asks pardon for those who ill-treat him and crucify him.
45.2 Christ crucified: our Redemption accomplished.
45.3 Jesus gives his Mother to be our Mother.

HOLY WEEK – HOLY SATURDAY
46. The Sepulchre of the Body of Jesus   307
46.1 Signs which followed the death of Our Lord. The
    lance. The deposition.
46.2 Preparation for the sepulchre. Valour and generosity
    of Nicodemus and Joseph of Arimathea.
46.3 The Apostles beside Our Lady.

EASTER SUNDAY
47. *Raised from the Dead*   313
47.1 The Resurrection of Our Lord is the basis of our
    faith. Jesus Christ lives: hence the great joy of all
    Christians.
47.2 The light of Christ. The Resurrection – a powerful
    call to the apostolate.
47.3 Appearances of Jesus: the encounter with his
    Mother. Living this liturgical time close to Her.

OCTAVE OF EASTER – EASTER MONDAY
48. The Joy of the Resurection   319
48.1 True joy has its origin in Christ.
48.2 Sadness is born of waywardness and distance from
    God. Being optimistic, serene and happy even in the
    midst of tribulation.
48.3 Giving peace and joy to others.

OCTAVE OF EASTER – EASTER TUESDAY
49. Jesus Christ lives forever   325
49.1 Appearance of Our Lord to Mary Magdalene. Jesus
    in our lives.
49.2 Presence of Christ in our midst.
49.3 Seeking and loving Christ. Mary Magdalene's
    example: whoever seeks Our Lord will find Him.

OCTAVE OF EASTER – EASTER WEDNESDAY
50. Letting oneself be helped 331
50.1 On the road to Emmaus. Jesus is alive and is at our side.
50.2 Jesus never abandons His own; let us not abandon Him. Fidelity. Being faithful in little things.
50.3 The virtue of fidelity should pervade all aspects of a Christian's life.

OCTAVE OF EASTER – EASTER THURSDAY
51. Meeting our Lord 337
51.1 Appearance to the Eleven. Jesus comforts the Apostles. The presence of Jesus Christ in our tabernacles.
51.2 *The Visit to the Blessed Sacrament* as a continuation of thanksgiving after Communion; a preparation for the next one. Our Lord awaits each one.
51.3 Fruits of this act of piety.

OCTAVE OF EASTER – EASTER FRIDAY
52. Constancy in apostolate 343
52.1 The miraculous catch of fish. Close to Our Lord the fruit is always abundant. Discovering Christ in the events of our life.
52.2 Apostolate presupposes patient work.
52.3 Apostolate requires time. The human and supernatural means to be employed.

OCTAVE OF EASTER – EASTER SATURDAY
53. Go out into the whole world 349
53.1 Our Lord sends us into the world to make his teaching known.
53.2 We too will meet with difficulties. Going against the current. Personal holiness.
53.3 *Cultivating souls one by one.* Optimism.

SECOND SUNDAY OF EASTER
54. The faith of St Thomas   356
54.1 Jesus' appearance to the Apostles in the absence of
Thomas. Apostolate with people who have known
Christ.
54.2 The act of faith of the Apostle Thomas. Our faith
has to be operative: acts of faith, confidential
relationship with Our Lord. Apostolate.
54.3 The Resurrection: a call to us to show with our lives
that Christ is alive. The need for formation.

SECOND WEEK OF EASTER – MONDAY
55. The imagination   362
55.1 Need for interior mortification in order to have a
supernatural life.
55.2 Mortification of the imagination.
55.3 Making good use of our imagination in our prayer.

SECOND WEEK OF EASTER – TUESDAY
56. The first Christians. Unity   368
56.1 Unity among Christians is a gift of God. Pray for it.
56.2 What destroys fraternal unity.
56.3 Charity unites, pride separates. The fraternity of the
first Christians. Avoid what could harm unity.

SECOND WEEK OF EASTER – WEDNESDAY
57. Love with deeds   374
57.1 Our Lord loved us first. Love is repaid with love.
Holiness in the ordinary duties of every day.
57.2 Genuine love. The Will of God.
57.3 Love and sentiment. Abandonment to God.
Fulfilment of our duties.

SECOND WEEK OF EASTER – THURSDAY
58. Doing good and resisting evil   380

Contents

58.1 The Apostles' resistance to obeying unjust
commands. Firmness in faith.
58.2 All earthly existence has to be directed to God.
Unity of life. The power of example.
58.3 The faith cannot be left aside when it comes to
evaluating earthly realities. Resisting evil.

SECOND WEEK OF EASTER – FRIDAY
59. Human means and Supernatural means **386**
59.1 Do whatever we can even if it is little. Our Lord
gives the increase.
59.2 Supernatural optimism: count on Our Lord and his
power.
59.3 Fruits of the apostolate depend on the combination
of human means and supernatural means. We are
God's instruments for doing things that surpass our
own capacities.

SECOND WEEK OF EASTER – SATURDAY
60. The Church will last till the end of time **392**
60.1 Indefectibility of the Church in spite of
persecutions, heresies and infidelities.
60.2 Attacks on the Church lead us to love her more and
to make acts of reparation.
60.3 Our own lives are not free either from moments of
darkness, of suffering or of trial. Assurance in Our
Lord's protection. Our Lady's help.

THIRD SUNDAY OF EASTER
61. The Lord's Day **399**
61.1 Sunday is the Lord's Day.
61.2 Feast days and holydays of obligation. Their
purpose. The Mass, centre of Catholic festivities.
61.3 Public worship. Sunday rest.

THIRD WEEK OF EASTER – MONDAY
62. Christian naturalness   **405**
62.1 Being coherent Christians in all the situations of
     life.
62.2 Apostolate in difficult environments.
62.3 Rectitude of intention.

THIRD WEEK OF EASTER – TUESDAY
63. Rectitude of intention   **411**
63.1 Purity of intention and presence of God. Acting with
     our minds on God.
63.2 Consciousness of praise, and learning to rectify. *For
     God all the glory.*
63.3 Examining the motives for our actions. Omissions in
     the apostolate on account of the lack of a right
     intention.

THIRD WEEK OF EASTER – WEDNESDAY
64. The fruits of difficulties   **417**
64.1 The apostolic spirit of the first Christians in spite of
     persecution. The fruits of tribulation and difficulties.
64.2 Fortitude in difficult circumstances.
64.3 Unity with God through costly moments.

THIRD WEEK OF EASTER – THURSDAY
65. The Bread of Life   **423**
65.1 The Blessed Eucharist announced at Capharnaum.
     The *Adoro te devote.*
65.2 The Mystery of Faith. Transubstantiation.
65.3 The effects of Communion on the soul: how it
     sustains, restores, delights.

THIRD WEEK OF EASTER – FRIDAY
66. The Communion of Saints   **429**
66.1 The communion of graces. The Church's treasury.

66.2 Available to all Christians. The incalculable echoes
    of our good deeds.
66.3 Indulgences.

THIRD WEEK OF EASTER – SATURDAY
67. The Particular Examination   **435**
67.1 We need to struggle daily to be faithful to Our Lord.
    The particular examination of conscience.
67.2 The aim and content of the particular examination.
67.3 Constancy in struggle. Faithfulness in difficult
    moments: the result of daily attention to small things.

FOURTH SUNDAY OF EASTER
68. The good shepherd. Love for the Pope   **441**
68.1 Jesus is the Good Shepherd, and entrusts Peter and
    his successors with the government of his Church to
    prolong his mission on earth.
68.2 The primacy of Peter. The love of the early
    Christians for Peter.
68.3 Faithful obedience to the Vicar of Christ; making
    his teaching known. *The Sweet Christ on earth*.
FOURTH WEEK OF EASTER – MONDAY
69. Desiring holiness   **447**
69.1 Wanting to be a saint – the first necessary step in
    persevering to the end of the way. Real and effective
    desires.
69.2 Softness and lukewarmness destroy desires for
    sanctity. The need for vigilance.
69.3 Counting on time and God's grace. Avoiding
    discouragement in the struggle to improve.

FOURTH WEEK OF EASTER – TUESDAY
70. The first Christians. Universality of the faith   **453**
70.1 The rapid spread of Christianity. The early
    Christians' holiness was through finding Christ in

their environment.
70.2 Exemplary citizens of the world. Bringing Christ to
all environments.
70.3 Christian family customs.

FOURTH WEEK OF EASTER – WEDNESDAY
71. Acts of Thanksgiving   459
71.1 Thanking God for all his benefits is a sign of faith,
hope and love. Countless reasons for thanksgiving.
71.2 Acknowledging God's goodness in our lives. The
virtue of gratitude.
71.3 Thanksgiving after Mass and Holy Communion.

FOURTH WEEK OF EASTER – THURSDAY
72. Learning to forgive   465
72.1 People can change. Avoid making definitive
judgements on people based on their external actions.
72.2 Forgive and forget. Making up with our friends.
72.3 Despite our ups and downs and other short-comings,
we can be good instruments of God if we are humble.

FOURTH WEEK OF EASTER – FRIDAY
73. Reading and Meditating on the Gospel   471
73.1 Reading the Gospel fruitfully.
73.2 Contemplating the most sacred humanity of Christ
in the Gospel.
73.3 God speaks to us in Scripture. His Word is always
meaningful.

FOURTH WEEK OF EASTER – SATURDAY
74. The Virtue of Hope   477
74.1 Human hope and the supernatural virtue of hope.
The certainty this virtue bestows. Our Lord always
gives us the necessary graces.
74.2 Sins against hope: despair and presumption.

74.3 The Blessed Virgin our Hope. Having recourse to
    her in moments of difficulty, and always.

FIFTH SUNDAY OF EASTER
75. The virtue of Justice 483
75.1 Being just with people and with society.
75.2 Promoting justice.
75.3 The basis and goal of justice.

FIFTH WEEK OF EASTER – MONDAY
76. We are temples of God 488
76.1 The indwelling of the Blessed Trinity in our souls.
    Looking for God within us.
76.2 Growth in God's friendship requires interior
    recollection. Mortification.
76.3 Friendship with the Holy Spirit.

FIFTH WEEK OF EASTER – TUESDAY
77. *My peace I give you* 494
77.1 The Lord gives his peace to his disciples.
77.2 True peace the fruit of the Holy Spirit. Bringing
    peace to the world, starting with our own soul, and
    then, our family, our place of work ...
77.3 Sowers of peace and joy.

FIFTH WEEK OF EASTER – WEDNESDAY
78. The vine and the branches 500
78.1 Christ is the true vine. Divine life in our souls.
78.2 Jesus prunes us so that we bear more fruit. The
    meaning of suffering and mortification. Frequent
    confession.
78.3 Union with Christ. Apostolate, overflow of interior
    life. The dry vine and its branches.

FIFTH WEEK OF EASTER – THURSDAY
79. Offering our daily actions   **506**
79.1 Through our Morning Offering we offer God our
     day from the very beginning. It is our first prayer.
79.2 How to offer our day. The *heroic minute*.
79.3 The Morning Offering and holy Mass. Offering our
     activity to our Lord many times throughout the day.

FIFTH WEEK OF EASTER – FRIDAY
80. The value of friendship   **512**
80.1 Jesus, *the friend who never betrays*. In him we learn
     the true meaning of friendship.
80.2 Friendship is a great human good which we can
     supernaturalize. Qualities of true friendship.
80.3 Apostolate with our friends.

FIFTH WEEK OF EASTER – SATURDAY
81. The Rosary   **520**
81.1 In the Rosary our Lady teaches us to contemplate
     the life of her Son.
81.2 The family Rosary, *a powerful weapon*.
81.3 Distractions during the Rosary.

SIXTH SUNDAY OF EASTER
82. The Hope of Heaven   **524**
82.1 We have been created for heaven. Fostering hope.
82.2 What God has revealed about eternal life.
82.3 The Resurrection of the Body. Thinking about heaven:
     to a determined and cheerful struggle to reach it.

SIXTH WEEK OF EASTER – MONDAY
83. The Gifts of the Holy Spirit   **530**
83.1 The supernatural virtues and the gifts of the Holy
     Spirit.
83.2 The seven gifts. Their influence in the Christian life.

Contents

83.3 Ten-day devotion to the Holy Spirit.

SIXTH WEEK OF EASTER – TUESDAY
84. May, Month of Mary   **536**
84.1 Devotion to our Lady draws down divine mercy.
     She is loved by the whole Christian people.
84.2 The month of May.
84.3 Visits to our Lady's shrines. Penitential and
     apostolic aspects.

SIXTH WEEK OF EASTER – WEDNESDAY
85. Fruits in the apostolate   **542**
85.1 Integral preaching of Christ's teaching. The
     example of St Paul and the first Christians.
85.2 Sowing the seed always. God gives the increase.
     Constancy in the apostolate.
85.3 Woman's unique role in evangelizing the family.

SIXTH WEEK OF EASTER: ASCENSION THURSDAY
86. Jesus awaits us in Heaven   **548**
86.1 Christ's glorious exaltation culminates in the
     Ascension.
86.2 His Ascension strengthens and nourishes our desire
     for heaven. The hope of heaven.
86.3 The Ascension and the Christian's apostolic mission.

SIXTH WEEK OF EASTER – FRIDAY
Decenary to the Holy Spirit
87. The Gift of Understanding   **554**
87.1 Understanding: necessary for a fully Christian life,
     to have a deeper knowledge of the mysteries of faith.
87.2 Given to all Christians: its development requires us
     to strive earnestly for personal holiness.
87.3 Need to purify our soul. Understanding and
     contemplative life.

SIXTH WEEK OF EASTER – SATURDAY
Decenary to the Holy Spirit
88. The Gift of Knowledge   **560**
88.1 This gift enables us to understand the world in the
     light of God's plan of creation and elevation to the
     supernatural order.
88.2 The gift of knowledge and the sanctification of
     temporal things.
88.3 True value and meaning of the world. Detachment
     and humility are needed to benefit from this gift.

SEVENTH SUNDAY OF EASTER
Decenary to the Holy Spirit
89. The Gift of Wisdom   **566**
89.1 Wisdom gives us a loving knowledge of God, and of
     people and created things insofar as they refer to him.
     Closely connected with the virtue of charity.
89.2 We share in Christ's love for the people we are in
     contact with. It teaches us to view events in the light
     of the providence of God, a loving Father.
89.3 The gift of wisdom and contemplative spirit in
     everyday life.

SEVENTH WEEK OF EASTER – MONDAY
Decenary to the Holy Spirit
90. The Gift of Counsel   **572**
90.1 The gift of counsel and the virtue of prudence.
90.2 The gift of counsel helps us have a true conscience.
90.3 Advice received in spiritual guidance. Ways to
     facilitate this gift.

SEVENTH WEEK OF EASTER – TUESDAY
Decenary to the Holy Spirit
91. The Gift of Piety   **578**
91.1 Piety enables us to appreciate our divine filiation,

Contents

giving our relationship with God the tenderness and affection of a son for his father.
91.2 Filial confidence in prayer. The gift of piety and charity.
91.3 Piety towards the Blessed Virgin, the saints, the souls in Purgatory and our parents. Respect for the goods of the earth.

SEVENTH WEEK OF EASTER – WEDNESDAY
Decenary to the Holy Spirit
92. The Gift of Fortitude   **584**
92.1 The Holy Spirit gives the soul the necessary strength to overcome obstacles and practise virtue
92.2 God expects us to be heroic in little things, in the fulfilment of our daily duties
92.3 Fortitude in our daily lives. How to facilitate the action of this gift.

SEVENTH WEEK OF EASTER – THURSDAY
Decenary to the Holy Spirit
93. The Gift of Fear   **590**
93.1 Servile fear and the holy fear of God. Effects of this gift in the soul.
93.2 The holy fear of God and readiness to reject all sin.
93.3 The link between this gift and the virtues of humility and temperance. Sensitivity of soul and the sense of sin.

SEVENTH WEEK OF EASTER – FRIDAY
Decenary to the Holy Spirit
94. The Fruits of the Holy Spirit   **596**
94.1 The fruits of the Holy Spirit in the soul, signs of the glory of God. Love, joy and peace.
94.2 Patience and longanimity. Their importance in apostolate.

94.3 The fruits more directly related to our neighbour's welfare: goodness.

SEVENTH WEEK OF EASTER – SATURDAY
Vigil of Pentecost
95. The Holy Spirit and Mary   **602**
95.1 Together with the Blessed Virgin we await the coming of the Holy Spirit.
95.2 The Holy Spirit in Mary's life.
95.3 The Virgin Mary, *heart of the nascent Church*, collaborates actively in the Holy Spirit's action in souls.

PENTECOST SUNDAY
96. The Coming of the Holy Spirit   **608**
96.1 The Jewish feast of Pentecost. The sending of the Holy Spirit. The rushing wind and the tongues of fire.
96.2 The Paraclete continually sanctifies the Church and every soul. Correspondence to the motions and inspirations of the Holy Spirit.
96.3 Correspondence: docility, life of prayer, union with the Cross.

Index to quotations from the Fathers and Popes   **615**

Subject Index   **629**

Table of Moveable Feasts

Year	Ash Wednes-day	Third Sunday of Lent	Easter	Ascension	Pentecost
2020	26 Feb	15 Mar	12 Apr	21 May	31 May
2021	17 Feb	7 Mar	4 Apr	13 May	23 May
2022	2 Mar	20 Mar	17 Apr	26 May	5 June
2023	22 Feb	11 Mar	9 Apr	18 May	28 May
2024	14 Feb	3 Mar	31 Mar	9 May	19 May
2025	5 Mar	23 Mar	20 Apr	29 May	8 June
2026	18 Feb	8 Mar	5 Apr	14 May	24 May
2027	10 Feb	28 Feb	28 Mar	9 May	16 May
2028	1 Mar	19 Mar	16 Apr	25 May	4 June
2029	14 Feb	4 Mar	1 Apr	10 May	20 May
2030	6 Mar	24 Mar	21 Apr	30 May	30 May

After Eastertide				
Year	Cycle	Begins in Week	From Monday	To Saturday in Week12
2020	A	9	1 June	27 June
2021	B	8	24 May	26 June
2022	C	10	6 June	25 June
2023	A	8	29 May	1 July
2024	B	7	20 May	29 June
2025	C	10	9 June	28 June
2026	A	8	25 May	27 June
2027	B	7	17 May	26 June
2028	C	9	5 June	24 June
2029	A	7	21 May	23 June
2030	B	10	10 June	29 June

LENT – ASH WEDNESDAY

1. CONVERSION AND PENANCE

1.1 Working towards a conversion of heart, especially during this time.

We are at the beginning of Lent, a time of penance and interior renewal to enable us to prepare for Easter.[1] The Church's liturgy unceasingly invites us to purify our souls and to begin again.

Yet, even now, says the Lord, *return to me with all your heart, with fasting, with weeping and with mourning; and rend your hearts and not your garments. Return to the Lord, your God, for He is gracious and merciful ...*,[2] as we read in the First Reading of today's Mass. Then as the priest places ashes on our forehead, he reminds us of the words of Genesis, after original sin. *Memento homo, quia pulvis es ...*, remember man that you are dust, and to dust you shall return.[3]

Memento homo ... Remember! Despite this reminder we sometimes forget that without God we are nothing. *Without God, all that remains of man's greatness is that little pile of dust, in a dish, at one side of the altar, on Ash Wednesday. It is what the Church marks us with on our forehead, as though with our own substance.*[4]

God wants us to detach ourselves from the things of the earth and return to him. He wants us to abandon sin, which makes us grow old and die, and for us to return to the fount of life and joy. *Jesus Christ himself is the most sublime grace of the whole of Lent. It is He who presents*

---

[1] cf Second Vatican Council, *Sacrosanctum Concilium*, 109
[2] Joel 2:12
[3] Gen 3:19
[4] J. Leclercq, *A Year with the Liturgy*

himself to us in all the wonderful simplicity of the Gospel.[5]

To turn our hearts towards God, to be converted, means that we must be prepared to use all the means to live as He expects us to live. We must be absolutely sincere with ourselves. We must try not *to serve two masters.*[6] We must love God with our whole heart and soul, and flee from any deliberate sin in our lives. Each of us must do this whatever his personal circumstances may be as regards work, health, family, age and so on.

Jesus is looking for a contrite heart within us, a heart that acknowledges its weaknesses and sins and is prepared to disencumber itself of them. *Then you will remember your evil ways, and your deeds that were not good ...*[7] God wants from us a genuine sorrow for our sins which we will manifest, above all, by going to sacramental confession, and by doing small deeds of mortification and penance out of love. *For us, conversion means seeking God's pardon and strength in the Sacrament of Reconciliation. This is the way to start again and to improve each day.*[8] In order to encourage our contrition the Church sets before us in today's liturgy the Psalm in which King David gave utterance to his repentance, and in the words of which so many saints have begged God for forgiveness. It can help us, too, in these moments of prayer, to say:

Have mercy on me, God, in your kindness,
in your compassion blot out my offence.
O wash me more and more from my guilt
and cleanse me from my sin.
My offences truly I know them;
my sin is always before me.

---

[5] St John Paul II, *Ash Wednesday Homily*, 28 February 1979
[6] cf Matt 6:24
[7] Ezek 35:31-32
[8] St John Paul II, Letter, *Novo incipiente*, 8 April 1979

Against you, you alone, have I sinned;
what is evil in your sight I have done.
A pure heart create for me, O God;
put a steadfast spirit within me.
Do not cast me away from your presence,
nor deprive me of your Holy Spirit.
Give me again the joy of your help;
with a spirit of fervour sustain me.
O Lord, open my lips
and my mouth shall declare your praise. (Psalm 50)

God will listen to us if today we repeat as an ejaculatory prayer:

A pure heart create for me O God; put a steadfast spirit within me.

1.2 Works of penance. Frequent confession, mortification, alms-giving.

True conversion is shown by the way we behave. We show that we really want to improve by the way we do our work or our study. We show it by the way we behave towards our family; by offering up to God, in the course of the day, little mortifications which make life for those around us more pleasant, and which make our work more effective. We can also show it by making a careful preparation for and going frequently to Confession.

Today God asks us also for a rather special mortification, which we offer up cheerfully: it is fasting and abstinence, which *strengthens our spirit as it mortifies our flesh and our sensuality.* [9] *It raises our soul to God. It gets rid of concupiscence by giving us the strength to overcome and to mortify our passions, and it disposes our heart that it may seek for nothing except to please God in everything.*

During Lent the Church asks for these signs of

---

[9] St Francis de Sales, *Sermon on Fasting*

penance (abstinence from the age of fourteen, and fasting between the ages of eighteen and the end of our fifty-ninth year), which bring us closer to God and give a special joy to the soul. She also asks us to be generous in giving alms. We should practise this with a merciful heart, wanting to console someone in need or to contribute, according to our means, to some work of apostolate for the good of souls. *All Christians can practise almsgiving – not only the rich and powerful, but those too who are no more than moderately well off and even the poor; in this way people who are unequal in their capacity to give alms are equal in the love and affection with which they give.*[10]

Detachment from material goods, mortification and abstinence purify us from our sins and help us to find God in our everyday life. For *whoever seeks God whilst wanting to hold on to his own likes and dislikes, may seek Him day and night, but will never find Him.*[11] Our daily duties are the principal source for this mortification: order, punctuality in starting our work, concentration and intensity we bring to it, etc. Through our contact with others we will find occasion to mortify our selfishness and help create a more pleasant atmosphere around us. *And the best mortification is that which overcomes the lust of the flesh, the lust of the eyes, and the pride of life in little things throughout the day. Ours should be mortifications which do not mortify others, and which give us more 'finesse', more understanding and more openness in our dealings with everybody. You are not mortified if you are touchy; if your every thought is for yourself; if you humiliate others; if you do not know how to give up what is unnecessary and, at times, what is necessary; if you become gloomy because things don't*

---

[10] *Divine Office, Second Reading, Thursday after Ash Wednesday*, St Leo the Great
[11] St John of the Cross, *The Spiritual Canticle*, 1,3

turn out the way you had hoped. On the other hand, you can be sure you are mortified if you know how to make yourself 'all things to all men, in order to save all' (1 Cor 9:22).[12]

Each one of us must draw up a specific plan of mortifications to offer to God every day during this Lent.

1.3 Lent, a time for coming closer to God.

We cannot let this day go without stimulating in our souls a deep and effective desire to go back once again, to return like the prodigal son, so as to be closer to God. In the Second Reading of today's Mass, St Paul tells us that this is an excellent time for us to bring about our conversion. *We entreat you not to accept the grace of God in vain ... Behold, now is the acceptable time; behold, now is the day of salvation.*[13] God says again, to each one of us, in the depths of our hearts, 'Return to me. Return to me with all your heart.'

Now is the time when this beginning again in Christ is going to be sustained by a special grace from God, proper to the liturgical season that has just started. That is why the Lenten message is replete with joy and hope, even though it is a message of penance and mortification.

When any one of us realises he is sad, he must think: 'It is because I am not close enough to Christ ...' When one of us becomes aware, for instance, of an inclination towards ill-humour, towards bad temper, he must similarly remind himself. If he throws the blame on things around him, he will be wide of the mark; he will be looking in the wrong direction.[14] Sometimes it is possible that a certain apathy or spiritual sadness may have its root cause in tiredness or sickness ... but it more frequently stems from a

---

[12] St J. Escrivá, *Christ is passing by*, 9
[13] *Second Reading of the Mass*, 2 Cor 5:20-6:2
[14] A. G. Dorronsoro, *Time to Believe*

lack of generosity in doing what God asks of us, from an effectually feeble struggle to mortify our senses, from a lack of concern for other people; in a word, it has its origins in a state of lukewarmness.

If we stay close to Christ we will always find the cure for our lack of possible ardour, and re-charge ourselves with the strength to overcome our lukewarmness and those defects that we could never overcome by ourselves. *When somebody says: 'I appear to be incorrigibly lazy. I am not tenacious; I don't seem to be able to finish the things I start', today he ought to think: 'I am not close enough to Christ'. That is why whenever we recognise something as a defect in our lives, as a weakness ..., we should immediately refer it to this type of intimate and direct examination: 'I do not seem to have the ability to persevere: I am not close to Christ. I am not cheerful: I am not close to Christ. And Christ is saying: Come on! Turn around! Return to me with all your heart!'*

It is time for each one of us to recognise that he is being urged on by Jesus Christ. Those of us who sometimes feel inclined to put off this decision should know that, now, the moment has come. Those of us who are pessimistic and who think there is no remedy for our defects should know that the moment has arrived. Lent is starting. Let us look on it as a time of change and hope.[15]

---

[15] *ibid*

2. THE CROSS OF EACH DAY

2.1 No true Christianity without the Cross. Our Lord's Cross a source of peace and joy.

Lent began yesterday, and the Gospel of today's Mass reminds us that if we are to follow Christ we have to carry our own Cross. *And He said to all, 'If any man would come after me, let him deny himself, and take up his cross daily and follow me'.*[1]

Our Lord, addressing himself to all men, speaks of the daily Cross. And these words of Jesus retain their fullest value. They are words spoken to all men who want to follow him. There is no such thing as a Christianity without the Cross, designed for soft and pusillanimous Christians with no sense of sacrifice. Our Lord's words state a condition that is absolutely necessary, a *sine qua non*. *Whoever does not take up his cross and come after me, cannot be my disciple.*[2] *A Christianity from which we tried to remove the cross of voluntary mortification and penance under the pretext that these practices are the remains of the Dark Ages or of an outworn Mediaeval era, quite inappropriate for a modern Humanistic Age, would be an insipid Christianity, a Christianity in name only. It would not have kept intact the doctrine of the Gospels, nor would it serve to induce men to follow in Christ's footsteps.*[3] It would be a Christianity without the Redemption, without Salvation.

One of the clearest symptoms of lukewarmness having

---

[1] Luke 9:23
[2] Luke 14:27
[3] J. Orlandis, *The Eight Beatitudes*, Pamplona

entered into a soul is precisely such an abandoning of the Cross, a contempt for little mortifications, a scorning of anything that in some way involves sacrifice and self-denial. On the other hand, to flee from the Cross is to turn one's back on holiness and joy; because one of the fruits of the mortified soul is just this capacity to relate to God and other people, and also a profound peace, even in the midst of tribulations and external difficulties. The person who abandons mortification is inevitably ensnared by his senses and becomes incapable of any supernatural thought.

There is no progress in the interior life without a spirit of sacrifice and mortification. St John of the Cross says that if few people reach a high state of union with God it is because so many do not want to. [4] And the same saint writes: *and if anyone wants one day to possess Christ, never let him seek him without the Cross.*[5]

We should not forget then that mortification is closely related to joy, and that when our heart is purified it becomes humbler, so that it can have closer dealings with God and other people. *This is the great paradox of Christian mortification. It would seem that accepting and, furthermore, seeking suffering ought to cause good Christians, in practice, to be the saddest of people, the men 'who have the worst time of it'.*

The reality is quite different. Mortification only produces sadness when there is in its practice too much selfishness and a lack of generosity and love of God. Sacrifice always brings with it joy in the midst of pain, the happiness of knowing that we are fulfilling God's will, and of making the effort to love him. Good Christians live 'quasi tristes, semper etiam gaudentes' (1 Cor 8:10) as

---

[4] St John of the Cross, *The Living Flame of Love*, II, 7
[5] *ibid*

though they were sad, but really always filled with joy.[6]

2.2 The Cross in the little things of each day.

The daily cross. 'Nulla dies sine cruce!' No day without its cross; not a single day in which we are not to shoulder the Cross of the Lord, no day during which we are not to accept his yoke ...

The way to our personal sanctification should daily lead us to the cross. This way is not a sorrowful one, because Christ himself comes to our aid, and in his company there is no room for sadness. I like to repeat, with my soul filled with joy, that there is not a single day without a cross – 'the' Cross.[7]

Our Lord's Cross, which we have to carry each day, is certainly not the cross produced by our selfishness, our envy, our laziness, etc. It is not to be found in the conflicts produced by our 'old man' and our disordered love of self. That does not come from God; it does not sanctify.

Occasionally we will meet the Cross in some great difficulty, in a serious and painful illness, in an economic disaster, in the death of a loved one. ... *do not forget that being with Jesus means we shall most certainly come upon his Cross. When we abandon ourselves into God's hands, He frequently permits us to taste sorrow, loneliness, opposition, slander, defamation and ridicule, coming both from within and from without. This is because He wants to mould us into his own image and likeness. He even tolerates our being called lunatics and our being taken for fools.*

This is the time to love passive mortification, which comes, hidden perhaps, or barefaced and insolent, when we least expect it.[8] Our Lord will give us the strength we

---

[6] R. M. de Balbin, *Sacrifice and Joy*, Madrid
[7] St J. Escrivá, *Christ is passing by*, 176
[8] ibid, *Friends of God*, 301

need to carry that Cross with elegance and He will fill us with unimaginable graces and fruits. We will understand that God conveys his benedictions in many ways, and frequently blesses his friends by making them share in his Cross and making them co-redeemers with him.

However, we will normally find the Cross each day in the sort of petty annoyances that may occur at work, and which usually present themselves to us through people around us. It may be something unexpected, the difficult character of a person with whom we have to live, plans perhaps that have to be changed at the last minute, stubborn materials or instruments of work that fail us when we most need them. Discomfort, maybe caused by cold, or heat, or noise … misunderstandings. A below-par seediness that impairs our efficiency on a particular day …

We have to accept these daily pinpricks courageously, offering them to God in a spirit of reparation without complaint. Those mortifications that crop up unexpectedly can help us, if we receive them well, to grow in the spirit of penance that we need so much, and to improve in the virtues of patience, of charity, of understanding: that is to say, *in holiness*. If we receive our setbacks with a bad spirit, it can cause us to rebel, or to become impatient or discouraged. Many Christians have lost their joy at the end of the day, not because of big reverses, but because they have not known how to sanctify the tiredness caused by work, or the little snags and minor frustrations which have arisen during the day. When we accept the Cross – little or great – it produces peace and joy in the midst of pain and is laden with merits for eternal life. Not accepting the Cross, the soul becomes thwarted or inwardly rebellious. This soon appears externally in the form of despondency and bad humour. *To carry one's Cross is something great. Great … It means facing up to life courageously, without weakness or meanness. It means that we turn into moral energy those difficulties which will never be lacking in our existence; it means understanding human sorrow; and, finally, it means knowing really how to love.*[9] The Christian who goes through life systematically avoiding sacrifice will not find God, will not find happiness. What he will have been taking care to avoid is his own sanctity.

2.3 Offering up disappointments. Little details of mortification.

If any man would come after me, let him deny himself .... As well as accepting the Cross that we meet on our way, often unexpectedly, we must look for other little mortifications so as to keep alive the spirit of penance that God asks us for. In order to make progress in the interior life it is a great help to have several little mortifications in mind, fixed, in advance, decided on beforehand, so that we do them every day.

These mortifications, intentionally sought out through love of God, will be of great value in helping us to overcome laziness, to counter that selfishness which seems ready to burst out at every moment, to beware of pride etc. Some will be of benefit to us in our work, having their effect on details of punctuality, order, intensity of concentration, and the care of the tools or equipment we use. Others will be aimed at enabling us to live charity better, particularly with the people we live and work with: knowing how to smile although we find it hard, showing appreciation for others, facilitating their work, having consideration for them in a pleasant manner, serving them in the little things of ordinary life, and never losing our temper with them. Other mortifications can be directed towards overcoming our desire for comfort, at keeping a guard over our internal and external senses, at overcoming

---

[9] St Paul VI, *Address*, 24 March 1967

our curiosity: we can have in mind specific mortifications at meals, in our personal appearance, etc. They do not have to be very big things, but we do need to acquire the habit of doing them with constancy and for love of God.

As the general tendency of human nature is in the direction of avoiding anything that demands effort, we must be very exacting in these matters, so as not to be satisfied simply with having good intentions. At times it will prove useful to write them down, so that we can go over them in the examination of conscience, or at other moments of the day, so as not to forget them. Let us remember too, that the mortifications most pleasing to God are those which have reference to charity, to the apostolate, and the faithful fulfilment of our duties.

Let us tell Jesus, as we finish our dialogue with him, that we are prepared to follow him, carrying our cross today and every day.

3. A TIME FOR PENANCE

3.1 Fasting and other signs of penance in Jesus' preaching and in the life of the Church.

The Gospel of today's Mass tells how the disciples of John the Baptist asked Jesus, *Why do we and the Pharisees fast, but your disciples do not fast?*[1]

Fasting was then, and always will be, one more sign of the spirit of penance that God asks of man. *In the Old Testament we can find gradually developing with ever-increasing richness, the religious sense of penance, as a personal religious act, which has as its end love for and abandonment in God.*[2] When it is accompanied by prayer it can be used to manifest humility before God.[3] The man who fasts turns towards God in an attitude of total dependence and abandonment. In Holy Scripture we see how fasting and other works of penance were performed before the commencement of any difficult task,[4] to implore forgiveness for sin,[5] to obtain the cessation of a calamity,[6] to gain the grace needed for the fulfilment of a mission,[7] to prepare oneself to come face to face with God etc.[8]

John the Baptist, who well knew the fruits of fasting, taught his disciples the importance and need of practising this penance. He coincided in this with the Pharisees who were pious and loved the law so that John's followers were

---

[1] Matt 9:14-15
[2] St Paul VI, Apostolic Constitution, *Paenitemini*, 17 February 1966
[3] cf Lev 16:29-31
[4] cf Jude 20:26, Esther 4:16
[5] 1 Kings 21:27
[6] Jude 4:9-13
[7] Acts 13:2
[8] Ex 34:28 , Dan 9:3

surprised that Jesus had not instilled it into his own
disciples. But Our Lord came to the defence of his own.
*Can the wedding guests mourn as long as the bridegroom
is with them?*[9] The *bridegroom*, according to the Prophets,
is God himself who manifests his love for men.[10]

Here Christ declares his divinity once again and calls
his disciples *the friends of the bridegroom*, his own friends.
They are with him and they do not need to fast.
Nevertheless, *When the bridegroom is taken away from
them, then they will fast.* When Jesus is no longer visibly
present, they will have need of mortification if they are to
see him with the eyes of their soul.

The whole penitential meaning of the Old Testament
*was no more than a shadow of what was to come. Penance
– a requisite of interior life confirmed as such by the
religious experience of mankind, and the object of a
special precept of divine revelation – takes on new
dimensions infinitely more vast and profound in Christ and
in the Church.*[11]

In early times the Church preserved penitential
practices in the spirit laid down by Jesus. The *Acts of the
Apostles* mention celebrations of the cult accompanied by
fasting.[12] Throughout his overflowing apostolic work, St
Paul is not satisfied with merely suffering hunger and thirst
when circumstances so demanded, but repeatedly added
the practice of deliberate fasting.[13] And the Church, as always, remains faithful to this penitential exercise, deter-
mining at each season the days when the faithful must fast,
and recommending this pious practice along with
opportune advice concerning it in spiritual direction.

---

[9] Matt 9:15

[10] cf Is 54:5

[11] St Paul VI, Apostolic Constitution, *Paenitemini*, 17 February 1966

[12] cf Acts 13:2 *et seq*

[13] cf 2 Cor 6:5, 11-27

Fasting, however, is only one form of penance. There are other forms of corporal mortification that make our conversion and our union with God easier. We can ask ourselves today how we live this spirit of penance that our Mother the Church wants us to live throughout our lives, but in a special way during the liturgical season of Lent in which we now find ourselves.

3.2 Contemplating the most holy humanity of Our Lord in the Way of the Cross. Eagerness to redeem.

Do penance, Jesus says at the beginning of his public life, just as John the Baptist had already preached, and as later the Apostles were to do at the beginning of the Church. We need penance for our life as Christians in order to make reparation for so many sins of our own and of others. We would be unable to come to know Jesus Christ without yet having attained a true spirit of penance and conversion; we would still be dominated by sin. We must not avoid it out of fear, or because we are sceptical about its usefulness, or because we lack supernatural outlook. *You are afraid of penance? ... Of penance, which will help you to obtain Life everlasting? And yet, in order to preserve this poor present life, don't you see how men will submit to all the cruel torture of a surgical operation?*[14] Avoiding penance would mean at the same time avoiding holiness and, perhaps, because of the consequences of this, rejecting salvation itself.

Our desire to identify ourselves with Christ will lead us to accept his invitation to suffer with him. Lent prepares us to contemplate the events of the Passion and Death of Jesus. Particularly on the Fridays of Lent, which remind us in a special way of that first Good Friday when Christ consummated the Redemption, we can meditate on the events of that day, which have been gathered together for

---

[14] St J. Escrivá, *The Way*, 224

us in the traditional devotion of The Way of the Cross. That is why St Josemaría Escrivá advises: *The Way of the Cross. Here indeed you have a sturdy and fruitful devotion. Spend a few moments each Friday going over those fourteen points of Our Lord's Passion and Death. I assure you that you will gain strength for the whole of the week.*[15]

In this devotion we will contemplate the most Sacred Humanity of Christ, who reveals himself to us suffering in his flesh as a man, but without losing the majesty of God. As we accompany Jesus along his *via dolorosa*, we will be able to re-live those central moments of the Redemption of the world, and contemplate Jesus as He is condemned to death and the Cross is laid upon him (2nd Station). We will see him set out on a path that we must follow. Each time Jesus sinks to the ground under the weight of the Cross we should be filled with horror, because it is our sins and the sins of all men that weigh God down. Then desires of conversion will spring to our hearts: *The exhausted body of Jesus staggers now beneath the huge Cross. His most loving Heart can barely summon up another breath of life for his flagging muscles, for his poor wounded limbs ... You and I can say nothing: now we know why the Cross of Jesus weighs so much. We weep over our wretched failings and also for the terrible ingratitude of the human heart. From the depths of our soul there comes an act of real contrition that lifts us up from the prostration of sin. Jesus has fallen that we might get up, once and for all.*[16]

Our contemplation of these sufferings of Jesus, and the voluntary mortifications we undertake in an endeavour to unite ourselves to Christ's eagerness to redeem, will also increase our apostolic spirit during this Lent. He gave his life in order to bring men close to God.

---

[15] *ibid*, 556
[16] *idem*, The Way of the Cross, Seventh Station

3.3 Our daily work the source of the little mortifications that God asks of us. Examples. Passive mortifications.

The source of the mortifications God asks of us is almost always to be found in our daily work. Mortifications right from the start of the day: getting up promptly at the time we have fixed for rising, overcoming laziness from the first moment; punctuality; our work finished down to the last detail; the discomfort of too much heat or cold; a smile even though we are tired or do not feel like smiling; sobriety in eating and drinking; order and care for our personal belongings and for the things we use; giving up our own opinion ... But for this we need above all to follow a particular piece of advice: *If you really want to be a penitent soul – both penitent and cheerful – you must above all stick to your daily periods of prayer, which should be fervent, generous and not cut short. And you must make sure that these minutes of prayer are not engaged in only when you feel the need, but at fixed times, whenever it is possible. Don't neglect these details. If you subject yourself to this daily worship of God, I can assure you that you will be always happy.*[17]

As well as those mortifications known as 'passive' – mortifications which present themselves to us without our looking for them – the mortifications that we propose to ourselves (and seek out) are called *active* mortifications. Amongst these, the mortifications which refer to the control of our internal senses are especially important for our interior progress and for enabling us to achieve purity of heart. These are: *mortification of the imagination* – avoiding that interior monologue in which fantasy runs wild, by trying to turn it into a dialogue with God, present in our soul in grace. We try to put a restraining check on that tendency of ours to go over and over some little happening in the course

---

[17] *idem, Furrow*, 994

of which we have come off badly. No doubt we have felt slighted, and have made much of an injury to our self-esteem, caused to us quite unintentionally. If we don't apply the brake in time, our conceit and pride will cause us to overbalance until we lose our peace and presence of God. *Mortification of the memory* – avoiding useless recollections which make us waste time[18] and which could lead us into more serious temptations. *Mortification of the intelligence* – so as to put it squarely to the business of concentrating on our duty at this moment[19] and, also, on many occasions of surrendering our own judgement so as to live humility and charity with others in a better way. To sum up, we try to get rid of those internal habits that we know we would not like to see in a man or a woman of God.[20] Let us make up our minds to keep close to Our Lord during these days by contemplating his most Sacred Humanity in the vivid and memorable scenes of The Way of the Cross. Let us see how, for our sakes, He walks along the Path of Sorrow.

---

[18] cf *idem*, *The Way*, 13
[19] cf *ibid*, 815
[20] cf *ibid*, 938

4. SAVING WHAT WAS LOST

4.1 Jesus comes as the Physician to cure the whole of mankind, for we are all sick. Humility in order to be cured.

Today's Gospel[1] tells us about Matthew's vocation; about how he was called by Our Lord, and the prompt way in which he responded: *And he left everything, and rose and followed him.* The new apostle wanted to show his gratitude towards Jesus with a feast that St Luke qualifies as a 'great' feast; *and there was a large company of tax collectors and others sitting at table with them.* All his friends were there.

The Pharisees were scandalised. They asked the disciples, *Why do you eat and drink with sinners?* The publicans were considered as sinners, because of the disproportionate benefits that they could obtain through their work and because of their dealings with the Gentiles.

Jesus answered the Pharisees with these consoling words: *Those who are well have no need of a physician, but those who are sick. I have not come to call the righteous, but sinners to repentance.*[2] Jesus comes to offer his kingdom to all men; his mission is universal. *The dialogue of salvation was not conditioned by the merits of those to whom it was directed; it was open to all men, without discrimination.*[3] Jesus comes for all, for we are all

---

[1] Luke 5:27-32
[2] Luke 5:31-32
[3] St Paul VI, Encyclical, *Ecclesiam Suam*, 6 August 1964

sick and we are all sinners; *No-one is good but God alone.*[4]
We must all seek God's mercy and forgiveness *in order to
have life*[5] and to reach salvation. Mankind is not divided
into two categories; those who are already justified by their
own efforts, and sinners. All of us need God, every day. If
anybody thinks he does not need God he will not be given
strength; he will go on being overshadowed by his interior
death or his sickness.

The words of Our Lord, who presents himself to us as
Physician, move us to ask humbly and confidently for
forgiveness for our sins and for the sins of all those *who
seem to want to remain far from God.* We say to him
today, with St Teresa: *Oh, what a hard thing I am asking of
you, my true God: that you should love one who does not
love you; that you should open the door to one who does
not knock; that you should give health to one who prefers
to be sick and chooses rather to walk in her infirmity! You
say, my Lord, that you have come to seek out sinners.
These, my Lord are the true sinners. Do not look on our
blindness, oh my God, but at the streams of blood that your
Son shed for us. May your mercy shine on such grave
wickedness; remember, Lord, that we were made by your
hands.*[6] If we turn to Jesus in this way, humbly, he will
always have mercy on us and on those we try to bring
closer to him.

4.2 Christ cures our sickness. Effectiveness of the Sacrament of Penance.

In the Old Testament the Messiah is described as the
shepherd who would come to care lovingly for his sheep,

---

[4] Mark 10:18
[5] cf John 10:28
[6] St Teresa, *Exclamations of the soul to God*, 8

binding up their wounds and healing those who were sick.[7]
He has come to seek what was lost, to call sinners, to give
his life as a ransom for many.[8] As had been prophesied, it
is He who *has borne our griefs and carried our sorrows ...
upon him was laid the chastisement that has made us
whole.*[9]

Christ is the one who cures all our infirmities; we are
all at least a little sick and this is why we need Christ. *He is
our physician and He heals our selfishness, if we let his
grace penetrate to the depths of our soul.*[10] We must go to
him as the sick man goes to the doctor, admitting what is
really wrong with him, wanting to be cured. *Jesus has
taught us that the worst sickness is hypocrisy, the pride
that leads us to hide our own sins. We have to be totally
sincere with him. We have to tell the whole truth, and then
we have to say: 'Domine, si vis, potes me mundare.'* Lord,
*if you will – and you are always willing – you can make me
clean. You know my weaknesses; I feel these symptoms, I
suffer from these failings. We show him the wound with
simplicity, and if the wound is festering, we show the pus
too. Lord, you have cured so many souls; help me to
recognise you as the divine physician, when I have you in
my heart or when I contemplate your presence in the
tabernacle.*[11] Sometimes our Lord will act directly in our
soul: *I will, be clean;*[12] keep going, be more humble, don't
be worried. On other occasions, and always when there is
grave sin, Our Lord says, *Go and show yourselves to the
priests.*[13] Go to the Sacrament of Penance, where the soul

---

[7] cf Is 61:1 *et seq*, Ezek 34:16 *et seq*
[8] cf Luke 19:10
[9] Is 53:4 *et seq*
[10] St J. Escrivá, *Christ is passing by*, 93
[11] *ibid*
[12] Matt 8:3
[13] Luke 17:14

always finds the opportune medicine. *By reflecting on the function of this Sacrament*, says St John Paul II, *the conscience of the Church discovers within it, as well as its judicial character, a therapeutic or medicinal character. This relates to the fact that Christ is frequently presented in the Gospels as the Physician, and at the same time his redeeming work is often called, from ancient days of Christianity, medicina salutis. 'I want to cure, not to accuse'* St Augustine used to say, *referring to this pastoral practice of penance. And thanks to the medicine of Confession, the experience of sin does not degenerate into despair.*[14] It brings with it great peace and immense joy.

We can be certain that God will always encourage us and help us to begin again. It is he who directs the struggle, and *an army Chief on the battlefield has more respect for the soldier who, having once given way to flight, returns and attacks the enemy bravely than for the soldier who never turned tail, but neither ever performed any act of valour.*[15] It is not only the person who never falls who sanctifies himself, but the person who always rises again. Having defects is not what is bad – all of us have defects – but making a pact with them and ceasing to fight. Christ then, the Physician, cures us and then helps us to struggle.

4.3 Hope in God when we feel our own weaknesses. 'Those who are well have no need of a physician, but those who are sick.' Hope in the apostolate.

If at some time we feel particularly discouraged by some spiritual ailment that seems to us incurable, don't let us forget these consoling words of Jesus: *Those who are well have no need of a physician, but those who are sick.*

---

[14] St John Paul II, Apostolic Exhortation, *Reconciliatio et Poenitentia*, 31, 2 December 1984
[15] St Gregory the Great, *Homilies on the Gospels*, 4, 4

There is a remedy for everything. He is always very close to us, but especially so at those very moments; however great the fault, however great our wretchedness may be; if we are truly sincere, that is enough.

Don't let us forget this, too, if sometimes in our personal apostolate it should seem to us that somebody has a sickness in his soul, a problem for which there is no apparent solution. There is one, always. Perhaps Our Lord wants more prayer and mortification, more understanding and affection from us. *All your sicknesses will be cured*, says St Augustine. *'But they are so many', you will say. The Physician is more powerful. For him, who is Omnipotent, there is no incurable illness; let yourself be cured, put yourself in his hands.*[16] We must approach him just as those simple people around him did. Just as the blind, the lame, the paralytics ... who so much longed for a cure. Only the person who knows he is tainted and is aware of his blemish experiences within himself the need to be cleansed; only the person who is conscious of his wounds and of his sores experiences a sense of urgency about being cured. We too must feel uneasiness until our ailments, those points that our particular or general examination of conscience shows us, are healed.

That day Matthew left his old way of life in order to start a new life with Christ. Today we can make our own this prayer of St Ambrose: *Like him* [Matthew], *I too want to leave behind my old life, and follow no-one but you, O Lord, who cure my wounds. Who will ever separate me from the love of God which I find in you ... ? I am bound to the Faith, nailed to the Faith; I am bound by the holy bonds of love. All of your Commandments will be like a cauterising iron whose touch I will bear always on my body ... medicine stings, but draws out the infection from*

---

[16] St Augustine, *Commentary on Psalm 102*

the wound. Cut away, O Lord Jesus, the putrefaction of my sins. For as long as you hold me bound by love, cut away any infection that is in me. Come soon to lance my many secret and hidden passions, and cut into the wound, so that the disease may not spread to the whole of my body ...

I have found a Physician who dwells in heaven, but who distributes his medicines on earth. He alone can cure my wounds because He does not suffer from them; He alone can take all sorrow away from my heart and all fear from my soul, because He knows me in the very depths of my being.[17] Many of Matthew's friends who were with Jesus at that feast would have felt welcomed and understood as a result of Our Lord's kindness towards them. Doubters he would have been particularly kind to. Later, they were to turn wholeheartedly towards him and accept his doctrine fully, even though it obliged them to change entirely many things in their lives. They were to form part of the first Christian community in Palestine. Matthew's friends met the Master at a feast. Jesus made use of all sorts of circumstances to bring people to salvation. We must imitate him in this in our own personal apostolate.

---

[17] St Ambrose, *Commentary on the Gospel of St Luke*, 5, 27

First Sunday of Lent

5. THE TEMPTATIONS OF JESUS

5.1 God allows us to be tempted so that we may grow in virtue.

Lent commemorates the forty days Jesus spent in the desert in preparation for his years of preaching, which culminated in the cross and in the triumph of Easter. Forty days of prayer and penance, and at the end of them the temptations of Christ, which the liturgy recalls for us in today's Gospel (cf Matt 4:1-11).

The whole episode is a mystery which man cannot hope to understand: God is here submitting to temptation, letting the evil one have his way. A mystery indeed. But we can meditate upon it, asking Our Lord to help us understand the teaching it contains.[1]

It is the first time the devil intervenes in Jesus' life, and he does so openly. He puts Our Lord to the test; perhaps he wants to find out whether the hour of the Messiah has actually arrived. Jesus allowed this intervention so as to give us an example of humility, and to teach us to overcome the temptations that we are going to have to undergo in the course of our lives. *As Our Lord did everything for our instruction,* says St John Chrysostom, *so he wished to be led out into the wilderness and there to enter into combat with the devil. He did this in order that the baptised should not be troubled if after Baptism they suffer still greater temptations, as though such were not to be expected.*[2] If we were not prepared to meet the temptations that we are to undergo, we would open the

---

[1] St J. Escrivá, *Christ is passing by*, 61
[2] St John Chrysostom, *Homilies on St Matthew*, 13, 1

door to a great enemy – discouragement and gloominess.

Jesus wanted to teach us by his example that no one should consider himself exempt from any type of trial. Ronald Knox has the following to say: *The temptations of Our Lord are also the temptations of his servants individually. But the scale of them, naturally, is different; the devil is not going to offer you and me all the kingdoms of the world. He knows his market; offers, like a good salesman, just as much as he thinks his customer will take. I suppose he thinks, with some justice, that most of us could be had for five thousand a year, and a great many of us for much less. Nor does he, to us, propose his conditions so openly; his offer comes to us wrapped up in all sorts of plausible shapes. But, if he sees the chance he is not slow to point out to you and to me how we could get the thing we want if we would be untrue to our better selves, and not infrequently if we would be untrue to our Catholic loyalties.*[3]

The Preface of today's Mass reminds us that Our Lord teaches us with deeds that we must overcome temptations and that we should derive benefit from all the trials that beset us. He *allows temptation, and uses it providentially to purify you, to make you holy, to detach you more from the things of earth, to lead you where He is and by the route he wants you to take, so as to make you happy (in a life which may not be comfortable); so as to give you maturity, understanding and effectiveness in your apostolic work with souls, and ... above all, to make you humble, very humble.*[4]

Blessed is the man who endures trial, says the Apostle St James, *for when he has stood the test he will receive the crown of life which God has promised to those who love him.*[5]

---

[3] R.A. Knox, *Pastoral Sermons*
[4] S. Canals, *Jesus as Friend*
[5] Jas 1:12

5.2 The temptations of Jesus. The devil tries us in a similar way.

The devil tempts us precisely by taking advantage of the needs and weaknesses of human nature.

After fasting for forty days and forty nights, Our Lord must have been very weak. Here He is in the wilderness; He feels hungry just like any other man in such circumstances. This is the moment the tempter chooses to come forward with the proposition that He should turn the stones that lie around him into the bread He needs and longs for so desperately.

Jesus *not only declines the food which his body requires, but also rejects a greater temptation: that of using his divine power to solve, if we can express it so, a personal problem ...*

How generous Our Lord is in humbling himself and fully accepting his human condition! He does not use his divine power to escape from difficulties or avoid effort. Let us pray that He will teach us to be tough, to love work, to appreciate the human and divine nobility of savouring the consequences of self-giving.[6]

This passage of the Gospel teaches us too to be particularly watchful over ourselves and over those whom we have a special obligation to help in their moments of weakness and tiredness: to be alert when we ourselves are going through a bad patch. It is at such moments that the devil chooses to tempt us more fiercely, so that our lives may turn away from God's will and follow a different path.

In the second temptation, *The devil took him to the holy city, and set him on the pinnacle of the temple, and said to him, If you are the Son of God, throw yourself down; for it is written: 'He will give his angels charge of you, and in their hands they will bear you up, lest you*

---

[6] St J. Escrivá, *loc cit*

strike your foot against a stone'. Jesus said to him: 'Again it is written: You shall not tempt the Lord your God'.

It seemed a very cunning temptation: if you refuse, you will demonstrate that you do not trust God completely; if you accept, you oblige him to send his angels to save you, to your own personal advantage. (The devil does not know that Jesus would not need any angel at all.)

Our Lord will hear a similar proposition, with an almost identical text, at the end of his life on earth: *He is the king of Israel; let him come down now from the cross, and we will believe in him.*[7]

Christ refuses to perform pointless miracles which would simply be a matter of vanity or ostentation. We too have to be on the alert so as to reject similar temptations that arise in our own circumstances. The wish to excel can be caused by even the holiest of things; we must be alert to false arguments claiming to be based on Holy Scripture, and not ask for (much less demand) proofs or extraordinary signs in order to believe. God indicates the path of faith to us with sufficient graces and testimonies in our everyday lives.

In the last of the temptations, the devil offers Jesus all the glory and temporal power that any man could wish for. The devil, *showed him all the kingdoms of the world and the glory of them, and he said to him, 'all these I will give you, if you will fall down and worship me'.* Our Lord now sent the tempter away once and for all.

The devil always promises more than he can give. Happiness is very far from being his gift. Any temptation is always a miserable deception. In order to test us, the devil takes advantage of our ambitions. Probably the worst of these is that of desiring one's own excellence at all costs, of systematically seeking ourselves in everything we do or

---

[7] Matt 27:42

plan. Our own self can often be the worst of all idols.

Neither should we fall down to worship ~~material~~ ~~things, making of them false gods~~ which will ultimately make slaves of us. Material goods cease to be good if they separate us from God and our fellow men.

We will have to keep up a constant watch, an unremitting struggle, because we still have the tendency to seek human glory, in spite of our having told Our Lord on many occasions that we want only his glory. Jesus speaks to us too: *You shall worship the Lord your God and him only shall you serve.* And that is what we want and what we ask for; to be able to serve God in the vocation to which he has called us.

5.3 Our Lord is always at our side. Arms with which to conquer.

God is always beside us. Whenever we are confronted with a temptation He says, *Be of good cheer, I have overcome the world.*[8] And we place all our trust in him because we know we would achieve very little by ourselves. *I can do all things in him who strengthens me.*[9] *The Lord is my light and my salvation; whom shall I fear?*[10]

We are able to arm ourselves against temptation through constant mortification in our work; in the way we live charity; in guarding our external and internal senses. As well as mortification we need prayer. *Watch and pray, that you may not enter into temptation.*[11] We must also guard against it by fleeing from the occasions of sin, (however marginal they may seem, for *Whoever loves danger will perish by it,*[12] and by having our time fully

---

[8] John 16:33
[9] Phil 4:14
[10] Ps 26:1
[11] Matt 26:41
[12] Sir 3:26

occupied, mainly in the fulfilment of our family, professional and social obligations.

If we are to overcome temptation we will have to repeat confidently over and over again the petition in the Our Father: *and lead us not into temptation*; grant us the strength to remain strong when faced with temptation. Since it is Our Lord himself who puts such a petition on our lips, it would be good for us to repeat it continually ...

We struggle against temptation by speaking openly about it to our spiritual director; making it thus known is almost overcoming it. He who reveals his own temptations to his spiritual director can be certain that God grants the spiritual director the grace needed to direct him well.[13]

We can always count on God's grace to overcome any temptation whatsoever. *But do not forget, my friend, that you need weapons in this spiritual battle. And your weapons have to be these: continuous prayer; sincerity and frankness with your spiritual director; the Holy Eucharist and the Sacrament of Penance; a generous spirit of Christian mortification which will bring you to flee from the occasion of sin and to avoid idleness; humility of heart, and a tender and filial devotion to Our Lady, Comforter of the Afflicted and Refuge of Sinners. Always turn confidently to Our Lady and say: 'My Mother, I trust in you'.*[14]

---

[13] B. Baur, *In Silence with God*
[14] S. Canals, *op cit*

6. THE EXISTENCE OF THE DEVIL AND HIS ACTIVITY

6.1 The devil exists and acts in people and society. His activity is mysterious, but real and effective.

Again the devil took him to a very high mountain ... Then Jesus said to him, 'Begone, satan!', we read in the Gospel of yesterday's Mass.[1]

The devil exists. Holy Scripture speaks of him from the first to the last of the revealed books, from Genesis to the Apocalypse. In the parable of the wheat and the weeds, Our Lord affirms that the weeds, whose purpose is to suffocate the wheat, were sown by *the enemy*.[2] In the parable of the sower, *the evil one comes and snatches away what is sown.*[3]

Some people are inclined towards a superficial optimism and think evil is merely an incidental imperfection in a world which is continually evolving towards better days. Nevertheless the history of mankind has been adversely affected by the devil's influence. We find in our day all the features of an intense evil which cannot be explained in terms of human behaviour alone. The devil, in all sorts of ways, wreaks havoc on mankind. There is no doubt that *the whole of man's history has been the story of dour combat with the powers of evil, stretching, so Our Lord tells us, from the very dawn of history up to the last day.*[4] The devil does this in such a way that *he provokes incalculable harm of a spiritual nature and, indirectly even of a physical*

---

[1] cf Matt 4:8-11
[2] Matt 13:25
[3] Matt 13:19
[4] Second Vatican Council, *Gaudium et spes*, 7

nature, to individuals and to society.[5]

The devil's activity is mysterious but at the same time real and effective. From the first centuries, Christians were conscious of diabolical activity. St Peter admonished the first Christians: *Be sober, be watchful. Your adversary the devil prowls around like a roaring lion, seeking someone to devour. Resist him firm in your faith.*[6]

With Jesus Christ, the devil's dominion has been reduced, for He *has freed us from the power of satan.*[7] As a result of the redeeming work of Christ, the devil can only cause real harm to those who freely allow him to, by consenting to evil and separating themselves from God.

In many passages of the Gospel Our Lord shows himself overcoming the devil, freeing many people from diabolical possession. We place our trust in Jesus, and he does not allow us to be tempted beyond our strength.[8] The devil will try to *reduce the human spirit and lead it to violate God's precepts, little by little darkening the hearts of those who try to serve him. This he will do to make them forsake the true God, turning to himself instead as though he were a god indeed.*[9] He does this at all times, in a thousand different ways. But God has given us the means to overcome all temptations; nobody sins necessarily. Let us consider, in depth, during this Lent what that means. As well as this, in order to free us from the devil's influence, God has given us an angel to help and protect us. *If you call upon your Guardian Angel at the moment of trial, he will protect you from the devil and will bring you holy inspirations.*[10]

---

[5] St John Paul II, *General Audience*, 13 August 1986
[6] 1 Pet 5:8
[7] Second Vatican Council, *Sacrosanctum Concilium*, 6
[8] cf 1 Cor 10:13
[9] St Irenaeus, *Adversus Haereses*, 5
[10] St J. Escrivá, *The Way*, 567

6.2 Who the devil is. His power is limited. We need divine help in order to conquer.

The devil is a personal, real and individual being, of a spiritual and indivisible nature, who separated himself from God forever by his sin, *because the devil and the other demons were created naturally good by God; but they became bad of themselves.*[11]

He is a liar and the father of lies[12] of sin, of discord, of affliction, of hatred, of all that is absurd and evil on earth.[13] He is the astute and envious serpent who brings death to the world,[14] the enemy who sows evil in man's heart[15] and the only being we have to fear if we are not close to God. His sole purpose in the world, which he has never renounced, is our perdition. Every day he will try to achieve that purpose through all the means at his disposal. *It all began with his rejection of God and God's kingdom, when he usurped his sovereign rights and tried to overturn the economy of salvation and the very ordering of creation itself. This attitude can be found reflected in the words of the tempter to our first parents: 'You will be like gods'. This is how the evil spirit endeavours to transplant into man the attitude of proud rivalry, of insubordination and opposition to God that has become the motivating force of his own whole existence.*[16]

The devil is the first cause of evil and of the disorders and ruptures which are produced in families and in society. *For instance, suppose,* says St J. H. Newman, *a sudden darkness were to fall upon the streets of a crowded city in day-time, you may fancy without my telling you what a*

---

[11] Fourth Lateran Council, Dz 800 (428)

[12] John 8:44

[13] cf Heb 2:14

[14] cf Wis 2:24

[15] cf Matt 13:28-39

[16] St John Paul II, *General Audience*, 13 August 1986

noise and clamour there would be, foot passengers, carriages, carts, horses all being mixed together. Such is the state of the world. The evil spirit, which worketh in the children of disbelief, the god of this world, as St Paul says, has blinded the eyes of them that believe not, and hence they are obliged to wrangle and debate, for they have lost their way; and they fall out with each other and one says this and one says that, because they do not see.[17]

In his temptations the devil has recourse to deceit, because he can present only a false good and a fictitious happiness, which inevitably turn into loneliness and bitterness. Outside of God true good or happiness do not exist; they cannot exist. Outside of God there is only darkness, emptiness and endless misery. But the devil's power is limited, and is also under the dominion and sovereignty of God, who is the only Lord of the Universe.

The devil – and our angels – cannot penetrate our innermost thoughts if we do not want them to. *The unclean spirits cannot know the nature of our thoughts, they can only conjecture at them from outwardly perceptible indications, or else by examining our dispositions, our words or the things they notice that we tend towards. On the other hand, what we have not chosen to exteriorise so that it remains hidden within our souls, is totally inaccessible to them. Even the very thoughts that they suggest to us, the reception we give them, the reaction they cause within us ... they cannot know any of this because of the very essence of our soul ... except, in every case, through our movements and external manifestations.*[18]

The devil is unable to violate our liberty so as to incline it towards evil. *It is a certain fact that the devil*

---

[17] St J. H. Newman, *Sermon for the Second Sunday of Lent – The world and sin*
[18] Cassian, *Conferences*, 7

cannot seduce anybody if he does not freely give to the devil the consent of his will.[19]

The holy Curé d'Ars says that *the devil is a great chained dog which puts people to flight, which makes a great noise, but which only bites those who come too close.*[20] To sum up: *No human power can be compared to his; only God's power can vanquish him and only God's light can unmask the snares that he lays. The soul that would overcome the power of the devil will not be able to do so without prayer, nor will it recognise his deceitful traps without the aid of mortification and humility.*[21]

6.3 Jesus Christ vanquishes the devil. Trust in Christ. Means that we have to use. Holy Water.

Jesus' life was summarised in the Acts of the Apostles in the words, *He went about doing good and healing all that were oppressed by the devil.*[22] And St John, speaking about the cause of the Incarnation, explains, *The reason the Son of God appeared was to destroy the works of the devil.*[23]

Christ is the true victor over the devil: *Now shall the ruler of this world be cast out,*[24] Jesus will say at the Last Supper, a few hours before his Passion. God *decided to enter into the history of mankind in a new and definitive manner by sending his own Son in human flesh, so that through him He might snatch men from the power of darkness and of satan (cf Col 1:3, Acts 10:38).*[25]

Nevertheless, the devil continues to retain a certain power over the world, in so far as men reject the fruits of

---

[19] *ibid*
[20] St Jean Vianney, (The Curé d'Ars), *Sermon on Temptations*
[21] St John of the Cross, *The Spiritual Canticle*, 3, 9
[22] Acts 10:39
[23] 1 John 3:8
[24] John 12:31
[25] Second Vatican Council, *Ad gentes*, 3

the Redemption. He has dominion over those who in one way or another voluntarily surrender themselves to him, preferring the kingdom of darkness to the kingdom of grace.[26] This is why we should not be surprised if we often see evil apparently triumph and justice cruelly wronged here and there.

It should give us great confidence to know that Our Lord has left us many means by which to conquer and to live in this world with the peace and joy of a good Christian. Amongst these means are prayer, mortification, the frequent reception of Holy Communion and the Sacrament of Penance, and love for Our Lady. We are always safe in Our Lady's company. The use of holy water is also an effective means of protection against the devil's influence. *You ask me why I always recommend, with such insistence, the daily use of holy water. I could give you many reasons. But there could be none better than that of the Saint of Avila: 'From nothing do evil spirits flee more precipitately, never to return, than from holy water'.*[27]

St John Paul II exhorts us, when we pray, to think more about what we say in the last petition of the Our Father; *Lead us not into temptation. Deliver us from Evil – from the Evil One. Do not let us give in, Lord, to the infidelity towards which the one who has been unfaithful right from the beginning entices us.*[28] The best way we have of showing that we want to replace the *non serviam* of the devil with our personal *Serviam: I will serve you, Lord,* is by making a special effort this Lent to improve in our faithfulness to what we know God wants of us.

---

[26] cf St John Paul II, *loc cit*
[27] St J. Escrivá, *The Way*, 572
[28] St John Paul II, *loc cit*

7. THE HELP OF THE GUARDIAN ANGELS

7.1 Existence of the Guardian Angels. The devotion of the first Christians.

St Matthew ends his narration of the temptations of Our Lord with this verse: *Then the devil left him and, behold, angels came and ministered to him.*[1]

Let us look for a moment at this appearance of angels in Jesus' life, for it will help us to understand their role – the role, that is, of their angelic mission – in all human life. Christian tradition describes the guardian angels as powerful friends, placed by God alongside each one of us, to accompany us on our way. And that is why He invites us to make friends with them and get them to help us.

In suggesting that we meditate on these passages of the life of Christ, the Church reminds us that during Lent, when we recognise our sins, our wretchedness and our need for purification, there is also room for our joy. Lent is a time for both bravery and joy; we have to fill ourselves with courage, for the grace of God will not fail us. God will be at our side and will send his angels to be our travelling companions, our prudent advisers along the way, our co-operators in all that we take on.[2]

Holy Scripture and Tradition rightly give the name of angels to those pure spirits who chose God, his kingdom and his glory when they were given the fundamental test of freedom.[3] They are charged with protecting all men. We

---

[1] Matt 4:11
[2] St J. Escrivá, *Christ is passing by*, 63
[3] St John Paul II, *General Audience*, 6 August 1986

read in the Epistle to the Hebrews: *Are they not all ministering spirits sent forth to serve, for the sake of those who are to obtain salvation?*[4]

It is common doctrine that each and every man, baptised or not, has his guardian angel. The angel's mission begins with the conception of a man and continues up to the moment of his death. St John Chrysostom affirms that *all the guardian angels will gather together at the universal judgement in order to bear witness themselves to the ministry that they exercised through God's command for the salvation of each man.*[5]

In the *Acts of the Apostles*, we find a number of passages which tell us about the intervention of these holy angels and about the confidence that the first Christians had in them.[6]

This trust and veneration of our first brothers in the Faith for the angels is particularly highlighted in the account of the freeing of St Peter from prison: *An angel of the Lord appeared, and a light shone in the cell, and he struck Peter on the side and woke him, saying, 'Get up quickly'. And the chains fell from off his hands. And the angel said to him, 'Dress yourself and put on your sandals'. And he did so. And he said to him, 'Wrap your mantle around you and follow me'.*[7]

As soon as he had been set free, Peter went to the house of Mary, the mother of Mark, *where many were gathered together and were praying.*

And when he knocked at the door of the gateway, a maid named Rhoda came to answer it. Recognising Peter's voice, in her joy she did not open the gate but ran in and

---

[4] Heb 1:14
[5] St John Chrysostom, *Catena Aurea*, vol III, p 238
[6] cf Acts 5:19-20, 8:26, 10:3-6
[7] Acts 12:7-11

told them that Peter was standing at the gate. They said to her, 'You are mad'. But she insisted that it was so. They said, 'It is his angel'.[8] This incident shows us what great affection the first Christians felt for Peter as well as the great naturalness of their faith in the guardian angels.

See on what intimate terms the early Christians were with their guardian angels. And you?[9]

We too have to get to know them in a natural and confident way, and we will often be amazed at the help they give us to overcome in our struggle against the evil one. *We receive valuable help from the good angels, messengers of God's love. We have been taught by the tradition of the Church to direct our prayer to them: 'Angel of God, you are my guardian, enlighten my mind, guard me, direct me and govern me, for I have been entrusted to your celestial care. Amen.*[10]

7.2 Ways in which they can help us.

Angels came and ministered to him. The guardian angels have the specific mission of helping every man to reach his supernatural end. *Behold, I send an angel before you,* the Lord says to Moses, *to guard you on the way and to bring you to the place which I have prepared.*[11] And the Catechism of the Council of Trent comments, *Just as fathers, when their sons have to travel among bad and dangerous roads, make sure they are accompanied by people who can guard them and defend them from danger, so in the same way does our heavenly Father, as we set out along this path that leads to our heavenly home. He gives each one of us an angel. He does this so that, strengthened*

---

[8] Acts 12:13-17
[9] cf St J. Escrivá, *The Way*, 570
[10] St John Paul II, *General Audience*, 20 August 1986
[11] Ex 23:20

by his power and help, we may be freed from the snares cunningly set by our enemies, and may repel the terrible assaults that they make on us. He wants us to walk straight along the path with such guides, so that no obstacle placed in our way by the enemy should turn us aside from the way that leads to heaven.[12]

Thus the mission of the guardian angels is to help men in the face of all temptations and dangers, and to bring good inspirations to their hearts. They are our intercessors, our guardians, and they give us their help whenever we invoke them. *The saints intercede for men. The guardian angels not only pray for men, but they carry out duties towards them. If intercession takes place through the blessed in Heaven, through the guardian angels there is both intercession and direct intervention; they are at the same time advocates for men before God and ministers of God before men.*[13]

The guardian angel can also give us material help if this is good for our supernatural end or for that of others. We should never hesitate to ask them for favours in the little material things that we need each day; finding a parking space; not missing a bus; help in an examination we have worked for, etc. They can co-operate with us especially in the apostolate; their assistance is invaluable in our struggle against temptations and against the devil, and in our prayer. *As well as taking our thoughts up to God, they bring God's help to our souls, and they watch over them like good shepherds, communicating sweet messages and divine inspirations. The angels defend us against those wolves which are the devils, and they protect us.*[14]

We have to treat our guardian angel as we would a

---

[12] *Catechism of the Council of Trent*, IX, 4
[13] G. Huber, *My Angel Will Go Before You*
[14] St John of the Cross, *The Spiritual Canticle*, 2, 3

good friend. He is always on the watch, constantly prepared to give us his aid, if only we would ask him. It is a great pity when, through ignorance or forgetfulness, we do not sense the company of such a faithful companion, or do not ask him for help whenever we need it. We are never alone at moments of temptation or difficulty. Our guardian angel helps us; he will remain by our side until the very moment we leave this world.

At the end of our lives, our guardian angel will accompany us before God's judgement seat, as the liturgy of the Church tells us in its prayers for the soul at the moment of death.

7.3 Devotion to the Guardian Angels and our friendship with them.

Have confidence in your guardian angel. Treat him as a lifelong friend – that is what he is – and he will render you a thousand services in the ordinary affairs of each day.[15]

So that our guardian angel can give us his help, we need to let him know, in some way, our intentions and desires. In spite of the great perfection of their nature, angels do not have God's power or infinite knowledge, so they cannot read what is in our consciences. We only have to speak to our guardian angel in our minds for him to understand and even to deduce from our inward thoughts more than we ourselves are able to express. That is why it is so important to treat our guardian angel as a friend.

As well as friendship, we owe our guardian angel veneration as one who is always in God's presence, who contemplates him face to face at the same time as he is by our side.

Devotion to our guardian angel will be an effective

---

[15] St J. Escrivá, *The Way*, 562

help in our relations with God, in our work and in our relationships with the people around us, in the small and not so small conflicts which may arise in the course of our lives. During this Lent we should be especially aware of, and moved by, the scene in the Garden of Gethsemane, where we see the most Holy Humanity of Our Lord comforted by an angel from Heaven.

We must learn to speak to the angels. Turn to them now; tell your guardian angel that these spiritual waters of Lent will not flow off your soul but will go deep, because you are sorry. Ask them to take up to the Lord your good will, which, by the grace of God, has grown out of your wretchedness like a lily grown on a dunghill. 'Sancti Angeli, Custodes nostri: defendite nos in proelio ut non pereamus in tremendo judicio.' Holy angels, our guardians, defend us in our fight so that we do not perish at the final judgement.[16] Let us ask Our Lady, *Regina Angelorum*, to teach us to get to know our angels, particularly during this Lent.

---

[16] St J. Escrivá, *Christ is passing by*, 63

8. CONFESSING OUR SINS

8.1 Sacramental Confession; a meeting with Christ.

Remember your compassion, O Lord, and your merciful love,[1] we read in the Entrance Antiphon of today's Mass.

Lent is the most opportune time for considering how we receive the sacrament of Penance, that meeting with Christ, who makes himself present in the priest. It is a meeting which is always unique and always different. In it He welcomes us as the Good Shepherd, He heals our wounds, He cleanses us and strengthens us. What Christ had promised through the Prophets is accomplished in this sacrament. *I myself will be the shepherd of my sheep, and I will make them lie down, says the Lord God. I will seek the lost; I will bring back the strayed, bind up the wounds of the cripples and strengthen the weak, and the fat and strong I will watch over.*[2]

When we go to receive this sacrament we must think of Christ above all else. We must make sure He is the centre of this sacramental act. God's glory and love must be more important than our sins. We need to look at Jesus much more than at ourselves. We must keep our eyes on his goodness rather than on our own wretchedness, because interior life is a dialogue of love in which God is always the point of reference.

The prodigal son who returns home – and that is who we are when we decide to go to Confession – sets out on his return journey because he is moved by the lamentable

---

[1] *Entrance Antiphon*, Ps 24:6
[2] Ezek 34:15-16

situation he finds himself in. All the same, he never loses his consciousness of his sin: *I am not worthy to be called your son.* However, as he approaches his father's house he begins to recall his affection for all the things to do with his home, the home he has always remembered as his true one. Then in the distance he sees the unmistakable figure of his father coming towards him. This is the most important moment – the meeting. Every contrite Confession is *a drawing near to the holiness of God, a rediscovery of one's true identity, which has been upset and disturbed by sin, a liberation in the very depth of one's self and thus a regaining of lost joy, the joy of being saved, which the majority of people in our time are no longer capable of experiencing.*[3] It is up to us to help others to be aware of, to experience, a sense of loss of God, so that they may draw close to him, for He is waiting for them.

We should feel a desire to be alone with Our Lord as soon as possible, just as his disciples looked forward to being with him after He had been absent for some days. We need to pour out before him all the sorrow we experience as we become aware of our weaknesses, our errors, our imperfections and sins, both in the way we have carried out our professional duties and in our relations with other people; in our apostolic activity, indeed, even in our life of piety.

This desire that we have to make Christ the centre of our Confession is important if we are to avoid routine, and if we are to draw out from the depths of our soul those things that are more weighty and which will only rise to the surface in the light of God's love. *Be mindful of thy mercy, O Lord, and of thy steadfast love.*

---

[3] St John Paul II, Apostolic Exhortation, *Reconciliatio et Poenitentia*, 2 December 1984, 31, III

8.2 We go to the sacrament of Penance to ask for forgiveness for our sins. Qualities of a good Confession: that it be concise, concrete, clear, complete.

Have mercy on me, O God, according to thy steadfast love. According to thy abundant mercy blot out my transgressions. Wash me thoroughly from my iniquity, and cleanse me from my sin![4]

In the course of our lives we have often asked God for forgiveness and many times He has forgiven us. At the end of each day, when we consider what we have done in the course of it, we should say *Have mercy on me, O God* ... Each one of us knows how much he is in need of God's mercy.

This is why we go to Confession: to ask for absolution for our faults as we would beg for alms which we would be far from deserving. But we go with confidence; trusting, not in our merits, but in his mercy, which is eternal and infinite and always ready to forgive. *The sacrifice acceptable to God is a broken spirit; a humble and contrite heart, O God, Thou wilt not despise.*[5] *'Cor contritum et humilitatum, Deus, non despicies.'*

He asks us only to acknowledge our faults; to humbly and sincerely acknowledge our debt. That is why we go to Confession – so that the person who takes God's place and acts on God's behalf can forgive us for him. It is not so much that he should understand or encourage us. We go to ask for forgiveness. That is why accusing ourselves of our sins *does not consist simply in recounting them*, because it is not a question of an historical account of our transgressions, but of sincerely and truly accusing ourselves of them: *I accuse myself of* ... It is a heartfelt accusation of something we wish had never happened. Neither do we try to find excuses in order to cover up our faults or diminish

---

[4] *Responsorial Psalm*, Ps 50:5
[5] Ps 50:17

our personal responsibility. Lord, *According to thy abundant mercy, blot out my transgression. Wash me thoroughly from my iniquity and cleanse me from my sin.*

With a simple and practical criterion St Josemaría Escrivá used to advise us that our Confession should be *concise, concrete, clear and complete.* The use of too many words frequently denotes a desire, whether conscious or not, to flee from direct and full sincerity. So as not to fall into this we need to make a good examination of conscience.

Concise: Confession with few words, just the words that are needed to say humbly what we have done or have failed to do, without any unnecessary elaboration or adornment.

Concrete: Confession without digression, without generalities. The penitent *will suitably indicate his situation, and also the time that has elapsed since his last Confession and the difficulties he finds in leading a Christian life.*[6] He declares his sins and the surrounding circumstances that have a bearing on his faults so that the confessor can judge, absolve and heal.[7]

Clear: A Confession where we make ourselves understood, declaring the precise nature of the fault, manifesting our wretchedness with the necessary modesty and delicacy.

Complete: Integral Confession, without leaving anything out through a false sense of shame so as not *to appear bad* in the confessor's eyes.

Let us examine whether, each time we prepare ourselves to receive this sacrament, we make sure that what we are going to say to the confessor has the characteristics just described.

---

[6] St Paul VI, *Ordo Poenitentiae*, 16
[7] cf *ibid*

8.3 Lights and graces we receive in this sacrament. Importance of our interior dispositions.

Lent is a particularly appropriate time to awaken and form the conscience. It is precisely at this time that the Church reminds us of the overwhelming necessity for sacramental Confession, so that we can all live Christ's resurrection, not only in the liturgy, but also in our own soul.[8]

Confession makes us share in the Passion of Christ, and through his merits, in his Resurrection. Each time we receive the sacrament with the necessary dispositions, a rebirth of the life of grace takes place in our soul. Christ's blood, lovingly shed, purifies and sanctifies the soul, and by its virtue the sacrament confers grace – if it has been lost – or increases it in different degrees according to the dispositions of the penitent. *The intensity of repentance is, sometimes, proportionate to a greater grace than that from which the penitent fell through sin; sometimes the same, sometimes less. For this reason the penitent rises sometimes with greater grace than he had before; sometimes with the same grace, and sometimes with less. We must say the same of the virtues which depend on and follow from grace.*[9]

In Confession, the soul receives greater light from God, and an increased strength – special graces to struggle against the inclinations which have been confessed and to avoid the occasions of sin so as not to fall again into the same faults. He asks for and receives help in his daily struggle. *See how good God is, and how easily He forgives sins; He not only restores what has been lost with his forgiveness but grants unhoped for benefits.*[10] How often

---

[8] St John Paul II, *Letter to the Faithful in Rome*, 28 February 1979

[9] St Thomas, *Summa Theologiae*, III, q89, a2 c

[10] St Ambrose, *Commentary on the Gospel of St Luke*, 2,73

have we received the greatest graces after Confession, after having told Our Lord that we have behaved badly towards him! Jesus always returns good for evil, to encourage us to be faithful. The punishment we have earned by our sins – like that which the inhabitants of Nineveh had earned, and of which the reading of today's Mass[11] speaks – is blotted out by God when he sees our contrition and our works of penance and atonement.

The sincere Confession of our faults always leaves great peace and joy in the soul. The sadness caused by sin and a lack of correspondence with grace turns into joy. *The moments of a sincere Confession may well be amongst the sweetest, the most comforting and the most decisive moments in life.*[12]

Now you realise how much you have made Jesus suffer, and you are filled with sorrow. How easy it is to ask his pardon and weep for your past betrayals! Such is your longing for atonement that you cannot contain it in your breast!

Fine ... but don't forget that the spirit of penance consists mainly in the fulfilment of the duty of each moment, however costly it may be.[13]

---

[11] *First Reading*, John 3:1-10
[12] St Paul VI, *Address*, 27 February 1975
[13] St J. Escrivá, *The Way of the Cross*, Ninth Station, 5

9. PRAYER OF PETITION

9.1 Petition and thanksgiving, two ways of coming to know God. Two ways of praying which please God. Rectitude of intention when we make our request.

Ask, and it shall be given you; seek, and you shall find; knock, and it shall be opened to you. For everyone who asks receives, and he who seeks finds, and to him who knocks it shall be opened.[1]

We spend a good part of our lives asking for things from people who have more than we have, or who have greater knowledge than ourselves. We ask because we are in need. Often the act of asking is the only contact we have with some people. If we never asked for anything we would end up in a sort of vacuum in a kind of false, impoverished self-sufficiency. The most important part of our life and of our being involves our asking and our giving. When we ask for things we acknowledge that we are in need. When we give we become aware of the limitless riches God has placed in our hearts.

The same thing happens in our relationship with God. A large part of our relationship with him is shaped by our petition, the rest depending on our gratitude towards him. When we ask him for things we are admitting and confessing our radical insufficiency. Asking makes us humble; what's more, we give our God the opportunity of showing us that He is our Father. In this way we come to know of the love God has for us. *Or what man of you, if his son asks him for bread, will give him a stone? ... How much more will your Father who is in heaven give good*

---

[1] *Gospel of the Mass*, Matt 7:7-12

things to those who ask him![2]

We must not be motivated by selfishness, pride, avarice or envy when we make our request. If, for example, we are asking for help in an examination; if what we want is a material favour, the cure of an illness, etc, we must examine, in the presence of God, the true motives behind our petition. From the depths of our soul we will ask him if what we are requesting will help us to love him more and to carry out his will better. Then we will often realise straightaway how unimportant is the thing we are about to ask for, the desired boon that has seemed to us a matter of life or death; and we will consider that what we have so set our heart on is not so important after all. We will know how to bring our will into line with God's will, and then we can be sure that our petition lies in the right direction.

We can of course ask God to cure us quickly of an illness. At the same time we must ask that if this does not come about because He has different plans – plans which are mysterious and hidden from us, but which are those of a Father – He should give us the grace we need to bear that particular suffering patiently. We shall ask for the wisdom to draw out from that illness fruits which will be for the good of our soul and for that of the whole Church.

The first condition for any petition to be effective is that we conform our will to God's will. God sometimes wills or allows things and events to happen that we do not want and do not understand, but which in the end will be of great benefit to us and to others. Each time we make that act of identification of our will with God's we shall have taken an important step forward in the virtue of humility.

There are countless good things that God wants us to ask him for, so that he can give them to us, material and spiritual goods, all of them ordered to our salvation and

---

[2] Matt 7:9, 11

that of our neighbour. *Won't you agree with me that, if we do not receive what we ask God for, it is because we do not pray with faith, with a sufficiently pure heart, with enough trust, or because we do not persevere in prayer as we should? God has never denied and never will deny anything to those who ask for his graces in the right way.*[3]

9.2 Humility and perseverance in our petition.

We should always endeavour to pray with the confidence of children. Then we will seek to identify our will with that of our Father God: *Not my will, but thine be done,*[4] is what we should add after each petition. For we do not want to affirm and insist on going ahead with our own projects in life; rather do we want to carry out God's will above all. The Gospels present us with many cases of this childlike, humble and persevering prayer. St Matthew tells us about a woman's petition[5] which can be an example for all of us. Jesus came to *the district of Tyre and Sidon*, the land of the Gentiles. He was looking for a place for his apostles to rest, because he could not find such a place in the desert region of Bethsaida. He wanted to spend a few days alone with them.

As they are on their journey, a woman comes up to them with an urgent petition. In spite of her perseverance in her request, Jesus keeps silent. *But he did not answer her a word*, says the Evangelist.

The disciples ask him to attend to her request so that she will go away. She is creating a nuisance with her insistence. But Jesus is thinking differently. After a while he breaks his silence; filled with tenderness at seeing her humility, he gives ear to her plea. He explains God's plan

---

[3] St Jean Vianney, (The Curé d'Ars), *Sermon on Prayer*
[4] Luke 22:42
[5] Matt 15:21-28

of salvation to her. *I was sent only to the lost sheep of the house of Israel.* It has been God's plan from all eternity. With his life and death on the Cross He will redeem all men, but the spreading of the Good News is to start in Israel. Later the apostles down the ages are to carry it, *to the ends of the earth,*[6] to all men.

But this Canaanite woman, who almost certainly had little understanding of the divine plan, is not discouraged by his reply; *But she came and knelt before him, saying, 'Lord help me!'* She knows what she wants and she knows she can obtain it from Jesus.

Our Lord explains again to her with a parable, what he has just said: *It is not fair to take the children's bread and throw it to the dogs.* (The 'children' were the people of Israel,[7] and she did not belong to them. The hour of the Gentiles had not yet come.)

But the woman does not give up in her determination. Her faith increases and overflows. She *brings herself* into the parable with great humility, like one more character in it: *Yes, Lord, yet even the dogs eat the crumbs that fall from their master's table.*

Such great faith, such humility, such constancy, cause Our Lord to exclaim, *O woman, great is your faith.* And in a tone in which is mixed solemnity and condescension he adds, *Be it done for you as you desire.*

The Evangelist is careful to note: *And her daughter was healed instantly.* For this exceptional miracle, exceptional faith, humility and constancy were necessary.

Jesus always hears us, even when it seems that he keeps silent. Perhaps it is then that he listens to us most attentively. Perhaps he is urging us on – with this apparent silence – to make sure we have the right dispositions for

---

[6] Acts 1:8

[7] cf Ex 4; Is 1:2; Jer 31:20; Os 11:1; etc

the miracle to take place; so that we ask him with trust, with faith, and without becoming discouraged.

When we feel we must have something, our prayer will so often be the same: *Lord, help me.* What a wonderful little prayer for so many needs, particularly those to do with the soul, which are so urgent for us!

But it is not enough just to ask. We have to persevere, like that woman, without giving up, so that our constancy may reach out much further than our merits. *The prayer of the righteous man has great power in its effects.*[8] God has foreseen all the graces and help that we need, but He has also foreseen our prayer. *Ask and it shall be given to you ... knock and it shall be opened to you.* And now we recall all our personal needs and those of the people who live close to us. God does not abandon us.

9.3 God always listens to us. Seeking also the intercession of our mother Mary and our guardian angel.

If on some occasion He has not granted us what we have trustingly asked for, it is because it would not have been good for us; *look well on him who does not give you, when you ask for it, what would not be in your best interests.*[9] He is the one who does know what is good for us! The prayer we offered with such insistence will perhaps have benefitted us in some other way, at some time when we needed it more. Our Father God will have used it well! *He always gives us more than we ask him for.*[10] Always.

So that our petition is heard more promptly, we can ask other people close to God for their prayers. This is what the Centurion from Capharnaum did. He sent some elders of the Jews to beg him to come and cure his servant.

---

[8] Jas 5:17
[9] St Augustine, *Sermon 126*
[10] St Teresa, *The Way of Perfection*, 37

Those friends performed their task well. They went up to Jesus and asked him with great earnestness and fervour to go down with them: *He is worthy,* they said, *to have you do this for him.*[11] Our Lord listened to their pleas.

When we do ask for prayers it would be useful for us to remember that, *Next to the prayer of priests and dedicated virgins, the prayer most pleasing to God is the prayer of children and that of the sick.*[12]

We will ask our guardian angel as well to intercede for us and present our petition before God, because *The special angel of each person – even of the most insignificant within the Church – as he always contemplates the face of God who is in heaven and sees the divinity of our Creator, unites his prayer to ours and co-operates as much as he can to obtain what we request.*[13]

We have another way, which the Church has always shown us, to make sure our petitions reach the presence of God more promptly. That way is through the mediation of Mary, Mother of God and our Mother. We turn to her now and at all times. *Remember, O most gracious Virgin Mary, that never was it known, that anyone who fled to thy protection, implored thy help and sought thy intercession, was left unaided. Inspired with this confidence I fly to thee*[14] ...

---

[11] Luke 7:3-4
[12] St J. Escrivá, *The Way,* 98
[13] Origen, *Treatise on Prayer,* 10
[14] St Bernard's prayer, *Memorare*

10. LENT – A TIME FOR PENANCE

10.1 Sin is something personal. Sincerity required in order to recognise our errors and weaknesses. The need for penance.

We can lose the effectiveness of true penance, which is the turning of the heart towards God, if we fall into the temptation, rife both in ages gone by and in our day, of failing to admit that sin is something personal. In the first Reading of today's Mass, the prophet Ezechiel warns the Jews of his time not to forget the great lesson taught by the Exile. They had begun to see it as the inevitable outcome of the sins others had committed in times past. The prophet declares that punishment is a consequence of the actual sins of each individual. Through his words the Holy Spirit speaks to us about our responsibility as individuals, and, consequently, about personal penance and personal salvation. *Thus says the Lord: The soul that sins shall die. The son shall not suffer for the iniquity of the father, nor the father suffer for the iniquity of the son; the righteousness of the righteous shall be upon himself, and the wickedness of the wicked shall be upon himself.*[1]

God wants the sinner to turn away from sin and to live,[2] but he has to cooperate with God by his repentance and works of penance. As St John Paul II says, *Sin is always a personal act, since it is an act of freedom on the part of an individual person, and not properly of a group or community.*[3]

---

[1] Ez 18:21
[2] cf Ez 18:23
[3] St John Paul II, Apostolic Exhortation, *Reconciliatio et paenitentia,*

To unload man of this responsibility, *would be to deny the person's dignity and freedom, which are manifested – even though in a negative and disastrous way – also in this responsibility for sin committed. Hence there is nothing so personal and untransferable in each individual as merit for virtue or responsibility for sin.*[4]

This is why it is a grace from God when we do not fail to repent of our past sins and when we make no attempt to cover up our present sins, even though they happen to be no more than imperfections, failures to love ... Let us too be able to say, *For I know my transgressions, and my sin is ever before me.*[5] It is true that one day we confessed our sins and Our Lord said: *Go, and do not sin again.*[6] But sins leave their mark on the soul. *When the fault has been forgiven, the remains of the sin – dispositions caused by the previous acts – remain. Nevertheless they are weakened and diminished, in such a way as not to dominate man. Indeed they persist more as dispositions than as habits.*[7] There also exist sins and faults which go unnoticed because of our lack of a spirit of examination, a lack of refinement of conscience. They are like tough weeds the roots of which have remained in the soul and which we need to eradicate by means of penance, to prevent them from springing up again and bringing forth bitter fruits.

There are many reasons for doing penance during this Lent, and we must seek out specific little ways of practising it: mortification at meals – such as the abstinence commanded by the Church; living punctuality; keeping guard over our imagination ... And, also, with the advice of our spiritual director, of our confessor, other

2 December 1984, 16
[4] *ibid*
[5] Ps 50:3
[6] cf John 8:11
[7] St Thomas, *Summa Theologiae*, 3, q86, a 5 c

bigger mortifications, which can help us to purify our soul
~~and to make amends~~ for our own sins and for those of
others.

10.2 Personal sin affects other people. Expiation for the sins of the world. Penance and the Communion of Saints.

Sins leave a mark on the soul that must be expunged
through sorrow and a great deal of love. Furthermore,
although sin is always a personal offence against God, it
still affects other people. For good or for evil we constantly
influence the people around us, people in the Church and in
the world. We influence them not only by the good or bad
example that we give, but by the direct results of our
actions: *This is the other aspect of that solidarity which on
the religious level is developed in the profound and
magnificent mystery of the Communion of Saints, thanks to
which it has been possible to say that 'every soul that rises
above itself, raises up the world'. To this law of ascent
there unfortunately corresponds the law of descent.
Consequently one can speak of a communion of sin,
whereby a soul that lowers itself through sin drags down
with itself the Church and, in some way, the whole world.
In other words, there is no sin, not even the most intimate
and secret one, the most strictly individual one, that
exclusively concerns the person committing it. With greater
or less violence, with greater or less harm, every sin has
repercussions on the entire ecclesial body and the whole
human family.*[8]

God asks us to be a cause of joy and light for the
whole church. It will be a great help to us if we go about
our work and our other daily occupations with the
knowledge that we are helping other people, and indeed the

---

[8] St John Paul II, *loc cit*

whole Mystical Body of Christ, through our penance. In particular, we help those people whom Christ has placed close to us on the path of life and to whom we are especially united. *If you experience the Communion of Saints – if you live it – you will gladly be a man of penance. And you will realise that penance is 'gaudium, etsi laboriosum,' joy, in spite of its hardship. And you will feel yourself 'allied' to all the penitent souls that have been, that are, and that ever will be.*[9] *You will find it easier to do your duty if you think of how your brothers are helping you, and of the help you fail to give them if you are not faithful.*[10]

The penance that God asks of us as Christians in the midst of the world should be discreet and cheerful. We should try to let it pass unnoticed, but we should not fail to practise it in a large number of specific deeds. In any case it does not matter very much if sometimes it is observed. *If they have witnessed your faults and weaknesses, will it matter if they witness your penance?*[11] If other people have witnessed our bad temper or our lack of love or our laziness, or other sins of ours, it should not matter to us if they know and see that we are making reparation for those weaknesses.

10.3 Penance in everyday life, and in serving the people around us.

A Christian's life can be filled with this penance that God sees. It could be the offering up of an illness or just tiredness; giving way and surrendering our own opinion; putting everything into our work, which we do well and finish off for love of God, imposing order on our effects

---

[9] St J. Escrivá, *The Way*, 548
[10] ibid, 549
[11] ibid, 197

and personal things ...

The type of penance that is particularly pleasing to
God is that which brings together many little acts of charity
and which tends to make the way towards God easier and
more pleasant for others.

In the Gospel of today's Mass, Our Lord says, *So if
you are offering your gift at the altar, and there remember
that your brother has something against you, leave your
gift there before the altar and go: first be reconciled to
your brother, and then come and offer your gift.*[12] Our
offering to God must be accompanied by charity. Some of
the best penances are those which refer to love for other
people: knowing how, for example, to say 'sorry' when we
have offended someone; making the sacrifice involved in
forming somebody we are responsible for; exercising
patience; seeing the need to forgive promptly and
generously. In this respect St Leo the Great says: *Although
we should endeavour to sanctify our bodies at all times,
now especially, during the Lenten fasts, you should perfect
yourselves through the practice of a more active piety.
Give alms; this is very effective in helping us correct
ourselves of our faults; but also forgive offences – and stop
complaining about those who have done you some harm.*[13]
Let us forgive always with a smile on our lips. Let us speak
clearly, without hard feelings, when in conscience we think
we ought to speak. And let us leave everything in the hands
of our Father God, with a divine silence – 'Jesus was
silent' (Matt 26:63) – if we are confronted with personal
attacks, no matter how brutal and shameful they might
be.[14]

When we approach the altar of our God, let us make

---

[12] Matt 5:23-24
[13] St Leo the Great, *Sermon 45 on Lent*
[14] St J. Escrivá, *Christ is passing by*, 72

sure we are not weighed down even slightly by sentiments of resentment or enmity or hard feelings. On the contrary let us endeavour to carry with us many deeds of understanding for others, courtesy, generosity and mercy.

This is how we will follow Christ along the Way of the Cross that he has marked out for us, and which led him to be crucified: *Father, forgive them, for they do not know what they are doing* (Luke 23:24).

It is love that has brought Jesus to Calvary. And once on the Cross, all his gestures and all his words are of love, a love both calm and strong ...

And we, our soul rent with sorrow, say to Jesus in all sincerity: I am yours and I give my whole self to you; gladly do I nail myself to your Cross, ready to be on the highways of this world a soul dedicated to you, to your glory, to the work of Redemption, the co-redemption of the whole human race.[15]

Our Mother, Mary, will help us to discover many opportunities in our everyday occupations of giving ourselves generously to the people around us.

---

[15] *idem, The Way of the Cross*, Eleventh Station

11. CALLED TO HOLINESS

11.1 God calls everyone to holiness, without distinction of profession, age, social standing, etc, in each one's walk of life.

You, therefore, must be perfect, as your heavenly Father is perfect,[1] we read at the end of to-day's Gospel. During these forty days of preparation for Easter the Church reminds us in many different ways that God expects much more of us – He expects a serious determination on our part to struggle for holiness.

Be perfect ... Our Lord speaks not only to the Apostles, but to all those who really want to be his disciples. We are expressly told that *when Jesus finished these sayings, the crowds were astonished at his teaching.*[2] Those crowds of people who listened to him would have been made up of mothers, fishermen, craftsmen, doctors of the law, young people... They all understood him and *they were astonished,* because Our Lord speaks to each one of them. Our Lord has great demands to make on each one of them, according to his or her own circumstances. The Master calls them to holiness without any distinction of age, profession, race or social standing. There are *no* followers of Christ who do not have a Christian vocation, a personal call to sanctity. *He chose us in him before the foundation of the world, that we should be holy and blameless before him,*[3] as St Paul was to repeat to the first Christians of Ephesus. If we are to reach this goal we will need to make an effort that will last

---

[1] Matt 5:48
[2] Matt 7:28
[3] Eph 1:4

for the whole of our life on this earth. *Let the ... righteous still do right, and the holy still be holy.*[4]

By divine inspiration, this teaching about the universal call to holiness is, since 1928, one of the central points of the preaching of St Josemaría Escrivá, who has reminded us again in our own times, in all possible ways, that – through Baptism the Christian is called to the fulness of Christian life – to holiness.

The Second Vatican Council has declared anew this ancient evangelical doctrine for the whole Church: a Christian is called to sanctity in the very place that he occupies in society: *All the faithful, whatever their condition or state – though each in his own way – are called by the Lord to that perfection of sanctity by which the Father himself is perfect.*[5] All, that is, *each and every one of the faithful*.

God calls all Christians to find him where they are, as they carry out their occupations in the middle of the world. He calls them to carry out that very task with human perfection, and at the same time with supernatural outlook; they are called to offer it to God; to live charity with the people around them; to do mortification; to live in the presence of God.

To-day we can ask ourselves as we talk to Our Lord in our prayer whether we often thank him for calling us to follow him closely; we can ask whether we are corresponding to the graces we have received by struggling to acquire all the virtues in a straightforward but rigorous way; whether we are on our guard against all comfort-seeking, which kills off any desire for sanctity and leaves the soul submerged in spiritual mediocrity, and in a state of lukewarmness. It is not enough to want to be merely good;

---

[4] Rev 22:11
[5] Second Vatican Council, *Lumen gentium*, 11

we have to make a determined effort to be *saints*.

11.2 *Sanctify work. Sanctify oneself through work. Sanctify others through work.* If we are to transform society there is a need for people who are holy.

You, therefore, must be perfect, as your heavenly Father is perfect. We can and we must attain to sanctity, with an increasing love for God and for other people for God's sake, through everyday things which we do over and over again, with apparent monotony. *To love and serve God there is no need to do anything strange or extraordinary. Christ bids all men without exception to be perfect as his heavenly Father is perfect. Sanctity for the vast majority of men implies sanctifying their work, sanctifying themselves in it, and sanctifying others through it. Thus they can encounter God in the course of their daily lives.*[6]

In order to turn work, any honest task, into a means of sanctity, it needs to be humanly well done, for you cannot offer God *anything that has a blemish, for it will not be acceptable for you.*[7] Work which is done well presupposes care taken over those little duties that are part and parcel of every profession. We have to live in strict accordance with the virtue of justice towards other people and towards society as a whole. We need to put things right promptly if in some way we have offended those we work with or for. We must make a constant effort to improve the way we do our work. This is equally important for the businessman, the workman or the student. It holds too for the doctor or the mother carrying out the usual household tasks in her home.

Sanctity will lead us to turn our work into an

---

[6] *Conversations with Monsignor Escrivá*, 55
[7] cf Lev 22:20

opportunity and a place to converse with God. In order to
do this we should offer up our work when we begin it, and
then frequently renew this offering, turning all its attendant
circumstances to good use. Whilst we are doing our work
we will discover many opportunities for offering up little
mortifications which will enrich our interior life, and for
offering up the very work that we are doing. It will provide
occasions, too, for practising the human virtues
(industriousness, for example, strength of character,
cheerfulness) and the supernatural virtues (faith, hope,
charity, prudence ...).

Our work can and should be the means of bringing
many people to know Christ. Some professions have
immediate repercussions on social life, such as teaching or
occupations related to the media, or those that involve the
exercise of civic duties in a country ... There are no jobs
that have nothing to do with the doctrine of Jesus Christ:
even for very technical problems within a firm, or in the
way a mother runs her house, a variety of solutions will
offer themselves. These solutions may be radically
different one from another, depending on whether one has
a Christian or a pagan outlook on life. The person without
faith will always have an incomplete view of the world,
whilst the Christian's way of behaving will sometimes
clash with the current fashion, or will not be in accord with
the accepted practices of colleagues within the same
profession. These circumstances are particularly favourable
for making Christ known, if we give a natural and firm
example of Christian living. The more the world declares
that it has no need of God, the more desperately it needs
him. If, as Christians, we struggle to follow Christ
seriously, we will make him known.

*A secret, an open secret: these world crises are crises
of saints. God wants a handful of men 'of his own' in every
human activity. And then ... 'pax Christi in regno Christi'*

the peace of Christ in the kingdom of Christ![8] We have to sanctify our work. We must sanctify ourselves in it and sanctify others through it.

11.3 Sanctity and apostolate in the middle of the world. The example of the first Christians.

The first Christians overcame many obstacles because of their determination and their love for Christ, and they have pointed out the way for us. Their faithfulness to God's teaching was stronger than the materialistic and frequently hostile atmosphere that surrounded them. Finding themselves in the very heart of that society, they did not seek to isolate themselves in order to avoid possible contagion or to ensure their own survival. They were fully convinced that they were God's leaven and their silent but effective action finally transformed that whole shapeless mass. *Above all, they knew how to be present in a serene way in the world and understood why they should not despise its values or disdain earthly realities. 'We already in our time fill the world and every aspect of it,' proclaimed Tertullian, and this Christian presence which extended to all environments and was genuinely interested in all worthwhile and honest realities has succeeded in imbuing those environments and realities with a new spirit.*[9]

With God's help, the Christian will endeavour to turn each ordinary everyday thing into something noble and of great value: he will try to turn everything he touches, not into gold, as in the legend of King Midas, but rather into grace and glory. The Church reminds us of the urgency of being present in the middle of the world, so as to guide all human realities back to God. This will only be possible if

---

[8] St J. Escrivá, *The Way*, 301

[9] J. Orlandis, *The Christian in the World*

we remain united to Christ through prayer and the sacraments. As the branch is united to the vine, so must we be united to him each day.[10]

Heralds of the Gospel are needed, who are experts in humanity, who know the depths of the heart of man in to-day's world, who share his joys and hopes, his concern and his sadness, and who at the same time are contemplatives, people in love with God. For this, new saints are needed. We must beg God to increase the spirit of sanctity in the Church and to send us saints to evangelise to-day's world.[11] This same idea was expressed by the Extraordinary Synod of Bishops in 1985 when they made an overall summary of the situation in the Church: *To-day we badly need to beg God, assiduously, for saints.*[12]

The Christian has to be *another Christ*. This is the great strength of the testimony of Christianity. It was said of Jesus by way of summarising his whole life, that He went about on earth *doing good,*[13] and it ought to be possible to say the same of each one of us if we really strive to imitate him. *The divine Teacher and model of all perfection preached holiness of life (of which He is the author and maker) to each and every one of his disciples without distinction: 'You, therefore must be perfect' (Matt 5:48) ... It is therefore quite clear that all Christians in any state or walk of life whatsoever are called to the fulness of Christian life and to the perfection of love, and that by this holiness a more human manner of life is fostered also in earthly society.*[14]

---

[10] cf John 15:1-7
[11] St John Paul II, *Address*, 11 October 1985
[12] Extraordinary Synod of Bishops, *Final Statement*, II, A, 4
[13] Acts 10:38
[14] Second Vatican Council, *Lumen gentium*, 40

SECOND SUNDAY OF LENT

12. FROM TABOR TO CALVARY

12.1 The important thing is to be always with Jesus. He will help us to progress.

Of you my heart has spoken: Seek his face. It is your face, O Lord, that I seek; hide not your face from me, we pray in the Entrance Antiphon of today's Mass.[1] The Gospel tells us what happened on Mount Tabor. Shortly before, in Caesarea Philippi, Jesus had declared to his disciples that he was to undergo suffering in Jerusalem, that he was going to die at the hands of the chief priests, the elders and the Scribes. The Apostles had been saddened and dismayed by this announcement. Now Jesus took with him Peter, James and John, and he led them apart[2] to pray.[3] They are the three disciples who later will witness his agony in the Garden of Olives. *And as he was praying, the appearance of his countenance was altered, and his raiment became dazzling white.*[4] They saw him talking to Elijah and Moses who appeared in glory and spoke of his death which he was to accomplish at Jerusalem.[5]

For six days the Apostles had been weighed down by sorrow by the announcement made in Caesarea Philippi. It is Jesus' tenderness that enables them to contemplate his glorification. St Leo the Great says that, *The principal aim of the Transfiguration was to banish from the disciples'*

---

[1] *Entrance Antiphon*, Ps 26:8-9
[2] cf Mark 9:2
[3] cf Luke 9:28
[4] Luke 9:29
[5] cf Luke 9:31

souls the scandal of the Cross.[6] The disciples would never forget this *drop of honey* that Jesus gave them in the midst of his grief. Many years later, St Peter would recall these moments in all their clarity: *And the voice was borne to him by the Majestic Glory, 'This is my beloved Son, with whom I am well pleased,' we heard this voice borne from heaven, for we were with him on the holy mountain.*[7] The Apostle was to remember them for the rest of his life.

Jesus always behaves in this way towards his own. In the midst of the greatest sufferings he gives us the consolation we need to keep going forward.

The flash of God's glory transported the disciples into a state of immense happiness. It made St Peter exclaim: *Master, it is well that we are here, let us make three booths* ... Peter wants to make that situation last longer. But, as the Evangelist was to say later, *not knowing what he said,* because what is good, what really matters, is not to be in this place or that, but always to be with Jesus, wherever we are, and to be able to see him behind all the circumstances in which we may find ourselves. If we are with him, it is all the same whether we find ourselves surrounded by the greatest consolations in the world, or in a hospital bed suffering indescribable pain. The only thing that matters is that we always see Him and live in his presence. It is the only really good and important thing in this life and in the next. If we remain with Jesus, we will be very close to other people and we will be happy in whatever place or situation we may find ourselves. *Vultum tuum, Domine, requiram.* I want to see you and I will seek your face, Lord, in the ordinary circumstances of each day.

_____

Sermon 51, 3

12.2 Often foster the Hope of Heaven, especially in difficult moments.

St Bede, commenting on today's passage of the Gospel, says that Our Lord, *in a loving concession allowed Peter, James and John to enjoy for a very short time the contemplation of the happiness that lasts forever, so as to enable them to bear adversity with greater fortitude.*[8] There is no doubt that the memory of those moments beside Our Lord on the mountain helped those apostles through many difficult moments in their lives.

Man's existence is a journey towards Heaven, our dwelling place.[9] It is a journey which is, at times, harsh and laborious because we often have to go against the current of opinion and we will have to struggle against many enemies both inside and outside of ourselves. But God wants to strengthen us with the hope of Heaven, in a special way at the more difficult moments or when the weakness of our condition makes itself more felt. *At the time of temptation think of the Love that awaits you in heaven: foster the virtue of hope – this is not a lack of generosity.*[10] There, *all is repose, joy and delight; all serenity and calm, all peace, splendour and light. It is not a light such as we enjoy now, and which, compared with that light, is no more than a lamp placed beside the sun ... For there there is no night, or twilight, heat or cold, or any change in one's way of being, but a state such as can be understood only by those who are worthy to possess it. There, there is no old age, or sickness, or anything allied to corruption, because it is the place and the home of immortal glory.*

And above all this the everlasting presence and

---

[8] St Bede, *Commentary on St Mark*, 8; 30:1,3
[9] cf 2 Cor 5:2
[10] St J. Escrivá, *The Way*, 139

possession of Christ, of the angels ... everyone perpetually of like mind, without any fear of Satan or the snares of the devil or the threats of hell or of death.[11]

Our life in Heaven will definitively be exempt from any possible fear. We will not have the worry of losing what we have, and we will not want to have anything different. Then, truly, we will be able to say with St Peter, *Master, it is well that we are here!* The glimpse of glory that the Apostle had will be fully ours in eternal life. *We are going to think about what heaven will be like. 'Eye has not seen, nor ear heard, neither has it entered into the heart of man those things that God has prepared for those who love him.' Can you imagine what it will be like to arrive there and meet God, to see that beauty, that love which is poured out into our hearts, which satisfies without satiating? I ask myself many times each day, 'What will it be like when all the beauty, all the goodness, all the infinite wonder of God is poured into this poor earthenware vessel that I am, that all of us are?' Then I will understand those words of the Apostle, 'Eye has not seen, nor ear heard ...' It is worthwhile my children, it is worthwhile.*[12]

The thought of the glory that awaits us should act as a spur in our daily struggle. Nothing is of such value as gaining Heaven: *and always bearing in mind this determination to die rather than to fail to reach the end of the way, if God ever causes you to suffer from thirst as he guides you through this life, it is because he will give you drink in plenty in the next life, without any fear of it ever failing you.*[13]

---

[11] St John Chrysostom, *Epistle 1 to Theodore*, 11
[12] St J. Escrivá, quoted in *Newsletter No.1* for the Cause of his beatification
[13] St Teresa, *The Way of Perfection*, 20, 2

12.3 The Lord does not distance himself from us. Living in this presence.

Immediately a cloud overshadowed them.[14] It reminds us of that other cloud that accompanies the presence of God in the Old Testament: *Then the cloud covered the tent of meeting, and the glory of the Lord filled the tabernacle.*[15] It was the sign that was the guarantee of divine intervention. *And the Lord said to Moses, 'Lo, I am coming to you in a thick cloud, that the people may hear when I speak with you, and may also believe you forever.'*[16] Now on Mount Tabor that cloud overshadows Christ, and the powerful voice of God the Father is heard coming from it: *This is my Son, my Chosen, listen to him.*

And God the Father speaks through Jesus Christ to all men of all ages. His voice is heard in every age, in a particular way through the teaching of the Church, who, *continually seeks ways of bringing this mystery of her Master and Lord to humanity – to the peoples, the nations, the succeeding generations, and every individual human being.*[17]

And when they lifted up their eyes, they saw no one but Jesus only.[18] Elijah and Moses were no longer there. They only see Our Lord. They see the Jesus they know, who is sometimes hungry, sometimes tired, who tries to make himself understood. They see Jesus without any special manifestations of glory. It was normal for the Apostles to see Our Lord like that: what was exceptional was to see him transfigured.

This is the Jesus we have to find in our ordinary life, in the midst of our work, out in the street, in the people around us, in our prayer. We have to find Him when he forgives us

---

[14] cf Mark 9:7
[15] Ex 40:34-35
[16] Ex 19:9
[17] St John Paul II, Encyclical, *Redemptor hominis*, 7
[18] Matt 17:8

in the Sacrament of Penance and, above all, in the Holy Eucharist where he is truly, really and substantially present. Normally he does not show himself to us with any special manifestations. Rather, *we have to learn to find Our Lord in what is ordinary*, every day, and we must flee from the temptation of ever wanting anything extraordinary.

We must never forget that that Jesus whom those three privileged men were with on Mount Tabor, is the same Jesus who is daily at our side. *When God grants you the grace of feeling his presence, and desires that you should speak to him as your most beloved friend, tell him about your feelings with all freedom and confidence. 'She hastens to make herself known to those who desire her.' (Wis 6:14) Without waiting for you to come close to him, he hastens towards you when you seek his love, and he presents himself to you, granting you the graces and remedies that you need. He only waits for one word from you in order to show you that he is beside you and wants to listen to you and console you. 'His ears are toward their cry' (Ps 33:16)* ...

Other friends, those who are friends in the world, have times that they spend talking together and other times when they are separated, but between God and yourselves, if you want, there need never be any time of separation.[19]

Would our lives not be different this Lent if we were to make this presence of God a reality in the habitual things of each day; if we tried to say more ejaculatory prayers, more acts of love and reparation, more spiritual communions? *Here is a point for your daily examination. Have I allowed an hour to pass, without talking with my Father God? Have I talked to him with the love of a Son? You can!*[20]

---

[19] St Alphonsus Liguori, *How to converse continually and familiarly with God*

[20] St J. Escrivá, *Furrow*, 657

SECOND WEEK OF LENT – MONDAY

13. CONSCIENCE THE LIGHT OF THE SOUL

13.1 Conscience throws light on all of one's life. It can be deformed and hardened.

O that to-day you would hearken to his voice! Harden not your hearts![1] The liturgy repeats this to us every day of this liturgical period. And each day, in very different ways, God speaks to the heart of each one of us.

Our prayer, during Lent, aims at awakening consciences, at making them sensitive to God's voice. 'Harden not your hearts,' the Psalmist says. In fact, the numbing of consciences, their indifference to good and evil, their deviations, are a great threat for man. Indirectly, they are also a great threat for society, because in the last analysis the level of morality of society depends on the human conscience.[2] Conscience is the light of the soul, of what is deepest in man's being; and if this light is put out, man is thrown into darkness and can commit the most dastardly abuses against himself and against others.

Your eye is the lamp of your body,[3] says the Lord. Conscience is the lamp of the soul, and if it is well formed it lights up the way, a way which leads to God, and man can make progress because of it. Although he may weaken and fall, he can raise himself and continue onward. But one who has allowed this interior sensitivity 'to drowse' or 'to die' to the things of God, is now without signposts and is lost. It is one of the great misfortunes in this life which can befall a soul: *Woe to those who call evil good and good evil, who put*

---

[1] *Divine Office*, Ps 94:8
[2] St John Paul II, *Angelus*, 15 March 1981
[3] Luke 11:34

darkness for light and light for darkness, who put bitter for sweet and sweet for bitter![4] proclaims the prophet Isaiah.

Jesus compares the function of conscience in our life to that of the eye. *When your eye is sound, your whole body is full of light; but when it is not sound, your body is full of darkness. Therefore be careful lest the light in you be darkness.*[5] When the eye is healthy, things are seen as they are, undistorted. A sick eye either does not see or it distorts reality; it deceives its own subject and he can come to think that events and people are in fact as his defective vision views them. When one makes a mistake in ordinary life, having falsely interpreted some facts, it can lead to problems and difficulties which are, at times, of little importance. But when the error refers to matters regarding eternal life, its consequences have no limit.

Conscience can be deformed through our not having used the means to get to know the Faith, or through an ill will dominated by pride, sensuality, laziness ... When Our Lord complains that the Jews were not receiving his message, He particularly notes the deliberate nature of their decision – they did not want to believe[6] – and He in no way accepted that the cause lay in a difficulty outside the will: this is a consequence of their refusal, freely chosen. *Why do you not understand what I say? It is because you cannot bear to hear my word.*[7] Passions and a lack of sincerity with oneself can come to force the intellect to think in a way more easily adapted to one's way of life, or to some defects or bad habits one does not want to give up. In such a case there is no good will; the heart is hardened, and conscience begins to drowse, for it no longer points in the

---

[4] Is 5:20-21
[5] Luke 11:34-35
[6] cf Luke 13:34; John 10:38
[7] John 8:43

right direction which would lead it to God. It is now like a broken compass which not only disorientates its owner but can also affect others. *The man whose heart is hardened and whose conscience is degenerate, even if he is in full possession of his strength and physical capacities, is sick spiritually, and everything must be done to restore him to health of soul.*[8]

Lent is a good time to ask the Lord to help us form our consciences really well, and for us to examine ourselves to see whether we are being radically sincere with ourselves, with God and with those people who in his name have the mission of advising us.

13.2 A well-formed conscience. Doctrine and life. Example.

The light which is in us does not spring up from within ourselves, from our subjectivity, but from Jesus Christ. *I am the light of the world,* He has told us, *he who follows me will not walk in darkness.*[9] His light brightens our consciences; but even more, it can turn us ourselves into a light that will illuminate the lives of others: *you are the light of the world.*[10] The Lord puts us Christians in the world so that, with the light of Christ, we can point the way to others. We will do so by word, but especially through our behaviour as regards professional, family and social obligations. We should therefore get to know very well the limits beyond which we cannot go with respect to our honour and Christ's morality: we should become aware of the good we can do and are doing, know clearly how an honest professional and a good Christian cannot permit himself to act, and to avoid any such action; if we have made a mistake we should know how necessary it is to

---

[8] St John Paul II, *ibid*
[9] John 8:12
[10] Matt 5:14

seek pardon, to make amends for it, and reparation also, if such is needed. The mother of a family, who has the running of her home as her sanctifying task, ought to ask herself in her prayer if she is exemplary in fulfilling her obligations towards God, if she lives sobriety, if she is managing to dominate any tendency to ill-humour, if she dedicates the necessary time to her children and to the home ... The businessman ought frequently to consider whether he is using all the means necessary to get to know the social doctrine of the Church, whether he makes the effort to put this teaching into effect in his business dealings, whether he pays just wages ...

Christian life is enriched when the teachings Our Lord conveys to us through his Church are put into effect in daily life. Doctrine then assumes all its inherent power. Doctrine and life are realities for a well-formed conscience. When, through a more or less culpable ignorance the doctrine is not known, or when although known it is not put into practice, Christian living becomes impossible, and real advance along the road to sanctity is out of the question.

We all need to form for ourselves a true and refined conscience, which readily listens to the voice of God in everyday matters. Doctrine (as regards the knowledge of moral and social teaching) and life (the effort to practise the Christian virtues) are two essential requisites for educating one's conscience. On occasion, faced with the 'grey areas', that are not unfamiliar in our professional work, we have to consider the situation in the presence of God: whenever necessary we should insist on receiving the best and most opportune advice from those who can clarify such matters for our conscience, and then put into practice the decisions we have made on our own responsibility.

We learn to be sincere with ourselves in the general and particular examination of conscience, to call our errors, weaknesses and faults against generosity by their real names, without masking them with false justifications or disregarding them as non-issues. A conscience which does not recognise its faults leaves man at the mercy of his own caprice.

13.3 Being a light for others. Responsibility.

Every traveller who is serious about wanting to reach his destination must know the route clearly. He is grateful for clear sign-posting, although these pointers may, at times, indicate a narrow path through a more difficult terrain; he will steer well clear of routes which although seeming to be quicker or less arduous lead nowhere – or to a precipice. We ought to have a great desire to form our conscience well, for it is the light that enables us to distinguish good from evil; it enables us to seek forgiveness and find our way back to the true path if we have lost sight of it. The Church offers us the means, but she does not exempt us from the effort required to use these means responsibly.

In our prayer to-day we can ask ourselves: Do I dedicate sufficient time to my religious formation, or do I allow myself to become absorbed by the other things that fill each day? Do I have a plan for reading, reviewed in spiritual guidance, which will help me make progress in doctrinal formation according to my age and background? Am I faithful to the Magisterium of the Church, knowing that there I find the light of truth rather than the contradictory opinions I often come across in matters of faith, social teaching etc? Do I try to get to know the teachings of the Popes and to make them known? Do I respect them with piety and docility? Do I frequently rectify my intention, offering up all my actions to God, taking into account our tendency to seek applause, recognition and praise for what we do? Am I constantly aware that this is often where the deformation of one's conscience begins?

We need light and clarity, both for ourselves and for those

around us. This is our big responsibility. The Christian has been placed by God as a lamp to light up, for others, the way towards God. We ought to educate ourselves *to face the rush of people who are going to press upon us with a specific and urgent question: 'Well then, what must I do?'*[11] Children, relatives, colleagues, friends – they all look to our behaviour, and we have the responsibility of leading them to God. And so that the blind person's guide is not himself also blind,[12] it is not enough to have second-hand knowledge or mere hearsay. To lead our friends and relatives to God, a vague and superficial knowledge of the route is not enough: we need to have walked it ourselves ... It is essential for us to have closer dealings with Our Lord, to get to know his doctrine better, to struggle against our own specific defects ... In a word, it means making progress ourselves in interior life and example. *Whoever has the mission of proclaiming great things,* says St Gregory the Great, *is also under obligation to practise them.*[13] And only if we personally put things into practice will we be effective when we come to talk about them.

When Jesus Christ wanted to teach his disciples how to acquire a spirit of service to one another, He wrapped a towel around himself and washed their feet.[14] This is what we have to do: to make Christ known, we ourselves have to be exemplary in our daily obligations, putting into practice the doctrine of Our Lord.

---

[11] St J. Escrivá, *Furrow*, 221
[12] cf Matt 15:14
[13] St Gregory the Great, *Pastoral Care*, 2,3
[14] cf John 13:15

14. HUMILITY & A SPIRIT OF SERVICE

14.1 Without humility we cannot serve others.

In the Gospel of today's Mass, Our Lord speaks of harsh realities, of those Scribes and Pharisees who *occupy the chair of Moses*. They are concerned only about themselves, having little regard for the people entrusted to them, those simple folk *harassed and helpless, like sheep without a shepherd.*[1] They are more interested in securing the places of honour at banquets, in their badges of rank, their phylacteries and their tassels, in being noticed and greeted in the market places and being called Rabbi.[2] Meant to be *salt and light* for the people of Israel, they have left their people without either salt or light. They themselves are in darkness, having preferred self-glorification to the glory of God. *Everything they do is done to attract attention.* Personal pride and the vainglorious search for prominence has led them to lose the humility and the spirit of service which should characterize those who wish to follow the Lord.

Christ warned his disciples: *You must not allow yourselves to be called Rabbi ... the greatest among you must be your servant.*[3] And He himself has repeatedly pointed out the way to us: *For which is the greater, the one who sits at table or the one who serves? Is it not the one who sits at table? But I am among you as one who serves.*[4]

Without humility and a spirit of service there can be

---

[1] Matt 9:36
[2] cf Matt 23:1-12
[3] cf Matt 23:8-11
[4] Luke 22:27

no effectiveness and it is quite impossible to practise charity. Without humility there is no holiness, for Jesus does not want conceited self-centred friends in his service: *the instruments of God are always humble.*[5]

In the apostolate and in the little acts of service we can offer others, there is no room for complacency or for arrogance, since it is the Lord who really does the work. When we serve, our capability bears no relationship to the supernatural fruits we seek. Without grace, one's best efforts are in vain: *no one can say 'Jesus is Lord' except by the Holy Spirit.*[6] Grace is the one thing that can raise the power of our human talents so as to achieve by them what would otherwise have been beyond our possibilities. *God opposes the proud, but gives grace to the humble.*[7]

When we struggle to attain this virtue we become effective and strong. *Humility will spur us on to carry out great tasks, but only on condition that we never lose sight of our inadequacy, and that we are all convinced, and more so each day, of our own helplessness.*[8] We ought to be constantly vigilant, because the worst kind of ambition is to strive for one's own exaltation, as the Scribes and Pharisees did – the ambition of seeking ourselves and our enhanced reputations in the things we do or plan to carry out. *Pride attacks on all flanks and its victim finds it all around.*[9]

If we are not humble we can make ourselves unfit for helping those around us, for pride infects everything. Where you have a proud person nothing goes right; nobody is treated properly: his family, his friends, his colleagues ... He expects and demands special treatment for himself because he considers himself different; one has to take care

---

[5] St John Chrysostom, *Homilies on St Matthew*, 15
[6] 1 Cor 12:3
[7] Jas 4:6
[8] St J. Escrivá, *Friends of God*, 106
[9] Cassian, *Institutions*, 11:3

to avoid hurting his very vulnerable sensibilities. The dogmatic tone of his utterances, his ironic or sarcastic contributions to any discussion – for he does not mind anyone else being shown up in a poor light if he himself is going to come out well – his tendency to cut short conversations which arise quite naturally, etc: all these are signs of something deep seated: it is the all-consuming egoism that takes possession of the personality when the limited horizons of one's life are centred on oneself.

These moments of prayer can be of use for us to examine, in the presence of God, the way we treat others, and to determine whether our behaviour towards them is imbued with a spirit of service.

14.2 Imitating the service given by Jesus, the supreme example of humility and dedication to others.

Jesus is the supreme example of humility and dedication to others. No one has ever had a greater dignity than He, and no one has served other men so diligently: *I am in your midst as one who serves*. This continues to be his approach towards each one of us. He is always ready to serve us, to help us, to lift us up from our falls. Do we make a point of serving others, in the family, at work, through those 'anonymous' favours for which in all probability we will never be thanked? Today, through the prophet Isaiah's lips. the Lord tells us: *Discite benefacere*.[10] Learn to do good ... and we will only learn if we concentrate on Jesus, our Model, and if we meditate frequently on his example and his teachings.

I have given you an example – Our Lord tells the disciples after he has washed their feet – *that you also should do to others as I have done to you.*[11] He gives us the

[10] Is 1:17
[11] John 13:15

best possible lesson for us to understand that if we are not humble, if we are not willing to serve, we will be completely unable to follow the Master. Our Lord invites us to follow him and to imitate him: He gives us a rule, which is simple but precise, and which will enable us to practise charity with humility and a spirit of sacrifice: *Whatever you wish that men would do to you, do so to them.*[12] The experience of what pleases or displeases me, or of what helps or hurts me, is a good measure of the things I ought to do or avoid in my relationships with others.

All of us would like a word of encouragement when things have not gone well, and would appreciate understanding from others when, once again, in spite of our best intentions we have made a mistake. We prefer others to have more regard to our positive deeds than to our shortcomings; we are glad to have a cordial atmosphere at our place of work or on coming home. We like to be stretched at work, but to be asked, nevertheless, with courtesy and in a kindly fashion to do what is required of us; we don't like anyone to speak badly of us behind our backs; and if someone does, we'd be grateful to have another defend us in our absence; we would like others to be concerned about us when we are ill; we would not be averse to receiving fraternal corrections when we do something badly, instead of having our blunder gossiped about with somebody else; we would be happy to know that our friends pray for us ... These are things which, with humility and a spirit of service, we have to do for others: *Discite benefacere.* If we behave in this way, the prophet Isaiah continues, *though your sins are like scarlet, they shall be as white as snow; though they are as red as crimson, they shall be like wool.*[13]

---

[12] Matt 7:12
[13] Is 1:18

14.3 We have to serve those amongst whom the Lord has placed us, learning in this matter from Our Lady.

The greatest among you must be your servant,[14] says the Lord. Thus we have to leave our egoism to one side and discover in ourselves those signs of charity which make others happy. If we do not make the daily effort to forget ourselves, we will pass by those who are near us over and over again without realising that they could do with a word of encouragement, that they need their work to be appreciated, and lack perhaps only a word of encouragement from us for them to be better.

Egoism blinds; it narrows our horizons when we look at others; humility constantly opens up a way to charity in practical details and suggests specific ways of serving. *This joyful spirit,* of openness to the others, *and the spirit of availability,* is capable of transforming any environment. Charity warms up as water in a rock fissure. *Love draws out love,*[15] says St Teresa; and St John of the Cross advises: *where there is no love, put love, and you will draw out love.*[16]

But we were gentle among you, like a nurse taking care of her children. So, being affectionately desirous of you, we were ready to share with you not only the Gospel of God but also our own selves,[17] exclaims St Paul to the Christians of Thessalonica. If we imitate him, our actions will bear similar fruit.

We have to practise this spirit of Christ with those nearest to us, within the family: *The husband ought not to seek only his own interests, but also those of his wife; and she, those of her husband. Parents should look after the*

---

[14] Matt 23:11

[15] St Teresa, *Life*, 22, 14

[16] St John of the Cross, *Letter to María de la Encarnación*

[17] 1 Thess 2:7-8

*interests of their children, and these in turn look after the
interests of their parents. The family is the only community
in which man 'is loved for himself', for what he 'is' and not
for what he 'has' ... Respect for this fundamental norm
explains, as the Apostle himself teaches, why nothing
should be done out of a spirit of rivalry or for vainglory,
but rather through humility, because of love. And this love,
which is opened up to others, makes members of the family
true servants of 'the domestic church', where all desire the
good and the happiness of each one; where each and every
one gives life to this love with an urgent search for that
good and that happiness.*[18]

If you act in this way, you will not be inclined to see,
as so often happens, *the speck in your brother's eye*
without seeing *the log in your own.*[19] The tiniest imperfections of others are magnified in our perspective and
our own graver faults tend to be minimised and all too
easily justified.

Humility, on the other hand, makes us recognise our
own weaknesses and defects. We are then in a position to
be understanding towards the shortcomings of other people
and to be able to extend to them a helping hand. We are
then also able to love them and to accept them with whatever defects they may have.

The Blessed Virgin, *handmaid of the Lord*, will teach
us to understand that to serve others is one of the ways of
finding joy in this life and one of the shortest routes to
Jesus.

---

[18] St John Paul II, *Homily of the Mass for families*, 2 November 1982
[19] Matt 7:3-5

15. TO DRINK OF THE LORD'S CHALICE

15.1 Identifying all our will with that of the Lord. Co-redeeming with him.

While Jesus was on his way to Jerusalem He spoke for the third time to his disciples about his passion and death, and of his glorious resurrection. At one of the places where they stopped on the journey He was approached by one of the group accompanying him, a woman, the mother of James and John. She sought to gain a favour for her sons. *Kneeling before him she asked him for something*, narrates St Matthew. She tells Jesus quite simply: *Command that these two sons of mine may sit one at your right hand and one at your left, in your kingdom.*[1] Our Lord replied immediately: *You do not know what you are asking. Are you able to drink the cup I am to drink? They said to him: 'We are able.'*[2]

The two brothers must not have grasped the reality of the situation, for a little earlier, as St Luke tells us, when Jesus spoke of his passion *they understood none of these things; this saying was hid from them, and they did not grasp what was said.*[3]

The language of the Cross is not easy to understand. Nevertheless, they were disposed, albeit with a general intention, to go along with whatever Jesus wanted. They had not placed any limits on how far they were willing to follow Our Lord; nor have we. And so, when we make petition for something, when we pray, we ought to be

---

[1] Matt 20:21-22
[2] Matt 20:22
[3] Luke 18:34

disposed towards accepting, above all, the Will of God;
even when it does not accord or run parallel with our
wishes, *His Majesty knows best what is suitable for us; it is
not for us to advise him what to give us, for He can rightly
reply that we know not what we ask.*[4] He wants us to ask
him for what we need and what we want, but above all he
wants us to conform our will to his. He will always give us
what is best.

James and John ask for a place of honour in the new
kingdom, and Jesus talks to them about redemption. He
asks them if they are ready to suffer with him. He uses the
familiar Hebrew image of a chalice, which symbolises the
will of God for an individual.[5] The Lord's is a bitter
chalice, which will turn to *a chalice of blessings,*[6] for all
men.

Drinking the cup of another was a sign of deep
friendship and of readiness to share a common destiny. It is
to this intimate relationship that Our Lord invites those
who wish to follow him. To take part in the glorious
resurrection one has to share the Cross with him. Are you
ready to suffer with me? Are you able to drink of my
chalice with me? *We can*, replied the two Apostles.

James died a few years later, beheaded on the orders of
Herod Agrippa.[7] St John underwent innumerable sufferings
and persecutions for love of his Lord. *He has called us too,
and asks us as he asked James and John: 'Are you ready to
drink the cup' – that cup which means giving yourself fully
to the will of the Father – 'which I am going to drink?'
'Possumus.' Yes! We are ready! (Matt 20:20-22) is the
reply of the sons of thunder. Are you and I really ready to*

---

[4] St Teresa, *The Interior Castle*, 2, 8
[5] cf Ps 16:5
[6] Is 51:17-22
[7] cf Acts 12:2

carry out, in everything, the will of our Father God? Have we given Our Lord our whole heart, or are we attached to our own self and to our own interests and comfort and self-love? Is there anything in our lives which is out of keeping with our Christianity, something which makes us unwilling to mend our ways? Today we are given a chance to see things straight.[8]

15.2 Offering up pain and voluntary mortification. A spirit of penance in ordinary life. Some examples of mortification.

When that woman made her motherly request, Jesus asked his disciples: *'Can you drink of the chalice ...?'* The Lord knew that they could imitate his passion; but nonetheless He asked them, so that for us too it is made clear that no one can reign with Christ who has not previously imitated his Passion. For highly-valued things are not obtained except at a high price.[9] Christian life cannot exist without sacrifice. This is its price. *The Lord has saved us with his Cross; with his death he has turned to give us hope, the right to life. We cannot follow Christ if we do not recognise him as our Saviour, if we do not honour him in the mystery of the Cross ... The Lord turned suffering into a means of redemption. With his pain, He has redeemed us, provided we never refuse to unite our sorrow to his, and to make it, together with his, into a means of redemption.*[10]

From now on, sorrow will always be able to associate itself with the Lord's chalice, to unite itself to his passion, for the redemption of all mankind. What previously was meaningless now makes sense in Christ. We too can say:

---

[8] St J. Escrivá, *Christ is passing by*, 15
[9] St John Chrysostom, *Homilies on St Matthew*, 35
[10] St Paul VI, *Address*, 24 February 1967

Therefore I endure everything for the sake of the elect, that they also may obtain the salvation which in Christ Jesus goes with eternal glory.[11] *By my pride in you which I have in Christ Jesus Our Lord, I die every day.*[12]

Mortification and a life of penance, to which Lent beckons us, have co-redemption as a principal reason – *a participation in the sufferings of Christ,*[13] taking part in the very chalice of the Lord. We are the first beneficiaries; but the supernatural effectiveness of our sorrow offered up and of our voluntary mortification reaches out to the whole church; and even to the entire world. This voluntary mortification is a means of purification and atonement. It is necessary if we are to be able to converse with the Lord in prayer, and it is indispensable for apostolic activity, for *action is worth nothing without prayer: prayer grows in value with sacrifice.*[14]

We practise a spirit of penance and of sacrifice in our daily lives, in the ordinary events of the day, without having to wait for extraordinary occasions. *Penance is fulfilling exactly the timetable you have fixed for yourself, even though your body resists or your mind tries to avoid it by dreaming up useless fantasies. Penance is getting up on time and also not leaving for later, without any real reason, that particular job that you find harder or most difficult to do.*

Penance is knowing how to reconcile your duties to God, to others and to yourself, by making demands on yourself so that you find enough time for each of your tasks. You are practising penance when you lovingly keep to your schedule of prayer, despite feeling worn out,

---

[11] 2 Tim 2:1
[12] 1 Cor 15:31
[13] St Paul VI, *Paenitemini*, 17 February 1966
[14] St J. Escrivá, *The Way*, 81

listless or cold.

Penance means being very charitable at all times towards those around you, starting with the members of your own family. It is to be full of tenderness and kindness towards the suffering, the sick and the infirm. It is to give patient answers to people who are boring and annoying. It means interrupting our work or changing our plans, when circumstances make this necessary, above all when the just and rightful needs of others are involved.

Penance consists in putting up good-humouredly with the thousand and one little pinpricks of each day; in not abandoning your job, although you have momentarily lost the enthusiasm with which you started it; in eating gladly whatever is served, without being fussy.

For parents and, in general, for those whose work involves supervision or teaching, penance is to correct whenever it is necessary. This should be done bearing in mind the type of fault committed and the situation of the person who needs to be so helped, not letting oneself be swayed by subjective viewpoints, which are often cowardly and sentimental.

A spirit of penance keeps us from becoming too attached to the vast imaginative blueprints we have made for our future projects, where we have already foreseen our master strokes and brilliant successes. What joy we give to God when we are happy to lay aside our third-rate painting efforts and let him put in the features and colours of his choice![15]

15.3 Mortifications which are born out of service to others.

The other disciples who had heard Jesus' conversation with the two brothers *were indignant.* Our Lord then told

---

[15] *idem, Friends of God, 138*

them: *You know that the rulers of the Gentiles lord it over them, and their great men exercise authority over them. It shall not be so among you; but whoever would be great among you must be your servant, and whoever would be first among you must be your slave, even as the Son of Man came not to be served but to serve, and to give his life as a ransom for many.*[16]

Christ's service to humanity is directed towards salvation. Our approach has to be one of service to God and to our neighbours, especially in matters referring to salvation, but also on the various occasions which arise in the course of each day. It has to mean serving the person one does not get on well with, expecting nothing in return. This is the best way of giving one's life for others, in an effective and hidden way which is hardly noticed, and which enables us to tackle that egoism of ours which deprives us of joy.

Most professions are 'a direct service': those, for instance, of housewives, sales-people, teachers, au pairs; and all honest professions, although perhaps less obviously and directly, are nevertheless a 'service'. May we not lose this view of the jobs we do so that we will be effectively helped to sanctify ourselves through work.

To serve others requires mortification, a continuing realisation of the presence of God, and a forgetting of self. On occasion, this spirit of sacrifice will clash with the mentality of those who think only of themselves. For us Christians it is *our pride* and our dignity. For in this way we are imitating Christ, and in thus serving willingly, out of love, many human and supernatural virtues are brought into play. *This dignity is expressed in readiness to serve, in keeping with the example of Christ, who 'came not to be served but to serve'. If in the light of this attitude of Christ,*

---

[16] Matt 20:24-28

'being a king' is truly possible only by 'being a servant', then 'being a servant' also demands so much spiritual maturity that it must really be described as 'being a king'. In order to be able to serve others worthily and effectively, we must be able to master ourselves, in order to be able to possess the virtues that make this mastery possible.[17]

We are delighted to serve and to help others at our side, although we may receive no remuneration for our service. To serve, beside Christ and for Christ, is to reign with him. Our Mother Mary, who served her Son and St Joseph, will help us give ourselves without measure, unstintingly.

---

[17] St John Paul II, *Redemptor hominis*, 21

SECOND WEEK OF LENT – THURSDAY

16. DETACHMENT

16.1 Detachment from things gives us the freedom we need to follow Christ. Goods are only the means.

In this period of Lent the Church in this regard calls out to us frequently so that we may disengage ourselves from the things of the earth, and thus fill our hearts with God. In today's First Reading, the prophet Jeremiah gives his message: *A blessing on the man who puts his trust in the Lord, and has the Lord for his hope. He is like a tree by the waterside that thrusts its roots to the stream: when the heat comes it feels no alarm; its foliage stays green; it has no worries in a year of drought and never ceases to bear fruit.*[1] The Lord looks after a soul which has placed its heart in him.

He who puts his confidence in earthly concerns, *whose heart turns from the Lord*, is condemned to be barren and ineffective with respect to what really matters. *He is like dry scrub in the wasteland; if good comes, he has no eyes for it; he settles in the parched places of the wilderness, a salt land, uninhabited.*[2]

The Lord wants us to be concerned about the things of earth and to love them in the right way: *fill the earth – and have dominion over every living thing.*[3] But one who in a *disorderly* fashion loves the things of the earth leaves no room in his soul for the love of God. Loving our Lord and such *attachment* are incompatible. *You cannot serve God*

---

[1] Jer 17:7-8
[2] Jer 17:6
[3] Gen 1:28

and mammon.[4] Things can become transformed into fetters which prevent one reaching out to Christ. And if we don't get to him, what is the purpose of our lives? *For us to reach God, Christ is the Way; but Christ is on the Cross, and to climb up to the Cross we must have our hearts free, not tied to earthly things.*[5] He led by example. He used the goods of this earth with perfect dominion over them and in the fullest freedom. *He became poor, so that by his poverty you might become rich.*[6]

For us to be able to follow him He has given us a necessary condition: *Whoever of you does not renounce all that he has cannot be my disciple.*[7] This is no less a necessity for those who wish to follow him in the midst of the world. Not renouncing his worldly possessions left the rich young man sad; he had many of them,[8] and he was attached to them. How much did that young man lose that day! He had had a fistful of things which would soon slip through his fingers.

Material goods are good since they come from God. They have been put by God at man's disposal since creation began, for his growth and development in society. We are administrators of these goods for a time, for only a short term. Everything should lead us to love God – Creator and Father – and the things He has made and given us. If we become too fond of *creatures*, and if we do not make effective acts of detachment from them, if they are not used to do good, they are converted into evil. Excluded from heaven are those who make riches the centre of their lives; St Paul calls avarice idolatry.[9]

---

[4] Matt 6:24
[5] St J. Escrivá, *The Way of the Cross*, Tenth Station
[6] 2 Cor 8:9
[7] Luke 14:33
[8] Mark 10:22
[9] Col 3:5

True interior life and a loving relationship with God are excluded by anyone who does not break off the ties that bind him to things, to people and to his own self in a disordered way – no matter how casual and tenuous such bonds may seem. *It makes little difference,* says St John of the Cross, *whether a bird is tied by a thin thread or by a cord. For even if tied by thread, the bird will be prevented from taking off just as surely as if it were tied by cord – that is, it will be impeded from flight as long as it does not break the thread. Admittedly, the thread is easier to snap, but no matter how easily this may be done, the bird will not fly away before first doing so.*[10]

Detachment increases our capacity for loving God, people and all the noble things of this life.

16.2 Detachment and generosity. Some examples.

In the Gospel of today's Mass we are presented with someone who makes poor use of his goods. *There was a rich man who used to dress in purple and fine linen and feast magnificently every day. And at his gate there lay a poor man called Lazarus, covered with sores, who longed to fill himself with the scraps that fell from the rich man's table.*[11]

This rich man had a conspicuous and familiar way of life: *he feasted.* He lived for himself, as if God did not exist, as if he did not need him. He lived comfortably; he had everything in abundance. The parable does not tell us that he denied God or that he had any particular animosity towards the poor man: only that he was blind to God and simply failed to notice his fellow man in need. He always lived for himself. He preferred to find his happiness in being self-centred rather than in generosity. And egoism

---

[10] St John of the Cross, *The Ascent of Mount Carmel*
[11] Luke 16:19-21

does blind; it degrades.

His sin? He simply did not notice Lazarus; he eliminated him from his consciousness. He did not use his goods according to God's wishes. *For it was not poverty that led Lazarus to heaven, but humility; nor was it wealth that prevented the rich man from attaining eternal rest but rather his egoism and his infidelity,*[12] says St Gregory the Great with profundity of insight.

Egoism and tepidity prevent one from seeing the needs of one's neighbour. People are then treated as things (it is a serious matter to see people as mere objects to be taken up or dropped as one sees fit), as valueless items. All of us have much to offer; such as affection, understanding, kindness and encouragement; and we can have work well done and completed, alms and good works for the needy, the daily smile, a piece of good advice, help for our friends in encouraging them to go to the sacraments ...

With the use we make of the riches – greater or less – which God has endowed us with, we will win eternal life. This is the time to merit it. Being generous, treating others as brothers and sisters, as children of God, we will be happy here on earth and, later, in the world to come. Charity, in its varied forms, is always a bringing to realisation of the kingdom of God on earth, and the only element which will give this passing world its real meaning.

This detachment has to be an *effective one*, with results which are clearly seen and are only to be obtained by sacrifice. It has also to be *natural and discriminating*, as befits Christians who live in the middle of the world and who have to use such goods as tools of their trade in their apostolic work. It is furthermore a matter of its being a *positive* detachment, for compared with the immense and infinite good which we are trying to acquire, everything on

---

[12] St Gregory the Great, *Homilies on the Gospel of St Luke*, 40:2

earth is ridiculously small and insignificant. Detachment has to be *internal*, too, for it must affect one's desires. It has also to be *current* and habitual, for we have to examine ourselves frequently to find out and make sure what it is that we have set our hearts on, and then to take specific measures to secure and retain the integrity of our interior freedom. *Cheerful* it has to be because our eyes are fixed on Christ, incomparable good – *quoniam bonus* – and because such detachment is not mere privation, but in fact real spiritual wealth, with dominion over things and true riches in abundance.

16.3 Detachment from the superfluous and the necessary, from preoccupation with health, God's gifts to us, etc.

Detachment is *born out of love* for Christ and, at the same time *makes it possible for this love to live and to grow*. God does not dwell in a soul filled with lumber, bric-a-brac and trinkets. Thus a constant vigil over interior order and cleanliness is needed. This lenten period is an opportunity to examine our attitude to things, to events and to ourselves. Do I have and carry around with me unnecessary impedimenta or superfluous items? Do I keep track of expenses or make a note of my outgoings so that I know where the money has been spent? Do I avoid what for me indicates impulsive spending, out of mere caprice or vanity, although this may well not be the case for others whose purchases are similar? Do I habitually give alms to people in need or to apostolic work, generously, without too much counting the cost? Do I support the traditional works of mercy and the divine worship of the Church, with donations proportional to my income and expenditure? Am I excessively fond of those elements or gadgets or implements which I have to use at work? Do I complain when I am lacking what seems to be necessary? Do I lead a life of sobriety, proper to one in search of holiness? Do I make superfluous purchases through haste or lack of foresight?

The detachment required of one who wishes to follow Our Lord closely includes, in addition to detachment from material goods, *a detachment from ourselves*: as regards our health, what others will think of us, noble ambitions, professional successes and triumphs ... *I would also include ... the high ideals which lead us to seek only the glory of God and to praise him. We can ensure our detachment by tailoring our will to this clear and precise rule: 'Lord, I want this or that only if it pleases you, because, if not, I am not in the slightest bit interested'. By acting in this way, we are dealing a mortal blow to the selfishness and vanity that lurk in every conscience. At the same time we will find true peace of soul through this selfless conduct that leads to an ever more intimate and intense possession of God.*[13] Are we thus detached from the fruits of our work?

Christians ought to possess goods *as though they had no goods.*[14] As St Gregory the Great suggests, *He who has what he needs for his use may possess these things, but he will possess them as if he possessed nothing; he foresees that suddenly he will have to leave them.* He who has available what he needs makes use of the things of this world as if he did not use them; he does not allow them to rule over his heart, so that they – never deflecting him from the way – are always of use to his soul, which tends towards higher things.[15]

And what of detachment from bodily health? *I have realised how important it is that we should not think of our own weak constitutions when we know that we are serving*

---

[13] St J. Escrivá, *Friends of God*, 114

[14] 1 Cor 7:30

[15] St Gregory the Great, *Homilies on the Gospels*, 36

the Lord ... What is the use to us of life and health if we cannot throw them away for so great a King and Lord? Believe me, sisters, you will never go wrong if you do this.[16]

Our hearts are for God, for He has made them, and only in him will our desire for eternal happiness be fulfilled. *Jesus is not satisfied 'going halves': he wants the lot.*[17] All other upright and noble loves – which go to form our life here on earth according to the specific vocation each one has received – are ordered to and fed by this our one great Love: Our Lord Jesus Christ.

God of love, bring us back to you. Send your Spirit to make us strong in faith and active in good works.[18]

Our Mother Mary will help us to purify and to bring order into the affections of our heart, so that only her Son reigns in it – now, and for all eternity. Most sweet heart of Mary, guard my heart and prepare a safe way for it.

---

[16] St Teresa, *Book of the Foundations*, 28, 18
[17] St J. Escrivá, *The Way*, 155
[18] *Entrance Antiphon*

17. ABHORRENCE OF SIN

17.1 Our Sins and Redemption. The true evil in the world.

> *God loved us and sent his Son as expiation for our sins.*[1]

The liturgy these days brings us closer, little by little, to the central mystery of the Redemption. It presents to us personalities of the Old Testament who are types of Our Lord. In the first reading of the Mass we are told about Joseph. Through the betrayal of his brothers he providentially came to be the saviour of his family and of the whole region.[2] He is a figure of Christ the Redeemer.

Joseph was the favourite son of Jacob, and at his father's request went in search of his brothers. He travelled a long way before finding them. He brought them good news of their father and also food. At first his brothers, who hated and envied him for being their father's favourite, considered killing him. Later, they sold him as a slave, and as such he was taken to Egypt. God made use of these circumstances so that years later he would come to hold a high position there. In a time of famine he would be the saviour of his brothers against whom he held no grudge despite their ill-treatment of him. He became a saviour too of Egypt, where through Joseph's good offices the tribes of Israel settled and became, as it were, a cradle for the chosen people. All those who approached Pharaoh for help were directed to Joseph: *Go to Joseph,* he would say to them.

Our Lord, sent by the Father, also came to bring light

---

[1] *Communion Antiphon,* 1 John 4:10
[2] Gen 3:4, 12:13, 17:28

to the world: *He came to his own and his own people received him not.*[3] *Finally he sent his son to them. 'They will respect my son', he said. But when the tenants saw the son, they said to each other: 'This is the heir. Come on, let us kill him and take over his inheritance.' So they seized him and threw him out of the vineyard and killed him.*[4] This is exactly what they did to Our Lord – they took him outside the city and crucified him.

The sins of men have been the cause of the death of Jesus Christ. Every sin bears an intimate and mysterious relationship to the Passion of Jesus. We will recognise the evil of sin only if we know how to relate it to the mystery of the Redemption. Only then will we really be able to purify the soul and to grow in contrition for our sins and transgressions. The conversion which Our Lord insistently asks for, and in a special way during this period of Lent as we approach Holy Week, ought to start with a firm rejection of all sin and with the determination to avoid every occasion that could put us in danger of offending God. Moral renewal, which this world so much needs, begins with this profound conviction: *On earth there is but one evil, which you must fear and avoid with the grace of God – sin.*[5] On the other hand, *the loss of the sense of sin is thus a form or consequence of 'the denial of God': not only in the form of atheism, but also in the form of secularism. If sin is the breaking off of one's filial relationship to God in order to situate one's life outside of obedience to him, then to sin is not merely to deny God. To sin is also to live as if He did not exist, to eliminate him from one's daily life.*[6] We do not wish to eliminate Our Lord from our lives, but

---

[3] John 1:11

[4] *Gospel of the Mass*, Matt 21:33-34, 45-46

[5] St J. Escrivá, *The Way*, 386

[6] St John Paul II, Apostolic Exhortation, *Reconciliatio et Poenitentia*, 18

rather to recognise and be more and more aware of his presence with each passing day.

We can very well say, says the Curé d'Ars, *that the Passion which the Jews made Christ suffer was almost nothing compared with what Christians make him undergo with their insults of mortal sins ... what horror there will be when Jesus Christ shows us the things for which we have abandoned him!*[7] What trash we will have preferred in exchange for so much good! Through divine mercy, with the help of grace, we will not leave him, and we will try to bring to him many who are separated from him.

17.2 Lent, an opportune occasion afforded us by the Church to help us in the fight against sin. The malice of venial sin.

The effort of personal conversion which the Lord asks of us is an effort for each day of our lives. But in special periods or situations, as in Lent, we receive special graces which we ought to make use of. This liturgical season is an extraordinary occasion for us to develop to a maximum the struggle against sin and to increase in ourselves the life of grace with good works.

To understand better the malice of sin we have to contemplate what Jesus Christ suffered for our sins. In the agony of Gethsemane, we see him suffering the indescribable. *For our sake he made himself to be sin who knew no sin,*[8] says St Paul: he burdened himself with all the atrocities we have committed, until his body ran with the sweat of blood. *Jesus, alone and sad, suffers and soaks the earth with his blood.*

Kneeling on the hard ground he perseveres in prayer ... He weeps for you ... and for me. The weight of the sins of

---

[7] St Jean Vianney, (The Curé d'Ars), *Sermon on Sin*
[8] 2 Cor 5:21

men overwhelms him.[9] It is a scene we should often recall, but especially when temptations get more severe.

Our Lord has called us to holiness for us to love with deeds. And on the approach we adopt towards deliberate venial sin will depend the progress we make in our interior life. For when we do not struggle to avoid venial sins or when there is not enough contrition for them, they damage the soul grievously. These venial sins make the soul insensitive to the inspirations and motions of the Holy Spirit. They weaken the life of grace and make the virtues more difficult to practise, and incline one towards mortal sin.

Many pious souls, says a present-day author, *are in an unfaithful state almost continuously as regards 'little things'; they are impatient, hardly charitable in their thoughts, judgements and words, false in their conversations and attitudes, slow and lax in their piety; they don't control themselves and are excessively frivolous in their language, or treat the good name of their neighbour lightly. They know their own defects and infidelities, and perhaps even accuse themselves in confession; but they do not seriously repent of them, nor do they make use of the means to avoid them in the future. They do not realise that each one of these 'imperfections' is like a leaden weight that drags them down. They do not realise that they are beginning to think in a purely human way and to work only for human reasons, or that they habitually resist the inspirations of grace and misuse them. The soul thus loses the splendour of its true beauty, and God is increasingly distanced from it. Little by little the soul loses contact with God: in him it does not see a loving and lovable Father to whom it should give itself with filial affection; something has been allowed to place itself between the two.*[10] This is the beginning of

---

[9] St J. Escrivá, *Holy Rosary*, First Sorrowful Mystery
[10] B. Baur, *In Silence with God*

the road to lukewarmness.

~~In a committed fight to banish all sin from our lives,~~ we will show Our Lord our love and our readiness to correspond with his grace. *How sad you make me feel when you are not sorry for your venial sins! For until you are, you will not begin to live a real interior life.*[11]

Let us ask Our Lady to grant us a loathing not only for mortal sin, but also for deliberate venial sin.

17.3 The fight against deliberate venial sin. Sincerity. Examination. Contrition.

The restoration of 'a proper sense of sin' is the first step that must be taken in facing the grave spiritual crisis looming over man today.[12]

To face up to this fight against venial sin in a determined way one must recognise venial sin for what it is: an offence against God which delays and can prevent union with Him. One must call it by its name, without excuses, without reducing the transcendental importance it has for a soul truly wishing to go to God. Flashes of anger, promptings of envy or sensuality not immediately rejected: a desire to be the centre of attention or attraction: not being concerned with anyone but oneself or with anything but our own interest and losing the capacity for being interested in others: acts of piety performed out of routine, with little attention and even less love: inconsiderately rash and less than charitable judgements about others ... these are not faults or mere imperfections, but *venial sins*.

We ought to ask the Holy Spirit to help us sincerely recognise our faults and our sins, to have a sensitive conscience which seeks pardon and does not look for ways to justify our errors. As St Augustine says: *He who has a*

---

[11] St J. Escrivá, *The Way*, 330
[12] St John Paul II, *loc cit*

healthy intuition of soul will feel how sins hurt.[13]

The saints have understood with noon-day clarity, in the light of love and of faith, that a single sin – especially mortal, but venial too – is a disorder greater than any cataclysm which lays waste the natural world, *for the goodness of grace in one single person is greater than the material good of the entire universe.*[14]

May we foster a sincere repentance for our faults and sins; may we fight to eradicate routine when we turn to the sacrament of Divine Mercy. *However small the sins that you may confess may be, always have sincere sorrow for them, together with a firm resolution to correct them in the future. Many who confess their venial sins out of custom and concern for order, but without thought of amendment, remain burdened with them for their whole lives and thus lose many spiritual benefits and advantages.*[15]

The Virgin Mary, *Refuge of Sinners*, will help us to have a refined conscience, to love Christ and all men, to be sincere with ourselves, and in Confession to recount our weaknesses and to know how to repent promptly for them.

---

[13] St Augustine, *Commentary on Psalm 37*
[14] St Thomas, *Summa Theologiae*, I-II, q113, a
[15] St Francis de Sales, *Introduction to the Devout Life*, II, 19

18. EACH OF US IS THE PRODIGAL SON

18.1 Sin, man's greatest tragedy. Consequences of sin in the soul. Without God happiness is impossible.

The Lord is kind and full of compassion, slow to anger, abounding in mercy. How good is the Lord to all, compassionate to all his creatures,[1] we recite in the Mass. In the Gospel, St Luke narrates[2] how one day, when a number of tax-collectors and sinners came to Jesus, the Pharisees began to gossip because He had welcomed all of them. It is then that Our Lord offers them this parable: *A man had two sons. The younger said to his father, 'Father, let me have the share of the estate that would come to me'.*

We are all children of God, and *being children, then heirs.*[3] The inheritance is the sum of incalculable good things God has prepared, and of the limitless happiness He has willed for us. It reaches its plenitude in heaven and only there will we secure it for ever. Until then we are liable to do what the younger son did with his inheritance: *A few days later, the younger son got together everything he had and left for a distant country, where he squandered his money on a life of debauchery. How many men over the centuries, how many in our own times, could find in this parable the basic characteristics of their own personal history!*[4] We are able to leave the family home and squander the goods we have been given in a way that is

---

[1] *Entrance Antiphon*, Ps 144:8-9
[2] Luke 15:1-3,11-32
[3] Rom 8:17
[4] St John Paul II, *Homily*, 16 March 1980

unworthy of our position as children of God.

When man sins gravely, he is lost to God and also in himself, for sin makes him lose his way to heaven. It is the greatest tragedy that can happen to a Christian. His honourable life, the hopes God had placed in him; his vocation to holiness, his past and his future have gone under. They are sunk. By loss of sanctifying grace he has moved away from the principle of life, which is God himself. The sinner whose offence is grave loses the merits he had acquired over the whole course of his previous life and is now incapable of any further merit, being subject in some way to the slavery of the Devil. As regards venial sin, St John Paul II reminds us that, although it does not cause the death of the soul, the person who commits it can cease to go forward or can stray from the way that leads to the knowledge and love of God. Thus it ought never to be considered as something trivial, or regarded as *a sin of little importance.*[5]

The estrangement from the Father causes havoc within the one who brings it about, whose will is weakened and who fritters away his inheritance which is none other than the dignity of the human being, the inheritance of grace.[6] He who, on leaving the house one day, enjoyed the prospect of worldly happiness outwith the boundaries of his father's farm, 'began to feel the pinch'. The world's delights are fleeting, and soon came to an end; sin does not produce true happiness, for the Devil does not possess it. Then comes loneliness and *the tragedy of lost dignity, the awareness of the divine sonship which has been squandered.*[7] The prodigal now had to tend the pigs, an

---

[5] St John Paul II, Apostolic Exhortation, *Reconciliatio et Poenitentia*, 17

[6] Second Vatican Council, *loc cit*

[7] St John Paul II, Encyclical, *Dives in misericordia*, 5

unseemly and degrading occupation for any Jew.

Be appalled, O heavens, at this; be shocked, be utterly desolate, says the Lord; for my people have committed two evils: they have forsaken me, the fountain of living waters, and have hewed out cisterns for themselves, broken cisterns, that can hold no water.[8] Without God, happiness is impossible, although for a time it may appear otherwise.

18.2 Returning to God. Sincerity and examination of conscience.

The son, far from his father's home, felt the pangs of hunger. *Then he came to his senses;* thinking things over, he decided to set out on his return journey. Thus begins every conversion, every repentance: it is man *coming to his senses,* calling to a halt his plunge to destruction, reflecting and considering where his ill-fated venture has led him; making, in fact, an examination of conscience, which looks at everything he has done from the time he left his father's house right up to the lamentable predicament in which he now finds himself. *Sociological analyses are not enough to bring about justice and peace. The root of evil is within man's own interior. The remedy, therefore, has also to come from the heart.*[9]

When one justifies sin, or ignores it, repentance and conversion are made impossible, for they have their root in the very depths of the person. To be able to examine one's life, one has to face one's actions courageously and sincerely, without casting around for false justifications. *Learn to call what is white, white, and what is black, black; call evil what is evil, and good what is good. Learn to call a sin, sin,*[10] St John Paul II advised us.

---

[8] Jer 8:12-13
[9] St John Paul II, *Homily to University Students,* Rome, 11 April 1979
[10] St John Paul II, *Homily to University Students,* Rome, 26 March 1981

In the examination of conscience, our life is compared with what we know was expected and what God expects of us. Many spiritual authors have compared the soul to a shuttered and closed room. As the window is opened and light comes flooding in, its imperfections, its disorder and dirt, everything shabby and broken becomes visible. In the examination, with the help of grace, we get to know the state we are in (that is to say, how we are in God's eyes). The saints have always recognised themselves as sinners; by their correspondence with grace they have opened wide the windows of their soul to the light of God; they have known how beneficial and necessary it is to examine well the whole room. In the examination we will discover also our omissions in the fulfilment of our promise of love for God and for men; and we will ask ourselves: to what can I attribute all this neglect and carelessness? When we do not find something to repent of, it will not be because of any lack of faults or sins, but because we have shut ourselves off from this light from God, which shows us at every instant the true condition of our soul. If the window is closed, the room remains in darkness and one cannot then see the grime, the dust, the chair upset and out of place, the lop-sided and cobwebbed pictures on the wall and all that is not right ... and even what is perhaps seriously wrong.

Pride also tries to prevent us seeing ourselves as we are: *their ears are hard of hearing, and their eyes are tight shut, lest they should perceive with their eyes and hear with their ears.*[11] The Pharisees, to whom Our Lord applies these words, chose to be deaf and blind, because in the end they were unwilling to change.

---

[11] Matt 13:15

18.3 The encounter with God our Father in a sincere and contrite confession. The joy of being in the Father's household.

So he left that place and went back to his father. He retraces his steps. In the plight he finds himself in, he feels homesick, and little by little his other senses begin to reassert themselves: the warmth of his home, the constant memory of his father's face, the old stirrings of filial affection begin to move him. Sorrow has been somehow ennobling, and the rehearsed phrases are very sincere: *Father, I have sinned against heaven and against you; I no longer deserve to be called your son. Treat me as one of your paid servants.*

Each of us too, called as we are to sanctity, is the prodigal son. *Human life is in some way a constant returning to our Father's house. We return through contrition, through that conversion of heart which means a desire to change. It means a firm decision to improve our lives, a decision which is to be expressed in sacrifice and self-giving. We return to our Father's house by means of that sacrament of pardon in which, by confessing our sins, we put on Jesus Christ again and become his brothers, members once more of God's family.*[12]

We have to come close to this sacrament desirous of confessing this or that fault, without misrepresenting it, without justifying it. *I have sinned against heaven and against you.* We accuse ourselves humbly and simply, without beating about the bush. Repentance for mistakes made is shown in sincerity.

The son arrives back, hungry, dirty and in rags. *While he was still a long way off, his father saw him and was moved with pity. He ran to the boy, clasped him in his arms and kissed him tenderly.*

---

[12] St J. Escrivá, *Christ is passing by*, 64

He ran to the boy ... While repentance often moves slowly, the mercy of God our Father speeds towards us when He sees from afar our least desire to return. This is why Confession is saturated with joy and hope. *It is the joy of God's pardon, conferred through his priests, when one who has had the misfortune to offend his infinite love repentantly returns to the arms of the Father.*[13]

So, too, do the words of God, who has recovered his lost and debased son erupt into joy. *Quick! Bring out the best robe and put it on him; put a ring on his finger and sandals on his feet! Bring the calf we have been fattening and kill it; we are going to have a feast, a celebration, because this son of mine was dead and has come back to life; he was lost and is found. And they began to celebrate.*

The best robe was raiment kept for the guest of honour; with *the ring* went the father's delegated power to seal, renewed authority and restoration of rights; *the sandals* declared him to be a free man. *It is in the Sacrament of Penance that you and I put on Jesus Christ and his merits.*[14] In Confession the Lord returns to us what we had culpably lost through sin – grace and the dignity of children of God. He has established this sacrament of his mercy so that we can always return to the family home. And our return always ends in joyful festivity. *Just so, I tell you, there is joy before the angels of God over one sinner who repents.*[15]

Having received absolution and having done the penance given to us by our confessor, *the penitent*, forgetting what lies behind,[16] enters once more into the mystery of salvation and journeys on towards his future happiness.[17]

---

[13] St John Paul II, *Address*, 24 March 1979
[14] St J. Escrivá, *The Way*, 310
[15] Luke 15:10
[16] Phil 3:13
[17] *New Rite of Penance*, note 6

19. THE MEANING OF MORTIFICATION

19.1 Truly following Christ implies practising a life of mortification and being close to the Cross.

If each of Christ's actions in his earthly life have redemptive value, the salvation of humanity culminates in the Cross. It is to this climactic point that all of Christ's life on earth is directed. *I have a baptism to be baptized with; and how I am constrained until it is accomplished!*[1] So He said to his disciples on the road to Jerusalem. He revealed to them his overwhelming desire to give his life for us, and He gave us an example of his love for the Will of the Father by dying on the Cross. It is on the Cross that the soul finds its full identification with Christ. This is the deepest meaning of acts of mortification and penance.

To be a disciple of Our Lord one needs to follow his measured words of advice: *If any man would come after me, let him deny himself, take up his cross and follow me.*[2] It is not possible to follow Our Lord without the Cross. Jesus' words are relevant in all ages, since they are directed to each and every man, for *he who does not bear his own cross and come after me cannot be my disciple.*[3] To take up the cross – the acceptance of sorrow and of the contradictions God permits for our purification, the costly fulfilment of our duties, Christian mortification voluntarily accepted – is the indispensable condition for following the Master.

What would become of a Gospel, of a Christianity, without the Cross, without pain, without the sacrifice of

---

[1] Luke 12:50
[2] Matt 16:24
[3] Luke 14:27

pain? asked Saint Paul VI. *It would be a Gospel, a Christianity, without Redemption, with no Salvatio; a Redemption and Salvation of which – and we ought to recognise it here with unmitigated sincerity – we stand in absolute need. The Lord has saved us with the Cross; with his death. He has given us hope again, the right to life ...*[4] It would be a valueless Christianity which would not be of use in our reaching Heaven, for *the world cannot be saved except with the Cross of Christ.*[5]

United to the Lord, voluntary mortification and passive mortification acquire their deepest meaning. They are not directed primarily to one's own perfection, nor are they a way of patiently bearing the contradictions of this life. They are *a participation* in the mystery of the Redemption.

Mortification can appear to some to be a sign of madness or of stupidity, some kind of relic left over from earlier epochs which no longer fits in with or is inappropriate to the progress and cultural development of our twentieth century day. It could also be a sign of contradiction or of scandal for those who have forgotten about God. But none of this should cause us surprise. St Paul had already written that *it is a stumbling block to the Jews and folly to the Gentiles.*[6] And in the very measure in which Christians lose sight of the supernatural meaning to their lives, they fail to understand that we can only follow Christ through a life of sacrifice, *juxta crucem*, beside the Cross. *If you don't deny yourself, you never will be a soul of prayer.*[7] And St Teresa adds: *To suppose that He would admit to his close friendship pleasure-loving people who*

---

[4] St Paul VI, *Address*, 24 March 1967
[5] St Leo the Great, *Sermon 51*
[6] 1 Cor 1:23
[7] St J. Escrivá, *The Way*, 172

want to be free from all trials is ridiculous.[8]

Although the very Apostles themselves, who followed Christ when He was acclaimed by the multitudes, love him deeply and are ready to give up their lives for him, they do not follow him to Calvary – for, not having as yet received the Holy Spirit, they are weak. There is a big difference between following Christ when this does not require a great deal from us, and identifying ourselves totally with him through the tribulations, great and small, of a life of sacrifice.

The Christian who journeys through life systematically opting out of sacrifice, who rebels in the face of pain, distances himself from holiness and happiness, which are found beside the Cross, very close to Christ the Redeemer.

19.2 On losing the fear of sacrifice.

The Lord asks each Christian to follow him closely; and for this, one has to accompany him to Calvary. We can never forget his words: *he who does not take up his cross and follow me is not worthy of me.*[9] Long before He had to suffer on the Cross Jesus had told his followers that they would have to carry it.

In mortification there is a paradox, a mystery, which can only be understood when love is present. Behind the apparent death is life, and he who egoistically tries to save his life for himself loses it: *Whoever would save his life will lose it; and whosoever loses his life for my sake will find it.*[10] To bear fruit, loving God and helping others in an effective way, sacrifice is necessary. There can be no harvest without a sowing season: *Unless a grain of wheat falls into the earth and dies, it remains alone; but if it dies,*

---

[8] St Teresa, *The Way of Perfection*, 18,2
[9] Matt 10:38
[10] Matt 16:24

it bears much fruit.[11] To be supernaturally effective one has to die to oneself through continuous mortification, forgetting completely one's comfort and eschewing egoism. *If a grain of wheat does not die, it remains unfruitful. Don't you want to be a grain of wheat, to die through mortification, and to yield a rich harvest? May Jesus bless your wheatfield!*[12]

We should lose our fear of sacrifice, of voluntary mortification, for it is a loving Father, who knows what is best for us, who wishes the Cross for us. He always wants the best for us. *Come to me all you who labour and are heavy laden, and I will give you rest. Take my yoke upon you, and learn from me; for I am gentle and lowly in heart, and you will find rest for your souls. For my yoke is easy and my burden is light.*[13] Close to Christ, tribulations and difficulties are not oppressive, they are not burdensome; on the contrary, they dispose the soul to prayer, to see God in the events of daily life.

Through mortification we raise ourselves up to the Lord; without it we remain at ground level. With voluntary sacrifice, with sorrow offered and borne patiently and with love, we unite ourselves firmly to the Lord. It is *as though he were to say: All you going about tormented, afflicted, and weighed down by your cares and appetites, think nothing of them. Come to me and I will refresh you; and you will find a rest for your souls that your preoccupation with your troubles takes away from you.*[14]

19.3 Other reasons for mortification.

To be convinced that we should practise generosity in

---

[11] John 12:24-25
[12] St J. Escrivá, *The Way*, 199
[13] Matt 11:28-30
[14] St John of the Cross, *The Ascent of Mount Carmel*, I, 7, 4

mortification, it is important to understand clearly the reasons that give it meaning. Some may find it very difficult to be mortified, precisely because they have not discovered this meaning. Many are the reasons which lead a Christian towards mortification. We have already considered the first one: to identify oneself with the Lord and to follow him in his desire to redeem on the Cross, offering himself in sacrifice to the Father. Our mortification thus has the same aims as the Passion of Christ and of the Holy Mass, and is daily converted into a deeper conformation of our will to the Will of the Father.

But mortification is also *a means to make progress, to advance in virtue*. The priest, in the dialogue which precedes the Preface of the Mass, raises his hands to heaven while he says: *Lift up your hearts*. And one hears the faithful respond: *We lift them up to the Lord*. Our hearts ought to be permanently turned towards God. The heart of a Christian ought to be full of love, with a hope always placed in his Lord. To be able to do this he cannot allow himself to be trapped by and be a prisoner of earthly things; he has to be constantly moving towards a greater purification. And this is not possible without penance, without continuous mortification, which is *the means to progress*.[15] Without it the soul remains subject to the thousand and one things which make their demands on and tend to disperse and dissipate the senses: attachment, impurity, tepidity, desires for an immoderate comfort ... mortification frees us from many entangling ties and gives us the capacity to love.

Mortification is *the indispensable means for doing apostolate*, for extending the Kingdom of Christ: *Action is worth nothing without prayer: prayer grows in value with*

---

[15] St J. Escrivá, *The Way*, 232

sacrifice.[16] We should be far off the track if we wished to attract others to God without supporting this action on a foundation of intense prayer, and if this prayer were not *reinforced* with mortification joyously offered up. And so it has been said, in many different ways, that interior life, shown especially in prayer and mortification, is *the soul of the apostolate.*[17]

Lastly, we do not forget that mortification also serves as *reparation for our past failures,* whether they have been great or small. Thus in many prayers do we ask the Lord to help us make up for lapses of our past life: *'emendationem vitae, spatium verae poenitentiae ... tribuat nobis omnipotens et misericors Dominus'* that the almighty and merciful God may grant us a change for the better in our lives and a time of true penance.[18] Thus through mortification, even our past faults are turned into a source of new life. *In the deep pit opened by your humility, let penance bury your negligences, offences and sins, just as the gardener buries rotten fruit, dried twigs and fallen leaves at the foot of the very tree which produced them. And so what was useless, what was even harmful, can make a real contribution to a new fruitfulness.*

From your falls learn to draw strength: from death, life.[19]

We ask the Lord that we may learn to use our life, from now on, in the best possible way. *When you look back on your life, which seems to have been marked by no great efforts or achievements, think how much time you have wasted, and how you can recover it with penance and greater self-giving.*[20]

---

[16] *ibid,* 81
[17] J. B. Chautard, *Soul of the Apostolate*
[18] Roman Missal, *Formula for Mass Intentions*
[19] St J. Escrivá, *loc cit,* 211
[20] *idem, Furrow,* 996

And when something costs us an effort, some of those thoughts which urge and encourage us to mortification will come to mind. *Reasons for penance? – atonement, reparation, petition, thanksgiving: means to progress – for you, for me, for others, for your family, for your country, for the Church ... And a thousand reasons more.*[21]

[21] idem, *The Way*, 232

20. DOCILITY AND GOOD DISPOSITIONS FOR MEETING JESUS.

20.1 Faith and correspondence with grace. Our souls need purification in order for us to see Jesus.

My soul is longing and yearning for the courts of the Lord. My heart and my flesh cry out to the living God,[1] we read in today's Mass. And to enter the dwelling of the Lord a soul has to be clean and humble. For us to be able to see Jesus, good dispositions are needed. Once again, this is what the Gospel of the Mass shows us.

Having spent some time preaching in the towns and cities of Galilee, Our Lord returned to Nazareth *where he had been brought up.* Everyone knew him there: he was the son of Joseph and Mary. *As his custom was,*[2] on Saturday Jesus attended the synagogue. He stood up to read the sacred text, and he chose the messianic passage of the prophet Isaiah. St Luke makes clear the extraordinary sense of expectation there was in the air: *Then He shut the book, and gave it back to the attendant, and sat down. All those who were in the synagogue fixed their eyes on him.* They had heard marvels about Mary's son and expected to see even more extraordinary things in Nazareth.

Nonetheless, although at the beginning *all bore testimony to him, and were astonished at the gracious words which came from his mouth,*[3] they did not have faith. Jesus explained to them that God's plans are not based on ties of blood or of nationality: it was not enough to have

---

[1] *Entrance Antiphon*, Ps 83:3
[2] Luke 4:16
[3] Luke 4:22

lived with Him. A great faith was needed.

He produced examples from the Old Testament. *In the prophet Elisha's time there were many lepers in Israel, but none of these were cured except the Syrian, Naaman*. The graces granted from Heaven, without any limits being placed by God, do not take into account one's race – Naaman did not belong to the Jewish people – one's age or social position. Jesus did not find the necessary dispositions in his hearers in the land where he was brought up; and so he did not work any miracle there. Those people saw in him only *the son of Joseph*, one who made tables and repaired chairs. *Is not this the son of Joseph?* they asked.[4] They did not know how to see beyond appearances. They did not discover the Messiah who had come among them.

On contemplating Christ we, too, ought to purify our soul. *That Christ you see is not Jesus. It is only the pitiful image that your blurred eyes are able to form ... Purify yourself. Clarify your sight with humility and penance. Then ... the pure light of Love will not be denied you. And you will have perfect vision. The image you see will be really his: his!*[5]

Lent is a good opportunity for intensifying our love with penitential deeds, which dispose the soul towards receiving lights from God.

20.2 The cure of Naaman. Docility and humility.

The First Reading of the Mass relates the cure of Naaman, a general in the army of the King of Syria.[6] This man, who suffered from leprosy, had heard a Hebrew slave say that in Israel there was a Prophet who could cure him

---

[4] *ibid*
[5] St J. Escrivá, *The Way*, 212
[6] 2 Kings 5:1-15

of his sickness. So, after a long journey, *Naaman came with his team and chariot and drew up at the door of Elisha's house. And Elisha sent him a messenger to say, 'Go and bathe seven times in the Jordan, and your flesh will become clear once more'.*

But Naaman did not understand the ways of God, so different were they from what he had imagined.

Here was I thinking, he said, *he would be sure to come out to me, and stand there, and call the name of the Lord his God, and wave his hand over the spot and cure the leprous part. Surely Abana and Pharphar, the rivers of Damascus, are better than any waters in Israel? Could I not bathe in them and become clean?*

The Syrian general did want to be healed and he had come a long way for this, but he had his own idea of what would effect his cure. And when he had returned, convinced that his journey had been in vain, his servants approached him and said: *If the prophet had asked you to do something difficult, would you not have done it? And the more reason then if he simply says to you, 'Bathe and you will become clean'.*

Naaman reflected on their words. He returned humbly to carry out the prophet Elisha's recommendations. *So he went down and dipped himself seven times in the Jordan, according to the word of the man of God; and his flesh was restored like the flesh of a little child, and he was clean.* He was humble and docile enough to take advice, which, humanly speaking, seemed useless. And he was cured. His interior dispositions made Elisha's prayer effective.

We, too, frequently have illnesses of the soul, with defects and shortcomings which we have not yet managed to uproot. Our Lord hopes we will be humble and docile to the indications and advice we receive from those whom God has placed to help us in the search for holiness in the midst of our work and family life. We cannot have our own

way when Our Lord points to a solution which goes
contrary to our own notions. In matters of the soul, we are
not our own best advisers, as we are not our own good
doctors. Normally, Our Lord makes use of other people.
*Christ himself called St Paul and spoke to him. He could
have revealed to Paul, there and then, the route to
holiness. But he preferred to direct him to Ananias, so that
from his lips would Paul learn the truth: 'Rise up, enter
into the city, and you will be told what you ought to do'.*[7] St
Paul allowed himself to be led. His strong personality, so
clearly shown on so many occasions and in so many ways,
helps him here to be docile. First, his fellow travellers take
him to Damascus. Then Ananias gives him back his sight
and he is now a man useful for fighting the battles of the
lord.

In spiritual guidance, the soul allows itself to find the
Lord, and to recognise him in ordinary matters.

20.3 Docility in spiritual direction.

Faith in the means God gives us works miracles. On
one occasion Our Lord asked a cripple to do something
which, from vast experience, the man knew he could not
do: it was to stretch out his withered hand. But again
docility, the sign of an operative faith, made the miracle
possible. *And the man stretched out his hand, and it was
restored, whole like the other.*[8] At times we too will be
asked to do things we think we are incapable of. But they
will become possible if we allow the grace of God to act
within us – a grace which, quite frequently, comes to us as
a result of docility in spiritual direction.

Our Lord asks us not to seek mere earthly supports
which would inevitably lead us to pessimism. He asks us

---

[7] Cassian, *Conferences*, 2
[8] Matt 12:9, *et seq*

for supernatural trust, for us to be *supernaturally realists* –
to count on Him, that is, being aware that Jesus Christ
continues to influence our lives.

Ten men find their cure because they are docile. Jesus
simply tells them: *Go and show yourselves to the priests.*[9]

On another occasion Our Lord has compassion on a
man born blind, and St John vividly relates the incident:
*Jesus spat on the ground and made a paste and anointed
the man's eyes with the clay, saying to him: 'Go, wash in
the pool of Siloam.'*[10] And the beggar did not doubt for an
instant. *So he went and washed, and came back seeing.*

*What an example of firm faith that blind man gives us!
His is a living, operative faith. Do you behave like this
when God commands, when so often you can't see, when
your soul is worried and the light is gone? What power
could the water possibly contain that when the blind man's
eyes were moistened with it they were cured? Surely some
mysterious eye-salve, or a precious medicine made up in
the laboratory of some wise alchemist, would have been
more efficacious? But the man believed; he acted upon the
command of God, and he returned with eyes full of light.*[11]

Blindness, defects, weaknesses: these are shortcomings that have a remedy. We ourselves cannot do
anything; Jesus Christ is all-powerful. The water of that
pool went on being water, and the clay continued to be
clay. But the blind man recovered his sight with a deeper,
living faith in the Lord. And thus, as so often in the Gospel,
we are shown the faith of those who have trusting relations
with Jesus. Without docility, spiritual guidance remains
fruitless. And one cannot be docile if he insists on being
stubborn, obstinate, incapable of assimilating an idea

---

[9] Luke 17:14
[10] John 9:1, *et seq*
[11] St J. Escrivá, *Friends of God*, 193

different from those he already holds, or which he has got into his head as a result of some negative experience when he has not counted on the help of grace. Pride makes one incapable of docility: for in order to understand one has to be convinced that there are still things which are outside our experience, and that we need someone to point them out to us. To achieve spiritual improvement, we have to realise that we are not as good as God expects us to be.

In matters related to our own interior life we ought to be forewarned, with a prudent mistrust in our own judgement, so as to be able to accept criteria different from or even opposed to our own. And we will allow God to mould and remould us through events and inspirations, through lights received in spiritual direction. We will permit ourselves to be shaped, to be moulded, to be formed with the docility of clay in the hands of the potter, without offering any resistance, with supernatural outlook, listening to Christ through the one who has the grace to direct. So Sacred Scripture tells us: *I went down to the potter's house, and there he was, working at his wheel. And the vessel he was making of clay was spoiled in the potter's hand, and he remade it into another vessel ... Like the clay in the potter's hand, so are you in my hand.*[12] With availability, with docility, we will allow ourselves to be reworked and reshaped by God as often as is necessary. This could be the resolution we make in our prayer today, a resolution which we will bring to fruition with the help of Our Lady.

---

[12] Jer 18:1-7

THIRD WEEK OF LENT – TUESDAY

21. TO PARDON AND FORGIVE

21.1 To forgive and forget the tiny offences.

It is almost inevitable in our daily dealings with others – at work, at home, in social relationships – that small frictions occur. It is also possible that someone may offend us, or treat us unfairly, and this may hurt us. And, perhaps, this may happen not infrequently. *Have I pardoned as often as seven times?* I might ask myself. That is to say 'do I always forgive?' It is the question Our Lord puts to Peter in the Gospel of today's Mass.[1] It is also the proposed theme for our prayer to-day. Do we know how to forgive on all occasions? Do we do so promptly?

We are aware of Our Lord's reply to Peter and to ourselves: *Not seven, I tell you, but seventy times seven.* That is to say, always, without limit. The Lord asks of those who follow him, of you and me, a forgiving approach and unlimited pardon. The Lord demands of his own friends a completely generous largeness of heart. He wants us to imitate him. *The omnipotence of God,* says St Thomas Aquinas, *is shown, above all, in the act of his forgiveness and the use of his mercy, for the way He has of showing his supreme power is to pardon freely ...*[2] And thus *nothing makes us so God-like as our willingness to forgive.*[3] It is where we also show our greatness of soul, our magnanimity.

Far be it from us, therefore, to remember who has offended us, or the humiliations we have endured – no

---

[1] Matt 18:21-35
[2] St Thomas, *Summa Theologiae*, I, q25, a3, ad3
[3] St John Chrysostom, *Homilies on the Gospel of St Matthew*, 30,5

matter how unjust, how uncivil or unmannerly they may have been – because it would not be right for a son of God to be preparing and keeping some kind of dossier from which to read off a list of grievances.[4] Although my neighbour may not improve, although over and over again he might commit the same offence or do something that offends me, I should avoid all bitterness. My heart should be pure and kept clean of all enmity.

The pardon we grant has to be sincere, from the heart, and be granted just as God pardons us. *Forgive us our trespasses* we say each day in the Our Father, *as we forgive those who trespass against us.* An immediate pardon, without allowing bitterness or a spirit of divisiveness to eat away at the heart – without either humiliating the other person or being in any way melodramatic. Often, in daily life, it is not even necessary to say 'you are forgiven': it is enough to smile, to change the direction of the conversation, to make an affectionate gesture – to forgive, once and for all, as if the offence had never taken place at all.

It is not necessary for us to suffer great injustice before we show such charity. Those little things which happen each day are opportunity enough: arguments in the home over trifling matters; sharp replies or disconcerting gestures (often caused by no more than tiredness) at work, in traffic jams or in the rush of public transport.

We would not be living our Christian life well if, at the least sign of friction, our charity began to grow cold and we began to feel distanced from others, or if we ourselves turned glum. Nor would it be very Christian if, when perhaps some serious damage were to cause us to lose our sense of the presence of God, our soul were to lose its peace and joy. We would not be behaving in a Christian way if we allowed ourselves to become touchy. We have to

---

[4] St J. Escrivá, *Friends of God*, 309

examine ourselves to see what our reactions are like when the irritations of the day crop up. Following Our Lord closely implies finding, even in the area of tiny contradictions or in the case of more serious injustices, the way to holiness.

21.2 Our forgiveness of others in comparison with that of Our Lord towards us.

And if thy neighbour does thee wrong seven times a day ... seven times thou shalt forgive him.[5] *Seven times* means times without number, even on the same day and, as it might be, over the same issue. *Charity is patient, is kind.*[6]

Forgiving, however, can cost us considerable effort, sometimes in little things as well as in big. The Lord knows this, and encourages us to turn to him; He will explain to us how this limitless forgiveness is compatible with a necessary just defence, since such a response has its origins in humility. When we turn to Jesus, He will remind us of the parable which to-day's Gospel relates: *A King decided to settle his accounts with his servants. When the reckoning began, they brought him a man who owed ten thousand talents.*[7] An enormous sum! The debt is of some seventy million denarii, a denarius being the daily wage of a labourer.

When one is sincere with oneself and with God, one immediately finds oneself to be that servant who *had no means of paying*. Not only because everything one is and everything one has is owed to God, but also because the offences which God has pardoned in us are countless. There is only one way out for us: to throw ourselves on God's mercy, so that He may do for us what he did for that

---

[5] cf Luke 17:4
[6] 1 Cor 13:7
[7] cf Matt 18:24 *et seq*

character in the parable – *The master felt so sorry for him that he let him go and cancelled the debt.*

But when that steward met one of his companions who owed him one hundred denarii, a comparatively trifling amount, he did not know how to forgive or be content to allow time for the debt to be paid, in spite of his colleague's pleading with all his might. *Then the master sent for him. You wicked servant,* he said, *I cancelled all that debt of yours when you appealed to me. Were you not bound, then, to have pity on your fellow servant just as I had pity on you?*

The humility of recognising the many debts we owe to God helps us to pardon and to forgive others. If we look to see what God has forgiven us, we realise that what we ought to forgive others – even in serious matters – is little: it does even not amount to *one hundred denarii.* Compared with ten thousand talents, it is nothing.

Our attitude to minor grievances has to be one of minimising their importance (an importance which, in reality, is what very often they don't have) and of forgiving with a good grace and without fuss. In forgiving and forgetting, it is we ourselves who have most to gain. Our life becomes more joyful and more serene, and trifles don't upset us. *It is true that life, which by its nature is already rather narrow and uncertain, sometimes becomes difficult. But that will help you to become more supernatural and to see the hand of God in everything. Then you will be more human and understanding with those around you.*[8]

We have to understand everyone; we must live peaceably with everyone; we must forgive everyone. We shall not call injustice, justice; we shall not say that an offence against God is not an offence against God, or that evil is good. When confronted by evil we shall not reply

---

[8] St J. Escrivá, *Furrow*, 762

with another evil, but rather with sound doctrine and good actions: drowning evil in an abundance of good (Rom 12:21).[9] We will not commit the error of that mean servant, who himself having been forgiven so much, was not capable of pardoning even a little.

21.3 Learning to see the good in others.

Charity changes the heart so that there is room in it for all men, even those who don't understand us or who fail to respond to our love. With the Lord beside us we will not feel anyone to be our enemy. Beside him we will learn not to judge the covert personal intentions of others.

We see only a few external signs which as often as not reflect the true motives for their actions. *Although you might see something bad, do not instantly judge your neighbour,* advises St Bernard, *but, rather, excuse him interiorly. Excuse the intention if you are unable to excuse the action. Consider it as if done in ignorance, or unawares, or through weakness. If the matter is so weighty that you cannot possibly overlook it, then try to believe the following and say to yourself: the temptation must have been very strong!*[10]

How many mistakes we make in the small clashes of each day. Many of these errors are made because our reactions are prompted by fear or suspicion. How many family arguments would resolve themselves in the recognition of responsibilities and duties if we were to concede that this ugly detail, that untimely event, has been due to the tiredness of the person concerned after a long and difficult day. *While you continue to interpret in bad faith the intentions of your neighbour, you have no right to*

---

[9] *idem, Christ is passing by,* 182
[10] St Augustine, *Sermon 40 on the Song of Songs*

demand that people should be understanding with you.[11]

Tolerance leads us to live a loving openness towards others, to look on them with constant kindness. It reaches the depths of the heart and knows how to look forward and find out that goodness which is in every person.

Only he who is humble is capable of maintaining an understanding attitude. Otherwise, the tiniest faults of others are magnified, and one tends to justify and minimise one's own greater faults and errors. Pride is like a curved mirror that distorts the reality of things.

He who is humble is objective, and thus can be respectful and tolerant towards others: forgiveness of others' faults comes easily to him. The humble person is not scandalized by these flaws in his neighbour. *There is no sin,* writes St Augustine, *or crime committed by another which I myself am not capable of committing through my weakness; and if I have not committed it, it is because God, in his mercy, has not allowed me to and has preserved me in good.*[12] Moreover, we *also learn to discover so many virtues in the people about us, who teach us by their hard work, their self-denial, their joy, that we shall not dwell too much on their defects; only when it is absolutely necessary shall we advert to them in order to help them with fraternal correction.*[13]

Our Lady will teach us, if we ask her, to know how to forgive – in Cana, Mary does not deplore or criticize the lack of wine, *but helps find a solution to the need* – and to struggle to cultivate in our personal lives these very virtues which, on occasion, may seem to us to be lacking in others. We will then be in an excellent position to lend them a hand.

---

[11] St J. Escrivá, *Furrow*, 635
[12] St Augustine, *Confessions*, 2:7
[13] St J. Escrivá, *Friends of God*, 20

THIRD WEEK OF LENT – WEDNESDAY

22. VIRTUES AND SPIRITUAL GROWTH

22.1 Virtues and holiness

You will show me the path of life; the fulness of joy in your presence, O Lord.[1]

Jesus uses different images to teach us that the path that leads to Life, to holiness, consists in the full development of the spiritual life. He speaks of the tiny mustard seed which grows into a great tree; in its branches the birds of the air come to rest. He speaks of the grain of wheat which reaches maturity and produces rich ears of corn ... That growth, not without its difficulties and sometimes seeming so slow, is in fact the increase of virtue. If we are to sanctify each day, we have to practise many human and supernatural virtues: faith, hope, charity, justice, fortitude – industriousness, loyalty, optimism ...

The virtues demand the repetition of acts in order to grow, because each act disposes the soul to perform the next one more easily. For example, if a person lives the 'heroic minute' when he wakes up, thus overcoming his laziness from the very first moment of the day,[2] he will find it easier to be diligent in going about his other duties whether they be large or small. In the same way, the sportsman improves his physical fitness by training, and acquires a greater aptitude for repeating his exercises. Virtues *make a man more perfect, and at the same time they make it easier for him to perform good works and to respond at every moment to God's will in a prompt and fitting manner.* Without virtues (those good habits acquired

---

[1] *Communion Antiphon*, Ps 15:11
[2] cf St J. Escrivá, *The Way*, 206

through the repetition of good acts, with the help of grace), it is difficult to perform any meritorious actions, and in any case such actions will be no more than random or isolated incidents. Without virtues it is easier to fall into imperfections and sins that widen the gap which separate us from God. The repetition of acts in a single direction leaves its mark on the soul in the form of habits which increasingly dispose the soul to behave for good or for evil in the future, depending on whether it is good or bad habits that are being formed. We can hope that a person who *habitually* acts well will continue to do so when he is confronted with difficulties; that habit, that virtue sustains him. This is why it is so important that we blot out the remains of the sins of our past life through penance. We must not allow them to incline us towards evil ever again. The more serious the falls and the longer a person has been separated from God, the more intense the penance should be, because the residual mark left by such sins will be so much the more difficult to erase.

The practice of virtue shows us at every moment which path it is that leads to God. When with the help of grace a Christian endeavours not only to avoid occasions of sin and resist temptations with fortitude, but also to reach the holiness that God asks of him, he becomes ever more aware that the Christian life demands both an increase in virtue and purification from past sins as well as from failures to correspond to grace. Especially during Lent the Church invites us precisely to grow in virtue: that is, in habits of doing good.

22.2 Human virtues and supernatural virtues. Practising them in everyday life.

Holiness conists in the exercise of the virtues, one day after another, in the environment and in the circumstances in which we live. *The human virtues provide the foundation for the supernatural ones. These in turn provide us with constant encouragement to behave in a more truly human way. In either case, it is not sufficient merely to 'want' to have these virtues. We have to learn how 'to practise' them. 'Discite benefacere' (Is 1:17), learn to do good. We need to make a habit of exercising each virtue, by actually being sincere, truthful, balanced, calm and patient ... for love is proved by deeds, and we cannot love God in words alone, but 'with deeds and in truth' (1 John 3).*[3]

The work of sanctification belongs entirely to God in his infinite goodness. Nevertheless, He has willed that correspondence on the part of human beings is necessary, and has consequently placed in our nature the capacity for disposing ourselves towards receiving the supernatural action of grace. Through cultivating human virtues – resilience, loyalty, truthfulness, affection, courtesy – we prepare our soul in the best possible way for the action of the Holy Spirit. Thus it is easy to understand that *it is not possible to believe in the sanctity of those who fail to live even the most elementary human virtues.*[4]

Christian virtues are what we must put into practice in our everyday lives, and in all circumstances, whether these be easy, troublesome, or very difficult. *Today, as yesterday, heroism is expected of the Christian – a heroism in great struggles, if the need arises. Normally, however, it will be heroism in the little skirmishes of each day.*[5] Just as a plant derives nourishment from the earth in which it is rooted, so too in the supernatural life the virtues of a Christian spread their roots out in whatever part of the world he is immersed in: work, family joys and sorrows, good and bad news ... Everything must help him to love

---

[3] *idem, Friends of God*, 91
[4] Bl. A. del Portillo, *On the Priesthood*
[5] St J. Escrivá, *Christ is passing by*, 82

God and do apostolate. Some occurrences are more likely to encourage acts of thanksgiving, whilst others will call for acts of divine filiation. Particular circumstances will bring about a growth in fortitude, others an increasing trust in God. If we bear in mind that the virtues form a single tapestry, a seamless robe, we can see that growth in one means a step forward in all the others. Besides, *it is charity that gives unity to all the virtues that make a man perfect.*[6]

We cannot wait for the arrival of ideal circumstances in order to seek sanctity and do apostolate ... *When a Christian carries out with love the most insignificant everyday action, that action overflows with the transcendence of God ... Stop dreaming! Leave behind false idealisms, fantasies, and what I usually call 'mystical wishful thinking' (If only I hadn't married. If only I didn't have this profession. If only I had better health. If only I were young. If only I were old ...) Instead, turn seriously to the most material and immediate reality, which is where Our Lord is.*[7]

Waiting for what we consider to be just the right situations and circumstances to arise in order to seek holiness would be the same as allowing our lives to pass us by in a meaningless and empty way. We can make use of our prayer today to ask ourselves in God's presence: Do I really want to identify myself more and more with Christ? Do I really make use of the actual happenings of each day to practise the human virtues, and, with God's grace, the supernatural virtues? Do I really try to love God more, doing the same things better each time and with greater rectitude of intention?

---

[6] St Alphonsus Liguori, *Practising the Love of Christ*
[7] *Conversations with Monsignor Escrivá*, 116

22.3 God always gives us his grace to live the Christian faith in all its fulness.

God doesn't ask anything impossible. He expects all Christians to live the christian virtues in their entirety, even if they find themselves in environments that seem to be moving farther and farther away from God. He will give the graces necessary for being faithful in such difficult situations. Furthermore, the good example He expects of all of us will often be the means of making Christ's doctrine attractive to others, and of evangelizing the world once again.

Many Christians, as they lose their supernatural outlook, and hence the real influence of grace on their lives, seem to think that the ideal proposed by Christ needs to be modified and adapted if ordinary people of our day and age are to be able to live it. They do not know how to stand their ground when confronted with moral dilemmas at work, or when discussions arise on the morality of marriage. They allow themselves to be influenced by the atmosphere of permissiveness and sensuality surrounding them. They give in to a more or less generalised pursuit of comfortable well-being, etc, just like everyone else. We must teach people through our own lives (we will have our faults but will be trying to overcome them), that the christian virtues can be lived in the midst of all honest undertakings, and that being understanding towards the defects and errors of others is not the same as lowering our own standards and sitting loose to the demands made by the Gospels.

So as to grow in the human and supernatural virtues, as well as in grace, we need to make a personal effort to develop the practice of these virtues in our everyday lives *until we acquire authentic habits, and not only the appearance of virtue. The facade appears full of strength and resilience. But how much softness and lack of will-*

power there is within! You must hold to your determination not to let your virtues become fancy dress but clothes that define your character.[8]

St John Chrysostom urges us to struggle in our interior life like *little children at school. First,* says the saint, *they learn the shape of the letters. Then they begin to distinguish the strokes; and thus, step by step, they learn to read. If we divide up the virtues into different parts, we can learn first, for example, not to speak badly of people. Then, passing to another letter, we can learn not to envy anybody: we can learn never under any circumstances to be a slave to the body: we can learn not to give way to gluttony. Passing on from there to the spiritual letters, we shall study continence, mortification of the senses, chastity, justice, and scorn for vainglory. We should try to be modest and of contrite heart. Let us link virtues together and write them on our souls. We have to do all this in our own home, with our friends, with our wives, with our children.*[9]

What is important is that we should make a definite and loving decision to strive after virtue in our everyday affairs. The more we practise performing these good acts, the easier we will find them to do next time. In this way we will identify ourselves more and more with Christ. Our Lady, *Model and school of all virtues*[10] will teach us to achieve our wish if we turn to her for help and advice. She will make it easier for us to reach the target we have set ourselves in our particular examination of conscience, in which we will often decide to aim at the acquisition of a very specific virtue.

---

[8] St J. Escrivá, *Furrow*, 777
[9] St John Chrysostom, *Homilies on the Psalms*, 11:8
[10] St Ambrose, *Treatise on Virginity*, 2

23. SINCERITY AND TRUTHFULNESS

23.1 The 'tongue-tied' devil. Need for sincerity.

To-day's Gospel tells us that Jesus *was casting out a devil that was dumb; when the demon had gone out, the dumb man spoke and the people marvelled.*[1]

Sickness, a physical evil that normally bears no relation to sin, can be a symbol of the state that a sinful man finds himself in; he is spiritually blind, deaf, paralysed. As well as being actual historical physical events, the cures that Jesus brings about are also symbolic: they represent the spiritual healing that He comes to effect in men's lives. Often in the way Jesus acts towards the sick He is giving us an image of the sacraments.

St John Chrysostom says about the Gospel passage from to-day's Mass that this man *was unable to present his request himself, because he was dumb; he was unable to ask others to do it either, because the devil had tied his tongue, and together with his tongue he had bound up his soul.*[2] The devil had him well and truly trussed up.

If we do not talk to Our Lord in our prayer about our wretchedness, and beg him to rid us of it; if we do not lay bare that wretchedness of ours in spiritual direction; if we keep silent because pride has sealed our lips, the sickness becomes practically incurable. Usually, if we do not talk about the way our soul is suffering, we also fail to listen; the soul becomes deaf to God's requests, we reject the argument and reason that could be the one clear light that will help us to return to the right road. On the other hand, it

---

[1] Luke 11:14; Matt 9:32-33
[2] St John Chrysostom, *Homilies on the Gospels*, 32, 1

will be easy for us to open our hearts sincerely if we try to accept this advice: ... *don't be frightened when you become aware of the burden of your poor body and of human passions. It would be silly and childishly naive to find out now that 'this' exists. Your wretchedness is not an obstacle, but a spur for you to become more closely united to God and to seek him constantly, because He purifies us.*[3]

As we repeat in the Responsorial Psalm of the Mass, *O that to-day you would hearken to his voice! Harden not your hearts!,*[4] let us make a resolution never to resist grace, and to be always very sincere.

23.2 Love for the truth. Sincerity, first of all with ourselves. Sincerity with God. Sincerity in spiritual direction and in Confession. Means of acquiring this virtue.

In order to live a life which is truly human, we must have a great love for the truth, which in a way is something that is sacred and must be treated with respect and love. The truth is sometimes so obscured by sin, by our passions and by a spirit of materialism, that if we did not live it we could never come to discern it. It is so easy to accept a lie when it comes to the aid of our laziness, flatters our vanity or our sensuality, or encourages in us a false sense of prestige! Sometimes the cause of insincerity is vainglory, pride, or even a fear of looking foolish.

Our Lord lived this virtue so much that he declared of himself, *I am the Truth.*[5] *The devil,* He said, *is a liar and the father of lies.*[6] Everything the devil promises is false. Jesus will ask the Father for us, for his own, that we may be *sanctified in the truth.*[7]

---

[3] St J. Escrivá, *Furrow*, 134
[4] Ps 94
[5] John 14:6
[6] John 8:44
[7] cf John 17, 17 *et seq*

There is a great deal of talk to-day about sincerity, authenticity and so on, but despite it people tend to hide themselves in anonymity and often disguise the true motives for their actions and conceal them from themselves and from others. They also try to remain anonymous before God, and flee from any personal encounter with him in prayer and in their examination of conscience. Nevertheless we will not be good Christians if we are not sincere with ourselves, with God and with other people. We men are sometimes afraid of the truth because it is demanding and inexorable. Sometimes the temptation may come to us to resort to pretence, to a small deception, to a half-truth or even a lie. On other occasions we may feel tempted to give another name to facts or to things so as not to upset people by telling the truth as it is.

Sincerity is a christian virtue of the highest order; we could not be good Christians if we did not live it with all its consequences. Sincerity with ourselves leads us to acknowledge our faults without any pretence and without seeking false excuses. Sincerity puts us on our guard against 'fabricating' the truth, or pretending that what suits us is true, like those who try to deceive themselves by saying that 'for them' something forbidden by God's law is not a sin. Subjectivity, our passions, lukewarmness, can all contribute towards our not being sincere with ourselves. The person who does not live this radical sincerity easily deforms his conscience and falls victim to interior blindness as regards the things of God.

Another common way of deceiving oneself is to be reluctant to accept the consequences of truth so as not to have to face up to them, or in such a case not to say the whole truth: *You never want to get to the heart of the matter. Sometimes, through politeness. Other times, most times, through fear of hurting yourself. Sometimes again, through fear of hurting others. And, always, through fear!*

As long as you are so afraid of the truth you will never be a man of sound judgement, a man of worth.[8]

The means that we first have to use in order to be sincere is prayer. Ask Our Lord to let us see our errors, the defects of our character ... ask him for strength to acknowledge them as such, and for the courage to ask his help in the inevitable struggle. Secondly, we have the daily examination of conscience, short but effective, by means of which we get to know ourselves. Next comes spiritual direction and Confession, really opening our souls, telling *the whole truth,* disclosing our innermost thoughts, so that those who direct us can help us on our way towards God. *Do not let even the smallest focal point of corruption take root in your souls, no matter how tiny it may be. Speak out. When water flows, it stays clean; blocked up, it becomes a stagnant pool full of repugnant filth. What was once drinking water becomes a breeding ground for insects.*[9] We will often find it helps us to be sincere if we say what we find most difficult first.

If with the help of grace we reject the 'tongue-tied' devil, we will find that one of the immediate fruits of sincerity is joy and peace in our souls. This is why we ask God for this virtue for ourselves, and for others as well.

23.3 Sincerity and truthfulness with others. The word of a Christian. *Loyalty and faithfulness* – virtues related to truthfulness. Other consequences of love for the truth.

Sincerity with God, with ourselves and with other people ... if we are not sincere with God we cannot love him or serve him. If we are not sincere with ourselves we cannot have a well-formed conscience which loves good and shuns evil. If we are not sincere with other people it

---

[8] St J. Escrivá, *The Way*, 33
[9] *idem*, *Friends of God*, 181

becomes impossible for us in any meaningful way to relate to them, and we do not please God.

The people around us have to know that we are truthful, that we never tell lies or ever practise deceit. Our word as Christians and honourable men and women has to be held in respect by others. *Let what you say be simply 'Yes' or 'No'; anything more than this comes from the devil.*[10] God wants to make the word of the person of good will, who is prepared to stand by what he says, stand out. The truth manifested in our dealings with others should also be a reflection of our relationship with God.

Love for truth will lead us to seek to put things right if we have blundered: *You must become accustomed never to tell a deliberate lie, whether to excuse yourself or for some other purpose, remembering always that God is the 'God of Truth'. If you happen to tell a lie inadvertently, correct it immediately by an explanation, or by making appropriate amends. An honest explanation always has more grace and force to excuse us than a lie has.*[11]

Another virtue closely related to truthfulness and sincerity is *loyalty*, which is truthfulness in one's behaviour. It means keeping one's word, one's promises, one's agreements. Our friends and acquaintances have to know us as men and women who are loyal. Faithfulness is loyalty to a strict commitment contracted with God or before God. Jesus *is called Faithful and True.*[12] Holy Scripture constantly speaks of God as the one who is faithful to his covenant with his people, the one who faithfully fulfils the plan of salvation that He has promised.[13]

Unfaithfulness is always false. Faithfulness, however,

---

[10] Matt 5:37
[11] St Francis de Sales, *Introduction to the Devout Life*, III:30
[12] Rev 19:11
[13] cf Rom 3:7

is an indispensable virtue in both one's private and social life. It is on faithfulness that marriage, the fulfilment of contracts, the ways in which governments act, etc., rely.

Love for the truth will lead us not to form hasty judgements, based on superficial information about people or events. We need to exercise a healthy critical spirit towards the news broadcast by radio, television, newspapers or magazines, for it is often biased or simply incomplete. Often objective facts are wrapped in opinions or interpretations that can give a deformed view of the reality. We have to be specially careful about news referring directly or indirectly to the Church. For love of truth itself we have to leave aside the sectarian channels of information which do nothing but muddy the waters. We have to look for information that is objective, true and discerning. At the same time we have to contribute towards giving others correct information. Then the promise of Jesus will become a reality, *The truth will make you free.*[14]

---

[14] John 8:32

24. LOVE OF GOD

24.1 The infinite love of God for each person.

Throughout Sacred Scripture one reads continually of the love of God for us. He lets us know this in various ways. He assures us that, though a mother might forget about the child of her womb, He will never forget about us. For *he leads us by the hand*[1] so as to have us always within sight.

The First Reading of the Mass, from the prophet Hosea, is a moving witness to the triumph of God's love over the repeated infidelities and hypocritical conversions of his people. Israel at last recognises that human alliances will not save her, nor will man-made gods,[2] or empty holocausts, but love, expressed in faithfulness to the Covenant. It is then that there is a glimmer of light and a glimpse of happiness without limit. That conversion itself is the fruit of God's love, for everything is born of him, who loves us with great generosity. *I will bring healing to their crushed spirits: in free mercy I will give them back my love; my vengeance has passed them by. I will be morning dew, to make Israel grow as the lilies grow, strike roots deep as the forest of Lebanon. Those branches shall spread; it shall become fair as a garden of olives, fragrant as cedar of Lebanon. None that dwells under the protection of that name but shall come back to me; corn shall be theirs in plenty, and they will prosper in growth like one of their own vineyards, farmed as the vintage of Lebanon itself.*[3]

We can never imagine how much God loves us. In order to save us, when we were lost, he sent his only-

---

[1] Is 49:15-17
[2] cf Hos 14:4
[3] *First Reading of the Mass*, Hos 14:2-10

begotten Son so that, in giving up his life, he would redeem us from the state we had fallen into. *God so loved the world that he gave his only-begotten Son, so that those who believe in him may not perish, but have eternal life.*[4] This very love moves him to give himself to us in a habitual way, dwelling in our soul in grace: *If a man has any love for me, he will be true to my word; and then he will win my Father's love, and we will then both come to him, and make our continual abode with him.*[5] And he communicates with us in the intimacy of our hearts, both during these periods of prayer and throughout the day.

I will serve you, because I came 'to serve and not to be served'. I am a friend, an associate and head, and a brother and sister, and a mother; I am everything, and all I want is an intimate friendship with you. I have become poor for you, a beggar for you, been crucified for you, buried in a sepulchre for you; in Heaven I intercede before God the Father for you; and on earth I am his ambassador to you. You are everything to me, brother, co-heir, friend and associate. What more do you want?[6] What more could we want? When we contemplate Our Lord in each one of the scenes of *The Way of the Cross* these words easily come to our lips, from the heart: *To know that you love me so much, my God, and yet ... I have not lost my mind!*[7]

24.2 His mercy shown even when we offend him.

Among the gods there is none like you, O Lord, for you are great and do marvellous deeds; you alone are God.[8] One of the greatest marvels is the love He has for us. He loves us with a singular and personal love, each one of us

---

[4] John 3:16
[5] John 14:23
[6] St John Chrysostom, *Homilies on St Matthew*, 76
[7] St J. Escrivá, *The Way*, 425
[8] *Entrance Antiphon*, Ps 85:8-10

separately, in particular. He has never stopped loving us, helping us, protecting us, talking to us – not even when we have been most ungrateful or committed the most serious sins. It is, perhaps, on such occasions that we have received the most attention from God as in the parables where he wished to express his mercy in a singular way: the lost sheep is the only one carried on the shoulders, the feast is laid on by the father for the one of his sons who has hurt him most, the lost drachma is carefully sought by its owner until she finds it ...[9]

God's attention to and his love for us have been constant throughout our lives. He has been aware of all the circumstances and events which we have had to live through. He is beside us in every situation and at every moment. *Behold I am with you all through the days that are coming, until the consummation of the world,*[10] until the final moments of our lives. How often He has continued an apparently chance meeting! In joy and in sorrow, through what at first sight seemed a misfortune, in a friend, in a colleague at work, in a priest who has looked after us ... *Just think about the wonder of God's love. Our Lord comes out to meet us, He waits for us: He is by the roadside where we cannot but see him, and He calls each of us personally, speaking to us about our own concerns – which are also his. He stirs us to sorrow, opens our conscience to be generous; He encourages us to want to be faithful, so that we can be called his disciples.*[11]

As a sign of his love He has left us the sacraments, *channels of divine mercy*. Among them, since we can receive some of the sacraments more frequently, what pleases him in a special way is Confession, where he

---

[9] cf Luke 15:1
[10] Matt 28:20
[11] St J. Escrivá, *Christ is passing by*, 59

pardons us our sins, and the Blessed Sacrament, where he has desired to remain in a most singular act of love for men.

It is for love of us that he has given his Mother to be our Mother. As a sign of this love He has also given us an angel who protects us, He advises us and showers us with a host of favours until we reach the end of our passage on earth, when He awaits us with the promised Heaven, a happiness without end and without limit. There we have had a place prepared for us.

We tell Him, with one of the prayers of to-day's Mass: *May your strength be at work in us, O Lord, pervading our minds and bodies, that what we have received by participating in this Sacrament may bring us the fulness of redemption.*[12] And we give thanks for so much Love, for such loving care, which we do not in any way merit. And we try to set ourselves aflame with desire to please him. Love is repaid with Love. A mystic expresses this idea poetically: *Had I a million lives I would give them to possess you, and a thousand ... a thousand more I would give ... to love You if I were able to ... with this love, pure and strong, with which You, being who you are ... love us continuously.*[13]

24.3 Our response. The first Commandment. Love of God in the incidents of each day.

The Gospel of the Mass tells us: *One of the scribes came up to Jesus and put a question to him: Which is the first of all the commandments? Jesus replied, This is the first: Listen, Israel, the Lord our God is the one Lord, and you must love the Lord your God with all your heart, with all your soul, with all your mind, and with all your strength.*[14]

He expects from each one of us an unconditional

---

[12] *Prayer after Communion*
[13] F.J. del Valle, *About the Holy Spirit*
[14] Mark 12:28-30

response to his love for us. Our love for God is shown in a thousand and one little incidents of each day: we love God through our work done well, the way we live our family life, our social intercourse, the use we make of our leisure time ... Everything can be converted into a deed of love. *While we carry out as perfectly as we can (with all our mistakes and limitations) the tasks allotted to us by our situation and duties, our soul longs to escape. It is drawn towards God like iron drawn by a magnet. One begins to love Jesus in a more effective way, with the sweet and gentle surprise of his encounter.*[15]

When we rise to respond to God's love, the obstacles disappear; on the other hand, without love even the tiniest difficulty seems insuperable. If there is union with the Lord, everything becomes tolerable. *While all sorts of setbacks are encountered as difficult by those who do not love; those who do love, on the contrary, find them trivial and easily manageable. There is no suffering, however cruel or violent it may be, which is not made bearable or even reduced to nothing by love.*[16] Cheerfulness, maintained even in the midst of difficulties, is the clearest sign that the love of God informs all our actions. For, comments St Augustine, *he who loves either does not feel the difficulty or he loves the very difficulty itself ... The works of those who love are never distressing.*[17]

Our love for God has to be supreme and absolute. Within this love all the noble loves of the earth find their place, according to the vocation each one has received, and each one fits in and is accommodated with naturalness. *It would not be fair to say 'either God or man'. They ought to love 'God and man'; love for the latter should never be*

---

[15] St J. Escrivá, *Friends of God*, 296
[16] St Augustine, *Sermon 70*
[17] St Augustine, *De bono viduitatis*, 21, 26

more than for God, or opposed to God or equal to the love for God. In other words; love for God is certainly dominant, but it is not exclusive. The Bible declares Jacob to be holy and loved by God: this is shown by the six years he spent winning over Rachael to be his wife. And those years seemed to him to be very few, such was his love for her. Francis de Sales comments on this: 'Jacob,' he writes, 'loved Rachael with all his might and with all his might did he love God. But he did not love Rachael in the way he loved God, nor did he love God in the way he did Rachael. He loved God as his God as more than all things and more than he loved himself. He loved Rachael as his wife above all other women and as he loved himself. He loved God with an absolute and sovereign love, and Rachael with his conjugal love. One love is not contrary to the other, because his love for Rachael did not impede the supreme transcendence of his love for God.' [18]

Love for God is necessarily shown in love for others. The way we love God is shown in the way we live charity with those who are beside us in our day-to-day lives. *In this they will know that you are my disciples ...* [19] the Lord has told us: in refinement in dealings with others; in mutual respect, in thinking in a way more favourable to others, in helping in little things in the home or at work, in a loving and appropriate fraternal correction, in prayer for the one who needs it most ...

Let us ask Our Lady to-day to teach us to respond to the love of her Son, so that we may also know how to love, with deeds, her other children who are our brothers.

---

[18] John Paul I, *General Audience*, 27 September 1978
[19] John 13:35

25. THE PHARISEE AND THE PUBLICAN

25.1 The need for humility. Pride perverts all.

Have mercy on me, O God ... For in sacrifice you take no delight; burnt offering from me you would refuse; my sacrifice, a contrite spirit. A humbled, contrite heart you will not spurn.[1] The Lord is moved and showers his graces on a humble heart.

In the Gospel of today's Mass[2] St Luke presents us with a scene with two men going up to the Temple to pray, one a Pharisee, the other a publican. The Pharisees considered themselves people who fulfilled the Law to perfection. The publicans were looked down upon for exacting taxes imposed by the occupying power, and were considered to be more in love with their detested profession than with fulfilling the Law. Before relating the parable the Evangelist goes out of his way to point out that Jesus was speaking to men who considered themselves to be just and who despised others.

The parable immediately makes clear that the Pharisee entered the Temple without humility and without love. He is the centre of his own thoughts and of his self-appraisal. *O God, I give you thanks because I am not like other men, thieves, unjust, adulterers; not one such as this publican here. I fast twice a week; I contribute a tenth of all I possess.* Instead of praising God he has begun, perhaps in a rather oblique fashion, to praise himself. Everything he did – the fasting, the paying of his tithes – was good. But all the goodness of these works was, however, undone by his pride: he attributed merit to himself and he had contempt for

---

[1] *Responsorial Psalm*
[2] Luke 18:9-14

others. Both humility and charity were lacking, and without these there can be neither good works nor any virtue.

The Pharisee stood where he could be seen. He prayed, he gave thanks for everything he did. But there is in his attitude a massive self-complacency, a great deal of 'self-satisfaction'. He compares himself with others and considers himself to have fulfilled the Law better, to be more just than they – to be altogether superior to them. Pride is the greatest obstacle man can put in the way of divine grace. It is the most dangerous capital vice: it is pervasive, and tends to insinuate itself even into good works, detracting from their value and depriving them of their supernatural merit. It is deeply rooted in man (in his disordered self-love), and there is nothing more difficult than to uproot it or even to recognise it for what it is. *To me, with the admiration I owe myself,* wrote Rousseau on the first page of a book. And many other miserable souls might easily inscribe the same thing on the last page of their own lives.

How sad it would be if you and I were to live or end up like this. Let us make a serious examination of conscience.[3] We ask the Lord to have compassion on us and not to allow us to fall into this state. Each day we implore him for the virtue of humility, and to-day we resolve to be more attentive to the many and varied signs which the capital sin of pride exhibits, and to rectify our intention in our deeds as often as is necessary.

25.2 The hypocrisy of the Pharisees. Signs of pride.

Some Pharisees were converted and became friends and faithful disciples of the Lord. But many others did not know how to recognise the Messiah who walked through their streets and squares. Pride led them to lose sight of the true meaning of their existence; their religious life, which

---

[3] St J. Escrivá, *Furrow*, 719

they were so proud of, was hollow and empty. Their
practices of piety were overshadowed by a purely external
formality and mere appearances, a meaningless playing to
the gallery. When they fasted they made sure others knew
of it by their distressed countenances;[4] when they prayed
they liked to stand up ostentatiously in the synagogue or in
the middle of the public squares;[5] when they gave alms
they announced what they were doing as if with a fanfare
of trumpets.[6]

Our Lord would warn his disciples: *Don't become like
the Pharisees.* And He would explain why they ought not to
follow their example. *All their deeds are done so as to be
seen by men.*[7] Using strong language so that they would react,
he called the Pharisees hypocrites, comparing them to white-
ned sepulchres – impressive to look at, but putrid within.[8]
The Pharisees were frauds. Their vainglory *was what
separated them from God: it made them look for another
theatre for their fights, and it saw to their being van-
quished. For, as one tries to please the spectators who see
what each one of us does, attention to the impression one
makes on such onlookers will be the kind of combat one is
really engaged in.*[9] To be humble, we can never forget that
the Spectator, the One who is present in our lives and who
witnesses all our deeds, is the Lord, whom at every
moment we have to try to please.

Through their pride, the Pharisees became severe,
inflexible, and demanding with their fellow-men, while
being complacent and indulgent towards themselves: *Woe
upon you for burdening men with packs too heavy to be*

---

[4] cf Matt 6:16
[5] cf Matt 6:5
[6] cf Matt 6:2
[7] Matt 23:5
[8] cf Matt 23:27
[9] St John Chrysostom, *Homily on St Matthew*, 72:1

borne, packs which you yourselves will not lift a finger to help carry.[10] To us the Lord says: *Among you, the greatest of all has to be the servant of all.*[11] And through St Paul, the Holy Spirit says: *Bear the burden of one another's failings; then you will be bearing the burden of Christ.*[12] One of the clearest signs of humility is that of serving and helping others, not occasionally or sporadically, but in a constant way.

Perhaps one of Our Lord's strictest reproaches was: *You have neither entered yourselves nor let others enter when they would.*[13] The Pharisees closed the road to those they were meant to guide. *Blind men leading the blind!*[14] he called them on another occasion. Pride cuts one off from supernatural light both for oneself and for others.

Pride makes itself felt in every aspect of life. *In dealings with one's neighbour, self-love makes us hyper-sensitive, inflexible, proud, impatient; it causes us to exaggerate our ego and our rights, to be cold, indifferent, unjust in our judgements and in word. One delights in speaking about one's actions, of one's insights and experiences, of difficulties, of sufferings, even when there is no need to do so. In practices of piety, one takes pleasure in looking at others, observing and judging them: one is inclined to make comparisons with them and to believe oneself better; to see only defects in them and deny their good qualities: to attribute to them intentions and aims which are not noble, and even to wish them ill. Self love ... leads us to feel offended when we are humiliated, insulted or passed over, or when we are not considered, esteemed or made a fuss of as*

---

[10] Luke 11:46
[11] Matt 23:11
[12] Gal 6:2
[13] Luke 11:52
[14] Matt 15:14

we had hoped for.[15]

We have to distance ourselves from the example and prayer of the Pharisee and learn from the publican. *My God*, he says, *have mercy on me, for I am a sinner.* It is an aspiration which can often be repeated, fostering as it does in the soul a love for humility, and bringing its importance to our attention when it is time for prayer.

25.3 Asking for humility.

The Lord is near to contrite hearts, so ready to defend the humbled spirit.[16] The publican addresses God in humble prayer, not trusting in his own merits, but in God's mercy: *The publican stood far off: he would not even lift his eyes up towards heaven; he only beat his breast, and said, 'God, be merciful to me; I am a sinner'.*

The Lord who *flouts the scornful, and gives the humble man his grace,*[17] pardons and forgives him. *I tell you, he went back home higher in God's favour than the other.*

The publican *'stood afar off', and so God the more easily approached him ... Whether he is far off from you or not depends on yourself. Love and He shall come closer; love and He will rest in you.*[18]

We too can learn from the publican that our prayer has to be humble, attentive and full of trust. We try *to avoid our prayers being a monologue centred on ourselves*, or concerned with virtues we believe ourselves to possess.

Behind this parable there is an idea which Our Lord is trying to instil in us: humility has to be the basis for the whole of our relationship with God and with other people. It is the foundation stone of the building under construction – our

---

[15] B. Baur, *In Silence with God*
[16] Ps 33:19
[17] Jas 4:6
[18] St Augustine, *Sermon 9*, 21

interior life. *Don't wish to be like a gilded weather-cock on top of a great building: however much it shines, and however high it stands, it adds nothing to the solidity of the building.*

Rather be like an old stone block hidden in the foundations, underground, where no-one can see you: because of you the house will not fail.[19]

When someone feels he has been disregarded in some insignificant matter, in what are really tiny details, he ought to realise that he is still falling short of being truly humble. It is an opportunity to accept one's own littleness and to become less proud. *You are humble not when you humble yourself, but when you are humbled by others and you bear it for Christ.*[20]

The help of Our Lady is the surest guarantee of progress in this virtue. *Mary is both Mother of mercy and of affection, to whom no one turns in vain; entrust yourself confidently to her, asking her to bring this virtue (of humility) within your reach, a virtue which She highly appreciated. Don't be afraid of not having your request heard by her. Mary will ask this of God, who exalts the humble and brings down the proud. And as Mary is all-powerful beside her Son, your prayer will certainly be answered.*[21] Having considered the Lord's teachings, and having contemplated the example of humility in Our Lady, we can finish with this petition: *Lord, take away my pride; crush my self-love, my desire to affirm myself and impose myself on others. Make the foundation of my personality be my identification with you.*[22]

---

[19] St J. Escrivá, *The Way*, 590
[20] *ibid*, 594
[21] J. Pecci, (Pope Leo XIII), *The Practice of Humility*, 56
[22] St J. Escrivá, *Christ is passing by*, 31

FOURTH SUNDAY OF LENT

26. JOY IN THE CROSS

26.1 Joy is compatible with mortification and pain. It is the opposite of sadness, not of penance.

Rejoice with Jerusalem and be glad for her, all you who love her ... we sing in the Antiphon of today's Mass: Rejoice with Jerusalem ....[1]

Joy is essentially a Christian characteristic, and in this liturgical season the Church does not fail to remind us that it should be present at every moment of our lives. There is a joy proper to the hope of Advent, then the joy of Christmas itself, so lively and warm. And as the year advances there is the joy of increasing closeness to the risen Christ. But today, as we approach the end of Lent, we meditate on the joy of the Cross. It is one and the same joy as that of being united to Christ: *only in him can each of us say truthfully with St Paul: He loved me and gave himself up for me* (Gal 2:20). This should be the source of our greatest happiness, as well as the source of our strength and support. Should we have the misfortune to encounter sorrow, undergo suffering, experience misunderstanding, or even to fall into sin, how quickly will our thoughts turn to the One who always loves us and who, with his infinite love as God, overcomes in every trial, fills our emptiness, forgives all our sins and eagerly impels us towards a new path that is safe and joyful.[2]

This Sunday is traditionally called *Laetare Sunday* from the opening words of the Entrance Antiphon. The strictness of the Lenten liturgy is interrupted on this

---

[1] Is 66:10-11
[2] St John Paul II, *Address*, 1 March 1980

Sunday with words that speak to us of joy. Today, rose-coloured vestments, if they are available, are permitted in place of purple,[3] and the altar can be decked with flowers as on no other day in Lent.[4]

In this way the Church wishes to remind us that *joy* is perfectly compatible with mortification and pain. It is *sadness* and not penance which is opposed to happiness. Taking part to the utmost in this liturgical season which reaches its climax in the Passion, and hence in suffering, we realise that approaching the Cross also means that the moment of our Redemption is coming ever closer. In this way, the Church and each of her children are filled with joy: *Rejoice with Jerusalem and be glad for her, all you who love her.*

The mortifications we do during these days should not cast a shadow over our interior joy. Rather, it ought to increase it, because our Redemption is near at hand; the pouring out of love for mankind, which is the Passion, is coming and the joy of Easter will soon be upon us. We therefore feel the need to be very closely united to Our Lord, so that our lives too may reflect once more the suffering He underwent for our sakes, as well as experiencing great happiness in the attainment of the glory and joy of the Resurrection through his Passion and his Cross.

26.2 Joy has a spiritual origin, arising from a heart that loves and feels itself loved by God.

Rejoice in the Lord always: again I say, Rejoice[5] – and this with a cheerfulness that is real happiness, an interior joy which cannot fail to be shown outwardly as well.

---

[3] Roman Missal, *General Instructions*, 308
[4] *Caeremoniale Episcoporum*, 1984, 48
[5] Phil 4:4

It is well known that there are different degrees of this 'joy'. Its most noble expression is the cheerfulness or 'happiness' in its strict sense, when someone at the level of his higher faculties finds satisfaction in the possession of a good which is recognised and loved ... All the more reason then, that such a one should experience spiritual joy and happiness when his spirit enters into the possession of God who is known and loved as his supreme and immutable good.[6] And Saint Paul VI went on to say: *Technological society has succeeded in multiplying the occasions of pleasure, but finds great difficulty in giving birth to happiness. For happiness has its origin elsewhere: it is a spiritual thing. Money, comfort, hygiene, material security etc, may often not be lacking, but nevertheless, despite these advantages, boredom, suffering and sadness are frequently to be found supervening in the lives of many people.*[7]

Christians understand these thoughts of the Pope very well. They are aware that joy and happiness stem from a heart that knows itself to be loved by God and which in its turn is madly in love with him. Moreover, it will be a heart that strives to express its love in deeds, since it knows that *deeds are love – not sweet words*[8]

A heart in union and at peace with God, even though it knows itself to be that of a sinner, goes to the source of all forgiveness, to Christ in the sacrament of Penance.

Lord, it is with great joy that we offer you the sacrifice that brings everlasting healing.[9] Suffering and tribulation are inevitably and eventually the lot of everyone on this earth. But suffering of itself alone neither transforms nor

---

[6] St Paul VI, Exhortation, *Gaudete in Domino*, 19 April 1975
[7] *ibid*
[8] St J. Escrivá, *The Way*, 933
[9] cf Heb 13:15

purifies. It may even be the cause of rebellion and hatred. Some Christians abandon Our Lord when they meet the Cross, because they seek a purely human happiness, free from pain and accompanied by material wealth.

God asks us to lose our fear of pain and tribulation and unite ourselves to him, as He waits for us on the Cross. Our soul will then be more purified, our love stronger. And we will realise that joy is inseparable from the Cross. Not only that, but we will also understand that we can never be happy if we are not united to Christ on the Cross, and that we will never know how to love if we do not at the same time love sacrifice. Those tribulations that appear to our poor human reasoning as unjust and meaningless are necessary for our personal holiness and for the salvation of many souls. Within the mystery of co-redemption, our sufferings united to those of Christ acquire an incomparable value for the entire Church and the whole of mankind. If we humbly have recourse to God, He will make us see that everything, even events and circumstances apparently least likely to do so, work together for the good of those who love him. Suffering, when seen in its true light, when it serves as a means of loving more, produces great peace and deep joy. That is why God often blesses us with the Cross.

That is how we must travel along *the way of self-giving: the Cross on our shoulders, a smile on our lips and light in our hearts.*[10]

26.3 God loves those who find joy in giving.

A Christian gives himself to God and to those around him. He makes demands on himself through mortification and in the way he faces up to difficulties. And he does all this most cheerfully, for he realises that these things lose

---

[10] St J. Escrivá, *The Way of the Cross*, Second Station, 3

their value if done under reluctant protest and with complaint. *God loves the cheerful giver.*[11] We should not be surprised to find that it hurts to do mortification and penance. What matters is knowing how to set about undergoing and accepting them manfully, in the secure knowledge that they please God, who is watching us.

Happy? – The question made me think. Words have not yet been invented to express all that one feels – in the heart and in the will – when one knows himself to be a son of God.[12] It is only logical that anyone who knows he is a son of God should feel such great inner happiness.

The experience that the saints have handed down to us is unanimous in this respect. It is enough to recall St Paul's confession to the Corinthians: *I am filled with comfort. With all our affliction, I am overjoyed.*[13] And it is useful to remember that St Paul's life was in no way easy or comfortable: *Five times have I received at the hands of the Jews the forty lashes less one. Three times I have been beaten with rods; once I was stoned. Three times I have been shipwrecked; a night and a day I have been adrift at sea; on frequent journeys, in danger from rivers, danger from robbers, danger from my own people, danger from Gentiles, danger in the city, danger in the wilderness, danger at sea, danger from false brethren; in toil and hardship, through many a sleepless night, in hunger and thirst, often without food, in cold and exposure.*[14] Still, in spite of all this, St Paul speaks the truth when he tells us: *I am filled with comfort. With all our affliction, I am overjoyed.*

As Holy Week and Easter draw near, so do for-

---

[11] 2 Cor 9:7
[12] St J. Escrivá, *Furrow*, 61
[13] 2 Cor 7:4
[14] 2 Cor 11:24-27

giveness, mercy, divine compassion and a superabundance of grace. A little while longer and the mystery of our salvation will be consummated. If at times we have been afraid of penance and atonement, we will be filled with courage at the thought of how short is the time involved, and how great the reward, a prize entirely disproportionate to our own little efforts. So let us cheerfully follow Jesus to Jerusalem, to Calvary, to the Cross. After all, *is it not true that as soon as you cease to be afraid of the Cross, of what people call the Cross, when you set your will to accept the Will of God, then you find happiness, and all your worries, all your sufferings, physical or moral, pass away?*[15]

---

[15] St J. Escrivá, *The Way of the Cross*, Second Station

27. PERSONAL PRAYER

27.1 The need for prayer. Jesus' example.

When he had found a place to pray in ...[1] There are many passages in the Gospel narrating that Jesus has withdrawn from the crowds and has gone on his own to pray.[2] And this is more clearly thrown into relief at the more important moments of his public ministry: at his Baptism,[3] at the election of the Apostles,[4] on the occasion of the first multiplication of the loaves,[5] at the Transfiguration,[6] etc. It was a normal thing for Jesus to do: *At times He spent the whole night in an intimate conversation with his Father. The Apostles were filled with love when they saw Christ pray.*[7] How it helps us too!

During this Lenten period we could perhaps concentrate especially on a scene we contemplate in the Rosary: the agony of Jesus in the Garden. Immediately before giving himself in the Passion, the Lord makes for the Garden of Gethsemane with the apostles. Jesus must often have prayed there, for St Luke says: *Now He went out, as his custom was, to Mount Olivet.*[8] But this time Jesus' prayer would be special: the moment for his agony had arrived.

Arriving at Gethsemane He tells them: *Pray that you*

---

[1] Luke 11:1-3
[2] cf Matt 14:23; Mark 1:35; Luke 5:16; etc
[3] cf Luke 3:21
[4] cf Luke 6:12
[5] cf Mark 6:46
[6] cf Luke 9:29
[7] St J. Escrivá, *Christ is passing by*, 119
[8] Luke 22:39

may not enter into temptation.[9] Before withdrawing a little to pray, Our Lord asks the Apostles too to pray. Jesus knows that they are soon to be subjected to the temptation of scandal on seeing the Master taken captive. He had already announced it at the Last Supper; but now He warns them that unless they are found vigilant and praying, they will not pass the test.

Prayer is indispensable for us, for if we neglect our dealings with God, little by little our spiritual life begins to languish. *If you abandon prayer you may at first live on spiritual reserves and, after that, by cheating.*[10] On the other hand, prayer unites us to God and He tells us: *Without me you can do nothing.*[11] It is good to pray with perseverance,[12] never vacillating. We have to speak with Him a great deal, insistently, in the various circumstances of our lives. Now, moreover, during Lent, we walk with Jesus along the Way of the Cross and *without prayer, how difficult it is to accompany him.*[13]

With the example of his own life, the Lord teaches us what our fundamental approach has to be: a continuous filial dialogue with God. *And mental prayer, in my view, is nothing but friendly intercourse, and frequent solitary conversation, with him Who we know loves us.*[14] We have always to try to have presence of God and to contemplate the mysteries of our Faith. This dialogue with God should not be interrupted. But even further, it ought to be carried on in the midst of all our activities. And what is indispensable is that it should be more intense during those periods we dedicate each day to mental prayer: we

---

[9] Luke 22:40
[10] St J. Escrivá, *Furrow*, 445
[11] John 15:5
[12] cf Luke 18:1
[13] St J. Escrivá, *The Way*, 89
[14] St Teresa, *Life*, 8, 2

meditate and we speak in his presence, knowing that He truly *sees us and hears us*. The need for prayer, together with the importance of charity, is one of the points most stressed by Our Lord in his ministry.

27.2 Personal prayer: confident dialogue with God.

Then he parted from them, going a stone's throw off, and knelt down to pray. 'Father,' he said, 'if it pleases thee, take away this chalice from before me; only as thy Will is, not as mine is.'[15]

When his spiritual suffering was so intense that it led him into agony, the Lord turns to his Father with a prayer brimming with confidence. He calls him *Abba,* Father, and says intimate things to him. This is the way we too should adopt. In our lives there will be moments of spiritual peace and others of more intense struggle, some moments perhaps of darkness and others of profound sorrow, with temptations to discouragement. The sight of Jesus in the Garden always points to the way we have to proceed – with a persevering and confident prayer. To move along the road to holiness, but especially when we feel the weight of our weaknesses, we have to recollect ourselves in prayer, in an intimate conversation with the Lord.

Public prayer (or prayer in common), in which all the faithful take part, is holy and necessary, for God also wishes to see his children praying together.[16] But the Lord's precept: *go into your inner room and shut the door upon yourself, and so pray to your Father in secret,*[17] should never be superseded. The liturgy is public prayer *par excellence: it is the summit toward which the activity of the Church is directed; it is also the fount from which all*

---

[15] Luke 22:41-42
[16] cf Matt 18:19-20
[17] Matt 6:6

her power flows ... The spiritual life, however, is not limited solely to participation in the liturgy. The Christian is indeed called to pray with others, but he must also enter into his inner chamber to pray to his Father in secret; furthermore, according to the teaching of the Apostle, he must pray without ceasing (1 Thess 5:17).[18]

Prayer in company with other Christians ought also to be personal prayer; while the lips recite it with the proper pace and pauses, the mind gives it all her attention.

In prayer one speaks with God just as one converses with a friend – knowing that he is present, always attentive to what we are saying, listening to us and replying. It is in such intimate conversation as the one we are just now trying to have with God, that we throw open our soul to the Lord, to adore him, to give him thanks, to ask him for help, to go more deeply – as the Apostles did – into the divine teachings.

You write: 'To pray is to talk with God. But about what?' About him, about yourself: joys, sorrows, successes and failures, noble ambitions, daily worries, weaknesses! And acts of thanksgiving and petitions: and Love and reparation.

In a word: to get to know him and to get to know yourself: 'to get acquainted'.[19]

Prayer ought never to be impersonal, anonymous, dispersed and lost in the crowd; because God, who has redeemed each individual person, wants to maintain a dialogue with each one: at the end of one's life, salvation or condemnation will depend on the personal response of each one. Prayer ought to be the dialogue of a particular person – one who has ideals, a job, friends, who has received specific graces from God – with his God.

---

[18] Second Vatican Council, *Sacrosanctum Concilium*, 10:12

[19] St J. Escrivá, *The Way*, 91

27.3 Using the means to pray in a recollected way.

When he rose from his prayer, he went back to his disciples and found that they were sleeping, overwrought with sorrow. 'How can you sleep?' he asked. 'Rise up and pray, so that you may not enter into temptation.' [20]

The apostles had ignored the Lord's command. He had left them there, close to himself, so that they would watch and pray, and thus not fall into temptation. But even now they do not love him enough, and allow themselves to be overcome by sleep and weakness, leaving Jesus unaccompanied, alone during that time of his agony. Sleep, the mental epitome of human weakness, has allowed an evil sadness to take hold of them: depression, lack of spiritual struggle, abandonment of a life of piety ...

We will not get into this situation if we maintain a living dialogue with God during each period of prayer. We will frequently resort to the Gospels or another book – like this one which you are reading – so that it may help us to channel our dialogue, to come closer to Our Lord, for whom no one or nothing can be a substitute. Thus many saints have been made. *During all these years,* says St Teresa, *except after communicating, I never dared begin to pray without a book; my soul was as much afraid to engage in prayer without one as if it were having to go and fight against a host of enemies. With this help, which was a companionship to me, and a shield with which I could parry the blows of my many thoughts, I felt comforted.* [21]

We have to use all the means at our disposal to do this mental prayer in a recollected way. We should do it in the best place, according to our circumstances; and, whenever possible, in front of Our Lord in the tabernacle. It should be done, too, at the time we have already planned in our

---

[20] Luke 22:45-46
[21] St Teresa, *Life*, 4, 3

FOURTH WEEK OF LENT – TUESDAY

28. PATIENT STRUGGLE AGAINST DEFECTS

28.1 The paralytic at Bethsaida. Constancy in the struggle and in the desire to improve.

The Gospel of to-day's Mass tells us about a man who has been ill for thirty-eight years, and who is hoping for a miraculous cure from the waters of the pool at Bethsaida. *When Jesus saw him and knew that he had been lying there a long time, he said to him, Do you want to be healed?* The sick man replied in all simplicity: *Sir, I have no one to put me into the pool when the water is troubled, and while I am going another steps down before me.* Jesus said to him, *Rise, take up your pallet and walk.* The paralytic obeyed. *And at once the man was healed, and he took up his pallet and walked.*[1]

The Lord is always willing to listen to us and to give us whatever we need in any situation. His goodness is always in excess of our calculations. But it requires a corresponding response on our part, with a desire to get out of the situation we are in. There can be no pact with our defects and errors, and we must make the effort to overcome them. We cannot ever 'get used to' the shortcomings and weaknesses which separate us from God and from others, on the excuse that they are part of our character, or that we have already tried several times over to tackle them without positive result.

It is the heart which moves us to improve in our interior dispositions through that conversion of the heart to God and to works of penance, thus preparing our souls to receive the graces God wishes to grant us.

Jesus asks us to persevere in the struggle, and to begin again as often as necessary, realising that it is in struggle that love grows. *The Lord does not ask the paralytic in order to learn – this would be superfluous – but to make his patience known to all, for that invalid for thirty-eight years had hoped, without ceasing, to be freed from his illness.*[2]

Our love for Christ is shown in our decisiveness and in the effort we make to root out as soon as possible our dominant defect, or to obtain a virtue which seems to us difficult to practise. But it is also shown *in the patience which we exercise in the ascetical struggle*: it is possible that the Lord will ask us to struggle over a long period, perhaps *for thirty-eight years*, to grow in a particular virtue or to overcome that particular negative aspect of our interior life.

A well-known spiritual author has taught the importance of being patient with one's own defects so as to develop *the art of profiting from one's faults.*[3] We ought not to be surprised – or disconcerted – when, having used all the means reasonably within our reach, we have not managed to reach the goal we had set ourselves. We must not simply *get used to it*, but *use our faults* to grow in true humility, in experience, in maturity of judgement.

The man the Mass presents to us was constant over thirty-eight years, and we may suppose that he could have so continued to the end of his days. The reward for his constancy was, above all, the meeting with Jesus.

[2] St John Chrysostom, *Homilies on the Gospel of St John*, 36

[3] J. Tissot, *The Art of Profiting from our Faults*

28.2 Patience in interior life. Return to the Lord as often as necessary.

Be patient, therefore, brethren, until the coming of the Lord. Behold, the farmer waits for the precious fruit of the earth, being patient over it until it receives the early and the late rain.[4]

It is necessary for one to know, to hope and to struggle with persevering patience, realising that this is what pleases God. St Francis de Sales used to say: One has to suffer, in patience, the setbacks to our perfection, doing whatever we can to make progress in good spirit. We hope with patience, and instead of getting frustrated at having done so little in the past, we try diligently to do more in the future.[5]

Moreover, virtue is not normally attained through sporadic bursts of effort. Rather is it in the continuity of the effort, the constancy of going on trying each day, each week, helped by grace. To win the battles of the soul, the best strategy often is to bide one's time and apply the suitable remedy with patience and perseverance. Make more acts of hope. Let me remind you that in your interior life you will suffer defeats, and you will have ups and downs – may God make them imperceptible – because no one is free from these misfortunes. But our all-powerful and merciful Lord has granted us the precise means with which to conquer ... All we have to do is to use them, resolving to begin again and again at every moment, whenever necessary.[6]

The heart of constancy lies in love: only with love can one be patient and struggle, without accepting failures and

[4] Jas 5:7

[5] J. Tissot, loc cit

[6] St J. Escrivá, Friends of God, 219

[7] cf St Thomas, Summa Theologiae, II-II, q136, a3

defeats as inevitable, as baffling difficulties that do not have a solution. We cannot become like those Christians, who, after many skirmishes and battles, find their strength has come to an end; their courage has failed them, when they *are only a couple of steps from the fountain of living water.*[8]

To be patient with oneself while uprooting unwholesome tendencies and defects in character implies both an unyielding approach and an acceptance of the fact that one will often have to present oneself before God like *the servant who had no resources with which to pay*[9] – with humility, seeking grace anew. On our way towards the Lord, many will be the defeats we suffer; many of these will be of no consequence, some will. But the atonement and contrition for these will bring us even closer to God. This sorrow and reparation for our sins and shortcomings, are not useless moods of gloom, for they are sorrow and tears born of love. It is the heavy thought of not returning as much love as our Lord merits; it is the sorrow of returning evil for good to one who so much loves us.

28.3 Patience, too, with others. Taking their defects into account. Patience and constancy in the apostolate.

In addition to being patient with ourselves, we have to exercise this virtue with those we most frequently deal with, and especially so if we have a special obligation to give formation, to help them in an illness, etc. We have to take into account the defects of those who are around us. Fortitude and understanding will enable us to remain calm, correcting when necessary and at the right time. Waiting a little while before correcting, giving a positive reply, smiling ... all this allows our words to touch the hearts of these people, hearts that would otherwise have remained closed.

8 cf St Teresa, *The Way of Perfection*, 19, 2
9 cf Mat 18:23

Now we can help them much more, with greater effectiveness.

Impatience makes mutual relationships difficult, and renders any possible help and correction ineffectual. *Continue making the same exhortation*, St John Chrysostom recommends, *and never lazily. Always act amiably and pleasantly. Do you not see how often painters will erase their sketches and at other times retouch them, when they are trying to portray a beautiful face? Don't let the painter be one up on you. For if they make so much of an effort for a bodily image, how much greater reason do we have when we try to form the image of a soul, leaving no stone unturned in trying to perfect it.*[10]

We ought to be particularly constant and patient in the apostolate. People need time, and God is patient: at every moment He gives his grace, He pardons offences and encourages progress. He has had, and continues to have, this limitless patience with us. And we ought to have it with those whom we wish to bring to Our Lord, although it might seem on occasions that they are not listening, or that the things of God do not interest them. We cannot abandon them just for this reason. On these occasions it will be necessary to intensify both our prayer and our mortification, our charity too and our sincere friendship.

None of our friends should ever be able to speak to Our Lord in the words of the paralytic: 'I do not have anyone to help me'.[11] This, unfortunately, could be said by many who are spiritually sick and paralytic, who could be useful and should be useful.

Lord: may I never remain indifferent to souls.

Let us examine ourselves to-day in our prayer, to see if we are sufficiently concerned about those who accompany

---

10 St John Chrysostom, *Homilies on the Gospel of St Matthew*, 30
11 St J. Escrivá, *Furrow*, 212

us on our journey through life; let us ask ourselves if we are concerned about their formation, or if we, on the other hand, have got used to their defects as something we have come to regard as incorrigible; are we really patient towards them?

It would also be good this Lent to recall that with mortification we can also atone for the sins of others and, in some way, merit for them the grace of faith, of conversion, of a greater dedication to God.

In Jesus Christ lies the remedy for all the evils of which humanity complains. In him everyone can find life and health. He is the fountain of those waters that give life to everything. This is what Ezekiel the prophet tells us in the readings of to-day's Mass: *This water flows east down to the Arabah and to the sea; and flowing into the sea it makes its waters wholesome. Wherever the river flows, all living creatures teeming in it will live. Fish will be very plentiful, for wherever the water goes it brings health, and life teems wherever the river flows.* [12] Christ converts into life everything which was previously death, and turns shortcomings and error into virtue.

FOURTH WEEK OF LENT – WEDNESDAY

29. UNITY OF LIFE

29.1 Christians as light of the world and salt of the earth.

God did not send his Son into the world to judge the world, but that the world might be saved through him.[1] He came into the world so that men might have light and stop thrashing about in the dark.[2] Having received the light, they can turn the world into a place where everything will be able to give glory to God and help man to achieve his ultimate goal. *The light shines in the darkness, and the darkness has not overcome it.[3]* These words are relevant for a good part of today's world which is in deep gloom, for without Christ men will never achieve peace, or happiness, or salvation. Outside of Christ only darkness and sin exist. Whoever rejects Christ remains without light and has no idea which way to go. In the innermost depth of his being he is disorientated.

For centuries, many have lived their lives (of work, study, business, research, social relationships, interests etc.) in separation from the faith. And as a consequence of this separation temporal realities have been adversely affected, existing, as it were, in the shadows on the fringes of the light of Revelation. Without this light many have come to consider the world as an end in itself, without any reference to God; therefore they have distorted the most elementary and basic truths. In western countries, particularly, it becomes necessary to correct this separation because many generations which should belong to Christ and the Church are being lost in these years, and because, unhappily, from these places the harmful influence of a new paganism is being sent into the whole world. Thus, contemporary paganism is characterised by the search for material well-being at any cost, and by the corresponding disregard – or, to put it more accurately, fear, genuine terror – of anything that could cause suffering. With this outlook, words such as God, sin, Cross, mortification, eternal life ... become incomprehensible to a great number of people, who are ignorant of their meaning and content. You have witnessed the incredible fact that many people began by putting God in parentheses, in some aspects of their professional lives. But then, as God demands, loves, and asks, they end up throwing Him out – like an intruder – from their civil laws and from the lives of their nations. With a ridiculous and presumptuous pride they want to lift up in his place the poor human creature, who has lost his supernatural and human dignity, and has become reduced – it is no exaggeration, one can see it everywhere – to a stomach, sex and money.[4]

The world remains in darkness because Christians, through lacking a unity of life, do not illuminate or give the realities of each day a special meaning. We know that the approach of true disciples of Christ towards the world is not one of separation; rather is it one of getting involved at the very core of things, as leaven within the lump – transforming it. The Christian, consistent with his faith, is salt which gives taste and preserves from corruption. And for this he relies, above all else, on his witness in the midst of his ordinary occupations with all the tasks he does fulfilled extraordinarily well. If we Christians really lived in accordance with our faith, the greatest revolution of all

[4] Bl. A. del Portillo, Pastoral Letter, 25 December 1985, 4

times would take place. The effectiveness of our co-redemption depends on each one of us. You should meditate on this.[5] Do I live, at every instant of my life, this unity of life – at work, in my leisure, at rest ...?[2]

29.2 Consequences of original sin. The Redemption. Redirecting all earthly realities to Christ.

Within the order established by the Creator, all creatures were placed at the service of man. Adam, with his pride, introduced sin into the world, breaking the harmony which existed between all created beings and man himself. In future, the intellect was to become dimmed, with the possibility of falling into error; the will weakened; and freedom immediately to love the good infected though not corrupted. Man became deeply injured, handicapped in his ability to learn and to achieve his true wellbeing. The Alliance with God was broken, leading on the one hand to internal disintegration and, on the other, to an inability to build up a union with others.[6] The disorder introduced by sin went beyond man – it affected nature too. The world is good, for it has been created by God so that in it man can achieve his ultimate end. But after the fact of original sin, material things – talents, techniques, laws – can be misdirected from their true goal and converted into evil for man, obscuring his ultimate end, and distancing him from God instead of taking him nearer to Him. Thus inequality, injustice and oppression are born, with sin as their origin. The sin of man, that is to say, his rupture with God, is the root cause of the tragedies which mark the history of freedom. To understand this, many of our contemporaries will have to discover again the sense of sin.[7]

---

5 St J. Escrivá, Furrow, 945
6 St John Paul II, General Audience, 6 August 1983
7 S.C.D.F., Instruction, Libertatis conscientiae, 22 March 1986, 37

In his infinite mercy, God has taken compassion on the state into which his creatures had fallen, and has redeemed us in Christ Jesus. He has brought us back into his friendship, and what is more, He has reconciled us with himself to such an extent that we are called children of God: *and so we are.*[8] He has destined us for life eternal, to dwell with Him forever in heaven.

It falls to us Christians, principally through turning our ordinary work into prayer, to make all earthly realities once again become a means of salvation. Only in this way will these truly be at the service of man. We have to impregnate every environment of society with a Christian spirit. Do not merely have the desire to do so: each of you, wherever you are working, has to give a divine content to the job you are doing, and through your prayer, mortification and well-finished professional work, you have to see to it that you are formed and form other souls in the truth of Christ, so that He may be proclaimed Lord of all earthly affairs.[9]

Am I doing everything I can to put this into practice? Am I aware that for this I need to have an ever deeper unity of life?

29.3 Life of piety and work. Sanctify in the middle of the world.

The mission entrusted to us by the Lord is by our approach to infuse a Christian spirit into society. Only then will structures, institutions, laws, leisure etc. have a Christian spirit and truly be at man's service. We, disciples of Jesus Christ, have to be sowers of fraternity at every moment and in every circumstance of our lives. When a man or woman lives the Christian spirit in a profound way, *all his or her activities and relationships reflect and*

---

8 1 John 3:1
9 Bl. A. del Portillo, *loc cit*, 10

communicate the charity of God and the goods of his Kingdom. It is necessary for us Christians to know how to put this Christian stamp on our daily relationships within the family, with our neighbours, at our work and in our leisure. This stamp or seal consists of simplicity, sincerity, fidelity, meekness, generosity, solidarity and joy.[10]

Personal practices of piety cannot be isolated from the rest of our daily concerns. Rather they should be moments when our constant turning to God is made more intense and more profound; the whole tone of our daily activity is then raised. It is clear that to seek sanctity in the middle of this world does not consist simply in *doing* or in *multiplying devotions or pious practices*. It lies in an effective union with the Lord which such actions promote and to which they are ordained. And when there is an effective union with the Lord, this affects the whole of one's activity. *These practices will lead you, almost without your realising it, to contemplative prayer. Your soul will pour forth more acts of love, aspirations, acts of thanksgiving, acts of atonement, spiritual communions and this will happen while you go about your ordinary duties, when you answer the telephone, get on a bus, open or close a door, pass in front of a church, when you begin a new task, during it and when you have finished it ...*[11]

Thus we will try to live, with Christ and in Christ, at each and every moment of our existence: at work, in the family, among friends. *This is unity of life.* It is then that personal piety is directed to action, giving it both encouragement and content, converting every task into another act of love for God. And in their turn, work and the tasks of each day make it easier to relate to God; they are the field where all the virtues are exercised. If we try to work well and to give our actions the transcendental dimension of the love of God, our deeds will be of use for the salvation of men and we will make the world more human. For it is not possible for man to be respected – and even less to be loved – if God is neglected or opposed, for man is only man when he is the true image of God. On the other hand, the presence of the devil in the history of humanity is increased in the measure that man and society are separated from God.[12]

We Christians are not alone in this work of sanctifying earthly realities. Re-establishing the order wished for by God, and leading the entire world to its fulness, is principally the work of the Holy Spirit, true Lord of history. *Non est abbreviata manus Domini*, the hand of God has not been shortened (Is 59:1): God is no less powerful today than he was in other times; his love for man is no less true. Our faith teaches us that all creation, the movement of the earth and the other heavenly bodies, the good actions of creatures and all the good that has been achieved in history, in short, everything, comes from God and is directed towards him.[13]

We ask the Holy Spirit to stir up the souls of many people – men and women, young and old, healthy and sick – so that they may be salt and light in earthly realities.

12 St John Paul II, *General Audience*, 20 August 1986
13 St J. Escrivá, *Christ is passing by*, 130

30. THE HOLY MASS AND PERSONAL SELF-SURRENDER

30.1 Christ's sacrifice on Calvary. He offered himself up for all men. Our personal self-surrender.

The first Reading of to-day's Mass relates the intercession of Moses before Yahweh so that He should not punish his People's infidelity. He invokes moving reasons: the good name of the Lord among the Gentiles, the faithfulness of his People to the Covenant made to Abraham and his descendants ... And, in spite of their infidelities and the inconstancy of the chosen People, God forgives once more. Moreover, God's love for his People, and through his People for the whole human race, will yet reach its supreme manifestation: *For God so loved the world that he gave his only Son, that whosoever believes in him should not perish, but have eternal life.*[1]

Christ's total self-surrender on our behalf, which reaches its culmination on Calvary, is an urgent call to us to correspond to his great love for each one of us. On the Cross, Jesus consummated his total self-surrender to his Father's will, and showed his love for all men, for each and every person. *He ... loved me and gave himself for me.*[2] Faced with this unfathomable mystery of Love, I should ask myself, what do I do for him? How do I correspond to his love?

On Calvary, Our Lord, Priest and Victim, offered himself to his heavenly Father, shedding his blood, which became separated from his Body. This is how he carried

---

[1] John 3:16
[2] Gal 2:20

out his Father's will to the very end.

It was the Father's will that the Redemption should be carried out in this way. Jesus accepts it lovingly and with perfect submission. This internal offering of himself is the essence of his Sacrifice. It is his loving submission, without limits, to his Father's will.

In every true sacrifice there are four essential elements: and all of them are present in the sacrifice of the Cross: *priest, victim, internal offering and external manifestation of the sacrifice.* The external manifestation must be an expression of one's interior attitude. Jesus dies on the Cross, externally manifesting (through his words and his deeds) his loving internal surrender. *Father, into thy hands I commend my spirit!*[3] I have finished the task you committed to me, I have fulfilled your Will. He is, both then and now, at once Priest and Victim. *Since, then, we have a great high priest who has passed through the heavens, Jesus, the Son of God, let us hold fast our confession. For we have not a high priest who is unable to sympathise with our weaknesses, but one who in every respect has been tempted as we are, yet without sinning.*[4]

This internal offering of Jesus gives full meaning to all the external elements of his voluntary sacrifice – the insults, the stripping of his garments, the crucifixion.

The Sacrifice of the Cross is a single sacrifice. Priest and Victim are one and the same divine person: the Son of God made man. Jesus was not offered up to the Father by Pilate or by Caiphas, or by the crowds surging at his feet. It was He who surrendered himself. At every moment of his life on earth Jesus lived a perfect identification with his Father's will, but it is on Calvary that the Son's self-surrender reaches its supreme expression.

---

[3] Luke 23:46
[4] Heb 4:14-15

We, who want to imitate Jesus, who want only that our life should be a reflection of his, must ask ourselves to-day in our prayer: do we know how to unite ourselves to Jesus' offering to the Father and accept God's will at every moment? Do we unite ourselves to him in our joys and our sorrows and in all the activities that make up each one of our days? Do we unite ourselves to him at the more difficult times, such as moments of failure, pain or illness, and at the easy times, when we feel our souls filled with joy?

My Mother and Lady, teach me how to pronounce a 'yes' which, like yours, will identify with the cry Jesus made before his Father: non mea voluntas ... (Luke 22:42) – not my will but God's be done.[5]

30.2 The Holy Mass, a renewal of the sacrifice of the Cross.

To help us to meditate to-day on the unity that exists between the Sacrifice of the Cross and the Holy Mass, let us fix our attention on the interior oblation that Christ makes of himself, with a total self-surrender and loving submission to his Father. The Holy Mass and the Sacrifice of the Cross are one and the same sacrifice, although they are separated in time. There is made present once again, not the sorrowful and bloody circumstances of Calvary, but the total loving submission of Our Lord to his Father's will. This internal offering of himself is identical on Calvary and in the Mass: it is Christ's oblation. It is the same Priest, the same Victim, the same oblation and submission to the Will of God the Father. The external manifestation of the Passion and Death of Jesus goes on – in the Mass, through the sacramental separation, in an unbloody manner, of the Body and Blood of Christ through means of the transubstantiation of the bread and the wine.

In the Mass, the priest is only the instrument of Christ,

---

[5] St J. Escrivá, *The Way of the Cross*, Fourth Station, 1

the Eternal and High priest. Christ offers himself in every
Mass in the same way as he did on Calvary, although now
he does so through a priest, who acts *in persona Christi*.
This is why *every Mass, even though it is celebrated
privately by a priest, is not a private action, but the action
of Christ and of the Church. In the sacrifice that she offers,
the Church learns to offer herself as a universal sacrifice,
and applies the unique and infinite redeeming virtue of the
sacrifice of the Cross for the salvation of the whole
world.*[6] Christ himself, in each Mass, offers himself up, thus
manifesting his loving surrender to his heavenly Father. This
is expressed now in the Consecration of the bread and,
separately, in the Consecration of the wine. This is the culmination – the essence, the very nucleus, of the Holy Mass.
Our prayer to-day is a good time to examine how we attend
Mass and how we take part in it. *Are you at Mass with the
same dispositions that Our Lady had on Calvary? Do we
realise that here it is the presence of the one and the same
God and the consummation of the same sacrifice?*[7] Perfect
Love, a total identification with God's will, will demand an
offering of oneself, a desire to co-redeem.

30.3 The Holy Mass, centre of the life of the Church and of every Christian.

As it is essentially identical with the Sacrifice of the
Cross, the Sacrifice of the Mass has an infinite value. In
each Mass there is offered to God the Father an infinite act
of adoration, thanksgiving and reparation, quite independent
of the specific dispositions of the people attending, or of
the celebrant. This is because Christ is at once the principal
Offerer and the Victim who offers himself. Thus there is no
more perfect way of *adoring* God than by offering the

---

[6] St Paul VI, Encyclical, *Mysterium Fidei*, 4, 3 September 1965
[7] St Jean Vianney, (The Curé d'Ars), *Sermon on Sin*

Mass, in which his Son, Jesus Christ, is offered as the Victim, and at the same time acts as High Priest.

There is no more perfect way of *thanking* God for everything that He is and for his continual mercy towards us: there is nothing on earth that can be more pleasing to God than the Sacrifice of the altar. Each time Holy Mass is celebrated, reparation is made for all the sins of the world, because of the infinite dignity of the Priest and of the Victim. We have here the only perfect and adequate *reparation*, to which we must unite our acts of sorrow. It is the only adequate sacrifice that we men can offer, and through it our daily occupations; our sorrows and our joys can take on in it an infinite value. The Holy Mass *is really the heart and the centre of the Christian world.*[8] In this holy sacrifice, *There is engraved whatever is most profound in the life of every human being: the life of the father, the mother, the child, the elderly person, the young man and the young woman, the teacher and the student, the man of culture and the uneducated man, the nun and the priest – of each one without exception. It is in this way that man's life becomes inserted, by means of the Eucharist, into the mystery of the living God.*[9]

The fruits of each Mass are infinite, but in us they are conditioned by our personal dispositions, and thus limited. Mother Church invites us to share conscientiously, actively and piously in the most sublime action which takes place each day.[10] We have to try to be attentive and recollected, particularly at the moment of the Consecration. For these moments we will try to penetrate into the soul of him who is at once Priest and Victim in his loving oblation to God the Father, just as on Calvary. This Sacrifice will then be the

---

[8] St John Paul II, *Homily at the Seminary of Venegono*, 21 May 1983
[9] idem, *Homily, 20th Italian National Eucharistic Congress*, 22 May 1983
[10] cf Second Vatican Council, *Sacrosanctum Concilium*, 48 and 11

central point of our daily life, as it is of the liturgy and of the life of the Church. Our union with Christ at the moment of the Consecration will be the more complete the greater our identification with God's will; the greater our dispositions of self-giving. In unity with the Son we offer the Holy Mass to the Father and, at the same time, we offer ourselves through him, with him and in him. This act of union must be so profound and true that it permeates the whole of our day and has a decisive influence on our work, on our relations with others, on our joys and failures: in fact, on everything we do.

If when the moment of Communion arrives and Jesus finds us with these dispositions of self-surrender, of loving identification with the will of God the Father, what will He do but pour out the Holy Spirit with all his gifts and graces on to us? We have many aids to enable us to live the Holy mass well. Amongst others we have the help of the angels, *Who are always present there in large numbers to give honour to this holy mystery. If we unite ourselves to them and their intentions we must indeed receive much favourable influence from their company. The choirs of the Church militant unite and join in with Our Lord in this divine act: in him, with him and through him, in order to win over the heart of God the Father and to make his mercy forever our own.*[11] Let us turn to them in order to help us avoid distractions. Let us make the effort to take more loving care of this unique moment in which we share in the Sacrifice of the Cross.

---

[11] St Francis de Sales, *Introduction to the Devout Life*

31. SEEING CHRIST IN ILLNESS

31.1 Jesus makes himself present in the sick.

Now when the sun was setting, all those who had any that were sick with various diseases brought them to him; and he laid his hands on every one of them and healed them.[1] The sick were so numerous that *the whole city was gathered together about the door.*[2] They brought the sick *when the sun was setting.*[3] Why not earlier? Certainly because that day was the Sabbath. After sunset a new day began and the obligation to observe the sabbath rest ceased; it was an obligation that pious Jews practised faithfully.

St Luke's gospel has recorded for us this homely detail about Christ; he cured them *laying his hands on every one of them.* Jesus pays great attention to each one of the sick and gives him the whole of his attention, because each person, and particularly a person who is suffering, is very important to him. Every single one is always welcomed by Jesus, who has a compassionate and merciful heart towards everybody, without exception, especially for those who are most in need.

Jesus characterises his presence among us by *preaching the gospel of the kingdom, and healing every disease and every infirmity.*[4] That is why *the throng wondered when they saw the dumb speaking, the maimed whole, the lame walking, and the blind seeing; and they glorified the God of Israel.*[5]

In his messianic activity in the midst of Israel, St John

---

[1] Luke 4:40
[2] Mark 1:33
[3] Mark 1:32
[4] Matt 9:35
[5] Matt 15:31

Paul II reminds us, *Christ drew increasingly closer to the world of human suffering. 'He went about doing good' (Acts 10:38), and his actions concerned primarily those who were suffering and seeking help. He healed the sick, consoled the afflicted, fed the hungry, freed people from deafness, from blindness, from leprosy, from the devil, and from various physical disabilities; three times he restored the dead to life. He was sensitive to every human suffering, whether of the body or of the soul. And at the same time he taught, and at the heart of his teaching there are the eight beatitudes which are addressed to people tried by various sufferings in the temporal life.*[6]

We, who want to be faithful followers of Christ, must learn from him how to treat the sick and how to love them. We have to approach them with great respect, affection and mercy. We should be happy when we are able to do some little service for them. Visiting them, keeping them company; making it possible for them to receive the Sacraments at the right time. In them especially, we see Christ. *Children. The Sick. As you write these words, don't you feel tempted to use capitals? The reason is that in children and in the sick a soul in love sees Him!*[7] There will be moments in our life when we perhaps are sick ourselves, or people around us are sick. This is a treasure that God gives us to look after. Our Lord comes close to us so that we may learn to love more and also to find him. In our dealings with people who suffer from various sicknesses the words of Our Lord become a reality in our lives, *As you did it to one of the least of these my brethren, you did it to me.*[8]

---

[6] St John Paul II, Apostolic Letter, *Salvifici Doloris*, 16, 11 February 1984
[7] St J. Escrivá, *The Way*, 419
[8] Matt 25:40

31.2 Sanctifying illness. Learning to be good patients.

Illness, when it is borne for love of God, is a means of sanctification, of apostolate; it is an excellent way of sharing in Christ's redeeming Cross. Physical suffering, which so frequently accompanies man's life on earth, can be a means that God uses to purify our faults and imperfections, to exercise and strengthen our virtues. It can be a unique opportunity to unite ourselves to the sufferings of Christ, who, although he was innocent, bore within himself the punishment merited by our sins.[9]

Particularly in times of illness we have to be close to Christ. *Tell me, my friend*, the beloved asked, *will you be patient if I redouble your sufferings? Yes*, replied the friend, *as long as you redouble my capacity to love.*[10] The more painful the illness, the more love we will need. At the same time we will receive more graces from God. Periods of illness are very special occasions that God allows so that we can co-redeem with Him and purify ourselves from the stains of sin that remain in our souls.

If sickness comes we must learn to be good patients. First of all we must accept the illness. *We need to suffer patiently not only the burden of being ill, but of being ill with the particular illness that God wants for us, among the people that He wants us to be with, and with the discomforts that He permits us to experience. I say the same of all other tribulations.*[11]

We have to ask God for help to bear our illness gracefully, whatever it is, trying not to complain, obeying the doctor. For *when we are sick we can get very tiresome. 'They aren't looking after me properly; nobody cares about me; I'm not getting the attention I deserve* nobody

---

[9] cf John 4:10
[10] R. Lull, *Book of the Friend and the Beloved*, 8
[11] St Francis de Sales, *Introduction to the Devout Life*

understands me ... !' The devil, who is always on the lookout, can attack from any angle. When people are ill his tactics consist in stirring up a kind of psychosis in them so as to draw them away from God and fill the atmosphere with bitterness, or destroy that treasure of merits earned (on behalf of souls everywhere) by pain – that is, when it is borne with supernatural optimism, when it is loved. Therefore, if God wills that we be struck down by some affliction, take it as a sign that He considers us mature enough to be associated even more closely with his redeeming Cross.[12]

The person who suffers united to Our Lord, 'completes' with his suffering what is lacking in the sufferings of Christ.[13] *The sufferings of Christ created the good of the world's redemption. This good in itself is inexhaustible and infinite. No man can add anything to it. But at the same time, in the mystery of the Church as his Body, Christ has in a sense opened his own redemptive suffering to all human suffering.*[14] With Christ, sickness and illness attain their full meaning. *Grant, Lord, that your faithful may become partakers in your Passion through their sufferings in this life, so that the fruits of your Salvation may be made manifest in them.*[15]

31.3 The Sacrament of the Anointing of the Sick.

Among the errands entrusted to the Apostles the task of preaching to and healing the sick stands out in particular. *And he called the twelve together and gave them power and authority over all demons and to cure diseases ... And they departed and went through the villages,*

---

[12] St J. Escrivá, *Friends of God*, 124

[13] cf Col 1:24

[14] St John Paul II, *loc cit*, 24

[15] ~~ne~~ *Office, Vespers, Friday of the Fourth Week in Lent*

preaching the gospel and healing everywhere.[16] The mission entrusted to the disciples after the Resurrection contains this promise: *And these signs will accompany those who believe ... they will lay their hands on the sick, and they will recover.*[17]

The disciples carried out this task, following the Master's example. The Acts of the Apostles and the Letters of the New Testament describe and lead us to meditate on the way the first Christians watched over the sick. The Sacrament of the Anointing of the Sick, instituted by Jesus Christ and proclaimed by the Apostle James in his Letter,[18] makes particularly present Our Lord's concern for all those who suffer a serious illness. *The presence of the presbyter beside the sick person is a sign of the presence of Christ, not only because he is the minister of the Anointing, of Penance and of the Eucharist, but because he is a special dispenser of the peace and consolation of Christ.*[19]

Illness, which came into the world because of sin, is also conquered by Christ in that it can be turned into a much greater good even than physical health. With the Anointing of the Sick we receive untold benefits that God confers through the Sacrament in order to sanctify grave illness. The first effect of this Sacrament is to increase sanctifying grace in the soul; that is why it is good to go to Confession before receiving this sacrament. However, if a person is not in the state of grace, and it has been impossible for him to go to Confession (for example, if he has had an accident and is unconscious) this holy Anointing blots out even mortal sin; it is sufficient for the sick person to make or to have previously made an act of

---

[16] Luke 9:1-6
[17] Mark 16:18
[18] Jas 5:14-15
[19] *Ritual of the Anointing of the Sick*, 6

contrition, even of imperfect contrition. As well as increasing grace, it removes the stain of sin from the soul, gives a special grace to overcome the temptations which may arise in that precise situation, and restores bodily health if that is for the good of salvation.[20] Thus the soul is prepared to enter Heaven. Reception of this Sacrament often produces great peace and serene joy in the sick person, as he considers that he is already very close to his Father God.

Mother Church recommends that the sick and elderly should receive this sacrament at the opportune moment, without delaying its administration out of false reasons of compassion, etc., in the last phases of life here on earth. It would be a pity if people who could have received the Anointing were to die without it through ignorance, carelessness, or a wrongly understood affection of friends and relations. Preparing the sick to receive it is a special sign of charity and sometimes of justice.

Our mother, Mary, is always very close. *The presence of Mary and her motherly help at these moments (of grave illness) must not be thought of as something marginal and simply parallel to the sacrament of the Anointing. It is, rather, a presence and a help which is set in motion and transmitted by the Anointing itself.*[21] We are in Lent. During this liturgical season let us open our eyes in a special way to the suffering around us. Christ wants to make himself present in his Passion, in that particular pain, in our own sickness or that of others, and to give it a redeeming value.

---

[20] cf Council of Trent, Dz 909, *Ritual of the Anointing of the Sick*
[21] A. Bandera, *Our Lady and the Sacraments*, Madrid

32. MAKING KNOWN THE DOCTRINE OF JESUS CHRIST

32.1 Every Christian should bear witness to Jesus' doctrine.

This is truly the prophet who was to come ... No man ever spoke like this man.[1] Our Lord speaks very simply about the most profound things, and he does so in an attractive and thought-provoking way. His words were understood as much by a doctor of the Law as by the fishermen from Galilee.

Jesus' way of speaking is pleasant and well suited to his hearers. He often repeated the same doctrine, but he sought to adapt his comparisons to the people who happened to be listening to him: the grain of wheat that must die in order to bear fruit; the joy of finding some coins that have been lost; the discovering of a hidden treasure ... Through images and parables He has taught us in the best possible way about the sovereignty of God the Creator, and at the same time has shown us that He is a Father who cares lovingly for each one of his children. Nobody has proclaimed as He did the fundamental truth of man – his freedom and his supernatural dignity, both of which come to him through the grace of his Divine filiation. The crowds sought him out to listen to him. Often it was necessary to tell the crowds to go away. Christ has *the words of eternal life,*[2] and He has given us the task of passing his teaching on to all generations, right to the end of time.

To-day, too, people thirst for the words of Jesus, the

---

[1] John 7:46
[2] John 6:68

only words that can bring peace to the soul; the only words that teach the way to heaven. All of us Christians have a share in this mission to make Christ known: *All the faithful, from the Pope to the last person to have been baptised, share in the same vocation, the same faith, the same Spirit, the same grace ... All share actively and with the same degree of responsibility (within the necessary plurality of ministries) in the one mission of Christ and of the Church.*[3]

There is a great urgency in making Christ's doctrine known, because ignorance is a powerful enemy of God in the world, and it is the *cause and, as it were, the root of all the evils that poison nations.*[4] This urgency is even greater in the countries of the West, as St John Paul II repeatedly pointed out: *We find ourselves in a Europe in which the temptation towards atheism and scepticism is becoming constantly stronger; in which there is taking root a grievous moral uncertainty with the falling apart of the family and the degeneration of morals; in which a dangerous conflict of ideas and movements dominates.*[5]

Every Christian must give testimony to the good doctrine of the gospel message, not only by example, but with words. And we must make use of every opportunity that presents itself (also knowing prudently how to find and make use of these opportunities) with our relatives, friends, colleagues, neighbours; with all those people we come across, even for a short time, on a journey, at a conference, whilst shopping, or whilst engaging in business. For the person who wants to travel along the way of sanctity, his life cannot be like a great avenue of missed opportunities, because God wants our words to echo his teachings in order to move hearts. *It is certain that God respects human*

---

[3] Bl. A. del Portillo, *Faithful and Laity in the Church*, Shannon
[4] St John XXIII, Encyclical, *Ad Petri cathedram*, 29 June 1959
[5] St John Paul II, *Address*, 6 November 1981

freedom, and that there may be people who 'do not want' to turn their eyes towards God's light. But the grace that God wants to pour out on earth is far stronger, more abundant and more plentiful. He makes use, now as before and always, of the co-operation of the apostles whom He himself has chosen to carry his light everywhere.[6]

32.2 Imitating Our Lord. Giving good example.

As we put into effect this re-evangelisation, this apostolate of giving doctrine, we will have to return time and again to the same ideas. We will endeavour to present Our Lord's teaching in an attractive manner (What could be more attractive?). God is waiting for the crowds who today, too, wander *like sheep without a shepherd*,[7] without a guide and without knowing in which direction to go, confused as they are by so many short-lived ideologies. No Christian should remain passive – in any way inhibited – in this task. It is the only really important task in the world. We must not make excuses (I'm no use. I can't. I haven't time.). The Christian vocation is a vocation to do apostolate, and God gives us the grace to correspond.

Are we really a ray of light in the midst of so much darkness, or are we still held fast bound by laziness or human respect? It will help us to be more apostolic and to overcome the obstacles if we consider, in the presence of God, that the people whose paths we have crossed during our lives had a right to expect us to help them to get to know Jesus better. Have we fulfilled this Christian duty of ours? Let us hope they will not be able to reproach us, in this life or the next, for having deprived them of that help: *hominem non habeo*,[8] I have had no one to give me a little

---

[6] Bl. A. del Portillo, *Pastoral Letter*, 25 December 1985, 7

[7] Mark 6:34

[8] John 5:7

light in so much darkness. *For the word of God is living and active, sharper than any two-edged sword.*[9] It reaches the very depths of the soul, right to the source of men's life and behaviour.

One day, the Gospel of today's Mass narrates, the Jews sent the temple guards to apprehend Jesus. When they returned and were questioned by their chiefs, *Why did you not bring him?* the guards answered, *No man ever spoke like this man.*[10] We can only suppose that those simple servants mingled for a while with the crowd, waiting for the moment to apprehend Our Lord, but they were filled with wonder at his teaching. What a lot of people would change their attitude if only we were able to show them the countenance of Christ, the true image that our Mother the Church presents for us! What great ignorance there is in our world after twenty centuries, even among many Christians!

St Luke says of Our Lord that he began *to do and to teach.*[11] The Second Vatican Council teaches that Revelation came about *gestis verbisque*, with deeds and words intrinsically intermingled.[12] The works of Jesus are the works of God done in his own name. And the simple people commented, *We have seen strange things.*[13]

We Christians must show people, with the help of God's grace, what really following Jesus means. *The man who has the mission of saying great things (and all of us as Christians have this sweet obligation) is equally obliged to practise them,*[14] said St Gregory the Great. Our friends, relatives, colleagues and acquaintances have to find us loyal, sincere, cheerful, optimistic, good at our job,

---

[9] Heb 4:12
[10] John 7:45-46
[11] Acts 1:1
[12] Second Vatican Council, *Dei Verbum*
[13] Luke 5:26
[14] St Gregory the Great, *Pastoral Care*, 2, 3

resilient, pleasant, courageous ... At the same time, in a
simple and natural way, we must make known our faith in
Christ. *We need*, says St John Paul II, *heralds of the Gospel
who are experts in humanity, who know the depths of the
heart of man to-day, who share in his hopes and joys, his
worries and his sadness, and at the same time are
contemplatives, in love with God. For this, new saints are
needed. The great evangelisers of Europe have been the
saints. We must implore God to increase the spirit of
holiness in the Church and to send us new saints to
evangelise to-day's world.*[15]

32.3 Not being surprised at difficult situations.

*Some people know nothing about God, because no one
has talked to them about him in terms they can
understand.*[16] There are many ways in which we can make
the person and teaching of Jesus and of his Church known,
so that people find them pleasant: through a family
conversation, giving Catechism classes, holding clearly,
charitably and firmly to Christian doctrine in conversation,
praising a good book or a good article. Sometimes it will
be our silence that others value, or our writing a simple
letter to the media of social communications thanking them
for a good piece of work. It always does good to somebody, perhaps in a way we could never have envisaged. In
any case, each of us should ask ourselves in these moments
of prayer: *How can I be a more effective and better
instrument? What obstacles am I putting in the way of
grace? What environments, what people could I reach if I
were less comfort-seeking, more in love with God! And
what if I had a greater spirit of sacrifice?*[17]

---

[15] St John Paul II, *Address to European Bishops*, 11 October 1985
[16] St J. Escrivá, *Furrow*, 941
[17] Bl. A. del Portillo, *Pastoral Letter*, 25 December 1985, 9

We must bear in mind that we will often have to go *against the current*, as so many good Christians have done throughout the centuries. With God's help we will be strong, so as not to be swept along by the errors that frequently come into fashion, or by morals of a permissive and licentious nature that militate against natural moral law and Christianity. Then too we will talk about God to our fellow men without missing a single opportunity. *I see all the circumstances of life – those of every individual person's existence as well as, in some way, those of the great cross-roads of history – as so many calls that God makes to men, to bring them face to face with truth, and as occasions that are offered to us Christians, so that we may announce, with our deeds and with our words strengthened by grace, the Spirit to whom we belong. (cf Luke 9:55).*

Every generation of Christians needs to redeem, to sanctify its own time. In order to do this, it must understand and share the desires of other men – one's equals – in order to make known to them, with a 'gift of tongues', how they are to correspond to the action of the Holy Spirit, to that permanent outflow of rich treasures that comes from our Lord's heart. We Christians are called upon to announce, in our own age, to this world to which we belong and in which we live, the message – old and at the same time new – of the Gospel.[18] The Holy Spirit will always give us light, especially in the more difficult situations, and we will know what to say, and how to act.[19]

---

[18] St J. Escrivá, *Christ is passing by*, 132
[19] cf Luke 12:11-12

33. A CRY FOR JUSTICE

33.1 Eagerness for justice and greater peace in the world. Living up to the demands of justice in our personal lives and within our sphere of relationships.

Give judgement for me, O God, and defend my cause against a godless people ... for you are my God and my strength,[1] we pray in the Entry Antiphon of to-day's Mass.

A loud clamour for justice can be heard throughout a large section of humanity, for *a better-assured peace within an atmosphere of mutual respect between men, and between the peoples of the world.*[2] This desire to construct a more just world in which greater respect is given to man, who has been created by God in his image and likeness, is a fundamental part of the *hunger and thirst for justice*[3] which must exist in the heart of a Christian.

All of Jesus' preaching is a call to justice (in its fullness and without diminution) and to mercy. Our Lord himself condemns the Pharisees, *who devour widows' houses and for a pretence make long prayers.*[4] And it is the Apostle St James who addresses this harsh reproach to those who grow rich through fraud and injustice: *Your riches have rotted ... Behold, the wages of the labourers who mowed your fields, which you kept back by fraud, cry out; and the cries of the harvesters have reached the ears of the Lord of hosts.*[5]

The Church, in faithfulness to the teaching of Holy

---

[1] Ps 42:1
[2] St Paul VI, Apostolic Letter, *Octogesima adveniens*, 14 May 1971
[3] cf Matt 5:6
[4] Mark 12:40
[5] Jas 5:2-4

Scripture, urges us to unite ourselves to this clamour of the world and to turn it into a prayer that reaches our Father God. At the same time she impels and urges us to live the demands that justice makes on our personal lives at a professional and social level, and to defend those who – because they are weaker – cannot avail themselves of their rights. The Christian is not expected to make sterile lamentations. Instead of complaining, Our Lord wants us to atone for the acts of injustice which are daily committed throughout the world: He wants us to try to remedy as many injustices as we can, starting with those that occur closest to us, in the sphere in which we move, just there where we live: the mother in her home with all those around her; the businessman in his firm; the professor in his university ...

The ultimate solution for restoring and promoting justice at all levels lies in the heart of each man. It is in the heart that every type of injustice imaginable comes into existence, and it is there also that the possibility of straightening out all human relationships is conceived. *By denying or trying to deny God, who is his Beginning and End, man profoundly disturbs his own order and interior balance and also those of society and even of visible creation.*

It is in their relationship to sin that Scripture regards all the different calamities which oppress man in his personal and social existence.[6] That is why, as Christians, we cannot forget that, when through our personal apostolate we bring men closer to God, we are building a world which is more human and more just. Moreover, our faith urges us never to avoid our personal commitment to the defence of justice, particularly in those aspects more

---

[6] S.C.D.F., *Instruction on Christian Freedom and Liberation*, 22 March 1986, 38

closely related to the fundamental rights of the person: the right to life, to work, to education, to good reputation ... *We have to uphold the right of all men to live, to own what is necessary to lead a dignified existence, to work and to rest, to choose a particular state in life, to form a home, to bring children into the world within marriage and to be allowed to educate them, to pass peacefully through times of sickness and old age, to have access to culture, to join with other citizens to achieve legitimate ends, and, above all, to enjoy the right to know and love God in perfect liberty.*[7]

Within our personal sphere of action we must ask ourselves the following questions: Do we do perfectly the work for which we are remunerated? Do we fully pay what we owe people for services rendered? Are we responsible in the way we exercise those rights and duties that can influence the activities of the institutions to which we belong? Do we make good use of our time at work? Do we defend other people's good name? Do we stand up for those who are weakest? Do we quash defamatory criticisms which may sometimes spring up in our midst? ... This is how we show our love for justice.

33.2 Fulfilment of our professional and social duties.

Our professional duties are an exceptional means of living the virtue of justice. Giving to each one his due, which is proper to this virtue, means in this case carrying out the terms of our contract. The owner of a business, the mistress of the household with domestics, the chief executive of an organisation, all assume an obligation to give just reward to the people who work under them. They are bound to reward them in accordance with just civil laws and, depending on right conscience, may sometimes go beyond what is laid down by law. For their part,

---

[7] St J. Escrivá, *Friends of God*, 171

workers and employees have the grave duty of working responsibly, in a professional manner, using their time well. Thus industriousness presents itself as a practical manifestation of justice. *I don't believe in the justice of idle people*, said St Josemaría Escrivá, *because ... they fail, sometimes seriously, in that most fundamental principle of equity, which is work.*[8]

The same principle can be applied to students. They have a serious obligation to study – it is their work – and they have an obligation of justice towards their family and society, who together support them economically, so that they may prepare themselves to give effective service.

Our professional duties are, as well, generally the most appropriate way of co-operating in social problems and attempting to build up a more just world.

The Christian who is eager to construct this world must be exemplary in the way he keeps the civil laws, because, so long as they are just laws, they are willed by God and constitute the very foundation of human brotherhood. As the ordinary citizens they are, they have to be exemplary in paying their taxes which are just and necessary for organised society to be effective and to reach far further than the individual alone could ever reach effectively.

Pay all of them their dues; taxes to whom taxes are due, revenue to whom revenue is due, respect to whom respect is due, honour to whom honour is due.[9] They do it, the Apostle says, *Not only to avoid God's wrath, but also for the sake of conscience.*[10] Christians have lived this ever since they first took on social obligations, even in the midst of persecution and the paganisation of public authorities.

---

[8] *ibid*, 169
[9] Rom 13:7
[10] cf Rom 13:7

As we learned from him [Christ], wrote St Justin the Martyr half way through the second century, *we strive to pay our taxes and contributions, fully and promptly, to your commissioners.*[11]

Among the social duties of a Christian, the Second Vatican Council reminds us that *every citizen ought to be mindful of his duty to promote the common good by using his vote.*[12] To shirk manifesting one's own opinion at the different levels where we should perform these social and civic duties would be a sin against justice, sometimes a grave sin, if that abstention were to favour candidates (whether for Members of Parliament, Parent/Teacher Associations, Boards of School Governors, Union representatives ...) whose outlook is opposed to the principles of Christian doctrine. With still greater reason would it be a lack of responsibility, and perhaps a grave sin against justice, to support organisations or persons – in any way at all – who by their activity do not respect the fundamental tenets of natural law and human dignity (as regards, for example, abortion, divorce, academic freedom, respect for the family, etc.).

33.3 Sanctifying society from within. Virtues which broaden and perfect the scope of justice.

The Christian who seeks to live his faith through political action conceived as service, may not adhere, without going against his own beliefs, to ideological systems which oppose – radically or substantially – his Faith and his perception of man. Therefore it is not licit to act in favour of the Marxist ideology with its atheistic materialism, its dialectic of violence, and the way in which that ideology understands individual freedom within

---

[11] St Justin, *Apology*, 1,7
[12] Second Vatican Council, *Gaudium et spes*, 75

collectivity. This same ideology denies any transcendence of man or of his personal and collective history. Neither may a Christian support that liberal ideology which claims to exalt individual liberty, removing from it any limitations, stimulating it to seek exclusively personal interest and power. At the same time it considers social solidarity as the more or less automatic consequence of individual initiatives, and not indeed as the primary end and cause of the value of social organisation.[13]

To-day we unite ourselves to this desire for greater justice, which is one of the principal characteristics of our age.[14] We ask our Lord for greater justice and greater peace; we pray for our rulers, as the Church always has done,[15] that they should be promoters of justice, peace, and a greater respect for the dignity of the person. We make the resolution to fulfil, so far as we are able, the demands the Gospel makes on our personal lives, with regard to the family and the world we live in and to which we belong.

As well as what belongs strictly to the virtue of justice, we will practise those other manifestations of natural and supernatural virtues which complement and enrich it: loyalty, courtesy, cheerfulness ... Above all, faith, which enables us to know the true value of the person, and charity, which leads us to go beyond what strict justice would demand in our dealings with others. We see other people as children of God, as did Christ himself, who says to us, *As you did it to one of the least of these my brethren, you did it to me.*[16]

---

[13] St Paul VI, *op cit*

[14] cf S.C.D.F., *loc cit*, 1

[15] cf 1 Tim 2:1-2

[16] cf Matt 25:40

34. *GO AND SIN NO MORE*

34.1 In the Sacrament of Penance it is Christ who forgives.

Woman, where are they? Has no one condemned you? No one, Lord. Neither do I condemn you; go, and do not sin again.[1] They placed her in the midst, says the Gospel.[2] They have humiliated her and shamed her in the extreme, without the slightest concern for her. They remind Our Lord that the Law imposed the severe penalty of death by stoning for this sin. *What do you say,* they ask him, disguising their ulterior motives so that *they might have some charge to bring against him.* But Jesus surprises them all. He does not say anything; *He bent down and wrote with his finger on the ground.*

The woman is terrified by them all. The Scribes and Pharisees go on asking questions. Then, *Jesus stood up and said to them, 'Let him who is without sin among you be the first to throw a stone at her.'* And once more He bent down and wrote with his finger on the ground.

They all went away, one by one, *Beginning with the eldest.* Not one of them had a clear conscience and they were trying to set a trap for Our Lord. All of them went away. *And Jesus was left alone with the woman standing before him. Jesus looked up and said to her, 'Woman, where are they? Has no one condemned you?'*

Jesus' words are full of gentleness and clemency, a manifestation of God's infinite mercy and forgiveness. She answered straight away, *No one, Lord.* And Jesus said to her, 'Neither do I condemn you; go, and do not sin again.'

---

[1] John 8:10-11
[2] cf John 8:1-11

We can imagine the enormous joy of that woman, her desire to begin again, her deep love for Christ.

Such a deep change has taken place in that woman's soul, stained by sin and suffused with her public shame, that we can only partly see the alteration in her with the light of faith. The words of the prophet Isaiah are fulfilled: *Remember not the former things, nor consider the things of old. Behold I am doing a new thing ... I will make a way in the wilderness and rivers in the desert ... to give drink to my chosen people, the people whom I formed for myself that they might declare my praise.*[3]

Every day, in every corner of the world, Jesus, through his ministers, the priests, continues to say *I absolve you from your sins ... 'Go', says our Lord, 'and do not sin again.'* It is Christ himself who forgives. *The sacramental formula, I absolve you ... and the imposition of the hand and the sign of the Cross made over the penitent show that at this moment the contrite and converted sinner comes into contact with the power and mercy of God. It is the moment at which, in response to the penitent, the Trinity becomes present in order to blot out sin and restore innocence. And the saving power of the Passion, Death and Resurrection of Jesus is also imparted to the penitent ... God is always the one who is principally offended by sin – 'tibi soli peccavi!' – and God alone can forgive.*[4]

The words pronounced by the priest are not just a prayer of supplication to ask God to forgive our sins, or a mere certification that God has deigned to grant us his pardon, but *at that moment every sin is forgiven and blotted out by the mysterious intervention of the Saviour.*[5]

---

[3] Is 43:16-21
[4] St John Paul II, Apostolic Exhortation, *Reconciliatio et Poenitentia*, 2 December 1984, 31, III
[5] *ibid*

Few words have ever produced more joy in the world than the words of absolution, *I absolve you from your sins* ... St Augustine affirms that the wonder they work is greater than the very creation of the world.[6] How glad are we to receive these words when we go to the sacrament of forgiveness? How grateful are we? How often have we thanked God for having this sacrament close at hand? In our prayer to-day we can show Our Lord our gratitude for this great gift.

34.2 Gratitude for absolution; the apostolate of Confession.

Through absolution, man is united to Christ the Redeemer, who willed to take our sins upon himself. Through this union the sinner shares once again in that fountain of grace that springs without ceasing from the open side of Jesus.

At the moment of absolution we will intensify our sorrow for our sins, saying perhaps one of the prayers from the ritual, such as the words of St Peter, *Lord, you know all things, You know that I love you.* We will renew our purpose of amendment. We will listen attentively to the priest's words which grant us God's forgiveness.

It is the moment of savouring the joy of having grace restored (if we have lost it) or of receiving an increase of grace and greater union with God. St Ambrose says: *See* [the Father] *comes out to meet you. He will fall on your neck and will give you a kiss, the pledge of love and tenderness. He will make them bring you a cloak, shoes for your feet ... You still fear a reprimand ... you are afraid of hearing words filled with anger, and he prepares a banquet for you.*[7] Our *Amen* turns into a longing to start again, even

---

[6] cf St Augustine, *Commentary on St John's Gospel*, 72
[7] St Ambrose, *Commentary on St Luke's Gospel*, 7

though we may have confessed only venial sins.

After each Confession we must *thank God* for his mercy towards us and stop, even though only momentarily, to decide exactly how we are going to put into practice the advice or indications we have received, or how to make our purpose of amendment more effective. Another manifestation of our gratitude is to make sure our friends, too, come to this well-spring of grace, and that we bring them closer to Christ, as the Samaritan woman did. She ran to tell her people so that they too should benefit from the unique opportunity that Jesus' journey through their town afforded them.[8]

It would be hard to find a greater act of charity than that of announcing to those who are covered in mud and lacking strength, the source of salvation that we have discovered, when we are purified and reconciled to God.

Do we use the means to carry out an effective apostolate of Confession? Do we take our friends to the Tribunal of divine mercy? Do we increase our own desire to purify ourselves by going frequently to the sacrament of Penance? Do we sometimes leave this meeting with God's mercy for 'later'?

34.3 The need to carry out the penance given by the Confessor. Generosity in our reparation.

Satisfaction is the final act which crowns the sacramental sign of Penance. In some countries the act which the forgiven and absolved penitent agrees to perform after receiving absolution is precisely called his penance.[9]

Our sins, even after they have been forgiven, deserve a temporal punishment which has to be undergone in this life, or after death in Purgatory, which is where those souls

---

[8] cf John 4:28
[9] St John Paul II, *loc cit*

go who die in a state of grace, but without having made full satisfaction for their sins.[10]

Moreover, after its reconciliation with God, there are still left in the soul the remains of sin; a weakness of the will to abide in good. There will remain also a certain facility for making wrong judgements: a certain disorder in the sensual appetite ... They are the weakened scars of actual sin and the disordered tendencies left in man by original sin, which are brought to a head by our personal sins. *It is not enough to remove the arrow from the body,* says St John Chrysostom; *We also have to heal the wound caused by the arrow. It is the same with the soul; after we have received forgiveness for our sins, we have to heal the wound that remains through penance.*[11]

Even after absolution, St John Paul II teaches, *there remains in the Christian a dark area, due to the wound of sin, to the imperfection of love in repentance, to the weakening of the spiritual faculties. It is an area in which there still operates an infectious source of sin which must always be fought with mortification and penance. This is the meaning of the humble but sincere act of satisfaction.*[12]

For all of these reasons we must put a lot of love into fulfilling the penance the priest gives us before granting absolution. It is usually easy to perform and, if we really love God, we will be aware of the great disparity there is between our sins and the penance we have been given. It is yet another reason for increasing our spirit of penance during this Lent, when the Church calls us to it in a special way.

'Cor Mariae perdolentis, miserere nobis!' – Invoke the Heart of Holy Mary, with the purpose and determination of

---

[10] cf Council of Florence, *Decree for the Greeks*, Dz 673

[11] St John Chrysostom, *Homily on the Gospel of St Matthew*, 3,5

[12] St John Paul II, *loc cit*, cf also *General Audience*, 7 March 1984

*uniting yourself to her sorrow, in reparation for your sins
and the sins of men of all times.*

*And pray to her – for every soul – that her sorrow may
increase in us our aversion from sin, and that we may be
able to love the physical or moral contradictions of each
day as a means of expiation.*[13]

---

[13] St J. Escrivá, *Furrow*, 258

35. CONTEMPLATING CHRIST. LIFE OF PIETY.

35.1 The enemies of grace. The remedy: to contemplate Christ.

When I am lifted up from the earth, I will draw all to myself, says the Lord.[1]

The first Reading of to-day's Mass brings us a passage from the Book of Numbers[2] which narrates how the people of Israel began to murmur against God and against Moses, because although they had been set free and brought out of Egypt, they were tired of travelling towards the Promised Land. As a punishment, the Lord *sent fiery serpents among the people, and they bit the people, so that many people of Israel died.* Then the people turned to Moses, acknowledging their sin, and Moses interceded with God that He might free them from the serpents. The Lord said to him, *Make a fiery serpent and set it on a pole; and every one who is bitten, when he sees it, shall live. So Moses made a bronze serpent, and set it on a pole; and if a serpent bit any man, he would look at the bronze serpent and live.*

This passage from the Old Testament, as well as being an historical narrative, is the type and image of what was to take place later with the coming of the Son of God. In his intimate conversation with Nicodemus Our Lord makes a direct reference to this narrative: *And as Moses lifted up the serpent in the wilderness, so must the Son of man be lifted up, that whosoever believes in him may have eternal*

---

[1] *Communion Antiphon*, John 12:32
[2] *First Reading*, Num 21:4-9

life.[3] Christ on the Cross is the salvation of the human race, the remedy for all our ills. He went voluntarily to Calvary, so that *whosoever believes may have eternal life*, so that he might draw all men to himself.

In no matter what age they attack God's people as they travel towards the promised land of Heaven, the serpents and the poison are much the same: selfishness, sensuality, doctrinal errors and confusion, laziness, envy, slander, calumny ... The grace we receive in Baptism, which is intended to reach its full development, is threatened by the same enemies as they always have been. In all ages we can perceive the wounds of original sin and of personal sins.

We Christians must seek the remedy and the antidote – just as the Israelites bitten by the serpents in the wilderness did – in the only place that it is to be found: in Jesus Christ and in his saving doctrine. We must not cease from contemplating him raised above the earth on the Cross, if we truly want to reach the Promised Land that comes at the end of this short journey. That is all this life really is. And as we do not want to reach our destination alone, we will strive to get many others to look at Jesus, in whom is salvation. Look at Jesus. Place before your eyes his most Holy Humanity, contemplate him in the Mysteries of the Holy Rosary, in the Way of the Cross, in the scenes that the Gospels narrate for us, or in the Tabernacle. Only if we have great piety will we be strong against the harassment of a world which seems to want to separate itself more and more from God, dragging with it anyone who is not on firm and sure ground.

We cannot turn our gaze away from God, because we see the havoc that the enemy wreaks around us every day. By himself, nobody is immune. *'Vultum tuum, Domine, requiram'*: *Thy face, Lord, do I seek; hide not thy face*

---

[3] John 3:14-15

from me.[4] We must grow in fortitude through our loving ~~and constant conversation with Jesus, through prayer,~~ through keeping presence of God throughout the day, and through our visits to the Blessed Sacrament. We must remember, too that Our Lord, Jesus, is not only the remedy for our weakness; He is also our Love.

35.2 Keeping presence of God in the midst of the world. 'Human devices'.

God wants ordinary Christians to be situated right in the midst of society – Christians who are diligent in their jobs, carrying out work that will generally occupy them from morning to night. Jesus expects that, as well as contemplating him and talking to him at the times expressly set aside for prayer, we should not forget the people we love or those things we consider important to us. That is why each of us must be a *soul of prayer at all times, at every opportunity and in the most varied circumstances, because God never abandons us. It is not a proper Christian attitude to look upon friendship with God only as a last resort. Do we think it normal to ignore or neglect the people we love? Obviously not! Those we love figure constantly in our conversations, desires and thoughts. We hold them ever present. So it should be with God.*[5]

Often, in order to keep Jesus present during the day, we will need to make use of those 'human devices', those ejaculations, acts of Love and reparation, spiritual Communions, 'glances' at a picture of Our Lady[6] and some human means to remind us that some time has gone by (too much for love) during which we have not turned to Our

---

[4] Ps 26
[5] St J. Escrivá, *Friends of God*, 247
[6] *idem,* cf *The Way*, 272

Lord, Our Lady, our guardian angel ... They are always simple things, but very effective ones. It happens to all of us that when we want to remember something during the day we find a means of ensuring that we do not forget it. If we take the same interest in remembering Our Lord, we will fill our day with little reminders, little ideas that will lead us to keep him present.

A father or mother away from home takes a photograph of the family so as to keep them in mind throughout the journey. How is it we don't carry an image of Our Lady in our wallet or handbag so that when we look at her we can say, Mother! My Mother! Why not have to hand a crucifix which will help us to offer atonement, to kiss it discreetly, to look at it when we find our study or our work more than usually trying?

Those possible reminders, the resources for keeping presence of God, are countless, because love is creative; they will be different for a doctor about to start an operation, and for a mother who, perhaps at the same time of day, is beginning to tidy up the house. One day, in Heaven, each of us will see how having had recourse to our guardian angel was a great help in carrying out our work. A bus driver will have his 'human devices' (he will know very well, for example, when he is closest to Jesus because he happens to be passing the walls of a church) and the dressmaker who stays in the same place all day will have hers. And all will be done with a matter-of-fact and cheerful spirit, without their being overwhelmed, but with love; *Ejaculatory prayers do not hinder your work, just as the beating of your heart does not impede the movements of the body.*[7]

Bit by bit, if we persevere, we will reach a point where being in the presence of God becomes our normal and

---

[7] St J. Escrivá, *Furrow*, 516

natural state, although we will always have to put up a
determined struggle to stay there.

35.3 Life of piety. Ejaculatory prayers.

Our Lord often withdrew to pray, perhaps for hours at
a time. *And in the morning, a great while before day, he
rose and went out to a lonely place, and there he prayed.*[8]
At other times he turned to his Father God with a short
loving prayer, an ejaculation: *I give thee praise, Father,
Lord of heaven and earth ...*[9] *I thank thee, Father, for thou
hast heard me ...*[10]

At another moment the Evangelist shows us how Jesus
is moved by the petitions of those who approach him. They
are prayers that we too can use as ejaculations: there is the
prayer of the leper who says, *Lord, if you will, you can
make me clean ...;*[11] the prayer of the blind man from
Jericho, *Jesus, Son of David, have mercy on me,*[12] and the
prayer of the good thief, *Jesus, remember me when you
come into your kingly power.*[13] Jesus is moved by these
prayers, filled as they are with faith, and he does not make
the people wait for an answer.

Sometimes we can use these expressions as a way of
asking for forgiveness, just as the tax collector did, he who
returned home justified – *God, be merciful to me a
sinner!*[14] Or I can repeat with St Peter after his denials,
Lord, you know everything; you know that I love you[15] – in
spite of my failings. Other expressions will help us to ask

---

[8] Mark 1:35
[9] Matt 11:25
[10] *ibid*
[11] Matt 8:2-3
[12] Luke 18:38-39
[13] Luke 23:42-43
[14] cf Luke 18:13
[15] John 21:17

for more faith: *I believe; help my unbelief,*[16] strengthen my faith: *My Lord and my God.*[17] says Thomas when Jesus appears to him after the Resurrection; it is a wonderful act of faith and self-surrender which perhaps we were taught to repeat as we genuflect before the Tabernacle. There are many ejaculations and short prayers that we can say with all our heart and soul, and which respond to the specific needs or situations that affect all of us.

Often we don't even have to put them into words. Sometimes a glance, a single word, a thought which is unarticulated but filled with love or sorrow ... a petition which does not fully take shape, but which Our Lord grasps straight away. For a soul closely united to God, ejaculations and such acts of love arise naturally, almost spontaneously, like a supernatural respiration which feeds the soul's union with God. This happens in the midst of the most absorbing occupations, because God expects everybody to live this life of union and prayer with Him.

St Teresa recalls the impression a particular ejaculation made in her life. *We often used to talk about this, and we loved to say very often, 'For ever and ever and ever ...' As I said this over a long period of time, Our Lord was pleased to impress on me, whilst still a child, the way of truth.*[18]

There is always the opportunity of saying an ejaculation. Our reading of the Holy Gospel, our meditation, will often be the source of ejaculatory prayers by which we can express our love for Jesus and his most Holy Mother.

As we finish our prayer we say to him, like the disciples of Emmaus, *Stay with us, for it is toward evening*

---

[16] Mark 9:23
[17] John 20:28
[18] St Teresa, *Life*, I,4

and the day is now far spent.[19]

Stay with us, Lord, because when you are not with us, night falls around us. Everything is darkness when you are not there. And we turn to Our Lady, to whom we know also how to direct ejaculations and acts of love: *Hail Mary ... Blessed art thou among women.*

---

[19] Luke 24:29

FIFTH WEEK OF LENT – WEDNESDAY

36. CO-REDEEMERS WITH CHRIST

36.1 The co-redemptive value of pain suffered for Christ.

God has brought us to the kingdom of his beloved Son, in whom we have redemption through his Blood, the forgiveness of our sins.[1]

To redeem means to set free by purchase or rescue. To redeem a prisoner meant paying a ransom for him so as to give him back his freedom. *Truly I say to you, everyone who commits sin is a slave to sin.* These are the words of Jesus in the Gospel we read in to-day's Mass.[2] After the original sin had been committed it was as if we were in a prison, slaves to sin and the devil and quite unable to reach Heaven. Jesus Christ, perfect God and perfect Man, paid the ransom for our freedom with his own blood, shed on the cross. He more than made up for the debt contracted by Adam when he committed the original sin as well as for all the sins which would be committed by men until the end of time. He is our Redeemer and his work is called our Redemption and Liberation since it has truly won the freedom of the children of God.[3]

Jesus Christ rescued us from sin and by so doing went to the root of all evil and cured it, in this way making possible the complete freedom of man. Now the words of the Psalm acquire their full meaning: *'Dominus illuminatio mea et salus mea, quem timebo?' The Lord is my light and my salvation; whom shall I fear? Though an army*

---

[1] *Communion Antiphon*, Col 1:13-14
[2] John 8:34
[3] cf Gal 4:31

encamp against me, my heart shall not fear; though war be waged against me, I shall be confident.[4] If evil had not been cured at its root, which is sin, man would never have been able to be truly free and feel himself strong in the face of evil. Jesus wanted to suffer pain and live in poverty himself in order to show us that physical suffering and the lack of material goods are not real ills. There only exists one true evil that we must fear and with God's grace reject – sin.[5] This is the worst kind of slavery, the only real disgrace for humanity and for each individual being.

It is only possible to overcome, partly in this life and completely in the next, all the other misfortunes which man suffers – starting from the basis of our freedom from sin. Moreover, physical sufferings – pain, illness, tiredness – if borne for Christ become true treasures for man. This is the great revolution brought about by Christ, and it can be understood only through prayer and with the light that faith gives. *I will tell you which are man's treasures on earth so that you won't let them go to waste: hunger, thirst, heat, cold, pain, dishonour, poverty, loneliness, betrayal, slander, prison ....*[6]

Therefore to-day we can consider whether or not we truly view pain, be it physical or moral, as a treasure which unites us with Christ. Have we learned to sanctify it or, on the contrary, do we complain about it? Do we know how to offer to God immediately and calmly those small mortifications which are foreseen and those which crop up in the course of the day?

To-day's liturgy proclaims: *Vultum tuum, Domine, requiram – Your face, Lord, I shall seek.*[7] The contemplation

---

[4] Ps 26
[5] cf St J. Escrivá, *The Way*, 386
[6] *op cit*, 194
[7] Ps 26

of God will satisfy our longing for happiness, and this consummation will take place when we wake up to reality, for as St Paul often commented, our life here is like a dream.[8]

36.2 Eternal life must come before all else.

My Kingdom is not of this world, the Lord had said. Therefore when He declared *I have come that you may have life – life in all its fulness*,[9] he was not referring to a comfortable earthly life without difficulties, but to eternal life, which begins in the one we are now living. He came to free us from what prevents us reaching definitive happiness; from sin, the only absolute evil, and from the damnation it leads to. *If the Son sets you free then you will be really free*, the Lord tells us in to-day's Gospel.[10] He also made it possible for us to overcome the consequences of sin – oppression, injustice, excessive economic differences, envy, hatred – or to suffer them cheerfully when they cannot be avoided.

Such is the value of the life that Christ has gained for us that all earthly goods must be seen as vastly inferior to it. This is by no means to say that we Christians should remain passive in the face of pain and injustice. On the contrary, it is for each and every one of us to accept our commitment, out of charity and a desire for justice, to make a more humane and just world, beginning in our homes and our places of work and always seeking above everything else the absolute good for man.

The price Christ paid for our freedom was his own life. Thus, He showed us the gravity of sin, how much our eternal salvation is worth and the way we can achieve it. St

---

[8] cf 1 Thess 4:14
[9] John 10:10
[10] John 8:36

Paul, too, reminds us: *You have been bought at a great price*, then adding, *glorify God and carry him in your body*.[11] But above all, the Lord wanted to go to such lengths precisely so as to show us his love, because no greater love has any man than that he *gives his life for his friends*.[12] Christ did this for us. He did not just agree to become one of us; he wanted to give his life as a ransom in order to save us. *He loved us and he gave himself up for us*.[13] *God has brought us to the Kingdom of his beloved Son, by whose blood we have received redemption and the forgiveness for our sins*.[14] Any man can rightly say: *The Son of God loved me and gave himself up for me*.[15]

How much do I value the life of grace which Christ obtained for me on Calvary? We could each ask ourselves this question to-day. Do I strive to increase this life of grace by frequenting the sacraments, through prayer and good works? Do I avoid occasions of sin, keeping up a resolute struggle against sensuality, pride, laziness? *I tell you that whoever commits sin is a slave of sin*.

36.3 Co-redeemers with Christ.

The apparent 'failure' of Christ on the Cross becomes a glorious redemption for all men when they decide that this is what they want. We receive in abundance the fruits of Jesus' love for us on the cross. *The work of salvation is taking place within the unfolding of the same human history that harbours evil*.[16] It goes forward in the midst of our failings and our denials, and secures its end by our loving response to Our Lord's heroic sacrifice.

---

[11] 1 Cor 6:20
[12] John 15:13
[13] cf Gal 2:20
[14] cf *Communion Antiphon*, Col 1:13-14
[15] Gal 2:2
[16] St J. Escrivá, *Christ is passing by*, 186

Lent is a good time to recall that the Redemption is being carried out daily, and for us to stop and consider the moments when Christ's victory is shown most clearly: *each time the Sacrifice of the Cross is celebrated, that sacrifice through which Christ offered himself as an oblation for us, the work of our redemption is being carried out.*[17] Each Mass is of infinite value; the fruits of it for each of the faithful depend upon their personal disposition. We can apply to the Mass and to our participation in it what St Augustine said: *It is not possible for me to love in a mean fashion ... since I should have engraved upon my heart that it was for me He died nailed to the cross.*[18] The Redemption was carried out just once in the Passion, the death and resurrection of Jesus, and is renewed in each of us in a particularly intense way when we intimately take part in the holy sacrifice of the Mass.

The Redemption is carried out also, albeit in a different manner from that of our actual participation in the Mass, in each one of our interior conversations with Our Lord, when we make a good confession, when we receive with piety the sacraments, which are like 'channels of grace'. Pain offered up to Our Lord in reparation for our sins – which deserve a far greater punishment – for our eternal salvation and for that of all the world, makes us co-redeemers with Christ. What was useless and destructive becomes something of incalculable value – the sickness of someone in hospital, the predicament of the mother of a family who faces up to problems which seem overwhelming, bad news which hurts us deeply, the problems we encounter each day, the mortifications we undertake or accept – all serve for the redemption of the world if we place them on the paten together with the bread

---

[17] Second Vatican Council, *Lumen gentium*, 3
[18] St Augustine, *On Holy Virginity*, 55

which the priest is offering in the Holy Mass. It might seem to us that these are very small things, and so taken separately they are, like the drops of water which the priest adds to the wine in the Offertory. However, in the same way that these drops of water join with the wine to become the Blood of Christ, the actions – even the little ones – which we offer, will acquire an immense value in the eyes of God, because we have joined them to Jesus' sacrifice.

The sinner who has been pardoned can with his own mortification, physical or spiritual, sought or unwelcome, unite himself to the Passion of Jesus, who has obtained the pardon for him.[19] Thus it is that we become co-redeemers with Christ.

We turn to the Virgin so that she may show us how to live our vocation as co-redeemers with Christ in our ordinary lives. *What did you feel*, we ask Our Lady in the intimacy of our prayer, *when you saw your Son crucified? I look at you and I can't find words to describe your pain. But I do understand when I see that your Son had need of it, when I understand that we your children need it, all the grief and pain and sorrow that you accepted without hesitation – 'Fiat' – it is a new 'be it done to me' in your life, a new way of accepting the work of co-redemption. Thank you, Mother of mine! Grant me this resolute attitude of surrender, of being completely forgetful of myself, so that by learning from you what the work of Co-redemption demands, all I may do to bring souls to God will seem to me to be very little. But remember to come and meet me as I go on my way, for alone I will not know how to go forward.*[20]

---

[19] St John Paul II, Apostolic Exhortation, *Reconciliatio et Poenitentia*, 31

[20] C. O'Shea, *The Way of the Cross*, 4

FIFTH WEEK OF LENT – THURSDAY

37. MEDITATING ON THE PASSION

37.1 The custom of meditating on Our Lord's Passion.

My people! What have I done, in what way have I offended you? Answer me. I gave you the water of salvation which flowed from my sorrow to drink and you gave me honey and vinegar. My people, what have I done to you?[1]

The liturgy of these days during Lent brings us closer to the fundamental mystery of our Faith – the Resurrection of the Lord. If the liturgical year is centred upon Easter then this period *demands an even greater devotion on our part, given its proximity to the sublime mysteries of divine mercy.*[2] *But we should not tread this path too hastily, lest we lose sight of a very simple fact which we might easily overlook. We will not be able to share in Our Lord's Resurrection unless we unite ourselves with him in his Passion and death (cf Rom 8:17). If we are to accompany Christ in his glory at the end of Holy Week, we must first enter into his holocaust and be truly united to him as he lies dead on Calvary.*[3] So during these days let us accompany Jesus, in our prayers, along his painful way to Calvary and his death on the cross. As we keep him company let us not forget that we too were protagonists in all those horrors, for Jesus *bore the burden of our sins,*[4] each and every one of them. We were freed from the hands of the devil and from eternal death *at a great price,*[5] that of the Blood of Christ.

The custom of meditating on the Passion began in the very earliest days of Christianity. Many of the faithful in

---

[1] Liturgy, *Good Friday*
[2] St Leo the Great, *Sermon 47*
[3] St J. Escrivá, *Christ is passing by*, 95
[4] cf 1 Pet 2:24
[5] cf 1 Cor 6:20

Jerusalem had themselves been present as Christ passed through the streets of the city on the eve of the Pasch. They would never forget Jesus' sufferings as he made his way to Calvary. The Evangelists dedicated a good part of their writings to the detailed account of those events. *We should read our Lord's Passion constantly*, said St John Chrysostom; *what great benefit we will gain by doing so. Even if you are as hard as stone, when you contemplate that He was sarcastically adorned, then ridiculed, beaten and subjected to the final agonies, you will be moved to cast all pride from your soul.*[6] How many people have been converted by careful meditation on the Passion!

St Thomas Aquinas said that *the Passion of Christ is enough to serve as a guide and model throughout our lives.*[7] One day while he was visiting St Bonaventure, St Thomas asked him where he had acquired such good doctrine as the one that he set out in his works. It is said that St Bonaventure showed him a crucifix, which was blackened from all the kisses he had given it, and explained *This is the book that tells me what I should write; the little I know I have learned from it.*[8] From the crucifix the saints learned how to suffer and truly love Christ. We too should learn from it. *Your crucifix ... As a Christian, you should always carry your crucifix with you. And place it on your desk. And kiss it before going to bed and when you wake up; and when your poor body rebels against your soul, kiss it again.*[9]

Our Lord's Passion should be a frequent theme in our prayer, but especially so in these days leading up to the central mystery of our redemption.

---

[6] St John Chrysostom, *Homilies on the Gospel of St Matthew*, 87,1
[7] St Thomas, *About the Creed*, 6
[8] St Alphonsus Liguori, *Meditations on Christ's Passion*, 1:4
[9] St J. Escrivá, *The Way*, 302

37.2 How we should meditate on the Passion.

In our meditation, the Passion of Christ comes out of its cold historical frame and stops being a pious consideration, presenting itself before our eyes as terrible, brutal, savage, bloody ... yet full of love.[10] We do well then to contemplate Our Lord's Passion: in our personal meditation, when reading the Gospel, in the sorrowful mysteries of the Holy Rosary, in The Way of the Cross ... sometimes we imagine ourselves to be there, present amongst those who witnessed those moments. We take a seat among the Apostles during the Last Supper, when our Lord washed their feet and spoke to them with infinite tenderness, at the supreme moment of the institution of the Sacred Eucharist. We picture ourselves as one more among the three who slept at Gethsemane when the Lord hoped that we would accompany him in his infinite loneliness; as one amongst those who heard Peter swear that he did not know Jesus; as one who heard the false testimonies at that travesty of a judgement and saw the Chief Priest make a great show of being shocked at Jesus' words; as one in the thick of the mob that screamed out for his death and saw him hoisted up on the cross on Calvary. We put ourselves among the onlookers and see the disfigured yet noble face of Jesus. Astonishingly, we feel his infinite patience.

With the help of grace, moreover, we can also try to contemplate the Passion of Christ as He himself lived it.[11] It seems impossible, and of course it will always be a very impoverished view compared with the reality of what in fact took place, but it can become for us an extraordinarily rich source of prayer.

St Leo the Great tells us that *Whoever truly wishes to venerate the Passion of the Lord should contemplate Jesus*

---

[10] St J. Escrivá, *Furrow*, 993
[11] cf R. A. Knox, *A Retreat for lay people*

crucified with the eyes of his soul, and in such a way that
he identifies his own body with that of Jesus.[12]

What would Jesus, in his infinite holiness, have felt at
Gethsemane, taking upon himself the burden of all the sin
of the world, all the acts of wickedness, of disloyalty, of
sacrilege? What loneliness must He have known when
three times He found fast asleep the disciples He had taken
with him for company that night? He saw too those among
his friends who, in the course of the centuries, would fall
asleep at their posts while the enemy remained wide
awake.

37.3 The fruits of such meditation.

If we are to know and follow Christ we must be moved
by his pain and helplessness; we must feel the lashes, the
thorns, the insults, the neglect, the degradation.

And this should be not as mere on-lookers, but as
protagonists; for it was our sins that led him to Calvary.
Therefore *It is good for us to try to understand better the*
meaning of Christ's death. We must get beyond external
appearances and clichés. We need to put ourselves really
and truly into the scenes which we are re-living; to witness
the sorrow of Jesus, his mother's tears, the disciples'
flight, the courage of the holy women, the daring of those
two Joseph and Nicodemus who ask Pilate for the body of
Our Lord.[13]

If it were only possible I would like to feel all that you
feel. But you are perfect man and your sensitivity is so
much greater than mine. At your side I see, yet again, that I
don't know how to suffer. And so I am amazed by your
ability to give everything without reserve. Jesus, I must tell
you just how cowardly I am. Yet seeing you nailed to the

---

[12] St Leo the Great, *Sermon 15 on the Passion*
[13] St J. Escrivá, *Christ is passing by*, 101

cross *'suffering all that can be suffered, your arms spread in one gesture of an eternal priest'* (Holy Rosary, J. Escrivá), *I am going to tell you something which may seem crazy; I want to imitate you, Lord. I want to give myself truly to you, once and for all, and be ready to do all that you ask of me. I know I am not nearly strong enough to be making such a request. But I know that I love you, Jesus.*[14]

Let us, *above all, come close to Jesus in his death, close to his cross which stands out in silhouette above the summit of Golgotha. But we must approach him sincerely and with the interior recollection that is a sign of Christian maturity. The divine and human events of the Passion will then pierce our soul as words spoken to us by God to uncover the secrets of our heart and show us what he expects of our lives.*[15]

By meditating on Christ's Passion we will gain countless rewards. Firstly, it will help us to maintain a great aversion to all sin, since *He was wounded for our iniquities, he was bruised for our sins.*[16] Jesus crucified should be the book which we, in the manner of the saints, read constantly so as to learn to detest sin and really grow in love for such a loving God; for it is in Christ's wounds that we learn of the evil of sin which condemned him to suffer such a cruel and ignominious death so that divine justice might be carried out. It is in Christ's wounds that we find proof of his great love for us, for He endured such terrible pain and suffering precisely so as to show us just how much he loved us.[17]

And we feel that *sin cannot be regarded as just a trivial mistake. To sin is to crucify the Son of God, to tear*

---

[14] C. O'Shea, *The Way of the Cross*, 11
[15] St J. Escrivá, *Christ is passing by*, 101
[16] Is 53:5
[17] St Alphonsus Liguori, *Meditations on Christ's Passion*, I,4

his hands and feet with hammer blows, to make his heart break.[18] A sin, therefore, is so much more than a simple 'human error'. Christ's sufferings will encourage us to avoid all that might be described as bourgeois attitudes, unwillingness and laziness. It will inflame our love and keep lukewarmness at bay. It will help us to mortify our soul and guard better all our senses.

If the Lord sometimes lets us suffer illness, pain or contradictions which are especially intense and serious, then it will be of great help and relief to consider the pain which Christ endured in his Passion. He experienced every kind of physical and moral pain since *He suffered at the hands of the Gentiles and the Jews, of men and of women – an example being the maids who accused Peter. He suffered at the hands of princes and their officials, and at the hands of the ordinary people too. He suffered at the hands of relatives and friends and acquaintances, on account of Judas who betrayed him and of Peter who denied him. In short, Christ suffered as much as it is possible for man to suffer. Christ suffered at the hands of his friends who abandoned him, He suffered as blasphemies were hurled at him; his honour and self-esteem suffered from all the taunts and jibes; He was even stripped of his clothes, the only possessions he had. In his soul he felt sadness, emptiness and fear; in his body, the wounds and the cruel lashes of the whip.*[19]

So let us make it our intention to come closer to the Virgin Mary in these days leading up to her Son's Passion, and let us ask her to show us how to meditate on these moments when He suffered so much for us.

---

[18] St J. Escrivá, *Furrow*, 993
[19] St Thomas, *Summa Theologiae*, III, q46 a5

FIFTH WEEK OF LENT – FRIDAY

38. THE AGONY IN THE GARDEN

38.1 Jesus at Gethsemane. The fulfilment of the will of the Father.

After the Last Supper, Jesus and the Apostles sing a psalm in an act of thanksgiving, as was the custom. Then the small group starts out towards a garden on the Mount of Olives which lies close at hand. Jesus had warned Peter and the others that that night all of them – in one way or another – would deny him, leaving him alone. They arrive at Gethsemane. Now Jesus says to his disciples *Sit here while I pray*, and taking with him Peter, James and John, he begins to be greatly distressed and troubled. He says to them *My Soul is very sorrowful, even to death; remain here and watch!*[1] And he withdraws from them about a stone's throw.[2] Jesus feels a tremendous need to pray. He stops beside some rocks and falls down, dejected – *He fell to the ground,*[3] writes St Mark. St Luke tells us: *He knelt down,*[4] and St Matthew states even more precisely: *He fell on his face,*[5] although Jews usually stood while praying. Jesus speaks to his Father in a prayer filled with confidence and affection, in which he abandons himself completely to Him. *My Father*, he says, *if it be possible let this cup pass from me; yet not as I will, but as thou wilt.*

Shortly before this he had told his disciples: *My soul is very sorrowful, even to death,* so intense was the sadness he was suffering that it could have killed him. This is how

---

[1] Mark 14:32-34
[2] Luke 22:41
[3] Mark 14:15
[4] Luke 22:41
[5] Matt 26:39

Jesus suffers. He who is innocence itself takes upon himself all the sins of man.

He took up man's sins as if they were his own and offered to pay personally all our debts incurred as a consequence of them. All of them: He would pay for those sins already committed, for the sins which were being committed at that moment in time, and for all the sins that would ever be committed till the end of time.

The Lord not only took responsibility for the sins of others, but made himself one with us, as the head is to the body; *He wanted our sins to be called his sins and for this He paid not only with his blood, but also with the shame of these sins.*[6] All those causes of suffering were captured in all their intensity by the soul of Christ.

In silence we watch how Jesus suffers: *And falling into an agony He prayed even more intensely.*[7] How we must thank the Lord for the voluntary sacrifice he offered to free us from sin and eternal death!

Jesus falls into such an agony that He sweats blood: *Jesus, sad and alone, suffers and soaks the earth with his blood. Kneeling on hard ground, he perseveres in prayer. He cries for you ... and for me: the weight of men's sins overwhelms him.*[8] But his confidence in the Father does not falter and he persists in his prayer. When his body seems able to resist no longer, an Angel comes to comfort him. The human nature of the Lord with all its capacity for suffering is shown to us in this scene.

In our lives there may be moments of intense struggle, perhaps darkness and deep pain, when we are tempted to lose heart and it is difficult to accept the will of God. The image of Jesus at the Mount of Olives shows us how we

---

[6] L. de la Palma, *The Passion of the Lord*
[7] Luke 22:43
[8] St J. Escrivá, *Holy Rosary*, First Sorrowful Mystery

must proceed in these moments; we must embrace the will of God, without putting any limit or condition whatsoever to our acceptance of it, and identifying ourselves with the love of God by means of persevering prayer.

Jesus prays in the Garden, Pater mi (Matt 26:39). Abba Pater! (Matt 14:36). God is my father, even though he may send me suffering. He loves me tenderly, even while wounding me. Jesus suffers to fulfil the most Holy Will of God. Following in the footsteps of the Master, can I complain if I too meet suffering along the way?[9]

38.2 The need for prayer in order to follow the Lord closely.

Jesus looks at us with a gaze of expressive simplicity on that night. He looks into souls and hearts in the revealing light of Divine Wisdom. The spectacle of all men's sins, of the sins of his brothers, files past before his eyes. He sees the deplorable opposition of so many who scorn the happiness he offers them, the uselessness of the generous sacrifice He will offer in vain for so many more. He feels great loneliness and moral pain because of this defiance and lack of response to such an outpouring of Divine love.

Three times he looks for those three disciples of his to accompany him in prayer; *Watch with me, be at my side, do not leave me alone!* he has asked them. *And again he came and found them sleeping, for their eyes were very heavy; and they did not know what to answer him.*[10] Perhaps in that state of tremendous helplessness He seeks a little company, a little human warmth. But his friends abandoned the Friend ... That was a night when they should have stayed awake, to have prayed. And they slept. They

---

[9] *idem, The Way of the Cross*, First Station, 1
[10] Mark 14:40

still did not love enough, and allowing themselves to be beaten by weakness and sadness, they left Jesus alone. In them the Lord found no support; they had been chosen for this and they had let him down ...

We must always pray, but there are moments when this prayer has to be intensified. To abandon it would be like abandoning Christ, leaving ourselves at the mercy of the enemy. *Why do you sleep?* He asks them – and he asks us too – *Rise and pray that you may not enter into temptation.*[11] For this reason we say to Jesus: *If you see me asleep, if you discover that I am afraid of pain, if you notice that I stop when I see the cross more closely, Do not leave me! Tell me, as you told Peter, James and John, that you need my affection, my love. Tell me that in order to follow you, in order never to abandon you again into the hands of those who plot your death, I have to overcome my drowsiness, my passions and my comfort ...*[12]

Our daily meditation, if it is true prayer, will keep us alert in the face of the enemy who never sleeps. And it will make us strong so as to endure and defeat temptations and difficulties. If we were to neglect it we would find ourselves in the hands of the enemy. We would lose our joy and we would be left without the strength to accompany Jesus.

Jesus wants us to accompany him today; *without prayer, how difficult it is to accompany him!*[13] Our own experience tells us so. Yet if we become strong through our daily relationship with Him, we will be able to tell him in all certainty: *Even though I die with you, I will not deny you.*[14] Peter could not fulfil his promise that night because,

---

[11] Luke 22:46
[12] C. O'Shea, *The Way of the Cross*
[13] St J. Escrivá, *The Way*, 89
[14] Mark 14:31

amongst other things, he did not persevere in prayer as the Lord had asked him to do. After his repentance, he would be faithful to his Master, even giving up his own life for him some years later.

38.3 The first sorrowful mystery of the Holy Rosary. Meditating upon it. This scene will help us to be strong in carrying out the will of God.

Meditating on this scene in the Passion can be of great help in making us strong so as never to omit our daily prayer and so as to carry out the will of God in the things we find difficult. Lord, may things be done not as I want, but as you want! *Jesus, whatever you want, I love,*[15] we tell him in all sincerity.

The souls of the saints have benefitted greatly from this passage in the life of Our Lord. St Thomas More shows us that Jesus' prayer in Gethsemane has strengthened Christians faced with great difficulties and tribulations. He too was strengthened by the contemplation of these scenes while he awaited decapitation and martyrdom for being true to his Faith. And it can help us to be strong in the face of the difficulties, both great and small, we encounter in our ordinary daily lives. While he was in prison this saint wrote: *Christ knew that many people would be filled with terror when faced with the threat of being tortured, and He wanted to encourage them with the example of his own pain, his own sadness, his own incomparable humiliation and fear.*

It seems that Christ is making use of his own agony to speak to those who find themselves in such a situation: Be brave, he seems to say, you who are feeble and weak. Do not give up hope. You are terrified and depressed, worn down by exhaustion and the dread of torture. Be confident,

---

[15] St J. Escrivá, *The Way*, 773

I have overcome the world and yet I was ever afraid and appalled, since my suffering grew in with the fearful knowledge of what was causi how I go before you along this path that is be many fears. Take hold of the edge of my cloak and you will feel flowing from it the power that will not allow your heart's blood to be contaminated with useless fears and anxieties.

It will hearten you and raise your spirits, especially when you remember that you are following closely in my footsteps. I am faithful, and will not allow you to be tempted beyond your strength, but give you the necessary grace to be able to bear the test; and it will fill you with gladness when you remember that this transient tribulation you are asked to bear will become a cargo of immense glory.[16] The saint wrote in these terms knowing he was to be beheaded a few days' later.

To-day we can resolve to contemplate frequently, perhaps every day, this moment in the life of Our Lord we know as the first sorrowful mystery of the Holy Rosary. In a special way it can provide suitable matter for our prayer when it is more than usually difficult to know just how to discover the will of God in events whose complexities we may not understand. Then, by way of an ejaculatory prayer, we can say *Volo quidquid vis, volo quia vis ... – I love what you love, I love because you love , I love it as you love it, I love it for as long as you love it.*[17]

---

[16] St Thomas More, *The Agony of Christ, in loc*
[17] Roman Missal, *Thanksgiving after Mass – Prayer of Clement XI*

39. THE ARREST OF JESUS

39.1 Judas' betrayal. Faithfulness in everyday things.

When he had finished his prayer in the Garden of Gethsemane the Lord rose to his feet and once again woke his three disciples who had fallen asleep through tiredness and discouragement. *Rise, let us be going*, he tells them. *See, my betrayer is at hand*. While he was still speaking, Judas came, one of the twelve, and with him a great crowd with swords and clubs.[1]

The betrayal is carried out with a show of friendship. *He came up to Jesus and said, 'Hail, Master!' And he kissed him.*[2] It seems impossible to us that a man who had known Christ so well could be capable of betraying him. What happened in Judas' soul? For he had been present at so many miracles, and knew so well Our Lord's goodness of heart for all men. Attracted by his word, he above all had experienced the predilection of Jesus, his special love for his most trusted friends, himself becoming one of the Twelve. He had been chosen and called to be an Apostle by the Lord himself. After the Ascension, when it was necessary to fill Judas' place, Peter would recall that 'he was numbered among us and was allotted his share in this ministry'.[3] He too was sent to preach and would have seen the abundant fruit of his apostolate. He may have performed miracles like the others. And he would have had very intimate and personal conversations with the Master, as did the other Apostles. What can have happened to his soul that

---

[1] Matt 26:46-47
[2] Matt 26:49
[3] Acts 1:17

he would now betray the Lord for thirty pieces of silver?

For it to be explicable, there must have been a long story behind the betrayal that night. For some time Judas would have been distant from Christ even though he was still in his company. On the surface he would have remained normal, but he must have changed inside and become distant. The split with the Master, the loss of his faith and his vocation must have taken place little by little, as he yielded in more and more important things. There is a moment when Judas protests because the little gestures of affection which others have made towards the Lord seem to him to be extravagantly excessive, and he even disguises his protest with his 'love of the poor'. But St John tells us the true reason: He was a thief, and as he looked after the common purse he took from what was put into it.[4]

He had allowed his love for the Lord to grow cold, and there remained only the mere external appearance of discipleship. His life of loving surrender to God had become a farce; more than once he would think it would have been better not to have followed the Lord at all. Now he does not remember the miracles, the cures, the happy moments with the Master, his friendship with the other apostles. He is now a man who has lost his way, out of touch, quite capable of committing the madness which will for us be so difficult to understand. The act now carried out has been preceded by increasingly greater acts of disloyalty. It is one final outcome of a long, interior process.

In contrast, perseverance is doing the small everyday things with faith; it is supported by the humility of beginning again when we go astray through weakness. *A house is not destroyed by a momentary impulse. More often it is because of an old defect in its construction. Sometimes it is the prolonged neglect by its inhabitants*

---

[4] John 12:6

that permits water to get in, at first drop by drop, imperceptibly, the damp eating away at the woodwork and rotting even the structure of stone. With time one tiny crack becomes larger, causing considerable damage. In the end, the rain pours in. The result is ruin.[5]

To persevere in our own vocation is to respond to the repeated calls the Lord makes in the course of our lives, even though there are obstacles and difficulties and, sometimes, the odd error, acts of cowardice and even defeats. As we contemplate these scenes from the Passion we consider our faithfulness in the tiny details of our own vocation. Is there any hint of a double life? Am I faithful to my own duties? Do I take care to ensure that my relationship with the Lord is sincere? Do I avoid becoming attached to material things – being drawn to the thirty pieces of silver?

39.2 Returning to the Lord with hope.

But the Lord did not waste the opportunity to do good to one who had done him wrong. After having saluted Judas with sincerity, he reproved him, not with the harshness which he deserved, but with the gentleness with which a sick person is treated. He called him by his name, which is a sign of friendship ... *Judas, would you betray the Son of Man with a kiss?* (Luke 22:48) With a sign of peace would you make war on me? And to move him to recognize his guilt even more, the Lord lovingly asked him another question: *Friend, why are you here?* (Matt 26:50) Because you have been my friend, the offence that you do me and the pain you cause me are all the greater. If it were an enemy who slandered me I could endure it, but you, my friend, my close friend, with whom I used to be so united ... (Ps 54:13) You have been a friend and you should still

---

[5] Cassian, *Conferences*, 6

be one; for my part, you can be a friend once again. I am ready to go on being your friend. Even though you do not love me, I love you. My friend, why do you do this? Why have you come?[6]

It is by mortal sin that the Christian betrays Jesus. All sin, even venial sin, is inextricably and mysteriously related to the Passion of the Lord. Our life is an affirmation or negation of Christ. But even after the most serious offences He is always ready to take us back into his friendship. Judas rejected the hand the Lord held out to him. His life, without Jesus, was ruined and was now bereft of meaning.

After betraying him, Judas must have followed the trial against Jesus with deep unrest. How would all this end? He soon found out that the Chief Priests had sentenced Jesus to death. Perhaps he never expected such a grave sentence; perhaps he saw now how the master was being treated ... what is certain is that when he saw Jesus sentenced, he regretted what he had done and gave back the thirty pieces of silver. He was sorry for his act of madness, but he did not exercise the virtue of hope – for he could still have gained Our Lord's forgiveness – and he lacked the humility to return to Christ. He could have been one of the twelve founders of the Church despite the enormity of his guilt if he had asked God for forgiveness.

For despite our sins and errors, the Lord waits for us when we return in trusting prayer and in Confession. He who forbids us to sin never gives up waiting for us, to grant us his forgiveness once a sin has been committed. See how He whom we spurn calls us. For although we separate ourselves from him, He does not separate himself from us.[7]

However great our sins may be, the Lord is always

---

[6] L. de la Palma, *The Passion of the Lord*

[7] St Gregory the Great, *Homily 34 on the Gospels*

waiting to forgive us. He takes into account human weakness, defects and mistakes. He is always ready to call us his friend again, to give us the necessary grace to go forward if we are sincere and willing to struggle. In the face of the apparent failure of so many of our attempts, we should remember that God asks not so much for success as for the humility to begin again without allowing ourselves to get discouraged and pessimistic, putting into practice instead the theological virtue of hope.

39.3 The flight of the disciples. The need for prayer.

It is moving to contemplate in this scene Jesus' concern for his disciples. When it was He himself who was in danger: *If you are looking for me*, he said to those who were with Judas, *let these men go.*[8] The Lord looks after his own.

Then they seized Jesus and took him to the high priest's house.[9] St John says that they bound Jesus.[10] And they did this violently, without any consideration whatsoever, the mob shoving him along with hurled insults and rude clamour. The disciples, frightened and bewildered, forgot their promises of loyalty during that memorable supper. *They all forsook him*, says the Evangelist, *and fled.*[11]

Jesus is left alone. One after the other the disciples have disappeared. *The Lord was flogged and nobody lifted a finger to help him. He was spat upon and nobody shielded him. He was crowned with thorns and nobody intervened. He was crucified and nobody prised out the nails.*[12] He is alone with all the sins and vileness of all times. And our sins and horrendous deeds were there

---

[8] John 18:8
[9] Luke 22:54
[10] John 18:12
[11] Mark 14:50
[12] St Augustine, *Commentary on Psalm 21*, 2, 8

before his eyes.

Peter followed him *from afar*.[13] And from afar off it is not really possible to follow Christ, as Peter after his threefold denial would come to understand. And we know this too. We either follow the Lord or we end up denying him. *We need only change a pronoun in the short evangelical phrase in order to discover the cause of our own desertions, be they small errors or serious falls, fleeting relaxations of effort or lengthy periods of lukewarmness. 'Sequebatur eum a longe': it is we then who follow him from afar ... Men follow Christ with maddening lack of generosity and with grudging lack of commitment to their Lord. There are too many Christians who, if they can be said to follow him at all, follow Jesus only from afar.*[14]

But now we assure him that we want to follow him closely. We want to stay with him and not leave him alone, in those moments and in those places when it is not easy to say that we are his disciples. We want to follow him in our work, in our studies, when we go along the street and when we are in the temple, with the family or during healthy recreation. But we know that by ourselves we cannot do anything: with our daily prayer, we can.

Perhaps one of his disciples went in search of the Holy Virgin and told her that they had taken her Son. And she, despite her immense pain, gave them peace in those bitter hours. We too can find refuge in her – *Refugium peccatorum* – if in spite of our good intentions we have not been brave enough to stand up for the Lord when he was counting on us. In her we will find the necessary strength to remain with the Lord in bad times, and to be reinforced by her in our desire to make amends.

---

[13] Luke 22:54
[14] G. Chevrot, *Simon Peter*

PALM SUNDAY

40. TRIUMPHAL ENTRY INTO JERUSALEM

40.1 The solemn, yet simple entry into Jerusalem.

Come, and as we make our way up to the Mount of Olives, let us go out to meet Christ, who is returning today from Bethany, and of his own will makes haste towards his most venerable and revered passion, whereby he will bring to fulfilment the mystery of the salvation of mankind.[1] Jesus leaves Bethany very early in the morning. Many fervent disciples of his had gathered there since the previous evening; some were natives of Galilee who had come on pilgrimage to celebrate the Passover, others were inhabitants of Jerusalem who had been won over by the recent miracle of the resurrection of Lazarus. Accompanied by this large gathering, as well as by others who joined them on the way, Jesus once more sets out along the old road from Jericho to Jerusalem towards the tiny summit of the Mount of Olives.

The circumstances favoured a great reception, because it was customary for the people to go out to greet the larger groups of pilgrims, who would enter into the city with songs and demonstrations of joy. Our Lord showed no opposition to the preparations for this jubilant entry. He himself would choose the sort of mount he would ride in on – a simple donkey which he had asked to be brought from Bethphage, a village very close to Jerusalem. People of importance had used the donkey as a form of travel in Palestine as far back as the time of Balaam.[2]

The procession was organised quite quickly. Some

---

[1] St Andrew of Crete, *Sermon 9 on Palm Sunday*
[2] cf Num 22:21 ss.

people spread a blanket on top of the animal and helped Jesus to mount upon it; others came forward to lay their garments on the ground to form a carpet for the donkey to pass over; many others ran along the roadside following the procession as it moved towards the city, laying down bits of green foliage along the route and waving olive and palm branches torn off the trees close by. And as they drew close to the city, *at the descent of the Mount of Olives, the whole multitude of the disciples began to rejoice and praise God with a loud voice for all the mighty works that they had seen, saying, 'Blessed is the King who comes in the name of the Lord! Peace in heaven and glory in the highest!'* [3]

Jesus makes his entry into Jerusalem as the Messiah upon a donkey, just as had been prophesied many centuries before.[4] The people, also, acclaim him in clearly messianic fashion. The pharisees knew these prophecies very well, but so also did the common people, and they were visibly overjoyed. Jesus accepts this homage and tells the pharisees, who were trying to dampen this demonstration of faith and joy, *I tell you, if these were silent, the very stones would cry out.*[5] In any case, the triumph of Jesus is a simple affair, he *makes do with a poor animal for a throne. I don't know about you; but I am not humiliated to acknowledge that in the Lord's eyes I am a beast of burden: 'I am like a donkey in your presence, but I am continually with you. You hold my right hand,' (Ps 72:23-24) you take me by the bridle.*[6]

Jesus also wants to enter triumphantly into the lives of men today, riding upon a humble animal; he would like us

---

[3] Luke 19:37-38

[4] Zach 9:9

[5] Luke 19:39

[6] St J. Escrivá, *Christ is passing by,* 181

to bear witness to him in the simplicity of our work done well, showing forth our cheerfulness, our serenity and our sincere concern for others. He wants to be close to us through the circumstances of normal human dealings. We too can tell him on a day like today, *Ut iumentum factus sum apud te ... I am like a little donkey before You. But You are always close to me, You have taken me by the bridle and brought me to do Your will; 'et cum gloria suscepisti me', and afterwards you have given me a big hug.*[7] *Ut iumentum ... I am like a donkey before You, Lord ... like a beast of burden, and I shall always remain close to You.* This could be an aspiration for us to use today.

Our Lord has entered triumphantly into Jerusalem. A few days later, in this same city, he will be nailed to a cross.

40.2 Correspondence to grace.

The triumphant procession of Jesus has now made its way from the top of the Mount of Olives and proceeds down the western slope towards the Temple looming ahead of them. Jesus can now see the whole city stretched out before him. On seeing this scene Jesus wept.[8] This weeping, amidst so many shouts of joy and such a solemn entry, must have been totally unexpected. Seeing Jesus, the disciples were completely at a loss. In a single moment all their joy was abruptly shattered.

Jesus sees how Jerusalem is sunk in sin, ignorance and blindness, *Would that even today you knew the things that make for peace! But now they are hid from your eyes.*[9] Our Lord sees how other days will fall upon it which will no longer be like this present day of joy and salvation, but rather of misfortune and destruction. A few years later the

---

[7] *idem*, A. Vazquez de Prada, *The Founder of Opus Dei*, Madrid
[8] Luke 19:41
[9] Luke 19:42

city will be razed to the ground. Jesus weeps over the impenitence of Jerusalem. How eloquent these tears of Christ! They are full of mercy, sorrowing over the city which has rejected him.

Every means had been tried, including miracles, actions and words, sometimes in a tone of severity, at other times with leniency, ... Jesus had tried everything with everyone, in the town and in the countryside, with simple people and with the learned doctors of the Law, in Galilee and in Judaea. Today, as well, and in every age, Jesus offers the riches of his grace to every man, because his will is always to save.

In our lives also, every means has been tried and every remedy has been made available. On so many occasions Jesus has sought those little encounters with us! How very many ordinary and extraordinary graces have been showered upon us in our lives! *For, by his incarnation, he, the son of God, has in a certain way united himself with each man. He worked with human hands, he thought with a human mind. He acted with a human will, and with a human heart he loved. Born of the Virgin Mary, he has truly been made one of us, like to us in all things except sin. As an innocent lamb he merited life for us by his blood which he freely shed. In him God reconciled us to himself and to one another, freeing us from the bondage of the devil and of sin, so that each one of us could say with the Apostle: the Son of God 'loved me and gave himself for me' (Gal 2:20).*[10]

The story of each man is the story of God's continual watchfulness over him. Each man is the object of the Lord's special love. Jesus was ready to do everything for Jerusalem, but the city was not willing to open up her gates to his mercy. This is the deep mystery of human freedom

---

[10] Second Vatican Council, *Gaudium et spes*, 22

which always retains that sad possibility of rejecting the grace of God. *Free man, subject yourself to a voluntary servitude, so that Jesus won't have to say of you what He is said to have told Saint Teresa about others: 'Teresa, I was willing. But men were not.'* [11]

How indeed are we responding to the countless promptings of the Holy Spirit, who seeks to make us holy in the midst of our ordinary duties and surroundings? Each day how often do we say 'yes' to God and 'no' to our selfishness, to our laziness and to everything that amounts to a lack of love, even if it is only something small.

40.3 The joy and sorrow of this day.

The children of Jerusalem welcomed Christ the King. They proclaimed the resurrection of life, and waving olive branches, they loudly praised the Lord: Hosanna in the highest. [12] We now realise that for many people this triumphant entry was very short-lived. Just five days later the enthusiastic hosannas gave way to angry shouts of *Crucify him!*. What accounts for such a sharp turn-about, and such inconsistent behaviour? If we are to understand at all, perhaps we only need to look a little into our own hearts. *How different the cries,* St Bernard comments, *'Away with him, away with him, crucify him,'* and then *'Blessed is he who comes in the name of the Lord, hosanna in the highest!' How different the cries are that now are calling him 'King of Israel' and then in a few days time will be saying, 'We have no king but Caesar!' What a contrast between the green branches and the cross, between the flowers and the thorns! Before they were offering their own clothes for him to walk upon, and so soon afterwards they are stripping him of his, and casting*

---

[11] St J. Escrivá, *The Way*, 761
[12] *Liturgy of Palm Sunday. Hymn to Christ the King.*

lots upon them.[13]

The triumphal entry of Jesus into Jerusalem asks for loyalty and perseverance from each one of us, it calls us to deepen in our faithfulness, and for our resolutions to be more than just bright lights that sparkle for a moment and then fade away. There are some striking contrasts in the depths of our hearts, for we are capable of the very greatest things and also the very worst, and so if we wish to possess the divine life and triumph with Christ, we need to be constant and through penance deaden within us anything that separates us from God and prevents us from following Our Lord unto the Cross. *The liturgy of Palm Sunday puts these words on our lips: 'Swing back, doors, higher yet; reach higher, immemorial gates, to let the king enter in triumph!'* (Antiphon during distribution of palms.) *Anyone who barricades himself in the citadel of his own selfishness will never come down onto the battlefield. But if he raises the gates of his fortress and lets in the king of peace, then he will go out with the king to fight against all that misery which blurs the eyes and numbs the conscience.*[14]

Also in Jerusalem is Mary, wanting to be close to her son in celebrating the Passover. It is to be the last Jewish Passover and the first Passover in which her Son is both Priest and Victim. Let us stay close to Her. Our Lady will teach us how to remain constant, how to struggle in little things, and to grow continually in love for Jesus. May She be close to our side as we contemplate the Passion, Death and Resurrection of her Son. We will not find a more privileged place.

---

[13] St Bernard, *Sermon on Palm Sunday* 2,4
[14] St J. Escrivá, *Christ is passing by*, 82

HOLY WEEK – MONDAY

THE PASSION OF OUR LORD

41. PETER'S DENIALS

41.1 Peter denies all knowledge of Our Lord. Our own denials.

As the trial of Jesus proceeds before the Sanhedrin, the saddest event in the life of Peter takes place. The one who had left everything to follow Our Lord, who had seen so many miracles worked and had received so many tokens of affection, now denies him utterly. He feels himself cornered and even swears he does not know Jesus.

And as Peter was below in the courtyard, one of the maids of the high priest came; and seeing Peter warming himself, she looked at him, and said, 'You also were with the Nazarene, Jesus.' But he denied it, saying, 'I neither know nor understand what you mean.' And he went out into the gateway. And the maid saw him, and began again to say to the bystanders, 'This man is one of them.' But again he denied it. And after a little while again the bystanders said to Peter, 'Certainly you are one of them; for you are a Galilean.' But he began to invoke a curse on himself and to swear, 'I do not know this man of whom you speak.'[1]

He denies that he knows his Lord, thereby denying the deepest meaning of his life, which is to be an Apostle and witness of the life of Christ and to proclaim that Jesus is the Son of the living God. His honour, his vocation to be an Apostle, all the hopes that had been placed in him by God, his past and his future, all came tumbling down. How could he possibly have said, *I know not this man*?

---

[1] Mark 14:66-71

A miracle worked by Jesus a few years before had had for him a deep and special significance. On seeing the miraculous draught of fishes (the first of them), Peter had understood everything; *he fell down at Jesus' knees, saying, 'Depart from me, for I am a sinful man, O Lord'. For he was astonished ...* [2] It seems that in a flash everything had become clear for him: the holiness of Christ and his own condition as a sinful man. Black stood in clear contrast with white, darkness with light, dirt with cleanness, sin with sanctity. In that moment, whilst his lips were saying that because of his sins he felt unworthy to be close to Our Lord, his eyes, however, and his whole attitude were asking that he might never ever depart from Him. That was such a happy day. That was when everything really began for him: *And Jesus said to Simon, 'Do not be afraid; henceforth you will be catching men.' And when they had brought their boats to land, they left everything and followed him.* [3] Peter's life from that moment on would have a most marvellous purpose, that of loving Christ and being *a fisher of men*. Everything else would serve as a means and an instrument to that end. Yet now, out of weakness and having allowed himself to be overcome by fear and human respect, everything had collapsed.

Sin, infidelity to a greater or lesser degree, always involves a denial of Christ and of that which is most noble within us, a denial of the highest ideals that Christ has sown inside us. Sin is the great downfall of man. This is why we need to struggle with determination, counting on grace, so that we avoid all grave sins, whether of malice, weakness or culpable ignorance, and then all deliberate venial sin.

---

[2] cf Luke 5:8-9
[3] Luke 5:10-11

But even from our sins, when we are unfortunate enough to commit them, we have to draw advantage, because contrition strengthens the bonds of our friendship with Our Lord. Our mistakes should never discourage us, provided we act with humility. A sincere act of repentance is always the occasion of a new encounter with Our Lord, from which we can derive some completely unsuspected consequences for our interior lives. If we sin, we have to come back again to Our Lord as often as is necessary, without getting anxious, although certainly with sorrow. *Peter took an hour to fall; but in an instant he rights himself and sets about raising himself higher than he was before his fall.*[4]

Heaven is full of great sinners who decided to repent. Jesus always welcomes us and rejoices to see us set out again upon the road we had abandoned, perhaps in small matters.

41.2 The look of Jesus and Peter's contrition.

Jesus, having been much ill-used, is led into one of the courtyards. He then *turned and looked at Peter.*[5] *Their looks meet. Peter would like to bow his head, but he cannot tear his eyes from Him, Whom he has just denied. He knows the Saviour's looks well; that look that had determined his vocation, he had not been able to resist either its authority or its charm; and that tender look of the Master's on the day He had affirmed, looking at His disciples, 'Here are my brethren, my sisters, my mother!' And that look that had made him tremble when he, Simon, had wanted to banish the Cross from Jesus' path! And the affectionately pitying look with which he had invited the too-rich young man to follow him! And His look, clouded*

---

[4] G. Chevrot, *Simon Peter*
[5] Luke 22:61

with tears, before Lazarus' tomb ... He knows them well, the Saviour's looks.

And yet never, never had he seen on the Saviour's face the expression he sees there at this moment, the eyes marked with sadness but without any severity. A look of reproach, without a doubt, but which becomes suppliant at the same time and seems to repeat to him, 'Simon, I have prayed for thee!'

This look only rests on him for an instant; Jesus is violently dragged away by the soldiers, but Peter sees Him all the time.[6] He sees that compassionate look of Jesus fixed upon the deep wound of his guilt. He now understands the enormity of his sin, and the fulfilment of Our Lord's prophecy about his betrayal. And Peter remembers the words of Our Lord, *'Before the cock crows today, you will deny me three times.' And he went out and wept bitterly.*[7] His going out *was to acknowledge his fault. He was able to weep bitterly because he knew how to love; the bitterness of sorrow in him quickly gave way to the sweetness of love.*[8]

Knowing that Our Lord had looked upon him prevented Peter from falling into despair. His look was one of encouragement in which Peter felt understood and forgiven. How it would remind him of the the parables of the Good Shepherd, the Prodigal Son and the Lost Sheep!

Peter went out. He moved away from that whole situation, in which he had imprudently placed himself, so as to avoid any possible relapses. He realised that this was not the place for him to be. He remembered his Lord and he *wept bitterly.* We see ourselves in the situation of Peter. *Sorrow of Love – Because He is good. Because He is your*

---

[6] G. Chevrot, *loc cit*

[7] Luke 22:61-62

[8] St Augustine, *Sermon 295*

Friend, Who gave His life for you. Because everything good you have is His. Because you have offended Him so much ... Because He has forgiven you ... He! Forgiven you! Weep, my son, with sorrow of Love.[9]

Contrition gives special strength to the soul; it restores hope, makes the Christian forget himself and draw close to God once more with a deeper act of love. Contrition proves the quality of interior life and always attracts God's mercy; *... this is the man to whom I will look, he that is humble and contrite in spirit ...* [10]

Christ found no difficulty in building his Church upon a man who was able to fall and who did fall. God also counts on weak instruments, provided they repent, to carry out his big project: the salvation of mankind.

It is very probable that after the denials and his repentance Peter would have gone to look for our Blessed Lady. This is what we do also at this moment as our own faults and denials come more vividly to mind.

41.3 True repentance. Acts of contrition.

As well as giving the soul great strength, true contrition also brings special happiness and enables us to be effective in our dealings with others. *The Master passes very close to us, again and again. He looks at us ... And if you look at him, if you listen to him, if you don't reject him, He will teach you how to give a supernatural meaning to everything you do ... Then you too, wherever you may be, will sow consolation and peace and joy.*[11]

Our Lord also looked at Judas, who was encouraged to come back in the moment of the betrayal and could hear Our Lord calling him friend. *Friend, why are you here?* In

---

[9] St J. Escrivá, *The Way*, 436
[10] Is 66:2
[11] St J. Escrivá, *The Way of the Cross*, Eighth Station, 4

this moment he did not repent, although later he did. When he *saw that he was condemned, he repented and brought back the thirty pieces of silver*[12]

What a contrast between Peter and Judas! Both in different ways betray their fidelity to their Master. Both repent. Peter, in spite of his denials, will become the rock upon which the Church of Christ will be set until the end of time. Judas *went and hanged himself.* Human repentance alone is not enough; it produces anxiety, bitterness and despair. Linked to Christ repentance is turned into a joyous sorrow, because a lost friendship is regained. Peter is united to Our Lord in an instant, and much closer than he had ever been before, because of his sorrow for his denials. Out of his denials is born a faithfulness that will take him even to martyrdom.

With Judas it is just the opposite, and he is left on his own: *What is that to us? See to it yourself,* the chief priests tell him. In the isolation brought about by sin, Judas would not go to Christ. He had lost hope.

We need to awaken frequently in our hearts a sorrow, born out of Love, for the sins we have committed. This we should do especially as we make our examination of conscience at the end of each day, and when we prepare ourselves for Confession.

You who tend to lose heart, I will tell you something that is very consoling: when a person does what he can, God will not deny his grace. Our Lord is a Father, and if, in the silence of his heart, one of his sons says to him: 'My Father in Heaven, here I am, help me ... ' If he goes to the Mother of God, who is our Mother, he will get through.[13]

---

[12] cf Matt 27:3-10
[13] St J. Escrivá, *The Way of the Cross*, Tenth Station, 3

THE PASSION OF OUR LORD

42. BEFORE PILATE: JESUS CHRIST, THE KING.

42.1 Jesus is condemned to death

Our Lord is led in chains to the residence of the Procurator, Pontius Pilate. They are in a hurry to get things over with. Jesus, with a silent dignity reflected in his walk, passes through the narrow streets which wind their way towards the house of Pilate. *It was already daylight and people in the city were awake and appearing at their doors and windows to see this man, famous and admired for his sanctity and deeds, now made prisoner. Our Lord had his hands bound together with a rope which was stretched also around his neck, for such was the punishment meted out to those who misused their freedom against the people. He would be cold so early in the morning and tired; his face was disfigured by blows and spittle, his hair dishevelled after having been pulled at, and his cheeks covered with bruises and blood, now become dry and hard. This is how Jesus appeared on the streets before the people, and they were all startled and frightened as they saw him. It was clear to everyone that the direction they were heading in and the manner of treating him all pointed towards his execution.*[1]

Jesus was passed from the Sanhedrin to the jurisdiction of the Romans, because the Jewish authorities were able to condemn a man to death but not to carry out the sentence. This is why they hurry along to the Roman

---

[1] L. de la Palma, *The Passion of the Lord*

authorities in the early hours of the morning to get the permission they need, by whatever means they can, for Jesus to be put to death. They want to get rid of him before the celebration of the feast begins. That which had been foretold about him was now beginning to be fulfilled to the letter: *For he will be delivered to the Gentiles, and will be mocked and shamefully treated and spit upon; they will scourge him and kill him, and on the third day he will rise.*[2]

Something very strange is taking place. Only a few days ago he had been speaking freely in the Temple with such majesty – *no one has ever spoken as this man* – and he had entered into Jerusalem acclaimed by all the people. Now he is a prisoner and is mistreated by the Jewish authorities. Once he had worked so many miracles and was followed by a whole crowd of his disciples; now he is dealt with as an evil-doer. The people would be amazed and the whole city would be talking about nothing else. They would call upon others to go and see such a surprising event. Jesus of Nazareth had been arrested!

They led Jesus to the square in front of the praetorium. His accusers, however, *did not enter the praetorium, so that they might not be defiled, but might eat the passover,*[3] since the Jews became legally impure if they entered the house of a foreigner. *What impious blindness!* exclaimed St Augustine. *They think they are going to get contaminated by going into the house of another, and yet they have no fear of impurity brought on by a crime of their own doing.*[4] Once again are fulfilled those very strong words which Our Lord had levelled at them on an earlier occasion: *You blind guides, straining out a gnat and swallowing a camel!*[5]

---

[2] Luke 18:32
[3] John 18:28
[4] St Augustine, *Commentary on the Gospel of St John*, 114,2
[5] Matt 23:24

So Pilate went out to them.[6] Jesus stood before Pilate,[7] who would be immediately aware of the peace and serenity of the accused, in sharp contrast with the agitation and impatience of those who were calling for his death.

Pilate asked him, *Are you the King of the Jews?*[8] Jesus replied, *'My kingship is not of this world; if my kingship were of this world, my servants would fight that I might not be handed over to the Jews; but my kingship is not from the world.'* Pilate said to him, *'So you are a king?'* Jesus answered, *'You say that I am a king.'*[9] This will be the last statement that Our Lord will make before his accusers; after this he will be silent, *like a sheep that before its shearers is dumb.*[10]

The Master now finds himself alone; his disciples no longer come to listen to the lessons he imparts, having abandoned him in the very moment when there is so much to learn. We should wish to accompany him in his sorrow and learn from him to have patience in the face of the small contradictions of each day, offering them up with love.

42.2 The King of the Jews. A kingdom of holiness and grace.

Thinking that in this way he might placate the hatred of the Jews, Pilate, *took Jesus and scourged him.*[11] This is the scene we contemplate in the second sorrowful mystery of the Rosary, *Bound to the pillar. Covered with wounds.*

The blows of the lash sound upon his torn flesh, upon his undefiled flesh, which suffers for your sinful flesh. More blows. More fury. Still more ... It is the last extreme of

---

[6] John 18:29
[7] Matt 27:11
[8] John 18:33
[9] John 18:36-37
[10] Is 53:7
[11] John 19:1

human cruelty.

Finally, exhausted, they untie Jesus. And the body of Christ yields to pain and falls limp, broken and half-dead.

You and I cannot speak. Words are not needed. Look at him, look at him ... slowly.

After this ... can you ever fear penance?[12]

When this has happened, *the soldiers plaited a crown of thorns, and put it on his head, and arrayed him in a purple robe; they came up to him, saying, 'Hail, King of the Jews!' and struck him with their hands.*[13] Today as we contemplate Jesus proclaiming his kingship before Pilate, we should also meditate upon that scene contained in the third sorrowful mystery of the Rosary.

The crown of thorns, driven in by blows, makes him a mock king ... And with their blows they wound his head. And they strike him ... and spit on him ...

You and I ... , haven't we crowned him anew with thorns and struck him and spat on him?

Never again, Jesus, never again ...[14]

Pilate went out again, and said to them, 'Behold, I am bringing him out to you, that you may know that I find no crime in him.' So Jesus came out, wearing the crown of thorns and the purple robe. Pilate said to them, 'Here is the man!'[15]

Jesus, adorned with the mock insignia of royalty, hides and yet at the same time gives a glimpse of his greatness as King of kings under this most tragic exterior. The entire creation is subject to his slightest gesture. The weaker he appears, the more promptly should we wish to affirm this title of his, which he possesses by his own right. His

---

[12] St J. Escrivá, *Holy Rosary*, Second Sorrowful Mystery
[13] John 19:4-5
[14] St J. Escrivá, *Holy Rosary*, Third Sorrowful Mystery
[15] John 19:4-5

kingdom is *a kingdom of truth and life, a kingdom of holiness and grace, a kingdom of justice, love, and peace.*[16] As we contemplate these scenes of the Passion, Christians cannot forget that Jesus Christ is *a king with a heart of flesh, like yours.*[17] Neither can we forget that there are many people who are ignorant about him and reject him.

This sad state of affairs makes me want to atone to Our Lord. When I hear that endless clamour – expressed more in ignoble actions than in words – I feel the need to cry out, 'He must reign!' (1 Cor 15:25)[18]

Many people are not aware that Christ is the only Saviour, the one who gives meaning to human events, to our lives. In him is found the joy and the fulness of desire of every heart; he is the true model, the brother of all, the irreplaceable friend, the only one worthy of all our confidence.

Contemplating the King crowned with thorns we should tell him that we want Christ to reign in our lives, in our hearts, in our works, in our thoughts, in our words, in all that we are.

42.3 Our Lord wants to reign in our souls.

Jesus Christ is king over all beings, since *all things were made through him,*[19] and in a special way over all men, who have been *bought with a price.*[20] The Angel had already told this to Mary: *you will ... bear a son ... and the Lord God will give to him the throne of his father David, ... and of his kingdom there will be no end.*[21] His kingdom, however, is not like those of this earth. During his public

---

[16] *Preface of the Mass of Christ the King*
[17] St J. Escrivá, *Christ is passing by*, 179
[18] *ibid*
[19] John 1:3
[20] 1 Cor 6:20
[21] Luke 1:32-33

ministry he never once accedes to the enthusiasm of the crowds, who viewed things too humanly and with a number of ambitions which were merely temporal. *Perceiving then that they were about to come and take him by force to make him king, Jesus withdrew again to the hills by himself.*[22] Nevertheless, he accepts the messianic act of faith made by Nathanael: *you are the Son of God! You are the King of Israel!*[23] In fact Our Lord recalls an ancient prophecy[24] in order to confirm and add depth to these words: *you will see heaven opened, and the angels of God ascending and descending upon the Son of man.*[25]

Jesus affirms his condition as Messiah and Son of God.[26] The Jewish authorities, blinded by their incredulity, even manage to acknowledge the exclusive political power of Caesar, the Roman, as long as they can reject the kingship of Christ and be rid of him. In spite of all of this, however, upon the wood of the Cross stands written for ever, 'Jesus of Nazareth, King of the Jews.'

He had told Pilate that his kingdom was not of this world. He tells us that his kingdom is one of peace, justice and love; God the Father *has delivered us from the dominion of darkness and transferred us to the kingdom of his beloved Son, in whom we have redemption.*[27]

Nevertheless, there are now many people who reject him. In many places you seem to hear that terrible cry, *We do not want him to reign over us.* It must have been with great heaviness of heart that Our Lord commented upon that parable, which reflects the attitude of many people, *But his citizens hated him,* Jesus tells us in the parable, *and*

---

[22] John 6:15
[23] John 1:49
[24] Dan 7:13
[25] John 1:51
[26] Matt 27:64
[27] Col 1:13

sent an embassy after him, saying, 'We do not want this man to reign over us.' [28] Sin is truly this great mystery of iniquity. We actually reject Jesus!

The reign of sin, wherever sin dwells, is a reign of darkness, sadness, loneliness, deception and lies. All the tragedies and calamities in this world, and our personal sorrows, find their origin in these words, *Nolumus hunc regnare super nos,* we do not want this man (Christ) to reign over us. We now finish our prayer, telling Jesus once again that *He is the King of my heart. He is the King of that intimate interior world of mine where no one can enter and where I alone am master. Here in my heart Jesus is King. This you well know, O Lord.* [29]

---

[28] Luke 19:14
[29] J. Leclercq, *A Year with the Liturgy*

43. THE WAY TO CALVARY

43.1 Jesus with the Cross on his shoulders passes through the streets of Jerusalem. Simon of Cyrene.

After a night of suffering, of insults and scorn, torn by the terrible torment of the scourging, Jesus is led out to be crucified. *Then he* [Pilate] *released for them Barabbas, and having scourged Jesus, delivered him to be crucified,*[1] says St Matthew's Gospel quite simply.

The people do not accept an exchange for Barabbas, an exchange of one who was innocent for one guilty of robbery and murder. Jesus is condemned to suffer a painful punishment followed by a savagely cruel death reserved for criminals. Very soon everyone can see that he is already far too seriously weakened to be able to carry the cross on his shoulders right up to Calvary. A man returning home, Simon of Cyrene, is forced to help. Where are the disciples? Jesus had spoken to them about carrying the cross;[2] and they had confirmed with great vehemence that they would go with Him even to death.[3] Now not even one of them is to be found to help him carry the piece of timber to the site of the execution. A stranger has to do it, and that under threat of force. There are no friendly faces around Our Lord, not even one willing to commit himself, to say a word in his favour, let alone champion him. Even those who were cured or who had received some benefit from him now do not wish to be conspicuous. What Isaiah had prophesied several centuries earlier is now fulfilled to the letter: *I have trodden the wine press alone, and from the peoples no one was with me ... I looked, but there was no one to help. I was appalled, but*

---

[1] Matt 27:26
[2] Matt 16:24
[3] Matt 26:35

there was no one to uphold.[4]

Simon gets hold of one end of the cross and lifts it onto his shoulders. The other end, more weighty, the one where there has been no response to love, the one freighted with the sins of each man – this end is carried by Christ, on his own.

There is one exception to the desertion which the Lord experiences. Tradition has handed the incident down to us. A woman by the name of Veronica steps forward with a piece of cloth to wipe the face of Jesus. And on the fabric there remains an impression of the face of the Lord. Veronica's veil is a symbol of the moving dialogue between Christ and the penitent soul. *Veronica responded to Christ's love with reparation; a reparation especially admirable because it came from a helpless woman who did not fear the ire of the enemies of Christ ... Will the image of Christ's face be imprinted on my soul as on the veil of Veronica?*[5]

Our Lord continues on his way. There has been some physical respite. But the path is tortuous and the ground uneven. His energy is dwindling; it is not at all to be wondered at that Jesus falls. Once, twice, three times – He falls and with increasing difficulty gets to his feet again. A few yards on and he stumbles again. Rising up he tells us how much he loves us; falling, he expresses the great need he has for us to love him. *It is not too late; nor is everything lost ... even though to you it may seem so – even though a thousand doom-laden voices keep saying so. Even though you are besieged by the furious faces of mocking and jeering onlookers. You have come at a good time to take up the Cross: the Redemption is taking place now! And Jesus needs many more Simons like the man from Cyrene.*[6]

---

[4] Is 63:3-5
[5] J. Aldewicz, *Be my witnesses*, (*The Way of the Cross*, Sixth Station)
[6] St J. Escrivá, *The Way of the Cross*, Fifth Station, 2

43.2 Jesus accompanied by two thieves on his route to Calvary. Ways of carrying the cross.

A little later on this journey to Calvary, Jesus passes by a group of tearful women, who are weeping for Him. He consoles them. *Here is the call to repentance, true repentance, genuine sorrow in the truth of the evil that has been committed. Jesus says to the daughters of Jerusalem, who weep at the sight of him: 'Do not weep for me, but weep for yourselves and for your children' (Luke 23:28). One cannot merely scrape away at the surface of evil; one has to get down to its roots, its causes, the inner truth of conscience ... Lord, let me know how to live and walk in the truth!*[7]

Forming part of the procession, their presence making his impending death yet more shameful, are two convicted criminals, described as two thieves. A recently-arrived spectator to the scene would see three men, each laden with a cross, walking towards death. But only one is the Saviour of the world. Only one of the crosses is the redeeming Cross.

Today, too, the cross can be carried in different ways. There is the cross carried furiously or sullenly, in a rage; man writhes and squirms, filled with hate, or at least, with a deep and burning resentment. It is a cross without meaning and without any explanation, useless; such a cross may even separate one from God. It is the cross of those in this world who seek comfort and material well-being, who will put up with neither suffering nor setbacks, for they have no wish to understand the supernatural meaning of pain. *It is a cross which does not redeem.* It is the cross carried by one of the thieves.

On the road to Calvary is a second cross, carried this time with resignation, perhaps even with some dignity, with an acceptance of the situation simply because there is no alternative to it. This is the one carried by the other

---

[7] K. Wojtyla, *Sign of Contradiction, The Way of the Cross, Eighth Station*

thief. Little by little he realises that close by him is the sovereign figure of Christ, who will radically change the final moments of his life on earth, and for eternity; he will be the one converted into *the good thief.*

There is a third way of carrying the cross. Jesus embraces the saving wood and teaches us how we ought to carry our own cross: with love, co-redeeming all souls with him, making reparation at the same time for our own sins. Our Lord has conferred on human suffering a deep meaning. Being able, as he was, to redeem us in a multitude of ways, he chose to do so through suffering, for *greater love has no man than this, that a man lay down his life for his friends.*[8]

Saintly people have discovered that sorrow, suffering and contradictions cease to be merely negative as soon as the cross is not seen to be on its own, but with Jesus who is passing by and coming to meet us. *My God! May I hate sin, and unite myself to you, taking the Holy Cross into my arms, so that I in my turn may fulfil your most lovable Will ... stripped of all earthly attachment, with no other glory but your glory ... generously, not keeping anything back, offering myself with you in a perfect holocaust.*[9]

Simon of Cyrene got to know Jesus through the Cross. Our Lord would reward him for his help by also giving the faith to his two sons, Alexander and Rufus.[10] Soon they would be among the outstanding Christians of the early years. We instinctively, as well as with reason, feel that Simon of Cyrene would later be a faithful disciple, held in esteem by the first Christian community in Jerusalem. *And it all started with the Cross.*

I went to those who were not looking for me; I was

---

[8] John 15:13
[9] St J. Escrivá, *loc cit*, Ninth Station
[10] cf Mark 15:21

found by those who sought me not (Is 65:1).

At times the Cross appears without our looking for it: it is Christ who is seeking us out. And if by chance, before this unexpected Cross which, perhaps, is therefore more difficult to understand, your heart were to show repugnance ... don't give it consolations. And filled with a noble compassion, when it asks for them, say to it slowly, as one speaking in confidence: Heart: heart on the Cross! Heart on the Cross![11]

Today's meditation provides us with an opportunity to ask ourselves how we have borne difficulties and sorrows. It is an occasion, too, to examine the question whether these have brought us closer to Christ, if we are co-redeeming with him, if we are making use of these contradictions to atone for our faults.

43.3 Meeting his Mother.

The Saviour walked, his body bowed down under the weight of the Cross, his eyes swollen and almost blinded by blood and sweat and tears; each step made painfully slow and difficult by his failing strength. His knees buckled as he virtually dragged himself along behind his two companions in punishment. The Jews laughed; the executioners and the soldiers pushed them forward.[12] In the Fourth Sorrowful Mystery of the Rosary we contemplate Jesus carrying his cross on the Via Dolorosa. *We are sad, living the Passion of Our Lord Jesus. See how lovingly He embraces the Cross. Learn from him. Jesus carries the Cross for you: you ... carry it for him.*

But don't drag the Cross ... Carry it squarely on your shoulder, because your Cross, if you carry it like that, will not just be any cross ... It will be the Holy Cross ... And

---

[11] St J. Escrivá, *loc cit*, Fifth Station
[12] L. de la Palma, *The Passion of the Lord*

surely you will find Mary on the way, as Jesus did.[13]

In *The Way of the Cross*, we meditate on the meeting of Jesus with his mother in one of the narrow thoroughfares through which the cruel procession passed. He stopped for a moment. *With immense love Mary looks at Jesus, and Jesus at his Mother. Their eyes meet, and each heart pours into the other its own deep sorrow. Mary's soul is steeped in bitter grief, the grief of Jesus Christ.*

O all you that pass by the way, look and see, was there ever a sorrow to compare with my sorrow? (Lam 1:12).

But no one notices, no one pays any attention: only Jesus ...

In the dark loneliness of the Passion, Our Lady offers her Son a comforting balm of tenderness, of union, of faithfulness; a 'yes' to the divine will.[14]

The Lord continues on his way, and Mary accompanies him a few yards behind, right up to Calvary. Simeon's prophecy is being fulfilled to the letter. What man would not weep seeing the Mother of Christ in such cruel torment?

Her Son so stricken ... and we, cowards, keep our distance, not wanting to accept the Will of God.

My Mother and Lady, teach me how to pronounce a Yes, which, like yours, will identify with the cry Jesus made before his Father: *non mea voluntas* ... (Luke 22:42): not my will but God's be done.[15]

When we suffer pain or affliction, when these are all the more piercingly severe, we turn to Our Lady, to the *Mater dolorosa,* to implore her to strengthen us, and so that we may learn to sanctify them with peace and serenity.

---

[13] St J. Escrivá, *Holy Rosary*, Fourth Sorrowful Mystery
[14] *idem, The Way of the Cross*, Fourth Station
[15] *idem*, Fourth Station, 1

44. THE LORD'S LAST SUPPER

44.1 Jesus celebrated the Last Supper with his Apostles.

Holy Thursday brings to mind the Lord's Last Supper with the Apostles. As in previous years, Jesus celebrates the Passover with his own disciples. But this time the celebration would have singular characteristics, as it was to be the last Passover of the Lord before *his transit to the Father* and because of the events which were to take place immediately following it. Every minute of this Last Supper reflects both the Majesty of Jesus, who knows He is to die the following day, and his love and affection for men.

The Passover was the principal Jewish feast and had been instituted to commemorate the liberation of the Jewish people from Egyptian domination. *This day shall be for you a memorial day, and you shall keep it as a feast to the Lord; throughout your generations you shall observe it as an ordinance for ever.*[1] Every Jew is obliged to celebrate this feast to keep alive the memory of the birth of the People of God.

For the special arrangements Jesus turned to his favourite disciples, Peter and John. These two made all the preparations with the greatest care. They took a lamb to the Temple and made a sacrifice of it. Then they returned to the house where the meal was to take place, to roast it. They also prepared water for the ablutions,[2] the *bitter herbs* (which represent the bitterness of slavery), the *unleavened bread* (in memory of their ancestors who had to interrupt their baking in the sudden flight from Egypt), the wine etc. They made a special effort so that everything would be just

---

[1] Ex 12:14
[2] John 13:5

right.

These preparations remind us of the great pains we should take to prepare ourselves for each Mass we attend. Here the very same Sacrifice of Christ is to be renewed, wherein he gave himself for us; we too are his disciples, taking the place of Peter and John in their reverent and careful preparations for the Solemnity.

The Last Supper begins with the setting sun. Jesus recites the psalms in a firm voice and in his familiar regional accent. St John has told us that Jesus ardently wished to have this meal with his disciples.[3]

Singular events took place in that period, which the evangelists have recorded for us: take, for instance, the rivalry between the Apostles, who began to discuss who was the greatest; think of Jesus' surprising example of humility and of service when he carried out the menial task of the lowest of the servants – *he began to wash their feet*; consider, too, how Jesus went out of his way to show his disciples his love and affection. *My little ones*, he actually calls them. *Christ himself wished to give that gathering such a fullness of significance, so rich in memories, scene of such moving words and sentiments, such new actions and precepts, that we will never come to an end of meditating on them and exploring them. It was, you might say, a testimonial dinner: it was an affectionate and yet a sombre occasion, a time mysteriously revealing divine promises and far-reaching visions. On top of that was the sad presentiment of death, with unprecedented omens of treason, of abandonment, of immolation; the conversation dies away, while Jesus' words flow continuously in his gentle and winning voice, though there is an unwonted tension in his grave allusion to profound revelations, the*

---

[3] John 13:1

matter of which hovers between life and death.[4]

What Christ did for his own may be summarised in a few words from St John: *he loved them to the end.*[5] To-day is a particularly appropriate day for meditating on the love Jesus has for each one of us, and how we respond to it: in regular dealings with him, in love for the Church, in acts of atonement and reparation, in charity towards others, in preparation and in thanksgiving for Holy Communion, in our desire to co-redeem with him, in our hunger and thirst for justice ...

44.2 Institution of the Holy Eucharist and priesthood.

And now, while they are eating, quite likely towards the very end, Jesus becomes at the same time serious and simple, simultaneously lucid and uttering deep truths in an attitude the Apostles recognise and know well. He remains silent for a few moments and then institutes the Holy Eucharist. Our Lord anticipates in sacramental form – *my Body ... given up: my Blood ... shed* – the sacrifice which is to be consummated the following day on Calvary. Until now God's covenant with his People has been represented by the paschal lamb's being sacrificed on the altar of holocausts, at the traditional feast for the entire family that they call the Paschal meal. Now the Lamb being offered up is Christ himself,[6] his, *the Blood of the new and everlasting covenant.* The Body of Christ is the new banquet for which all the family congregate: *Take this and eat.*

In the Cenacle Our Lord anticipated sacramentally what on the following day He would carry out on the hill of Calvary – the offering and immolation of himself – Body and Blood – to the Father, as the sacrificial lamb

---

[4] St Paul VI, *Homily, Holy Thursday*, 27 March 1975
[5] John 13:1
[6] 1 Cor 5:7

which inaugurates the new and definitive Covenant between God and man, and which redeems everyone from the slavery of sin and from eternal death.

Jesus gives himself to us in the Eucharist to strengthen us in our weakness, to accompany us in our loneliness, and as a foretaste of Heaven itself. At the door leading to his Passion and Death, he ordains things in such a way that this Bread will never be lacking until the end of the world. For Jesus, on that memorable evening, gave his Apostles and their successors, the bishops and priests, the power to renew this marvel until the end of time. *Do this in memory of me.*[7] Together with the Holy Eucharist, which has to last *until He comes,*[8] he instituted the ministerial priesthood.

Jesus will always remain really, truly, and substantially present with us in the Blessed Eucharist. The Jesus of the Cenacle is the same Jesus who is in the Tabernacle. That night the disciples enjoyed the physical presence of Christ, when he gave himself to them and to all men. This evening, when we go to adore him publicly at the *Altar of Repose*, we too will find him again. He sees us and recognises us. We can speak to him as the Apostles did, and recount to him what concerns us and what gives us great joy; and we can thank him for being amongst us, and we can accompany him while recalling his generous self-giving. Jesus always awaits us in the tabernacle.

44.3 The 'New Commandment' of Our Lord.

This is how all will know that you are my disciples: if you have love for one another.[9] Jesus tells the Apostles of his imminent departure. He is going to prepare a place for

---

[7] Luke 22:19, 1 Cor 11:24
[8] 1 Cor 11:26
[9] Liturgy, *Washing of the Feet, Fifth Antiphon*, John 13:35

them in Heaven;[10] meanwhile, they will be united to him in faith and through prayer.[11]

It is then that he announces the New Commandment, which has already been proclaimed on every page of the Gospel. *This is my commandment, that you love one another as I have loved you.*[12] Since then we have learned that *charity is the way to follow God most closely*[13] and the quickest way to find him. The soul understands God better when it lives charity with greater refinement, for God is love; and it is enobled more and more in the measure in which it grows in this theological virtue.

The way we treat those around us is the feature by which we will be known as his disciples. Our degree of union with him will be seen in our understanding for others and in the way we are of service to them. For recognition as his followers, *He does not speak of their reaction to his being raised from the dead, or any other obvious proof, but of this one: that you love one another.*[14] *Many ask themselves if they are in love with Christ, and go searching for signs to be able to discover and prove that they love him; the sign that never deceives is fraternal charity ... It is also the measure of the condition of our interior life, especially of our life of prayer.*[15]

A new commandment I give you ...[16] It is a new commandment because the reasons for it are new: the neighbour is one with Christ, the neighbour is the object of the special love of the Father. It is new because the Model is always current, and because it establishes a new

---

[10] John 14:2-3

[11] John 14:12-14

[12] John 15:12

[13] St Thomas, *Commentary on the Epistle to the Ephesians*, 5,1

[14] *idem*, On Charity

[15] B. Baur, *In Silence with God*

[16] John 13:34

relationship between men. And it is new, too, because the degree of its fulfilment is new: *as I have loved you;* because it is directed to new peoples; because it needs new hearts; because it lays the foundations of a new order, one which has been unknown heretofore. It is new because it will always result in a freshness of approach between men, accustomed as they are to their egoism and routine. This *Holy Thursday* we can ask ourselves, as we come to the end of this period of prayer, if those people around us where we spend the greater part of our lives know that we are disciples of Christ by the amiable, understanding and welcoming approach we have in dealing with them; if we try never to lack charity in thought, word or deed; if we know to make things up with them when we have treated others badly; if we show those around us many signs of affection, such as warmth, appreciation, words of encouragement, fraternal correction when necessary, the habitual smile and good humour, details of service, and a little help of the sort that goes unnoticed ... *This love is not something reserved for important matters, but must be exercised above all in the ordinary circumstances of daily life.*[17]

With the Passion of Our Lord so close, let us recall both Mary's dedication to the accomplishment of God's Will and her service to others. So great is Mary's love for all mankind that she, too, fulfilled Christ's words when he affirmed: *Greater love has no man than this, that he should lay down his life for his friends (John 15:13).*[18]

---

[17] Second Vatican Council, *Gaudium et spes*, 38
[18] St J. Escrivá, *Friends of God*, 287

45. JESUS DIES ON THE CROSS

45.1 Jesus asks pardon for those who ill-treat him.

Jesus is nailed to the Cross. And the liturgy sings: *Sweet nails, sweet tree where life begins.*[1]

The whole of Jesus' life is directed towards this supreme moment. He has barely managed, gasping and exhausted, to get to the top of that hillock called 'the place of skulls'. The executioners stretch him out on the ground and begin nailing him to the wood. They place the nails first into his palms, piercing his torn flesh. Then he is hoisted up until he hangs straight from the vertical shaft of wood which has been fixed into the ground. The feet are then nailed. Mary, his Mother, contemplates the scene.

The Lord is firmly nailed to the cross. He has waited for this for many years, and this day He is to fulfil his desire to redeem all men ... What until now has been an instrument of infamy and dishonour, has been converted into the tree of life and the stairway of glory. A deep joy fills him as he extends his arms on the cross, for all those sinners who will approach him will now know that he will welcome them with open arms ...

He saw – and this filled him with joy – how the cross was to be loved and to be adored, because he was going to die on it. He saw the witnessing saints who for love and in defence of the truth were to suffer a similar martyrdom. He saw the love of his friends; he saw their tears at the foot of the cross. *He saw the triumph and the victories Christians would achieve under the standard of the cross. He saw the great miracles which, with the sign of the cross, would be*

---

[1] Hymn, *Crux fidelis*, Adoration of the Cross

*performed throughout the world. He saw so very many men
who, with their lives, were going to be saints, because they
would know how to die like him, overcoming sin.*[2] He
reflected on the many occasions we would kiss the
crucifix; on our beginning again so often ...

Jesus is raised on the cross. Around him is a
distressing scene. Some pass by, and jeer; the chief priests,
more scathing and sarcastic, scoff at him; others,
indifferent, are mere spectators. There is no reproach in
Jesus' eyes – only pity and compassion. He is offered harsh
wine and myrrh. *Give strong drink to him who is perishing,
and wine to those in bitter distress; let them drink and
forget their misfortune, and remember their misery no
more.*[3] It was the custom to make such humanitarian
gestures with condemned men. The drink – a strong rough
wine with some myrrh – had a numbing effect and made
the suffering more bearable.

Our Lord tasted it as a sign of gratitude towards the
person who offered it to him, but wished to take no more,
so as to drain the chalice of suffering. *Why so much
suffering?* asks St Augustine. And he replies: *Everything
he suffered was the price of our ransom.*[4] He was not
content to suffer a little; he wished to drink the chalice to
the dregs without leaving a single drop behind, so that we
might learn the greatness of his love and the baseness of
sin, so that we may be generous in self-giving, in
mortification and in the service of others.

45.2 Christ is crucified: our Redemption is accomplished.

Crucifixion was the most cruel and insulting form of
execution which was known in ancient times. A Roman

---

[2] L. de la Palma, *The Passion of the Lord*

[3] Prov 31:6-7

[4] St Augustine, *Commentary on Psalm 21*, 11, 8

citizen could not be crucified. Death followed after a prolonged agony. At times, the executioners hastened the end of the Crucifixion by breaking the legs of the crucified. From apostolic times till to-day, there have been many who cannot accept a God made man who died on a piece of timber to save us: the drama of the cross continues to be a *scandal for the Jews and folly to the gentiles.*[5] There has always been, and there still is to-day, a temptation to detract from the value of the Cross.

The intimate union of each Christian with his Lord requires a full knowledge of his life, this chapter of the Cross included. Here the Redemption is accomplished; here one finds the key to suffering in the world; here we learn a little about the malice of sin and the love of God for each man. We do not remain indifferent in front of a crucifix.

By now they have fastened Jesus to the wooden cross. The executioners have ruthlessly carried out the sentence. Our Lord, with infinite meekness, has let them have their way.It was not necessary for him to undergo so much torment. He could have avoided those trials, those humiliations, that ill-usage, that iniquitous judgement, and the shame of the gallows, and the nails and the lance ... But he wanted to suffer all this for you and for me. And we, are we not going to respond?

Very likely there will be times when, alone in front of a crucifix, you find tears coming to your eyes. Don't try to hold them back ... But try to ensure that those tears give rise to a resolution.[6]

45.3 Fruits of the Cross. 'The good thief.'

The fruits of the Cross were not long in coming. One of the thieves, acknowledging his sins, turns to Jesus: *Lord,*

---

[5] 1 Cor 1:23
[6] St J. Escrivá, *The Way of the Cross*, Eleventh Station, 1

remember me when you are in your Kingdom. He speaks to him with the confidence of a companion in anguish. He would certainly have previously heard of Christ, of his life and of his miracles. But now he has met up with Jesus, just when it seems that his divinity is most obscurely hidden. And he has seen Jesus' behaviour since they began their march up to Calvary: his silence is impressive, as is his compassionate gaze at the faces He encounters on the way. He has observed his great majesty despite his exhaustion and so much suffering. The words he now utters are not extemporized. They express the end result of a process which began within him when he first met Christ. He has not needed to see any miracle to be converted into a disciple of Christ; to be a first-hand witness to Christ's suffering has been sufficient. Many others were to be converted on meditating these same events of the passion related in the Gospels.

Our Lord is moved when, amidst all the insults, he hears that voice which recognises him as God. After so much suffering they would have filled his heart with joy. *I assure you*, he replies, *that this day you will be with me in Paradise.*[7]

The efficacy of the Passion is limitless. It has filled the world with peace, with grace, with forgiveness, with happiness in souls, with salvation. The Redemption which Christ carried out just once, is applied to each person who freely accepts it. Each one of us can truly say: The Son of God *loved me and gave himself up for me.*[8] No, not *for all of us*, but *for me*, as if I were the only one. The salvific action of the Redemption is carried out whenever Holy Mass is celebrated.[9]

---

[7] Luke 23:43
[8] Gal 2:20
[9] cf Second Vatican Council, *Lumen gentium*, 3 and *Prayer over the*

Jesus Christ wishes to submit himself out of love, fully conscious, totally free, and with a sensitive heart ... No one has ever died like Jesus Christ, because he was Life itself. No one has expiated for sin like Him, for He was purity itself.[10] Now we receive the copious fruits of the love of Jesus on the Cross. Only our 'not wanting' can waste for ourselves the Passion of Christ.

Very close to Jesus is his Mother, with the other holy women. There too is John, the youngest of the Apostles. *When Jesus saw his Mother and the disciple whom he loved standing near, he said to his Mother, 'Woman, behold your son!' Then he said to the disciple, 'Behold your Mother!' And from that hour the disciple took her into his own home.*[11] Jesus, after giving himself in the Last Supper, now wishes to give us what he loves most on earth, the most precious thing that still remains to him. They have stripped him of everything else. And He gives Mary to us to be our Mother.

This gesture has a double significance. On the one hand, Jesus takes care of his Mother, totally fulfilling the Fourth Commandment of the Decalogue. On the other, he declares her to be our Mother. *Thus the Blessed Virgin advanced in her pilgrimage of faith, and faithfully persevered in her union with her Son unto the cross, where she stood, in keeping with the divine plan, enduring with her only-begotten Son the intensity of his suffering, associating herself with his sacrifice in her mother's heart, and lovingly consenting to the immolation of this victim which was born of her. Finally, she was given, by the same Christ Jesus, dying on the Cross, as a mother to his disciple.*[12]

Gifts, Second Sunday of Ordinary Time
[10] R. Guardini, *Our Lord*
[11] John 19:26-27
[12] Second Vatican Council, *Lumen gentium*, 58

The sun's light is extinguished and the earth is left in darkness. It is close on three o'clock, when Jesus cries out: 'Eli, Eli, lamma sabacthani?' That is, 'My God, my God, why hast thou forsaken me?' (Matt 27:46).

Then, knowing that all things are to be accomplished, that the Scriptures may be fulfilled he says: 'I am thirsty.' (John 19:28).

The soldiers soak a sponge in vinegar and, placing it on a reed of hyssop, they put it to his mouth. Jesus sips the vinegar, and exclaims: 'It is accomplished.' (John 19:30)

The veil of the temple is rent, and the earth trembles, when the Lord cries out in a loud voice: 'Father, into thy hands I commend my spirit' (Luke 23:46). And he expires.

Love sacrifice; it is a fountain of interior life. Love the Cross, which is an altar of sacrifice. Love pain, until you drink, as Christ did, the very dregs of the chalice.[13]

With Mary, our Mother, it will be much easier, and so we sing with the liturgical hymn:

O dear Mother, fount of love,
Touch my spirit from above;
Make my heart with yours accord.
Let me mingle tears with you,
Mourning him who mourned for me,
All the days that I may live,
By the cross with you to stay,
There with you to weep and pray,
Is all I ask of you to give ...[14]

---

[13] St J. Escrivá, *The Way of the Cross*, Twelfth Station
[14] Hymn, *Stabat Mater*

46. THE SEPULCHRE OF JESUS' BODY

46.1 Signs following the death of Our Lord.

After three hours of agony Jesus died. The evangelists narrate that the sky was darkened while Our Lord was still hanging on the Cross. And extraordinary events occurred, for it was the Son of God who was to die. *The curtain of the temple was torn in two, from top to bottom,*[1] signifying that the death of Christ had caused the cult of the old covenant to lapse.[2] Now the pleasing cult offered to God would be through the Humanity of Christ, who is both Priest and Victim.

Good Friday evening was approaching; it was necessary to take the bodies away – they could not remain there on the Sabbath. Before the first star shone in the heavens, the bodies had to be buried. As it was the eve of the Pasch (the day of Preparation for the Passover), *in order to prevent the bodies from remaining on the Cross on the Sabbath (for the Sabbath was a high day), the Jews asked Pilate that the legs might be broken, and that they might be taken away.*[3]

Pilate sent some soldiers to break the legs of the two thieves, so that they would die quickly. Jesus was already dead. *But one of the soldiers pierced his side with a spear, and at once there came out blood and water.*[4] This event, besides being an historical fact witnessed by St John, has deep significance. St Augustine and Christian tradition see

---

[1] Matt 27:51
[2] cf Heb 9:1-14
[3] John 19:31
[4] John 19:33

the sacraments and the Church itself flowing from the open breast of Jesus. *There it was that the gate of life was opened, from there the sacraments of the Church flow; without these one does not enter true life.*[5] *The Church grows visibly through the power of God in the world. The origin and growth of the Church are symbolized by the blood and water which flowed from the open side of the crucified Jesus.*[6] The death of Christ pointed to the supernatural life we were to receive through the Church.

This wound, which strikes one's breast and passes through it, is a result of the superabundance of love, and it is added to all the others. It is a way of expressing what no words can say. As Co-redemptrix, Mary understands and suffers. Her Son can no longer feel; she can. Thus to the end, is the prophecy of Simeon fulfilled: *a sword shall pierce your own soul.*[7]

They lower Christ from the Cross with love and veneration. With great care they lay him in the arms of his Mother. Although his Body is all wounded, his countenance is serene and majestic. Slowly and with piety we gaze at Jesus, as the most blessed Virgin would. Not only has he ransomed us from sin and death, but he has taught us to put the will of God above all personal plans, to live detached from everything, to know how to pardon, even when the offender has not repented, to know how to forgive others, to be apostles until the very moment of death, to suffer without sterile lament, to love men although one is suffering because of them ... *Don't hinder the work of the Paraclete: seek union with Christ, so as to be purified, and feel with him the insults, the spitting, the blows, and the thorns, and the weight of the Cross ..., the*

---

[5] St Augustine, *Commentary on the Gospel of St John*, 120, 2
[6] Second Vatican Council, *Lumen gentium*, 3
[7] Luke 2:35

nails tearing through the flesh, the agony of a forsaken death. And enter through our Lord's open side until you find a refuge there in his wounded heart.[8] There we will find peace. St Bonaventure speaks of this mystical life within the wounds of Christ. *O how good it is to be with Christ crucified! I wish to make three resting places in him. One, in the feet; another, in the hands; the third, perpetually in his precious side. Here I would like to rest and relax, to pray and to sleep. Here I will speak to his heart and he will grant me everything I ask. O, how lovable are the wounds of our Holy Redeemer! ... In them do I live, and from their special dishes do I receive sustenance.*[9]

Let us look at Jesus slowly, and in the intimacy of our hearts say to him: Kind Jesus, hear my prayer! *Hide me within your wounds, and keep me close to you. Defend me from the evil enemy. Call me at my death to the fellowship of your saints, that I may sing your praise with them through all eternity. Amen.*[10]

46.2 Nicodemus and Joseph of Arimathea.

Joseph of Arimathea, a rich man, a disciple of Jesus, with influence in the Sanhedrin who has remained hidden while our Lord is acclaimed throughout Palestine, now presents himself to Pilate to take charge of the Body of the Lord. He is willing to ask *for the great demand that ever has been made – the Body of Jesus, Son of God, treasure of the Church, its riches, its teaching and exemplar, its consolation, the Bread which will sustain one until life eternal. In that moment Joseph, with his petition, represents the desires of all men, of the whole Church,*

---

[8] St J. Escrivá, *The Way*, 58
[9] *Prayer of St Bonaventure*
[10] Roman Missal, *Act of Thanksgiving after the Mass*

which needs Him to keep eternally alive.[11]

In this disconcerting period, when all the disciples except John have fled, another disciple of great social standing, who has not been present in the triumphant hours, now comes forward. *With him comes Nicodemus, the same who earlier visited Jesus by night; he brings with him a mixture of myrrh and aloes, about one hundred pounds weight.*[12]

How grateful Our Lady is for the help from these two men, for their generosity, their valour, their piety! How grateful we too are to them!

The small group which, with the Blessed Virgin and the women who receive special mention in the Gospel, takes charge of burying the Body of Jesus has little time because of the following day's feast, which begins with sunset on this day. The Body is washed with special piety. It is embalmed (the amount of sweet smelling herbs which Nicodemus bought is considerable: *about one hundred pounds in weight*; it is wrapped in a new linen shroud supplied by Joseph;[13] it is laid in a sepulchre hewn out of a rock. The sepulchre belonged to Joseph and had not previously been used.[14] They covered his head with a napkin.[15]

How we envy Joseph of Arimathea and Nicodemus! How we would have loved to be able to care, with immense piety, for the Body of our Lord. *With them I too will go up to the foot of the Cross; I will press my arms tightly around the cold Body, the corpse of Christ, with the fire of my love ...; I will unnail it, with my reparation and mortifications ...; I will wrap it in the new winding-sheet of*

---

[11] L. de la Palma, *The Passion of the Lord*
[12] John 19:39
[13] Mark 15:46
[14] cf Matt 27:60
[15] cf John 20:5-6

my clean life, and I will bury it in the clean rock of my
~~*breast, where no one can tear it away from me, and there,*~~
Lord, take your rest! Were the whole world to abandon you
and to scorn you ... serviam!; I will serve you, Lord.[16]

We ought not to forget, even for a day, that Jesus is in
our tabernacles – alive! But He is defenceless, as on the
Cross, or, as later, in the sepulchre. Christ gives himself to
the Church and to each Christian so that with *the fire of our*
love we may look after him and attend to him in the best
way we can; and so that *our clean life* may envelop him as
did Joseph's linen cloth. But, in addition to such signs of
our love, there ought to be others that require some of our
money, of our time, of our effort: Joseph of Arimathea and
Nicodemus were not niggardly with these other signs of
love.

46.3 The Apostles beside Our Lady.

The Body of Christ lay in the tomb. The world was in
darkness. Mary was the only light still burning on earth. *The*
Mother of Our Lord – my Mother – and the women who have
followed the Master from Galilee, after taking careful note of
everything, also take their leave. Night falls.

Now it is all over. The work of our Redemption has
been accomplished. We are now children of God, because
Jesus has died for us and his death has ransomed us.
'Empti enim estis pretio magno!' (1 Cor 6:20), you and I
have been bought at a great price.

We must bring into our own life, to make them our
own, the life and death of Christ. We must die through
mortification and penance, so that Christ may live in us
through love. And then follow in the footsteps of Christ,
with a zeal to co-redeem all mankind. We must give our life
for others. That is the only way to live the life of Jesus

---

[16] St J. Escrivá, *The Way of the Cross*, Fourteenth Station, 1

Christ, and to become one and the same with him.[17]

We don't know where the Apostles were that evening while the Body of Christ was being buried. Perhaps they were hovering around, disorientated and confused: aimless, distraught, filled with sadness. If we see them together again on the Sunday, united once more,[18] it is because on the Saturday, or perhaps on the Friday evening, they had turned to Our Lady. With her faith, her hope and her love, she protected the nascent Church, still weak and startled. Thus was the Church born – under the mantle of Mary. Thus from the beginning has she been the Comforter of the afflicted, of those under pressure. This Saturday, when everyone fulfilled the festival day of rest *as the law required,*[19] was not a sad day for Our Lady: her Son had stopped suffering. She serenely awaited the moment of the Resurrection: for this reason she did not accompany the holy women who went to embalm the dead Body of Jesus.

We ought always to have immediate resort to that end-lessly burning light in our lives, which is the Blessed Virgin. And more so, if, on occasion, we have left Christ and found ourselves lost, having abandoned sacrifice and the Cross, as did the Apostles. She will bring hope back to us. *Our Lady is rest for those who work, consolation for those who weep, medicine for the sick, a harbour for those assailed by tempests, pardon for sinners, sweet relief for the sad, succour for those who implore.*[20] Beside her we are able to live the immense joy of the Resurrection.

---

[17] *ibid*
[18] cf Luke 24:9
[19] Luke 23:56
[20] St John Damascene, *Homily on the Dormition of the Blessed Virgin Mary*

47. RAISED FROM THE DEAD

47.1 The Resurrection of Our Lord, the basis of our faith. Jesus Christ lives: hence the great joy of all Christians.

The Lord is truly risen, alleluia. To him be glory and power for all the ages of eternity, alleluia, alleluia.[1]

'*When the Sabbath was over, Mary Magdalen and Mary, the mother of James, and Salome brought spices with which to go and anoint the dead body of Jesus.' Very early on the following day, just as the sun is rising, they come to the tomb (Mark 16:1-2). And on entering it they are dismayed, for they cannot find the body of our Lord. A youth, clothed in white, says to them: 'Do not be afraid. I know you seek Jesus of Nazareth: non est hic, surrexit enim sicut dixit – he is not here, for he has risen, as he said (Matt 28:5).' He has risen! Jesus has risen: He is not in the tomb. Life has overcome death.*[2]

The glorious resurrection of the Lord is the key to interpreting his whole life, and the ground of our faith. Without this victory over death, says St Paul, all our preaching would be useless and our faith in vain.[3] Furthermore, the guarantee of our future resurrection is secured upon the resurrection of Christ, because although we were dead through sin, God, full of mercy, moved by the infinite compassion with which he loved, gave us Christ ... and He raised us with him.[4] Easter is the

---

[1] *Entrance Antiphon*, cf Luke 24:34, cf Rev 1:6
[2] St J. Escrivá, *Holy Rosary*, First Glorious Mystery
[3] cf 1 Cor 15:14-17
[4] Eph 2:4-6

celebration of our Redemption, and therefore the
celebration of thanksgiving and joy.

The Resurrection of the Lord is a central reality of the
Catholic faith, and has been preached as such since the
beginning of Christianity. The importance of this miracle is
so great that the Apostles are, above all else, witnesses of
Jesus' resurrection.[5] They announce that Christ is alive,
and this becomes the nucleus of all their preaching. After
twenty centuries this is what we announce to the world:
Christ lives! The fact of the resurrection is the supreme
argument for the divinity of Our Lord.

After arising by his own power, Jesus, glorious, was
seen by the disciples, who were able to ascertain that it was
He: they were able to talk with him, they saw him eat, they
saw the marks of the nails and the lance ... The Apostles
declare that He manifested himself to them with numerous
proofs,[6] and many of these men died testifying to this truth.

Jesus Christ lives. And this crowns us with happiness.
This is the great truth which fills our faith with meaning.
Jesus, who died on the cross, has risen. He has triumphed
over death; he has overcome sorrow, anguish and the
power of darkness ... In him we find everything. Outside of
him our life is empty.[7]

He appeared to his most holy Mother. He appeared to
Mary of Magdala, who is carried away by love. And to
Peter and the rest of the Apostles. And to you and me, who
are his disciples and more in love than Mary Magdalen ...
the things we say to him!

May we never die through sin: may our spiritual
resurrection be eternal ... You have kissed the wounds in
his feet ... and I, more daring – because I am more a child

---

[5] cf Acts 1:22; 2:32; 3:15; etc.

[6] Acts 1:3

[7] St J. Escrivá, *Christ is passing by*, 102

– have placed my lips upon his open side.[8]

47.2 The light of Christ. The Resurrection – a powerful call to the apostolate.

St Leo the Great says in a beautiful way[9] that Jesus hastened to rise as soon as possible because He was in a hurry to console His Mother and the disciples: He was in the tomb strictly as long as was necessary to comply with the three days that had been foretold. He rose on the third day, as soon as He could, just before sunrise, *when everything was still dark,*[10] in advance of the dawn with his own light. The world was benighted. Only the Virgin Mary was a light amid such darkness. The Resurrection is the great light for the world: *I am the Light,*[11] Jesus had said; light for the world, for all ages of history, for every society, for each man.

Last night, while we were taking part – if were able to – in the liturgy of the Easter Vigil, we saw how at the outset there was total darkness inside the church, this being the image of the profound darkness in which humanity was plunged without Christ, without the revelation of God. Then, in an instant, the celebrant proclaimed the exhilarating, wonderful news: *May the light of Christ, rising in glory, dispel the darkness of our hearts and minds.*[12] And from the light of the Easter candle, symbolizing Christ, all the faithful received the light: the darkened church was now illuminated with the light of the Easter candle and the candles of all the faithful. It is the light the Church lets flood over the earth, submerged as it was in darkness.

---

[8] *idem, Holy Rosary*, First Glorious Mystery
[9] St Leo the Great, *Sermon 71*, 2
[10] John 20:1
[11] John 8:12
[12] *Roman Missal, Easter Vigil*

The Resurrection of Christ is a powerful call to apostolate: to be light and to carry the light to others. To do this we must be united to Christ. *St Paul gave a motto to the Christians at Ephesus: 'Instaurare omnia in Christo' (Eph 1:10), to fill everything with the spirit of Jesus, placing Christ at the centre of everything. 'Si exaltatus fuero a terra, omnia traham ad meipsum', when I am lifted up from the earth, I will draw all things to myself. Through his Incarnation, through his work at Nazareth and his preaching and miracles in the lands of Judaea and Galilee, through his death on the Cross, and through his Resurrection, Christ is the centre of the universe, the First-born and Lord of all creation.*

Our task as Christians is to proclaim the kingship of Christ, announcing it through what we say and do. Our Lord wants men and women of his own in all walks of life. Some he calls away from society, asking them to give up involvement in the world, so that they remind the rest of us by their example that God exists. To others he entrusts the priestly ministry. But he wants the vast majority to stay right where they are, in all earthly occupations in which they work: the factory, the laboratory, the farm, the trades, the streets of the big cities and the trails of the mountains.[13]

47.3 Appearances of Jesus: the encounter with his Mother, to whom He appears first. Living this liturgical time very close to Our Lady.

The Blessed Virgin, who was accompanied by the holy women through those hours of the crucifixion, did not go with them in their pious attempt to finish embalming the dead body of Jesus. Mary Magdalen and the other women who had followed Jesus from Galilee had forgotten the words of the Lord concerning his Resurrection on the third

---

[13] St J. Escrivá, *Christ is passing by*, 105

day. Our Lady knew He would rise. In a spirit of prayer that we can scarcely imagine and cannot describe, she awaited her glorified Son. *The gospels do not tell us of the appearance of the risen Christ to Mary. Nevertheless, since she was so specially close to the Cross of her Son, she must also have had a privileged experience of his Resurrection.*[14] It is an ancient tradition of the Church that Jesus appeared first of all to his Mother in solitude. It could not have been otherwise, because she is the first and principal co-redeemer of the human race, in perfect union with her Son. Alone she would have been, since this appearance would be for a reason very different from the reason for the other appearances to the women and the disciples. He had to reassure and comfort them, and win them to him definitively in the faith. The Blessed Virgin, who had become the Mother of the human race now reconciled with God, did not at any time cease to be in perfect union with the Blessed Trinity. Every last vestige of hope in the Resurrection of Jesus that remained on earth had been gathered into her heart.

We do not know how Jesus appeared to his Mother. He appeared to Mary Magdalen in a form she did not immediately recognise. He joined the two disciples making for Emmaus as a traveller catching up with them on the road. To the Apostles assembled in the cenacle he appeared behind closed doors ... In an intimacy we can barely comprehend, He showed himself to his Mother in such a form that she would have known him instantly in his glorious state. He would also have shown her that He would not continue the same life as he had done before on earth.[15] After the pain she had endured, Our Lady was filled with an immense joy. *The star of the morning shines*

---

[14] St John Paul II, *Homily*, Guayaquil, 31 January 1985

[15] cf F.W. Willam, *The Life of Mary*

not so lovely, says Fr Luis de Granada, *as the Mother's eyes shone in that gracious face of hers, the unblemished mirror of divine splendour. She sees the body of her Son risen and glorious, the disfigurement of his Passion gone, the grace of those divine eyes returned, his previous loveliness restored and increased. The openings of the wounds which had been sword-thrusts of pain for the Mother – to see them now as fountains of love; to see the One who had suffered between thieves, attended now by angels and saints; to see the One who commended her to the disciple from the Cross reach out his loving arms now, his visage radiant with unutterable peace ... Take her, do not leave her. Embrace her and ask her not to let go. Then, stricken with anguish, she had not known what to say; now, mute with joy, she cannot speak.*[16] We join in this immense joy.

It is said that each year on this holy day St Thomas Aquinas counselled his hearers not to fail to congratulate the Blessed Virgin on the Resurrection of her Son.[17] And this is exactly what we do, beginning today, by reciting the *Regina Coeli* which will take the place of the *Angelus* during Eastertide. *Queen of Heaven, Rejoice. Alleluia! For He whom you did merit to bear has risen as He said ...* And we ask to be raised up forever from all sin, to remain in intimate union with Jesus Christ. Let us resolve to live this Easter period very close to Our Lady.

---

[16] Fr Luis de Granada, *Book of Prayer and Meditation*
[17] Fr J.F.P., *Life and Mercies of Our Lady, according to St Thomas Aquinas*

48. THE JOY OF THE RESURRECTION

48.1 True joy has its origin in Christ.

The Lord has risen from the dead, as he said; let us all exult and rejoice, for he reigns for all eternity, alleluia.[1]

Joy is never lacking during any part of the liturgical year, because the entire cycle is related in one way or another with the Easter solemnity. It is in these days, though, that this joy is particularly made manifest. By the Crucifixion and Resurrection of Christ we have been saved from sin, from the power of the devil and from eternal death. Easter reminds us of our supernatural birth at our baptism, when we were made children of God, and it is the guarantee of our own resurrection. St Paul tells us that *God has made us alive through Christ, and raised us up with him.*[2] Christ, the first-born of men, has become the true exemplar for us and the beginning of our future glorification.

Our Mother the Church introduces us in these days to the joy of Easter through the texts of the liturgy – readings, psalms, antiphons ...; in them she asks above all that this joy be the early solid assurance of our eternal happiness in Heaven. From ancient times fasting and other bodily mortifications were dispensed from, as an external symbol of a joy at once spiritual and physical. *The fifty days of Easter,* says St Augustine, *exclude fasts, since it is in anticipation of the banquet that awaits us on high.*[3] But this invitation of the liturgy will not be worth anything if a true

---

[1] *Entrance Antiphon*
[2] Eph 2:6
[3] St Augustine, *Sermon 252*

encounter with the Lord does not occur in our lives, if we do not live with greater fulness the meaning of our divine filiation.

The writers of the gospels have left us evidence in each of his recorded appearances of how the Apostles rejoiced at seeing the Lord. Their joy increased when they had seen Christ, knowing with certainty now that He lives, for they have been with Him.

True joy does not depend on mere physical or material wellbeing, is not diminished by the presence of difficulties, by the absence of health ... Deep joy originates in Christ, in the love that God has had for us and in our correspondence with this love. The Lord's promise is fulfilled – today: *I will give you a joy which no one will take from you.*[4] Nobody can. Nor can pain take it away, nor calumny, nor abandonment ... nor even weaknesses and falls, if we turn promptly to the Lord. This is the sole condition of our remaining in it: not to separate ourselves from God, not to allow things to divide us from him; to know at all times that we are his sons and daughters.

48.2 Sadness is born of waywardness and distance from God. Being optimistic, serene and happy even in the midst of tribulation.

The Gospel of the Mass tells us: *the women came quickly away from the tomb and ran to tell the disciples. And there, coming to meet them, was Jesus. 'Greetings', he said. And the women came up to him, and falling down before him, clasped his feet.*[5]

The liturgy of the Easter season repeats these same words in a thousand different texts. *Rejoice*, never lose

---

[4] John 16:22
[5] Matt 28:8-9

your peace and joy. *Serve the Lord with gladness,*[6] for there is no other way to serve him. *You are enjoying a few days of great happiness, and your soul seems to be filled with light and colour. And funnily enough, the reasons for your joy are the same ones that at other times disheartened you!*

It is always the same: it all depends on the point of view. 'Laetetur cor quaerentium Dominum!' – *when you seek the Lord, your heart always overflows with happiness.*[7]

At the Last Supper Our Lord did not conceal from the Apostles the contradictions that awaited them. He promised them, however, that their despondency would turn to joy. *So you have sorrow now, but I will see you again and your hearts will rejoice, and no one will take your joy from you.*[8] These words, that at the time may have been incomprehensible, were not completely fulfilled right away. But a short time later, those who had become cowards would now be seen taking leave of the Sanhedrin happy to have suffered something for their Lord.[9] In the love of God, who is our Father and the Father of all men, and in the consequent forgetfulness of ourselves, lies the origin of that profound joy which is the Christian's.[10] And this is usual for those who follow Christ. A pessimistic sadness must always be something foreign to the Christian. It is something that, should it ever occur, will require urgent remedy.

Remoteness from God, waywardness, is the only thing that can disturb us and take away this wonderful gift. Let us struggle, therefore, to seek the Lord in our work and in

---

[6] Ps 99:2
[7] St J. Escrivá, *Furrow*, 72
[8] John 16:22
[9] Acts 5:40
[10] *The Navarre Bible*, Introduction to the Gospel of St John

all our undertakings; let us chastise our caprices and our egotism whenever the occasion arises, each day if necessary. This effort keeps us alert and attentive to the things of God, and on the lookout for everything that can make life more pleasant for others. This interior struggle gives the soul a special youthfulness of spirit. There is no greater youthfulness than the youthfulness of one who knows he is a son of God and acts accordingly.

If on any occasion we should have the misfortune to be separated from God, we should remember the prodigal son and with the Lord's help return again to the Father with a repentant heart. In Heaven there will be a great feast on that day of home-coming; its echo will resound in our soul. This is what happens every day in little ways and small things. So it is that, with many acts of contrition, the soul is habitually at peace and in serenity.

We must always foster joy and optimism and reject sadness, which is sterile and leaves the soul at the mercy of many temptations. When one is happy, one is a stimulus and an encouragement for others; sadness, on the other hand, obscures and causes damage.

48.3 Giving peace and joy to others.

To be happy is a form of giving thanks to God for the innumerable gifts He gives us. Joy is *the first tribute we owe him, the simplest, most sincere way of showing that we are aware of the gifts of nature and grace He showers upon us, and which we thank him for.*[11] God the Father is pleased with us when he sees us happy and joyful with true gladness.

We do great good around us with our joy, for this brings others to God. Joy is frequently the best example of charity for those around us. Let us remember the first

---

[11] P. A. Reggio, *Supernatural Spirit and Good Humour*

Christians. Their life was attractive because of the peace and joy with which they did the commonplace things of ordinary life. They were *families who lived in union with Christ and who made him known to others, small christian communities which were centres for the spreading of the Gospel and its message. They were families no different from other families of those times, but living with a new spirit, which spread to all those who were in contact with them. This is what the first Christians were, and this is what we have to be: sowers of peace and joy, the peace and joy that Jesus has brought to us.*[12] Many people will find God behind our optimism, in the customary smile, in a cordial attitude. This example of charity to others – of forcing ourselves to flee from gloomy moods and sadness at all times and to remove their cause – is particularly communicated to those closest to us. To be more precise, God wants the home where we live to be *a bright and cheerful home*, never a dark unhappy place, full of tension due to egocentricity and lack of mutual comprehension.

A Christian household must be happy, because supernatural life leads us to practising those virtues (generosity, cordiality, a spirit of service ...) to which joy is so intimately united. A christian home makes Christ known in an attractive way among families and throughout society.

We must also try to take this serene, kindly joy to our work-place, out into the street and into all our social relations. The world is apprehensive and anxious. It is in need, above all, of the *gaudium cum pace*,[13] of the peace and joy the Lord has given us. So many people have found the road to God in the cordial, smiling conduct of a good Christian! Joy is an enormous help in the apostolate

---

[12] St J. Escrivá, *Christ is passing by*, 30
[13] *Roman Missal, Preparation for Mass*

because it leads us to give Christ's message in a cheerfully benevolent and positive way, as the Apostles did after the Resurrection. Jesus Christ must always have demonstrated his infinite interior peace. We need it for ourselves too, in order to grow internally. St Thomas Aquinas says expressly that *everyone who wants to make progress in the spiritual life needs to have joy.*[14] Sadness debilitates us. It is like the heavy clay accumulating on the boots of a walker which, as well as befouling them, makes each step more difficult for him.

This interior joy is also the state of mind necessary for perfectly complying with our obligations. And *the greater these are the greater must be our joy.*[15] The greater our responsibility (parents, teachers, priests, superiors ...), the greater also our obligation to have this peace and joy to give to others, and the greater the urgency of recovering it when its habitual possession has been interrupted or disturbed.

Let us think of the joy of the Blessed Virgin. She is *unreservedly open to the joy of the Resurrection ... She recapitulates all joys, lives the perfect joy promised to the Church: 'Mater plena sanctae laetitiae' she is,* and with every reason her children on earth, turning their eyes toward the Mother of hope and the Mother of grace, invoke her as the Cause of their Joy – 'causa nostrae laetitiae'.*[16]

---

[14] St Thomas, *Commentary on the Letter to the Philippians*, 4, 1

[15] P. A. Reggio, *op cit*

[16] St Paul VI, Apostolic Exhortation *Gaudete in Domino*, 9 May 1975.

49. JESUS CHRIST LIVES FOREVER

49.1 Appearance of Our Lord to Mary Magdalene. Jesus in our lives.

Mary Magdalene has returned to the tomb. Her affection and devotion for Jesus even after His death are deeply moving. She had remained faithful in the terrible moments of Calvary, and the love of her who had been possessed by seven devils[1] continues to be very great. Grace had taken root and borne fruit in her heart after it had been freed from so many evils.

Mary remains outside the tomb weeping. Some angels, whom she does not recognize as such, ask her why she is crying. *Because they have taken away my Lord*, she says to them, *and I do not know where they have laid him.*[2] It is the only thing that matters to her in the whole world. And for us too it is the only thing that interests us above anything else whatever.

Saying this – the Gospel of the Mass continues – *she turned around and saw Jesus standing, but she did not know that it was Jesus.* Mary had not ceased to weep for her absent Lord. And her tears prevented her from seeing him now that He was so close beside her. Jesus said to her: *Woman why are you weeping? Whom do you seek?* Here we see the risen Christ, smiling, friendly, welcoming. But she, thinking it was the gardener, said to him: *Sir, if you have removed him, tell me where you have laid him, and I will take him away.*

One word from Christ was enough to dry her eyes and

---

[1] cf Luke 8:2
[2] John 20:13

lighten her heart. *Jesus said to her: Mary!* The word had that unique inflection which Jesus gives to every name – ours too! – and which goes hand in hand with a vocation, with a very special friendship. Jesus calls us by our name and the tone of his voice is unmistakable.

Jesus' voice has not changed. The risen Christ continues to have all the features of the Jesus who suffered: the tone of his voice, his manner of breaking bread, the marks of the nails in his hands and in his feet.

She turned; she saw Jesus and she threw herself at his feet and cried out in Aramaic: *Rabboni (which means Teacher).* Her tears, which now pour out like a river that has burst its banks, are tears of joy and happiness. St John chose to record for us the original Hebrew word – *Rabboni* – which was used and which had been used so often to address Jesus. It was a sort of family word that should not be tampered with. Jesus is not just one more *teacher* among so many others, but is *the Teacher*, the only one capable of teaching the true meaning of life, the only one who has the words of eternal life.

Mary went to the Apostles to fulfil the task that Jesus had given her and told them: *I have seen the Lord.* Reflected in her words is an immense joy. What a difference it makes to her life now that she knows that He is risen, in contrast to the time when she was only seeking to honour the dead body of Jesus!

What a difference it makes to our existence, also when we seek to live in accordance with this consoling reality: Jesus Christ continues to live among us! He is the same one whom Mary Magdalene took that morning to be the local gardener! *Christ is alive. He is not someone who has gone, someone who existed for a time and then passed on, leaving us a wonderful example and a great memory ... His resurrection shows us that God does not abandon his own. He promised He would not: 'Can a woman forget her baby that is still unweaned, pity no longer the son she bore in her womb? Even these may forget, yet I will not forget you'* (Is 49:14-15). And He has kept his promise. *His delight is still to be with the sons of men (cf Prov 8:31).*[3]

Jesus often calls us by our name, in his unmistakable tone of voice. He is very close to each one of us. May external circumstances – tears, maybe, like those of Mary Magdalene, because of sorrow, or failure, or deception, or pain, or discouragement – never prevent us from seeing the Jesus who calls us. May we always be able to purify anything that could be the cause of our vision's becoming clouded.

49.2 Presence of Christ in our midst.

Jesus Christ, the Second Person of the Blessed Trinity, who was made man in the virginal womb of Mary, is now in Heaven with that same body which He assumed in the Incarnation and which died on the Cross and rose again on the third day. One day we too, like Mary Magdalene, will contemplate the Sacred Humanity of Our Lord, and in the meantime we have to foster the desire of seeing him: *Seek ye my face. My heart says to thee, 'Thy face, Lord, do I seek.'*[4] In Heaven we shall see Jesus as He is without any imperfection of image; it will be a meeting with someone who knows us and whom we know because we have already been with him on many occasions.

As well as being in Heaven, Christ is also really present in the Blessed Eucharist. *The unique and indivisible existence of Christ the Lord whereby He lives in the glory of Heaven is not multiplied by the Sacrament but rendered present in every place on earth where the Eucharistic Sacrifice is celebrated. And this same existence*

---

[3] St J. Escrivá, *Christ is passing by*, 102

[4] Ps 26:8

remains present after the Sacrifice in the Most Blessed Sacrament which is reserved in the tabernacle, the living heart of our churches. It is, then, our bounden and loving duty to honour and adore in the Blessed Bread, which we see with our eyes, the Word Incarnate himself, whom we cannot see, but who nonetheless, without leaving Heaven, is made present before us.[5]

The presence of the living Christ in the host is the guarantee, the source and the culmination of his presence in the world.[6] Christ lives, and he is present too with his power in the Sacraments. He is present in his Word whenever Sacred Scripture is read in the Church. He is present whenever the Church prays and comes together in His name.[7] He lives also in each Christian in an intimate, deep and ineffable way. He has fulfilled the promise that He made to the Apostles when He was taking leave of them at the Last Supper: *If a man loves me, he will keep my word, and my Father will love him, and we will come to him and make our home with him.*[8] God dwells in our souls in grace and we should seek him there; we should listen to him there, because He does speak to us and we will understand him if we keep our ears attentive and our hearts clean. It is this presence St Paul is referring to when he says that each one of us is a Temple of the Holy Spirit.[9]

When he considered the unspeakable presence of God in the soul, St Augustine exclaimed: *Late have I loved you, O Beauty so ancient and so new; late have I loved you! For behold you were within me, and I outside; and I sought you outside ... You were with me and I was not with you. I was kept from you by those things, yet had they not been in you,*

---

[5] St Paul VI, *The Creed of the People of God*
[6] St J. Escrivá, *loc cit*
[7] cf Second Vatican Council, *Sacrosanctum concilium*, 7
[8] John 14:23
[9] cf 2 Cor 6:16-17

they would not have been at all. You called and cried to me and broke open my deafness: and you sent forth your beams and shone upon me and chased away my blindness.[10]

Within our soul in grace Our Lord is closer to us than a person standing beside us, closer than a child in its mother's arms or a brother or sister walking hand in hand; He is closer than our own very heart. Let us not neglect to speak with him constantly.

49.3 Seeking and loving Christ. Mary Magdalene's example teaches us that whoever seeks Our Lord sincerely will always end up finding him.

Christ lives and in various ways is present among us, and even within us. We should therefore set out to meet him, as it were, and try to be more aware of his ineffable presence so that, being more conscious of his presence, we will speak with him more and his love will grow in us. *We must seek Christ in the word and in the bread, in the Eucharist and in prayer. And we must treat him as a friend, as the real living person he is – for he is risen. Christ, we read in the Letter to the Hebrews, 'holds his priesthood permanently, because he continues forever ... consequently he is able for all time to save those who draw near to God, since he always lives to make intercession for them' (Heb 7:24-25).*

Christ, the risen Lord, is our companion and friend. He is a companion whom we can see only in the shadows – but the fact that he is really there fills our whole life and makes us yearn to be with him forever.[11] If we contemplate the risen Christ, if we try to look at him with an unclouded vision, we shall understand in a profound way that it is

---

[10] St Augustine, *Confessions*, 10, 27-38
[11] St J. Escrivá, *Christ is passing by*, 116

possible now also to follow him closely, to live our lives close beside him in such a way that they expand and acquire a new meaning.

After doing this for some time a personal relationship will gradually become established between Jesus and ourselves – a loving faith – that can be today, after the passing of twenty centuries, just as authentic and strong as the faith of those who contemplated him risen and glorious and still bearing the signs of his Passion in his Body. We will notice that, with ever-greater naturalness, we will find ourselves referring to our Lord everything that forms part of our existence and see that we wouldn't be able to live without him. Finding Our Lord will mean for us at times a patient and laborious search, beginning and beginning again every day, perhaps even having a distinct impression that we are only at the very beginning of our interior life. Nevertheless, if we struggle, we will always grow closer to Jesus. But it is important that we should never allow discouragement to enter our souls through possible setbacks, which will often be only apparent anyway.

The example of Mary Magdalene, who persevered in fidelity to our Lord in moments of difficulty, teaches us that whoever sincerely and constantly seeks Jesus will end up finding him. And in any circumstances whatever of our lives we will find him much more easily if we start out on our search led by the hand of Our Lady, our Mother, to whom we say in the 'Hail Holy Queen': *Show unto us the blessed fruit of thy womb, Jesus*.

50. LETTING ONESELF BE HELPED

50.1 On the road to Emmaus: Jesus, alive and at our side.

The Gospel of today's Mass presents us with another appearance of Jesus on the evening of his Resurrection. Two disciples are making their way to the village of Emmaus, having lost all hope because Christ, in whom they had placed the whole meaning of their lives, was dead. Our Lord catches up with them, as if He too were just another traveller on the road, and walks with them without being recognized.[1] They engage in broken conversation, as happens when people talk as they are going along. They speak about their preoccupation: what has happened in Jerusalem on the Friday evening – the death of Jesus of Nazareth. The Crucifixion of Our Lord had been a very severe test for the hopes of all those who considered themselves to be his disciples and who to some extent or another had placed their trust in him. Things had all taken place very quickly and they still hadn't got over all they had seen with their very eyes.

These men who are returning to their home village after having celebrated the Paschal feast in Jerusalem show by the tone of their conversation their great sadness and how discouraged and disconcerted they are: *We had hoped that he was the one to redeem Israel.* But now they speak of Jesus as a reality belonging to the past: *Concerning Jesus of Nazareth, who was a prophet mighty in deed ... Notice the contrast. They say 'who was!' ... And He is there*

---

[1] Luke 24:13-35

by their side. He is walking with them, in their company, trying to uncover the reason, the most intimate roots of their sadness!

'Who was!', they say. We too, if only we would examine ourselves sincerely, with an attentive examination of our sadness, our discouragement, our being a little tired of life, would find a clear link with this Gospel passage. We would discover how we spontaneously remark 'Jesus was', 'Jesus said', because we forget that, just as on the road to Emmaus, Jesus is alive and by our side at this very moment. This is a discovery which enlivens our faith and revives our hope, a finding that points to Jesus as a joy that is ever present: Jesus is, Jesus prefers, Jesus says, Jesus commands now at this very moment.[2] Jesus lives.

These men did know about Christ's promise of rising on the third day. They had heard that morning the message of the women who had seen the empty tomb and the angels. Things had been sufficiently clear for them to have nourished their faith and their hope; but instead, they speak of Christ as belonging to the past, as a lost opportunity. They are a living picture of discouragement. Their minds are in darkness and their hearts are numbed.

Christ Himself – whom they did not at first recognize but whose company and conversation they accept – interprets those events for them in the light of the Scriptures. Patiently He restores in them their faith and their hope. And the two of them recover also their joy and their love: *Did not our hearts burn within us,* they say later, *while he talked to us on the road, while he opened to us the scriptures?*[3]

It is possible that we too may sometimes meet with discouragement and lack of hope because of defects that

---

[2] A. G. Dorronsoro, *God and People*, Madrid
[3] Luke 24:32

we cannot manage to root out, or of difficulties in the apostolate or in our work that seem to be insurmountable ... On these occasions, provided we allow ourselves to be helped, Jesus will not allow us to be parted from him. Perhaps it will be in spiritual direction, once we open our souls in all sincerity, that we will come to see Our Lord again. And with him there will always come joy and the desire to begin again as soon as possible: *And they rose that same hour and returned to Jerusalem.* But it is essential that we allow ourselves to be helped, and that we be ready to be docile to the advice that we receive.

50.2 Fidelity. Being faithful in little things.

Hope is the virtue of us wayfarers who have not yet reached the goal but who know that we will always have the means to be faithful to Our Lord and to persevere in our vocation, each of us in the fulfilment of his or her duties. For this we need to be attentive to Christ, who draws near to us in the course of our occupations, and *to grasp hold of the strong hand which God never ceases to reach out to us, to keep us from losing our supernatural point of view. Let us persevere even when our passions rear up and attack us, attempting to imprison us within the narrow confines of our selfishness; or when puerile vanity makes us think we are the centre of the universe. I am convinced that unless I look upward, unless I have Jesus, I will never accomplish anything. And I know that the strength to conquer myself and to win comes from repeating that cry, 'I can do all things in him who strengthens me' (Phil 4:13), words which reflect God's firm promise not to abandon his children if they do not abandon him.*[4]

In the Gospels Our Lord often speaks about fidelity:

---

[4] St J. Escrivá, *Friends of God*, 213

He gives us the example of the faithful and prudent servant, of the valet who is good and loyal even in the smallest things, of the faithful steward etc. So deeply has the notion of fidelity permeated the Christian that the title 'faithful' is sufficient of itself to identify the disciples of Christ.[5]

The opposite of perseverance is inconstancy, which inclines a person to break off easily from doing good or from the practice of virtue as soon as difficulties or temptations arise. Among the most frequent obstacles to faithful perseverance, the first one of all is pride, which attacks the very foundations of fidelity and weakens the will to fight difficulties and temptations. Without humility, perseverance becomes feeble and shaky. At other times what will render continued commitment difficult will be the very environment itself, the behaviour of people who should be exemplary and are not, and who for that very reason seem to wish to create the impression that to be faithful is not one of the fundamental values of the person.

On other occasions, obstacles can have their origin in carelessness concerning little things. Our Lord himself said: *He who is faithful in very little is faithful also in much.*[6] The Christian who takes care of even the smallest duties of his or her work (punctuality, order, etc), who struggles to keep presence of God throughout the day, who guards his senses with naturalness ..., the married person loyal to his or her spouse in the small things of daily life, the student who prepares his classes every day ... these are the ones who are on the right road to being faithful when the time comes for their commitment to the call for genuine heroism.

Fidelity to the end of our life demands fidelity in the

---

[5] cf Acts 10:45; 2 Cor 6:15; Eph 1:1
[6] Luke 16:10

little things of every day and readiness to begin again whenever there has been any falling away through weakness. Persevering in one's vocation is a matter of responding to the calls that God makes in the course of a lifetime, even though obstacles and difficulties may arise – and even, at times, of coping with isolated incidents of cowardice or defeat. Christ's call requires a firm and constant response and, at the same time, a deeper penetration into the meaning of the Cross and into the greatness and demands of one's own particular way.

50.3 The virtue of fidelity should be manifested in all aspects of a Christian's life.

This virtue of fidelity should pervade all the different areas and expressions of a Christian's life: one's relationship with God, with the Church, with one's neighbour; it should be active in work, in duties of state, and in attitudes towards oneself. What is more, a person lives fidelity in all its forms by being faithful to his or her vocation, and it is on fidelity to Our Lord that fidelity to all true commitments is based, and that to which everything in its turn can be reduced. Failure, then, in the vocation that God has desired for us means failure in everything. When fidelity to Our Lord is missing then everything is disunited and broken, though it can still happen that in his mercy God can put everything together again if only we humbly ask him.

God himself continually supports our fidelity and always takes human weakness, defects and mistakes into account. He is always ready to give us the necessary graces, as He did with the disciples of Emmaus, to keep going forward with constancy, provided there is sincerity of life and the desire to struggle. And whenever our efforts apparently meet with failure (if this should happen), we should remember that God looks with loving eyes more on the continuous effort to struggle rather than on the 'success' obtained.

In this way, having persevered with God's help in the little things of every day, at the end of our lives we will hear with unutterable joy those words of Our Lord: *Well done, good and faithful servant; you have been faithful over a little, I will set you over much; enter into the joy of your master.*[7] It is very possible that we too may meet people who have lost the supernatural meaning of their lives and to whom we have to bring back – in the Lord's name – light and hope. There is great lukewarmness and darkness in the world, and the Christian's apostolic mission is a continuation of Jesus' mission in the lives of the people around him.

As we finish our prayer we too say to Jesus: *Stay with us, for it is toward evening* ... Stay with us, Lord, because without you all is darkness and our life has no meaning. Without you, we are disoriented and lost on our journey. On the other hand, with you everything takes on a new meaning: even death itself becomes totally different. *Stay with us, for it is toward evening and the day is now far spent.* Stay with us Lord ... remind us always of the essential things of our existence ... help us to be faithful and to know how to listen attentively to the wise counsel of those people in whom You make yourself present to us as we constantly travel towards you. *'Stay with us because it is getting dark.' The prayer of Cleopas and his companion was truly effective. How sad it would be if you and I were not able to detain Jesus who is passing by! What a shame not to ask him to stay!*[8]

---

[7] Matt 25:21-23
[8] St J. Escrivá, *Furrow*, 671

51. MEETING OUR LORD

51.1 The presence of Jesus Christ in our tabernacles.

In the Gospel of today's Mass[1] we read how Jesus, having appeared to Mary Magdalene, to the other women, to Peter and to the disciples from Emmaus, appears also to the Eleven: *And he said to them, Why are you troubled, and why do questionings rise in your hearts? See my hands and my feet that it is I myself; handle me and see; for a spirit has not flesh and bones as you see that I have.*

He then showed them his hands and his feet, and ate with them. The Apostles will be forever convinced that their faith in the Risen One is not a result of mere credulity, of enthusiasm or of imagination, but of facts which they themselves were able to confirm repeatedly. Jesus, in His appearances, adapts with marvellous condescension to the state of mind and the varied situations of those to whom He reveals himself. He does not treat them all in the same way; but by different ways He leads them to certainty about His Resurrection and about the fact that He is the cornerstone of the Christian faith. Our Lord wishes to give every possible guarantee to those who constitute the newly emerging Church so that throughout the centuries our faith will rest on solid foundations: *The Lord is risen indeed.* Jesus is alive.

Peace to you, Jesus said when he presented himself to his disciples, who were filled with fear. They immediately saw his wounds and were filled with joy and astonishment. This too should be our refuge. It is here that we will always

---

[1] cf Luke 24:35-48

find peace of soul and the necessary strength to follow Him all the days of our life. *We will go there like the doves which, in the words of Scripture (cf Cant 2:14), find shelter from the storm in the crevices in the rocks. We hasten to this refuge to find the intimacy we seek with Christ. We find his conversation soothing and his countenance comely, because 'those who know that his voice is gentle and pleasing are those who have welcomed the grace of the Gospel, which makes them say: You have the words of eternal life' (St Gregory of Nyssa, In Canticum Canticorum homiliae, 5).*[2]

Jesus is very near to us: in Christian countries where there are so many tabernacles we are hardly ever more than a few miles from Him. How difficult it is not to see the walls or at least the spire of some church whether we are in the middle of a crowded city or travelling by road or by train. Christ is there! It is the Lord![3] our faith and our love exclaim. We can say it because Our Lord is present there really and substantially: He is the same one who appeared to the disciples and who has always shown such interest in everybody. Jesus has remained in the Blessed Eucharist. In this memorable Sacrament there is contained, really, truly and substantially, his Body and Blood together with his Soul and Divinity and, consequently, the whole Christ. The presence of Christ in the Blessed Eucharist is real and permanent, because once Mass is over, Our Lord remains in each one of the consecrated hosts that has not been consumed.[4] He who is present is He who was born, died and rose again in Palestine, the one who is at the right hand of God the Father.

We meet with Him in the tabernacle and he sees us and knows us. We can speak to him as the Apostles did and

---

[2] St J. Escrivá, *Friends of God*, 302
[3] cf John 21:7
[4] cf Council of Trent, Canon 4 *On the Eucharist*, Dz 886

tell him what things we are enthusiastic about and what things are causing us concern. There we always find true peace, of the kind that endures in spite of all sorrow and every obstacle.

51.2 The Visit to the Blessed Sacrament.

Eucharistic piety, St John Paul II said, *should be centred above all on the celebration of the Lord's Supper, which perpetuates the pouring out of His love on the Cross. But it has a logical prolongation ... in the adoration of Christ in this divine Sacrament, in the Visit to the Blessed Sacrament, in prayer beside the Tabernacle, as well as in those other exercises of devotion both personal and collective, private and public, which you have been practising for centuries ... Jesus waits for us in this Sacrament of Love. Let us not be mean with our time when it comes to going to meet him in adoration, in contemplation that is filled with faith, and disposed to make reparation for the grave faults and crimes of the world.*[5]

Jesus is there in the nearest Tabernacle. Perhaps just a few miles away or even perhaps a few yards ... How could we not go to see him, to love him, to tell him about our affairs, to ask him for things? What a lack of consistency on our part if we were not to do this with faith? How easy it is to understand that centuries-old custom of *the daily visits to the divine tabernacles?*[6] There the Master has been waiting for us for the past twenty centuries,[7] and we can be together with him like Mary, the sister of Lazarus – the one who chose the better part[8] – in that house in Bethany. *I will tell you*, says St Josemaría Escrivá, *that for me the tabernacle*

---

[5] St John Paul II, *Address*, 31 October 1982
[6] Pius XII, *Mediator Dei*, 20 November 1947
[7] cf St J. Escrivá, *The Way*, 537
[8] cf Luke 10:42

*has always been a Bethany, a quiet and pleasant place
where Christ resides: a place where we can tell him about
our worries, our sufferings, our desires, our joys, with the
same sort of simplicity and naturalness as Martha, Mary
and Lazarus. That is why I rejoice when I stumble upon a
church in town or country; it's another tabernacle, another
opportunity for the soul to escape and join in intention our
Lord in the Sacrament.*[9]

Jesus is waiting for us to visit him. It is, in a way, a
return of his visit to us in Holy Communion, and it is *a
proof of gratitude, an expression of love, an acknowledgement of the Lord's presence.*[10] It is a continuation of our act
of thanksgiving for the previous Communion and a
preparation for the next.

When we find ourselves before the tabernacle we can
indeed say in all truth and accuracy: God is here! And in
the presence of this mystery of faith there is no room for
any other attitude except that of adoration – *Adoro te
devote ... O hidden God, devoutly I adore You*; of respect
and astonishment; and, at the same time, of unlimited
confidence. *Dwelling with Christ Our Lord, the faithful
enjoy his intimate friendship and pour out their hearts
before him for themselves and their dear ones, and pray for
the peace and salvation of the world. They offer their entire
lives with Christ to the Father in the Holy Spirit, and
receive in this wonderful exchange an increase of faith,
hope and charity. Thus they nourish those right
dispositions which enable them with all due devotion to
celebrate the memorial of the Lord and receive frequently
the bread given us by the Father.*[11]

---

[9] St J. Escrivá, *Christ is passing by*, 154
[10] St Paul VI, *Mysterium Fidei*, 3 September 1965
[11] cf *Instruction on the Eucharistic Mystery*, 50

51.3 Fruits of this act of piety.

You have started to visit the Blessed Sacrament every day ... I am not surprised to hear you say, 'I have come to love the Sanctuary light madly.'[12] The Visit to the Blessed Sacrament is an act of piety that only takes a few minutes; nevertheless, what a lot of graces and what fortitude and peace does Our Lord give through it. There we find that our sense of presence of God throughout the day is improved and we gather new strength to take the difficulties of the day in our stride. There our desire to work better is enkindled and we are provided with a good supply of peace and joy to take with us to our family life. Our Lord, who always pays generously, is grateful for the fact that we have gone to visit Him. *And as to paying us, he is so careful about this that you need to have no fear he will leave us without our reward if only we raise our eyes to Heaven and remember Him.*[13]

In the Visit to the Blessed Sacrament we go to keep Jesus company for a few minutes. It could be that on a particular day not many have gone to visit him even though He was expecting them. Therefore He is all the more pleased to see us there. We shall say some of the usual prayers to him as well as making the spiritual Communion. We'll ask him for help – both spiritual and material; we'll tell him what is causing us concern and what we are happy about; we'll tell him that, in spite of our miseries, He can count on us for the re-evangelization of the world and we'll tell him, perhaps, that we want to bring a friend close to him. *What shall we do, you sometimes ask, in the presence of Jesus in the Blessed Sacrament? Love him, praise him, thank him and ask him for things. What does a thirsty*

---

[12] St J. Escrivá, *Furrow*, 688
[13] St Teresa, *The Way of Perfection*, 23,3

person do when he sees a pure clean fountain?[14] When we leave the Church after these moments of prayer, we will have in us greater peace, a determination to help others, an eager longing to receive Holy Communion, because the only way that intimate union with Jesus can be fully realized is in the Eucharist. It will effectively have helped us to increase our presence of God in the course of our work and our daily tasks. It will be easy for us to keep up a relationship of friendship and confidence with him throughout the day.

The first Christians from the moment they began to have churches and to reserve the Blessed Sacrament had already started to live this pious custom. This is how St John Chrysostom commented on that passage of Scripture: *and Jesus entered the Temple. This was proper to a good son: to enter immediately into the house of his Father to render due honour to Him there – just as you, who should imitate Jesus, whenever you enter a city should first of all go to the church.*[15]

Once we are in the church, we can easily find out where the tabernacle is – which is the first place we should direct our attention to – because it should be located in a *truly prominent place ... suited to private prayer.* And there the presence of the Blessed Eucharist will be indicated by the small lamp which as the sign of honour to Our Lord, will be continuously burning before it.[16]

As we finish our prayer we ask our Mother Mary to teach us how to love Jesus really present in the tabernacle as she loved Him all those years of His life in Nazareth.

---

[14] St Alphonsus Liguori, *Visits to the Blessed Sacrament*, 1
[15] St John Chrysostom, *Catena Aurea*, III
[16] cf *Instruction on the Eucharistic Mystery*, 53, 57; *Code of Canon Law*, can. 938 & 940

52. CONSTANCY IN APOSTOLATE

52.1 Discovering Christ in the events of our life.

Jesus Christ ... is the stone which has become the head of the corner. And there is salvation in no one else, for there is no other name under heaven given among men by which we must be saved.[1] The Apostles have left Jerusalem for Galilee as the Lord had told them to.[2] They are there beside the lake: at the same place or at one similar to the one where Jesus found them and invited them to follow him. Now they have gone back to the old occupations they had when the Lord first called them. Jesus finds them again immersed in their work. *And He revealed himself in this way. Simon Peter, Thomas called the Twin, Nathanael of Cana in Galilee, the sons of Zebedee, and two others of his disciples were together.*[3] There are seven of them altogether. It is just twilight. Other boats have already gone out fishing. *Simon Peter said to them, 'I am going fishing'. They said to him, 'we will go with you'. They went out and got into the boat; but that night they caught nothing.*

At dawn *Jesus stood on the beach.* The risen Jesus comes seeking his own, to strengthen them in the Faith and in his friendship and to continue explaining to them the great mission that awaits them. *His disciples did not know that it was Jesus;* they still don't recognize Him. They are about a hundred yards from land. At this distance, at daybreak, they cannot make out the man's features very well, but they can hear as soon as He began to speak: *Friends, have you caught anything?* the Lord asks them.

---

[1] *First Reading of the Mass*, Acts 4:12
[2] cf Matt 28:7
[3] John 21:2 ff

They answered him, 'No'. He said to them, 'Cast the net on the right side of the boat, and you will find some'. And Peter obeys. *So they cast it, and now they were not able to haul it in, for the quantity of fish.* John confirms Peter's inner conviction. Bending towards him he says *It is the Lord.* Peter, who has been holding himself back until that moment, suddenly takes a leap as if he has been given a push. He doesn't wait till the boats get to the shore. As soon as Simon Peter heard that it was the Lord he girded up his tunic and threw himself into the sea. *But the other disciples came in the boat, dragging the net full of fish, for they were not far from the land, but about a hundred yards off.*

John's love immediately recognized the Lord on the shore: It is the Lord! *Love, love is farsighted. Love is the first to appreciate kindness. The adolescent Apostle, who felt a deep and firm affection for Jesus, because he loved Christ with all the purity and tenderness of a heart that had never been corrupted, exclaimed: 'It is the Lord'!*[4]

During the night, on their own, in the absence of Christ, they had laboured in vain. They had been wasting their time. In the morning, when it was light, when Jesus was present, when He gave light with his word, when He directed the operation, the nets were completely filled as they were brought to land.

The same thing happens to us every day. In the absence of Christ the day becomes night, an empty night, just another day in our life. Our efforts are not enough by themselves; we need God for them to bear fruit. By the side of Christ, when we have him with us, our days are enriched. Pain and illness are converted into a treasure that lasts beyond death: with Jesus by our side the question of living with those who surround us becomes a whole world of possibilities for doing good: opportunities for attention,

---

[4] St J. Escrivá, *Friends of God*, 266

encouragement, cordiality, prayer for others ...

The real tragedy for a Christian starts when he can no longer see Jesus in his life; when because of lukewarmness or sin or pride, the horizon becomes clouded over; when things are done as if Jesus were not by his side, as if the Lord had never risen from the dead.

We should pray a lot to Our Lady asking her to help us to discover Our Lord in the midst of all the events of our lives; so that we may be able to say very often, *It is the Lord!* And this, too, whether it be a case of suffering or of joy, whatever the circumstances. By Christ's side, always near him, we will be apostles in the middle of the world, in all circumstances and situations.[5]

52.2 Apostolate presupposes patient work.

When they came to land they saw some coals already prepared and some fish and some bread placed upon them. Jesus said to them: *Bring some of the fish that you have just caught. So Simon Peter went aboard and hauled the net ashore, full of large fish, a hundred and fifty-three of them; and although they were so many, the net was not torn.* The Fathers of the Church have often commented on this incident, seeing the boat as representing the Church, whose unity is symbolised by the net that does not break; the sea is the world; Peter in the boat symbolizes the supreme authority of the Church; the number of fish signifies those who are called.[6] We, like the Apostles, are the fishermen who have to bring people to the feet of Christ, because souls belong to God.[7]

Why did the Lord include so many fishermen among his Apostles? ... What were the good points that He saw in

---

[5] cf F. Fernandez, *Lukewarmness – the Devil in disguise*
[6] cf St Augustine, *Commentary on St John, in loc.*
[7] cf St J. Escrivá, *Friends of God*, 267

them? I think there was one thing which He specially appreciated in those who were to be his Apostles: an unshakeable patience ... They had worked all night and had caught nothing; long hours of waiting after which the grey light of dawn was to bring them their reward, but there was none ... What a lot of waiting the Church of Christ has had to endure throughout the centuries ... patiently extending her invitation and leaving grace to do its work! ... What does it matter if she has worked very hard in one place or another and reaped very little for her Master? On the basis of his word, in spite of everything, she will launch her nets again until such time as his grace, the limits of which are in no way proportioned to human efforts, brings her again a new catch of fish.[8] We don't know how or when, but all apostolic effort bears fruit, even though it often happens that we do not see it. Our Lord asks from us Christians the same capacity for patient waiting as he found in the fishermen. He asks us to be constant in our personal apostolate with our friends and acquaintances, never to abandon them or to give up anybody as being impossible.

Patience is a principal part of fortitude; it leads us to know how to wait when that is what the situation requires, to use more human and supernatural means, to begin again many times, to take into account our own defects and those of the people we want to bring to God. *An indispensable requirement in the apostolate is faith, which is often shown by constancy in speaking about God, even though the fruits are slow to appear.*

If we persevere and carry on in the firm conviction that the Lord wills it, signs of a Christian revolution will appear around you, everywhere. Some will follow the call,

---

[8] R.A. Knox, *Sermon preached on the Feast of Ss Peter and Paul*, 29 June 1947

others will take their interior life seriously, and others – the weakest – will at least be forewarned.[9]

52.3 Apostolate requires time, human and supernatural means.

Jesus already knew the defects of his Apostles when he called them. He wants them as they are. To Peter he would say after He had eaten with them that morning: *Simon, son of John, do you love me more than these? ... Feed my lambs ... Feed my sheep.*[10] He counts on them for the founding of his Church. He gives them the power to perform the Sacrifice of the Altar in his name, the power to pardon sins. He entrusts his doctrine and his teachings to their care. He places his full confidence in them and patiently forms them. He allows for the necessary time to make them suitable for the mission they will have to carry out.

Our Lord has also foreseen the time and the manner of each person's sanctification, while fully respecting each one's personal correspondence with his grace. On our part we are called upon to be good channels through which his grace will flow and to facilitate the action of the Holy Spirit in ourselves, in friends, relatives, acquaintances and colleagues ... If Our Lord never gets tired of giving his help to everybody, how can we who are only instruments ever become discouraged? Once the carpenter's hand is firmly placed on the wood, how can the tool ever have any reservations about doing its work?

The path that leads to Heaven is not a short one. And God does not usually grant graces that immediately and definitively bestow holiness. Normally our friends will draw close to Our Lord little by little. We will meet with

---

[9] St J. Escrivá, *Furrow*, 207
[10] John 21:15-17

resistance, often a consequence of original sin leaving its mark on the soul, and also of personal sins. For us, it is a matter of facilitating God's action with our prayer and mortification, of truly caring for those concerned, of giving example, of speaking the right word at the right moment, of sincere friendship, of understanding, of overlooking their defects. If our friends are slow in responding to grace, we should be all the more generous with our signs of friendship and affection, thus reinforcing the human basis of apostolate. To intensify our relationship with a person who seems not to want to be committed to something which could bring him or her closer to Jesus is a sign of true friendship on our part and of rectitude of intention, and of the fact that we are motivated by the desire that God may have many friends here on earth, as well as by concern for the good of our friends.

The Gospels show us how Our Lord was a Friend to his disciples, giving them as much time as was necessary: He asks them, in order to start the conversation, whether they have anything to eat. He then prepares a meal for them on the shore of the lake. He goes away with Peter and asks him, while John follows behind, to continue trusting him. It ought not to surprise us that some friends treated in this way by the Friend should afterwards give their lives for him in martyrdom, for the salvation of the world. Let us pray to Our Lady that she will help us to imitate Jesus in such a way that in friendship we may not be *just passive. You have to become a real friend to your friends. You can help them first with the example of your behaviour and then with your advice and with the influence that a close friendship provides.*[11]

---

[11] St J. Escrivá, *Furrow*, 731

53. GO OUT INTO THE WHOLE WORLD

53.1 Our Lord sends us into the world to make his teaching known.

The Resurrection of Our Lord constitutes a call to apostolate until the end of time. Every one of his appearances ends with an apostolic command. To Mary Magdalene Jesus says: *Go to my brethren and say to them, I am ascending to my Father and to your Father;*[1] and to the other women, *Go and tell my brethren to go to Galilee and that they shall see me there.*[2] The disciples of Emmaus feel the need of communicating to others that same night that Jesus is alive.[3] In the Gospel of today's Mass St Mark reports the great apostolic mandate which will continue to be in force for all time: *Afterwards he appeared to the eleven themselves as they sat at table ... And he said to them, 'Go into all the world and preach the gospel to the whole creation'.*[4]

From that time onwards the Apostles began to bear testimony to that which they had heard and seen and to preach *repentance and forgiveness of sins ... in his name to all nations, beginning from Jerusalem.*[5] What they preach and bear testimony to are not mere speculations but salvific facts which they themselves have witnessed. When as a result of the death of Judas it becomes necessary to complete the number of the twelve apostles, one condition is that the candidate be someone who was a witness to the

---

[1] John 20:17
[2] Matt 28:10
[3] cf Luke 24:35
[4] Mark 14:15-16
[5] cf Luke 24:44-47

Resurrection.[6]

In those Eleven the Church is represented. In them, all Christians of all time receive the joyful mandate of communicating to whomsoever we meet on our way that Christ is alive, that in him sin and death have been conquered, that He calls us to a share in the divine life, that all the problems that beset us can be solved. Christ himself has given us this right and this duty. *The Christian vocation is by its very nature a vocation to the apostolate,*[7] and *all the faithful, from the Pope to the child who has just been baptized, share one and the same vocation, the same faith, the same Spirit, the same grace ... They all have an active and appropriate share ... in the single mission of Christ and of the Church.*[8]

Nobody should prevent us from exercising this right in the fulfilment of this duty. The First Reading of the Mass tells us how the Apostles reacted when the Chief Priests and the Scribes absolutely forbade them to preach and teach in the name of Jesus. Peter and John replied: *Whether it is right in the sight of God to listen to you rather than to God, you must judge; for we cannot but speak of what we have seen and heard.*[9]

We cannot remain silent either. There is a great deal of ignorance around us, there is a great deal of error, and the number of people who go through life lost and confused because they don't know Christ is beyond counting. We have to communicate the doctrine and the faith that we have received to many people in the course of our daily contact with them. *'Nor do men light a lamp and put it under a bushel, but on a stand, and it gives light to all in*

---

[6] cf Acts 1:21-22
[7] Second Vatican Council, *Apostolicam actuositatem*, 2
[8] Bl. A. del Portillo, *Faithful and Laity in the Church*
[9] Acts 4:20

the house. Let your light so shine before men, that they may see your good works, and give glory to your Father who is in heaven'.

And at the end of his time upon earth, Christ commanded: 'euntes docete' – go out and teach. He wants his light to shine in the behaviour and words of his disciples, and in yours too.[10]

53.2 We too will meet with difficulties. Going against the current. Re-evangelization of the world. Personal holiness.

As soon as the Apostles began with courage and daring to teach the truth about Christ, the obstacles also began to present themselves. And in the course of time persecution and martyrdom followed. But before long belief in Christ had extended beyond Palestine, arriving in Asia Minor, Greece and Italy, and reaching men of every culture, social position and race.

We too can expect to meet with misunderstanding, a sure sign of divine predilection, and can be sure that we are following the footsteps of Our Lord, because *a disciple is not above his teacher.*[11] We accept our setbacks joyfully as being permitted by God. We welcome them as opportunities to activate our faith and hope and love. They help us to increase our prayer and mortification, confident that prayer and sacrifice always produce fruit,[12] because *the Lord's chosen ones will not labour in vain.*[13] And we always treat other people well, with understanding, drowning evil in abundance of good.[14]

It should not surprise us that very often we have to go

---

[10] St J. Escrivá, *Furrow*, 930
[11] Matt 10:24
[12] cf St J. Escrivá, *The Way*, 694-7
[13] Is 65:23
[14] cf Rom 12:21

against the current, in this world that seems to distance itself every day more and more from God, that has material wellbeing as its end, giving no importance to spiritual values or simply relegating them to a secondary plane. It is a world some would like to organise with its back turned completely against its Creator. Along with the deep and disordered attraction which material goods exercise on those who have lost all contact with God, there is added the bad example of some Christians; through this, *when religious education is neglected, doctrine misleadingly expounded or shortcomings made evident in the religious, moral and social life of believers, then we must admit that the true face of God and of religion is veiled rather than revealed.*[15]

The apostolic field in which the Apostles and the first Christians had to do their sowing was one with hard ground, rocks, thistles and thorns. Nevertheless the seed which they scattered bore fruit abundantly. In some places it yielded a hundredfold, in others sixty and in others thirty. It is enough for there to be just a minimum of correspondence for the fruit to come, because the seed is from God, and it is He who makes the divine life grow in souls.[16] It is for us to do the apostolic work of preparing them: first of all, with prayer, mortification and the works of mercy which always attract divine favour; then with friendship and understanding and the power of example.

Our Lord awaits us in the family, in the university, in the factory, in the most diverse associations, disposed to rechristianize the world once again: *Go into all the world and preach the gospel to the whole creation*, Our Lord continues saying to us. Ours is an age when Christ needs men and women who are able to stand beside the Cross,

---

[15] Second Vatican Council, *Gaudium et spes*, 19
[16] cf 1 Cor 3:6

strong, daring, simple, hard workers, without any human respect when it comes to doing good; men and women who are cheerful, who have as the foundation of their lives prayer – a relationship with Jesus that is full of friendship.

Our Lord counts on our resolutions to be better, to struggle more against our defects and against everything, no matter how small it might be, that separates us from Him. He counts on our doing an extensive apostolate among those people with whom we have more frequent dealings. We should consider today in our prayer whether there are around us; as happened with the first Christians, groups of people who are drawing closer to God through us. We should ask ourselves if our life is having an influence for good on the people with whom we have more frequent contact because of friendship, work, relationship, etc.

53.3 Supernatural optimism.

The Church is born from the Paschal Mystery of Christ, and is made present to the men of their times with an apparent smallness, like leaven, but with a divine power capable of transforming the world, making it more human and drawing it closer to its Creator. Many men of good will are responding today to the frequent calls of the Successor of Peter to give light to the many consciences immersed in darkness in countries where formerly Christ was loved.

Just as in the days of the early Christians, *what is truly important is to deal with souls one by one so as to draw them close to God.*[17] That is why we ourselves should also be very close to Our Lord, united to Him as the branch is to the vine.[18] Without personal holiness apostolate is impossible; the leaven becomes a useless lump. We will simply become absorbed by the pagan atmosphere that we

---

[17] Bl. A. del Portillo, *Letter*, 25 December 1985, 9
[18] cf John 15:5

often find surrounding people who perhaps were formerly good Christians.

The first reading of the Mass tells us that *when the rulers, elders and scribes saw the boldness of Peter and John, and perceived that they were uneducated, common men, they wondered; and they recognized that they had been with Jesus.*[19] The Apostles are seen to be sure of themselves, without any complexes, with the optimism that comes from being friends of Christ. That is a friendship that grows day by day, in prayer and in contact with Him.

The Christian will always be optimistic if he is united to Our Lord, *with a supernatural optimism that sinks its roots in the faith, that is nourished on hope and is given wings by love ...*

Faith: avoid defeatism and sterile lamenting about the religious situation of your countries, and get on with the job with effort and move ... many people.

Hope: 'God does not lose battles' (J. Escrivá, passim). If the obstacles are great, then divine grace is also more abundant. He will be the one to remove them, making use of each one of us as a lever.

Charity: work with great rectitude for love of God and souls. Have affection and patience with your neighbour, look for new ways of doing things, for new initiatives: love sharpens ingenuity. Make use of all possible approaches ... in this task of building up a more Christian and a more human society.[20]

Holy Mary, Queen of Apostles, will set us aflame with faith and hope and love for her Son so that we may contribute effectively, in and from our own environment, to the christianization of today's world, just as the Pope is asking us to do. The words of Our Lord, *Go therefore into*

---

[19] Acts 4:13
[20] Bl. A. del Portillo, *ibid*, 10

the whole world continue to echo in our ears. Then it was only Eleven who were involved; now we are much more numerous. Let us pray for the faith and the love that they had.

54. THE FAITH OF ST THOMAS

54.1 Jesus' appearance to the Apostles in the absence of Thomas. Apostolate with people who have known Christ but who do not keep up their relationship with Him.

The first day of the week,[1] the day on which Our Lord rose from the dead, the first day of the new world, is a day full of incident: from *very early*[2] in the morning when the women go to the tomb, until *very late*[3] at night, when Jesus comes to comfort his closest friends: *Peace be with you*, he says to them. *When he had said this, He showed them his hands and his side.* On that occasion, Thomas was not with the other Apostles: he was not able to see the Lord or to hear his consoling words.

This is the Apostle who had said on one occasion: *Let us go too and die with him.*[4] At the Last Supper he had expressed his ignorance to Our Lord in the simplest possible terms: *Lord we do not know where you are going; how can we know the way?*[5] Filled with the deepest joy, the Apostles would have looked for Thomas throughout Jerusalem on that very same night or the next day. As soon as they found him they would not be able to tell him quickly enough: *We have seen the Lord.* But Thomas, like all the others, had been deeply affected by what his own eyes had seen: he would never forget the Crucifixion and Death of the Master. He doesn't give the slightest credence to what the others have to tell him: *Unless I see in his*

---

[1] John 20:1
[2] Mark 16:2
[3] John 20:19
[4] John 11:16
[5] John 14:5

hands the print of the nails, and place my finger in the mark of the nails, and place my hand in his side, I will not believe.[6] Those who had been his companions during those three years and with whom he was united by so many bonds, would have repeated to him in a thousand different ways that same truth which was their joy and their certainty: *We have seen the Lord.*

Thomas thought the Lord was dead. The others assure him that He is alive, that they themselves have seen and heard him, that they have been with Him. That's what we have to do also; for many men and women Christ is, as it were, dead, because He hardly means a thing to them. He counts for almost nothing in their lives. Our faith in the risen Christ impels us to go to those people, to tell them in a thousand different ways that Christ is alive, that we unite ourselves to him by faith and love every day, that he guides and gives meaning to our lives.

In this way, fulfilling that obligation of faith to make the truth known with our example and our word, we contribute personally to the building up of the Church, like those first Christians who are mentioned in the Acts of the Apostles: *And more than ever believers were added to the Lord, multitudes both of men and women.*[7]

54.2 Our faith has to be operative: acts of faith, confidential relationship with Our Lord. Apostolate.

Eight days later, his disciples were again in the house, and Thomas was with them. The doors were shut, but Jesus came and stood among them, and said, Peace be with you. Then he said to Thomas, 'Put your finger here, and see my hands; and put your hand, and place it in my side; do not

---

[6] John 20:25
[7] Acts 5:14

be faithless, but believing. [8]

Thomas's reply is an act of faith, of adoration and of self-surrender without limits: *My Lord and my God.* These five words of his are inexhaustible in their significance. His faith springs not so much from the evidence of seeing Jesus as from an immense sorrow. It isn't so much the proof, as his love, that leads him to adoration and to renewing his apostolate. Tradition tells us that the Apostle Thomas died a martyr for his faith in Our Lord. He spent his life in His service.

These preliminary doubts of Thomas have served to confirm the faith of those who were to believe in Him later on. *What conclusion, dear brethren, do you come to?*, asks St Gregory the Great. *Surely it was not by chance that this chosen disciple was missing in the first place? Or that on his return he heard, that hearing he doubted, that doubting he touched, and that touching he believed? It was by divine dispensation and not by chance that things so fell out. God's mercy worked wonderfully, for when that doubting disciple touched his Master's wounded flesh he cured the wound of our disbelief ... So this doubting disciple, who actually touched, became a witness to the reality of the resurrection.* [9]

If our faith is firm, then that of many others will be supported by it. It is essential that our faith in Jesus Christ increases every day, that we learn to look upon happenings and persons as He looks on them, that our activity in the middle of the world be animated by Jesus' doctrine. But, at times, we too find ourselves lacking in faith like the Apostle Thomas. We have need of greater confidence in Our Lord in the face of difficulties in the apostolate, of events that we don't know how to interpret from the

---

[8] John 20:26-27
[9] St Gregory the Great, *Homilies on the Gospels*, 26,7

supernatural point of view, in times of darkness that God permits so that we may grow in other virtues.

The virtue of faith is one that gives us the true dimension of events and permits us to form a correct judgement about everything. *Only by the light of faith and by meditation on the word of God can one always and everywhere recognize God in whom 'we live and move and have our being' (Acts 17:28), seek His will in every event, see Christ in everyone whether he be a relative or a stranger, and make correct judgements about the true meaning and value of temporal things both in themselves and in their relation to man's final goal.*[10]

Let us meditate on the Gospel of today's Mass. *Let us take another look at the Master. You too may find yourself now hearing his gentle reproach to Thomas: 'Let me have your finger; see, here are my hands. Let me have your hand; put it into my side. Cease your doubting, and believe' (John 20:27); and, with the Apostle, a sincere cry of contrition will rise from your soul: 'My Lord and my God' (John 20:28). I acknowledge you once and for all as the Master. From now on, with your help, I shall always treasure your teachings and I shall try to follow them loyally.*[11]

My Lord and my God! These words have served as an aspiration for many Christians, and as an act of faith in the Real Presence of Jesus Christ in the Blessed Sacrament, when passing in front of a tabernacle or at the Consecration of the Mass. They can also help us to deepen our faith and our love for the risen Christ, really present in the Sacred Host.

---

[10] Second Vatican Council, *Apostolicam actuositatem*, 4
[11] St J. Escrivá, *Friends of God*, 145

54.3 The Resurrection constitutes a call to us to show with our lives that Christ is alive. The need for formation.

The Lord replied to Thomas: *Have you believed because you have seen me? Blessed are those who have not seen and yet believe.*[12] *This expression makes special reference to us,* says St Gregory the Great, *for we have not seen him in the flesh but know him in the mind. So, if we put our faith to the proof by good works, we are blessed. He who gives expression to his faith is a genuine believer.*[13]

The Resurrection of Our Lord is a call to us to show with our lives that he lives. The deeds of a Christian should be the fruit and the manifestation of his love for Christ. In the early centuries the spread of Christianity was brought about mainly by the personal testimony of Christian converts. It was a straightforward preaching of the Good News: person to person, family to family, among people with the same kind of job, between neighbours; within a given area of a city or town, in the market place, in the streets. Today, too, Our Lord wishes that the world, the street, the workplace and the family be channels for the transmission of the faith.

In order to be able to profess our faith by word, it is necessary to know its content clearly and with precision. That is why throughout the centuries our Mother the Church has given such importance to studying the Catechism, in which, in a brief and simple way, the essentials of what we have to know are contained, so as to be able to live it afterwards. St Augustine was already reminding the catechumens who were about to receive Baptism: *So, then, on Saturday next, on which we shall*

---

[12] John 20:29
[13] St Gregory the Great, *ibid*, 26,9

celebrate the Vigil, God willing, you will have to render not the Prayer (the Our Father), but the 'Symbolum' (the Creed); because if you do not learn it now, afterwards you will not be hearing it every day in the Church from the people. And, in learning it well, say it every day so as not to forget it: when getting up from bed, when you are going to sleep, pronounce your 'Symbolum'; pronounce it to God, striving to learn it by heart, and don't be lazy about repeating it. It is a good thing to repeat so as not to forget. Don't say: 'I have already said it yesterday, I am saying it today and I say it every day: I have it well engraved in my memory.' Let it be for you as a reminder of your faith and a mirror in which you see yourself reflected. Look at yourself, then, in it; check to see if you continue believing all the truths that you say in words that you believe, and rejoice daily in your faith. Let them be your riches; let them be as an apparel for the adornment of your soul.[14] What a number of Christians there are who would need to have these same words said to them because they have forgotten the essentials of their faith ...*

Christ also asks that we confess him with deeds before our fellow men. Therefore we should consider: should we not be more valiant on this or that particular occasion? Should we not have a greater spirit of sacrifice when it comes to getting some of our tasks completed? We should think too about our work, about the environment that surrounds us: are we known to be people who live a life of faith? Do we lack daring in apostolate? Do we have a deep knowledge of the essential elements of our faith?

Let us finish our prayer by asking Our Lady, Seat of Wisdom, Queen of Apostles, to help us to show with our behaviour and our words that Christ is alive.

---

[14] St Augustine, *Sermon 58*,15

SECOND WEEK OF EASTER – MONDAY

55. THE IMAGINATION

55.1 Interior mortification needed for supernatural life.

The Gospel of today's Mass[1] tells us of the intimate dialogue that took place one night between Jesus and Nicodemus. This man is moved by the preaching and the miracles of the Master and feels the need to know more. He shows great respect towards Jesus: Rabbi, Master, he calls Him.

Nicodemus asks Jesus about His mission, perhaps still uncertain whether He is just another prophet, or if He is the Messiah: *Rabbi*, he says to him, *we know that you are a teacher come from God; for no one can do these signs that you do, unless God is with him.* And Jesus replies in quite an unexpected way: Nicodemus asks about his mission and Jesus reveals to him an astonishing truth: *a man must be born again.* He is speaking of a spiritual birth by water and the Holy Spirit: a whole new world is unfolding before the eyes of Nicodemus.

Jesus' words also open up an unlimited horizon for the spiritual advancement of any Christian who allows himself to be led with docility by the inspirations and motions of the Holy Spirit, because interior life does not consist solely in acquiring a series of natural virtues or observing certain pious practices. It is a question of a complete transformation – of, in fact, *being born again*, which Our Lord asks from us: *you must rid yourselves of the old self according to which you lived your past life,*[2] St Paul said to the faithful of Ephesus.

---

[1] John 3:1-8
[2] Eph 4:22

This interior transformation is, above all, a work of grace in the soul, but it requires our collaboration also by way of mortification of the intellect, of memory and of imagination, so as to purify our potencies in order for the life of Christ to develop freely within us. Many Christians don't make any progress in their dealings with God in prayer because they neglect interior mortification, without which exterior mortification loses its foundation.

The imagination is undoubtedly a very useful faculty, because the soul, which is united to the body, cannot think without the help of images. Our Lord spoke to the people by means of parables, expressing the most profound truths by means of images, and we have seen how he follows this same procedure with Nicodemus. In the same way the imagination can be a great help in the interior life, for contemplating the life of Our Lord or the mysteries of the Rosary. *But for it to be beneficial and useful, the imagination has to be directed by right reason illuminated by faith. Otherwise it could become what has been called 'the lunatic of the house'; it takes us away from the consideration of divine things and draws us towards those that are vain, frivolous, fantastic and even prohibited. Even in the best of cases it can lead us to day-dreaming, from whence arises sentimentalism, which is so opposed to true piety.*[3]

Given our condition after original sin, the subjection of the imagination to reason can usually be achieved only through mortification, *with the result that it ceases to be the lunatic of the house and confines itself to its own specific purpose, which is that of serving the intelligence enlightened by faith.*[4]

---

[3] R. Garrigou-Lagrange, *The Three Ages of the Interior Life*
[4] ibid

55.2 Mortification of the imagination.

Allowing our imagination to roam freely means in the first place wasting time which is a gift from God and part of the inheritance left to us by Our Lord. *Get rid of those useless thoughts which, at best, are but a waste of time,*[5] is the advice of the author of *The Way*. Besides, the imagination which is lost thus in fantastic and sterile dreams is a fertile field in which a great number of voluntary temptations are sure to appear to convert our useless thoughts into a real occasion of sin.[6]

When this interior mortification is lacking, the dreams of the imagination are often centered upon our own talents, on how well we performed a particular action, on the admiration – unreal too, perhaps – which we provoked in certain people or in our own environment ... And so what started out as a useless thought evolves into a loss of that rectitude of intention which up to then had been intact. Then pride, which is always at the ready, takes shape from something that appeared at first to be totally innocent, and if it is not stopped in time it destroys anything good it finds. In particular, it destroys a large part of that attention which is due to others, preventing us from noticing their needs and practising charity. *The proud person's horizon is terribly limited: it stops at himself. He can see no further than himself, his qualities, his virtues, his talent. His is a godless horizon. Even other people have no place on this cramped horizon: there is no room for them.*[7]

At other times the imagination entertains itself by judging other people's way of acting, and often makes judgements that are negative and lacking in objectivity, because when one does not look upon others with

---

[5] St J. Escrivá, *The Way*, 13
[6] St J. Escrivá, *Furrow*, 135
[7] S. Canals, *Jesus as friend*

understanding and with the desire of helping them, one takes an unjustly partial view of them. When one examines somebody without the charity of understanding, one judges his behaviour coldly without taking into account the motives he may have had for acting in that way, or one gratuitously attributes something bad or something less good to another's action without any foundation for doing so. Only God can penetrate hidden things, and read the heart's truth and give their true value to all circumstances. Through a blameworthy superficiality these useless thoughts lead to rash judgement, which springs from a heart with little rectitude and no presence of God. Interior mortification in regard to these useless thoughts would have avoided this interior lack of charity which separates a person from God and from others. *The reason for so many rash judgements is that they are considered to be of little importance; nevertheless, if it is a question of grave matter, they can lead to the committing of grave sins.*[8]

It often happens, if we are not alert in cutting off useless thoughts and offering this mortification to Our Lord, that our imagination will rotate around ourselves, creating fictitious situations that are little or in no way compatible with the Christian vocation of a son of God who should have his heart set on him. These thoughts cool the heart; they separate from God and afterwards make it difficult to maintain the right climate of dialogue with Our Lord in the midst of our affairs.

Let us examine ourselves today in our prayer as to how we are getting on with this interior mortification which helps so much to keep the presence of Our Lord in our lives and which avoids so many inappropriate things, temptations and sins. It is worth our while to meditate seriously on this, in a deep fashion and with the desire to

---

[8] St Jean Vianney, (The Curé d'Ars), *Sermon on rash judgement*

make effective resolutions.

55.3 Making good use of our imagination in our prayer.

Mortification of the imagination brings with it countless benefits for the soul. It's not just a matter of a purely negative task, nor does it lie on the frontiers of sin but in the area of presence of God and of Love. In the first place, it purifies the soul and disposes it towards living presence of God better; it causes us to make good use of the time dedicated to prayer, because it is the imagination and its fancies that often inhibit dialogue with Our Lord, and which distract us when we should be more attentive – for example, in Holy Mass and Communion. Mortification of the imagination permits us to make better use of our time at work, to do it conscientiously and sanctify it. In the area of charity it facilitates our being attentive to others instead of being wrapped up in ourselves and immersed in dreams.

The imagination that is purified by means of constant mortification, in which useless thoughts are promptly rejected, has an important role to play in the interior life, in our dealings with God: it helps us meditate on the scenes of the Gospel, accompanying Jesus in his years at Nazareth with Joseph and Mary, in his public life with the Apostles. In particular, it is of great help when contemplating the Passion of Our Lord and the mysteries of the Rosary.

Make it a habit to mingle frequently with the characters who appear in the New Testament. Capture the flavour of those moving scenes where the Master performs works that are both divine and human, and tells us, with human and divine touches, the wonderful story of his pardon for us and his enduring Love for his children. Those foretastes of Heaven are renewed today, for the Gospel is always true.[9]

---

[9] St J. Escrivá, *Friends of God*, 216

If at times you don't feel strong enough to follow in the footsteps of Jesus Christ, say a few loving words to those who knew him well during his life on earth. To Mary, first of all, for she it was who brought him to us. Then to the Apostles. "And there were certain Gentiles who approached Philip, the man from Bethsaida in Galilee, and made a request of him: 'Sir', they said, 'we desire to see Jesus'. Philip came and told Andrew, and together Andrew and Philip went and told Jesus (John 12:20-22)." Don't you find this scene encouraging? Those foreigners didn't dare to approach the Master directly, so they looked for a good intercessor ...

My advice is that, in your prayer, you actually take part in the different scenes of the Gospel, as one more among the people present. First of all, imagine the scene or mystery you have chosen to help you recollect your thoughts and meditate. Next apply your mind, concentrating on the particular aspect of the Master's life you are considering – his merciful Heart, his humility, his purity, the way he fulfills his Father's Will. Tell him then what happens to you in these matters, how things are with you, what is going on in your soul. Be attentive, because he may want to point something out to you, and you will experience suggestions deep in your soul, realising certain things and feeling his gentle reprimands.[10]

And so we shall imitate Our Lady, who kept all these things – the events of the life of Our Lord – and pondered them in her heart.[11]

---

[10] *idem*, 252-253
[11] Luke 2:19

SECOND WEEK OF EASTER – TUESDAY

56. THE FIRST CHRISTIANS. UNITY

56.1 Unity among Christians is a gift of God. Pray for it.

The company of those who believed were of one heart and soul.[1] These words of the Acts of the Apostles are like a summary of the deep unity and fraternal love of the first Christians, which attracted so much attention from their fellow citizens. *The disciples bore testimony to the Resurrection not only with their words but also with their virtues.*[2] What stands out among them is the attitude – born of charity – of seeking harmony always.

The unity of the Church from its very beginnings is an express wish of Christ. He speaks to us of one sole Pastor,[3] and he highlights the unity of the Kingdom which cannot be divided,[4] of the building that has one single foundation.[5] This unity was always founded on the profession of one sole faith, on the observance of a single form of worship and on submission to a sole hierarchical authority, constituted by Jesus Christ himself. *There is only one Church of Jesus Christ*, St John Paul II taught in his catechesis in Spain, *which is like a big tree into which we are all grafted. It's a matter of a deep vital unity which is a gift from God. It is not merely, nor above all, an external unity; it is a mystery and a gift ...*

This unity then is shown around him who in each diocese has been constituted as Shepherd, the Bishop. In the universal Church it is shown around the Pope, the

---

[1] *First Reading of the Mass*, Acts 4:32
[2] St John Chrysostom, *Homilies on the Acts of the Apostles*, 11
[3] cf John 10:16
[4] cf Matt 12:25
[5] cf Matt 16:18

Successor of Peter.[6]

The unity of faith was, among the first Christians, the support of their fortitude and of the inner life which flowed over into the exterior. The same Christian life has been lived since then by very different peoples, each with their own specific individual, social, racial and linguistic characteristics. There, wherever there were Christians, *they shared, experienced and transmitted one single doctrine with the same soul and the same heart and identical voice.*[7]

The first Christians defended this unity of theirs to the point of facing persecution and even martyrdom. The Church has always encouraged her children to watch over their precious unity and pray for it. Our Lord prayed for it at the last Supper for the whole Church: *that they all may be one; even as thou, Father, art in me, and I in thee, that they also may be one in us.*[8]

Unity is a very great benefit that we should implore every day because *every kingdom divided against itself cannot last and every city or house divided against itself cannot stand.*[9] And St John Chrysostom comments: *a house or city once divided is destroyed quickly; and it is the same with regard to the Kingdom, which is the strongest entity that there is, since it is the union of their subjects that gives strength to kingdoms and houses.*[10] So there should be unity with the Pope, unity with the Bishops, unity with our brothers in the Faith – and with all men to attract them to faith in Christ.

56.2 What destroys fraternal unity.

The one, says St Thomas, *is not opposed to the*

---

[6] St John Paul II, *Homily*, Madrid, 3 November 1982
[7] St Irenaeus, *Adversus Haereses*, 1,10,2
[8] John 17:21
[9] Matt 12:25
[10] St John Chrysostom, *Homilies on St Matthew*, 48

*multitude, but to division; and neither does the multitude
exclude unity: what it excludes is the division of each thing
into its components.*[11] What divides is whatever separates
from Christ: any sin, for example, although this separation
is more perceptible in those faults of charity which isolate
one from others, and the faults in obedience towards the
Shepherds whom Christ has established to rule the Church.
The variety of characters, races, customs, or ways of being
is not opposed to unity. It is for this reason that the Church
can be Catholic, universal and one and the same in all
times and places. It is *this interior unity*, Saint Paul VI
said, *which endows her with the surprising capacity of
uniting men of the greatest diversity, respecting or, even
more, giving a new value to their specific characteristics,
providing they are positive, that is, truly human; which
endows her with the capacity of being catholic, of being
universal.*[12]

The Apostles and their successors had to bear the pains
provoked by those who spread errors and divisions. *They
speak of peace and they make war,* regretted St Irenaeus;
*they swallow the camel while they strain out the fly. The
reforms they preach can never remedy the ills of disunity.*[13]

The first Christians were convinced that if their faith
enjoyed good health, they had nothing to fear.[14] We should
pray a lot for unity for the whole Church: that we all may
be one, that we may be faithful to the faith we have
received, that we may obey promptly all the commands
and indications of the Roman Pontiff and of the Bishops in
communion with him.

Unity is closely linked to personal ascetic struggle to

---

[11] St Thomas, *Summa Theologiae*, I, q30, a3
[12] St Paul VI, *Address*, 30 March 1965
[13] St Irenaeus, *Adversus Haereses*, 4,33,7
[14] Tertullian, *De praescriptione haereticorum*,

be better, to be more united to Christ. *There is very little we can do in our work for the whole Church ... if we have not attained this close intimacy with Our Lord Jesus: if we are not really with him and like him sanctified in the truth; if we do not preserve his word in us trying to discover its hidden riches every day.*[15]

The unity of the Church, whose vital principle is the Holy Spirit, has as its central point the Blessed Eucharist, which is *the sign of unity and the bond of love.*[16] Removing discord and praying for unity *is never more appropriately achieved than when the Body of Christ, which is the Church, offers the very body and blood of Christ in the Sacrament of bread and wine.*[17]

56.3 Charity unites, pride separates. The fraternity of the first Christians. Avoid anything that could harm unity.

St Paul calls frequently for unity: to the Christians of Ephesus he writes: *I beg you to lead a life worthy of the vocation to which you have been called, with all lowliness and meekness, with patience, with forbearing for one another in love, eager to maintain the unity of the Spirit in the bond of peace.*

He continues, referring to an ancient acclamation, possibly used in the early Liturgy during baptismal ceremonies, which highlights the unity of the Church as the fruit of the oneness of the divine essence and of the action of the Three Persons of the Blessed Trinity, who act in the Church and are the cause of its unity:[18] *There is one body and one Spirit, just as you were called to the one hope that belongs to your call, one Lord, one faith, one baptism, one*

---

[15] St John Paul II, *Message for Church Unity Octave*, 23 January 1981
[16] St Augustine, *Commentary on St John*, 26
[17] *Divine Office, Second reading*, St Fulgentius
[18] cf *The Navarre Bible*, Captivity Epistles

God and Father of us all, who is above all and through all and in all.[19]

St Paul lists different virtues: humility, gentleness, longanimity, various manifestations of charity, which is the bond of unity in the Church. *The temple of the King is not ruined, or cracked or divided: the cement of the living stones is charity.*[20] Charity unites, pride separates.

The first Christians showed their love for the Church through a charity which overcame all barriers, whether social, economic, racial or cultural. Whoever possessed material goods shared them with those who had none,[21] and they all prayed for one another and encouraged each other to persevere in the faith of Christ. One of the earliest Apologists, in the second century, described the behaviour of the first Christians as follows: *they love one another, they do not despise widows and they rescue orphans from those who treat them with violence; and he who has, gives unbegrudgingly to him who has not.*[22]

However, the greatest charity was directed towards fortifying the brethren in the faith. The *Acts of the Martyrs* recount in almost every page specific details of this concern for the fidelity of the others. Truly *it was Love that enabled them to make their way through that corrupt pagan world.*[23] It was love for the brethren in the faith and love for the pagans. We also will bring our world to God if we can imitate the first Christians in our understanding and affection for everybody, even if at times our concern for and attention to others meet with no response. And we shall strengthen in the faith any who are growing weak, with our example and our word and our dealings that are

---

[19] Eph 4:1-6
[20] St Augustine, *Commentary on Psalm 44*
[21] cf Acts 4:32 ff
[22] Aristides, *Apology*, XV, 5-7
[23] St J. Escrivá, *Friends of God*, 172

always friendly and open. *A brother helped by a brother is like a strong city.*[24]

Out of love for the Church, let us use all possible means so as not to damage, not even remotely, the unity of Christians: *you should always avoid complaining, criticising, gossiping ... avoid absolutely anything that could bring discord among brothers.*[25] On the contrary, we should always foster everything that is an occasion for mutual understanding and concord. If on some occasion we are not able to praise, we should say nothing.[26] In the words of the Liturgy: *May we overcome today all envy and dissension.*[27]

In order to learn how to safeguard the unity of the Church let us have recourse to our Mother Mary. *May she, the Mother of love and unity, bind us closely, in order that, like the first community born from the Cenacle, we may be 'one heart and one soul.' May she, the 'Mother of Unity', in whose womb the Son of God was united with humanity, inaugurating mystically the nuptial union of the Lord with all men, help us to be 'one' and to become instruments of unity, among Christians and among all men.*[28]

---

[24] Prov 18:19
[25] St J. Escrivá, *Furrow*, 918
[26] *idem*, *The Way*, 443
[27] *Divine Office, Morning Prayer, intercessions*
[28] St John Paul II, *Homily*, 24 March 1980

SECOND WEEK OF EASTER – WEDNESDAY

57. LOVE WITH DEEDS

57.1 Our Lord loved us first. Love is repaid with love. Holiness in the ordinary duties of every day.

God so loved the world that he gave his only son, that whoever believes in him should not perish but have eternal life.[1]

With these words of the Gospel of the Mass we are shown how the Passion and Death of Jesus Christ is the supreme manifestation of God's love for men. He took the initiative in love, surrendering for us him whom He loves most, in whom He is well pleased[2] – his own Son. Our faith *is a revelation of his goodness, of the mercy, of the love of God for us. God is love (cf 1 John 4:16), that is to say, love which is diffusive and is lavish: and everything is summarised in this great truth which explains everything and illuminates everything. It is necessary to see the history of Christ in this light. 'He loved me', writes St Paul and each one of us can and should repeat the same to himself: 'He loved me and sacrificed Himself for me' (Gal 2:20).*[3]

The love of God for us reaches its climax in the Sacrifice of Calvary. God held back Abraham's arm when he was on the point of sacrificing his only son, but He did not hold back the arm of any of those who were nailing His Only-Begotten Son to the Cross. Therefore St Paul exclaims, filled with hope: *He who did not spare his own Son ... will he not give us all things with him?*[4]

---

[1] John 3:15
[2] cf Matt 3:17
[3] St Paul VI, *Homily on the Feast of Corpus Christi*, 13 June 1975
[4] Rom 8:32

The self-giving of Christ constitutes a pressing call for correspondence with that love: love is repaid with love. Man was created in the image and likeness of God.[5] *And God is Love.*[6] Therefore the heart of man is made for love and the more he loves the more he becomes identified with God; only when he loves can he become happy. And God wishes us to be happy, here on earth too. Man cannot live without love.

Personal holiness is not centred in the fight against sin but in love for Christ, who shows Himself to us as being truly human, fully aware of everything about us. The love of God for men and of men for God is a love of mutual friendship. And one of the specific characteristics of friendship is relationship. In order to love Our Lord it is necessary to know Him, to speak to Him. We get to know Him by meditating on His life in the Holy Gospels. In them He shows Himself to us as being endearingly human and very close to our life. We meet Him in prayer and in the Sacraments, especially in the Blessed Eucharist.

Meditation on the Most Sacred Humanity of Our Lord – especially when we read the Gospel and when we consider the Mysteries of the Rosary – constantly nourishes our love of God and constitutes a living teaching as to how we have to sanctify our day. In his hidden life, Jesus wished to descend to the most common things of human existence, to the daily life of a manual worker who supports a family. And so we see him during almost the whole of His life working day after day, caring for his tools in the small workshop, dealing simply and in a friendly way with the neighbours who came to ask Him to make a table for them or a rafter for a new house, caring for his Mother with great affection. That is how He fulfilled the

---

[5] cf Gen 1:27
[6] 1 John 4:8

will of his Father God during those thirty years. When we look at his life, we learn to sanctify our own work, our family, our friendships. Everything that is truly human can be holy, can be a channel for our love of God, because Our Lord on assuming our human nature, sanctified it.

57.2 Genuine love. The Will of God.

Knowing that God loves us with an infinite love is the good news that gives joy and meaning to our lives, and it is the marvellous announcement that the risen Christ sends us to announce to all men. We too can say that *we know and believe the love that God has for us.*[7] And faced with this love we feel ourselves incapable of expressing that which our hearts can't manage to feel either: *To know that you love me so much, my God, and yet ... I haven't lost my mind.*[8]

All that Our Lord has done and is doing for us is an outpouring of his attention and of his grace: his Incarnation, his passion and death on the Cross which we have been contemplating in recent days, the constant pardoning of our sins, his continuous presence in our tabernacles, the help He sends us every day. Considering all He has done and does for men, our correspondence with such love should never seem sufficient to us.

The greatest proof of this correspondence is fidelity, loyalty, the unconditional adherence to the Will of God. In this regard Jesus teaches us by showing his infinite desire to do the Will of his Father, telling us that his food is to do the Will of him who sent him.[9] *I have kept my Father's commandments*, he says, *and abide in his love.*[10]

---

[7] 1 John 4:16
[8] St J. Escrivá, *The Way*, 425
[9] cf John 15:10
[10] John 15:10

The will of God for us is found principally in the faithful fulfilment of the commandments and the other teachings proposed to us by the Church. It is there that we find what God wishes for us. And in their fulfilment, done with human nobility and with awareness of the constant presence of God, we find God's love, and holiness. Love for God does not consist in sensible feelings, although these too may be given to us by Our Lord so as to help us to be more generous. It consists essentially in the full identification of our will with that of God. That is why we should ask ourselves frequently: Am I doing what I ought to be doing at this moment?[11] Do I offer my activity to God on starting it and during its accomplishment? Do I rectify my intention when vanity and the thought of 'what people will say' tend to intervene? Do I try to do my work with human perfection? Am I a constant source of joy for those who live or work with me? Does my daily presence among them draw them closer to God?

Love is repaid with love, but it must be genuine love, which is seen in specific ways in the fulfilment of our duties towards God and towards others, even when our feelings do not incline us in this direction, and it may be for us an uphill struggle. *The highest perfection consists not in interior favours or in great raptures*, wrote St Teresa, *but in the bringing of our wills so closely into conformity with the Will of God that, as soon as we realize that he wills anything, we desire it ourselves with all our might.*[12]

Love should continue to survive even when there is total dryness, if Our Lord should permit this to happen. In general, it is on occasions like this that our relationship with Our Lord is purified and strengthened.

---

[11] cf St J. Escrivá, *The Way*, 772
[12] St Teresa, *Book of the Foundations*, 5,10

57.3 Love and sentiment. Abandonment to God. Fulfilment of our duties.

In the service of God, a Christian should be guided by faith and in this way overcome the ups and downs of moods. *To guide myself by mere sentiment would be like putting a servant in charge of the household and causing the master to relinquish his position. Sentiment is not what is bad, but the importance that is given to it ... In certain souls the emotions constitute all their piety, to such an extent that they are convinced that they have lost it whenever the feeling goes away ... If only these souls could understand that this is precisely the moment in which to begin to have it.*[13]

Love that is true, whether the senses have a part in it or not, includes all aspects of our existence, in a true unity of life; it leads us *to insert God into everything, which otherwise would be insipid without him. A pious person whose piety is not superficial strives to fulfil his duty: sincere devotion leads to work, to the willing fulfilment of the duties of each day – even when this is hard; there is an intimate union between this interior supernatural reality and the external manifestations of human activity. Professional work, human relationships of friendship and companionship, striving – shoulder to shoulder with our fellow citizens – to achieve the wellbeing and progress of society, are the natural fruits, a logical consequence, of this sap of Christ which is the life of our soul.*[14] False piety does not make any impact on the ordinary life of a Christian. It does not become transformed into improved behaviour or into helping others.

The fulfilment of the will of God in the duties – generally small – of every day is the most sure guide for

---

[13] J. Tissot, *The Interior Life*
[14] St J. Escrivá, *In memoriam*, EUNSA, Pamplona

the Christian who has to find holiness in the midst of earthly realities. There are very different ways in which these duties may be carried out: with resignation, like somebody who has no alternative but to do them; accepting them, which involves a deeper and more thoughtful commitment; agreeably, wanting what God wants because, even though it may not be seen at this moment, the Christian knows that God is our Father and that He wants the best for His children; or even better, with complete abandonment, embracing the Will of God at all times, without laying down any limits whatever. This last is what Our Lord asks from us: to love him without any conditions, without waiting for more favourable situations, in the ordinary things of every day and, if he should so permit, in more difficult and extraordinary circumstances. *As soon as you truly abandon yourself in the Lord, you will know how to be content with whatever happens. You will not lose your peace if your undertakings do not turn out the way you hoped, even if you have put everything into them, and used all the means necessary. For they will have turned out the way God wants them to.*[15]

With the words of a prayer that the Church suggests to us for use after Mass, let us say to Our Lord: *Volo quidquid vis, volo quia vis, volo quomodo vis, volo quamdiu vis: I want whatever you want, I want because you want, I want as you want, I want as long as you want.*[16]

Our Blessed Lady who pronounced and put into practice that *be it done unto me according to thy word,*[17] will help us to fulfil the Will of God in everything.

---

[15] St J. Escrivá, *Furrow*, 860
[16] *Roman Missal, Prayer of Pope Clement XI*
[17] Luke 1:38

58. DOING GOOD AND RESISTING EVIL

58.1 The Apostles' resistance to obeying unjust commands. Firmness in faith.

In spite of a severe prohibition from the High Priest and from the Sanhedrin that they should not preach again or *teach at all in the name of Jesus,*[1] the Apostles preached every day more freely and with more determination the doctrine of the faith. And there were many who were converted and who were baptized. Then, as we are told in the First Reading of the Mass, *they set them before the council. And the high priest questioned them saying, 'We strictly charged you not to teach in this name, yet here you have filled Jerusalem with your teaching'. Peter and the Apostles answered, 'We must obey God rather than men.*[2] And they continued to announce the Good News.

The Apostles' resistance to obeying the commands of the Sanhedrin was not a matter of pride or lack of knowledge of the social duties towards lawful authority. They resisted them because the council wished to impose on them a command which was against the law of God. They reminded their judges courageously and simply that obedience to God comes first. They were fully convinced *that for those who fear God there is no danger but only for those who don't fear Him,*[3] and that it is worse to commit an injustice than to suffer it.

The Apostles showed by their behaviour their firmness of faith, how deeply they had absorbed the Master's

---

[1] cf Acts 4:18
[2] Acts 5:27-29
[3] St John Chrysostom, *Homilies on the Acts of the Apostles*, 13

teaching after having received the Holy Spirit, and the weight they attached to God's honour.[4]

The fortitude and conviction of the first Christians is what Our Lord is also asking from his followers today, when, in certain environments, there breathes a climate of indifference or even direct attack, more or less veiled, on true human and Christian values. A well-formed conscience will lead a Christian to be as law-abiding as the best of his fellow citizens, at the same time as he is ready to take a stand against anything contrary to the natural law. The State is not juridically omnipotent; it is not the source of good and of evil.

It is an obligation for Catholics who are present in political institutions to exercise a critical role within their respective institutions so that their programmes and activities correspond every day more to the aspirations and criteria of Christian morality. In some cases it could even be obligatory to object in conscience to activities or decisions that go directly contrary to some precept of Christian morality.[5]

The effective protection of fundamental individual rights, the right to life from the very first moment of conception, the protection of marriage and the family, equality of opportunities in education and in work, freedom of education and of speech, religious freedom, personal security, contribution to world peace, all form part of the common good for which Christians should be prepared to fight.[6]

Passivity in the face of such important affairs would really be a lamentable error and omission – at times grave – of the duty to contribute to the common good. They would form part of *the sins of omission* for which – as well

---

[4] cf *The Navarre Bible*, Acts of the Apostles
[5] Spanish Episcopal Conference, *Witnesses to the living God*, 28 June 1985
[6] *ibid*, *Catholics in public life*, 22 April 1986

as those of thought, word and deed – we ask Our Lord for pardon every day at the start of the Mass. *Many things, whether they be material, technical, economic, social, political or cultural, when left to themselves, or left in the hands of those who lack the light of the faith, become formidable obstacles to the supernatural life. They form a sort of 'closed shop' which is hostile to the Church.*

You as a Christian and perhaps as a research worker, writer, scientist, politician, or labourer, have the duty to sanctify those things. Remember that the whole universe – as the Apostle says – is groaning as in the pangs of labour, awaiting the liberation of the children of God.[7]

58.2 All earthly existence has to be directed to God. Unity of life. The power of example.

All around us there is a constant movement, an ebbing and flowing of currents of opinion, of doctrines, of ideologies, of very distinct interpretations of man and of life. And this happens not just in books for specialists, but through fashionable novels, illustrated magazines, newspapers and television programmes, all of them accessible to old and young. In the midst of all this doctrinal confusion there is need for a norm of discernment, a clear, steady and profound criterion which allows us to see everything with the unity and consistency of the Christian view of life which knows that everything derives from God and is ordained to God.

The Faith provides us with a stable criterion of guidance and the firmness of the Apostles in putting it into practice. It gives us a clear vision of the world, of the value of things and of people, of true and false goods. Without God and without knowledge of the ultimate end of man the world ceases to be intelligible or is seen only from a partial

---

[7] St J. Escrivá, *Furrow*, 311

and deformed angle. Precisely *the most perniciously typical aspect of the modern era consists in the absurd attempt to reconstruct a solid and fruitful temporal order divorced from God, the only foundation on which it can endure.*[8]

The Christian should not leave his faith aside in any circumstance. *Non-sectarianism. Neutrality. Old myths that always try to seem new.*

Have you ever stopped to think how absurd it is to leave one's Catholicism aside on entering a university, a professional association, a cultural society, or Parliament, like a man leaving his hat at the door?[9] This attitude is equivalent to saying – in politics, in business, in leisure or in entertainment, when I am with my friends, when it comes to choosing a school for my children – that here in this situation God has nothing whatever to do with it; in these affairs my Christian faith must not exert any influence, for none of this comes from God or is ordained to God.

Nevertheless, the faith casts light on the whole of existence. Everything is ordained to God. But this ordination must respect the particular nature of each thing. It is not a matter of turning the world into one big sacristy, or homes into convents, or the economy into a benevolent institution. Without naive simplifications, the faith should inform a Christian's thought and action, because he should never in any circumstance, in any moment of the day, cease to be a Christian and to behave and think as such.

Therefore *Christians will exercise their respective professions moved by the spirit of the Gospel. He is not a good Christian who subjects his way of acting professionally to the sole desire of earning money or of*

---

[8] St John XXIII, Encyclical, *Mater et Magistra*, 15 May 1961, 217
[9] St J. Escrivá, *The Way*, 353

obtaining power as the supreme and definitive value.
Christian professionals should be, in any area of life
whatever, an example of industriousness, competence,
honesty, responsibility and generosity.[10]

58.3 The faith cannot be left aside when it comes to evaluating earthly realities. Resisting evil.

A Christian should not set aside the light of the faith
when trying to evaluate a political or social programme or
a work of art or of culture, nor will he consider just a single
aspect of it – economic, political, technical or artistic – in
order to reach the conclusion that it is good. If in a
particular political or social event, or work of art or
whatever, its proper ordination to God – as shown by the
demands of the divine law – is not preserved, then the
overall evaluation cannot but be negative, in spite of its
having certain merits in some limited way.

One cannot praise a political action or social
regulation or work of art when it becomes transformed into
an instrument for evil. It is a question of strict morality and
therefore of common sense. Who would praise an insult to
his own mother just because it was composed in verse
which had perfect rhythm? Who would broadcast it and
praise it for its perfections even with the advertence that
these were only 'formal'? It is clear that the technical
perfection of the means does nothing but aggravate the evil
of the thing which is in itself disordered and which
otherwise would perhaps pass unnoticed or be less virulent.

Faced with *abominable crimes*, as the Second Vatican
Council described those of abortion, the rightly-formed
Christian conscience requires that one should in no way
take part in them, should vigorously discourage them,
prevent them if possible and, besides, participate actively

---

[10] Spanish Episcopal Conference, *Witnesses to the living God*

in efforts to avoid or correct this moral abuse of the legal system. In regard to these very grave matters and others of a similar kind which are directly opposed to morality, nobody can think that there is nothing he can do. Whatever little each person is able to do, he should do it, especially should he be in public life. *By exercising our vote we entrust certain institutions and specific people with the management of public affairs. On this collective decision very important aspects of social, family and personal life depend, not only in the economic and material order but also in the moral order.*[11] It lies in the hands of everybody, of each individual, provided he acts with supernatural outlook and with common sense, to make this world, which God has given us to live in, into a more human place and a means of sanctification. If we strive to fulfil our social duties, whether we live in a big city or in a little out-of-the-way village, with an important job in society or a lowly one, even though we may think our contribution is tiny, we shall be faithful to Our Lord. And the same applies if it should happen that one day the Lord were to ask us for a more heroic action: *He who is faithful in a very little is faithful also in much.*[12]

---

[11] *ibid, Catholics in public life*
[12] Luke 16:10

59. HUMAN MEANS AND SUPERNATURAL MEANS

59.1 Do whatever we can even if it is little. Our Lord gives the increase.

We read in the Gospel of the Mass that Jesus retired to a solitary place with his disciples, *to the other side of the Sea of Galilee, which is the Sea of Tiberias.*[1] But, as we know from the Gospel accounts, the multitudes followed him as soon as they realized it. Our Lord welcomed these people who were seeking him: *Jesus spoke to the crowds of the Kingdom of God, and cured those who had need of healing.*[2] Jesus is compassionate towards suffering and towards ignorance.

Now the day began to wear away.[3] Our Lord had spent a long time unveiling the mysteries of the Kingdom of Heaven and giving peace and consolation. The Apostles, concerned by the lateness of the hour and by the fact that the place was very remote, felt the need to draw the Master's attention: *Send the crowd away, to go into the villages and country round about to lodge and get provisions; for we are here in a lonely place.*[4]

The Lord surprises them with his question: *How are we to buy bread so that these people may eat?* He makes them see their lack of financial means: *Philip answered him, 'Two hundred denarii would not buy enough bread*

---

[1] John 6:1-15
[2] Luke 9:11
[3] Luke 9:12
[4] *ibid*

for each of them to get a little. [5] But the Apostles do what they can: they find five loaves and two fish. They have no other means, and there were five thousand men – too many for what was available.

Sometimes Jesus makes us, too, see that the problems are too great for us, that there is little or nothing we can do about the situation that confronts us. He asks us not to pay too much attention to the material resources, because they may only cause us to be pessimistic, and that instead, we should place more reliance on the supernatural means. He asks us to be supernaturally realistic; that is to say, to count on him and his power.

Our Lord wants us to avoid thinking that the solution lies in human effort alone; and He also wants us to avoid passivity, which under the pretext of total abandonment in the hands of God, converts hope into a disguised spiritual laziness.

Jesus makes use of whatever is available: a few loaves and a few fish; it was all the Apostles could collect. He added the rest. But He did not wish to do without the human means, even though they were few. That is how Our Lord acts in our lives: He does not wish us to remain without doing anything if the instruments which we have at our disposal are insufficient or even scarce. Jesus asks us for faith, obedience, daring and always to do whatever we can; not to omit using any human means that is available to us and at the same time to count on him, conscious that our possibilities will always be very small. *The farmer too, as he proceeds to turn over the furrows of his field with the plough, or scatter seed, suffers cold, bears the discomfort of rain, looks at the sky and sees it overcast and, nevertheless, continues sowing. The only thing he fears is that he may be held up by consideration of the woes of this present life and the time will go by, leaving him with*

---

[5] John 6:5-7

nothing to harvest. Don't put it off till later; do your sowing now.[6] And this even if it seems that the field will not yield any fruit. Don't wait until we have all the human means, don't wait till all the difficulties disappear. On the supernatural plane there is always fruit: Our Lord sees to that; He blesses our efforts and He multiplies them.

59.2 Supernatural optimism: count on Our Lord and his power.

When Jesus sends his disciples on their first apostolic mission He says to them: *Take no gold, nor silver, nor copper in your belts, no bag for your journey, nor two tunics, nor sandals, nor a staff; for the labourer deserves his food.*[7] He urges them to set off without delay to fulfil their work. And so that from the beginning they may learn to put their trust in supernatural means, He takes away all human help from them.

The Apostles set out in this way – with nothing – so that it can be seen that the cures, the conversions, the miracles which they perform are not their own; that their human resources and qualities are not enough to ensure that people will be prepared to accept the Kingdom of God. They shouldn't be concerned about the lack of material goods, or of extraordinary human gifts; God will provide as much as may be needed of whatever is missing.

This holy daring repeats itself again and again in all apostolate. What great things have been achieved when even the most indispensable human means were lacking! That's how the saints worked! They knew very well that *Christ, sent by the Father, is the source and origin of the whole apostolate of the Church.*[8] Once a Christian is

---

[6] St Augustine, *Commentary on Psalm 125,5*, PL 36, 164
[7] Matt 10:9-10
[8] Second Vatican Council, *Apostolicam actuositatem*, 4

convinced about what God wants, he should delay just long enough to survey the means available. *In your apostolic undertakings you are right — it's your duty — to consider what means the world can offer you (2 + 2 = 4), but don't forget — ever! — that, fortunately, your calculations must include another term: God + 2 + 2 …*[9]

We can draw the same lesson from the first reading of today's Mass which includes the words of Gamaliel, who was St Paul's teacher, to the Sanhedrin, advising them as to what they should do with the Apostles. After having recalled some examples of purely human initiatives — the risings of Theudas and Judas the Galilean — which collapsed with the deaths of their leaders, he adds, *So in the present case I tell you, keep away from these men and let them alone; for if this plan or this undertaking is of men it will fail; but if it is of God, you will not be able to overthrow them. You might even be found opposing God!*[10] Our security and optimism as we work for God are founded on the fact that He does not abandon us: *Si Deus pro nobis, quis contra nos — if God is with us who can be against us?*[11]

To count on God always in the first place is a good sign of humility. The Apostles learned this lesson well and they put it into practice in their evangelizing work after the Resurrection. *What then is Apollo? What is Paul? Servants through whom you believed, as the Lord assigned to each. I planted, Apollo watered, but God gave the growth,*[12] St Paul will say.

Nevertheless, Our Lord will also ask us to employ all the human means available to us, as if the whole success of the undertaking were to depend on them alone.

---

[9] St J. Escrivá, *The Way*, 471
[10] Acts 5:38-39
[11] Rom 8:31
[12] 1 Cor 3:5-6

59.3 Apostolic fruits depend on the combination of human means and supernatural means. We are God's instruments for doing things that surpass our own capacities.

In the first sending of the Apostles our Lord expressly told them: *You are not to carry purse or wallet.* They were to understand in that first apostolic venture that it is Jesus who gives effectiveness: the cures, the conversions, the miracles would be due not to their own human qualities but to their Master's divine power.

Before the final journey to Jerusalem Jesus completed the lesson of that first apostolic journey. He asked them: *When I sent you out with no purse or bag or sandals, did you lack anything? They said, 'Nothing'. He said to them, 'But now let him who has a purse take it, and likewise a bag. And let him who has no sword sell his mantle and buy one.'*[13] Although the supernatural means come first in all apostolate, Our Lord still wants us to use all the human possibilities we can. Grace does not replace nature and we cannot ask Our Lord for extraordinary assistance or help when, through the ordinary channels, God has placed the necessary instruments in our hands. *A person who would not try to do everything in his power, and who expected divine help for everything, would be tempting God,*[14] and the grace of God would cease to act.

Hence the importance of cultivating the human virtues, which support the supernatural ones and are a necessary means to fulfil our ambition of bringing others closer to God. How can we present the Christian life in an attractive way if we are not cheerful, hardworking, sincere, good friends? *There are some people who, when they speak about God or the apostolate, seem to feel the need to*

---

[13] Luke 22:35-36
[14] St Thomas, *Summa Theologiae*, II-II, q53, a4 ad 1

apologise. Perhaps it is because they hav _____
the value of human virtues, but, on the _____
been greatly deformed spiritually, and ar _____

In doing apostolate we have to use _____ which in themselves are good, because God mad the service of man: *For all things are yours,* St Paul ten us, *whether the world, or life or death or the present or the future.*[16] At the same time, we have to keep in mind that we are pursuing an objective which surpasses these means infinitely: that is, to bring men to Christ, to be converted and begin a new life.

That is why we will not wait to have all the means (perhaps we will never have them), or neglect to do certain works or to begin others. *Begin by making the best use of what you have.*[17] The Lord will bless us, especially when He sees our faith, our confidence in him and our interest and effort in trying to have all the necessary means available. God, if He wanted to, could do without these means, but He counts, nevertheless, on our will to put them at his service.

Do you see? With him you could do it. Why are you surprised? Be convinced: there is nothing to be surprised about. If you trust in God – really trust – things work out easily. And, what is more, you always go further than you imagined you could.[18]

---

[15] St J. Escrivá, *Furrow*, 37
[16] 1 Cor 3:22
[17] cf St J. Escrivá, *The Way*, 488
[18] St J. Escrivá, *Furrow*, 123

60. THE CHURCH WILL LAST TILL THE END OF TIME

60.1 Indefectibility of the Church in spite of persecutions, heresies and infidelities.

Immediately after the multiplication of the loaves and fishes, when the multitude had already had their fill, Jesus himself sent them away and ordered the disciples to set off in the boats. The evening was already far advanced.

The Gospel of the Mass[1] tells us that the Apostles were heading towards the other shore, towards Capharnaum. It grew dark and Jesus was not with them. From St Matthew's Gospel we know that He also took leave of them and went up into the hills to pray.[2] The sea had become rough because of the strong wind that was blowing,[3] and the boat was being strongly buffeted by the waves because the wind was against them.[4]

Tradition has seen this boat as an image of the Church[5] in the midst of the world, tossed about in the course of the centuries by the waves of persecution, of heresies and of infidelities. *That wind*, comments St Thomas Aquinas, *is a figure of the temptations and the persecutions that the Church is to suffer because of lack of love. Because, as St Augustine says, when love grows cold the waves get bigger ... However, the wind and storm and waves and darkness will not cause the ship to be diverted from its course and*

---

[1] cf John 6:16-21
[2] cf Matt 14:23
[3] cf John 6:18
[4] cf Matt 14:24
[5] cf Tertullian, *De Baptismo*, 12

be destroyed.[6] From the very beginning contradictions had to be dealt with, coming from inside and from outside. Our Mother the Church suffers these attacks now in our own times also, and her children with her. *This is nothing new. Since Jesus Christ Our Lord founded the holy Church, this mother of ours has suffered constant persecutions. In times past the attacks were delivered openly. But today, as yesterday, the Church continues to be buffeted from many sides ...*

When we hear heretical voices about us ..., when we see that the sanctity of marriage and the priesthood are attacked without fear of rebuke. We see people deny the Immaculate Conception and the perpetual Virginity of our Mother holy Mary, along with all the other privileges and gifts with which God adorned her. We see the perpetual miracle of the Real Presence of Jesus Christ in the Holy Eucharist, the primacy of Peter and even the Resurrection of Our Lord put in doubt. How can anyone not feel tempted to sadness? But have confidence, for the Holy Church is incorruptible.[7]

The attacks on the Church make us suffer, but at the same time the knowledge that Christ is in the boat fills us with an immense sense of security and a great peace. He lives forever in the Church and therefore the gates of Hell will not prevail against her;[8] she will last till the end of time. Everything else, everything human, passes away; but the Church remains always, just as Our Lord willed her to do. Christ is present in her and the boat will not sink even though it is rocked too and fro. This divine assistance is the foundation of our unshakeable faith: the Church in the face

---

[6] St Thomas, *Commentary on St John, in loc.*

[7] St J. Escrivá, *Homily, The Supernatural Aim of the Church,* 28 May 1972

[8] Matt 16:18

of all human uncertainties will remain ever faithful to Christ in the midst of all the storms, and it will be the universal sacrament of salvation. Her history is a permanent moral miracle in which we can always strengthen our faith.

Already in St Augustine's time the pagans were saying: *The Church is going to perish; the Christians are already finished.* To which the Saint replied: *Nevertheless, I can see you dying every day and the Church continues to remain standing, announcing the power of God to the succeeding generations.*[9]

What little faith we have if doubts begin to creep in because the storm has become stronger against her, against her institutions or against the Pope and the Bishops. Let us not be over-impressed by adverse circumstances, because if we allowed this to happen, we would lose our serenity, our peace, and our supernatural vision. Christ is always very close to us and asks us for confidence. He is beside each one of us, and we should fear nothing. We have to pray more for the Church, be more faithful to our own vocation, do more apostolate among our friends and make more reparation.

60.2 Attacks on the Church lead us to love her more and to make acts of reparation.

The indefectibility of the Church means that she is imperishable. That is to say, she will last till the end of the world; and likewise it means that she will not undergo any substantial change in her doctrine, in her constitution or in her worship.

The First Vatican Council says the Church possesses *an invincible stability,* and that *founded on a rock she will subsist firmly until the end of time.*[10]

---

[9] Quoted by G. Chevrot, *Simon Peter*
[10] *Dz* 1824

The reason for the permanence of the Church lies in her intimate union with Christ, who is her Head and Lord. After going up to Heaven He sent the Holy Spirit to his own to teach them all truth,[11] and when He charged them to preach the Gospel to all nations He assured them that He would be with them all days even to the consummation of the world.[12]

The Church demonstrates her fortitude when she resists immovably all the assaults of persecutions and heresies. *The Lord himself looks after her, enlightening and fortifying her rulers so that they may faithfully and fruitfully discharge their functions; and (especially in circumstances of greater difficulty) raising up in the bosom of Mother Church men and women of outstanding sanctity to give example to other Christians and so promote the increase of his mystical Body. Moreover Christ looks down from heaven always with singular love upon his immaculate Bride as she labours in this earthly exile, and when He sees her in peril He saves her from the waves of the tempest, either himself directly, or through his angels, or through her whom we invoke as Help of Christians, and through other heavenly protectors; and having calmed the sea, he consoles her with that peace 'which surpasses all knowledge' (Phil 4:7).[13]* The Faith bears testimony to the fact that this firmness in her constitution and her doctrine will last forever until He comes.[14]

In certain surroundings, especially in the intellectual sphere, one sees and feels a sort of conspiracy of 'cliques', not infrequently aided and abetted by Catholics. With cynical perseverance they maintain and spread slanders to

---

[11] 1 Cor 10:17
[12] cf Matt 28:20
[13] Pius XII, *Mystici Corporis*, 29 June 1943
[14] cf 1 Cor 11

*cast a shadow over the Church, or over certain individuals
and organisations within it. All this is done in the face of
all truth or reason.*

*Pray each day with faith: 'ut inimicos Sanctae
Ecclesiae' – enemies, because that is what they proclaim
themselves to be – 'humiliare digneris, te rogamos audi
nos!' Confound, Lord, those who persecute you, with the
charity of your light, which we are ready to spread.*[15]

The attacks on the Church, the bad example, the
scandals, will lead us to love her more, to pray for those
who are doing the damage and to make reparation. Let us
remain firm always in communion with her, faithful to her
teaching, united to her sacraments and docile to the
guidance of the Hierarchy.

**60.3 Our own lives are not free either from moments of
darkness, of suffering or of trial. Assurance in Our
Lord's protection. Our Lady's help.**

When the Apostles had rowed about three miles, Jesus
came to them unexpectedly, walking on the water, to
strengthen their weak faith and to give them heart in the
midst of the tempest. He drew near to them and said: *It is I;
do not be afraid. Then they were glad to take him into the
boat, and immediately the boat was at the land to which
they were going.*[16]

In our own life, perhaps there will be no shortage of
tempests and threatening skies, of interior darkness, of
misunderstandings – and, with more or less regular
frequency, situations in which we should correct our course
because we have gone astray. Then we should strive to see
Our Lord, who always comes in the storm of suffering. Let
us learn to accept the setbacks with faith, as blessings from

---

[15] St J. Escrivá, *Furrow*, 936
[16] John 6:20-21

heaven to purify us and draw us closer to God.

It is I; do not be afraid. Whoever recognizes the reassuring voice of Our Lord in the events that may sour our lives, of whatever kind they may be, immediately discovers the security of reaching dry land: *They were glad to take him into the boat, and immediately the boat was at the land to which they were going*, where Jesus wished them to go. It is enough to be in his company for us to feel secure always. Insecurity arises when our faith is weakened, when we don't have recourse to Our Lord because it seems that He doesn't hear us or doesn't care for us. He knows very well what is happening to us and He wants us to go to him to ask for help. He will never leave us in a tight spot. What confidence the words of Jesus contained in the Communion Antiphon for today should inspire in us: *Father, I desire that they also, whom thou hast given me, may be with me where I am.*[17]

It could seem on some occasions of greater or less duration that Christ is not there, as if He had abandoned us or did not hear our prayer. But He is never the one who abandons. *The Lord looks on those who revere him*, we read in the Responsorial Psalm, *to rescue their souls from death.*[18]

If we remain close to Our Lord in personal prayer and the Sacraments, we will be able to do everything. With Him the storms – interior and exterior – are converted into occasions for increasing our faith and hope and charity and fortitude. With the passage of time we may come to understand the meaning of these difficulties.

We will emerge from all the trials, temptations and tribulations through which we have to pass if we are close to Christ, more purified, with more humility, and with

---

[17] John 17:24
[18] Ps 32

more love of God. And we shall always be able to count on the help of Our Mother in Heaven. *You are not alone. Suffer that tribulation joyfully. It's true, poor child, that you don't feel your Mother's hand in yours. But ... have you never seen the mothers of this earth, with arms outstretched, following their little ones when, without anyone's help, they venture to take their first shaky steps? You are not alone: Mary is close beside you.*[19] She is there all the time, but especially when for whatever reason we are experiencing difficulties. Let us not cease to have recourse to her.

---

[19] St J. Escrivá, *The Way*, 900

THIRD SUNDAY OF EASTER

61. THE LORD'S DAY

61.1 Sunday is the Lord's Day.

On Sundays there is an assembly of all who live in towns or in the country ... This is the first day, on which God transformed darkness and matter and made the world; the day on which Jesus Christ our Saviour rose from the dead.[1] The Jewish Sabbath gave way to the Christian Sunday from the very beginning of the Church, and from then on, every Sunday we celebrate the Lord's Resurrection.

Saturday was the day dedicated to Yahweh in the Old Testament. God himself instituted it[2] and commanded the Israelites to abstain from certain tasks on that day in order to honour him properly.[3] It was also the day on which the family got together to celebrate the end of the captivity in Egypt. As time passed, the rabbis complicated the divine precept, so that by the time of Jesus there had come into being a series of oppressive and meticulous prescriptions that bore no relation to what God had laid down about the Sabbath.

The Pharisees clashed frequently with Jesus on these points. In spite of this, Our Lord did not look down on the Sabbath, did not suppress it as a day dedicated to Yahweh; on the contrary, it would seem to have been his favourite day. On that day he went to the synagogues to preach, and many of his miracles were performed on the Sabbath.

Sacred Scripture everywhere presents a lofty and noble

---

[1] *Divine Office, Second reading*, St Justin, *First Apology*, 67
[2] Gen 2:3
[3] Ex 20:8-11, 21:13; Deut 5:14

idea of the Sabbath. It was the day established by God so
that his people might devote to him public cult, and the
complete dedication of the day to this purpose appears as a
grave obligation.[4] The importance of this command is also
deduced from its repetition in Scripture. Sometimes the
prophets point out as a cause of God's punishments the fact
that people have not kept the Sabbath.

The Sabbath rest was a strictly religious event, which
is why it always culminated in the offering of a sacrifice.[5]

The feastdays of Israel, and particularly the Sabbath,
were a sign of the Divine Covenant and the people's way
of expressing their joy at being God's property and the
object of his election and his love. That is why every
feastday was linked to a salvation event.

Yet these feastdays contained only the promise of a
reality which still had to take place. With the Resurrection
of Our Lord the Sabbath gives way to the reality which it
had foreshadowed, the Christian celebration. Our Lord
himself speaks of the kingdom of God as a great banquet
offered by a king on the occasion of the wedding of his
son,[6] through whom we are invited to share in the
messianic benefits.[7] With Christ there arises a new and
superior cult, because now we have also a new priest, and a
new victim is offered.

61.2 Feast days and holydays of obligation. Their purpose. The Mass, centre of Catholic festivities.

After the Resurrection, the first day of the week was
commemorated by the Apostles as the Lord's day,
dominica dies,[8] the day on which He had won victory over

---

[4] cf Ex 31:14-15
[5] cf Num 28:9-10
[6] cf Matt 22:2-13
[7] cf Is 25:6-8
[8] Apoc 1:10

sin and death for us through His Resurrection. For that reason the first Christians had their meetings on a Sunday. And that has been the constant and universal tradition up to the present day. *The Church, following an apostolic tradition which began with the Resurrection of Christ, celebrates the paschal mystery once a week, on the day which is fittingly called the 'day of the Lord' or Sunday.*[9]

This precept of sanctifying holy days regulates one of man's essential duties with regard to his Creator and Redeemer. We render cult to God on this day dedicated to him specially, through participation in the sacrifice of the Mass. There is no other celebration which could fill the meaning of this precept.

In addition to Sunday, the Church established holy days to commemorate the chief events of our salvation: Christmas, Easter, the Ascension, Pentecost and other feasts of our Lord, and the feasts of Our Lady. Alongside these, from earliest times the Church has celebrated the *dies natalis* or anniversary of the martyrdom of the first Christians. These Christian holidays eventually became the basis of the civil calendar. In her calendar, the Church *commemorates the mysteries of Redemption, opens the riches of the sanctifying power and merits of our Lord in such a way that in a certain sense these become present at every moment, so that the faithful can put themselves in contact with them and become filled with the grace of salvation.*[10]

The centre and origin of the joyfulness of Christian feasts is to be found in the presence of Our Lord in his Church. He is the pledge and anticipation of definitive union in the celebration which will have no end.[11] From it

---

[9] Second Vatican Council, *Sacrosanctum concilium*, 106
[10] *ibid*, 102
[11] cf Apoc 21:1ff; 2 Cor 1:22

there springs the joy that characterizes our Sunday celebration: this rejoicing is seen in today's prayer over the offerings: *Lord, receive these gifts from your Church. May the great joy you give us come to perfection in heaven.* That is why a holy day is not merely a remembrance of past events, an historical anniversary: rather is it a sign which shows Christ and makes him present amongst us.

The Mass makes Jesus present in his Church: it is a sacrifice of infinite value offered to God the Father in the Holy Spirit. All other human, cultural and social values of holy days have to take second place to this: they cannot be allowed at any moment to obscure or substitute for what is fundamental. Alongside the Mass, other expressions of liturgical and popular piety such as Benediction, processions, chants, special care in dress, etc. are particularly important.

We must try through example and apostolate to make Sunday into *the Lord's day, a day of adoration and glorification of God, of the Holy Sacrifice, of prayer, of rest, of recollection, of cheerful meetings in the family.*[12]

61.3 Public worship. Sunday rest.

Let the earth cry out to God with joy; praise the glory of his name; proclaim his glorious praise, we read in the Entrance Antiphon.[13]

The precept of sanctifying holy days responds also to the need to give public cult to God. We cannot be satisfied on such occasions with merely private cult. Some people try to relegate dealing with God to the realm of conscience, as if it did not necessarily have to have external expression. However, man has the right and the duty of giving public and external cult to God. It would be gravely harmful if

---

[12] Pius XII, *Address*, 7 September 1947
[13] Ps 65:1-2

Christians were obliged to hide away in order to practise their faith and worship God, which is their primary right and duty.

Sundays and Church holy days are, above all, days set aside for God, days particularly well suited to looking for Him and finding Him. *'Quaerite Dominum.' We can never cease to look for him: however, there are moments which demand doing so with more intensity, because during those periods Our Lord is particularly close, and so it is easier to find and meet him. This nearness constitutes Our Lord's answer to the Church's invocation, which is expressed continuously by means of the liturgy. Even more so, it is the liturgy which precisely actualises the nearness of the Lord.*[14]

Holydays of obligation are of great importance in helping Christians to receive the action of grace more fully. During these days the believer is asked to interrupt his work in order to dedicate himself the better to Our Lord. But there is no festivity without celebration, since a holiday does not consist simply in refraining from working. Neither can there be a Christian feastday without the faithful coming together to give thanks, to praise the Lord, to remember his deeds. And so it would be very unchristian to plan to spend the weekend or a 'holiday' of obligation in such a way as to make impossible or very difficult one's dealings with God. It happens to certain lukewarm Catholics that they end up thinking they have insufficient time to hear Mass, or they rush through it as if freeing themselves from a burdensome obligation.

Rest is not only an opportunity to recuperate energies, but is also the sign and the anticipation of the definitive repose of that celebration which is heaven. That is why the Church wishes to celebrate her feastdays by including in

---

[14] St John Paul II, *Homily*, 20 March 1980

them a rest from work. On the other hand, Catholics, like anyone else, have a right to that rest, a right which the State must guarantee and protect.

This holy day rest must not be interpreted as a simple doing nothing, a mere passing of the time, but rather as a positive involvement in something which enriches the personality in different ways. There are many ways of resting, and it is important not to take the easiest way out, which often is not the one that rests us most in any case. If we know how to limit the use of television on feast days as well, for example, we will not be repeating so much the false excuse of not having time. On the contrary, we will see that during those days we can spend more time with our family, look after the education of our children, develop social relationships and friendships, make a visit or two to people in need, or to those who are alone or sick. Perhaps this will be our chance to have a longer conversation with a friend. Or it may be the moment that a mother or father needs to speak with one of their children on their own, and listen to them. In general terms one must know how to have *one's whole day taken up with a flexible schedule in which, besides the daily norms of piety, an important place should be given to rest, which we all need, to family get-togethers, to reading, and to time set aside for an artistic or literary hobby or any other worthwhile pastime. We live poverty by filling the hours of the day usefully, doing everything as well as we can, and living little details of order, punctuality and good humour.*[15]

---

[15] *Conversations with Monsignor Escrivá,* 111

62. CHRISTIAN NATURALNESS

62.1 Being coherent Christians in all the situations of life.

The trial of Stephen unleashed a great persecution against the Church. In today's reading, the story of his apostolate and his martyrdom is told.[1] *Stephen was filled with grace and power and began to work miracles and great signs among the people.* The same means, almost the same words, as were used against Jesus were used against him. *We have heard him say that Jesus the Nazarene is going to destroy this place and alter the traditions that Moses handed down to us.*

Stephen proclaimed bravely his belief in the risen Jesus. And even if Our Lord does not ask us for our lives as he asked Stephen, he is an example to us of a coherent Christian life, lived naturally and openly, undeterred by false scandals or by what people might say. We have to expect that at times people will judge us in a twisted manner because they fail to understand the nature of a Christian way of acting or many of the loving demands of Christ's doctrine. We would then have to imitate Our Lord and his faithful followers, even if it meant giving our life for him – acting with serenity, leading a Christian life with all its consequences. Doubtless it would be more comfortable to adapt ourselves to these pagan situations and lifestyles, but if we did we could not continue to be faithful disciples of Jesus. Such situations, in which we need firmness of character and fortitude in the faith can arise anywhere – in the university, at work, or in the place

---

[1] cf Acts 6:8-15

where we go on holiday with the family.

In their public activities Catholics should be inspired by the criteria and Gospel objectives lived and interpreted by the Church. Legitimate diversity of opinion in temporal matters should not detract from the necessary agreement of Catholics in defending and promoting values and projects of life derived from the morality of the Gospel.[2] Catholics must reject any fear of causing upset if, on account of living as faithful disciples of our Lord, their behaviour is adversely interpreted or clearly rejected. One who would hide his Christian personality in the midst of an environment of pagan customs would be giving in to human respect, and would do well to remember to hear those words of Jesus: *He who denies me before men, I will also deny him before my Father who is in heaven.*[3]

Do you know what is the first temptation the devil presents to someone who has begun to serve God better? asks the Curé d'Ars – *It is human respect.*[4] What is our behaviour like when we are with our friends, at work, at a social gathering? Do we show our condition as sons and daughters of God with simplicity and daring?

62.2 Apostolate in difficult environments.

Sometimes it seems to go down well to speak without warmth of the real truths of life, or else not to speak about them at all. And there is a tendency to describe as a fanatic someone who speaks enthusiastically about a noble cause – such as the right to life from conception, freedom in education – or else there is a tendency to brand a person with certain adjectives if he or she has deep convictions about the meaning of life and tries to put them into practice.

---

[2] Spanish Episcopal Conference, *Witnesses to the living God*, 28 June 1985
[3] Matt 10:32
[4] St Jean Vianney, (The Curé d'Ars), *Homily on Temptations*

Without being intemperate, which would be alien to the lovable example that Jesus left us, we should try to live our lives, with the help of grace, in a way that is replete with profound and firm Christian conviction. We are well aware, for example, that indifference in the face of God's marvels is a great evil, the consequence of lukewarmness or of a dead or sleeping faith, no matter how much people try to disguise their indifference as *objectivity*.

In Baptism we receive the grace which saves and which gives meaning to our earthly pilgrimage. With such a great good to hand, a Christian is naturally cheerful and optimistic, and seeks to communicate his happiness to those around him with an unceasing apostolate.

Jesus always did good. *I ask you*, he once said to some Scribes and Pharisees who were spying on him, *is it right to do good or evil?* after which he cured the man with the withered hand. We must do good everywhere, communicate in every environment the joy of knowing Christ. We feel the need to win souls for Truth, for Love, for Christ. *This is called, in a correct use of terminology, 'proselytism'. Word-manipulation intervenes at this point. The word 'proselytism' has been tarred by some people with the notion of furthering selfish interests, with the use of dishonourable means to fascinate, to coerce or trap those to whom it is directed. Such an attitude must be condemned. But what must be condemned is sectarian proselytism, which is mercenary, which makes use of other people's ignorance, of their material poverty, of their emotional loneliness.*

But does that mean that we Christians have therefore to renounce apostolic fruitfulness, the communicative fraternity of genuine proselytism?[5]

Our certainty of the truths of our faith – only a person

---

[5] C. Lopez Pardo, in *Palabra Magazine*, 245

with convictions is capable of convincing others – and the love of Christ lead us to communicate in a fruitful manner what we ourselves have found: this is true proselytism. And we must carry it out everywhere.

62.3 Rectitude of intention.

The place where we look for holiness is in our work, in our relationships with the people who share the same tasks with us, in our social contacts, and in our families.

When we come across obstacles, lack of understanding or unjust criticism, we will ask Our Lord for his grace to keep us calm, and, normally, we will not stop doing apostolate. Our Lord did not always find well-intentioned people when he was spreading the Good News. This never stopped him from talking about the marvels of the kingdom of God. The Apostles, at the beginning of the Church, and the first Christians also, found themselves in situations and environments which, at least at first, completely rejected the doctrine of salvation they had in their hearts, but they still managed to convert the ancient world. *Why are you so apathetic? If you come across a group at work who are a bit difficult, you lose interest in them. Perhaps they have become difficult because you have neglected them. Yet you throw in the towel and think of them as a dead weight which holds back your apostolic ideals because they do not understand you ... You may love and serve them with your prayer and mortification, but how do you expect them to listen to you if you never speak to them?*[6]

On the other hand there is no such thing as an unchangeable or definitive situation. The passage of time always shows in a true light the person who works and deals honourably with everyone, with a right intention and without seeking personal interest.

---

[6] St J. Escrivá, *Furrow*, 954

Only those of unsteady character with a superficial formation, and without clear criteria to guide them, allow themselves to be influenced by what people say. Often this attitude, which even humanly speaking is unattractive, is backed up by the desire to avoid having a hard time, or the fear of putting one's job in danger, for example, or the desire not to be different from others in any way.

We read in the Responsorial Psalm: *Even though princes sit plotting against me, thy servant will meditate on thy statutes. Thy testimonies are my delight, they are my counsellors.*[7]

In order to get over worrying about what people will say, we need to have a right intention, being more concerned about God's opinion than anyone else's. We also need strength to ignore small criticisms in a cheerful and imperturbable manner, and be ready to communicate the treasure which each disciple of the Lord has found. We need, too, to give good example, which is simply living coherently with the grace our Lord has placed in our hearts. It is one thing we will never regret. Even in the most difficult environments we can win souls for Christ if we really want to make those friends, colleagues and acquaintances of ours happy. *Before wanting to make saints out of all those people we love, we must make them happy and joyful, for nothing better prepares a soul for grace than joy.*

You already know that when you have in your hands the hearts of those whom you wish to make better, if you are able to attract them through the meekness of Christ you have already gone halfway on your apostolic road. When they love you and trust you, when they are content, the field is ready for the sowing. For their hearts are open like fertile ground, ready to receive the white grain of your

---

[7] Ps 118:23-24

word as an apostle or educator.

If you know how to speak without wounding, although you may have to correct or reprimand, hearts will not close themselves to you. The seed will fall on truly fertile ground and the harvest will be plentiful. If things were otherwise your words would find, not an open heart, but a brick wall; your seed would not fall on fertile ground but 'on the side of the road' of indifference or distrust; or 'on the rocky ground' of a soul that is ill-disposed; or 'among the thorns' of a wounded and resentful heart.

We must never lose sight of the fact that our Lord has promised his effectiveness to friendly faces, to cordiality, good manners, and clear, persuasive words which direct and form without wounding. We should never forget that we are men relating to other men, even when what we want is to do good to souls. We are not angels. And therefore our appearance, our smile, our manners, are factors which condition the effectiveness of our apostolate.[8]

In the Blessed Virgin we find, as the Apostles found, the necessary strength to speak about God without worrying about what people might say. *The Master, before ascending to the right hand of the Father, told the disciples: 'Go and preach to all the nations', and they had remained full of peace. But they still had doubts: they did not know what to do, and they gathered around Mary, Queen of Apostles, so as to become zealous preachers of the Truth which will save the world.*[9]

---

[8] S. Canals, *Jesus as friend*
[9] St J. Escrivá, *Furrow*, 232

63. RECTITUDE OF INTENTION

63.1 Purity of intention and presence of God. Acting with our minds on God.

The life of the first Christians and their witness to the world make known to us their quality and their character. Their norm of conduct was not to take the easy way out, or opt for the more comfortable line, or the more popular decision, but rather did they seek to fulfil completely the will of God. *They ignored the danger of death ... they forgot how few they were, they never noticed how many were against them, or the power or strength or wisdom of their enemies. Their power was greater than all of that: theirs was the power of him who had died on the Cross and risen again.*[1] They had their gaze riveted on Christ, who gave his life for all men. They were not seeking their own personal glory, nor the applause of their fellow citizens. They always acted with a right intention, because they had their eyes fixed on the Lord. That is what allows St Stephen to say at the moment of his martyrdom: *Lord do not take their sin into account*, as we read in to-day's Mass.[2]

Our intention is right when Christ is the end and motive of all our actions. *Purity of intention is no more than presence of God: God our Lord is present in all our intentions. How free our heart will be of every earthly obstacle, how clear our vision and how supernatural our way of doing things when Jesus Christ really reigns in our intimate world and presides over all our plans and purposes.*[3]

---

[1] St John Chrysostom, *Homilies on St Matthew*, 4
[2] Acts 7:59
[3] S. Canals, *Jesus as friend*

, the person who is always seeking the
plause of others can easily deform his own
rule of action then becomes *what people*
than the Will of God. Concern for the
can easily become fear of the environ-
ment. It is easy then to neutralise the apostolic activity of
Christians, *who have taken upon themselves the urgent task
to fulfil on earth*[4] the evangelization of the world.

Sometimes, in order not to appear out of step, one
easily begins not to be consistent with one's principles.
One falls into the temptation of leaning to the side from
which approving smiles and handshakes more readily
come, or at least in the direction of mediocrity. This is
what happened to the Pharisees. *Vanity and cowardice
were what led them away from God. That is what led them
to seek another theatre for their struggles, and is what lost
them: because once you begin to try pleasing your
spectators, the battles you fight are the ones they want to
see.*[5] On the contrary, those who truly seek Christ have to
accept that their conduct will be unpopular and often
criticised, particularly if they live in an environment that is
not very Christian.

The first thing we have to do with our actions is to
please Christ. *If I were still concerned about pleasing men,
I would not be a servant of Christ.*[6] And St Paul also
replies to some Corinthians who were criticising his
apostolate: *Not that it makes the slightest difference to me
whether you, or indeed any human tribunal, find me worthy
or not. I will not even pass judgement on myself ... The
Lord alone is my judge.*[7]

---

[4] Second Vatican Council, *Gaudium et spes*, 93
[5] St John Chrysostom, *o.c.*, 72
[6] Gal 1:10
[7] 1 Cor 4:3-4

Human judgements are often wrong. Only God can judge our actions and our intentions. *Among the surprises which await us on the day of judgement, not least will be the silence with which Our Lord will greet those actions of ours which merited the applause of men ... On the other hand it can happen that he will weigh in positive terms some actions which have drawn down criticism and censorship upon us. Our Judge is the Lord. It is He whom we have to please.*[8] We must ask ourselves many times each day: Am I doing what I should be doing now? Do I seek the glory of God, or am I trying to show off, to make sure people like me? If we are sincere on those occasions we will obtain light to rectify our intention if necessary, and direct it towards God.

63.2 Consciousness of praise, and learning to rectify. *For God all the glory.*

A wrong intention destroys the best of actions: the deed can be well done, it can even be beneficial, but, since it is corrupted at source, it loses all its value in the eyes of God. Vanity or self-seeking can destroy, sometimes completely, what could have been a deed meriting holiness. Without a right intention we go astray.

On some occasions, receiving some praise is a sign of friendship and can help us along the path of goodness. But we should direct this praise towards God in all simplicity; besides, it is one thing to receive a word of praise, a sign of being well received; another thing altogether is to look for praise. And we must always be careful and attentive when we are praised or commended, since *many times our poor soul goes off the right path, as soon as it is applauded ... thus it finds its delight more in being called happy than in actually being so. And that thing which should have been a*

---

[8] G. Chevrot, *In Secret*

reason for praising God becomes instead a cause of our separation from him.[9]

In the Gospel Our Lord points out the result of good deeds done without a right intention: *They have received their reward*, he says, referring to the Pharisees, who wanted to be praised and well thought of. They got what they wanted: a glance of approval, a gesture of admiration, some words of praise. And shortly there would be nothing left but dust, and nothing at all for eternal life. What a terrible failure to lose so much for so little. God accepts our actions, even small ones, if we offer them to him with a pure intention: *Do everything for the glory of God,*[10] St Paul advises us. The two small coins that the poor widow threw into the offering box of the Temple[11] became a great treasure in heaven.

Our Lord contemplates our lives and has his hand outstretched each day for what we can offer him: he accepts whatever we really do for him. We get our own sad recompense for the rest here below. *Purity of intention. The suggestions of pride and the impulses of the flesh are not difficult to recognize ... and you fight and, with grace, you conquer.*

But the motives that inspire you, even in the holiest actions, do not seem clear; and deep down inside you hear a voice which makes you see human reasons in such a subtle way that your soul is invaded by the disturbing thought that you don't act as you should – for pure Love, solely and exclusively to give God all the glory.

React at once each time and say: 'Lord, for myself I want nothing. All for your glory and for Love.[12]

---

[9] St Gregory the Great, *Moralia*, 10, 47-48
[10] 1 Cor 10:31
[11] Mark 12:42
[12] St J. Escrivá, *The Way*, 788

There we have a marvellous aspiration to say over and over again: *Lord, for myself I want nothing. All for your glory and for Love.* It will help us to practise detachment from many things and to rectify our intention on many an occasion.

63.3 Examining the motives for our actions. Omissions in the apostolate on account of the lack of a right intention.

In order to be people who act for the right intention, we must examine the motives of our actions. We must consider in the presence of God what it is that leads us to behave in one way or another. Why is it, for example, that we omit to carry out apostolate? Is it because we are afraid of what people will say? Or why do we adapt ourselves so easily to non-Christian surroundings? In the light of faith we will be able to identify the points of cowardice or vanity which are present in our behaviour.

Our Lord gives us a clear rule: *When you give alms, do not sound a trumpet before you.*[13] We shouldn't advertise our good actions; we must not stop to consider at length the things we have done well. *Your left hand must not know what your right hand is doing* – we must not stop to analyse our good acts while we are doing them – or afterwards. We should not omit what we are supposed to do either.

We have a first-class witness to our actions. Nothing we do goes unnoticed by our Father God. Nothing is a matter of indifference to him. That should already be sufficient recompense for us, a great motive to rectify our intention in our work and in our apostolate.

An impatient and disordered anxiousness to climb up the professional ladder can mask self-love under the appearances of 'serving souls'. It is a lie – and I really mean that – when we seek to justify our actions by sayir

---

[13] Matt 6:2-4

that we must not miss certain opportunities, certain favourable chances.

Turn your eyes back to Jesus; he is 'the Way'. During his hidden years there were also 'very favourable' chances to advance his public life – when he was twelve years old for instance, and the doctors of the law were in amazement at his questions and at the answers He gave. But Jesus Christ fulfilled the Will of his Father, and he waited. He obeyed.

Do not lose that holy ambition of yours to lead the whole world to God, but when certain possibilities present themselves (they might show, perhaps, a desire to desert ...) remember that you too have to be obedient and work away at that obscure job, which does not seem at all brilliant, for as long as God asks nothing else of you. He has his own times and paths.[14]

Our Lord asks us to be watchful, because if we are careless we will slip into the habit of looking for rewards here below, and we will avoid doing good out of cowardice, human respect, or fear of what other people will think of us. We must not be like the ship *which has made many voyages, escaped many storms, only to run aground on a rock in the very harbour, with all its treasures lost overboard. This is the case of the person who, after a considerable amount of work, does not reject the temptation of seeking praise, and is shipwrecked in the harbour itself.*[15]

We are freer when we do things for God alone. Thus, we are not dependent on what people will say, or on human gratitude, which is always a fragile thing anyway. Rectitude of intention helps us carry out a more fruitful ...stolate in any environment or circumstances; it points ... the path of interior freedom.

———————
...row, 701
...tom, *Homily on Evangelical perfection*

64. THE FRUITS OF DIFFICULTIES

64.1 The apostolic spirit of the first Christians in spite of persecution. The fruits of tribulation and difficulties.

After the martyrdom of St Stephen there arose a persecution against the Christians of Jerusalem which caused them to scatter throughout other areas of the Middle East.[1] Providence made use of that circumstance to carry the seed of the faith to other places which otherwise would have taken longer to get to know Christ. *Those who had been driven away spread the gospel as they went from place to place.*[2] *Notice how,* says St John Chrysostom, *the Christians even in the midst of misfortune kept up their preaching instead of neglecting it.*[3]

Our Lord always has more complete plans, and what seemed to some the end of the primitive Church in fact led to its strengthening and expansion. So those who persecuted the Church, whose objective was to stifle the recently-born seed of faith, were the indirect cause why so many more people, otherwise unreachable on account of their dwelling in faraway places, got to know the doctrine of Jesus Christ. The apostolic spirit of the Christians was expressed both during times of peace, which were the majority, and in times of calumny and persecution. They never ceased to announce the Good News which they had in their hearts, convinced as they were that the doctrine of Jesus Christ gives eternal salvation; besides, it is the only doctrine that can make this world a more just and humane place.

---

[1] Acts 8:1-8
[2] Acts 8:4
[3] St John Chrysostom, *Homilies on the Acts of the Apostles*, 18

These early Christians were fervent, firm, coherent in their faith, full of goodness, and always friendly and smiling with those around them. These features must have been, on innumerable occasions, the basis of that first impulse which led people to the faith.

The first Christians would doubtless remember – perhaps they had heard it from the lips of the Apostles themselves – what our Lord had repeated often and in different ways: *If the world hates you, know that it hated me first of all.*[4] They would be filled with optimism then, on considering that they would be given the grace to face their difficulties and tribulations, knowing that God arranges all things for the good of those who love him.[5]

The Apostles themselves, together with numerous converts, came up against resistance and opposition from the first moment. But they were not unduly worried about the environment, being primarily interested in the salvation of souls.

Encountering difficulties of one type or another should not occasion surprise. *Beloved, when God tests you with the fire of tribulation, do not be surprised as if something strange were happening,* St Peter says.[6] And St James the Apostle adds: *Consider yourselves happy indeed, my brethren, when you encounter trials of every sort.*[7] We can draw great good from them. These trials and difficulties can differ considerably. Some arise because of a materialist and anti-Christian environment which opposes Christ's reign in the world – calumnies, professional discrimination, anti-Catholic fanaticism. On other occasions Our Lord permits sickness, financial disaster, failures, absence of

---

[4] John 15:18
[5] cf Rom 8:28
[6] 1 Pet 4:12
[7] Jas 1:2

fruits in an apostolic enterprise after many efforts or lack
of understanding.

In any case, we should understand in the depths of our
hearts that God is very close to us. He helps us, with more
graces, to mature in virtue and to bear fruit in the
apostolate. On these occasions God wants to purify us like
gold in the furnace, cleansing our soul of its dross, leaving
it more refined and valuable.

64.2 Fortitude in difficult circumstances.

*And every day, both in the temple and from house to
house, their teaching and their preaching was continually
of Jesus Christ.*[8] In our own circumstances, when attitudes
become sectarian or draw people away from God, we must
feel a call from Our Lord to show with our words and with
the example of our lives that the Risen Christ is among us,
and that without him, man and this world will always be
disoriented and unhinged. The greater the darkness, the
greater the need for light. We must struggle against the
current, relying on a life of personal prayer, strengthened
by the presence of Jesus Christ in the Tabernacle. Our
interior struggle to reject bourgeois values has to be more
purposeful. One of the greatest fruits we must draw from
difficulties, whatever they are, is the need to be more
aware of Our Lord, to be more generous in prayer and
sacrifice.

Contradiction leads us to purify our intention, doing
things for God without seeking human rewards.

If, out of cowardice or lack of fortitude, or because of
not asking Our Lord for help, we were to give way in the
face of difficulties, our soul would then retrogress in terms
of unity with God. It would become full of sadness, and
indicate clearly a superficial interior life, one that has but

---

[8] Acts 5:42

little love of God. The devil usually makes good use of these occasions to intensify his attacks, and the soul then can either draw nearer to God, being united to the Cross, or draw away from him, falling into lukewarmness, lacking in love and in vitality. The same difficulty – sickness, calumny, a hostile environment – will have different effects according to the dispositions of the soul. We cannot forget that the supernatural objective we are seeking is an arduous good, a difficult one to attain, which demands a vigorous response on our part, full of fortitude. Fortitude is a cardinal or key virtue: it helps clear away obstacles and the fears which can hinder the will from following Our Lord resolutely.[9] God always gives the necessary graces at every moment and in all circumstances.

When we face contradictions in our environment we should be nonetheless serene and cheerful. It will be the same joy as the Apostles had, *because they had been worthy to suffer for the name of Jesus.*[10] St John Chrysostom points out: *it does not say that they did not suffer, but that the suffering caused them joy. We can see this in the account of the freedom which they immediately put to good use; immediately after being scourged they gave themselves up to preaching with admirable intensity.*[11] *They say this and that about you.. But what does your good name matter?*

In any case, don't feel ashamed or sorry for yourself, but for them: for those who ill-treat you.[12]

64.3 Unity with God through costly moments.

When we feel the weight of the Cross, our Lord invites

---

[9] cf St Thomas, *Summa Theologiae*, II-II, q122, a3

[10] Acts 5:41

[11] St John Chrysostom, *ibid* 14

[12] St J. Escrivá, *Furrow*, 241

us to go to him. *Come, not to give an account ... don* ̣
~~*afraid to hear talk of a yoke, because it is gentle;*~~ *don't ι*
afraid if I speak of burden, because it is light.[13] And then,
by the side of Christ, all the struggles of life, everything
that can be annoying and difficult, becomes lovable.
Sacrifice and sorrow borne with Christ is neither bitter nor
crushing, but rather in accord with our will. *Everything
hard is made bearable through love ... What can love not
do ...? Look how people in love work: they do not feel what
they suffer; they increase their efforts as the difficulties
increase.*[14]

Unity with God through adversity, of whatever kind, is
a grace that God is always ready to grant us. However, like
all grace, it demands the use of our freedom, our response.
We must not reject the means that God places within our
reach. We must be particularly prepared to open our hearts
in spiritual guidance, if on some occasion the Cross gets
particularly heavy. *A gentle wind is not the same as a
hurricane. Anyone can resist the first: it is child's play, a
parody of struggle.*

*Gladly you bore small contradictions, shortages and
little worries. And you enjoyed the interior peace of
thinking: now I am really working for God, because here
we have the Cross ...*

*But now, my poor son, the hurricane has come, and
you feel you are being shaken by a force that could uproot
century-old trees. You feel this from without and within.
But you must remain confident, for your Faith and your
Love cannot be uprooted, nor can you be blown from your
way, if you remain with the 'head', if you maintain unity.*[15]

Our Lord waits for us in the Tabernacle, to encourage

---

[13] St John Chrysostom, *Homilies on St Matthew*, 37,2

[14] St Augustine, *Sermon 96*, 1

[15] St J. Escrivá, *Furrow*, 411

to inform us that the heaviest part of the
carried by him, on the road to Calvary.
we learn how to carry peacefully and
seemed most difficult and demanding.
*......ng may collapse and fail. Events may turn out
contrary to what was expected and great adversity may
come. But nothing is to be gained by being perturbed.
Furthermore, remember the confident prayer of the
prophet: 'The Lord is our judge, the Lord gives us our
laws, the Lord is our king; it is he who will save us'.*

*Say it devoutly every day, so that your behaviour may
agree with the designs of Providence, which governs us for
our own good.*[16]

From the persecution which those first faithful
suffered there arose new conversions in unexpected places.
From the difficulties and obstacles which Our Lord permits
in our lives innumerable apostolic fruits are born, our love
becomes more refined and strong, and our soul emerges
purified from these trials if we manage to bear them
peacefully and united to Christ. As we finish our prayer we
say to Our Lord that we want to seek him in all the
circumstances of our life – of profession, age, health or
environment – whether they be favourable or not, and in
the midst of whatever external or internal difficulties we
may have come up against.

*In the hour of rejection at the Cross, the Virgin Mary
is there by her Son, willing to go through the same fate. Let
us lose our fear of behaving like responsible Christians
when the environment in which we move is not easy. She
will help us.*[17]

---

[16] *idem*, 855
[17] *idem*, 977

65. THE BREAD OF LIFE

65.1 The Blessed Eucharist announced at the Synagogue of Capharnaum. Our Lord asks us for a living faith. The *Adoro te devote*.

I am the bread of life. Your fathers ate manna in the desert and yet they died. The bread which comes down from heaven is such that he who eats it never dies.[1] We read in today's gospel this marvellous and astounding announcement which Jesus made in the synagogue at Capharnaum. Our Lord went on: *I myself am the living bread which has come down from heaven. If anyone eats this bread he shall live forever; and the bread which I shall give is my flesh for the life of the world.*[2]

Jesus reveals the great mystery of the Blessed Eucharist. His words have such realism that they exclude any other interpretation. Without faith, his words have no meaning. On the other hand, when the presence of Christ in the Eucharist is accepted by faith, then the revelation of Jesus turns out to be clear and unmistakable, and he shows us the infinite love which God has for us.

'*Adoro te devote, latens deitas, quae sub his figuris vere latitas*': *Godhead here in hiding, whom I do adore, Masked by these bare shadows, shape and nothing more,* we say with St Thomas Aquinas in that hymn which was adopted by the Church's Liturgy many centuries ago. It is an expression of faith and of piety that can help us express our love, because it forms a summary of the principal points of catholic doctrine on this sacred Mystery.

---

[1] John 6:48-50
[2] John 6:51

Godhead here in hiding, whom I do adore ... we repeat in the intimacy of our hearts, slowly, with faith, hope and love. The people who were present on that day in the synagogue understood the proper and literal meaning of our Lord's words. If they had understood him in a symbolic or figurative manner, they would not have been as confused and amazed as St John shows them to have been on hearing what Jesus said. And these words would not have been the occasion of many of them leaving Our Lord on that day. *This is a harsh saying, and who can bear it?*[3] they said as they went away. It is a harsh saying, and continues to be so, for those who are not well-disposed, for those who do not admit without the shadow of a doubt that Jesus of Nazareth, God, who became man, communicates out of love in this way with men. I adore you, hidden Godhead, we say to Him in our prayer, expressing our love, our gratitude and the humble assent with which we receive him. This attitude is essential if we are to approach this mystery of Love.

'*Tibi se cor meum totum subiicit, quia te contemplans totum deficit*': *See, Lord, at thy service low lies here a heart, Lost, all lost in wonder at the God thou art.* We feel the need of repeating this many times to Our Lord, because the number of unbelievers is great. He also asks us, and all who want to follow him very closely, *Do you also want to go away?*[4] And on seeing the lack of direction, the confusion of so many Christians whose souls are asleep to the supernatural life, our love has to re-affirm itself. *Tibi se cor meum totum subiicit* ... Our faith in the real presence of Christ in the Eucharist has to be firm: *We believe that as the bread and wine consecrated by Christ at the Last Supper were converted into his Body and his Blood, which*

---

[3] John 6:60
[4] cf John 6:67

were immediately offered for us on the Cross, thus also the bread and wine consecrated by the priest are converted into the Body and Blood of Christ, sitting gloriously in heaven; and we believe that the mysterious presence of Our Lord, under the appearance of those elements, which continue appearing to our senses in the same fashion as before, is a true, real and substantial presence.[5]

65.2 The Mystery of Faith. Transubstantiation.

The words of Our Lord cannot be watered down: *the bread which I shall give is my flesh for the life of the world. This is the mystery of Faith*, we proclaim immediately after the Consecration at Mass. It has been and is the touchstone of the Catholic faith. By transubstantiation, the species of bread and wine *are no longer common bread and common drink, but rather the sign of something sacred and the sign of spiritual food. But they take on a new expressiveness and a new purpose for the very reason that they contain a new 'reality', which we are right to call 'ontological'. For beneath these appearances there is no longer what was there before but something quite different ... since on the conversion of the bread and wine's substance, or nature, into the Body and Blood of Christ, nothing is left of the bread and wine but the appearances alone. Beneath these appearances Christ is present whole and entire, bodily present too, in his physical 'reality', although not in the manner in which bodies are present in a place.*[6]

We look at Jesus present in the Tabernacle, perhaps just a few yards away, and we tell him that we know, through faith, that he is present. We believe firmly in the promise which he made at Capharnaum and fulfilled shortly afterwards in the Cenacle. *'Credo quidquid dixit*

---

[5] St Paul VI, *The Creed of the People of God*, 24
[6] St Paul VI, *Mysterium Fidei*, 3 September 1965

Dei Filius: nihil hoc verbo veritatis verius': What God's Son has told me, take for truth I do; Truth himself speaks truly or there's nothing true.

In Holy Communion Christ himself, perfect God and perfect man, gives himself to us; he is mysteriously hidden, but wishes to communicate divine life to us. When we receive him in this sacrament, his Divinity acts on our soul by means of his glorious Humanity, with a far greater intensity than when he was here on earth. None of the people who were cured – Bartimaeus, or the paralysed man of Capharnaum, or the lepers – were as close to Christ, to Christ himself, as we are every time we go to Holy Communion. The effects produced by that Living Bread, Jesus, in our soul are immeasurable and of an infinite richness. The Church expresses it clearly in the following words: *All the effect which material food and drink have with regard to the life of the body, sustaining, restoring and delighting it, is carried out by this sacrament with regard to the spiritual life.*[7]

Hidden under the sacramental species, Jesus waits for us. He has remained there so that we can receive him and be strengthened in his love. We must examine our faith today; let us ask ourselves what our love is like, how do we prepare ourselves for Communion, when so many people neglect Our Lord entirely. We must say with Peter: *we have known and believed that you are the Christ.*[8] You are our Redeemer, our *raison d'etre.*

65.3 The effects of Communion on the soul: how it sustains, restores, delights.

Communion sustains the life of the soul in a way similar to that in which food sustains the body. The

---

[7] Council of Florence, *Exultate Deo*, *Dz* 1322-698
[8] John 6:70

reception of the Blessed Eucharist keeps Catholics in God's grace, since the soul recovers its energies from the continual wear and tear it suffers through the wounds of original sin and of personal sins. It maintains the life of God in the soul, freeing it from lukewarmness; and it helps us to avoid mortal sin and struggle effectively against venial sins.

The Blessed Eucharist increases supernatural life also: it makes it grow and develop. And while it fills the soul spiritually, it gives it an increasing desire for eternal goods: *Those who eat me will never be hungry, those who believe in me will never be thirsty.*[9] *Material food first of all turns itself into the person who eats it, and as a consequence, restores his losses and increases his vital energies. Spiritual food, on the other hand, turns the person who eats it into Itself, and thus the proper effect of this sacrament is the conversion of man into Christ, so that he may no longer live for himself, but that Christ may live in him. And as a consequence it has the double effect of restoring the spiritual losses caused by sins and defects and of increasing the power of the virtues.*[10]

Finally, the grace we receive in each Communion delights the person who receives with good dispositions. Nothing can be compared to the joy of the Holy Eucharist, to the friendship and nearness of Jesus, present within us. *Jesus Christ, during his life on earth, never passed by anywhere without pouring out his abundant blessings, from which we can deduce how great and precious must be the gifts which those who have the happiness of receiving Him in Holy Communion must share; or rather, that all the happiness we can have in this life consists in receiving Our*

---

[9] John 6:35
[10] St Thomas, *Commentary on Book IV of the Sentences*, d12, q2, a1

Lord in Holy Communion.[11]

Communion is *the remedy for our daily needs,*[12] *medicine of immortality, antidote against death, and food by which to live forever in Jesus Christ.*[13] It grants to the soul the peace and joy of Christ which is truly a *foretaste of eternal happiness.*[14]

Among all the practices of piety there is none whose sanctifying effectiveness can be compared to the worthy reception of this sacrament. In it, not only do we receive grace, but the Source and Fountainhead from which all grace flows. All the sacraments are ordained towards the Blessed Eucharist: it is the pivotal sacrament.[15]

Hidden under the accidents of bread, Jesus wants us to come and receive him frequently. The banquet, he tells us, is ready.[16] Many indeed are those who are absent, and Jesus waits for us to tell all those others that he is also waiting for them in the Tabernacle.

We must ask Our Lady to help us go to Communion every day with better dispositions.

---

[11] St Jean Vianney, (The Curé d'Ars), *Sermon on Holy Communion*
[12] St Ambrose, *On the Mysteries*, 4
[13] St Ignatius of Antioch, *Letter to the Ephesians*, 20
[14] cf John 6:58; *Dz* 875
[15] St Thomas, *Summa Theologiae*, III, q65, a3
[16] cf Luke 14:15 ff

66. THE COMMUNION OF SAINTS

66.1 The communion of graces. The Church's treasury.

St Paul refers in his writings to the fundamental event of his life, which we read about in today's first reading at Mass. It had remained forever ingrained in his mind. *Then on his journey, when he was nearly at Damascus, a light from heaven shone suddenly about him. He fell to the ground, and heard a voice saying to him: 'Saul, Saul, why do you persecute me?' 'Who are You, Lord?' he asked. And He said, 'I am Jesus whom you persecute.'*[1] In this first revelation, Jesus shows himself as personally and intimately united to his disciples whom Paul is persecuting.

Later on, the doctrine of the Mystical Body of Christ, one of the central topics in his preaching, would show this profound unity among Christians, on account of their being united to their Head, who is Christ. *If one part is suffering, all the rest suffer with it; if one part is treated with honour, all the rest find pleasure in it.*[2] This unbreakable faith in the union of the faithful with one another led the Apostle to ask for prayers from the first Christians at Rome, whom he did not yet know personally, in order to be freed from the unbelievers he was going to meet in Judaea.[3] He always felt very united with his brothers in the Faith, whom he always addressed as 'saints' in his letters: *Paul and Timothy, servants of Jesus Christ, to all the saints in Christ Jesus, who are at Philippi.*[4] From the earliest times of the

---

[1] Acts 9:3-5
[2] 1 Cor 12:26
[3] Rom 15:30-31
[4] Phil 1:1

Church, Christians have professed as one of the principal truths of faith in the Apostles' Creed: *I believe in the Communion of Saints.* It consists in a community of spiritual qualities, of spiritual possessions from which everyone benefits. It is not a sharing in worldly benefits, of a material, cultural or artistic nature, but a community of imperishable goods, with which we can offer one another help of an incalculable value. Today, offering Our Lord our work, our prayer, our joy and our difficulties, we can do an immense good to people who are far from us, and to the entire Church.

Live a special Communion of Saints: and, in the moments of interior struggle, just as in the hours of professional work, each of you will feel the joy and the strength of not being alone.[5] St Teresa, aware of the destruction caused by Protestant errors in the Church, knew also of this support we can give one another: *The things of God's service are so bad,* she said, *that those of us who do serve Him have to stand back to back in order to make progress at all.*[6] This doctrine was always practised throughout the history of the Church.[7]

What does the Communion of Saints mean for us in practice? It means that all of us who are united in Christ – the saints in Heaven, the souls in purgatory, and we upon earth – must be mindful of the the needs of one another ... The saints 'must' love the souls whom God loves. The love that the blessed in Heaven have for the souls in Purgatory and the souls on earth is not a passive love. We might call it an active, 'hungry' love. The saints long to help onward to Heaven all souls, whose precious value they now realize

---

[5] St J. Escrivá, *The Way*, 545

[6] St Teresa, *Life*, 7-8

[7] cf St Ignatius of Antioch, *Letter to the Ephesians* 2,2-5; St Cyprian, *Letter 60*; St Clement of Rome, *Letter to the Corinthians* 36,1 ff; St Ambrose, *Treatise on Cain and Abel* 1 ff

*as never before. And if the prayer of a good man on earth
has power with God, there is no estimating the power of
the prayers which the saints offer for us. They are God's
heroes, his intimate friends and familiars.*[8]

66.2 Available to all Christians. The incalculable echoes of our good deeds.

The Communion of Saints extends even to the most
unfortunate Christian: however much he finds himself on
his own, he knows that he never dies alone: the whole
Church stands beside him to give him back to the God who
created him.

The Communion of Saints is a fact that goes beyond
time. Each act which we perform in charity has limitless
repercussions. On the Last Day we will be given to
understand the incalculable reverberations which the
words, actions or institutions of a saint, and of ours, have
had in the history of the world.

We all need one another. We can all help one another.
In fact we are continually sharing in the spiritual goods
common to the whole Church. At this moment, someone is
praying for us, and our soul is being vitalised by the
suffering, the work or the prayer of people whom we
perhaps do not even know. One day, in the presence of
God, at the moment of the particular judgement, we will
see these immense contributions which kept us afloat on
many occasions, and on others helped us draw a little
closer to God.

If we are faithful, we will also contemplate with
immense joy how our sacrifices, work and prayers were
effective in helping other people. Perhaps we will see the
salvation of others as due in great measure to our prayer,
our mortification, our good deeds ...

---

[8] L. Trese, *The Faith Explained*, p. 146

We share in this communion of spiritual benefits in a singular manner through the Holy Mass. The unity of all the members of the Church, even of those furthest away, is perfected every day around the Body of the Lord, which is offered for his Church and for the whole of humanity. *All Christians, by the Communion of Saints, receive the graces of every Mass, whether the celebrant offers it before thousands of people, or is helped by a server who is a child, perhaps distracted.*[9]

St Gregory the Great expresses in a graphic and pedagogic manner the marvellous effectiveness of the Mass. *It seems to me*, he says in one of his homilies, *that many of you know the story I am going to tell you now. It is said that not very long ago a man was taken prisoner by his enemies and led to a distant part of the country. Since he was a long time there, and his wife did not see him coming home, she thought he was dead. So she had Mass said for him every week. And as many times as his wife had Mass offered for the forgiveness of his sins, on each occasion, the chains of his captivity loosened. When he came back later to his own town, he told his wife with wonderment how on certain days of the week, the chains which bound him in his cell loosened by themselves. When his wife thought of the times and the days this happened, she recognized that he was freed when the Holy Sacrifice was being offered for his soul, as far as she could remember.*[10] Many chains are broken for us every day, thanks to the prayer of others.

66.3 Indulgences.

The invisible unity of the Church has many visible expressions. A privileged moment of that unity takes place

---

[9] St J. Escrivá, *Christ is passing by*, 89
[10] St Gregory the Great, *Homilies on the Gospels*, 37

in the sacrament whose name is precisely Communion, in that august Sacrifice which is the same all over the world. One is the priest who offers it, one the Victim, one the people also who offer it, one the God to whom it is offered, and one the result of the offering. *The one bread makes us one body, though we are many in number; the same bread is shared by all.*[11] Just as yesterday that bread was a handful of separate grains of wheat, so too Catholics, in the measure of their unity with Christ, are fused into one body, even though they come from very different conditions and places. *In the Sacrament of the Eucharistic Bread,* says the Second Vatican Council, *the unity of the faithful is represented and reproduced.*[12] It is the sacrament of charity,[13] which presupposes unity among the brethren.

It is also a truth of faith that the same interchange of spiritual benefits exists between the faithful who make up the Church triumphant in Heaven, the Church suffering in Purgatory and the Church militant on earth. We can commend ourselves to, and so receive help from, the saints in Heaven (whether canonized or not), from the angels, from the souls who are still being purified in Purgatory (and we can help them to alleviate their burden from where we are on earth) and from our brothers and sisters who, like us, are still on pilgrimage towards our ultimate homeland.

When we fulfil the pious duty of praying and offering suffrages for the souls of the faithful departed, we must take particularly into account those with whom we had stronger bonds on earth: parents, brothers and sisters, friends and relations. They count on our prayers. The Holy Mass is also the best suffrage we can offer for the faithful departed.

---

[11] 1 Cor 10:17
[12] Second Vatican Council, *Lumen gentium*, 3
[13] St Thomas, *Summa Theologiae*, III, q73, a3

On this dogma of the Communion of Saints the doctrine of indulgences is based. Through indulgences the Church administers authoritatively the graces gained by Christ, Our Lady and the Saints; under certain conditions, the Church makes use of these graces to make up for the punishment due our sins, and also to make up for what the souls in Purgatory need.

This doctrine on the exchange of spiritual benefits has to be a great stimulus for us to fulfil our duties faithfully, in order to be able to offer all our deeds to God and to pray devoutly, knowing that all our tasks, sicknesses, difficulties and prayers are a considerable help to others. Nothing we do with rectitude of intention is ever lost. If we were to put that reality of our faith into practice better, our lives would be more fruitful.

Here is a thought to help you in difficult moments: 'The more my faithfulness increases, the better will I be able to contribute to the growth of others in that virtue.' How good it is to feel supported by each other.[14]

If we remind ourselves that someone is interceding for us at this moment, and that someone else will be hoping for our prayer in order to overcome a bad situation or to help him make up his mind to stay closer to Our Lord, then we will be inspired to practise our Faith more deeply today.

---

[14] St J. Escrivá, *Furrow*, 948

67. THE PARTICULAR EXAMINATION

67.1 We need to struggle daily to be faithful to Our Lord. The particular examination of conscience.

Many of Our Lord's followers became argumentative or were scandalized when he promised the Eucharist in the synagogue at Capharnaum. At the announcement of something so wonderful a large number of his followers left him: St John says in the Gospel of today's Mass: *After this many of his disciples drew back and no longer went about with him.*[1]

Seeing his wonderful self-giving to men in Eucharistic Communion, their reply was to turn their backs on him. It was not the crowd as such but his own disciples who abandoned him. The Twelve remained faithful to their Master and Lord. They, perhaps, had not understood much about Our Lord's promise; however, they remained by his side. Why did they remain? Why were they loyal at that moment of disloyalty? It was because they were his friends, because through living with him day after day they had come to understand that he had *the words of eternal life*, because they loved him deeply. *Lord, to whom shall we go?* is Peter's reply to Jesus' query as to whether they too were leaving: *Lord, to whom shall we go? You have the words of eternal life; and we have believed, and have come to know, that you are the Holy One of God.*[2]

We Christians live in privileged times for giving testimony to faithfulness, a virtue at times undervalued. We can frequently see infidelity in marriage, promises

---

[1] John 6:66
[2] John 6:69

dishonoured, betrayal of the doctrine and person of Christ. The Apostles show us that this virtue is founded on love; they are faithful because they love Christ. It is love which induces them to remain in the midst of defections. Only one of them will betray him later – because he stopped loving. That is why St John Paul II gave this advice to all: *Make a particular effort to seek Jesus and attain a deep personal faith which influences and directs your whole life; but above all may your commitments and plans consist in loving Jesus, with a sincere, genuine and personal love. He should be your friend and your support along the way of life. He alone has the words of eternal life.*[3] Nobody but He.

As long as we live in this world our life is a constant struggle between love for Christ or giving in to lukewarmness, to our passions, or to comfort-seeking, which destroys love. Faithfulness to Christ is forged each day by struggling against whatever separates us from him, and by an effort to make progress in virtue. Then we will be faithful both when times are good and when they are difficult, when it seems few remain by Our Lord's side.

To remain steadfastly faithful to Our Lord we must always struggle cheerfully, even though the battles may be small ones. The particular examination of conscience is one of the ways we have of getting closer to God, of loving him in an ever greater way. It helps us to struggle effectively against the defects and obstacles separating us from Christ and from our fellow men, and it makes it easier for us to acquire virtues and habits which will smooth away any roughness in our relationship with Jesus.

The particular examination specifies the targets for our interior life, and helps us to rise, with the help of God's grace, to a definite and particular altitude on the mountain of holiness, or to repulse an enemy, who though perhaps

---

[3] St John Paul II, *Address*, 30 January 1979

small is well-armed and causes widespread damage and setbacks. *The general examination implies defence. The particular, attack. The first is your armour. The second, your sword.*[4]

Today, as we say to Our Lord that we want to be faithful to him, we should ask ourselves in his presence: Are my desires to grow in love really all that great? Do I turn these desires to struggle into something which can be a target for my particular examination? Am I docile to the indications I receive in spiritual guidance?

67.2 The aim and content of the particular examination.

We become aware of the basic motivations of our actions through the general examination; with the particular examination we seek the effective remedies for combating particular defects or for progressing in virtue. This repeated and brief examination throughout the day at fixed times has a very precise aim: *Your particular examination should be directed towards the acquisition of a definite virtue or the rooting out of your dominant defect.*[5] At times this examination has the purpose of *defeating the Goliath of the dominant passion,*[6] the most evident of our defects which does most harm to our relationship with Our Lord and to charity with those around us. *When someone is particularly hampered by a defect, he should take up arms against this enemy alone and try to combat it before all else ... because as long as we have not achieved victory over it we will have lost the fruits of victory over everything else.*[7] This is why self-knowledge is so important and why we should make

---

[4] St J. Escrivá, *The Way*, 238
[5] *ibid*, 241
[6] J. Tissot, *The Interior Life*
[7] St John Climacus, *The Ladder to Heaven*, 15

ourselves known in spiritual guidance where we normally
set the topic of this examination.

As we don't all have the same defects *each one has
necessarily to wage his battle with an eye to the specific
nature of the attack.*[8]

The following could be matter for the particular
examination: presence of God at work, in family life, while
walking along the street; being more alert in discovering
the presence of tabernacles and greeting Our Lord with an
aspiration, perhaps even though we cannot visit him at that
moment; care of punctuality right from the time of getting
up in the morning, on starting the prayer, at Holy Mass;
having patience with ourselves, with the defects of our
fellow workers or in the family; rooting out any tendency
to gossip and trying to see that nobody gossips in our
company; brusqueness in dealing with others; indifference
to our neighbour's needs; developing the virtue of being
thankful so that we can express gratitude even for small
favours and services in our daily life; being more ordered
in our use of time, with our books and work materials; our
relationship with our Guardian Angel. One topic for
particular examination that can leave a deep impression on
our soul if we work at it will be to attend Mass and receive
Holy Communion with greater love.

Even though in some instances the objective of the
particular examination might appear to be negative,
opposition to a particular evil, the best mode of combat is
to practise the virtue contrary to the defect we are trying to
uproot – practising humility, for example, by overcoming
the tendency to be the centre of everything or to wish to be
always receiving praise and acknowledgement; again, we
can practise serenity in order to avoid hastiness. In this way
interior struggle becomes more effective and attractive.

---

[8] Cassian, *Conferences*, 5, 27

The tendency of the soul towards good is greater than that
~~*towards the avoidance of evil.*~~[9]

Before deciding on the subject of our particular
examination we should ask Our Lord for light to know
what he wants us to struggle in. We can say to him like the
blind man of Jericho, *Domine, ut videam – Lord, let me
see,*[10] and ask help through spiritual guidance.

67.3 Constancy in struggle. Faithfulness in difficult moments is the result of daily attention to small things.

Each person has to work out the details of his or her
own examination. Some people – because of their character
or temperament – have to be especially specific and keep
careful track of progress because of their tendency to
vagueness and generalities; for others this may only create
problems where there shouldn't be any. We can be helped
in spiritual guidance if we let ourselves be known.

It shouldn't surprise us if it takes time to attain the
proposed objective in our struggle. If our target is well
chosen, normally it will be a fairly deep- rooted defect
which requires a patient struggle, beginning again and
again without getting discouraged. In beginning again with
God's help we strengthen the foundations of our humility.
Fortitude, constancy and humility are needed to keep the
particular examination alive. Love, always resourceful, will
find a way of making our daily struggle seem new, because
through it, rather than self-mastery, we are seeking to love
Our Lord, removing every barrier which causes a difficulty
in the growth of our friendship with him and therefore
separates us from others. Love gives us an opportunity to
make many acts of contrition for failures, and acts of
thanksgiving for the successes we manage to achieve.

---

[9] St Thomas, *Summa Theologiae*, I-II, q29, a3
[10] cf Mark 10:48

A daily struggle in a given particular examination is the best remedy for lukewarmness and softness. What a wonderful thing it would be if our Guardian Angel could testify at the end of our life that we struggled each day even though we weren't always victorious! *We must convince ourselves that the worst enemy of a rock is not a pickaxe or any other such implement, no matter how sharp it is. No, its worst enemy is the constant flow of water which drop by drop enters the crevices until it ruins the rock's structure. The greatest danger for a Christian is to underestimate the importance of fighting skirmishes which ... can, little by little, leave him soft and weak.*[11]

As we finish our prayer we say to Our Lord, like Peter: Lord, to whom shall we go? You have the words of eternal life. Without you we have no Way, no Truth and no Life.

It is a beautiful aspiration to repeat often, but especially at the moment of struggle. We ask Our Lady, *Virgo fidelis*, Virgin most faithful, to help us to be faithful, trying to remove daily the very definite obstacles that separate us from her Son.

---

[11] St J. Escrivá, *Christ is passing by*, 77

68. THE GOOD SHEPHERD. LOVE FOR THE POPE

68.1 Jesus is the Good Shepherd, and entrusts Peter and his successors with the government of his Church to continue his mission on earth.

The Good Shepherd has risen, who laid down his life for his sheep and willingly died for his flock, alleluia.[1]

This Sunday's liturgy centres upon the image of the Good Shepherd. The Shepherd's sacrifice gave life to his sheep and brought them back to the fold. Years later St Peter confirmed Christians in their faith by reminding them in the midst of persecution what Christ had done and suffered for them: *By his wounds you have been healed. For you were straying like sheep, but have now returned to the Shepherd and Guardian of your souls.*[2] And so the whole Church prays that *the renewal constantly at work with us may be the cause of our unending joy,*[3] and asks God the Father to *lead us to a share in the joys of heaven, so that the humble flock may reach where the brave Shepherd has gone before.*[4]

The early Christians had a special affection for the image of the Good Shepherd, and have left us countless testimonies of it in the catacombs and on many well-known ancient buildings through murals, reliefs, gravestone etchings, mosaics and sculptures. This Sunday's liturgy invites us to meditate on our Saviour's merciful tenderness,

---

[1] *Communion Antiphon*
[2] 1 Pet 2:25
[3] *Prayer over the Offerings*
[4] *Collect*

so that we recognize the rights he acquired over each one of us by his death. It is also a good opportunity to consider in our prayer our love for the good shepherds whom he has left to guide us and keep us in his name.

The Old Testament frequently refers to the Messiah as a good Shepherd who must feed, rule and govern God's people, often abandoned and scattered. The prophecies of the awaited shepherd are fulfilled in Jesus, but in him with new features. He is the Good Shepherd who gives his life for his sheep and provides other shepherds to continue his mission. As opposed to thieves who seek their own interests and destroy the flock, Jesus is the door of salvation;[5] he who enters will find abundant pasture.[6] There is a tender relationship between Jesus the Good Shepherd and his sheep: he calls each by his name; he leads them; the sheep follow because they know his voice; he is the one and *only shepherd* who has only one flock,[7] protected by the Father's love.[8] He is the *chief Shepherd.*[9]

In his last appearance before the Ascension, the risen Christ made Peter the shepherd of his flock,[10] the Church's guide. In this way the prophecy made to Peter before the Passion was fulfilled: *but I have prayed for you that your faith may not fail; and when you have turned again, strengthen your brethren.*[11] Then he prophesied that as a good shepherd he would die for his flock.

Christ trusts Peter despite the denials. He simply asks for his love the same number of times that He had been denied. Our Lord doesn't mind entrusting his Church to a

---

[5] cf John 10:10
[6] cf John 10:9-10
[7] cf John 10:16
[8] cf John 10:29
[9] 1 Pet 5:4
[10] cf John 21:15-17
[11] Luke 22:32

weak man who repents and loves with deeds.

Peter was grieved because he said to him the third time, 'Do you love me?'. And he said to him, 'Lord, you know everything; you know that I love you'. Jesus said to him, 'Feed my sheep.'

The shepherd symbol which Jesus has claimed for himself is passed on to Peter: he must continue Our Lord's mission and be his representative on earth.

Jesus' words to Peter – *feed my lambs, feed my sheep* – explain Peter's mission as one of guarding Our Lord's whole flock without limitations. *Feed* is equivalent to 'direct and govern'. Peter is made the shepherd and guide for the whole Church. As the Second Vatican Council points out, Jesus Christ *put Peter at the head of the other Apostles, and in him he set up a lasting and visible source and foundation of the unity of both faith and communion.*[12]

Ubi Petrus ibi Ecclesia – where Peter is, there is Christ's Church. In union with him we know with certainty the way that leads to salvation.

68.2 The primacy of Peter. The love of the early Christians for Peter.

The Church is built on the primacy of Peter, as on a rock, until the end of the world. Peter's stature is immeasurably enhanced since Christ is the real foundation of the Church[13] and Peter now takes his place. That is why his successors have since acquired the title of Vicar of Christ, that is, one who takes Christ's place.

Peter is the Church's strong defence against the storms she has suffered and will suffer throughout the centuries. Built on him, as foundation and with his watchfulness as good shepherd, its victory is assured despite trials and

---

[12] Second Vatican Council, *Lumen gentium*, 18
[13] 1 Cor 3:11

temptations. Peter must eventually die but as regards his role of supreme shepherd *Our Lord will assure it lasts eternally for the perpetual health and perennial good of the Church, which, being founded on rock, must remain stable to the end of time.*[14]

Love for the Pope goes back to the Church's beginnings. *The Acts of the Apostles*[15] tell us movingly of the early Christians' reaction to the imprisonment of St Peter by Herod Agrippa, who planned to kill him when the Paschal feast was over. Meanwhile the Church prayed unceasingly to God for him. *Look at how the faithful feel for their pastors,* says St John Chrysostom. *They don't resort to protest or rebellion, but to prayer as an unfailing remedy. They did not say: as we are powerless men, it is useless to pray for him. They never reasoned in this way, but prayed with love.*[16]

We ought to pray a lot for the Pope and his intentions, since he bears the heavy weight of the Church on his shoulders. For example, we could use the following liturgical prayer: *Dominus conservet eum, et vivificet eum, et beatum faciet eum in terra, et non tradat eum in animam inimicorum eius: may the Lord keep him and give him life, make him happy on earth and save him from deliverance into the hands of his enemies.*[17] Every day the clamour of the entire Church spread over the world rises to God in petition *with him and for him.* No Mass is celebrated without his name being mentioned and prayers said for him and his intentions. Our Lord will be very pleased to see that throughout the day we remember to offer prayers, hours of work or study and some mortification for his Vicar on earth.

---

[14] First Vatican Council, *Pastor aeternus*, chap 2
[15] cf Acts 12:1-12
[16] St John Chrysostom, *Homilies on the Acts of the Apostles*, 26
[17] *Enchiridion Indulgentiarum*, 1986, 39: prayer *pro Pontifice*

*Thank you, my God, for that love for the Pope you
have placed in my heart;*[18] it would be wonderful if we
could say this more meaningfully each day. This love and
veneration for the Roman Pontiff is one of the great gifts
Our Lord has left us.

68.3 Faithful obedience to the Vicar of Christ; making his teaching known. The *sweet Christ on earth*.

Along with showing him love and respect, we also
pray for the one who takes Christ's place on earth. *Love for
the Roman Pontiff must be in us a beautiful passion, for in
him we see Christ.*[19] Therefore *we will not fall into the all
too easy temptation of setting one Pope against another,
having confidence only in those whose actions respond to
our personal feelings. We are not among those who
nostalgically look back to a former Pope or look forward
one in the future who will eventually dispense us from
obeying the present one. Read the liturgical texts for the
coronation of Pontiffs and you will notice that nowhere is
there a reference to a conferral of powers proportionate to
the dignity of the person elected by the conclave. Christ
gives these powers directly to Peter's successor. Therefore
in speaking of the Roman Pontiff we exclude from our
vocabulary any expressions derived from parliamentary
assemblies or the polemics of newspapers; let it not be said
that people not of our faith should be the ones who explain
the prestige of the head of Christendom in the world to
us.*[20]

And there would be no true love and respect for the
Pope without faithful internal and external obedience to his
teaching and doctrine. Good children listen with profound

---

[18] St J. Escrivá, *The Way*, 573
[19] *idem*, *Homily, Loyalty to the Church*, 4 June 1972
[20] G. Chevrot, *Simon Peter*

respect to even the simplest advice of the common Father and try sincerely to put it into practice.

In the Pope we should see somebody who is in Christ's place in the world – the *sweet Christ on earth,* as St Catherine of Siena used to say – loving and listening to him because his voice is the truth. We try to see that his words reach all the corners of the earth without distortion, so that, just as when Christ was on earth, many people disoriented by ignorance and error can discover the truth and many afflicted people recover their hope. It is part of the Christian's apostolic task to make the Pope's teaching known.

Jesus' very words can be applied to the Pope: *He who abides in me ... he it is that bears much fruit, for apart from me you can do nothing.*[21] Without this union all fruit is only apparent and empty and, in many cases, brings bitterness and damages the whole Mystical Body of Christ. On the other hand, if we are very united to the Pope, we will only have reasons for optimism in the task before us; this is reflected in these words of St Josemaría Escrivá: *Joyfully I bless you, son, for that faith in your mission as an apostle which inspired you to write: 'There's no doubt about it: the future is certain, perhaps in spite of us. But it is essential that we should be one with the Head – 'ut omnes unum sint', that all be one! – through prayer and sacrifice.*[22]

---

[21] John 15:5
[22] St J. Escrivá, *The Way*, 968

69. DESIRING HOLINESS

69.1 Wanting to be a saint – the first necessary step in persevering to the end of the way. Real and effective desires.

My soul thirsts for God, for the living God. As a hart longs for flowing streams, so longs my soul for thee, O God ... When shall I come and behold the face of God?[1] We pray thus in the liturgy of the Mass. The deer attempting to slake his thirst with water is the psalmist's symbolic way of describing the desire for God present in the heart of an upright person: a thirst and vehement desire for God! Such is the aspiration of one who is not content to accept worldly success as the satisfaction for human ambitions. *For what will it profit a man, if he gains the whole world and forfeits his life?*[2] Jesus' question forces us to take a radical look at the broad horizon of our life to which only God gives ultimate meaning. My soul thirsts for God! The saints were men and women with a great desire to belong to God completely, despite their defects. We could each ask ourselves: have I a true desire to be a saint? The answer would most assuredly be in the affirmative: yes. But our reply should not be as to a theoretical question, because for some holiness is *unattainable, something to do with ascetical theology – but not a real goal for them, a living reality.*[3] We want to make it happen with the help of God's grace.

So longs my soul for thee, O God. We must start by

---

[1] *Responsorial Psalm*, Ps 41
[2] Matt 16:26
[3] St J. Escrivá, *Christ is passing by*, 96

making the desire for holiness flourish in our own soul, telling Our Lord: 'I want to be a saint'; or at least 'When I experience my softness and weakness, I *want* to want to be a saint'. To banish doubt and make holiness more than an empty word let us turn and look at Christ: *The Lord Jesus, divine teacher and model of all perfection, preached holiness of life (of which he is author and maker) to each and every one of his disciples without distinction: 'You, therefore, must be perfect, as your heavenly Father is perfect.' (Matt 5:48)*[4]

He has taken the initiative. If He had not, the possibility of being a saint would never have occurred to us. Jesus puts it to us as a command: *be perfect!*, and so it is not surprising that the Church makes sure her children hear the following resounding words: *Therefore all the faithful are invited and obliged to holiness and the perfection of their own state of life.*[5]

Consider then how vehement our desire for holiness has to be! In Holy Scripture the prophet Daniel is called *vir desideriorum*, a man of desires.[6] Wouldn't it be wonderful if we all were worthy of such a title! The first thing that souls must do if they embark on the path of holiness is really to want to be saints *whatever may come, whatever may happen to them, however hard they may have to labour, whoever may complain of them, whether they reach their goal or die on the road.*[7]

Allow your soul to be consumed by desires – desires for loving, for forgetting yourself, for sanctity, for Heaven. Do not stop to wonder whether the time will come for seeing them accomplished, as some pseudo-adviser might

---

[4] Second Vatican Council, *Lumen gentium*, 40
[5] *ibid*, 42
[6] Dan 9:23
[7] St Teresa, *The Way of Perfection*, 21,2

suggest. Make them more fervent each day, for the Holy Spirit says that he is pleased with men of desires.

Let your desires be operative, and put them into practice in your daily tasks.[8]

Therefore, we should examine our conscience to see if our desires of holiness are sincere and effective, and furthermore, to see if we take them as something *obligatory* for a faithful Christian – as we have seen the Second Vatican Council state – in response to God's desires. This examination could reveal the reason for so much weakness and apathy in interior struggle. *You tell me, yes, you want to. Very good: but do you want as a miser longs for gold, as a mother loves her child, as a worldling craves for honours, or as a wretched sensualist seeks his pleasure?*

No? Then, you don't want to![9]

Let us develop these desires with the virtue of hope: one can only effectively desire something when there is hope of attaining it. If we consider some aim to be impossible and not for us, we will not really desire it; our theological hope rests on God.

69.2 Softness and lukewarmness destroy desires for sanctity. The need for vigilance.

The conversion of Cornelius the Centurion mentioned in the first reading at Mass shows that God is no respecter of persons. St Peter explains to the others what has happened: *the Holy Spirit fell upon them just as on us at the beginning.*[10]

There are no limits or barriers to the power of the Holy Spirit. This is true in our case, just as it was for Cornelius,

---

[8] St J. Escrivá, *Furrow*, 628
[9] St J. Escrivá, *The Way*, 316
[10] Acts 11:15-17

who was not a Jew by race or nation. On the one hand we have to want to be saints, but we must also take into account that *unless the Lord builds the house, those who build it labour in vain.*[11] Humility leads us to count always above all on God's grace. To this we add our efforts to acquire virtues and practise them continuously, and our apostolic zeal, since our concept of personal holiness should not be one which ignores others or which is indifferent to charity: that would be contradictory. Lastly, there is our desire to be with Christ on the Cross, that is, to be mortified, not rejecting sacrifice in small things and, if need be, in big things.

We should be forewarned about approaching God with reservations and without renunciation, trying to make the love of God compatible with what is not pleasing to him. We should be alert in developing our desires for holiness continually through prayer, by asking God for the ability to struggle each day, to discover in examination of conscience the places where our love is growing cold. Desire for holiness is real when we fulfil our acts of piety with refinement, not omitting them or delaying them for any reason whatever, refusing to be led by our moods and feelings, because *the soul truly in love with God never fails through laziness to do all in its power to seek God's Son, the Beloved. And having done all it could it is still not satisfied as it thinks it has done nothing.*[12]

The virtue of humility enables us to avoid a sense of self-satisfaction with what we have done, and not to be content with ineffectual desires. It lets us see how we can do more to show the sincerity of our desires with deeds of love, ensuring that our sins, offences and negligences don't frustrate our expectations. Humility doesn't clip the wings

---

[11] Ps 126:1
[12] St John of the Cross, *The Spiritual Canticle*, 3,1

of our desires, but rather helps us understand the need to have recourse to God to make them come true. With God's grace we can do all in our power to make virtue grow in our soul, by removing obstacles, fleeing from occasions of sin and bravely resisting temptations.

69.3 Counting on time and God's grace. Avoiding discouragement in the struggle to improve.

My soul thirsts for God, for the living God. Is this thirst compatible with our experience of our defects and even our falls? Yes, because saints are not those who have never sinned, but those who have always got up again. Refusal to pursue holiness at seeing ourselves full of defects is a hidden form of pride and obvious cowardice which will end up stifling our desires for God. *Feeling easily deflated and lying down under adversity is characteristic of cowardly souls lacking the firm virtue of trusting in God's promises.*[13]

Abandoning God, ceasing to struggle because of our defects when there is opposition is a serious mistake, a very subtle and dangerous temptation which can lead us to that form of pride called pusillanimity, lack of courage and strength to bear misfortune or undertake large enterprises. Perhaps we need to rid ourselves of false illusions in wanting to be saints in a day: that would be impossible unless God decided to perform a miracle, which he has no reason to do since he gives us all the graces we need – by ordinary means – in a continuous and progressive way.

An effective desire for holiness consists in a conscious and determined effort to use the necessary means to attain holiness. If desire is lacking nothing can be done; one doesn't even try. Desires alone are not enough. *We must be patient, then, and not try to banish in a day the many*

---

[13] St Basil, *Homily on Joy*

habits we have picked up in neglecting our spiritual health.[14]

God counts on time and is patient with each one of us. If we get discouraged at the slowness of our spiritual improvement, we should remember how disastrous it is to leave good undone, to hold back in face of difficulties and get discouraged by our defects. God can obviously give us more light to see with a clearer conscience, and to undertake the struggle on new battle-fronts with greater optimism, remembering that the saints have always considered themselves great sinners; that is why they tried harder to be united to God through prayer and mortification, relying on the divine mercy: *let us patiently hope for our improvement, and instead of being anxious about having done little in the past let us diligently try to do more in the future.*[15]

As the deer longs for flowing streams, so longs my soul for thee, O God. Let us keep our desire for God alive; let us enkindle the flame of faith and hope in the fire of the love of God, enlivening our virtues and burning away our miseries, and we will assuage our thirst for holiness with the water that springs up to eternal life.[16]

---

[14] J. Tissot, *How to Profit from your Faults*
[15] *ibid*
[16] cf John 4:14

70. THE FIRST CHRISTIANS.
UNIVERSALITY OF THE FAITH

70.1 The rapid spread of Christianity. The early Christians' holiness was through finding Christ in their environment.

Our Lord founded the Church on the weakness – but also on the fidelity – of a few men, the Apostles, to whom he promised the constant assistance of the Holy Spirit ...

The preaching of the Gospel does not arise in Palestine through the personal initiative of a few fervent individuals. What could the Apostles do? They were nothing in their time. From a human point of view they were neither rich, nor learned, nor heroes. Jesus places on the shoulders of a handful of disciples an immense, divine task.[1] An observer devoid of supernatural vision and seeing the initial apostolate of that small group would have considered it destined to failure from the start. However, that group of men of faith were faithful and began to preach that novel teaching everywhere, clashing head-on with many pagan ways; in a short time the world knew that Jesus Christ was the Redeemer of the world.

The Good News is preached to all men from the beginning without discrimination. Those exiled in the persecution arising from Stephen's death – as we read in today's Mass[2] – travelled as far afield as Phoenicia, Cyprus and Antioch. In the latter city there were so many of them that it was there that the followers of Jesus were first called Christians. A few years later we find Christ's followers in

---

[1] St J. Escrivá, *Homily, Loyalty to the Church*, 4 June 1972
[2] cf Acts 11:19-20

Rome and throughout the Empire.

At the beginning the Christian faith took root mainly among simple people: ordinary soldiers, labourers in the woollen industry, slaves, and merchants too.

For consider your call, brethren; not many of you were wise according to worldly standards, not many were powerful, not many were of noble birth.[3]

God is no respecter of persons, and those who were called at the beginning – being humanly speaking ignorant and weak – were to be the instruments he would use to spread the Church. Thus the effectiveness would be seen to be more clearly divine.

Among the early Christians there were also cultured and educated people who were important by human standards, like the Ethiopian minister, centurions, men like Apollo and Dionysius the Areopagite, women like Lydia; but they were a minority among the vast number of converts to the new faith. St Thomas comments that *it is further to God's glory that the leaders of society were brought to him by simple people.*[4]

The early Christians worked at all the normal occupations of their time, with the exception of any professions that might present a danger to their faith like 'interpreters of dreams', diviners, temple-keepers, and so on. And despite the fact that pagan religious practices were part of public life, each stayed in the place and profession where he met the faith, trying to give his tone to society, striving to be exemplary in conduct, never rejecting – quite the opposite in fact – the task of getting closer to his neighbours and fellow citizens. They were involved in the forum, the market place and the army. Tertullian would say: *We Christians don't turn our backs on the world; we*

---

[3] 1 Cor 1:26
[4] St Thomas, *Commentary on 1 Corinthians, ad loc.*

are present in the forum, at the baths, in the workshops, the bazaars, the market places and public squares. We are sailors, soldiers, farm hands, businessmen.[5]

Our Lord reminds us that today too he is calling all, without discrimination of profession, social standing or race. *What compassion you feel for them! ... You would like to cry out to them that they are wasting their time ... Why are they so blind, and why can't they perceive what you – a miserable creature – have seen? Why don't they go for the best?*

Pray and mortify yourself. Then you have the duty to wake them up, one by one, explaining to them – also one by one – that they, like you, can find a divine way, without leaving the place they occupy in society.[6]

This was what our first brothers and sisters in the faith did.

70.2 Exemplary citizens of the world. Bringing Christ to all environments.

By the end of the second century Christians are found throughout the Empire: *There is no race among men, whether barbarian or Greek or of any other name, whether among the housed or among the homeless nomads, or those in shepherd's tents, who do not offer prayers and thanksgiving to the Father and maker of all things in the name of Jesus Christ crucified.*[7]

The Christian faithful do not flee from the world in order to seek Christ fully: they consider themselves as part of the world's structure to which they try to give form from within by their prayer, their example and their magnanimous charity: *what the soul does for the body is*

---

[5] Tertullian, *Apology*, 42
[6] St J. Escrivá, *Furrow*, 182
[7] St Justin, *Dialogue with Tryphon*, 117, 5

what Christians do for the world.[8] They gave life to a world which had lost the sense of human dignity in many ways, while still remaining citizens like the others, and without any special distinction in dress or insignia, or by changing their nationality.[9]

They were not only citizens, but exemplary ones: *obeying the laws, but by their lives surpassing its demands,*[10] they fulfilled them to the letter for the good of all. St Paul had already taught that they should pray for those in authority.[11]

As exemplary citizens they respected the civil authorities, they paid their taxes and fulfilled their other social obligations. In peace and war as well as in times of open hatred it was all the same. St Justin Martyr tells us of a case of heroic virtue in civic matters by the early Christians: *Just as we learned from him (Christ), we try to pay our taxes and dues promptly and in full to your agents ... So while adoring God alone, we willingly obey you in everything else, openly recognizing you as kings and governors of mankind and asking in our prayer that both you and the imperial power would possess in full wisdom the skill of government.*[12] In a forceful attack on the degeneration of the pagan world Tertullian wrote that the faithful in their meetings used to pray for the emperors, their ministers and those in authority, for temporal well-being and for peace.[13]

In any age we Christians should not be indifferent to the society of which we form part. We try to act responsibly in our temporal affairs so as to transform them

---

[8] *Letter to Diognetus*, 6, 1
[9] cf *ibid*, 5,1-11
[10] *ibid*, 5,10
[11] cf 1 Tim 2:1-2
[12] St Justin, *First Apology*, 17
[13] cf Tertullian, *Apology*, 39,1 ff

from inside with a new spirit. The further removed it seems Christ is from a place, the more urgently do Christians need to be present there so as to bring, as the first ones in the Faith did, the salt of Christ, and give back to man his human dignity, so often lost. *To follow in Christ's footsteps, today's apostle does not need to reform anything, but even less has he to take no part in contemporary affairs going on around him. He has only to act as the first Christians did, and give life to his environment.*[14]

70.3 Christian family customs.

There were many roads leading to the Faith, some of them extraordinary ones, as with St Paul.[15] Our Lord called others through the example of a martyr; mostly the Good News got known through a work-companion, a neighbour, a fellow-prisoner or traveller and so on. Already in apostolic times it was customary to baptize children before they reached the use of reason. St Paul baptized whole families and, like the other Apostles, passed on the practice to the whole Church. Origen was able to write two centuries later: *The Church has inherited from the Apostles the practice of baptizing even infants.*[16]

The Christian homes of the early faithful were no different on the outside from any others. Parents passed on the Faith to their children and these in their turn did likewise. In this way the family became the main pillar for the grounding of Christian faith and morality. Christian homes being steeped in love were havens of peace, often in the midst of misunderstandings, calumnies and persecutions from without. In the home children learned the morning offering, how to be thankful and bless the table, how to

---

[14] St J. Escrivá, *Furrow*, 320
[15] cf Acts 9:1-19
[16] Origen, *Commentary on the Letter to the Romans*, 5,9

turn to God in good times and in bad.

What parents taught their children came with the naturalness of life itself, and so the family thus fulfilled its mission as educator. The following is the advice given by St John Chrysostom to Christian couples: *Show your wife you appreciate her company a lot and that you prefer to be at home rather than outside, because she is there. Show her a preference among all your friends and even above the children she has given you; love them because of her ... Pray all together ... Learn the fear of God; everything else will flow from this like water from a fountain and your house will be filled with bounty.*[17] At other times it is a son or daughter who is the one responsible for spreading Christianity in their family: they attract other brothers and sisters to the Faith; then perhaps their parents, who in turn bring the uncles and aunts ... even the godparents end up being involved.

There are many Christian devotions which can be practised in the home: reciting the Rosary, having pictures and statues of Our Lady, making cribs at Christmas, blessing the table ... and many more. If these are looked after they will help to make the home always a friendly place, characteristic of a Christian family where people are taught from their earliest years to speak to God and his Most Holy Mother with naturalness.

---

[17] St John Chrysostom, *Twentieth homily on the Letter to the Ephesians*

71. ACTS OF THANKSGIVING

71.1 Thanking God for all his benefits is a sign of faith, hope and love. Countless reasons for thanksgiving.

The Entrance Antiphon for today's Mass says: *I will praise you, Lord, among the nations; I will tell of your name to my kin, alleluia.*[1]

Sacred Scripture constantly encourages us to give thanks to God. The hymns, psalms and the words of all just men are filled with praise and thanksgiving to God. The Psalmist says *Bless the Lord, O my soul, and forget not all his benefits.*[2] The expression of thanks is an extraordinarily beautiful way of relating to God and men. As a form of prayer it is very pleasing to God and in some way an anticipation of the praise we will give him eternally. We call the sacrament of the Holy Eucharist precisely *thanksgiving* as a foretaste of the union of eternal happiness.

In the Gospel we see Our Lord saddened at the ingratitude of lepers who were not thankful: having been cured they forgot the person who had restored them their health, their families, their work, their lives. Jesus kept on waiting for them.[3] On another occasion he is grieved at Jerusalem's lack of awareness of God's infinite mercy in visiting it[4] and of his attempts to care for it like a hen sheltering her chickens under her wing.[5]

---

[1] *Entrance Antiphon*, Ps 17:50; 12:23
[2] Ps 102:2
[3] cf Luke 17:11 ff
[4] cf Luke 19:44
[5] cf Matt 23:37

Thankfulness is a way of expressing our faith because we recognise God as the source of all good; it is a sign of hope because we accept that all good comes through him; and it leads to love[6] and humility because we acknowledge our poverty and our need. St Paul makes a special exhortation to the early Christians to be thankful: *Give thanks in all circumstances; for this is the will of God in Christ Jesus for you,*[7] and he considers ingratitude as one of the causes of paganism.[8]

St John Chrysostom points out that *St Paul in all his letters gives thanks for all the good things of the earth. Let us likewise give thanks for the benefits received by ourselves and others, whether big or small.*[9] One day when we are in God's presence eternally, we will comprehend with full clarity not only that we owe our existence to him but that our lives were full of his care, his graces and benefits, *more numerous than the sands of the sea.*[10] We will realise that we have only reason to be thankful to God and to others. Only when faith is dead can a person be unaware of these benefits and this pleasant obligation.

Get used to lifting your heart to God, in acts of thanksgiving, many times a day. Because he gives you this and that. Because you have been despised. Because you haven't what you need or because you have.

Because he made his Mother so beautiful, his Mother who is also your Mother. Because he created the sun and the moon and this animal and that plant. Because he made that man eloquent and you he left tongue-tied ...

Thank him for everything, because everything is good.[11]

---

[6] cf St Thomas, *Summa Theologiae*, II-II, q101, a3
[7] 1 Thess 5:17
[8] cf Rom 1:18-32
[9] St John Chrysostom, *Homilies on St Matthew*, 25, 4
[10] *ibid*
[11] St J. Escrivá, *The Way*, 268

71.2 Acknowledging God's goodness in our lives. The virtue of gratitude.

Our Lord taught us how to be thankful for even the least of favours: *And whoever gives to one of these little ones even a cup of cold water because he is a disciple, truly, I say to you, he shall not lose his reward.*[12] The Samaritan who returned to thank Our Lord went away with an even greater gift: faith and Our Lord's friendship: Jesus said to him *Rise and go your way; your faith has made you well.*[13] The nine ungrateful lepers were left without getting the best part of all. Our Lord expects us Christians to go and say to him many times each day *Thank you, Lord!*

The virtue of gratitude forms a real bond among men and reveals fairly clearly the interior quality of the person. As popular wisdom puts it: *breeding and thankfulness go together.* Human relationships suffer in the absence of this virtue.

When we are grateful to others we remember their favour affectionately no matter how small it may be, and we wish to repay it in some form. Many times we can only say something like *thank you.* The joy shown in such a gesture contains our thanks. Our whole day is filled with acts of service and favours from those around us. It costs little to show our gratitude and it does so much good by creating a better atmosphere, improving relationships and making charity easier to practise.

Whoever is thankful to God is thankful to those around him. He is more prompt to appreciate and be thankful for any small favours. The proud person who is always absorbed with his own things cannot be thankful; he feels that everything is his due.

If we are thinking of God and others, in our own

---

[12] Matt 10:42
[13] Luke 17:19

homes we will appreciate that the house is clean and tidy, that somebody has closed the windows to keep the temperature right, that our clothes are cleaned and ironed ... And if on some occasion one of these things were not as we had hoped, we should be able to overlook it, because the number of times things are pleasant and favourable is immeasurably greater.

When we leave our apartment the porter deserves our thanks for his vigilance, the lady in the chemist shop who gave us our medicine, those who have worked all night to compile our newspaper, the bus driver also ... Human life is full of small acts of service. How different life would be if we were to thank people whenever we paid or charged our bills! Gratitude is a human sign of big-hearted people.

71.3 Thanksgiving after Mass and Holy Communion.

In our relationship with Our Lord we should thank him many times every day, because he surrounds us with his care and his gifts: *my soul will be filled to overflowing.*[14] However, there is a very special moment in which Our Lord fills us with his gifts and during which we should particularly grateful, namely thanksgiving after Mass.

Our dialogue with Jesus at these moments should be specially intimate, simple and joyful. There should be acts of adoration, of petition, of humility, of atonement and thanksgiving. *The saints ... have constantly told us that the most precious moment of our spiritual lives should be the thanks we give for receiving the Eucharist.*[15]

At these moments we should shut our hearts to everything that is not Jesus, no matter how important it may be or may seem to be. At times we will feel alone with him and words are unnecessary; it is enough to believe that

---

[14] C. Journet, *The Meaning of Grace*
[15] R. Garrigou-Lagrange, *The Three Ages of the Interior Life*

He is there in our soul and we in him. It is not hard to feel deeply grateful and happy and experience our Friend's true friendship. The angels are present and adore him in our souls. At those moments the soul is as near Heaven as it is possible to be in this world. How can we be thinking about other things ...?

On other occasions we can make good use of those prayers found in devotional books which generations of Christians have used to nourish their piety throughout many centuries: the *Te Deum*, *Trium puerorum*, *Adoro te devote*, *Anima Christi* and many more which have been left to us by saints and good Christians truly devoted to the Blessed Sacrament.

If we love Christ, who offers himself for us, we will feel compelled to find a few minutes after Mass for an intimate personal thanksgiving, which will prolong in the silence of our hearts that other thanksgiving which is the Eucharist. How are we to approach him, what are we to say, how should we behave?

Christian life is not made up of rigid norms ... Still, I feel that, on many occasions, the central theme of our conversation with Christ, in our thanksgiving after Holy Mass, can be the consideration that Our Lord is our king, physician, teacher and friend.[16]

Our King, because he has ransomed us from sin and brought us to the kingdom of light. We ask him to reign in our hearts, in the words we say today, with the work we have offered him, in our thoughts, in each of our actions.

In Communion we see Jesus the Physician, and he has the remedy for all our illnesses. We approach Communion as he was approached by the blind, the deaf, the paralytic ... And let us not forget that we have the Source of all life putting himself at our disposal within our souls. He is the

---

[16] St J. Escrivá, *Christ is passing by*, 92

Life.

Jesus is the Teacher whom we recognise as having the words of eternal life ... and in ourselves there is so much ignorance! He is constantly teaching – but we must be attentive. If our imagination, our memory and senses are let loose ... we will fail to hear him.

Through Communion we look at our Friend, the true Friend, from whom we learn about friendship. We tell him what is happening in our life, and we always find an encouraging word, a consoling word ... At times we ask the help of our Guardian Angel: *Thank him for me; you know how to do it better.*

There is nobody better than Our Lady, who carried God's Son in her womb for nine months, to teach us how to treat him better in our thanksgiving after Communion. Let us have recourse to her.

72. LEARNING TO FORGIVE

72.1 People can change. Avoid making definitive judgements on people based on their external actions.

The first reading of the Mass tells us of an event that took place among St Paul's missionary companions. They had sailed from Paphos and arrived in Perga in Pamphylia; but there John left them *and returned to Jerusalem.*[1] The others continued their apostolic journey and reached Antioch of Pisidia. John, also called Mark, was a cousin of Barnabas, Paul's inseparable apostolic partner and one of the pillars of the work of spreading the faith among the Gentiles. Since early youth Mark had known the fervent apostolate of the early Christians at Jerusalem gathered around Our Lady and the Apostles, whom he had known intimately. Mark's mother had been among the first women to help Jesus and the Twelve. It seems natural that Barnabas should have thought specially of initiating his cousin John Mark as a partner in the task of spreading the Gospel under his joint authority with St Paul.[2]

John lost heart and went home, leaving his partners. He felt unable to cope and turned back. This event must have weighed heavily on the others who went ahead. However, in preparing the second great apostolic journey to visit the brethren who had received the faith, *Barnabas wanted to take with them John called Mark. But Paul thought it best not to take with them one who had withdrawn from them in Pamphylia, and had not gone with*

---

[1] Acts 13:13
[2] cf *The Navarre Bible*, Introduction to St Mark's Gospel

466   FOURTH WEEK OF EASTER • Thursday

them to the work.[3]

St Paul was not of a mind to take someone with him who had already let him down once. Such a difference arose then between them that they parted from each other. *Barnabas took Mark with him and sailed away to Cyprus, but Paul chose Silas and departed, being commended by the brethren to the grace of the Lord.*[4] The arguments and the differences of viewpoints must have been substantial to cause such a separation. St Jerome says, *Paul was the more strict and Barnabas the more lenient in maintaining their views. Nevertheless this argument showed up clearly human frailty.*[5]

Despite everything, Paul being a man of immense heart, and a fervent apostle who sacrificed himself to the utmost for his brethren, did not make a definitive judgement on Mark. On the contrary, years later we find Mark described as one of the Apostle's closest partners[6] and a deep source of consolation for him.[7] *Aristarchus, my fellow prisoner, greets you, and Mark the cousin of Barnabas (concerning whom you have received instructions – if he comes to you, receive him), and Jesus who is called Justus ... they have been a comfort to me.*[8] Later on, Paul asks Timothy to go with Mark because *he is very useful in serving me.*[9] Within a few years Mark was once more a friend and an effective partner of the Apostle in his hardship. Perhaps once Paul had thought Mark was of no use; now he wants him by his side. People can change, and when we have to judge them by their outward

---

[3] Acts 15:37-38
[4] Acts 15:39-40
[5] St Jerome, *Dialogue against the Pelagians* 11, 17
[6] Philem 24
[7] cf Col 4:10ff
[8] cf Col 4:10-11
[9] cf 2 Tim 4:11

behaviour – God alone can know their intentions – we should never make judgements that are fixed and unchangeable. Our Lord loves us as we are, with our defects too, when we struggle to overcome them, and he counts on time and grace to change us. Seeing the defects of those around us – sometimes very evident and undeniable ones – we should never lack the charity which enables us to understand and to help them. *From now on, couldn't we look at others in such a way as not to be disheartened by their defects? The time will come when the wounds are forgotten ... Perhaps many things which have saddened us today or in recent times will be forgotten. We have defects, but we can love each other! This is because we are brethren and because Christ loves us truly ... as we are.*[10] The fundamental reason is that although Christ does not love our shortcomings, he loves us despite our many defects. Let defects not be a cause of distancing ourselves from those with whom we are living, with those around us at the office, in the university or in our place of work.

72.2 Forgive and forget. Making up with our friends.

St Paul gives us an example of how to forget, of how to repair breakdowns in our relationships, of how to be a real friend. As regards St Mark he is a magnificent example to us of humility and hope. The event in which he was the subject of the argument dividing Barnabas and Paul must have deeply impressed and greatly hurt the Evangelist. He must have been deeply hurt at seeing himself rejected by Paul, who had a well-won reputation as a tireless evangelizer of great wisdom and holiness. He in his turn was able to forget, and was there where he was needed, comforting Paul and being extremely helpful in the ministry.

---

[10] A. G. Dorronsoro, *God and People*

St Mark managed to forgive and forget because he had a great soul. That is why later on he was such a marvellous instrument of grace. *Those who zealously keep a list of grudges show themselves to be very narrow-minded. Such poor wretches are impossible to live with.*

True charity neither keeps account of the necessary services it renders all the time, nor takes note of the effronteries it has to put up with. 'Omnia suffert' – it endures all things.[11]

If we lack humility we will tend to draw up our list of small grudges which, despite being small, take away our peace with God, waste a lot of energy and make us incapable of undertaking the great plans Our Lord has in mind each day for those close to him. The heart of the humble person is set on God and is thus filled with joy, becoming, as it were, less vulnerable. It doesn't matter to him what people say or might have said. He forgets immediately, and doesn't give too much consideration to the humiliations which every man or woman experiences in one way or another in the course of their daily life.

Such simplicity and humility, not getting complicated when pride suggests our reputation is being maligned, leaving aside possible grudges, gives us the ability to begin again when we have been cowardly or have failed. We see Mark take up his work immediately again with Barnabas after the cowardice and fatigue of the first journey – ready this time to be unconditionally faithful.

The humble person finds it easy to be fraternal with others and so looks for ways to relate to those around him. He restores friendship if it has been for any reason broken or has cooled off, and is always ready to lend a brotherly hand and be helped himself. The relationships necessary for social life are formed in this way. *In closeness there is*

---

[11] St J. Escrivá, *Furrow*, 738

*mutual support and on this charity is built ... If I then fail
in putting up with your character and you don't want to
bear with mine, how can charity grow between us since
patience does not unite us in mutual love? As we have said,
in a building each stone is both supportive and a support.*[12]

72.3 Despite our ups and downs and other short-comings, we can be good instruments of God if we are humble.

Besides St Mark's apostolic work of expansion and
consolidation among the new converts, he worked in very
close cooperation with Peter, Paul and Barnabas.
According to the most reliable tradition he was St Peter's
interpreter in Rome, probably translating both the
preaching and oral teachings of the Prince of the Apostles.
Above all he was a very docile instrument of the Holy
Spirit in leaving us the priceless jewel of the second
Gospel.

It is a great source of consolation and hope to us when
we look at the person of this Evangelist, from his very first
steps up to his becoming an invaluable instrument for the
early Church and for all time. Despite our shortcomings,
the possible failures and hesitations of our past, like him
we can be assured, with the help of grace, of being able to
give a selfless and useful service to the Church. Despite
everything, we too can become effective instruments.

What help and care he must have given at Rome to the
elderly St Paul in prison. Both had made their own the
words written by the Apostle of the Gentiles to the
Christians at Corinth: *Love is patient and kind ...*[13] Love
overcomes all.

Charity can overcome all our defects, smooth out the

---

[12] St Gregory the Great, *Homilies on Ezechiel*
[13] cf 1 Cor 13:1

differences between characters, and remove anything that might be an obstacle in relationships. Charity can overcome all resistance. How different everything would have been if Paul had given in to the prejudice that Mark couldn't be relied on for anything, because he had once been cowardly or exhausted, or had allowed himself to become discouraged and gone back to Jerusalem! How different things would also have been if Mark had harboured a grudge because the Apostle didn't want to have him on his second journey!

Let us today ask Mary our Mother that we may never hold anything against anybody, for it would do great damage to our heart, to our love for God and our neighbour. Let us learn from St Mark how to begin again, a thousand times if necessary, if we for any reason have to go through a similar bad experience of failure or cowardice.

73. READING AND MEDITATING ON THE GOSPEL

73.1 Reading the Gospel fruitfully.

Jesus Christ is *the way, the truth and the life*[1] for each person, the Gospel of today's Mass tells us. In knowing him we know the purpose of life and of all things; our life is an ongoing journey towards him. It is in the Gospel we must learn *the supreme knowledge of Jesus Christ*,[2] how to imitate him and follow in his footsteps. *And to learn from him, you must try to know his life – reading the Gospel and meditating on the scenes of the New Testament – in order to understand the divine meaning of his life on earth. In our own life we must reproduce Christ's life. We need to come to know him by reading and meditating on Scripture.*[3]

We want to identify ourselves with our Lord, our daily living to be a reflection of him. *But to be Christ himself, we must 'see ourselves in him'. It's not enough to have a general idea of the spirit of Jesus' life; we have to learn the details of his life and, through them, his attitudes. Especially, we must contemplate his life, and from it derive strength, light, serenity and peace.*

When you love someone, you want to know all about him, his life and his personality, so as to become like him. That is why we have to meditate on the life of Jesus, from his birth in a stable right through to his death and resurrection.[4]

---

[1] cf John 14:6
[2] Phil 3:8
[3] St J. Escrivá, *Christ is passing by*, 14
[4] *ibid*, 107

We should read the Gospel with a longing to know him so as to love him. We can't read Scripture as though it were just another book. *In the sacred books the Father who is in Heaven comes lovingly to meet his children, and talks with them.*[5] Prayer has to accompany our reading, because we know that God is the principal author of those books. In them, and in the Gospels in particular, we find *food for the soul, and a pure and lasting fount of spiritual life.*[6] *We should listen to the Gospel* – St Augustine writes – *as though Christ were present and talking to us. We shouldn't say: those who knew him in real life were very fortunate, for many of those who knew him, did in fact crucify him; and many who did not know him believed in him. The words which our Lord spoke were written down; they have been safeguarded and preserved for us.*[7]

To read and meditate on the Gospel fruitfully we have to do so with faith, knowing that it contains the truths of salvation, and contains them without error; we also have to read it with piety and holiness of life. The Church, with the help of the Holy Spirit, has preserved intact and free from all error the priceless treasure of our Lord's life and doctrine; by meditating on it we can easily draw close to him and strive to become saints. We will discover the intimate truths contained in those books only insofar as we desire to be saints; only thus will we taste the divine fruit which they contain. Do we truly appreciate this tremendous treasure which we have so readily to hand? Are we trying to grow in knowledge and love for the sacred humanity of our Lord each day through our Gospel reading? Do we ask the Holy Spirit to help us each time we begin reading the Gospel?

---

[5] Second Vatican Council, *Dei Verbum*, 21
[6] *ibid*
[7] St Augustine, *Commentary on St John*, 30

73.2 Contemplating the most sacred humanity of Christ in the Gospel.

We only love what we know well. That's why we need to have the life of Christ *in our heart and mind, so that at any time, without any book, we can close our eyes and contemplate his life, watching it like a film. In this way the words and actions of our Lord will come to mind in all the different circumstances of our life.*

In this way we become involved in his life. It is not a matter of just thinking about Jesus, of recalling some scenes of his life. We must be completely involved and play a part in his life. We must follow him as closely as Mary his Mother did, as closely as the first twelve, the holy women, the crowds that pressed about him. If we do this without holding back, Christ's words will enter deep into our soul and will really change us ...

If we want to bring other men and women to our Lord, we must first go to the Gospel and contemplate Christ's love.[8]

We read the Gospel eager to know our Lord just as his disciples knew him, to observe his reactions, his behaviour, his words; to see him full of compassion at the sight of so many people in need; to see him tired after a long day's journey; impressed by the faith of a mother or of a centurion; patient with the defects of his most faithful followers; we also contemplate his habitual closeness to his Father, the trusting way he turns to Him, in his nights of prayer, in his ceaseless love for all.

To love him more, to know his most blessed humanity, to follow him closely, we should read the New Testament and meditate on it slowly, with love and piety. The Second Vatican Council *forcefully and specifically exhorts all the Christian faithful ... to frequently read sacred Scripture.*

---

[8] St J. Escrivá, *Christ is passing by*, 107

Ignorance of Scripture is ignorance of Christ, said St Jerome. Therefore, let them go gladly to the sacred text itself, whether in the sacred liturgy, which is full of his divine words, or in devout reading.[9]

Through the shedding of your Son's Blood, we ask God in today's Mass for *life through you.*[10] Well, this food for our soul, which we should try to receive daily, is easy to take. Three or four minutes a day is enough, but doing it with love. *I advised you to read the New Testament and to enter into each scene and take part in it, as one more of the characters. The minutes you spend in this way each day enable you to 'incarnate' the Gospel, reflect it in your life and help others to reflect it.*[11]

73.3 God speaks to us in Scripture. His Word is always meaningful.

How sweet are your words to my taste, sweeter than honey in my mouth![12]

St Paul taught the early Christians that the word of God is *living and active.*[13] It is always relevant, always new for each person, new each day, and besides, it is personal because it is destined expressly for each of us. As we read the Gospel, we will recognise ourselves in some character in a parable, or we will feel that certain words are aimed at us in a particular way. *In many and various ways God spoke of old to our fathers by the prophets; but in these last days He has spoken to us by a Son.*[14] These times are also our times. Jesus Christ continues speaking to us. As his words are divine and eternal, they are always

---

[9] Second Vatican Council, *Dei Verbum*, 25
[10] *Collect*
[11] St J. Escrivá, *Furrow*, 672
[12] Ps 118:103
[13] cf Heb 4:12
[14] cf Heb 1:1

relevant and up-to-date. In a certain sense, what the Gospel narrates is happening today, now, in our lives. The prodigal son is leaving home or returning to his Father today; likewise sheep wander off today and get lost, and the shepherd goes looking for them; leaven is needed today to transform the lump, and light to enlighten the darkness of sin.

The Gospel reveals to us the meaning of our life and its value, and shows us the path we ought to follow. *The true light – the Word – that enlightens every man was coming into the world.*[15] And that Word is addressed to every man without exception. That is why the Gospel should be for us a source of aspirations which feed our presence of God during the day, and it is also why we should bring it to our prayer often.

If we meditate on the Gospel we will find peace. *Power came forth from him and healed them all,*[16] St Luke tells us on one occasion. That power continues coming forth from Jesus each time we have contact with him and his words, which last eternally.

For a Christian, the Gospel should be the most important book: for us it is essential if we are to come to know Jesus Christ. We must look at him and contemplate him until we know him thoroughly, every aspect of his personality. The Gospel allows us to become fully immersed in the mystery of Jesus: this is particularly important today as you hear so many confusing ideas about this most transcendental topic for mankind: Jesus Christ, the Son of God, the corner stone. *Don't go astray in the mist and the fog, but rather listen to the voice of the shepherd. Fall back on holy Scripture, there you will find the delight of your heart; you will find nothing there that*

---

[15] John 1:9
[16] Luke 6:19

will harm or poison you; rich is the food you will find there.[17]

Frequently it's good to do our Gospel reading first thing in the morning, trying to focus on some practical point which can help us in our presence of God during the day, or help us imitate our Lord in some aspect of our activity: for example, trying to be more cheerful, being more kind to others, more attentive to those who are suffering, accepting tiredness, etc. Thus, almost without realising it, that great desire could become a reality in us: *How I wish your bearing and conversation were such that, on seeing or hearing you, people would say: This man reads the life of Jesus Christ.*[18]

That would be a great benefit not only for ourselves, but also for those who live or work with us, or who have contact with us.

---

[17] St Augustine, *Sermon 46 on Shepherds*
[18] St J. Escrivá, *The Way*, 2

74. THE VIRTUE OF HOPE

74.1 Human hope and the supernatural virtue of hope.

We read in the Gospel of today's Mass these consoling words of our Lord: *If you ask anything in my name, I will do it.*[1] The Communion antiphon has equally consoling words of our Lord: *Father, I desire that they also, whom you have given me, may be with me where I am, to behold my glory.*[2]

Jesus himself is our intercessor in Heaven, and he promises us that everything we ask for in his name He will grant us. To ask in his name means, in the first place, to have faith in his resurrection and in his mercy; and it means asking for those human and supernatural things which are good for our salvation, which is the fundamental object of the Christian virtue of hope, and of man's very life itself.

The farmer has natural hope when he sows the seed; the sailor 'hopes' when he sets out on a sea journey, and the business man 'hopes' when he sets up a business. They hope to obtain an earthly goal: a good harvest, to reach a particular port, to obtain a good income.

Christian hope is essentially supernatural, and hence is far superior to the natural desire for happiness and to natural confidence in God. Through this virtue we tend towards eternal life, to supernatural happiness, which is nothing other than the possession of God himself: to see God as He sees himself, to love him as He loves himself. We tend towards God by using the means which God

---

[1] John 14:14
[2] John 17:24

himself promised us; means which are always available to us if we do not reject them. We are confident we will obtain that limitless good, but the main reason for that confidence is God himself: in his mercy and infinite love He offers us his helping hand, and we respond with our good will, lovingly accepting the hand He stretches out to us.[3]

With the virtue of hope, the Christian is not guaranteed salvation, unless he is granted an extraordinary grace by God, but he does tend with certainty towards his goal in much the same way as, in the human order of things, a person who undertakes a journey is not certain of reaching his goal but can confirm that he is on the right road and be reasonably certain of reaching his goal if he does not go astray. *The certitude of Christian hope is not, therefore, as yet the certitude of salvation, but it is the firmest kind of certitude that we are tending toward salvation.*[4] We are confident that God *never asks the impossible of us, but he does expect us to do what we can, and to ask for help to do what is beyond our means.*[5]

The Magisterium of the Church teaches that *everybody should have firm hope in God's assistance. For if we are faithful to grace, just as God began in us the work of our salvation, he will bring it to completion, 'working in us both the will to do it and the accomplishment of that will' (Phil 2:13).*[6] Our Lord will not leave us if we do not leave him, and he will give us all the means we need to go forward in all circumstances, in every time and place. He listens to us every time we humbly have recourse to him. He gives us the means to become holy through our

---

[3] cf R. Garrigou-Lagrange, *The Three Ages of the Interior Life*, Vol II
[4] *ibid*
[5] St Augustine, *De Gratia*, 43,5
[6] Council of Trent, *Decree on justification*, chap 13, Dz 806

ordinary activity, in the midst of our work and in the circumstances in which we find ourselves. He gives us more grace if the difficulties are greater, and more strength if our weaknesses are more pronounced.

74.2 Sins against hope: despair and presumption.

Christian hope should be laborious, to avoid the presumption which expects the divine reward without working for it; and it should be firm and invincible, to avoid discouragement.[7]

There is presumption when one relies more upon one's own resources than on the help of God, forgetting that grace is needed for every good deed one does; or when one is expecting something from God's mercy which he cannot give us because of our bad disposition; for example, to expect to be pardoned when true repentance is lacking, or to expect eternal life without making any effort to merit it.

It is not unusual for a person to slip rather quickly from a state of presumption into a state of despair when faced with trials and difficulties; it is as though that difficult good, which is the object of hope, were impossible to attain. That discouragement leads first to pessimism, and then to lukewarmness,[8] a lukewarmness which feels that the struggle for personal holiness is too difficult a task; what happens next is that all effort is abandoned.

The cause of discouragement is not the existence of difficulties, but rather the absence of a genuine desire for holiness and of reaching Heaven. When we love God and want to love him more, we avail ourselves of difficulties to show him our love and to grow in virtue. Lack of hope creeps in when bourgeois attitudes are allowed to flourish in the soul; when one becomes attached to things of this

---

[7] R. Garrigou-Lagrange, *op cit*
[8] cf St J. Escrivá, *The Way*, 988

world, regarding them as the only things that are worth while.

The lukewarm person becomes discouraged because through a good deal of culpable negligence he has lost sight of his goal, which is personal holiness and a desire to know and love God more. Then material things take on an absolute value, if not in theory at least in practice. *If we make temporal projects into absolute goals, eliminating from our horizon our eternal dwelling and the goal for which we have been created – to love and praise God and to possess him afterwards in Heaven – then our noblest efforts betray us and lead to our defilement.*[9]

We should go through life with clearly-determined goals, with our eyes on God, which is what helps us to carry out our daily work enthusiastically, whether we feel like it or not. Then we appreciate that all the good things of this world – although genuinely good in themselves – are only relatively so and should always be subordinate to eternal life and what relates to it. The goal of Christian hope transcends absolutely everything earthly.

This attitude towards life requires a cheerful daily struggle, because the tendency of every man and woman is to make this life into a *lasting city*, when in actual fact we are only passing through. How can we ensure that our hope is firm and strong? By striving in our interior life, in areas which are clearly spelt out for us in spiritual guidance, by examining our conscience daily, by beginning and re-beginning, humbly and without discouragement: that is what guarantees our hope. Our Lord promises us, as we read in the Gospel of today's Mass, that every time we go to him for help he will look after us.

---

[9] cf F. Fernandez, *Lukewarmness – the Devil in Disguise*

74.3 The Blessed Virgin our Hope. Having recourse to her in moments of difficulty, and always.

I am the Mother of Fair Love ... in me is all hope of life and vigour:[10] for centuries the Church has put these words on the lips of Our Lady. The patriarchs and the prophets lived the virtue of hope in a special way in the Old Testament, as did all the devout Israelites. They lived and died with their eyes on *the prize the whole world treasures*[11] and on the goods which its arrival in the world would bring with it; *they looked forward to them and welcomed them at a distance, considering themselves to be no better than strangers and exiles on earth.*[12] Over many generations that hope sustained the people of Israel in the midst of countless trials and tribulations.

With greater strength than the patriarchs and the prophets and all mankind together, the Blessed Virgin Mary added to that clamour of hope, of longing for the prompt arrival of the Messiah. That hope was greater in Mary because she was confirmed in grace and, therefore, preserved from all presumption and from any lack of confidence in God. Even before the Annunciation, Mary had penetrated into sacred Scripture more than any human intellect had ever done; and that clarity in the knowledge of what the prophets had announced went on increasing until it reached a point of total confidence that what had been announced would come about. That hope was growing as the certainty of *the sailor grows – he has taken the necessary precautions to ensure that he reaches his goal – and his certainty increases as he draws closer.*[13]

Mary lived the virtue of hope when in her youth she

---

[10] cf Sir 24:24
[11] Hag 2:8
[12] Heb 11:13
[13] R. Garrigou-Lagrange, *The Mother of the Saviour*

ardently desired the arrival of the Messiah; later, she hoped that the secret of her virginal conception of our Lord would be revealed to Joseph, her spouse; she exercised the virtue of hope when they were in Bethlehem and they had no place for the Messiah to be born; and she had hope during her hasty flight into Egypt. Later on, when all seemed lost on Calvary, she awaited – and hoped for – the glorious Resurrection of her Son, while the whole world was plunged in darkness. Now, as the Ascension of Jesus into Heaven draws close, she is ready to sustain the new-born Church in spreading the Gospel and converting the pagan world.

Over the centuries Our Lord has multiplied the signs of his merciful assistance, and he has left us Mary as a powerful beacon so that we will always know which way to turn when we get lost. *If the winds of temptation blow, if you run against the reefs of temptation, look at the star, call on Mary. If the waves of pride, of ambition or of envy are breaking over you, look at the star, call on Mary. If anger, greed or impurity are violently shaking the ship of your soul, turn to Mary. If you are dismayed at the thought of your sins, confounded by the ugliness of your conscience, fearful at the idea of judgement, and you begin to sink into a bottomless abyss of sadness or of despair, think about Mary.*

When in danger, anguish, or in doubt, think about Mary, invoke Mary. Let Mary always be on your lips, may she never be absent from your heart. To obtain her help and intercession, always follow the example of her virtues. You will not go astray if you follow her. You will not despair if you call to her. You will not get lost if you think about her. If she is holding you by the hand you will not fall. If she is protecting you, you have nothing to fear. You will not grow weary if she is your guide. You will reach port safely if she is looking after you.[14]

---

[14] St Bernard, *Homily 2 on the 'missus est'*, 7

75. THE VIRTUE OF JUSTICE

75.1 Being just with people and with society.

The Lord's word is true, he is faithful in all his dealings; faithfulness he loves, and the just award, the whole earth overflows with the Lord's goodness.[1]

Justice is the cardinal virtue which allows men to live together in a seemly and truly human manner. Without it, living together would be impossible. Society, family life and the world of business would cease to be human; they would become situations where men trod other men underfoot. Justice regulates life in society taking human nature into account – that is to say, respecting the rights of the individual. *Justice is the fundamental principle of life, and of men living together, of human communities, of societies and of peoples.*[2]

One aspect of this virtue has to do with our relations with our neighbour, our friends, our colleagues, and everybody in general: it regulates our relations with other people in society, so that we give every man his due. Another aspect of this virtue has to do with the duties of society itself towards the individual. Finally, justice also regulates the duties of the citizen towards the society to which he belongs.

Justice in society comes from the people who make up that society. They project on to society their own justice or their lack of justice; this applies particularly to those who have greater responsibility. This is true in the family, in business, in national and international affairs. If we really want justice to be the order of the day in our society, then

---

[1] *Responsorial Psalm*: Ps 33:4-5
[2] St John Paul II, *General Audience*, 8 November 1978

let us make the individual members of our society just. Let
each of us begin by ourselves being just on three different
planes: with those with whom we come into contact each
day, with those who depend upon us, and by contributing
to our society as we ought. That is the primary moral
obligation of justice: we must practise it in every aspect of
our lives. We must live upright, noble lives; we must be
just with our family, with our neighbours, with the State.
The struggle to ensure that our society is more just must
express itself in a series of personal decisions which shape
the soul of the individual, little by little. Through specific
deeds of justice, we find ourselves moved more and more
readily by *an established and unhesitating will to give to
every man his due*;[3] that is the essence of this virtue.

It is up to the members of society to work with
personal responsibility for a more just, more upright and
altogether healthier society. And there is no task more
attractive and nobler than that.

75.2 Promoting justice.

*God calls us through what happens during our day:
through the suffering and happiness of the people we live
with, through the human interests of our colleagues and
the things that make up our family life. He also calls us
through the great problems, conflicts and challenges of
each period of history, which attract the effort and
idealism of a large part of mankind.*[4] Our faith urges us to
be present, to play an active part in the noble interests, *in
the things that make up our family life*, and *in the conflicts
and challenges of each period of history* so as to sanctify
ourselves and to sanctify those realities, making them more
human, more just, and bringing them to God. *It is easy to*

---

[3] St Thomas, *Summa Theologiae*, II-II, 58, 1
[4] St J. Escrivá, *Christ is passing by*, 110

understand the impatience, anxiety and uneasiness of people whose naturally Christian soul (cf Tertullian, Apology, 17) stimulates them to fight the personal and social injustice which the human heart can create. So many centuries of men living side by side and still so much hate, so much destruction, so much fanaticism stored up in eyes that do not want to see and in hearts that do not want to love.[5]

Our faith urges us on because the need for justice in the world is great indeed. *The good things of the earth, monopolised by a handful of people; the culture of the world, confined to cliques. And, on the outside, hunger for bread and education. Human lives – holy, because they come from God – treated as mere things, as statistics. I understand and share this impatience. It moves me to look at Christ, who is continually inviting us to put his new commandment of love into practice.*

All the circumstances in which life places us bring a new message, asking us to respond with love and service to others.[6]

Out of love for Jesus Christ and love for his fellow men, the Christian strives to rectify unjust situations. The just person, in the fullest meaning of the term, is one who generates everywhere an atmosphere of cheerfulness and love, and, at the same time, who does not compromise with injustice. The normal ambit for this is one's own social circle: our family, our workplace, the city or locality where one lives. If we examine our conscience we may possibly find injustices which need to be rectified: hasty judgements against people or institutions, lack of honest effort in our work, treating some people unjustly ...

75.3 The basis and goal of justice.

Love for Jesus Christ is the great motivating source of

---

[5] *ibid*, 111
[6] *ibid*

the just person's actions. The more faithful we are to our Lord the more just we will be, the more committed we will be to true justice. A Christian knows that his neighbour, the *other person*, is Christ himself, present in others, especially in the needy. *Only with the light of faith can we appreciate what is at stake in the justice or injustice of our actions: it is a matter of accepting or of rejecting Jesus Christ himself.*[7] That is the great driving force of our actions. That is something that Christians alone can see, with the light of faith: Christ is waiting for us in our fellow men. *For I was hungry and you gave me no food; I was thirsty ...* Omissions: *Truly, I say to you, as you did it not to one of the least of these, you did it not to me.*[8]

Our Lord is in each person who is in need. *The poor of society – individual poor people – should receive special attention from the Church and from Christians; and certain areas of our towns and cities, the sick and the marginalised and certain ethnic and cultural groups, should also be given special and continuing attention. We need to increase our effort to be with them and to share in their difficulties; we should feel God calling us in the needs of our brothers and sisters, and change the whole of society so that it is more just and more welcoming to the poor.*[9]

We must learn to recognise Christ when he comes out to meet us in our brothers, the people around us.[10] It would be good to see how much we respect justice, how much attention we give it, how keen are we on justice; and we should further enrich justice through the Christian virtue of charity: all that would tell us how faithfully we are following Christ. It's also true the other way around: if we

---

[7] P. Rodriguez, *Faith and Life of Faith*, Pamplona
[8] cf Matt 25:45
[9] Spanish Episcopal Conference, *Witnesses to the living God*, 28 June 1985, 59
[10] St J. Escrivá, *op cit*, 111

are friends of Christ and love him, that love and friendship will overflow into our relationship with others.

The spiritual and material responsibilities of the Christian towards others are demanding: he must know how to serve others willingly, with his heart, and in deeds. When faced with those responsibilities, with the help of God's grace, the Christian will neither be cowed, on the one hand, nor get caught up in a frenzy of confused, 'strange' activity, on the other. But he mustn't give in to passivity either: 'caritas enim Christi urget nos': the love of Christ urges us on (2 Cor 5:14).[11] It brings us beyond the demands of simple justice, but, obviously, it presupposes justice.

If this exercise of charity is to be above all criticism, and seen to be so ... – the Second Vatican Council tells us *– the demands of justice must first of all be satisfied; that which is already due in justice is not to be offered as a gift of charity.*[12]

Through the exercise of justice we are constantly being brought into contact with Christ. In the final analysis, *To treat another person justly is to acknowledge God's presence in that person.*[13]

Hence, the Christian cannot live true justice if he is not in the state of grace;[14] his justice would be flat, dwarfed. In our dealings with others, Christ expects more of us. Let us ask him *to give us a good heart, capable of having compassion for the pain of others. Only with such a heart can we realize that the true balm for suffering and anguish in this world is love, charity.*[15]

---

[11] F. Ocariz, *Love for God, Love for men*, Madrid
[12] Second Vatican Council, *Apostolicam actuositatem*, 8
[13] P. Rodriguez, *op cit*
[14] cf St Thomas, *Summa Theologiae*, II-II, 4, 7
[15] St J. Escrivá, *op cit*, 167

FIFTH WEEK OF EASTER – MONDAY

76. WE ARE TEMPLES OF GOD

76.1 The indwelling of the Blessed Trinity in our souls. Looking for God within us.

We frequently see in the Gospel the friendship the Apostles had with our Lord: they spend time chatting with him, asking him about things they don't understand. The Gospel of today's Mass mentions one of those incidents: it's a topic which must have come up often, especially towards the end of our Lord's life.

Our Lord said to them: *He who has my commandments and keeps them, he it is who loves me; and he who loves me will be loved by my Father, and I will love him and manifest myself to him.*[1] In Jesus' day it was commonly held among the Jews that when the Messiah arrived he would reveal himself to everybody as King and Saviour.[2] The Apostles thought that our Lord's words referred to them, to those who were close to him, those who loved him. Judas Thaddaeus understood what our Lord was saying, and he asked *Lord, how is it that you will manifest yourself to us, and not to the world?*

In the Old Testament, God revealed himself on different occasions and in different ways, and he promised that he would dwell in the midst of his people.[3] But now our Lord is referring to a very different kind of presence: his presence in the people who love him, in each person who is in a state of grace. *If a man loves me, he will keep my word, and my Father will love him, and we will come to*

---

[1] John 14:21
[2] cf *The Navarre Bible*, St John
[3] cf Ex 29:45; Ez 37:26-27

him and make our home with him.[4] This is the presence of the Blessed Trinity in the soul which has been reborn through grace. This is a fundamental teaching of the Christian life frequently repeated by St Paul: *For we are the temple of the living God,*[5] he says to the first Christians of Corinth.

Quoting this passage, St John of the Cross comments: *What more desirest thou, O soul, and what more seekest thou without thyself, since within thyself thou hast thy riches, thy delights, thy satisfaction ... thy Beloved, Whom thy soul desires and seeks? Rejoice thou and be glad in thy inward recollection with Him, since thou hast Him so near.*[6]

We should learn to become better and better friends of God who is dwelling within us. Through this divine presence, our soul becomes a miniature heaven. Reflection on that thought can help us enormously. At Baptism the three Persons of the most Blessed Trinity came into our soul: they want to be closer to us throughout our lives than the closest of friends. This presence – which is quite unique – is lost only through mortal sin. But we Christians should not be content with simply not losing God's presence within us: we should recall his presence within us in the midst of our daily activity, when we're going from place to place, to thank him, to ask him for help, to atone for the sins we commit against him each day.

At times we think that God is far away, whereas in fact he is very close to us. He is more interested in what we're doing than the best of friends. Reflecting on this ineffable closeness of God, St Augustine exclaimed: *Late have I loved you, O Beauty so ancient and so new, late have I*

---

[4] John 14:23
[5] cf 2 Cor 6:16
[6] St John of the Cross, *The Spiritual Canticle*, 1, 8

*loved you. For behold you were within me, and I outside;
and I sought you outside ... You were with me, but I was
not with you. I was kept from you by those things, yet had
they not been in you, they would not have been at all. You
called and cried to me and broke open my deafness. You
sent forth your beams and shone, and chased away my
blindness.*[7]

But to talk to God, really present in our soul in grace,
we need to control our senses, as they tend to scatter and
become attached to all sorts of things. We need to be aware
that we are *temples of God* and to behave accordingly. We
need to surround with love, with resounding silence, that
intimate presence of the Blessed Trinity in our soul.

76.2 Growth in God's friendship requires interior recollection. Mortification.

The presence of the three divine Persons in our souls
in grace is a living presence, which is open to our
friendship: they are inviting us to get to know them and to
love them. It is up to us to correspond. *Why climb the
mountains or go down into the valleys of the world looking
for him who dwells within us?*[8] St Augustine asks. But St
Gregory tells us: *As long as our mind is giddy with carnal
images it will never be able to contemplate ... because
there are as many obstacles blinding it as there are
thoughts pulling it hither and thither. Hence, for the soul to
contemplate the invisible nature of God, the first step must
be: let it be recollected within itself.*[9]

God asks some people to withdraw from the world to
achieve that recollection. But he wants the majority of
Christians (housewives, students, employees) to find it in

---

[7] St Augustine, *Confessions*, 10, 27-38
[8] St Augustine, *De Trinitate*, 8, 17
[9] St Gregory the Great, *Homilies on Ezechiel*, 2, 5

the midst of their daily activities. We keep our senses for God by means of ongoing mortification throughout the day; that's also the way to interior contentment. We mortify our imagination by putting aside useless thoughts; our memory, by not entertaining memories which don't bring us closer to God; our will, by fulfilling our timetable of work and our duties, however small they may be.

Concentrated work, if it is offered to God, not only does not obstruct our conversation with God but rather facilitates it. The same applies to our external activity: social relations, family life, leisure time, journeys ... Everything in life – except when superficiality predominates – has a profound, intimate dimension; it takes on that dimension when we are recollected and brings it into our friendship with God. Recollection means *bringing together what was scattered*, re-establishing interior order, controlling our senses as they tend towards dispersion even in things which are good or indifferent; it means having God as the centre of our intentions in what we're doing and planning.

The opposite to interior recollection is dissipation and superficiality. The senses and faculties dip into whatever pool they meet along the way, and the result is unsettled purpose, scattered attention, deadened will and quickened concupiscence.[10] Unless we are recollected we cannot pay attention to God.

The more we purify our heart and our senses, the more recollected we are, the more our soul will long for contact with God, *like the deer that yearns for running streams.*[11] *Our heart then needs to distinguish and adore each one of the divine Persons. The soul is, as it were, making a discovery in the supernatural life, like an infant opening*

---

[10] cf St J. Escrivá, *The Way*, 375

[11] cf Ps 51:2

his eyes to the world about him. The soul spends time lovingly with the Father and the Son and the Holy Spirit, and readily submits to the work of the lifegiving Paraclete, who gives himself to us without any merit on our part.[12]

76.3 Friendship with the Holy Spirit.

Although the indwelling of the most Blessed Trinity in our soul pertains to the three persons – the Father, the Son and the Holy Spirit – it is attributed in a particular way to the Third Person. And during this period, as Pentecost Sunday draws closer, the liturgy invites us to give more attention to our friendship with the Holy Spirit.

The Counsellor, the Holy Spirit, whom the Father will send in my name, he will teach you all things, and bring to your remembrance all that I have said to you,[13] our Lord tells us in today's Gospel. This he promised on a number of occasions,[14] as though he wished to point out to us the enormous importance it would have for the entire Church, for the world, and for each person who would follow him. It is not a passing gift, limited to the moment we receive the Sacraments or to some other particular time; rather is it a stable, permanent Gift. *The Holy Spirit dwells in the hearts (of the faithful) as in a temple.*[15] He is the *Sweet Guest of the soul,*[16] and the more the Christian grows in good deeds, the more he purifies himself, the happier the Holy Spirit is to dwell in him and to give him new graces for his holiness and for his apostolate.

The Holy Spirit is present in the soul of the Christian in grace so as to make him more and more like Christ, to urge him to fulfil the will of God and to help him in that task.

---

[12] St J. Escrivá, *Friends of God*, 306
[13] John 14:26
[14] cf John 14:15-17; 15:36; 16:7-14; Matt 10:20
[15] Second Vatican Council, *Lumen gentium*, 9
[16] *Sequence of the Mass of Pentecost Sunday*

The Holy Spirit comes as a remedy to our weaknesses,[17] and intercedes before the Father on our behalf, with groans beyond all utterance.[18] Now He fulfils his mission of guiding, protecting and giving new life to the Church, because, as Saint Paul VI said, Christ promised two different elements for the continuation of his work on earth, and brought them into being: *the apostolate, and the Spirit. The apostolate takes an external and objective form; it constitutes, so to speak, the material body of the Church. It gives it its visible and social structure. Whereas the Holy Spirit, the second element, is active internally, within each person, and also in the community as a whole, raising up, giving new life, sanctifying.*[19]

Let us ask our Lady to help us appreciate this most blessed reality, because our life will then be very different. Why should we feel alone when the Holy Spirit is with us? Why should we ever feel anxious or insecure, even for a single day of our lives, when the Paraclete is so attentive to us and to everything we do? Why go chasing madly after an apparent happiness, when there is no greater happiness than friendship with this sweet Guest who dwells within us? How different our conversation or behaviour would be on occasion if we were only conscious of the fact that we are temples of God, temples of the Holy Spirit.

As we finish our prayer, let us turn to Mary, our Mother: *Hail Mary, temple and tabernacle of the most Blessed Trinity, help us.*

---

[17] Rom 8:26
[18] *ibid*
[19] St Paul VI, *Opening address*, 3rd Session of the Second Vatican Council, 14 September 1964

FIFTH WEEK OF EASTER – TUESDAY

77. *MY PEACE I GIVE YOU*

77.1 The Lord gives his peace to his disciples.

The Gospel of today's Mass relates one of the promises our Lord made to his apostles at the Last Supper, a promise which became a reality after the Resurrection: *Peace I leave with you; my peace I give to you; not as the world gives do I give to you.*[1] Later on, at the same Supper, he repeated: *I have said this to you, that in me you may have peace. In the world you will have tribulation; but be of good cheer, I have overcome the world.*[2] Now, after the resurrection, our Lord stands in the midst of the apostles and says to them: *Pax vobis. Peace be with you.*[3] Our Lord would have spoken those words with that warm voice of his which the apostles knew so well. His friendly greeting dispelled the fear and the shame the apostles felt after the cowardly way they had behaved during his passion. Our Lord's greeting and his warm expression recreates that personal atmosphere in which he communicates his peace to them.

To wish one another peace was the way Jews usually greeted one another. The Apostles continued this custom, as we see in their letters;[4] and so did the early Christians, as can be seen in many inscriptions dating back to that period. The Church uses the same greeting in the liturgy on certain occasions; before holy Communion, for example, the priest wishes peace to the people, because peace is a prerequisite in order to share worthily in the holy sacrifice.[5] *Pax Domini*, the peace of the Lord.

---

[1] John 14:27
[2] John 16:33
[3] John 20:19-21
[4] cf 1 Pet 1:3; Rom 1:7
[5] cf Matt 5:23

Over the centuries Christians put more meaning into their words of greeting, making them more spiritual. Supernatural outlook permeated the lives of the people, and its positive influence can be seen in generation after generation; those greetings are an external sign of a society which had a Christian heart. In today's world, we seem to be losing that supernatural outlook in the greetings we use. But it could be very helpful to our interior life to try to give a Christian tone to our greetings of welcome and farewell; it would add to our sense of the presence of God in our lives.

If we develop the habit, for example, of greeting the Guardian Angel of the people we meet, it will be easier for us to raise our dealings with them to a higher level. It would be a consequence of the presence of God dwelling in our soul. Let us strive not to lose supernatural outlook in the ordinary things of each day: *Peace be with you*, our Lord said to them. In the words of St Gregory Nazianzen, *we should be ashamed if we are not using that greeting of peace which our Lord left us when he was about to depart from this world.*[6] But whatever our normal greeting may be, it can always be an occasion to live our fraternity with others better, to pray for them and to bring them peace and joy, as our Lord did with his disciples.

'For behold, when the voice of your greeting came to my ears, the babe in my womb leaped for joy' (Luke 1:44) ... This joy of Elizabeth reminds us of what a treasure a greeting is when it comes from a heart which is filled with God. How often the shadows of loneliness engulfing a soul can be blown away by the light and warmth of a smile, or of a pleasant word.[7]

---

[6] St Gregory Nazianzen, *Catena aurea*, VI
[7] St John Paul II, *Homily*, 11 November 1981

77.2 True peace, the fruit of the Holy Spirit.

In the mouth of our Lord the ordinary Jewish greeting takes on its deepest meaning, because peace was one of the Messianic gifts *par excellence*.[8] When bidding farewell to somebody who had done some good, our Lord often said: *Go in peace*.[9] He entrusts a mission of peace to his disciples. *Whatever house you enter, first say: Peace be to this house*.[10] To desire peace for others and to foster it in our surroundings is a great human good, and when it is inspired by charity, it is also a great supernatural good. When our soul is at peace it is a clear sign that God is close to us; besides it is one of the fruits of the Holy Spirit.[11] St Paul frequently exhorted the first Christians to live peaceful and happy lives: *agree with one another, live in peace, and the God of love and peace will be with you*.[12]

True peace is the result of holiness, the result of the struggle not to allow our love to be smothered by our disordered tendencies and our sins. When we love God, the soul is like a good tree, which is known by its fruits. Our actions reveal the presence of the Paraclete, and, insofar as they cause spiritual joy, they are called fruits of the Holy Spirit.[13] One of these fruits is *the peace of God, which passes all understanding*,[14] the true peace that Christ desired for the Apostles and for Christians of every era. *When God comes to you, you will feel the truth of these greetings: My peace I give to you ..., peace I leave you ..., peace be with you ..., and you will feel it even in the midst*

---

[8] cf Is 9:7; Mic 5:5
[9] cf Luke 7:50, 8:48
[10] Luke 10:50
[11] Gal 5:22
[12] 2 Cor 13:11
[13] cf St Thomas, *Summa Theologiae*, I-II, 70, 1
[14] Phil 4:7

of troubles.[15]

St Augustine describes true peace as *tranquillity in order*;[16] order between God and ourselves, order within ourselves and order in our relationships with others. If we live that threefold order we will have peace, and we will transmit peace to others. Order towards God means that we are firmly determined to root all sin out of our lives, and to centre everything on Christ. Order towards others means, in the first place, being very refined in the way we live justice (justice in our words, in our judgements and in our actions), because peace is the result of justice.[17] And then, going beyond justice, there is mercy; on so many occasions, mercy moves us to help, to console, to be a support to those in need. *Where justice is loved, where the dignity of the human person is respected, where one is not looking to one's own caprice or personal interest, but rather to serve God and others – that's where you'll find peace.*[18]

Our Lord has entrusted to us the task of bringing peace to the world, starting by having peace in our own souls, and then, in our family and in our place of work. We should work actively to bring animosity and conflict to an end, to create an atmosphere of cooperation and mutual understanding. Peace in a family, or in any group of people, isn't simply the absence of arguments or quarrels; that could be a sign simply of mutual indifference. Peace means helping others in areas of personal or common interest; true peace means being concerned about others, being interested in their plans and projects, their joys and sorrows. Our Lord wants us to foster in our hearts

---

[15] St J. Escrivá, *The Way*, 258
[16] St Augustine, *The City of God*, 19, 13, 1
[17] Is 32:17
[18] Bl. A. del Portillo, *Homily*, 30 March 1985

ambitious longings for peace and harmony in this world of ours, which seems to lack that peace more and more, because at times men don't want to have God in their hearts. God wants us Christians to bring peace and joy with us wherever we go.

77.3 Sowers of peace and joy.

Christable is our peace.[19] For twenty centuries he has been saying to us: *Peace I leave you, my peace I give you*. He wants each of us to proclaim this to the whole world, by the way we live; to the world in which we live, even if at times it may seem rather small.

The life of the first Christians helped many to discover the meaning of their existence. They brought peace to their families and to the society in which they lived. In many inscriptions from that period we find greetings with which they desire peace to others. This peace – which is from God – will be found on earth as long as there are *men and women of good will*.[20] A significant part of our apostolate will be bringing serenity and joy to the people around us; the more anxiety and sadness we meet, the more urgent this apostolate of ours will be. *Every Christian has the duty to bring peace and joy to his own surroundings on earth. This cheerful crusade of manliness will move even shrivelled or rotten hearts, and raise them to God.*[21]

Even though in life they suffered trials and tribulations as others do, every Christian should be remembered as a man or woman who gave an example of smiling self-sacrifice, a serene, cheerful person, because he or she lived as a child of God. Our resolution from today's prayer could be the following: *May no one read sadness or sorrow in*

---

[19] Eph 2:14
[20] Luke 2:14
[21] St J. Escrivá, *Furrow*, 92

your face, when you spread in the world around you the sweet smell of your sacrifice: the children of God should always be sowers of peace and joy.[22] This is possible only when we remember our divine filiation.

Remembering that we are children of God will give us that solid peace, which isn't disturbed by the ups and downs of our emotions or the events of the day: it will give us the serenity and steadiness which we need so much. To ensure that we are open and friendly to everyone, we need to stamp out any kind of antipathy or animosity; it would indicate that we were not very supernatural in our dealings with others. We also need to fight against any roughness or sharpness in our character, which could upset others and would indicate that we were not sufficiently mortified. We need to fight against selfishness, against softness and against love of comfort. These are serious obstacles to friendship and to effectiveness in the apostolate.

The sincere desire for peace which Our Lord has placed in our hearts should urge us to do everything possible to avoid anything that might cause disunity or conflict – for example, being critical of others or having a negative attitude towards them, talking about people behind their backs or complaining about them.

Let us have recourse to Mary, our Mother, so that we may never lose our joy and our serenity. *Mary is the Queen of peace, and thus the Church invokes her. So when your soul or your family are troubled, or things go wrong at work, in society or between nations, cry out to her without ceasing. Call to her by this title: 'Regina nobis' – Queen of peace, pray for us. tried it when you have lost your c surprised at its immediate effect.*[23]

---

[22] *ibid*, 59
[23] *ibid*, 874

78. THE VINE AND THE BRANCHES

78.1 Christ is the true vine. Divine life in our souls.

I am the vine, you are the branches. He who abides in me, and I in him, he it is that bears much fruit, we read in the Gospel of the Mass.[1]

Because of their ingratitude the chosen people had often been compared to a neglected vineyard: Scripture speaks of the ruin and the restoration of the vineyard uprooted from Egypt and planted in a new land;[2] Isaiah expresses God's complaint that his vineyard, after so much care, expecting that it would give grapes, yielded wild grapes.[3] Jesus also uses the image of the vineyard to signify the Jews' rejection of the Messiah and the call of the Gentiles.[4]

But here Our Lord uses the image of the vine and the branches in a totally new sense. Christ is *the true vine*, which communicates its own life to the branches. It is the life of grace which flows from Christ and is communicated to all the members of his body, which is the Church. Without this new sap, they produce no fruit, because they are dead and withered.

His is a life of such great value that Jesus shed His blood, down to the last drop, so that we could receive it. All his words, actions and miracles introduce us progressively to this new life, teaching us how it begins and grows within us, how it dies and how it is restored to us if we have lost it.[5] *I have come*, he tells us, *so that they*

---

[1] n 15:1-8
[2] 79
[3] 1-5
[4] 33-34
[5] ix, *Spiritual Testimony of St John*, Madrid

may have life and have it more abundantly.[6] *You have only to live on in me, and I will live on in you.*[7]

He makes us sharers in the very life of God! Man, at the moment of Baptism, is transformed at the deepest level of his being, to such an extent that he undergoes a new birth, which makes us sons of God, brothers of Christ and members of his Body which is the Church. This life is eternal, if we do not lose it through mortal sin. Death no longer has real power over the one who has this life – he will never die; he will move house,[8] to go and live permanently in Heaven. Jesus wants us to share in something of which he has the fulness. *The life which had flowed forth from the adorable Trinity overflows once more; it spreads and propagates itself. From the head it descends to the members ... The stem and the branches form one single being, they are nourished and act together, producing the same fruits because they are fed by the same sap.*[9]

I write this to you who believe in the name of the Son of God, St John tells us, having recounted for us indescribable wonders, *that you may know you have eternal life.*[10] This new life we receive, or is strengthened, particularly by means of the sacraments, which Our Lord chose to institute so that the Redemption could reach all men in a simple and accessible manner. In these seven efficacious signs of grace we discover Christ, the fountain of all graces. *There He speaks to us, there He forgives us, there He strengthens us, there He sanctifies us, there He gives us the kiss of reconciliation and of friendship; there He gives us His own merits and His own power; there He gives us Himself.*[11]

---

[6] John 10:10
[7] John 15:4
[8] cf *Preface of the Dead I*
[9] M.V. Bernadot, *The Eucharist and the Trinity*, Madrid
[10] 1 John 1:50
[11] E. Boylan, *This Tremendous Lover*, pp. 128-129

78.2 Jesus prunes us so we bear more fruit. The meaning of suffering and mortification. Frequent Confession.

The branch that yields no fruit in me, he cuts away; the branch that does yield fruit he trims clean, so that it may yield more fruit.[12]

The Christian who breaks away from the channels along which grace reaches him (prayer and the sacraments) is left without food for the soul, which *ends up dying at the hands of mortal sin, because its reserves are exhausted, and the moment comes when even a light temptation is sufficient to make it fall: he falls by himself because he has not the strength to remain standing. He dies because his life is finished. But if the channels of grace are not cleared because a heap of carelessness, negligence, laziness, softness, human respect, influences from the environment, haste and other considerations obstruct them, then the life of the soul languishes and a person lives badly until he eventually dies. And, naturally, his sterility is total, because he does not yield any fruit.*[13]

It is God's will however, that we *give fruit and give it more abundantly.*[14] Therefore he prunes the vine so that it may give more fruit. And Jesus continues: *You are already made clean by the word which I have spoken to you.*[15] Our Lord has used the same word for the pruning of the vine as he did for the cleansing of his disciples. Literally the translation should run: *He cleanses him who bears fruit so that he bear more fruit.*[16]

We have to tell Our Lord sincerely that we are ready for him to remove everything in us which is an obstacle to his action: character defects, attachment to our own

---

[12] John 15:2
[13] F. Suarez, *The Vine and the Branches*, Madrid
[14] cf John 15:8
[15] John 15:3
[16] *The Navarre Bible*, St John, note to 15:2

opinion or to material goods, human respect, details of softness or of sensuality ... Even though it hurts, we are resolved to let ourselves be cleansed of all the dead weight, because we want to yield more fruit of holiness and apostolate.

Our Lord cleans us and purifies us in many ways, at times permitting disasters, illness, slander etc. *Have you not heard the Master himself tell the parable of the vine and the branches? Here you can find consolation. He demands much of you, for you are the branch that bears fruit. And he must prune you 'to make you bear more fruit'. Of course: that cutting, that pruning, hurts. But afterwards, what richness in your fruits, what maturity in your actions.*[17]

Our Lord has also wished us to have easy access to the sacrament of Penance, to purify ourselves of our frequent faults and sins. The frequent reception of this sacrament, with true sorrow for sins, is very much related to that cleansing of the soul so necessary for all apostolate.

78.3 Union with Christ. Apostolate, the overflow of interior life. The dry vine and its branches.

Abide in me and I in you. As the branch cannot bear fruit by itself, unless it abide in the vine, neither can you, unless you abide in me.[18]

In our personal dealings with Jesus Christ we prepare and learn to be effective, to understand, to be cheerful, to love others truly and to bring them closer to God; in short, to be good Christians. *Therefore*, remarks St Augustine, *united to Christ our head, we are all strong, but separated from our head we are worth nothing ... Because, united to our head we are vine; without our head ... we are cut branches, destined not for use by the farmers, but for the*

---

[17] St J. Escrivá, *The Way*, 701
[18] John 15:4-6

*fire. Whence Christ tells us in the gospel: 'Without me you
can do nothing'. O Lord! Without you, nothing, with you
everything ... Without us he can do a lot, nay, everything;
we without him can do nothing.*[19]

The fruits which Our Lord expects from us are of
many kinds. But everything would be useless if we had no
life of prayer, if we were not united to Our Lord. It would
be like trying to collect good bunches from a vine that got
separated from the main stem. *See how full of fruit are
those vines, because they are getting the sap which comes
from the main trunk. Only in this way have those tiny buds
of a few months ago been able to change into sweet,
mature fruit which gladden the sight and the heart of
people* (cf Ps 103:15). *On the ground perhaps a few single
twigs remain, half buried. They were vines too, but dry and
withered. They are the most graphic symbol of sterility.*[20]

The life of union with Our Lord goes outside the
personal sphere and can be seen in our way of working, in
our dealings with others, in our care for our family – in
everything. From that union with Our Lord springs a
wealth of apostolate, because *the apostolate, of whatever
kind it be, must be an overflow of the interior life.*[21] Christ
is *the source of the Church's whole apostolate. Clearly
then, the fruitfulness of the apostolate of lay people
depends on their union with Christ. As our Lord himself
said: 'Whoever dwells in me and I in him, bears much fruit,
for separated from me you can do nothing'* (John 15:5).
*This life of intimate union with Christ in the Church is
maintained by the spiritual helps common to all the faithful
... Laymen should make such a use of these helps that,
while meeting their human obligations in the ordinary*

---

[19] St Augustine, *Commentary on Psalm 30*, II, 1, 4
[20] St J. Escrivá, *Friends of God*, 254
[21] ibid, 239

conditions of life, they do not separate their union with Christ from their ordinary life; but through the very performance of their tasks, which are God's will for them, actually promote the growth of their union with him.[22]

In all walks of life the same thing happens: nobody gives what he hasn't got. Good fruits can only come from a good tree. *The branches of the vine are most despicable if they are not joined to the vine; and are most noble if they are ... If they are cut off they are of use neither to the vinedresser nor to the carpenter. The branches are for one of two things: the vine or the fire. If they are not on the vine, they go to the fire; to avoid the fire they must be united to the vine.*[23]

Are we yielding the fruit Our Lord expects from us? Have many of our friends come close to Our Lord as a result of our dealings with them? Have we helped any of them to go to the sacrament of Confession? Do we yield fruits of peace and cheerfulness among those with whom we spend most of our day? These are questions which could help us to make some specific resolution before finishing our prayer. And we do this along with Mary, who tells us: *Like a vine I caused loveliness to bud, and my blossoms became glorious and abundant fruit.*[24] *He who finds me finds life and obtains favour from the Lord.*[25] She is the short cut to get to Jesus, who fills us with his divine life.

---

[22] Second Vatican Council, *Apostolicam actuositatem*, 4
[23] St Augustine, *Commentary on St John*, 81, 3
[24] Sir 24:23
[25] Prov 8:35

79. OFFERING OUR DAILY ACTIONS

79.1 Through our Morning Offering we offer God our day from the very beginning. It is our first prayer.

God has given us days and nights so that we may order our lives. *Each day echoes its secret to the next, each night passes on to the next its revelation of knowledge.*[1] As we leave behind the previous day, each new day reminds us that we must continue the work which night interrupted, and carry on with our projects and hopes. *Man goes forth to his work and to his labour until the evening; then night comes, and with a kindly smile bids us put away all the toys we poor mortals make such a fuss over; shuts our books for us, hides our distractions from us, draws a great black coverlet over our lives ... As the darkness closes round us, we go through a dress-rehearsal of death; soul and body say good night to one another ... And then morning comes, and with morning, a re-birth.*[2]

Each day, in a certain sense, begins with a birth and ends with a death; each day is a life in miniature. In the final analysis, our journey through the world will have been holy and pleasing to God if we have tried to ensure that each day was pleasing to God, from sunrise to sunset. The same can be said for the night, because we offer that to God also. 'Today' is the only time we can offer to God. *Each day echoes its secret to the next*; yesterday whispers to today, and on God's behalf says to us: begin well. *Do your duty 'now', without looking back on 'yesterday',*

---

[1] Ps 18:2
[2] R.A. Knox, *A Retreat for Lay People*, pp.21-22

which has already passed, or worrying over 'tomorrow', which may never come for you.[3] Yesterday has disappeared forever, with all its possibilities and all its dangers. All that remains are reasons for contrition for the things we didn't do well, and reasons for gratitude for the countless graces, benefits and attention we have received from God. And 'tomorrow' is still in our Lord's hands.

What we must sanctify is the present day. And how are we going to do that if we don't start by offering it to God? It is only those who don't know God and lukewarm Christians who start their day off in any old way. The Morning Offering is an act of piety which focuses the day properly from the outset, directing it towards God just as a compass points towards the north pole. Our Morning Offering disposes us to listen to the Holy Spirit, and to heed the many inspirations and graces he sends us throughout the day. *If you should hear his voice this day, harden not your hearts.*[4] And God does talk to us each day.

Let us tell our Lord that we want to serve him this day, that we want to be conscious of his presence. *Renew your decision each morning, with a very determined 'Serviam', I will serve you, Lord. Renew your resolution not to give in, not to give way to laziness or idleness; to face up to your duties with greater hope and more optimism, convinced that if we are defeated in some small skirmish we can overcome this setback by making a sincere act of love.*[5]

Our actions will be all the more pleasing in the eyes of God if our offering is made through his Mother, who is also our Mother. *Try to put whatever you wish to offer to God into the hands of Mary – her hands are most gracious and worthy of all esteem – so that your offering will be*

---

[3] St J. Escrivá, *The Way*, 253
[4] Ps 94:7-8
[5] St J. Escrivá, *Friends of God*, 217

happily accepted by our Lord.[6]

79.2 How to offer our day. The 'heroic minute'.

The first Christians used to live the custom of offering their day to God. An early Christian wrote: *as soon as they wake up, before facing back into the hurly-burly of life, before making any plans or even thinking about their family duties, the Christians offer their thoughts, and everything, to God.*[7]

Writing to the Corinthians, St Paul exhorts them and us to offer our whole day to God: *Whether you eat or drink, or whatever you do, do all for the glory of God.*[8] And to the Colossians he writes: *Whatever you do, in word or deed, do everything in the name of the Lord Jesus, giving thanks to God the Father through him.*[9]

Many good Christians develop the habit of giving their first thought of the day to God. The 'heroic minute' follows: it facilitates the Morning Offering and getting the day off to a good start. *The heroic minute. It is the time fixed for getting up. Without hesitation: a supernatural reflection and ... up. The heroic minute: here you have a mortification that strengthens your will and does no harm to your body.*[10] *If, with God's help, you conquer yourself, you will be well ahead for the rest of the day.*

It's so discouraging to find oneself beaten at the first skirmish.[11]

Although we don't have to follow any particular formula when saying the Morning Offering, it's good to opt for some habitual way of living this practice of piety.

---

[6] St Bernard, *Homily on the birth of the Blessed Virgin Mary*, 18
[7] Cassian, *Conferences*, 21
[8] 1 Cor 10:31
[9] Col 3:17
[10] St J. Escrivá, *The Way*, 206
[11] *ibid*, 191

Some people like to recite some simple prayer they learned as children or as adults. The following prayer to our Lady is well known; it is both a Morning Offering and a daily consecration of oneself to Mary: *O Mary, my Mother, I offer myself entirely to you. And to prove my filial affection, this day I consecrate to you my eyes, my ears, my tongue, my heart; in short, my whole being. And now, my good Mother, as I am entirely yours, look after me and protect me as someone who belongs to you. Amen.*

Apart from the Morning Offering, it's up to each of us to decide what other prayers we'd like to say when we get up: perhaps some other prayer to our Lady, and a prayer to St Joseph and to our Guardian Angel. It's also a good moment to call to mind the resolutions we made at the examination of conscience the previous night, asking God for the grace to put them into effect that day.

Almighty Lord and God, protect us by your power throughout the course of this day, even as you have enabled us to begin it: do not let us turn aside to any sin, but let our every thought, word and deed aim at doing what is pleasing in your sight.[12]

79.3 The Morning Offering and Holy Mass. Offering our activity to our Lord many times throughout the day.

We ought to turn to our Lord each day asking him to help us remember his presence. To talk to our Lord only during those periods which we set aside for prayer is not enough: we should also remember him during our normal daily activities, because not only would we like these activities to be well done but we would like them to be prayer, to be pleasing to God. That's why we say with the Church: *Lord, be the beginning and end of all that we do and say. Prompt our actions with your grace, and complete*

---

[12] *Divine Office, Morning prayer, Monday, Week 2*

them with your all-powerful help.[13]

During holy Mass we have a fitting opportunity to renew the offering of our life and of our actions of the day to God. When the priest is offering the bread and the wine, we offer everything we are and everything we possess, and everything we have in mind to do that day. On the paten we place our memory, our intellect, our will, our family, our work, our joys and sorrows, all our concerns ... and the aspirations and acts of atonement, the small mortifications, and the acts of love which we hope will fill our day. These offerings of ours are always small and poor, but as we unite them to the offering of Christ in the Mass they become immeasurable and eternal. Speaking of the laity, the Second Vatican Council says: *For all their works, prayers and apostolic undertakings, family and married life, daily work, relaxation of mind and body, if they are accomplished in the Spirit – indeed even the hardships of life if patiently borne – all these become spiritual sacrifices acceptable to God through Jesus Christ (cf 1 Pet 2:5). In the celebration of the Eucharist these may most fittingly be offered to the Father along with the body of the Lord.*[14]

On the altar, beside the bread and the wine, we leave all that we have, all that we are: our hopes and dreams, all that we love, all that's on our mind. At the consecration of the Mass we give it all definitively to God. So now, none of all these things is ours alone, and, as children of God, aware that everything we have is on loan, we should use it for the purpose for which we have intended it: that is, for the glory of God and for the good of those close to us.

Offering everything we do to God helps us to do things better, to be more effective in our work, to be more cheerful in family life even though we may be tired, to get

---

[13] *ibid, Divine Office, Morning prayer, Monday Week 1*
[14] Second Vatican Council, *Lumen gentium*, 34

on better with everybody, to be better citizens.

We can renew the offering of our work throughout the day; for example, when we are beginning a new task, or when we're finding the job we are at particularly difficult. Our Lord also accepts our tiredness, and when we offer it to him, then it too acquires redemptive value.

Let us live each day as though it were the only day we had to offer to God, trying to do things well, and rectifying things when we do them badly. And one day it *will* be our last day, but we will have offered that day too to God our Father. Then, if we have tried to offer our life continually to God, we will hear Jesus saying to us, as he said to the good thief: *Truly, I say to you, today you will be with me in Paradise.*[15]

---

[15] Luke 23:43

FIFTH WEEK OF EASTER – FRIDAY

80. THE VALUE OF FRIENDSHIP

80.1 In Jesus we learn the true meaning of friendship.

Greater love has no man than this, that a man lay down his life for his friends. You are my friends ... No longer do I call you servants ... I call you friends.[1] Our Lord tells us this in the gospel of today's Mass.

Jesus is our friend. In him the apostles found their greatest friendship. He was someone who loved them, someone to whom they could speak of their joys and sorrows, someone they could question with complete confidence. They well knew what he meant when he told them: *Love one another, even as I have loved you.*[2] The sisters of Lazarus can find no better description than that of friendship when asking him to come: *your friend is sick,*[3] is the message they send him. It is the best argument they can think of.

Jesus sought and encouraged the friendship of all he met on the roads of Palestine. He always made use of conversation in order to get to the bottom of their souls and fill them with love. And apart from his infinite love for all men, he openly showed his friendship with particular people: the Apostles, Joseph of Arimathea, Nicodemus, Lazarus and his family and others. Nor did he deny the title of *friend* to Judas himself at the very moment the latter was handing him over to his enemies; he asks Peter after the denials: *Do you love me?*[4] Are you my friend? Can I rely

---
[1] John 15:13-15
[2] John 13:34
[3] John 11:3
[4] John 21:6

on you? And he gives him his Church: Feed my lambs, feed my sheep.

Christ, the risen Christ, is our companion and friend. He is a companion whom we can see only in the shadows – but the fact that he is really there fills our whole life, and makes us yearn to be with him forever.[5] He, who has partaken of our life, also wants to share in our burdens: *I will give you rest,*[6] he tells us all. He is the same one who ardently wishes us to share in his glory for all eternity.

Jesus Christ is the friend who never betrays,[7] who, when we go to see him or to speak to him, is always ready to receive us. He awaits us with a welcome that is always the same, even though there may have been forgetfulness or coldness on our part. He always helps, encourages and consoles us.

Friendship with Our Lord, which is born and grows through prayer and worthy reception of the sacraments, helps us to understand better the significance of human friendship. Sacred Scripture describes it as a treasure: *a faithful friend is a sturdy protector* – we are told by Sirach – *he that has found one has found a treasure. There is nothing so precious as a faithful friend; and no scales can measure his excellence.*[8] The apostles learned the true meaning of friendship from Christ himself. And the Acts of the Apostles show us how St Paul had many friends, whom he loved dearly. He misses them when they are not there, and he is filled with joy when he gets news of them.[9] Early Christianity has left us testimonies of great friendships among our early brethren in the faith.

---

[5] St J. Escrivá, *Christ is passing by*, 116
[6] Matt 11:28
[7] cf St J. Escrivá, *The Way*, 8
[8] Sir 6:14-15
[9] cf 2 Cor 2:13

80.2 Friendship is a great human good which we can supernaturalize. Qualities of true friendship.

Our daily conversation and friendship with Christ lead us to have an open, sympathetic attitude, which increases our capacity for having friends. Prayer refines the soul and makes us particularly apt to understand other people. Also, it increases our generosity, our optimism, our affability in social relations, and our gratitude – all being virtues which facilitate the way of friendship for the Christian.

True friendship is without self-interest, because it consists more in giving than in receiving. It does not seek its own interests, but those of the friend. *The true friend cannot have two sides for his friend: friendship, if it is to be loyal and sincere, demands renunciation, probity, exchanges of favours and of noble, licit acts of service. A friend is strong and sincere, in the measure that he thinks generously of others, with personal sacrifice on his part – always, of course, in the context of supernatural prudence. In the climate of trust which arises where there is true friendship, a corresponding reaction is to be expected from the other party; one expects a recognition of what we are, and, when necessary, a clear defence without palliatives.* [10]

For there to be true friendship, a response is required; the affection and good will have to be mutual. [11] If the friendship is true, it always tends to become stronger. It doesn't permit envy to spoil it. It doesn't grow cold with suspicion. It grows when there are difficulties, [12] *up to the point of considering the friend as one's other self, whence St. Augustine says: 'Well did he speak of his friend who called him the other half of his soul.'* [13] Then they share

---

[10] St J. Escrivá, *Letter*, 11 March 1940
[11] cf St Thomas, *Summa Theologiae*, II-II, 23, 1
[12] cf St Aelred of Rievaulx, *Treatise on spiritual friendship*, 3
[13] St Thomas, *loc cit*

their joys and sorrows naturally.

Friendship is, at the same time, a human quality and an occasion for developing many human virtues, because it creates *a harmony of feelings and tastes which are quite distinct from sense-love; rather it develops the dedication of one friend to the other, to very high levels – even that of heroism. We believe that meetings ... provide the opportunity for noble and virtuous souls to enjoy this human and Christian relationship which is called friendship. It both requires and develops generosity, selflessness, sympathy, solidarity, and, especially, the possibility of making mutual sacrifices.*[14]

The good friend does not run away when difficulties arise; a good friend never turns traitor, never speaks badly of the other, and never allows his friend to be criticized when absent. Rather he stands up for him. Friendship involves sincerity, trust, sharing of joys and sorrows, encouragement, consoling, and helping by example.

80.3 Apostolate with our friends.

Down through the centuries, friendship has been (and still is) a pathway along which many men and women have come close to God and gone to heaven. It is a natural and simple path which eliminates many obstacles and difficulties. Our Lord frequently bears it in mind as a means of letting himself be known. The first few who met him went to tell the good news to the ones they loved. Andrew brought Peter, his brother; Philip, his friend Nathanael; and John probably brought his brother James.

This was the way that faith in Christ spread in the early days of Christianity: from brother to brother, from father to son, from slave to master and vice versa, from friend to friend. Friendship is a unique basis for letting

---

[14] St Paul VI, *Address*, 26 July 1978

Christ be known, because it is the natural medium for communicating feelings, for sharing the joys and sorrows of those who are near us by reason of family, our work or mutual interests.

It is characteristic of friendship to give our friend the best we have. Our greatest treasure, beyond all compare, is having found Christ. We would not have true friendship if we were not to communicate the immense gift of our Christian faith. Our friends have to find in us – Christians who want to follow Jesus closely – support, strength and a supernatural meaning for their lives. The certainty of finding understanding, interest, and attention will lead them to open their heart trustingly, knowing that we love them and are prepared to help them. All this we will do in the performance of our normal daily activities, trying to be exemplary in our profession or studies, fostering friendship at all times, dealing warmly and openly with people, and urged on by charity.

Friendship leads us to start our friends off on a true Christian life if they are far from the Church, or to get them back onto the path they left one bad day, if they have stopped practising the faith they had received. With patience and constancy, without hurry, without pause on our part, they will gradually get closer to Our Lord, who is waiting for them. Sometimes we can do a period of prayer with them, perform an act of mercy by visiting a sick or needy person, or invite them to make a visit to the Blessed Sacrament with us. Then when the time is ripe, we will talk to them about the sacrament of divine mercy, Confession, and we will help them to prepare for receiving it. Those trusting relationships, under the shelter of friendship, become open channels for apostolate, through the Holy Spirit. *Those well-timed words, whispered into the ear of your wavering friend; the helpful conversation that you managed to start at the right time; the ready professional advice that improves his university work; the discreet indiscretion by which you open up unexpected horizons for his zeal. This all forms part of the 'apostolate of friendship'.*[15]

Friendship can do everything with the help of grace; it helps move us to beseech Our Lord with prayer and mortification. As we have never hidden our faith in Christ from them, they will find it natural that we often talk to them about the most important thing in our life, in just the same way that they talk to us about the things they consider the most important.

Our Lord wants us to have many friends because his love for mankind is infinite, and our friendship is an instrument for getting through to them. Among the people we deal with every day, what a great number are waiting – even without their knowing it – for the light of Christ to get to them! And how happy we are every time a friend of ours becomes a friend of The Friend!

Jesus, who *went about doing good,*[16] and who won the hearts of such a great number of people, is our model. Likewise we have to go about among our relations, colleagues, neighbours and friends. Today is a good day for us to ask ourselves: Do the people who usually come in contact with us feel the need to come closer to Our Lord as a result of our example and words? Are we concerned about their soul? Can it really be said of us that we, like Jesus, are passing through their life doing good?

---

[15] St J. Escrivá, *The Way*, 973
[16] Acts 10:38

81. THE ROSARY

81.1 In the Rosary our Lady teaches us to contemplate the life of her Son.

Love for our Lady is shown in our life in many different ways. The Holy Rosary has been the Marian prayer most recommended by the Church down through the ages. In it, piety gives us a summary of the principal truths of the Christian faith; as we consider each of the mysteries, our Lady teaches us to contemplate the life of her Son. She, intimately united to Jesus, at times takes first place; other times, it is Christ himself who is the first to attract our attention. Mary always talks to us about Jesus: of the joy of his birth, of his death on the Cross, and of his glorious Resurrection and Ascension.

The Rosary is our Mother's favourite prayer. *To say the Holy Rosary, considering the mysteries, repeating the 'Our Father' and 'Hail Mary', with the praises to the Blessed Trinity and the constant invocation of the Mother of God, is a continuous act of faith, hope and love, of adoration and reparation.*[1]

Etymologically, the Rosary is a *crown of roses, a delightful custom which among all peoples represents an offering of love and a symbol of joy.*[2] *It is the most excellent means of meditated prayer, constituted in the manner of a mystical crown, in which the angelic salutation, the Lord's Prayer and the doxology to the August Trinity are intertwined with the consideration of the highest mysteries of our faith. In it, by means of many*

---

[1] St J. Escrivá, *Holy Rosary*, Preface
[2] Pius XII, *Address*, 16 October 1940

scenes, the mind contemplates the drama of the Incarnation and of the Redemption of our Lord.[3]

In this Marian prayer, vocal prayer is combined with the meditation of the Christian mysteries, which is as it were the soul of the Rosary. Thanks to this unhurried meditation it is possible for all to say the same words, while at the same time each one can do his or her own personal prayer. To imagine oneself as a participant in the scenes being considered helps one to say it well. In this way, *we shall live the life of Jesus, Mary and Joseph.*

Each day we shall do something new for them. We shall hear their family conversation. We shall see the Messiah grow up. We shall admire his thirty years of hidden life ... We shall be present at his Passion and Death ... We shall be amazed at the glory of his resurrection ... In a word: carried away by Love (the only real love is Love), we shall contemplate each and every moment of the life of Christ.[4]

In considering the mysteries, vocal prayer – the *Our Fathers* and the *Hail Marys* – comes to life; our interior life is enriched with deep content, which becomes a source of prayer and contemplation throughout the day. Little by little, it identifies us with Christ's feelings and enables us to live in a climate of intense devotion: we rejoice with Christ joyful, we suffer with Christ suffering, and we look forward in hope to the glory of Christ risen. Saint Paul VI said that the liturgy and the Rosary, *although existing on essentially different planes of reality, have as their object the same salvific events wrought by Christ. The former presents anew, under the veil of signs and operative in a hidden way, the great mysteries of our redemption. The latter, by means of devout contemplation, recalls these*

---

[3] St John XXIII, Encyclical, *Grata recordatio*, 26 September 1959
[4] St J. Escrivá, *op cit*, p. 9

same mysteries to the mind of the person praying and stimulates the will to draw from them the norms of living.[5]

81.2 The family Rosary, 'a powerful weapon'.

The Second Vatican Council asks *all the sons of the Church that the cult, especially the liturgical cult, of the Blessed Virgin, be generously fostered, and the practices and exercises of piety, recommended by the Magisterium of the Church towards her in the course of centuries, be highly esteemed.*[6] And we are well aware of how insistently the Church has recommended saying the Rosary. It is *one of the best and most efficacious prayers in common that the Christian family is invited to recite,*[7] and in many cases it will be an aim of Christian life for many families. Sometimes it is enough to begin by saying just one mystery, perhaps using such signal opportunities as the month of May or a visit to a shrine or chapel of our Lady. Much has been achieved if children are taught to say it from an early age.

The family Rosary is a source of good for everyone, for it attracts God's mercy to the home. *The saying of the Angelus and of the Rosary*, said St John Paul II, *must be for every Christian and even more for Christian families, like a spiritual oasis during the course of the day, from which we can get strength and confidence.*[8] And just a few days later, the Holy Father once again remarked: *Guard jealously that tender and confident love for our Lady, which characterizes you. Don't ever let it get cold ... Be faithful to the traditional exercises of Marian piety in the Church: the saying of the Angelus, the month of Mary, and*

---

[5] St Paul VI, *Marialis cultus*, 48
[6] Second Vatican Council, *Lumen gentium*, 67
[7] St Paul VI, *op cit*, 54
[8] St John Paul II, *Angelus*, in Otranto, 5 October 1980

in a special way, the Rosary. Would that there be a resurgence of that beautiful custom of praying the Rosary in the family.[9]

Today in our prayer we can see whether we approach the Holy Rosary as a *powerful weapon*[10] to get from the Blessed Virgin those graces and favours which we need so much, whether we say it with the necessary attention, whether we try to deepen in its rich content, especially stopping and meditating each of the mysteries for a few moments, and whether we try to get our family and friends to start saying it and so to have more dealings with our Mother in Heaven, and to love her more.

81.3 Distractions during the Rosary.

Sometimes, when we Christians try to spread the saying of the Rosary as a form of talking to our Lady every day, we come across people, even good people, who make the excuse that they are frequently distracted in saying it and that, therefore *not to say it is better then saying it badly*, or words to that effect. Pope John XXIII used to say that *the worst Rosary is the one that doesn't get said*. We can tell our friends that, instead of omitting it, it is more pleasing to our Lady that we say it as well as we can, even though we have distractions. It can also happen that *if you have many distractions at prayer, that prayer of yours may well be upsetting the devil a great deal.*[11]

The Rosary has sometimes been compared to a song: our Lady's song. So, although we may not always follow the words consciously, the melody will lead us, almost imperceptibly, to keep our thoughts and our hearts on our Lady.

---

[9] St John Paul II, *Homily*, 12 October 1980
[10] St J. Escrivá, *op cit*, p. 5
[11] St Alphonsus Liguori, *Treatise on Prayer*

Involuntary distractions do not cancel the fruits of the Rosary, or of any other vocal prayer, provided one is struggling to avoid them. St Thomas points out that a vocal prayer may be the object of a threefold attention: correct pronunciation of all the words; special concentration on the meaning of the words; and attention to the final goal of our prayer, namely God and the thing we are praying for. This last is the most important and necessary kind of attention, and can be had by people who are not very well educated or who don't understand clearly the meaning of the words they are saying, and *can be so intense that it transports the mind to God.*[12]

If we try, we can say the Rosary well each time: watching our pronunciation, pauses, attention, stopping a few moments to consider the mystery we are about to say, offering a decade perhaps for a specific intention – the Universal Church, the Roman Pontiff, the intentions of the bishop of the diocese, our family, priestly vocations, the apostolate, peace and justice in a particular country, or some matter that worries us – trying to ensure that these *roses* offered to our Lady never become bedraggled or faded through routine, or allowing more or less voluntary distractions to take over ... Avoiding all distractions is very difficult, on occasions practically impossible, but our Lady knows that too and accepts our good will and our efforts.

To say the Rosary devoutly, it is important to say it at a suitable time. *A sad way of not praying the Rosary is leaving it for the end of the day.*

If you say it when going to bed, it will be done at best badly and with no meditation on the mysteries. It will be difficult then to avoid routine, which is what drowns true piety, the only piety worth the name.[13] *You always leave the*

---

[12] St Thomas, *Summa Theologiae*, II-II, 83, 3
[13] St J. Escrivá, *Furrow*, 476

Rosary for later, and you end up not saying it at all because you are sleepy. If there is no other time, say it in the street without letting anybody notice it. It will, moreover, help you to have presence of God.[14]

The Rosary has the advantage that it can be said anywhere: in the church, in the street, in the car, alone or in family, while in a doctor's waiting room or queuing to get some forms. Very few Catholics can say sincerely that they don't have time to say *the prayer most beloved and recommended by the Church.*

One day our Lord will show us the consequences of having prayed devoutly, albeit with some distractions too, the Holy Rosary: disasters that were avoided by our Lady's special intercession, assistance to loved ones, conversions, ordinary and extraordinary graces for ourselves and for others, and the many people who benefitted from this prayer and whom we didn't even know.

This prayer which is so efficacious and pleasing to our Lady will in many moments of our life be the most effective channel for petition, for thanksgiving, and for making atonement for our sins: *'Immaculate Virgin, I know very well that I am only a miserable wretch, and all I do is increase each day the number of my sins ... ' You told me the other day that was how you spoke to Our Mother.*

And I was confident in advising you with assurance to pray the Holy Rosary. Blessed be that monotony of 'Hail Marys' which purifies the monotony of your sins![15]

---

[14] *ibid*, 478
[15] *ibid*, 475

82. THE HOPE OF HEAVEN

82.1 We have been created for Heaven. Fostering hope.

During this forty-day period between Easter and the Ascension of Our Lord, the Church asks us to keep our eyes on Heaven, our final dwelling place, to which Our Lord is calling us. This invitation becomes more pressing as we approach the day on which Jesus went up to the right hand of his Father.

Our Lord had promised his disciples that in a little while he would be with them forever. *Yet a little while, and the world will see me no more, but you will see me.*[1] Our Lord has kept his promise in this period when he stays close to his loved ones. But this presence will not end when he goes up with his glorious body to his Father, because, by his Passion and Death he has prepared for us a place in his Father's house, where there are many mansions.[2] *I will come again*, he tells them, *and will take you to myself, that where I am you may be also.*[3]

The Apostles, who had been saddened by the prediction of Peter's denials, are comforted by the hope of Heaven. The return to which Our Lord is referring includes his second coming at the end of the world,[4] and the meeting with each soul when it leaves the body. Our death will be just that: a meeting with Christ, whom we have tried to serve throughout our lifetime. He will bring us to the fulness of glory, the meeting with his Heavenly Father,

---

[1] John 14:19-20
[2] cf John 14:2
[3] John 14:3
[4] cf 1 Cor 4:5; 11:26

who is also our Father. There in Heaven, where we have a place prepared for us, Jesus awaits us, the same Jesus who is with us, who awaits us in prayer and with whom we have often been in intimate friendly conversation.

From our regular conversations with Our Lord is born the desire to be with him. Faith sweetens much of the bitterness of death. Our love for Jesus completely changes the meaning of that last moment which comes for everybody. *Those in love try to see each other. People in love have eyes only for their love. That's logical, isn't it? The human heart feels this need. I would be lying if I denied my eagerness to contemplate the face of Jesus Christ. 'Vultum tuum, Domine, requiram!' I will seek your countenance, O Lord.*[5]

The thought of Heaven will help us to be detached from the things of this world and to overcome difficult situations. We make God very happy when we foster that theological virtue of hope, which is united with faith and love. There will be times when we need it a lot. *At the time of temptation think of the love that awaits you in Heaven: foster the virtue of hope – this is not a lack of generosity.*[6] It will be likewise at moments of great sorrow and trial, and when we find it very hard to be faithful or persevering in our work or apostolate. The reward is a big one, and it is just around the corner, not long from now.

Meditating on Heaven, which is our destination, ought to spur us on to be more generous in our daily struggle, *because hope of the reward comforts the soul unto doing good works.*[7]

The thought of that final meeting of love to which we are called will help us to be on our guard in big things and

---

[5] St J. Escrivá, quoted in *Newsletter No.1* for the Cause of his beatification
[6] *ibid, The Way*, 139
[7] St Cyril of Jerusalem, *Catechesis*, 348, 18, 1

in little things, giving them the finishing touch, as if each one were to be the last before going to meet our Heavenly Father.

82.2 What God has revealed about eternal life.

Words are altogether inadequate for describing our life in Heaven, that life which God has promised to his children. The Church reminds us that *we will be with Christ and 'we shall see God' (cf 1 John 3:2), and it is in these promises and marvellous mysteries that our hope essentially consists. Our imagination may be incapable of reaching these heights, but our heart does so, instinctively and completely.*[8]

What we now but poorly discern by revelation, and can barely imagine in our present state, will one day become a joyful reality. In the Old Testament the happiness of Heaven is portrayed by evoking the Promised Land, which is reached after a very long, hard journey through the desert. There, in our new and permanent resting place, are to be found all benefits;[9] there, the exhaustion caused by such a long and difficult pilgrimage will come to an end.

Our Lord spoke to us in many ways of the incomparable happiness awaiting those who, in this life, love God with deeds. Eternal happiness is one of the truths which our Lord preached with most insistence ... *For this is the will of my Father, that everyone who sees the Son and believes in him should have eternal life, and I will raise him up at the last day.*[10] Later, at the Last Supper, he says: *Father, I desire that they also, whom thou hast given me,*

---

[8] S.C.D.F., *Letter on some questions concerning Eschatology*, 17 January 1979
[9] cf Ex 3:17
[10] John 6:40

may be with me where I am, to behold my glory which thou hadst given me in thy love for me before the foundation of the world.[11]

Everlasting happiness is compared to a banquet which God prepares for men; a banquet at which all the longings of the human heart for happiness will be unimaginably satisfied.[12]

The Apostles often talk to us of that happiness which awaits us. St Paul teaches that now we see God *in a mirror dimly, but then face to face,*[13] and that the happiness which we will enjoy there is indescribable.[14]

The happiness of eternal life lies principally in the direct, immediate vision of God. It involves not only a perfect intellectual knowledge of God, but also a sharing of life with God, One and Triune. To see God is to live with him, and to be happy with him. And so, from this loving contemplation of the three divine Persons, an unlimited joy will arise in us. All the hunger for happiness and love of our poor heart will be satisfied unendingly, eternally. *Let us imagine what Heaven will be like. 'Eye has not seen, nor ear heard, neither has it entered into the mind of man to imagine the things that God has prepared for those who love him'. Can you imagine what it will be like to arrive there, and meet God, and see that beauty which pours into our hearts and satisfies without satiating our desire? I ask myself many times a day: what will it be like when all the beauty, all the goodness, all the infinite wonder of God pours into this poor clay vessel that I am, that we are. And then I understand well why the Apostle wrote: 'Eye has not seen, nor ear heard' ... It is worth every effort, my children,*

---

[11] John 17:24
[12] cf Luke 13:29; 14:15
[13] 1 Cor 13:12
[14] 1 Cor 2:9

it is indeed worth while.[15]

82.3 The Resurrection of the Body. Thinking about Heaven should lead us to a determined and cheerful struggle to reach it.

Apart from the immense joy of beholding God and of seeing and living with the risen, glorified Christ, there is also an *accidental* happiness, by means of which we will enjoy those created goods to which we aspire: the company of those blessed whom we most loved down here – members of our family and friends; and also the glory of our risen bodies, because our risen body will be identical in all respects to our present body. St Paul tells us that *this perishable nature must put on the imperishable, and this mortal nature must put on immortality.*[16] This body, not another one the same, or very similar. The Trent Catechism says *it is of vital importance to be fully convinced that the identical body, which belongs to each one of us during life, shall, though corrupt and dissolved into its original dust, be raised up again to life.*[17] St Augustine states clearly that *this flesh will rise, the same which was buried ... The flesh which now falls ill and suffers, this same flesh will rise again.*[18] Our personality will continue to be the same, and we will have our own body, but vested with glory and splendour, if we have been faithful. Our body will have the properties characteristic of glorious bodies: agility and subtlety, that is, not subject to the limitations of space and time; impassibility – *he will wipe away every tear from*

---

[15] St J. Escrivá, quoted in *Newsletter No. 1* for the Cause of his beatification
[16] 1 Cor 15:53
[17] *Catechism of the Council of Trent*, I, XI, 7; cf S.C.D.F., *Declaration concerning the translation of the article 'carnis resurrectionem' of the Apostles' Creed,* 14 December 1983
[18] St Augustine, *Sermon 264,* 6

their eyes, and death shall be no more, neither shall there be mourning nor crying nor pain any more;[19] and finally, brightness and beauty.

I believe in the resurrection of the body, we say in the Apostles' Creed. Our bodies in Heaven will have characteristics which are different from the present ones, but they will continue being bodies and will occupy a space,[20] as the glorious body of Christ and Our Lady do now. We do not know where that place is, nor how it comes about. The present earth will have been transformed: *Then I saw a new Heaven and a new earth; for the first Heaven and the first earth had passed away ... Behold I make all things new.*[21] Many Fathers and Doctors of the Church, and also many saints, have thought that the renewal of the whole created order arises from revelation itself.

Now that the day of Our Lord's Ascension is close, the thought of Heaven should lead us to a more determined and cheerful struggle to get rid of the obstacles which separate us from Christ. It also encourages us to seek in the first place the goods which last instead of craving for those that perish.

The thought of Heaven gives great serenity. Nothing here is irreparable, nothing is definitive, all wrongs can be righted. The only definitive defeat would be to miss the door which leads to Life. Our Lady is there too, waiting for us.

---

[19] Apoc 21:4
[20] cf M. Schmaus, *Dogmatic Theology*, VII, Madrid
[21] cf Apoc 21:1ff

83. THE GIFTS OF THE HOLY SPIRIT

83.1 The supernatural virtues and the gifts of the Holy Spirit.

We live surrounded by God's gifts. Everything we have that is good, all our spiritual and bodily qualities, and countless other gifts, all of them are God's gifts to make us happy in this life and to enable us reach Heaven safely. But it was first and foremost in Baptism that our Father God filled us with innumerable gifts. He erased the stain of original sin from our soul. He enriched us with the gift of sanctifying grace, by which he made us sharers in his own divine life, and he made us his sons and daughters. He also made us members of the Church.

Along with grace, God adorned our soul with the supernatural virtues and the gifts of the Holy Spirit. The virtues give us the power or capacity of acting in a supernatural way, of judging the world and events from a higher point of view – that of faith – and of behaving as true children of God. They give us the power of knowing God intimately, of loving him as he loves himself and of performing actions which are meritorious for eternal life. Under the influence of these virtues, our work becomes a treasury of merits for Heaven, although, humanly viewed, it may seem to have little importance.

The supernatural virtues give us power, in the same way that our feet give us the power of walking and our eyes the power of seeing the world around us. Even so, it is not enough for us to have feet for travelling, or eyes for looking at a picture. The cooperation of our own freedom is necessary as well our desire and our effort to embark on the journey, or to apply our mind to the picture in order to appreciate its beauty.

The gifts of the Holy Spirit are a new present which God bestows on the soul so that it can more perfectly, and effortlessly, carry out the good works in which our love of God – our holiness – is seen.[1] It is characterized by, for example, acts of presence of God, charity, acts of offering of our work, and small mortifications throughout the day.

Under the influence of these gifts, *the soul is equipped and strengthened so that it more easily and more promptly obeys His voice and impulse. These gifts, moreover, are so effective that they lead the just soul to the highest point of sanctity, and they are of such excellence that they continue to exist in Heaven, though in a more perfect way. By the help of these charisms, the soul is aroused and helped to seek after, and to obtain, the evangelical beatitudes, which, like flowers blossoming in the springtime, are tokens and heralds of eternal beatitude.*[2]

The gifts of the Holy Spirit proceed to configure our life according to the way of being of a son of God. They endow us with a greater finesse and awareness to detect the motions and inspirations of the Paraclete and put them into practice. In this way, he proceeds to govern our life, promptly and with ease; and so our life is guided by the Will of God, and not by our own tastes and whims.

Today we ask the Holy Spirit to *bend the stubborn heart and will*, especially the stubbornness of pride; to *melt the frozen, warm the chill* – that is, our lukewarmness in dealing with God; to *guide the steps that go astray,*[3] because our earthly attachments are numerous – for example, the weight of past sins, the weakness of our will, our ignorance of what would so often be more pleasing to

---

[1] cf St Thomas, *Summa Theologiae*, I-II, 68, 1
[2] Leo XIII, *Divinum illud*, 9 May 1897
[3] *Sequence of the Mass of Pentecost*

God. These are the source of our defeats, weaknesses and tiredness. And so, we ask him, in our prayer, to rid our soul of *the dead weight which still remains from all its impurities and drags it down to the ground ... so that it can rise up to God's Majesty and be enveloped in the living flame of his Love.*[4]

83.2 The seven gifts. Their influence in the Christian life.

But when the Counsellor comes, whom I shall send to you from the Father, even the Spirit of truth, who proceeds from the Father, he will bear witness to me.[5] Our Lord announces this news in the Gospel of today's Mass, and the liturgy of the Church invites us, in various ways, to get our souls ready for the action of the Holy Spirit.

A resolute battle against every deliberate venial sin prepares us to receive the light and the protection of the Paraclete, by means of his gifts. The light which is bestowed on our intellect makes us know and understand the things of God; the assistance to our will permits us to use successfully the opportunities for doing good which we encounter every day, and to reject the temptations of everything that would separate us from God.

The gift of understanding shows us the riches of the Faith with greater clarity. The gift of knowledge enables us to judge created things in an upright manner, and to keep our heart fixed on God, and on things insofar as they lead us to him. The gift of wisdom enables us to comprehend the unfathomable wonder of God, and it urges us to seek him in preference to all other things, amid our ordinary work and obligations. The gift of counsel points out the paths of holiness to us – God's Will in our ordinary daily life – and encourages us to choose the option which most

---

[4] cf St J. Escrivá, *The Way*, 886
[5] John 15:26

closely coincides with the glory of God, and the good of our fellow man. The gift of piety inclines us to treat God with the intimacy with which a child treats his father. The gift of fortitude uplifts us continually, helping us to overcome the difficulties which we inevitably meet on our journey to God. The gift of fear induces us to flee the occasions of sin, resist temptation, avoid every evil which could sadden the Holy Spirit,[6] and to fear above all the loss of the One whom we love, and who is the reason of being of our life.

These are days to prepare for the celebration of the solemn sending out of the Holy Spirit on the Church, represented by the Apostles foregathered in the Cenacle, along with Mary the Mother of God. We pray constantly that we may be docile to the work of the Holy Spirit in our soul, and that he may not cease to move and inspire the people of these times in which we live, who are *particularly hungry for the Spirit*,[7] and so much need his protection and his help. We tell him:

> *Come, O Holy Spirit, come,*
> *And from thy celestial home*
> *Shed a ray of light divine!*
> *Come, thou Father of the poor,*
> *Come, thou source of all our store,*
> *Come, within our bosoms shine!*
> *Thou on those who ever more*
> *Thee confess and thee adore*
> *In thy sevenfold gifts descend;*
> *Give them virtue's sure reward,*
> *Give them thy salvation, Lord,*

---

[6] cf Eph 4:30
[7] St John Paul II, *Redemptor hominis*, 4 March 1979, 18

Give them joys that never end.[8]

83.3 Ten-day devotion to the Holy Spirit.

To increase our devotion to the Holy Spirit, we can begin by practising the human and Christian virtues, at work and in our daily dealings with others. If a Christian *fights to acquire these virtues, his soul is preparing to receive the grace of the Holy Spirit fruitfully. The Third Person of the Blessed Trinity, the soul's sweet guest* (Sequence: Come Holy Spirit) *pours out his gifts: wisdom, understanding, counsel, fortitude, knowledge, piety and the fear of the Lord* (cf Is 11:2).[9]

The Holy Spirit desires (far more than we could ever desire) to give us his gifts in such abundance that they form a torrential river in our supernatural life, and produce their wonderful fruits in us. He is waiting only for us to rid our souls of any possible obstacles, to ask him to give us a greater desire of purification, and to tell him from the depth of our soul: *Come, Holy Spirit, fill the hearts of your faithful. Enkindle in them the fire of your love.* It is his only wish to fill us with his grace and his gifts. *If you, then, who are evil, know how to give good gifts to your children, how much more will the Heavenly Father give the Holy Spirit to those who ask him!*[10]

Throughout these days of preparation for the Feast of Pentecost, we have to implore humbly *the Father of lights*[11] to send the Spirit of his Son into our hearts, *crying, Abba! Father.*[12] We should ask Christ to send forth, from the bosom of his Father, the one who is thus praised:

---

[8] *Sequence of the Mass of Pentecost*
[9] St J. Escrivá, *Friends of God*, 92
[10] Luke 11:30
[11] Jas 1:17
[12] Gal 4:6

> *Thou of all consolers best,*
> *thou the soul's delightful guest,*
> *dost refreshing peace bestow.* [13]

In the ten-day preparation which begins on the feast of the Ascension, we want to become more receptive to the graces which the Paraclete pours out on us continually. Let us each ask him for his gifts, so that we may be his good instrument in our family circle, at work, and in society. *A sure way to be humble is to contemplate how, even without talents, fame or fortune, we can be effective instruments if we go to the Holy Spirit so that he may grant us his gifts.*

The Apostles, though they had been taught by Jesus for three years, fled in terror from the enemies of Christ. But after Pentecost, they let themselves be flogged and imprisoned, and ended up giving their lives in witness to their faith. [14]

Our faithfulness to the inspirations and graces which we receive from the Holy Spirit will often be revealed in our readiness to respond to spiritual guidance, and in our daily effort to work toward the goals and the implementation of the suggestions which have been indicated to us.

Recourse to our Lady, the spouse of the Holy Spirit, is the surest way for us to dispose our soul for whatever new gifts the Paraclete wishes to give us.

---

[13] *Sequence of the Mass of Pentecost*
[14] St J. Escrivá, *Furrow*, 283

SIXTH WEEK OF EASTER – TUESDAY

84. MAY, MONTH OF MARY

84.1 Devotion to our Lady draws down divine mercy. She is loved by the whole Christian people.

Month of sun and flowers ... month of Mary, at the crowning of the Paschal time. Since Advent our thoughts have followed Jesus; now that the great peace that follows the resurrection is in our souls, how can we not return to her who gave Him to us?

She appeared on earth to prepare His coming; she lived in His shadow, to such an extent that we do not see her intervening in the Gospel except as the mother of Jesus, following Him, watching Him. And when Jesus leaves us, she effaces herself.

She effaces herself, but she remains in the memory of the people because we owe Jesus to her.[1]

As on other occasions, we see Jesus talking about the mysteries of the Kingdom of God. The crowds are all about him, looking at him and observing a deep silence. All of a sudden, unexpectedly, a woman shouts with all her strength: *Blessed is the womb that bore you, and the breasts that you sucked.*[2]

The prophecy contained in the *Magnificat* begins to be fulfilled. *Henceforth all generations will call me blessed,*[3] Mary had exclaimed, under the motion of the Holy Spirit. On this occasion, with popular spontaneity, a woman's words have begun something which will not cease until the end of the world. Those words of Our Lady at the outset of

---

[1] J. Leclercq, *A Year with the Liturgy*
[2] Luke 11:27
[3] Luke 1:48

her vocation were to have their most complete fulfilment down through the centuries. Poets, intellectuals, kings, warriors, craftsmen, mothers, mature men and women, and children scarcely able to talk; in the fields, in cities, on mountain-tops, in factories and on the highways; amid sorrows and joys; on the most transcendental of occasions – consider how innumerable individuals have given up their soul to God while looking at a picture of Our Lady, or with the sweet name of Mary on their lips or in their mind; or on the most ordinary of occasions – like turning a corner and catching a fleeting glimpse of an image of our Lady; on so many occasions of such different kinds, millions of voices in all languages have sung the praises of the Mother of God. It is a ceaseless cry all across the world, which daily calls down God's mercy on the earth – a cry which we cannot explain except in terms of an express wish of God. The Second Vatican Council reminds us that *from earliest times the Blessed Virgin has been honoured under the title of Mother of God, under whose protection the faithful took refuge in all their dangers and necessities.*[4]

The whole Christian people have always known how to go to God through his Mother. With the constant experience of her graces and favours, they have called her *All-powerful in supplication* and they have found, in her, the short-cut to God. Love has found many ways of addressing her and honouring her. The Church has constantly recommended and blessed this devotion to the Blessed Virgin Mary as a sure way to get to our Lord, *because Mary is always the way that leads to Christ. Every encounter with her cannot but end in a meeting with Christ himself. And what more does a continuous recourse to Mary signify than the quest for Christ, who is in her arms, in her, through her and with her – Christ, our Saviour, to*

---

[4] Second Vatican Council, *Lumen gentium*, 66

whom men, amid the discouragements and dangers here below, have the duty and feel the need to seek as a harbour of salvation and transcendent source of life.[5]

84.2 The month of May.

In the month of May, Catholics show their devotion to the Blessed Virgin in many wonderful ways which enliven all the days of the month, following closely the Second Vatican Council's recommendation that *the entire body of the faithful pour forth instant supplications to the Mother of God and Mother of men that she, who aided the beginnings of the Church by her prayers, may now, exalted as she is above all the angels and saints, intercede before her Son in the fellowship of all the saints,*[6] and are urged to value highly *the practices and exercises of piety, recommended by the Magisterium of the Church towards her in the course of centuries.*[7]

Let us ask ourselves today in our prayer what resolutions we have made and how we are putting them into practice, with regard to increasing our prayer to our Lady, throughout this month when Catholics traditionally honour her most.

The dedication of the month of May to Mary was born from a love that was forever seeking new ways of expressing itself, and from a reaction against pagan customs which were to be found in many places during *the month of flowers.* Among the 13th century *Canticles to Mary* of King Alfonso the Wise of Castille, we find one which starts with the words: *Welcome, month of May.* In it the poet extols the return of May, because it invites us to entreat Mary with greater veneration, to free us from evil

---

[5] St Paul VI, *Mense maio,* 29 April 1965
[6] Second Vatican Council, *Lumen gentium,* 69
[7] *ibid,* 67

and to fill us with gifts.

In our own times, we Catholics, wanting to be close to her always, offer her special presents in May: pilgrimages, visits to churches dedicated to her, little sacrifices in her honour, periods of study and well-finished work offered up to her, and a more attentive recitation of the Rosary.

How does a normal son or daughter treat his mother? In different ways, of course, but always affectionately and confidently, never coldly. In an intimate way, through small, commonplace customs. And a mother feels hurt if we omit them: a kiss or an embrace when leaving or coming home, a little extra attention, a few warm words.

In our relationship with our mother in heaven, we should act in just the same way. Many Catholics have the custom of wearing the scapular; or they have acquired the habit of greeting those pictures – a glance is enough – which are found in every catholic home and in many public places; or they recall the central events in Christ's life by saying the Rosary, never getting tired of repeating its words, just like people in love; or they mark out a day of the week for her, Saturday ... doing some special little thing for her and thinking particularly about her motherhood.[8]

84.3 Visits to our Lady's shrines. Penitential and apostolic aspects.

A traditional manifestation of love for our Mother is the pilgrimage to a Marian shrine or church, done in a spirit of penance – which consists of some little voluntary sacrifice; for example, going on foot from an appropriate point along the route, denying ourselves some items of food or drink, saying the Rosary with special piety ... all with the apostolic aim of bringing the person with us a

---

[8] St J. Escrivá, *Christ is passing by*, 142

little closer to God.

May pilgrimages can be very suitable moments for doing a fruitful apostolate with our friends. In those Marian shrines and churches, numerous people have received ordinary graces – and also extraordinary ones – from the Mother of God. Some of them have started out on a new life, having made a good confession, perhaps for the first time in many years; others have discerned our Lord's call to a fuller self-surrender in the service of God and of souls; others have obtained help to overcome grave difficulties of body or soul ... Nobody has ever gone away empty-handed. Saint Paul VI pointed out how Providence, *often along wonderful pathways, has distinguished the Marian shrines by a special seal.*[9]

Those places, big and small, where there is a special presence of our Lady, are visited by people who come to give thanks to Mary, to praise her, to ask things of her, and also to begin the Christian life again, having lived, perhaps many years, far from God. Think what a great number of requests our Lady must have heeded from those in urgent need who fled in hope to her at those places. In such centres of Marian devotion, St John Paul II said, speaking at Saragossa, the heritage of the Marian faith of countless generations is not a mere memory of the past, but rather a point of departure towards God. *The prayers and sacrifices offered, the living heartbeat of a people which tells Mary of its natural joys, sorrows and hopes, are new stones which raise up the sacred dimension of a Marian faith. Because in that religious continuity, virtue gives birth to new virtue. Grace attracts grace.*[10]

These pilgrim shrines, which date from early times, are today all beyond all counting. They have been the fruit of

---

[9] St Paul VI, *Letter to the Rectors of Marian Shrines*, 1 May 1971
[10] St John Paul II, *Homily* in Saragossa, 6 November 1982

Christians' love for their Mother down through the centuries. Let us plan our own pilgrimage now in our prayer – a pilgrimage characterized by apostolate and by an attitude of penance, which facilitates prayer and more readily raises it up to God; a pilgrimage that is full of Marian devotion, expressed by the devout recitation of the Rosary. We should not forget that we are now fulfilling that prophecy which our Lady made one day: *all generations will call me blessed*. And let us not forget to show special signs of love to our Lady every day of this month.

SIXTH WEEK OF EASTER – WEDNESDAY

85. FRUITS IN THE APOSTOLATE

85.1 Integral preaching of Christ's teaching. The example of St Paul and the first Christians.

Today's reading at Mass shows us the apostolic spirit of St Paul in the heart of pagan society. In the Areopagus in Athens the Apostle preached the essential elements of the faith, attuned to the outlook and ignorance of his hearers but without omitting fundamental truths. He knew well that what he taught might sound very strange and unacceptable to the Athenians, but he did not adapt his teaching, watering it down to make it more 'understandable'. In fact, *when they heard of the resurrection of the dead, some mocked; but others said: 'We will hear you again about this'.*[1]

St Paul left Athens and made his way to Corinth. For quite some time he felt keenly what had happened in the Areopagus for, in the words of St John Chrysostom, *the Athenians were partial to new discourses, but then ignored them and paid no attention to their content. They were only interested in having something new to talk about.*[2] This event reminds us Christians today that we must make known Christ's teaching, the one doctrine that can save; not necessarily the most popular one or the one that may be most 'successful' in human terms, or the one that suits the mood of the day or tones in with the tastes of the times.

The Apostles preached the Gospel in its entirety. So too has the Church through the ages. As Pope Benedict XV reminded us: *What St Paul taught was all the truths and*

---

[1] Acts 17:32
[2] St John Chrysostom, *Homilies on the Acts of the Apostles*, 39

precepts of Christ, even the most demanding ones, without silencing or watering down any. He spoke of humility, of self-denial, of chastity, of detachment from earthly goods, of obedience ... And he did not fear to stress that one had to choose between serving God and serving Belial, because it is not possible to serve the two together. He taught that after death all had to undergo a woeful judgement; that no one can bargain with God; that one can only expect eternal life if one has kept God's laws; that seeking pleasures by breaking these laws one can only expect eternal damnation ... Never did the Preacher of the truth think he had to omit these things because they might seem harsh to his listeners, especially in view of the corruption of the times.[3] We must act in like manner.

The person who announces Christ must be willing to be unpopular at times, to forgo 'success' in human terms, to row against the current, without glossing over the more demanding aspects of Christ's teaching: things like mortification, uprightness and honesty in business and professional matters, generosity in having children, chastity and purity in and outside marriage, the value of virginity and celibacy for the sake of the kingdom of heaven ... There is no other prescription for curing this sick world of ours. As Pope Benedict XV also said: *Since when does a doctor give useless medicine to his patients, being afraid to prescribe useful ones?*[4]

In a world which in many ways is estranged from God and at odds with a Christian way of thinking, *on all Christians, accordingly, rests the noble obligation of working to bring all men throughout the whole world to hear and accept the divine message of salvation.*[5] Ordinarily our

---

[3] Benedict XV, Encyclical *Humanum genus*
[4] *ibid*
[5] Second Vatican Council, *Apostolicam actuositatem*, 3

first obligation will be to direct our apostolic activity towards those whom God has placed near us, those with whom we are in frequent contact. We should be opportunely apostolic, presenting Christ's teaching in an attractive and heart-warming way. We will not attract anyone to the faith if we are rash and impetuous; we will if we are kind, patient and loving.

85.2 Sowing the seed always. God gives the increase. Constancy in the apostolate.

Very often God allows our prayer and efforts to bear fruit in unexpected ways. *My chosen ones shall not labour in vain*:[6] such is his promise. In the Communion antiphon of today's Mass we read these consoling words: *You did not choose me, but I chose you and appointed you that you should go and bear fruit and that your fruit should abide.*[7]

At times the apostolic mission is to sow without seeing the fruits; at other times it is to reap, perhaps, what others have sown by word, or by silent suffering in a hospital bed, or by doing well a job that was humdrum and unspectacular. Whichever of the two, God wants both sower and reaper to rejoice together.[8]

If the fruits are long in coming and we are tempted to judge the worth of our efforts by their immediate results, we ought not to forget that at times we will not see the grain ripen, that others will harvest it. What God expects of us is that we sow tirelessly, that we experience the joy of sowing, certain that the seed sown in the furrow will one day sprout and bear fruit. Thus we will avoid being discouraged. Discouragement can often be a sign of having sown without an upright intention, of not working for God

---

[6] Is 65:23
[7] John 15:16
[8] cf John 4:36

but for oneself. What we cannot finish others will finish.

Nor should we try to harvest the fruit before it is ripe. *Let us not spoil the flower in trying to open it with our fingers. The flower will open, the fruit will ripen in the season and in God's own time. As for us, let us sow, plant, water, and then wait.*[9] Constancy and patience are essential virtues in the apostolate. Both are expressions of the virtue of fortitude.

The patient person is like the sower who falls in with the course of nature and carries out each task at the proper time – ploughing, sowing, watering, fertilising, weeding and harvesting. All this must be done before the wheat is ready to be made into bread for the family table. The impatient person wants to eat the bread before the wheat is grown. If we neglect our struggle for holiness and do not help others achieve sanctity as well, we will see no fruits. To act thus is to have a too human vision of things and to be in open contradiction with the patient figure of Jesus. He is able to wait for days and weeks and months and years for the conversion of a sinner. Souls need time, and it is not for us to know exactly how much. Let us carry out a good sowing, and then wait patiently; let us ask God for the fortitude to be constant.

85.3 Woman's unique role in evangelizing the family.

St Paul's preaching in Athens gave rise to the first Christian community in the city. *Some men joined him and believed, among them Dionysius the Areopagite and a woman named Damaris and others with them.*[10] They were the first seed sown by the Holy Spirit and from them would come at a later date many men and women who were faithful to Christ.

---

[9] G. Chevrot, *The Well of Life*
[10] Acts 17:34

Damaris is one of the many women who appear in the pages of the Acts of the Apostles. Her conversion shows the universality of the Gospel. The Apostles followed in the footsteps of Jesus who, unmindful of the prejudices of the times, announced the coming of the kingdom to men and women alike.[11]

St Luke has also informed us that the evangelization of Europe began with a mother, Lydia, who immediately evangelized her own family and brought them all to be baptized.[12] Among the Samaritans it was a woman who first heard Christ's message and later spread it to her neighbours.[13]

The Gospel shows us how women followed and ministered to Christ; how they were present at the foot of the Cross; how they were the first to go to the empty tomb. We find in them no sign of hypocrisy, or wrongdoing or betrayal.

St Paul had a deep insight into the role of the Christian woman as mother, spouse and sister in spreading the Christian message. This view is reflected in his preaching and letters. Some of these women are especially commended for the sacrifices they made to help him in his work of evangelization.

At all times, and no less in ours, Christian women play a most important part in the apostolate and in the handing on of the faith. *Women are called to bring to the family, to society and to the Church, characteristics which are their own and which they alone can give: their gentle warmth and untiring generosity, their love for detail, their quick-wittedness and intuition, their simple and deep piety, their*

---

[11] cf *The Navarre Bible*, Acts of the Apostles
[12] cf Acts 16:14
[13] cf John 4:1 ff

constancy.[14] The Church expects from women commitment and witness to all that contributes to the dignity of the human person and furthers their true happiness.

When these qualities with which God has endowed woman grow and develop, *her life and work will be really constructive, fruitful and full of meaning, whether she spends the day dedicated to her husband and children or whether, having given up the idea of marriage for a noble reason, she has given herself fully to other tasks.*

Each woman in her own sphere of life, if she is faithful to her divine and human vocation, can and in fact does achieve the fulness of her human personality. Let us remember that Mary, Mother of God and Mother of men, is not only a model but also a proof of the transcendental value of an apparently unimportant life.[15] We ask her to pray for the fruits of Christian women's labours in the family, society and the Church. We ask her that there always be an abundance of vocations in the Church, of many people totally committed to God.

[14] *Conversations with Monsignor Escrivá*, 87
[15] *ibid*

86. JESUS AWAITS US IN HEAVEN

86.1 Christ's glorious exaltation culminates in the Ascension.

According to the Gospel of St Luke the last gesture of our Lord on earth was to give a blessing.[1] The Eleven had gone, as Jesus had told them to, from Galilee to the Mount of Olives near Jerusalem. On seeing the risen Christ once more they fell down before him as their Master and their God and *worshipped him*.[2] Now they are much more conscious of what they had for some time believed in their hearts and confessed with their lips: that their Master was the Messiah.[3] They were delighted and full of joy at having their Lord and their God so near. After the forty days spent in his company they could be witnesses to what they had seen and heard. The Holy Spirit would confirm in them the teachings of Jesus and would lead them to the complete truth.

The Master spoke to them as only God could: *Jesus came and said to them, 'All authority in Heaven and on earth has been given to me'.*[4] Jesus confirmed the faith of those who worshipped him and taught them that the power they were to receive was a sharing in his own divine power. The power to forgive sins, and to bring about a rebirth through Baptism is the power of Christ himself, given now to his Church. The mission of the Church is to

---

[1] Luke 24:51
[2] cf Matt 28:17
[3] cf Matt 16:18
[4] Matt 28:18

continue always the work of Christ, to teach men divine truths and make known the demands these truths impose, to help men follow God's way through the grace of the sacraments.

He said to them ... 'You shall receive power when the Holy Spirit has come upon you; and you shall be my witnesses in Jerusalem and in all Judaea and Samaria and to the ends of the earth'. And when he had said this, as they were looking on, he was lifted up, and a cloud took him out of their sight.[5] Thus does St Luke describe for us the Ascension in the *Acts of the Apostles.*

He withdrew from their sight little by little. The Apostles remained for a long while, looking up as Jesus ascended majestically *until a cloud took him out of their sight.* It was the cloud that signifies the presence of God.[6] In John Chrysostom's words: *It was a sign that Jesus had entered Heaven.*[7]

Jesus' life on earth finished not with his death on the Cross but with his Ascension into Heaven. It is the last of the mysteries of his life here on earth. It is a redemptive mystery which together with his Passion, Death and Resurrection makes up the Paschal Mystery. It was fitting that those who saw Christ die amid insults, scoffing and mockery on the Cross should see him now exalted. They see fulfilled now the words Jesus had one day spoken to them: *I am ascending to my Father and your Father, to my God and your God.*[8] And again: *Now I am no more in the world, but they are in the world, and I am coming to thee.*[9]

We meditate on the Ascension of our Lord into Heaven in the Second Glorious Mystery of the Rosary. In

---

[5] *First reading of the Mass*, Acts 1:7-9
[6] cf Ex 13:22; Luke 9:34 ff
[7] St John Chrysostom, *Homilies on the Acts of the Apostles*, 2
[8] John 20:17
[9] John 17:11

the words of the Founder of Opus Dei: *Jesus has gone to the Father. – Two Angels in white approach us and say, Men of Galilee, why do you stand looking up to Heaven? (Acts 1:11).*

Peter and the others go back to Jerusalem – 'cum gaudio magno' – with great joy (Luke 24:52). It is fitting that the Sacred Humanity of Christ should receive the homage, praise and adoration of all the hierarchies of the Angels and of all the legions of the Blessed in Heaven.[10]

86.2 His Ascension strengthens and nourishes our desire for Heaven. The hope of Heaven should be fostered.

In a sermon to commemorate today's solemnity St Leo the Great said: *Today we are not only made possessors of Paradise but with Christ we have ascended, mystically but also really, to the highest Heavens and have won through Christ a grace more wonderful than the one we had lost.*[11]

The Ascension strengthens and nourishes our hope of attaining Heaven. It invites us always to lift up our heart, as the preface of the Mass says, and seek the things that are above. Our hope is very great because Christ himself has gone to prepare a dwelling place for us.[12]

Jesus is in Heaven with his glorified Body, with the signs of his redemptive sacrifice[13] and with the marks of his Passion, marks which Thomas could see and touch, marks which bring about our salvation. The Sacred Humanity of Christ has its natural place in Heaven but he who gave his life for us awaits us there. *Christ awaits us. We are 'citizens of Heaven' (Phil 3:20), and at the same*

---

[10] St J. Escrivá, *Holy Rosary*, Second Glorious Mystery
[11] St Leo the Great, *Homily I on the Ascension*
[12] cf John 14:2
[13] cf Apoc 5:6

*time fully-fledged citizens of this earth, in the midst of
difficulties, injustices and lack of understanding, but also
in the midst of the joy and serenity that comes from
knowing that we are children of God ...*

*If, in spite of everything, Jesus' ascension into Heaven
leaves a certain taste of sadness in our souls, let us go to
his Mother, as the Apostles did. 'They returned to
Jerusalem ... and they prayed with one mind ... together
with Mary, the Mother of Jesus'.*[14]

The hope of Heaven will fill our day with joy. We will
imitate the Apostles who, in the words of St Leo the Great,
benefitted so greatly from the Ascension of our Lord that
all that beforehand had caused them fear now caused them
joy. From that moment on, their souls were fixed in
contemplation on the divinity seated at the right hand of
the Father; the very vision of his body was no obstacle to
their believing with their minds illumined by faith that
Christ had not separated himself from his Father when he
descended, and had not separated himself from his
disciples when he ascended.[15]

86.3 The Ascension and the Christian's apostolic mission.

*And while they were gazing into Heaven as he went,
behold, two men stood by them in white robes, and said,
'Men of Galilee, why do you stand looking into Heaven?
This Jesus, who was taken from you into Heaven, will come
in the same way as you saw him go into Heaven'.*[16] *Like the
Apostles, we remain partly perplexed and partly saddened
at his departure. It is not easy, in fact, to get accustomed to
the physical absence of Jesus. I am moved when I think*

---

[14] St J. Escrivá, *Christ is passing by*, 126
[15] St Leo the Great, *Sermon 74*, 3
[16] Acts 1:11

that, in an excess of love, he has remained with us, even when he has gone away. He has gone to Heaven and, at the same time, he gives himself to us as our nourishment in the sacred host. Still, we miss his human speech, his way of acting, of looking, of smiling, of doing good. We would like to go back and regard him closely again, as he sits down at the edge of the well, tired from his journey (cf John 4:6); as he weeps for Lazarus (cf John 11:35); as he prays for a long time (cf Luke 6:12); as he feels pity for the crowd (cf Matt 15:32; Mark 8:2).

It has always seemed logical to me that the most holy humanity of Christ should ascend to the glory of the Father. The ascension has always made me very happy. But I think that the sadness that is particular to the day of the ascension is also a proof of the love we feel for Jesus Christ, our Lord. He is God made man, perfect man, with flesh like ours, with blood like ours in his veins. Yet he leaves us and goes up to Heaven. How can we help but miss his presence?[17]

The angels told the Apostles that it was now time for them to begin the task before them, that there was not a minute to be wasted. With the Ascension Christ's earthly mission comes to a close, and ours, as his disciples, begins. It is good that, today in our prayer, we hear the words with which Jesus intercedes for us before his Father: *I do not pray that thou shouldst take them out of the world,*[18] out of our proper place in society, out of our job or family, *but that thou shouldst keep them from the evil one.* Jesus wishes each of us to remain in his place, sanctifying the world from within, improving it and placing it at the feet of God. Only thus will the world be a place where human dignity is valued and respected, a place where men live in

---

[17] St J. Escrivá, *Christ is passing by*, 117
[18] John 17:15

peace, in true peace, the peace which is so closely linked to God.

Today's feast reminds us that our concern for souls is a response to a command of love given to us by our Lord. As he goes up to Heaven, Jesus sends us out as his witnesses throughout the whole world. Our responsibility is great, because to be Christ's witness implies first of all that we should try to behave according to his doctrine, that we should struggle to make our actions remind others of Jesus and his most lovable personality.[19]

Those we live and work with, those we come in contact with, should find us loyal, sincere, joyful and hard-working. We should behave as people who fulfil their duties honestly and live as children of God in the ups and downs of each day. The ordinary norms of courtesy (how we greet others, our cordiality and spirit of service), which for many are merely conventional and external, have to be in us the fruit of charity and an expression of real interest in someone else.

Jesus departs, but he remains close to each of us. In a special way we find him in the Tabernacle, perhaps in one not far from where we live or work. Let us have recourse to him there, even though often we cannot go physically but only with our heart, and ask him to help us in our apostolic endeavours. Let us tell him that he can count on us to make known his teaching everywhere we go.

The Apostles returned to Jerusalem in the company of Mary. With her they awaited the coming of the Holy Spirit. Let us too prepare for the coming of Pentecost staying close to our Lady.

---

[19] St J. Escrivá, *Christ is passing by*, 122

SIXTH WEEK OF EASTER – FRIDAY

DECENARY TO THE HOLY SPIRIT

87. THE GIFT OF UNDERSTANDING

87.1 Through this gift, which is necessary for living a fully Christian life, we come to have a deeper knowledge of the mysteries of faith.

Every page of Holy Scripture shows us how God cares for us and gently leads us to holiness. In the Old Testament God is seen as the true light of Israel, without which the people would lose their way and stumble in the darkness. Time and time again the outstanding figures of the Old Testament turn to Yahweh so that he may guide them at difficult moments. *Show me now thy ways*[1] was Moses prayer as he led the people towards the promised land. Without God's guiding light he felt himself lost. And King David asked: *Give me understanding, that I may keep thy law and observe it with my whole heart.*[2]

Jesus promises us the Spirit of truth whose mission it is to illumine the whole Church.[3] Jesus *completed and perfected Revelation and confirmed it with divine guarantees. He did this by the total fact of his presence and self-manifestation, by words and works, signs and miracles ... and by sending the Spirit of truth.*[4] The Apostles themselves only understood later the full meaning of Jesus' words. As Saint Paul VI said: *The Holy Spirit is the soul of the Church. It is he who explains to the faithful the deep*

---

[1] Ex 33:13
[2] Ps 119:34
[3] cf John 16:13
[4] Second Vatican Council, *Dei Verbum*, 4

meaning of the teaching of Jesus and of his mystery.[5]

The Holy Spirit brings us to an initial understanding of the truths of faith and then *constantly perfects faith by his gifts, so that Revelation may be more and more profoundly understood.*[6] Through the gift of understanding the faithful come to have a fuller grasp of the truths of faith. The Holy Spirit illumines the mind with a most powerful light and enables us to see more clearly what until then was only dimly seen. It often happens that *we know some mystery for quite a while; we have heard something and thought about it; but all of a sudden we see it in a new light. It is as if we had not understood it at all until then.*[7] Under the influence of the Holy Spirit a Christian has greater certainty in believing; everything is much clearer. Under his light supernatural truths give an indescribable joy, a joy which is a foretaste of Heaven.

Thanks to this gift, says St Thomas, *God is glimpsed here below.*[8] This happens to those who are pure and docile to the inspirations of the Paraclete. Nevertheless the mysteries of faith remain enveloped in a certain obscurity.

To reach this knowledge the ordinary light of faith is insufficient. We need a special outpouring of the Holy Spirit, which we will receive in the measure in which we respond to grace, are pure of heart and desirous of reaching holiness. The gift of understanding enables us to see all things with supernatural vision. It brings us to reverence the greatness of God, to pay him filial affection and to judge created things rightly. *Little by little, in the measure in which love grows in the soul, a person's mind reflects more and more the splendour of God*[9] and becomes more

---

[5] St Paul VI, *Evangelii nuntiandi*, 75

[6] Second Vatican Council, *Dei Verbum*, 5

[7] A. Riaud, *The Action of the Holy Spirit in souls*, Madrid

[8] St Thomas, *Summa Theologiae*, I-II, 69, 2

[9] M.M. Philipon, *The Gifts of the Holy Spirit*, Madrid

familiar with the hidden mysteries of God.

On this day of the *decenary* – ten days of prayer (\em
to the Holy Spirit we could examine how seriously (we
want to be purified, and see whether this desire is
expressed in our using well the graces of Confession. Do
we go to Confession regularly; do we make a sincere
examination of conscience before going; do we ask the
Holy Spirit to help us be contrite; do we foster the desire to
avoid all sin and all deliberate faults?

87.2 This Gift is given to all Christians, but its development requires us to live in the state of grace and strive earnestly for personal holiness.

Through the gift of understanding the Holy Spirit
makes us plumb the depths of the mysteries of revelation.
In a supernatural and therefore in a gratuitous way he
teaches us the meaning of the deepest truths of faith. As St
Teresa says: *It is like one who, without having learned
anything, or having taken the slightest trouble in order to
learn to read, finds himself in possession of all existing
knowledge; he has no idea how or whence it has come,
since he has never done any work, even so much as was
necessary for the learning of the alphabet.*

*This last comparison, I think, furnishes some sort of
explanation of this Heavenly gift, for the soul suddenly
finds itself learned, and the mystery of the Most Holy
Trinity, together with other lofty things, is so clearly
explained to it that there is no theologian with whom it
would not have the boldness to contend in defence of the
truth of these marvels.*[10]

The gift of understanding enables us to grasp the
deeper meaning of the Scriptures, the life of grace, the
presence of Christ in each sacrament and in a real

---

[10] St Teresa, *Life*, 27, 8-9

substantial way in the Blessed Eucharist. It gives us, as it were, an instinct for what is supernatural in the world. For the eyes of one of Christ's faithful, illumined by the Holy Spirit, there is a whole new universe to be discovered. The mysteries of the Most Blessed Trinity, the Incarnation, the Redemption, and the Church become living realities affecting the day-to-day life of the Christian. They have a decisive influence on his work, on his family life and friendships. Prayer becomes deeper and easier.

Those who are docile to the Holy Spirit are purified in soul, awakened in faith and can discover God in all created things and in the daily events of ordinary life. The lukewarm person does not heed these touches of grace because his soul is closed to the divine. He has lost his sense of faith, and of the demands and details of faith.

The gift of understanding allows us to contemplate God in the midst of ordinary matters and events, whether pleasant or sorrowful. The way to achieve the fulness of this gift is by personal prayer in which we contemplate the truths of faith; by a joyful, loving struggle to maintain presence of God throughout the day; by fostering acts of contrition whenever we have cut ourselves off from God. This gift is not something extraordinary given only to exceptional persons. No. It is given to all those who want to be faithful to God wherever they find themselves, sanctifying their joys and sorrows, toils and rest.

87.3 Need to purify our soul. Understanding and contemplative life.

To make progress on the road of holiness we must foster interior recollection. This means not having our senses restless, not being curious about everything going on, not being oblivious of God. We need mortification of the internal senses (imagination, memory, keeping useless thoughts at bay), and of the external senses, struggling to be conscious of God's presence, seeing the hand of God behind the ups and downs of life.

We need to purify our heart, for only the pure of heart can see God.[11] Lack of purity, attachment to the goods of the earth and giving the body all that it wants dull the soul's interest for the things of God. *The unspiritual man does not receive the gifts of the Spirit of God, for they are folly to him, and he is not able to understand them because they are spiritually discerned.*[12]

The spiritual man is the Christian who bears the Holy Spirit in his soul in grace and has his heart and mind fixed on Jesus. His pure, sober and mortified life is the best preparation for being a worthy dwelling place for the Spirit, a place where the Paraclete can dwell with all his gifts.

When the Holy Spirit finds the soul well disposed He takes it over and leads it along paths of deep prayer. *We start with vocal prayers which many of us have been saying since we were children ... First one brief aspiration, then another, and another ... till our fervour seems insufficient, because words are too poor ... : then this gives way to intimacy with God, looking at God without needing rest or feeling tired. We begin to live as captives, as prisoners. And while we carry out as perfectly as we can (with all our mistakes and limitations) the tasks allotted to us by our situation and duties, our soul longs to escape. It is drawn towards God like iron drawn by a magnet. One begins to love Jesus, in a more effective way, with the sweet and gentle surprise of the encounter.*[13]

St Josemaría Escrivá is describing the path followed by souls who live a normal life in normal circumstances, no matter what their educational background, job or state

---

[11] cf Matt 5:8

[12] 1 Cor 2:14

[13] St J. Escrivá, *Friends of God*, 296

in life. For many, this way begins with frequent consideration of the Sacred Humanity of Christ, reached through the Blessed Virgin and passing necessarily through the Cross, to the Blessed Trinity.

Our heart now needs to distinguish and adore each one of the divine Persons. The soul is, as it were, making a discovery in the supernatural life, like a little child opening his eyes to the world about him. The soul spends time lovingly with the Father and the Son and the Holy Spirit, and readily submits to the work of the lifegiving Paraclete, who gives himself to us with no merit on our part, bestowing his gifts and the supernatural virtues![14]

As we finish our prayer let us turn to Mary, who had the fulness of grace and the gifts of the Holy Spirit, and ask her to teach us to come close to and love the Paraclete always, but in a special way during this decenary. We ask her to help us not remain stuck halfway along the road that leads to the holiness we are called to.

---

[14] *ibid*, 306

88. THE GIFT OF KNOWLEDGE

88.1 This gift enables us to understand the world in the light of God's plan of creation and elevation to the supernatural order.

Creatures are, as it were, a trace of the passing of God, whereby are revealed His greatness, power, wisdom and other Divine virtues.[1] Things are like a mirror which reflect the splendour, beauty, goodness and power of God. In the words of the psalmist: *The heavens are telling the glory of God; and the firmament proclaims his handiwork.*[2]

And yet, frequently, because of original sin and subsequent personal sins, men are unable to perceive the signs of God in the world and do not know him as the source of all good. In the book of Wisdom we are told: *For all men who were ignorant of God were foolish by nature; and they were unable from the good things that are seen to know him who exists, nor did they recognize the craftsman while paying heed to his works ... If through delight in the beauty of these things men assumed them to be gods, let them know how much better than these is their Lord, for the author of beauty created them.*[3]

The gift of knowledge enables man to understand created things as signs which lead to God, and the meaning of their elevation to the supernatural order. Through the world of nature and grace the Holy Spirit enables us to

---

[1] St John of the Cross, *The Spiritual Canticle*, 5, 3
[2] Ps 19:1
[3] Wis 13:1-3

perceive and contemplate the infinite wisdom, power and goodness of God. God's nature is reflected in created things. *Like the gifts of understanding and of wisdom, the gift of knowledge is a contemplative gift enabling us to see into the very mystery of God.*[4]

Through this gift a Christian perceives and understands that *all creation, the movement of the earth and the other heavenly bodies, the good actions of creatures and all the good that has been achieved in history, in short, everything, comes from God and is directed toward him.*[5] This gift is a supernatural disposition whereby the soul participates in God's knowledge, grasps the relationship between creatures and their Creator, and perceives how and in what way creation serves man's last end.

The hymn of the three young men in the book of Daniel, which many Catholics use for thanksgiving after Holy Communion, is a clear expression of the gift of knowledge. All created things are asked to bless and give glory to God. *Benedicite, omnia opera Domini, Domino ...: all works of the Lord, bless the Lord; praise and bless him forever.* Angels of the Lord ... heavens ... waters above the heavens ... sun and moon ... stars of heaven ... rain and dew ... all winds ... winter cold and summer heat ... nights and days ... light and darkness ... mountains and hills ... plants ... springs ... seas and rivers ... whales and fish ... birds of the air ... wild beasts and cattle ... priests of the Lord ... spirits and souls of the righteous ... the holy and humble in heart: praise and thank him because his mercy is everlasting.[6]

In this wonderful hymn all creation, animate and inanimate, gives glory to its Creator. It is *one of the purest*

---

[4] M.M. Philipon, *The Gifts of the Holy Spirit*, Madrid
[5] St J. Escrivá, *Christ is passing by*, 130
[6] cf Dan 3:52-90

*and most burning expressions of the gift of knowledge: that
the heavens and all creation should give glory to God.*[7]
Often it will help us give thanks to God after sharing in the
Mass, the work which gives him most glory.

88.2 The gift of knowledge and the sanctification of temporal things.

Through the gift of knowledge the Christian who is
docile to the Holy Spirit will learn to discern perfectly
between what leads to God and what separates from him,
in the field of arts, of fashion, and in the world of ideas.
Truly he will be able to say that wisdom *guided him on
straight paths; she showed him the kingdom of God, and
gave him knowledge of angels.*[8] The Holy Spirit himself
will warn us when what is good and true in itself is in
danger of becoming bad by leading us away from our last
supernatural end. It could be a disordered desire for
material possessions, or an attachment to these goods in a
way that does not leave the heart free to serve God.

Christians who must sanctify themselves in the middle
of the world have a particular need of this gift so as to
direct all temporal activities to God, making them a means
of holiness and apostolate. Through it a housewife discovers how her work at home is a way to God if it is done
with an upright, honest intention and with a desire to please
God; a student learns that study is the ordinary way to love
God, do apostolate and serve society; for an architect the
way to God is through plans and drawings; for a nurse, her
care of the sick. We understand that we must love the
world and temporal affairs, and come to discover the truth
of those words of St Josemaría Escrivá: *There is 'something holy', something divine hidden in the most ordinary*

---

[7] M.M. Philipon, *op cit*
[8] Wis 10:10

situations, and it is up to each one of you to discover it.[9]
~~When a Christian carries out with love the most insignifi-~~
cant everyday action, that action overflows with the transcendence of God. That is why I have told you repeatedly,
and hammered away once and again at the idea, that the
Christian vocation consists in making heroic verse out of
the prose of each day.[10] The epic poetry we men and
women write for God is comprised of the ordinary events
of the day, the problems and joys we meet along our way.

   We love the things of earth, but we value them
correctly, that is, as God values them. Thus we give the
utmost importance to being *temples of the Holy Spirit*
because *if God is dwelling in our soul, everything else, no
matter how important it may seem, is accidental and
transitory, whereas we, in God, stand permanent and
firm.*[11] We treasure our faith more than material goods and
even life itself, and would be ready to abandon all else to
preserve it. In the light of this gift we see the value of
prayer and mortification and appreciate the importance
they have in our life. Thus we would never dream of
omitting them.

88.3 True value and meaning of the world. Detachment and humility are needed to benefit from this gift.

   By this gift the Christian understands the littleness of
the value of earthly things if they do not lead to the things
of Heaven; the shortness of human life on earth; the limited
happiness this world can give when compared with that
which God has promised to those who love him; the
pointlessness of so much effort if it is not carried out in
God's presence ... When the soul recalls its past life, in

---

[9] *Conversations with Monsignor Escrivá*, 114
[10] *ibid*, 115
[11] St J. Escrivá, *Friends of God*, 92

which perhaps God was not given first place, it feels a deep sorrow for so much evil and for so many lost opportunities, and there is born in it the desire to make up for lost time by being more faithful to God.

Everything in this world – which we love and in which we have to sanctify ourselves – appears in the light of this gift as marked with perishability, while in all its clarity we see our supernatural end, to which we ought to subordinate all earthly things.

This vision in faith of the world, of events and of individuals can become darkened, and even totally obscured, by what St John calls the *concupiscence of the eyes*.[12] The mind then seems to reject the true light, and becomes unable to direct earthly affairs to Him; instead, these become its end. The disordered desire for material goods, the determination to reduce the search for happiness to affairs here below, impedes or frustrates the action of this gift. The soul then falls into a species of blindness in which it is unable to recognize and to taste the true goods, those which do not perish, and its supernatural hope is replaced by an ever greater desire for material well-being, fleeing from any suggestion of mortification and sacrifice.

This purely natural vision of the world eventually degenerates into total ignorance of the truths about God, or else they are seen as something purely theoretical, without practical relevance to everyday life and normal behaviour. The sins against this gift leave one without light. This is the explanation for the great ignorance of God that there is in the world. At times it is a question of real incapacity to understand or assimilate the supernatural, because the eyes of the soul have been turned completely towards partial and illusory goods and have been closed to the true ones.

To dispose us to receive this gift we need to ask the

---

[12] 1 John 2:16

Holy Spirit to help us exercise freedom and detachment from material goods and to be more humble, so that we can learn the true value of things. Together with these dispositions we need to foster and increase our sense of the presence of God, which helps us to see him in our work. Let us make the firm resolution to bring to our prayer the events of our life and the realities of our every day: family, colleagues working beside us, the thing that concerns us most ... Prayer is always a powerful searchlight to illuminate the true reality of things and happenings.

To obtain this gift, to make us capable of possessing it in greater fullness, we have recourse to the Blessed Virgin. She is the *Mother of fair love, of fear, of knowledge, and of holy hope.*[13]

Mary is also the Mother of knowledge, for it is with her that we learn the most important lesson of all, that nothing is worth while if we are not close to Our Lord. All the wonders of this earth, the fulfilment of our every ambition, all this is worthless unless the living flame of love burns within us, unless there is the light of holy hope giving us a foretaste of never-ending love in our true homeland in Heaven.[14]

---

[13] Sir 24:24
[14] St J. Escrivá, *Friends of God*, 278

89. THE GIFT OF WISDOM

89.1 Wisdom gives us a loving knowledge of God, and of people and created things insofar as they refer to him. This gift is closely connected with the virtue of charity.

There exists a knowledge of God and of what refers to God which only comes with holiness of life. Through the gift of wisdom the Holy Spirit places this knowledge within the reach of simple souls who love God. *I thank thee, Father, Lord of heaven and earth, that thou hast hidden these things from the wise and understanding and revealed them to babes.*[1] It is a knowledge not learned from books but given by God who illumines and fills our mind and heart, will and understanding with love. By means of this light of love, the Christian has a more intimate and joyful knowledge of God and his mysteries.

We appreciate the flavour of some fruit much more when we taste it than when we read a description of it in a botany book. What description comes near the actual taste we get when we bite into fruit? So too, when we are united to God and savour him by personal experience we know divine things much better than when we read things written by learned men.[2] This knowledge is given especially by the gift of wisdom.

Just as a mother knows her child by the love she has for it, so too, through charity, a soul attains a deep

---

[1] Matt 11:25
[2] L.M. Martinez, *The Holy Spirit*, Madrid

knowledge of God who lovingly bestows light and the ability to know divine mysteries. It is a gift of the Holy Spirit because it is the fruit of charity given by him to each one. This gift is a sharing in God's infinite wisdom. St Paul prayed that the first Christians *be strengthened with might through his Spirit in the inner man ... that you, being rooted and grounded in love, may have the power to comprehend with all the saints what is the breadth and length and height and depth, and to know the love of Christ which surpasses knowledge, that you may be filled with all the fulness of God.*[3] To understand, being rooted in love, says the Apostle. This kind of knowledge is deep and loving.

St Thomas Aquinas teaches[4] that the object of this gift is principally God himself and divine things but it also includes the things of this world insofar as they come from God and are ordered to him.

No higher knowledge of God is possible than this joyful knowledge which enriches and facilitates our prayer and life of service to God and men. *Wisdom is better than jewels, and all that you may desire cannot compare with her,*[5] we read in the Book of Proverbs. And the Book of Wisdom tells us: *I preferred her to sceptres and thrones, and I accounted wealth as nothing in comparison with her. Neither did I liken her to any priceless gem, because all gold is but a little sand in her sight, and silver will be accounted as clay before her. I loved her more than health and beauty, and I chose to have her rather than light, because her radiance never ceases. All good things came to me along with her, and in her hands uncounted wealth. I rejoiced in them all, because wisdom leads them; but I did*

---

[3] Eph 3:16-19
[4] cf St Thomas, *Summa Theologiae* I, 45, 2
[5] Prov 8:11

not know that she was their mother ... [Wisdom] *is an unfailing treasure for men; those who get it obtain friendship with God.*[6]

The gift of wisdom is closely connected with the virtue of charity. It bestows a special knowledge of God and others, and prepares the soul for *a certain experience of the sweetness of God,*[7] both in himself and in created things insofar as these refer to him.

By this gift, so closely united with charity, we are better able to live in harmony with others. Every day we have very many opportunities to serve and help those around us. Today in our prayer let us see whether we serve as we ought to, whether we try to make the lives of other people pleasant and joyful.

89.2 Through this gift we share in Christ's love for the people we are in contact with. It teaches us to view events in the light of the providence of God who is always a loving Father.

Among the gifts of the Holy Spirit, I would say that there is one which we all need in a special way: the gift of wisdom. It makes us know God and rejoice in his presence, thereby placing us in a perspective from which we can judge accurately the situations and events of life.[8] With the vision this gift bestows, the soul who wishes to follow Christ closely contemplates reality from a higher perspective, because it shares in some way in the vision which God himself has of creation. Everything is judged with the clarity given by this gift.

We see in our dealings with other people a chance to be merciful, doing an effective apostolate and bringing

---

[6] Wis 7:8-14
[7] St Thomas, *Summa Theologiae*, I-II, 112, 5
[8] St J. Escrivá, *Christ is passing by*, 133

them closer to God. A Christian understands better the great need men have to be helped on their way to Christ. Others are seen as persons in need of God, and that is the way Jesus sees them.

Illumined by this gift, the saints have understood the real meaning of the events of this life, whether small or great. And so they do not consider illness a misfortune, nor do they rail against the sufferings they endure because they understand that God blesses in different ways, and frequently he blesses with the Cross. They know that all things, even those which are inexplicable from the purely human viewpoint, work for the good of those who love God.[9]

The gift of wisdom, the principle of a living contemplation that directs action, enables the soul to taste the goodness of God, to see it manifested in all events, even in the most painful, since God permits evil only for a higher good, which we shall see later and which it is sometimes given us to glimpse on earth.[10]

Through this gift the motions of grace will bring us and our neighbours and friends great peace. We will be helped to bring joy wherever we go, and to find the right word to reconcile those who are at odds with one another. Thus does this gift tie in with the beatitude: *Blessed are the peacemakers*. Those who have peace in themselves can bring peace to others. This peace which the world cannot give results from seeing all within the providential plan of God, who never for a moment forgets his children.

89.3 The gift of wisdom and contemplative spirit in everyday life.

The gift of wisdom gives us a loving, penetrating faith,

---

[9] cf Rom 8:28
[10] R. Garrigou-Lagrange, *The Three Ages of the Interior Life*, II

and a clarity and understanding of the unfathomable mystery of God which we never thought possible. It can have to do with the presence and nearness of God, or the Real Presence of Christ in the tabernacle, which produce an extraordinary happiness. As a spiritual writer has told us: *The soul remains there, without saying anything, or saying only a few simple words of love, in deep contemplation, with its eyes fixed on the Sacred Host, never tiring of looking at him. It seems as if Jesus were seeing into its very depths.*[11]

The more usual thing, however, will be to find God in everyday life, with no special effects but with the intimate certainty that God watches over us, sees what we are doing, cares for us as for his children, at work or at home. The Holy Spirit teaches us that if we are faithful to his grace, our everyday affairs are the normal way to God, there we serve him in this life and prepare ourselves to contemplate him in Heaven for all eternity.

In the measure in which we purify our heart we will understand better the real meaning of the world, of other people whom we will see as children of God and of what goes on around us, sharing in the very vision God has of the world, always of course in accordance with our status as creatures.

The gift of wisdom illumines our intellect and inflames our will so as to discover God in the ordinary things of each day, in sanctifying our work, in the love with which we finish what we have begun, in the effort we need to make to be always ready to serve others.

This loving action of the Holy Spirit in our lives will only be possible if we take good care of the times especially set aside for God: Mass, times of personal prayer, visits to the Blessed Sacrament. These items must

---

[11] A. Riaud, *The Action of the Holy Spirit in souls*, Madrid

be given priority in our normal day, and even at times when we seem to have far too much to do; when we are full of fervour and when we are spiritually dry; when journeying, or resting or suffering ill health. Besides taking care of these special times set aside for God, we also need to be mindful of what makes up the backdrop of our life: we need a good awareness of God's presence. This can be achieved by saying aspirations, making acts of thanksgiving and contrition, offering up small sacrifices, whether voluntarily sought or which simply crop up throughout the day.

May the Mother of God and our Mother protect us, so that each one of us may serve the Church in the fullness of faith, with the gifts of the Holy Spirit and with our contemplative life. May each one of us joyfully honour the Lord by carrying out his own duties, those which are properly his; each one of us, in his job or profession and fulfilling the obligations of his state in life.[12]

---

[12] St J. Escrivá, *Friends of God*, 316

90. THE GIFT OF COUNSEL

90.1 The gift of counsel and the virtue of prudence.

There are many moments when we could stray from the path which leads to God. There are many side tracks we could wander down. But God has reassured us with these words: *I will instruct you and teach you the way you should go; I will counsel you with my eye upon you.*[1] The Holy Spirit is our best Adviser, our best Teacher, our best Guide. Our Lord's promise to his Apostles for when they might find themselves in very difficult situations, is very heartening: *When they deliver you up, do not be anxious how you are to speak or what you are to say; for what you are to say will be given you in that hour; for it is not you who speak, but the Spirit of your Father speaking through you.*[2] They were to have the special assistance of the Holy Spirit as would Christians through the centuries when placed in similar circumstances.

The behaviour of so many Christian martyrs shows how the promise Jesus made has been fulfilled in the life of the Church. It is moving to see related in documents which have come down to us the serenity and wisdom of people with little learning, and even of children. The Holy Spirit, who assists us in even the smallest difficulties, will do so in a special way in times of stress when we have to confess our faith.

Through the gift of wisdom, the Holy Spirit perfects

---

[1] Ps 32:8
[2] Matt 10:19-20

the acts of the virtue of prudence, and prudence in turn tells us which means to use in any given situation. Frequently we must make a decision; sometimes it is an important matter, at other times much less so. But in all of them, our holiness is in some way involved. God grants the gift of wisdom to those who are docile to the action of the Holy Spirit, so that they may make decisions quickly and correctly. This gift is like a supernatural instinct for knowing which way gives most glory to God. Just as prudence is present in all our actions, so too the Holy Spirit, through the gift of counsel, is the Light and permanent guiding Principle of our actions. The Paraclete inspires us when we choose the means to carry out God's will. He leads us along paths which involve charity, peace, joy, sacrifice, fulfilment of duty and faithfulness in small things. He marks out the path for us at every instant.

The first area where this gift must be lived is in our own interior life. There, in our soul in grace, the Paraclete acts in a silent way, gently but forcefully. *This most wise Teacher has such skilful ways of teaching us that they are wonderful to watch. They are all sweetness, all affection, all goodness, all prudence, all discretion.*[3] From those teachings and from the light we bear in our soul come those impulses, those calls to improve and respond ever better to God. From him come those firm resolutions that can change a life or give rise to greater effectiveness in our dealings with God, at work, and in the network of activities which comprise our day.

To allow ourselves be advised and guided by the Paraclete, we should want to belong entirely to God, not placing any limitations on the action of grace. We should want to seek God for what he is in himself, infinitely worthy of our love, and without expecting other rewards or

---

[3] F.J. del Valle, *About the Holy Spirit*

compensations. This we should do both in times of spiritual fervour as well as in times of spiritual dryness. *We must seek, serve, and love God unselfishly, not in order to be virtuous, nor to acquire holiness or grace or even Heaven itself, nor for the happiness of possessing him, but solely for the sake of loving him. And when he offers us graces and gifts, we should tell him that the only gift we want is the gift of love, in order to love him; if he says to us: Ask me for anything you like, we should ask for nothing except love and more love, in order to love him and to love him more.*[4] With that love of God comes everything else a person may desire in his heart.

90.2 The gift of counsel helps us have a true conscience.

The gift of counsel presupposes that we have used all the other means necessary to act prudently: to obtain the necessary data; to foresee the possible consequences of our actions, to learn from the experience of similar situations in the past, to ask advice when the moment comes. This is natural prudence which is then reinforced by grace. Along with supernatural prudence we receive this gift of counsel which allows us to make a sure and quick decision regarding the means to be used, or the reply to be given, or the way to be followed. There are times when it is impossible to put off a decision because circumstances demand an immediate and sure reply, as that which our Lord gave the Pharisees when, in bad faith, they asked whether it was lawful to pay tribute to Caesar or not. Jesus asked for a coin with which the tribute was paid and, on being given it, asked: *Whose likeness and inscription is this? They said, Caesar's. Then he said to them, Render therefore to Caesar the things that are Caesar's, and to God the things that are God's. When they heard it, they*

---

[4] ibid

marvelled; and they left him and went away.[5]

The gift of counsel is a great help in keeping a true conscience, and not letting it be deformed. If we are docile, the Holy Spirit will illumine our conscience with light and advice. Our soul will not deviate or make excuses for faults and sins. Rather it will react with contrition, with a greater sorrow at having offended God. This gift illumines brightly the soul which is faithful to God, in such a way that it does not apply moral laws wrongly, does not allow human respect to sway it, is not carried away by fashions and trends of the moment, but is ruled always by God's will. The Paraclete counsels us, directly or through others, regarding which is the right path to follow, a path which may well be different from the one suggested by *the spirit of the world*. A person who ceases to apply moral norms to his behaviour, whether in important or not so important matters, does so because he places his own will before the will of God.

To be docile to the lights and interior motions which the Holy Spirit inspires in our heart does not by any stretch of the imagination mean excluding *our consulting others or listening humbly to the teachings of the Church. Quite the contrary. The saints have always been anxious to obey their superiors, convinced that obedience is a royal highway, the surest and quickest way to the greatest holiness. The Holy Spirit himself inspires such filial submission to the lawful representatives of Christ's Church: 'He who hears you hears me, and he who rejects you rejects me' (Luke 10:16).*[6]

---

[5] Matt 22:21-22
[6] M.M. Philipon, *The Gifts of the Holy Spirit*, Madrid

90.3 Advice received in spiritual guidance. Ways to facilitate this gift.

The gift of counsel is particularly needed by those whose mission it is to guide and direct other people. St Thomas teaches that *every good piece of advice regarding men's salvation comes from the Holy Spirit.*[7] The advice we receive in spiritual guidance, where clearly and frequently the touch of the Holy Spirit is evident, ought to be received with the joy a wayfarer has at finding the path, giving thanks to God and to the person who represents him, and with the determination to put into practice what we have been advised. At times this advice can have a special echo in the person who receives it, inspired directly by the Holy Spirit.

The gift of counsel is necessary for everyday living, both for ourselves and to be able to advise our friends in their spiritual lives and in their undertakings. This gift corresponds to the beatitude about the merciful,[8] because *one has to be merciful to know how to give helpful advice discreetly to those who need it; such advice, far from disheartening them will encourage them gently and forcefully.*[9]

Today we ask the Holy Spirit to help us to be docile to his inspirations, because the greatest obstacle to the gift of counsel taking root in our souls is attachment to our own judgement, not knowing how to give way, lack of humility and hastiness in acting. We facilitate this gift if we become accustomed to bring to our prayer any important decisions we have to make. *Never make a decision*, we are told in *The Way*, *without first stopping to consider the matter in*

---

[7] St Thomas, *Commentary on the Lord's Prayer*
[8] *ibid*, *Summa Theologiae*, II-II, 52, 4
[9] R. Garrigou-Lagrange, *The Three Ages of the Interior Life*, II

the presence of God;[10] *and if we try to be detached from our own opinion: Don't waste the opportunity of yielding your own judgement;*[11] if we are completely sincere when we ask for advice in spiritual guidance or when seeking guidance in some moral matter which affects us directly. It may have to do with professional ethics, or judging before God whether we should have a larger family ... If we are humble, if we recognize our own limitations, we will feel the need to seek advice at particular times. Then we ought not simply go to the first person we meet but *to a person with the right qualities, to someone who wants to love God as sincerely as we do and who tries to follow him faithfully. It is not enough to ask just anyone for their opinion. We must go to a person who can give us sound and disinterested advice ... As we go through life we find ourselves coming across people who are objective and know how to weigh things up, who don't get heated or try to tip the balance towards that which favours them. Almost instinctively, we find ourselves trusting such people, because, unassumingly and quietly, they always act in a good and upright manner.*[12]

He who follows me will not walk in darkness, but will have the light of life.[13] If we try to follow Jesus each day of our life, we will not be wanting in the light of the Holy Spirit at every moment. If we are upright in our intention, he will not allow us fall into error. Mary, Mother of Good Counsel, will win for us the graces we need if we have recourse to her with the humility of those who know that on their own they will often stumble and lose their way.

---

[10] St J. Escrivá, *The Way*, 266
[11] *ibid*, 177
[12] *ibid*, *Friends of God*, 86 & 88
[13] John 8:12

SEVENTH WEEK OF EASTER – TUESDAY

DECENARY TO THE HOLY SPIRIT

91. THE GIFT OF PIETY

91.1 Piety enables us to appreciate our divine filiation, giving our relationship with God the tenderness and affection of a son for his father.

Divine filiation is an effect of the gift of piety that causes us to relate to God with the tenderness and affection of a good son towards his father, and to relate to the rest of mankind as brothers of the same family.

In the Old Testament this gift is seen in many ways, particularly in the constant prayer of the Chosen People to God: sentiments of praise and petition; adoration of God's divine majesty; intimate confessions which express to the Heavenly Father with all simplicity their joys, sorrows and hopes ... Especially in the psalms we can find all the sentiments that fill the soul in its confident dialogue with God.

When the fulness of time had come, Christ taught us the proper tone in which we ought to address God. *When you pray, say: Father ...*[1] In all circumstances of life we have to direct ourselves to God with this filial trust: Father, *Abba*. In many passages of the New Testament the Holy Spirit has wanted us to find the aramaic word *abba*, which was the affectionate name by which Hebrew children addressed their father. This word expresses our attitude and channels our prayer to God. *He is not a distant being who contemplates indifferently the fate of men – their desires, their struggles, their sufferings. He is a Father who loves his children so much that he sends the Word, the Second*

---

[1] Luke 11:2

Person of the most Blessed Trinity, so that by taking on the nature of man he may die to redeem us. He is the loving Father who now leads us gently to himself, through the action of the Holy Spirit who dwells in our hearts.[2]

God wants us to go to him with total confidence, like little children who are in need. All our piety is nourished by this fact: we are children of God. And the Holy Spirit, through the gift of piety, teaches us and facilitates for us this trusting relationship of a son with his Father.

See what love the Father has given us, that we should be called children of God; and so we are.[3] It seems as if after the words 'that we should be called children of God', St John paused to allow his spirit to penetrate deeply into the immensity of the love which the Father has shown us, not limiting himself simply to calling us children of God, but making us so in the most authentic sense. This is what makes St John cry out: 'and so we are'.[4] The Apostle invites us to consider the immense benefit of divine filiation which we receive with the grace of Baptism, and encourages us to second the action of the Holy Spirit that causes us to treat our Father God with great trust and tenderness.

91.2 Filial confidence in prayer. The gift of piety and charity.

This filial confidence is seen particularly in the prayer which the Spirit himself places in our hearts. *Likewise the Spirit helps us in our weakness; for we do not know how to pray as we ought, but the Spirit himself intercedes for us with sighs too deep for words.*[5] Thanks to these motions we

---

[2] St J. Escrivá, *Christ is passing by*, 84
[3] 1 John 3:1
[4] B. Perquin, *Abba, Father*
[5] Rom 8:26

can address God in many different ways, in a rich and varied prayer, like life itself. On occasions we will speak to our Father God in tones of filial complaint: *Why dost thou hide thy face?*;[6] or we may express our desires for greater holiness: *I seek thee, my soul thirsts for thee; my flesh faints for thee, as in a dry and weary land where no water is*;[7] or our union with Him: *there is nothing upon earth that I desire besides thee*;[8] or our unshakeable hope in his mercy: *thou art the God of my salvation; for thee I wait all the day long.*[9]

This filial disposition of the gift of piety is seen also in our readiness to ask again and again like needy children until we are granted what we want. In prayer, our will is identified with the Will of our Father, who always wants the best for his children. This trust in prayer makes us feel secure, unwavering, daring; it dissipates anxiety and the unease that comes from depending solely on our own strength, and helps us to be serene in the face of difficulties.

The Christian who is moved by the spirit of piety understands that our Father God wants the best for each of his children. He has everything arranged to our best advantage. That is why happiness consists in finding out what God wants for us in each moment of our lives and putting it into effect without delay. From this confidence in God's fatherliness we get serenity, because we know that even what seems to be unmitigated evil can contribute to the good of those who love God.[10] Our Lord will teach us one day the necessity for such and such a humiliation, this or that financial collapse, or sickness ...

---

[6] Ps 43:24
[7] Ps 62:1
[8] Ps 72:25
[9] Ps 24:5
[10] cf Rom 8:28

This gift of the Holy Spirit enables us to carry out promptly and easily our obligations of justice and charity. It helps us to see, as children of God, the people whom we live with and meet every day, individuals who have an infinite value because He loves them with a limitless love and has redeemed them with the Blood of his Son shed on the Cross. The gift of piety moves us to have a great respect for our neighbours, to share their sufferings and try to help them. Moreover, the Holy Spirit makes us see Christ in our fellow men for whom we perform these services: *Truly I say to you: as you did it to one of the least of these my brethren, you did it to me.*[11]

Piety towards others leads us to judge them always with kindness *which walks hand in hand with a filial affection for God our common Father.*[12] It disposes us to forgive easily any offences received, even very painful ones. This is what our Lord has commanded us: *Love your enemies and pray for those who persecute you, so that you may be sons of your Father who is in heaven; for he makes his sun rise on the evil and on the good, and sends rain on the just and on the unjust.*[13] If our Lord refers here to serious offences, are we not going to forgive and excuse the little slights which living with others involves? A generous and unconditional spirit of forgiveness is a characteristic sign of the sons and daughters of God.

91.3 Piety towards the Blessed Virgin, the saints, the souls in Purgatory and our parents. Respect for the goods of the earth.

This gift of the Holy Spirit causes us to have a filial love for our heavenly Mother, for whom we have a most

---

[11] Matt 25:40
[12] R. Garrigou-Lagrange, *The Three Ages of the Interior Life*, I
[13] Matt 5:44-45

tender affection; and moves us to have great devotion to the angels and saints, particularly to those who have a special charge over us,[14] as well as for the souls in Purgatory, beloved souls who have need of our suffrages. It makes us love the Pope, the common Father of all Christians ... The virtue of piety, which is perfected by this gift, inclines us also to render honour and reverence to persons in positions of lawful authority – in the first place to our parents.

Earthly fatherhood is seen to be a participation in and a reflection of, God's paternity *from whom every family in heaven and on earth is named.*[15] From our parents *we have received existence; God made use of them to infuse into us a soul and reason; by them we were led to the Sacraments, instructed in our religion, schooled in right conduct and holiness, and trained in civil and human knowledge.*[16]

The awareness of our divine filiation moves us to love and honour our parents ever more and more, to respect our elders (our Lord will greatly reward our care for the aged) and all lawful authority.

The gift of piety extends and goes further than the acts of the virtue of religion.[17] By means of this gift the Holy Spirit activates all the virtues which in one way or another are related to justice. Its field of activity includes our relations with God, with angels and with men. It includes also all created things, *considered as family belongings of God's household*[18] : the gift of piety makes us treat them always with respect because of their relation to their Creator.

Moved by the Holy Spirit, Christians read Holy

---

[14] cf St Thomas, *Summa Theologiae*, II-II, 121
[15] Eph 3:15
[16] *Catechism of the Council of Trent*, III, 5, 9
[17] cf M.M. Philipon, *The Gifts of the Holy Spirit*, Madrid
[18] *ibid*

Scripture with love and veneration, because it is as it were a letter which our Heavenly Father sends us: *in the sacred books, the Father who is in heaven meets his children with great love and speaks with them.*[19] And likewise we are moved to have great affection for sacred things, especially anything that has to do with divine worship.

Among the fruits that the gift of piety produces in souls responsive to the graces of the Paraclete can be counted: serenity in all circumstances of life; trusting abandonment in divine Providence, because if God cares for all his creatures, in a particular way does he care for his children;[20] cheerfulness, which is a proper characteristic of the children of God: *May no one read sadness or sorrow in your face when you spread in the world around you the sweet smell of your sacrifice: the children of God should always be sowers of peace and joy.*[21]

If we consider often each day that we are sons and daughters of God, the Holy Spirit will encourage and foster more and more this filial and trusting relationship with our Heavenly Father. Charity towards everyone also facilitates the growth of this gift in our souls.

---

[19] Second Vatican Council, *Dei Verbum*, 21
[20] cf Matt 6:28
[21] St J. Escrivá, *Furrow*, 59

SEVENTH WEEK OF EASTER – WEDNESDAY

DECENARY TO THE HOLY SPIRIT

92. THE GIFT OF FORTITUDE

92.1 The Holy Spirit gives the soul the necessary strength to overcome obstacles and practise virtue.

The history of the people of Israel is a continuous manifestation of God's protection. The mission of the individuals entrusted with guiding and protecting the chosen people in their journey to the Promised Land was greatly superior to their strength and their possibilities. When Moses expresses to God his incapacity to appear before Pharaoh in order to liberate the Israelites from Egypt, God says to him: *I will be with you.*[1] This same divine assistance is guaranteed to the prophets and all those who receive special tasks. The thanksgiving songs always acknowledge that only through the strength they have received from on high have they been able to carry out their task. The psalms never cease to exalt God's protective power. Yahweh is the Rock of Israel, its strength and its security.

Our Lord promises the Apostles, the pillars of the Church, that they will be *clothed with power from on high.*[2] The Paraclete himself assists the Church and each of her members until the end of time. The supernatural virtue of fortitude, God's direct help, is absolutely necessary for Christians to fight and overcome the obstacles that appear in their interior battle to love God more every day and

[1] Ex 3:12
[2] Luke 24:49

fulfil their duties. The virtue of fortitude is perfected by the gift of fortitude, which makes the acts of the virtue quick and easy to perform.

To the extent to which we manage to purify our souls and are docile to the action of grace, each of us can say with St Paul: *I can do all things in him who strengthens me.*[3] Under the action of the Holy Spirit, the Christian feels capable of the most difficult actions and bearing the hardest trials for love of God. The soul, moved by this gift, does not trust its own strength, because if it is humble, none better than itself is aware of its own weakness and its incapacity to carry out the task of its sanctification and the mission which God entrusts to it in this life; but it hears, especially in difficult moments, the voice of God saying: I will be with you. And it dares to reply: *If God is for us, who is against us? ... Who shall separate us from the love of Christ? Shall tribulation, or distress, or persecution, or famine, or nakedness, or peril, or sword? ... No, in all these things we are more than conquerors through him who loved us. For I am sure that neither death, nor life, nor angels, nor principalities, nor things present, nor things to come, nor powers, nor height, nor depth, nor anything else in all creation, will be able to separate us from the love of God in Christ Jesus our Lord.*[4] This is a cry of fortitude and of optimism which is based on God.

If we allow the Paraclete to take possession of our lives, our confidence will be limitless. Then we will understand in a deeper way that God chooses what is weak, *what is low and despised in the world ... so that no human being might boast in the presence of God,*[5] and that he doesn't ask his sons and daughters for anything other than

---

[3] Phil 4:13
[4] Rom 8:31-39
[5] cf 1 Cor 1:27-29

their readiness to place all that they can at his disposal, in order to enable Him to perform wonders of grace and of mercy. Then nothing appears too difficult, because we rely on God for everything and we will not place all our trust in whatever resources we happen to use, but only in the grace of God. The spirit of fortitude gives the soul renewed energy when faced with obstacles, interior or exterior, and for practising virtue in its environment and in its deeds.

92.2 God expects us to be heroic in little things, in the fulfilment of our daily duties

Tradition associates the gift of fortitude with *hunger and thirst for righteousness.*[6] *The vivid desire of serving God in spite of all difficulties is indeed that hunger which our Lord arouses in us. He produces it and hears it, according to the words spoken to the prophet Daniel: 'I come to instruct you, for you are a man of desires' (Dan 9:23).*[7] This gift produces in the soul that is docile to the Holy Spirit an ever greater desire for holiness, that never wavers in the face of obstacles and difficulties. St Thomas says that we ought to desire that holiness in such a way that *in this life we are never satisfied, as a miser is never satisfied.*[8]

The example of the saints inspires us to grow more and more in fidelity to God in the midst of our obligations, loving him all the more insofar as we experience greater difficulties, placing our desire for holiness on a firmer foundation, not being discouraged by lack of resources in our apostolate or in suspecting perhaps that we are not making progress, at least in appearance, in the targets we set ourselves. As St Teresa has written: *It is most important – all-important, indeed – that they should begin well by*

---

[6] Matt 5:6
[7] R. Garrigou-Lagrange, *The Three Ages of the Interior Life*, II
[8] St Thomas, *Commentary on St Matthew*, 5, 2

making an earnest and most determined resolve not to rest until they reach their goal, whatever may come, whatever may happen to them, however hard they may have to labour, whoever may complain of them, whether they reach their goal or die on the road or have no heart to confront the trials which they meet, whether the very world dissolves before them.[9]

The virtue of fortitude, perfected by the gift of the Holy Spirit, enables us to overcome the obstacles that in one way or another we encounter along the path of holiness, but it doesn't remove the weakness of human nature, the fear of danger, pain or weariness. A person who is strong can still experience fear, but can overcome it thanks to love. Precisely because of love, a Christian is able to face greater risks, even though one may feel repugnance not only at the beginning, but also for as long as the trial lasts or the desired-for object is still being sought. Fortitude does not always eliminate the deficiencies inherent in all created beings.

This virtue can bring one to offer one's life willingly in witness to the faith if our Lord so desires it. Martyrdom is the supreme act of fortitude, and God has demanded it of many of the faithful throughout the history of the Church. The martyrs have been – and are – the Church's crown, another testimony to her divine origin and her holiness. Every Christian ought to be prepared to give his or her life for Christ if circumstances demand it. The Holy Spirit would then give one the strength and courage to face this supreme test. Normally, though, what is asked of us is heroism in little things, in the daily fulfilment of our duties.

Every day we need the gift of fortitude, because every day we have to practise the virtue of fortitude in order to overcome our whims, our selfishness and laziness. We

---

[9] St Teresa, *The Way of Perfection*, 21, 2

have to be unwavering when facing an atmosphere that is often hostile to Christ's doctrine, so as to overcome human respect, so as to give a simple yet eloquent witness to our Lord, as the Apostles did.

92.3 Fortitude in our daily lives. How to facilitate the action of this gift.

We need to ask often for the gift of fortitude to overcome our resistance to doing what we find difficult to do, to face up to the normal obstacles of living, to bear with sickness patiently when it comes, to persevere in our daily work, to be constant in apostolate, to bear adversity with serenity and supernatural outlook. We have to ask for this gift in order to have that interior fortitude that lets us forget about ourselves and be more aware of the people around us, to mortify our tendency to look for attention, to serve others without their scarcely noticing it, to overcome impatience, in order not to give too much importance to our own problems and difficulties, in order not to complain when faced with difficulty or discomfort, to mortify our imagination by rejecting useless thoughts ... We need fortitude in apostolate so as to speak about God without fear, to behave always in a Christian way even though it goes against the trend in a pagan environment, to make fraternal correction when necessary ... Fortitude is necessary for us to fulfil our duties effectively: to help unreservedly the people who depend on us, to be demanding with gentleness and with the firmness that each case requires ... In this way the gift of fortitude becomes our great recourse against lukewarmness, which would give rise to neglect and laziness.

The gift of fortitude sees difficulties as exceptional conditions in which to grow and develop, if when they arise we stay close to our Lord. *Trees that grow in shady and sheltered places, while externally they develop with a healthy appearance, become soft and yielding, and they are easily damaged by anything at all; whereas trees that grow on the tops of very high mountains, buffeted by strong winds and constantly exposed to all types of weather, agitated by storms and frequently covered by snow, become stronger than iron.*[10]

This gift is obtained through humility – accepting our own weakness – and having recourse to God in prayer and the sacraments.

The sacrament of Confirmation gave us the strength to fight as *milites Christi*, as soldiers of Christ.[11] Holy Communion – *food for our strength*[12] – restores our energies. The sacrament of Penance fortifies us against sin and temptation. In the sacrament of Anointing our Lord gives us his help to conquer in the last battle, the one in which our eternal destiny is decided.

The Holy Spirit is a sweet and wise Master, but he is also demanding, because he doesn't give us his gifts unless we are prepared to take up our Cross and correspond to his graces.

---

[10] St John Chrysostom, *Homily on the glory of tribulation*

[11] cf 2 Tim 2:3

[12] cf St Augustine, *Confessions*, 7, 10

93. THE GIFT OF FEAR

93.1 Servile fear and the holy fear of God. Effects of this gift in the soul.

St Teresa says that God bestows two remedies for all the temptations and trials that we have to endure: *Love and fear ... Love will make us quicken our steps, while fear will make us look where we are setting our feet so that we shall not fall.*[1]

But not every fear is good. There is the worldly fear[2] of those who fear physical evil above all else, or the social disadvantages which can beset them in this life. They flee from all earthly inconveniences; as soon as they foresee that fidelity to a Christian way of living can cause them any hardship, they show themselves ready to abandon Christ and his Church. From this fear springs *human respect* and it is the origin of countless surrenders and of betrayal itself.

That fear which is called servile is quite different. This turns the soul from sin because of fear of the punishment of hell or for some other self-interested supernatural motive. This is a good fear, since for many who are far from God, this can be the first step toward their conversion, and the beginning of love.[3] This should not be the chief motive of the Christian, but in many cases, it will be a great defence against temptation and the allurements of evil.

---

[1] St Teresa, *The Way of Perfection*, 40,1
[2] cf M.M. Philipon, *The Gifts of the Holy Spirit*, Madrid
[3] Sir 25:12

He who fears is not perfected in love,[4] writes the Apostle St John, because the true Christian acts through love and is created to love. The holy fear of God, gift of the Holy Spirit, is that which dwelt, with the other gifts, in the most holy Soul of Christ and which also filled the Most Blessed Virgin. It is the gift of holy souls, which persists eternally in heaven and leads the blessed, together with the angels, to give continual praise to the Most Blessed Trinity. St Thomas teaches that this gift is a consequence of the gift of wisdom and is, as it were, its outward sign.[5]

This filial fear is proper to children who feel themselves protected by their Father, whom they do not wish to offend. Its results are twofold. An immense respect for God's majesty, a deep discernment of what is sacred and a limitless rejoicing in his goodness as a Father, is the more important of the two, since it was the only one present in Christ and in our Lady. This gift enables holy souls to acknowledge their nothingness before God. We may also repeat frequently, recognising our nothingness, perhaps as an aspiration, those words so often repeated by St Josemaría Escrivá: *I am worth nothing, I have nothing, I can do nothing, I know nothing, I am nothing, nothing at all!*[6] at the same time as he realized the incalculable grandeur of knowing oneself and of being a child of God.

During our life on earth there is another effect that derives from this gift: a great horror of sin, and the liveliest contrition if one has had the misfortune to commit it. By the light of faith, illumined by the splendour of the other gifts, the soul grasps something of the transcendence of God and of the infinite distance and the abyss which sin opens between man and God.

---

[4] John 4:18
[5] St Thomas, *Summa Theologiae*, II-II, 45, 1 and 3
[6] Quoted by A. Vazquez de Prada, *The Founder of Opus Dei*.

The gift of fear enlightens us to understand that *sin is at the root of the moral evils which divide and ravage society.*[7] And the gift of fear leads us also to a hatred for deliberate venial sin and to an energetic reaction against the first symptoms of lukewarmness, carelessness or mediocrity. At particular moments of our life we may feel the need to repeat insistently, as an urgent petition: *I don't want to be lukewarm, 'confige timore tuo carnes meas'. Grant me, my God, a filial fear that will make me react!*[8]

93.2 The holy fear of God and readiness to reject all sin.

Love and fear. These must be the accompaniments of our way. *When love banishes fear, fear itself is changed into love.*[9] It is the fear of a child who loves his Father without reserve, and who will allow nothing in the world to distance him from that Father. Then the soul understands better the infinity which separates it from God and at the same time its condition as a child of God. Never until now has it trusted more in God; never, either, has it respected and venerated him more. When the holy fear of God is lost, the sense of sin becomes diluted or vanishes. Then tepidity easily enters the soul. It fails to discern the power and majesty of God, and the honour due to him.

We cannot bring the supernatural world nearer by trying vainly to eliminate God's transcendence. The way to do it is through the divinization wrought in us by grace, through humility and love expressed in the struggle to banish all sin from our life.

If we are to banish this evil ... we must first try to ensure that our dispositions, both habitual and actual, are

---

[7] St John Paul II, *Letter* presenting the *Instrumentum laboris* of the VI Synod of Bishops, 25 January 1983
[8] cf St J. Escrivá, *The Way*, 326
[9] St Gregory of Nyssa, *Homily 15*

*those of a clear aversion to sin. Sincerely, in a manly way,
we must develop, both in our heart and in our mind, a
sense of horror for mortal sins. We must also cultivate a
deep-seated hatred of deliberate venial sin, those
negligences which while they don't deprive us of God's
grace, do serve to obstruct the channels through which
grace comes to us.*[10] Nowadays, many people seem to have
lost the holy fear of God. They forget who God is and who
they are, they forget divine justice and so they are
encouraged to persist in their follies.[11] The consideration of
our final end, of the Last Things, of that reality which we
will encounter perhaps before long, the definitive meeting
with God, disposes us to receive more fully from the Holy
Spirit this gift which is so near to love.

93.3 The link between this gift and the virtues of humility and temperance. Sensitivity of soul and the sense of sin.

Our Lord tells us in many ways that we should be
afraid of nothing except sin, which takes away our friendship with God. Confronted with any difficulty, any situation,
an uncertain future, we shouldn't feel afraid. We should be
strong and courageous as befits children of God. A
Christian cannot live in terror, but should have in his heart
a holy fear of God, whom nonetheless he loves madly.

Throughout the Gospel, *Christ repeats several times
'Do not fear ... do not be afraid'. And at the same time,
together with these appeals for fortitude resounds the
exhortation: 'rather fear him who can destroy both body
and soul in hell' (Matt 10:28). We are called to fortitude
and at the same time to fear of God, and this should be a
fear that comes of love, a filial fear. And only when this*

---

[10] St J. Escrivá, *Friends of God*, 243
[11] cf St J. Escrivá, *The Way*, 747

fear sinks into our hearts can we be really strong with the strength of the apostles, the martyrs and the confessors.[12]

Among the principal effects which the fear of God works in the soul are detachment from created things, and an interior attitude of vigilance to avoid the least occasion of sin. The soul acquires a particular sensitivity to discern whatever *can grieve the Holy Spirit.*[13]

The gift of fear lies at the root of humility since it shows the soul its own fragility and teaches it the need of maintaining a will faithfully and lovingly subjected to the infinite Majesty of God. So we do not want to oust God from his place; happy to stay in ours, we do not want honours which are for his glory. One of the signs of pride is ignorance of the fear of God.

The gift of the fear of God, like humility, has an affinity with the virtue of temperance. It leads us to use human goods in moderation, in secondary place to our supernatural end. The root of sin is most frequently found in the disordered search for sense pleasures or for material things. And here this gift is active, purifying the heart and keeping it entire for God.

The gift of fear is above all the struggle against sin. All the other gifts help in this specific mission: the insight bestowed by the gifts of understanding and wisdom show one the greatness of God and the true meaning of sin. The practical directives of the gift of counsel maintain one in an untiring battle against evil.[14]

This gift, which was infused along with the others in Baptism, increases in the measure in which we are true to the graces the Holy Spirit grants us. It does so specifically when we consider the greatness and majesty of God, when

---

[12] St John Paul II, *Address to the new Cardinals*, 30 April 1979
[13] Eph 4:30
[14] cf M.M. Philipon, *op cit*

we conduct an examination of conscience in depth, discovering our faults and sins and giving them the importance which they have. The holy fear of God will lead us easily to contrition and repentance arising from filial love. *Love and fear of God! These are two strong castles whence we can wage war on the world and on the devils.*[15]

The holy fear of God will gently lead us to a prudent mistrust of ourselves, to flee quickly from the occasions of sin. And it will incline us to a greater sensitivity for God and all that refers to God. Let us ask the Holy Spirit to help us by means of this gift to recognize our faults sincerely and to feel true sorrow for them. May He make us react as the Psalmist: *My eyes shed streams of tears, because men do not keep thy law.*[16] Let us pray that, with a sensitive soul, we always keep alive our sense of sin.

---

[15] St Teresa, *op cit*, 40, 2
[16] Ps 118:136

Seventh Week of Easter – Friday

Decenary To The Holy Spirit

94. THE FRUITS OF THE HOLY SPIRIT

94.1 The fruits of the Holy Spirit in the soul, signs of the glory of God. Love, joy and peace.

When the soul is docile to the inspirations of the Holy Spirit, it becomes that good tree which is known by its fruits. These fruits enrich the Christian's life and are manifestations of the glory of God: *By this my Father is glorified, that you bear much fruit,*[1] Jesus says at the Last Supper.

These supernatural fruits are countless. St Paul, by way of example, indicates twelve fruits, result of the gifts which the Holy Spirit has infused in our soul: love, joy, peace, patience, kindness, goodness, gentleness, self-control, faithfulness, modesty, continence, chastity.[2]

First is love or charity, the first sign of our union with Christ. This is the most excellent of these fruits, making us feel that God is near and drawing us to lighten the burden others carry. The first manifestation of the action of the Holy Spirit in our soul is a sensitive and operative charity towards those who live with us or with whom we work. *There is no sign or mark which distinguishes the Christian and the lover of Christ greater than the care of our brothers and sisters and zeal for the salvation of souls.*[3]

This first and chief fruit of the Holy Spirit is *followed necessarily by joy, since the lover rejoices in union with his*

---

[1] John 15:8
[2] cf Gal 5:22-23
[3] St John Chrysostom, *Homilies on the incomprehensible*, 6, 3

beloved.[4] Joy is the result of love; therefore the Christian is distinguished by his joy, which persists through sorrow and failure. How much good has been wrought in the world by the joy of Christians. *To rejoice under trial, to smile in sufferings ..., to sing in our heart ever more clearly, the longer and sharper the thorns ... and all this for the sake of love ... this is, together with love, the fruit that the divine Vinedresser wishes to gather from the branches of the mystic Vine. These are fruits which only the Holy Spirit can produce in us.*[5]

Love and joy leave in the soul the peace of God *which passes all understanding.*[6] St Augustine defines it as *tranquillity in order.*[7] There is a false peace based on disorder, such as that which reigns in a family where the parents always yield to the children's whims, with the excuse of *having peace.* The same applies in a city where, on the pretext of not wishing to upset anyone, criminals would be allowed to commit their misdeeds. Peace, the fruit of the Holy Spirit, is the absence of unrest, and the repose of the will in the stable possession of good. This peace supposes a constant battle waged upon the disordered tendencies of one's own passions.

94.2 Patience and longanimity. Their importance in apostolate.

Only in heaven shall we find the fulness of love, joy and peace. Here we have a foretaste of eternal happiness in the measure in which we are faithful. When there are obstacles, the souls which allow themselves to be guided by the Paraclete produce the fruit of patience. So they are

---

[4] St Thomas, *Summa Theologiae*, I-II, 70, 3
[5] A. Riaud, *The Action of the Holy Spirit in souls*, Madrid
[6] Phil 4:7
[7] St Augustine, *The City of God*, 19, 13, 1

led to bear with serenity, without sterile complaint or protest, the physical and moral sufferings which everybody experiences in life. Charity is full of patience; and patience is frequently the support of love. *Charity*, wrote St Cyprian, *is the bond which unites brothers, the cement of peace, the crossbeam which gives solidity to unity ... Only take patience from it, however, and it will remain desolate; take from it the sap of suffering and of resignation and it will lose its roots and its vigour.*[8] Christians should see the loving hand of God, who uses sufferings and sorrows to purify those whom He loves most and to sanctify them. This is why they do not lose their peace when they meet with illness, contradiction, the defects of others, calumnies ... not even with their own spiritual failures.

Longanimity is like patience. It is a stable disposition by which we wait serenely without complaint or bitterness and for as long as God wishes, the deferrals willed or permitted by him, before we reach the ascetic or apostolic targets which we set ourselves.

This fruit of the Holy Spirit gives the soul the full certainty – if it uses the means, if there is ascetic struggle, if it begins again always – that these objectives will be attained, in spite of the real obstacles which are there, in spite of weaknesses, errors and sins, if such were the case.

In the apostolate the patient person always has high targets, to the measure of God's Will, although the immediate results may seem small, and uses all the human and supernatural means available, with a holy persistence and constancy. *An indispensable requirement in the apostolate is faith, which is often shown by constancy in speaking about God, even though the fruits are slow to appear.*

If we persevere and carry on in the firm conviction that the Lord wills it, signs of a Christian revolution will

---

[8] St Cyprian, *The good of patience*

appear around you, everywhere. Some will follow the call, others will take their interior life seriously, and others – the weakest – will at least be forewarned.[9]

The Lord is counting on this daily unremitting effort for the apostle's task to give fruit. If sometimes this is slow in appearing, if the effort we have put into bringing a relative or colleague closer to God should seem in vain, the Holy Spirit will make us understand that no one who works for God with rectitude of intention can work in vain. *My chosen shall not labour in vain.*[10] Longanimity is seen to be the perfect unfolding of the virtue of hope.

94.3 The fruits more directly related to our neighbour's welfare: goodness, kindness, faithfulness, modesty, continence and chastity.

These are the fruits which bind the soul more directly to God and to its own holiness. Next, St Paul enumerates others which are aimed chiefly at the good of our neighbour: *Put on then, as God's chosen ones, holy and beloved, compassion, kindness, lowliness, meekness and patience, being forbearing with one another and, if one has a complaint against another, forgiving each other.*[11]

The goodness which the Apostle is telling us about is a stable disposition of the will which makes us desire all kinds of goods for others, without distinction – friends and enemies, relatives or strangers, neighbours or those far away. The soul feels itself beloved by God. This prevents it from feeling jealousy or envy: in others it sees children of God, whom He loves and for whom Christ has died.

It is not enough just to have a theoretical desire of good for others. True charity is an efficacious love which is

---

[9] St J. Escrivá, *Furrow*, 207
[10] Is 65:23
[11] Col 3:12-13

transformed into actions. Charity is beneficent,[12] St Paul tells us. Kindness is precisely that disposition of the heart which inclines us to do good to others.[13] This fruit is shown in myriad works of mercy, both corporal and spiritual, which Christians carry out all over the world without excluding anyone. In our own life it is shown in the thousand details of service which we offer to those with whom we live and work daily. Kindness inspires us to bring peace and joy wherever we go and to have a constant disposition to be understanding and affable.

Gentleness is intimately united to goodness and perfection, and is, as it were, its finishing and perfection. It opposes those barren outbursts of anger, which really are a sign of weakness. Charity is not irritable or resentful,[14] but is always gentle and refined, maintained by a great fortitude of spirit. The soul which possesses this gift of the Holy Spirit is not impatient, nor does it harbour resentment for the offences or insults received from others, although it may feel – sometimes very vividly because of its greater sensitivity derived from its friendship with God – the bitterness and harshness, the humiliations they inflict. It knows that God uses all this to purify souls.

Faithfulness follows gentleness. The faithful person fulfils all duties, even the smallest, and is trusted by others. Sacred Scripture tells us: *There is nothing so precious as a faithful friend, and no scales can measure his excellence.*[15] To be faithful is one way of living justice and charity. Faithfulness constitutes a summary of all the fruits which refer to our relations with our neighbour.

The three last fruits which St Paul indicates refer to the

---

[12] 1 Cor 13:4
[13] cf A. Riaud, *op cit*
[14] 1 Cor 13:5
[15] Sir 6:15

virtue of temperance. This, under the influence of the gifts of the Holy Spirit, produces fruits of modesty, continence, and chastity.

A modest person knows how to behave serenely and properly in each situation, appreciating the talents he or she possesses without magnifying or minimizing them, knowing them to be God's gift for the service of others. This fruit of the Holy Spirit is reflected in that person's outward carriage, in his mode of speech and dress, in his dealings with people and social relations. Modesty is attractive because it bespeaks simplicity and inner order.

The two last fruits which St Paul indicates are continence and chastity. As if by instinct, the soul is extremely vigilant to avoid what might damage interior and exterior purity, so pleasing to God. These fruits which give beauty to Christian life and dispose the soul to understanding what refers to God, can be gathered even in the midst of great temptations, if one avoids the occasion and struggles with decision, knowing that the grace of God will never be lacking.

As we finish our prayer, we draw near the Most Blessed Virgin, because God uses her so that, by the influence of the Paraclete, she will produce abundant fruit in souls. *I am the Mother of fair love, of fear, of knowledge and of holy hope. Come to me, you who desire me, and eat your fill of my produce. For the remembrance of me is sweeter than honey and my inheritance sweeter than the honeycomb.*[16]

---

[16] Sir 24:19-20

Seventh Week of Easter – Saturday

Vigil of Pentecost

95. THE HOLY SPIRIT AND MARY

95.1 Together with the Blessed Virgin we await the coming of the Holy Spirit.

While they awaited the coming of the promised Holy Spirit *all with one accord devoted themselves to prayer, together with Mary, the Mother of Jesus.*[1] All are in the same place, in the Cenacle, inspired by the same love and the same hope. In their midst is the Mother of God. In this scene Tradition sees mirrored Mary's motherhood for the whole Church. *The era of the Church began with the 'coming', that is to say, with the descent of the Holy Spirit on the Apostles gathered in the Upper Room in Jerusalem, together with Mary, the Lord's Mother.*[2]

Our Lady lives what is like a second Advent, an expectation which prepares the Holy Spirit's full communication of his gifts to the newborn Church. This Advent is at once very like and very different from the first, the one which prepared for the birth of Jesus. Very similar, because in both we find prayer, recollection, faith in the promise and a burning desire that the promise be fulfilled. Mary, bearing Jesus in her womb, remained in the silence of her contemplation. Now our Lady lives deeply united to her glorified Son.[3]

This second waiting is very different from the first. In the first Advent, the Virgin is the only one to live the

---

[1] Acts 1:14

[2] St John Paul II, *Dominum et vivificantem*, 18 May 1986, 25

[3] cf M.D. Philippe, *The Mystery of Mary*, Madrid

promise fulfilled in her womb. Here she waits accompanied by the Apostles and the holy women. This is a shared expectation, that of the Church which is about to manifest itself publicly around our Lady. *Mary, who conceived Christ through the workings of the Holy Spirit, the love of the living God, presides over the birth of the Church on the day of Pentecost, when the Holy Spirit Himself descends upon the disciples and pours out life in unity and in charity upon the Mystical Body of Christians.*[4]

The resolution of our prayer today, the eve of the great solemnity of Pentecost, is to await the coming of the Paraclete, closely united to our Mother *by her prayers imploring the gift of the Spirit, who had already overshadowed her in the Annunciation,*[5] changing her into the new Tabernacle of God. She, who at the start of the Redemption gave us her Son, now *by her most powerful intercession obtained for the newborn Church the prodigious Pentecostal outpouring of that Spirit of the Divine Redeemer who had already been given on the Cross.*[6]

It was St Luke who related this fact, the evangelist who gave us the longest account of Jesus' childhood. It is as if he wanted us to understand that just as Mary had a major role in the Incarnation of the Word, she was intimately involved in the beginning of the Church, Christ's body.[7]

Mary is our path to a better disposition for greater friendship with the Paraclete and greater docility to his inspirations. The Apostles understood this: that is why we see them beside her in the Cenacle.

Let us examine the quality of our habitual relationship with Mary, and make some practical resolution today. Let

---

[4] St Paul VI, *Address*, 25 October 1969
[5] Second Vatican Council, *Lumen gentium*, 59
[6] Pius XII, *Mystici Corporis*, 29 June 1943
[7] St J. Escrivá, *Christ is passing by*, 141

us take greater care when we recite the Holy Rosary, contemplating its mysteries; let us offer her some little sacrifice, different from those we are accustomed to make during the week. Let us show greater affection when we greet her, through her images which we see in the street, or in our room.

95.2 The Holy Spirit in Mary's life.

The Blessed Virgin received the Holy Spirit at Pentecost with a unique fulness. This was so because her heart was the purest, the freest, the heart which most incomparably loved the Most Blessed Trinity. The Paraclete came down upon the soul of the Blessed Virgin and filled it in a new way. He is the *sweet Guest* of Mary's soul. Our Lord had promised to him who loved God: *we will come to him and make our home with him.*[8] This promise is fulfilled above all in Our Lady.

She, *God's masterpiece,*[9] had been prepared with immense care by the Holy Spirit to be the living tabernacle of the Son of God. Therefore the Angel greets her: *Hail, full of grace.*[10] And, already possessed by the Holy Spirit and filled with his grace, she received yet another new and singular fulness of that grace: *The Holy Spirit will come upon you and the power of the Most High will overshadow you.*[11] *Redeemed, in a more exalted fashion, by reason of the merits of her Son and united to him by a close and indissoluble tie, she is endowed with the high office and dignity of the Mother of the Son of God, and therefore she is also the beloved daughter of the Father and the temple of the Holy Spirit. Because of this gift of sublime grace, she*

---

[8] John 14:23
[9] St J. Escrivá, *Friends of God*, 292
[10] Luke 1:28
[11] Luke 1:35

far surpasses all creatures, both in

During her life our Lady grev
God the Father, God the Son (her
Holy Spirit. She corresponded to
motions of the Paraclete, and eac
those inspirations she received
offered the least resistance, nev
Her growth in human and s
continuous, under a special influe

For all who are led by the
God.[13] No creature allowed itsel
the Holy Spirit as did our holy
divine filiation as she did.

The Holy Spirit, who had
mystery of her Immaculate Conc
Pentecost to dwell in her in a r
Jesus had made about the Parac
in the soul of the Blessed Vir
remembrance all that I have s
you into all the truth.[15]

The Blessed Virgin is the c
for us, if in spite of so many of
father receives the prodigal son
loves us with an infinite love an
as we correspond with his grac
those who have offended him,
his immaculate Mother, the
always?

If the love of God can ach
the response from our human

[12] Second Vatican Council, *Lumen g*
[13] Rom 8:14
[14] John 14:26
[15] John 16:13

Heaven and on earth.[12]
w continually in love for
Son Jesus) and God the
all the inspirations and
h time she was docile to
new graces. She never
er denied God anything.
upernatural virtues was
nce of grace.
Spirit of God are sons of
f to be led and guided by
Mother Mary. None lived

lived in Mary since the
eption, came on the day of
new way. All the promises
lete are fully accomplished
gin: *He will bring to your*
id to you.[14] *He will guide*

reature God loves most. As
fences He receives us as the
, though we are sinners He
d fills us with gifts as often
es. *If He is so generous with*
what won't He do to honour
most Holy Virgin, faithful

-

ieve such great results, when
heart – which is frequently a

_____

entium, 53

And just as he who was in darkness, when the sun rises receives its light through his bodily eyes, and contemplates in all clarity what he could not see before, so he who is found worthy of the gift of the Holy Spirit finds his soul full of light, and, raised above natural reasoning, sees that which he formerly did not know.

After Pentecost our Lady is *as it were, the heart of the infant Church!*[20] The Holy Spirit, who had prepared her to be the Mother of God, now at Pentecost disposes her to be Mother of the Church and of each one of us.

The Holy Spirit never ceases to act within the Church. On every side He awakens new desires of holiness, new and at the same time better children of God, who have their finished Model in Jesus Christ, the first-born of many brethren. Our Lady, collaborating actively with the Holy Spirit in souls, exercises her maternity over all her children. And so she is proclaimed by the title of Mother of the Church, *that is to say, Mother of the whole People of God, as much of the faithful as of the Pastors, who call her loving Mother. And we wish* – proclaimed Saint Paul VI – *that from now on she be honoured and invoked by the whole Christian people with this most pleasing title.*[21]

Holy Mary, Mother of the Church, pray for us and help us to prepare, the coming of the Paraclete into our souls.

---

[20] R. Garrigou-Lagrange, *The Mother of the Saviour*
[21] St Paul VI, *Address to the Council*, 2 September 1964

PENTECOST SUNDAY

96. THE COMING OF THE HOLY SPIRIT

96.1 The Jewish feast of Pentecost. The sending of the Holy Spirit. The rushing wind and the tongues of fire.

The love of God has been poured into our hearts through the Spirit of God dwelling within us, Alleluia.[1]

Pentecost was one of the three great Jewish feasts. Many Israelites used to go as pilgrims to Jerusalem during these days, to adore God in the Temple. The feast originated from a very ancient thanksgiving celebration, in gratitude to God for the yearly harvest about to be reaped. Later, another motive was added to this day's celebration with the remembrance of the promulgation of the Law given by God on Mount Sinai. This was celebrated fifty days after the Pasch. So the material harvest which the Jews celebrated with such joy became a feast of immense rejoicing, by God's design, in the New Dispensation: the coming of the Holy Spirit with all his gifts and fruits.

When the day of Pentecost had come, they were all together in one place. And suddenly a sound came from heaven like the rush of a mighty wind, and it filled all the house where they were sitting.[2] The Holy Spirit shows [h]imself in those elements which usually accompanied the [pr]esence of God in the Old Testament: wind and fire.[3]

Fire appears in Sacred Scripture as love which pene[trate]s all things and as a purifying element.[4] These are [imag]es which help us to understand better the action which

---

[1] *Antiphon*, Mass of the Vigil, Rom 5:5, 8:11
[2] [...]

[...]ilippe, *The Mystery of Mary*, Madrid

the Holy Spirit carries out in souls: *Ure igne Sancti Spiritus renes nostros et cor nostrum, Domine*: Lord, with the fire of the Holy Spirit, purify our inmost being and our heart.

Fire also produces light and signifies the new brightness which the Holy Spirit sheds on the doctrine of Jesus Christ: *When the Spirit of truth comes, he will guide you into all the truth ... He will glorify me, for He will take what is mine and declare it to you.*[5] On this occasion Jesus had already forewarned his disciples: *The Counsellor, the Holy Spirit ... will teach you all things, and bring to your remembrance all that I have said to you.*[6] It is the Holy Spirit who leads us to a full understanding of the truth taught by Christ, who *completed and perfected Revelation and confirmed it by divine guarantees ... finally by sending the Spirit of truth.*[7]

In the Old Testament the action of the Holy Spirit is often intimated by the word *breath*. This expresses both the gentleness and the strength of divine love. There is nothing subtler than the wind, which manages to penetrate everywhere, even to reach inanimate bodies and give them a life of their own. The rushing wind of the day of Pentecost expresses the new force with which divine love invades the Church and souls.

When St Peter sees the multitudes of people gathered near the Cenacle, he convinces them that this is the fulfilment of what had been foretold already by the Prophets.[8] *And in the last days it shall be, God declares, that I will pour out my Spirit upon all flesh.*[9] Those who receive the outpouring of the Spirit are no longer a

---

[5] cf John 16:13-14
[6] cf John 14:26
[7] Second Vatican Council, *Dei Verbum*, 4
[8] Joel 2:28
[9] Acts 2:17

privileged few, like the companions of Moses[10] or the prophets. No, these are all mankind, in the measure in which they receive Christ.[11] The action of the Holy Spirit was to produce, in the disciples and those who heard them, such an admiration that they were all enraptured, full of love and joy.

96.2 The Paraclete continually sanctifies the Church and every soul. Correspondence with the motions and inspirations of the Holy Spirit.

The coming of the Holy Spirit on the day of Pentecost was not an isolated event in the Church's life. The Paraclete sanctifies it continually as He also sanctifies every soul. This He does through the innumerable inspirations which are all *the attractions, motions, rebukes and interior compunctions, lights and intuitions which God works in us. So He strengthens our heart with his blessings, with his care and fatherly love, so as to arouse us, move us, impel us and draw us to holy virtues, to heavenly love, to good resolutions: in short, to all that leads us to our eternal life.*[12] *His action in the soul is gentle and mild ... He comes to save, to cure, to enlighten.*[13]

At Pentecost, the Apostles were strengthened in their mission as witnesses to Jesus, to announce the good news to all peoples. But not only the Apostles. All who believe in Him will have the happy duty of announcing that Christ has died and is risen for our salvation. *And in the last days it shall be, God declares, that I will pour out my Spirit upon all flesh, and your sons and daughters will prophesy, and your young men shall see visions, and your old men*

---

[10] cf Num 11:25
[11] cf John 7:39
[12] St Francis de Sales, *Introduction to the Devout Life*, III, 18
[13] St Cyril of Jerusalem, *Catechesis 16 on the Holy Spirit*, 1

shall dream dreams; yea, and on my men-servants and my maid-servants in those days I will pour out my Spirit; and they shall prophesy.[14] So Peter preaches on the morning of Pentecost and so begins the epoch of the last days, the days in which the Holy Spirit has been lavished newly upon those who believe that Jesus is the Son of God and who fulfil his doctrine.

All we Christians have since then the mission of proclaiming and singing the *magnalia Dei*,[15] the marvels which God has worked in his Son and in all those who believe in him. We are already a holy people, bound to make known the greatness of God, who brought us *out of darkness into His marvellous light.*[16]

When we realize that our sanctification and the apostolic effectiveness of our lives depend upon our correspondence with the motions of the Holy Spirit, we feel the need to ask Him often to *wash what is stained, water our dryness, heal our infirmity, enkindle our tepidity, and direct our straying steps,*[17] since we know that within us there are many defects – lukewarmness, stains, areas which do not give the fruit they should because they have dried up, elements which are diseased, as well as little deviations which must be corrected.

We need too to ask for a greater docility, an active docility that leads us to welcome the inspirations and the touches of the Paraclete with purity of heart.

96.3 Correspondence: docility, life of prayer, union with the Cross.

If we want to grow in fidelity to the constant motions

---

[14] Acts 2:17-18
[15] Acts 2:11
[16] 1 Pet 2:9
[17] cf *Sequence for the Mass of Pentecost*

and inspirations of the Holy Spirit in our soul, *we can fix our attention on three fundamental points : docility, life of prayer and union with the Cross.*

First of all docility, because it is the Holy Spirit who, through his inspirations, gives a supernatural tone to our thoughts, desires and actions. It is He who leads us to be receptive to Christ's teaching and to assimilate it in a profound way. It is He who gives us the light by which we perceive our personal calling and the strength to carry out all that God expects of us.[18]

The Paraclete never ceases to act in our soul. Not a single aspiration do we say that is not inspired by the Holy Spirit,[19] as St Paul tells us in the second reading of the Mass. He is present and moves us in prayer, as we read the Gospel, when we discover new light through a piece of advice we have received, as we ponder upon a truth of faith which already perhaps we have often considered. We realise that this clarity does not depend upon our will. It does not come from us, but from God. It is the Holy Spirit who leads us gently to the Sacrament of Penance to confess our sins, to raise our heart to God at an unexpected moment, to carry out some particular work. It is He who suggests to us to make some small sacrifice, or finds for us the right words to inspire someone to be better.

In the second place, a life of prayer, because the giving of one's self, the obedience and meekness of a Christian, are born of love and lead to love. And love leads to a personal relationship, to conversation and friendship. Christian life requires a constant dialogue with God, One in three Persons, and it is to this intimacy that the Holy Spirit leads us ... Let us acquire the habit of conversation with the Holy Spirit, who is the one who will make us holy.

---

[18] St J. Escrivá, *Christ is passing by*, 135
[19] cf 1 Cor 12:3

*Let us trust in him and ask his help and feel his closeness
to us. In this way our poor heart will grow: we will have a
greater desire to love God and to love all creatures for
God's sake.*[20]

*And finally, union with the Cross, because in the life of
Christ, the Resurrection and Pentecost were preceded by
Calvary. This is the order that must be followed in the life
of any Christian ... The Holy Spirit comes to us as a result
of the Cross – as a result of our total abandonment to the
will of God, of seeking only His glory and of renouncing
ourselves completely.*[21]

We can end our prayer by making our own the
petitions of the hymn which is sung in the sequence of the
Mass of this day of Pentecost: Come, O Holy Spirit, send
from heaven a ray of your light. *Come, O father of the
poor; come, O giver of graces; come, O light of hearts.
Best of all Consolers, welcome. Guest of the soul, cool
refreshment. You are rest in our labour, peace in
difficulties and solace in our grief. O most holy Light! Fill
the inmost being of the hearts of your faithful ... Grant to
your children who trust in you your seven sacred gifts.
Give them the merit of your virtue, the port of salvation;
give them everlasting joy.*[22]

If we want to have a deeper friendship with the Holy
Spirit, nothing is so effective as a close friendship with
Mary. She it was who seconded, as no other creature ever
did, the inspirations of the Holy Spirit. The Apostles,
before the day of Pentecost, *with one accord devoted
themselves to prayer, together with the women and Mary,
the Mother of Jesus.*[23]

---

[20] St J. Escrivá, *op cit*, 136

[21] *ibid*, 37

[22] *Sequence for the Mass of Pentecost*

[23] cf Acts 1:14

INDEX TO QUOTATIONS FROM THE FATHERS, POPES AND THE SAINTS

Note: References are to **Volume**/Chapter.Section

Acts of Thanksgiving
St Augustine, **5**/39.2
St Bede, **5**/78.1
St Bernard, **5**/10.1, **5**/39.3
St Francis de Sales, **4**/84.1
St John Chrysostom, **2**/71.1
St Thomas Aquinas, **5**/78.2

Advent
St Bernard, **1**/1.3

Almsgiving
St Leo the Great, **5**/67.2
St Thomas Aquinas, **3**/17.3

Angels
Origen, **2**/9.3
St Bernard, **7**/30.3
St John Chrysostom, **2**/7.1
St John of the Cross, **2**/7.2
St Peter of Alcantara, **3**/51.2
St John Paul II, **2**/7.1, **2**/30.3, **7**/27

Apostolate
Benedict XV, **2**/85.1
Bl. Alvaro, **2**/29.1,
John Paul I, **3**/3.2
Letter to Diognetus, **2**/70.2
St Ambrose, **4**/87.1
St Augustine, **1**/8.3, **2**/59.1, **4**/92.3, **5**/52.1, **5**/87.3
St Cyril of Alexandria, **5**/62.1
St Gregory the Great, **3**/88.2,

4/69.1
St Ignatius of Antioch, **5**/37.3
St J. H. Newman, **3**/3.2
St John Chrysostom, **1**/4.3, **2**/85.1, **2**/94.1, **3**/88.2, **3**/89.3, **4**/87.1, **7**/42.2
St John Paul II, **1**/45.3, **2**/11.3, **3**/13.3, **4**/37.3, **4**/69.1, **4**/87.3, **5**/10.2, **5**/20.1, **5**/57.1, **5**/68.3, **6**/57.3, **7**/2.3
St Paul VI, **6**/57.2, **7**/25.3
St Teresa, **5**/68.3
St Thomas Aquinas, **1**/9.2, **3**/5.2, **7**/4.3
St Thomas of Villanueva, **4**/40.3
Tertullian, **2**/70.1, **4**/40.2

Ascetical struggle
Cassian, **2**/67.2
St Ambrose, **2**/22.3
St Augustine, **3**/3.1, **3**/18.2, **4**/25.1, **4**/80.2
St Bernard, **5**/50.2, **6**/12.2
St Cyprian, **5**/34.2
St Francis de Sales, **1**/12.3, **4**/25.1
St Gregory the Great, **2**/4.2, **4**/25.2
St Ignatius of Antioch, **4**/96.1

St John Chrysostom, **1**/12.2,
2/22.3, **4**/14.1, **4**/59.1,
5/34.2, **5**/50.2, **5**/61.2
St John Climacus, **2**/67.2
St John Paul II, **4**/14.3, **6**/20.1
St Peter Damian, **3**/92.2
St Peter of Alcantara, **1**/13.2
St Teresa, **1**/1.3, **2**/12.2
St Vincent of Lerins, **1**/6.3

Aspirations
St Teresa, **2**/35.3

Atonement
St Bernard, **6**/50.2

Baptism
Origen, **2**/70.3
St Augustine, **1**/51.1
St Cyril of Alexandria, **1**/50.1
St John Chrysostom, **2**/5.1
St John Paul II, **5**/43.2,
5/59.2, **6**/3.2
St Leo the Great, **1**/51.1
St Thomas Aquinas, **6**/3.3

Blessed Trinity
St Augustine, **6**/40.3
St John of the Cross, **6**/40.1
St Teresa, **6**/40.2, **6**/40.3

Catechism
St John Paul II, **3**/13.2, **4**/86.2

Character
Cassian, **1**/11.1

Charity
St Alphonsus Liguori, **2**/22.2
St Augustine, **3**/52.2, **5**/23.1,
5/52.1
St Bernard, **4**/85.3
St Cyprian, **2**/94.2, **5**/94.3
St Francis de Sales, **3**/100.1
St Jerome, **5**/23.1

St John Chrysostom, **4**/21.2
St Teresa, **3**/100.1
St Thomas Aquinas, **2**/44.2,
4/1.2, **5**/15.3
Tertullian, **6**/4.3, **6**/52.3

Chastity
St Jean Vianney, **1**/23.3
St John Chrysostom, **1**/23.3,
4/62.2, **4**/62.3
St John Paul II, **1**/23.1,
4/62.2, **4**/83.2, **4**/83.3,
5/90.3, **6**/22.1
St Leo the Great, **1**/16.3

Christ
Origen, **5**/31.2
Pius XI, **5**/91.1
Pius XII, **5**/52.2, **6**/49.3,
6/50.1
St Ambrose, **5**/91.3
St Augustine, **1**/2.2, **1**/32.2,
5/3.2, **5**/31.1, **5**/56.2
St Bernard, **5**/56.1
St Hippolytus, **5**/47.1
St John Chrysostom, **5**/6.1
St John of the Cross, **5**/96.2
St John Paul II, **5**/2.3, **5**/31.1,
5/64.1, **6**/49.1, **6**/50.3
St Leo, **7**/12.2
St Paul VI, **5**/18.3
St Teresa, **5**/61.3, **7**/35.2
St Thomas Aquinas, **1**/40.1,
7/12.1

Church
Bl. Alvaro, **6**/18.3
Gregory XVI, **4**/73.3
Pius XI, **3**/10.2, **6**/8.2
Pius XII, **4**/37.3, **6**/8.2
St Ambrose, **4**/73.3, **5**/5.2
St Augustine, **5**/5.2
St Cyprian, **3**/10.2, **4**/13.3

St Cyril of Jerusalem, 3/10.2
St Gregory the Great, 3/10.2
St John Chrysostom, 5/31.2
St John Paul II, 4/37.2,
  5/28.1, 5/41.2, 7/40.3
St John XXIII, 3/10.2
St Leo the Great, 4/73.2
St Paul VI, 4/18.3, 5/47.2,
  6/8.1

Civic Duties
St Ambrose, 4/58.1
St Justin, 2/33.2, 2/70.2, 4/58.2
St John Paul II, 5/21.3
Tertullian, 4/58.2

Communion of saints
St Ambrose, 5/68.1
St John Paul II, 1/10.3, 5/68.1
St Teresa, 2/66.1
St Thomas Aquinas, 5/71.3,
  6/8.3

Compassion
St Augustine, 1/4.3
St John Paul II, 1/3.2, 1/10.1,
  1/10.2, 5/15.1, 5/31.3
St Paul VI, 5/15.1
St Thomas Aquinas, 4/64.2

Confession
Bl. Alvaro, 3/7.2, 5/27.2
St Ambrose, 2/34.2
St Augustine, 3/7.3, 4/60.2
St Bede, 3/4.1
St Gregory the Great, 2/39.2
St Jean Vianney, 2/55.2
St John Chrysostom, 2/21.1,
  2/34.3
St John Paul II, 1/4.2, 2/1.1,
  2/18.3, 2/34.1, 2/34.3,
  4/46.3, 5/5.3
St Paul VI, 5/27.2
St Thomas Aquinas, 2/8.3,

2/21.1

Conscience
St John Paul II, 2/13.1

Contrition
St Augustine, 2/41.2
St John Chrysostom, 4/60.1
St Teresa, 5/16.2

Conversation
St Augustine, 5/15.3
St Gregory of Nyssa, 3/19.2
St John Chrysostom, 5/9.3
St John Paul II, 5/6.2

Conversion
St Augustine, 7/20
St John Paul II, 1/10.1

Cowardice
St Basil, 2/69.3
St John Chrysostom, 3/89.3

Cross
St Athanasius, 3/56.3
St Augustine, 4/82.1
St Gregory the Great, 2/12.1
St Irenaeus, 5/28.3
St John Damascene, 7/23.1
St John Paul II, 4/82.1, 5/22.2
St Thomas Aquinas, 5/19.3

Death
Bl. Alvaro, 5/97.3
Leo X, 5/80.3
St Bede, 4/2.2
St Ignatius Loyola, 5/80.3
St Jerome, 4/2.3
St John Paul II, 4/2.1

Dedication
St Augustine, 5/9.2, 5/12.1
St Jerome, 3/86.2
St John Paul II, 3/104.2

Detachment
St Augustine, 5/21.3

St Francis de Sales, 5/24.2
St John of the Cross, 2/16.1
St John Paul II, 5/21.3, 5/38.3
St Teresa, 2/16.3
St Thomas Aquinas, 7/50.3

Devil
Cassian, 2/6.2
St Irenaeus, 2/6.1
St J. H. Newman, 2/6.2, 4/19.1
St Jean Vianney, 2/6.2
St John of the Cross, 2/6.3
St John Paul II, 2/6.1, 2/6.3,
    5/42.1
Tertullian, 5/42.2

Difficulties
Bl. Alvaro, 4/54.2
John Paul I, 5/44.3
Pius XII, 2/60.2, 5/53.2
St Alphonsus Liguori, 5/69.2
St Athanasius, 4/3.1
St Augustine, 1/32.1, 2/24.3,
    2/64.3, 3/98.3, 4/8.1,
    4/25.1, 5/16.2
St Bernard, 4/96.1, 7/43.2
St Cyprian, 1/36.3
St Francis de Sales, 4/25.1,
    6/30.2
St Gregory Nazianzen, 1/13.1
St Gregory the Great, 3/98.2,
    4/96.3, 5/9.2, 5/85.1
St J. H. Newman, 4/5.3, 4/96.3
St Jean Vianney, 5/61.1
St John Chrysostom, 1/32.1,
    1/43.3, 2/5.1, 2/64.1,
    2/64.2, 2/92.3, 4/50.3
St John of the Cross, 4/25.1
St John Paul II, 2/29.3
St Paul VI, 2/2.1
St Teresa, 1/32.3, 4/25.3
St Theophilus of Antioch,

5/53.2
St Thomas Aquinas, 2/60.1

Divine filiation
St Athanasius, 5/59.1
St Cyprian, 5/33.1
St Cyril of Jerusalem, 6/3.2
St Hippolytus, 6/3.2
St John Chrysostom, 4/24.3,
    7/5.2
St John Paul II, 1/17.1, 4/32,
    5/59.1, 5/59.2
St Teresa, 5/60.3
St Thomas Aquinas, 1/24.3,
    1/36.2, 1/36.3, 4/32.1,
    4/98.1, 5/33.1, 5/59.1,
    5/59.2, 5/64.2, 5/75.3
Tertullian, 5/33.2

Docility
St John Paul II, 7/5.1

Doctrine
St J. H. Newman, 3/18.2
St Pius X, 7/5.1

Duties
John Paul I, 5/51.2
St Gregory the Great, 2/13.3

Early Christians
St Clement, 6/58.2
St John Chrysostom, 5/79.1,
    6/58.1
St John Paul II, 5/2.1, 5/8.2
St Justin, 2/70.2

Ecumenism
St John Paul II, 6/4.3
St Paul VI, 6/5.2

Eucharist
Bl. Alvaro, 3/46.2
Cassian, 6/47.2
St Alphonsus Liguori, 1/2.1,
    6/44.2, 6/47.1

St Ambrose, **5**/40.2, **5**/40.3, **6**/46.2

St Augustine, **2**/56.2, **4**/47, **6**/42.2, **6**/45.2, **6**/47.1

St Cyril of Jerusalem, **4**/47.2, **4**/56.2, **6**/43.1

St Fulgentius, **2**/65.3

St Gregory the Great, **4**/70.3

St Ignatius of Antioch, **2**/65.3

St Irenaeus, **4**/65.2

St Jean Vianney, **2**/65.3, **4**/65.3

St John Chrysostom, **1**/2.1, **4**/70.1

St John of the Cross, **5**/7.3

St John Paul II, **2**/51.2, **4**/46.3, **4**/47.1, **4**/65.3, **4**/70.2, **4**/70.3, **6**/41.1, **6**/41.2

St Paul VI, **1**/2.2, **1**/2.3, **2**/44.1, **2**/49.2, **2**/65.1, **2**/65.2, **3**/4.3, **4**/43.2, **4**/56.2, **5**/89.3, **6**/5.1, **6**/41.3, **6**/43.1, **6**/45.3

St Pius X, **1**/2.3

St Teresa, **6**/45.2

St Thomas Aquinas, **2**/65.3, **3**/4.1, **3**/103.2, **4**/43.3, **6**/43.2, **6**/46.1 **6**/46.3, **6**/47.1

Evangelisation

St John Paul II, **2**/32.1, **2**/32.3, **4**/87.3, **5**/12.2, **6**/12.3, **6**/18.2

St Paul VI, **5**/20.2, **5**/20.3, **6**/9.2, **6**/13.2

Examination of conscience

Bl. Alvaro, **4**/93.1

St Augustine, **1**/19.2

St John Chrysostom, **4**/57.2

St John Climacus, **4**/93.2

St John of the Cross, **4**/93.1

St Teresa, **4**/93.3

Example

St Ambrose, **5**/13.2

St Gregory the Great, **2**/32.2

St Ignatius of Antioch, **5**/1.2

St John Chrysostom, **4**/40.2, **4**/72.1, **4**/72.2, **5**/62.2

St John Paul II, **4**/4.3, **4**/73.1

St Teresa, **5**/62.2

Faith

Bl. Alvaro, **6**/18.3

Pius XII, **3**/55.2, **5**/53.2

St Ambrose, **1**/6.1, **4**/13.1, **5**/64.2

St Augustine, **2**/54.3, **4**/54.1, **4**/55.3, **5**/4.2, **5**/48.3, **5**/51.3

St Gregory Nazianzen, **5**/26.1

St Gregory the Great, **2**/54.2, **2**/54.3, **6**/45.1

St Jean Vianney, **3**/44.2

St John Chrysostom, **2**/63.1, **3**/55.1, **3**/89.1, **4**/55.3

St John Paul II, **1**/44.3, **2**/67.1, **6**/6.2, **6**/13.2, **7**/1.3, **7**/12.2

St Justin, **6**/52.1

St Paul VI, **6**/6.2

St Vincent of Lerins, **6**/6.1

St Teresa, **4**/55.1

Family life

St Augustine, **7**/19.1

St John Chrysostom, **2**/70.3

St John Paul II, **1**/31.2, **2**/14.3, **3**/95.1, **4**/91.1, **4**/91.3, **5**/29.3, **7**/6.2, **7**/19, **7**/28.2, **7**/54.3

St Thomas Aquinas, **5**/29.3

Fear

St Augustine, **3**/99.1

St J. H. Newman, 3/99.1
St John Chrysostom, 6/12.3
St John Paul II, 2/93.3, 5/82.2
St Teresa, 2/93.1, 2/93.3

Forgiveness
St Ambrose, 3/5.1
St Augustine, 1/37.2
St John Chrysostom, 3/54.2,
    4/61.3, 5/41.3
St John of the Cross, 5/1.1
St John Paul II, 5/1.3
St Therese of Lisieux, 5/3.1
St Thomas Aquinas, 4/60.2

Fraternity
St Augustine, 3/52.2
St Cyprian, 5/41.3
St Francis de Sales, 5/78.3
St Gregory the Great, 5/78.2
St John Chrysostom, 5/79.1,
    5/88.3
St John Paul II, 5/78.3,
St Leo the Great, 4/10.2
St Paul VI, 5/20.3
Tertullian, 4/79.2

Freedom
St John Paul II, 4/74.2, 4/74.3

Friendship
St Ambrose, 4/41.2, 4/41.3,
    4/89.3
St Bernard, 4/89.1
St Paul VI, 2/80.2
St Teresa, 1/36.1
St Thomas Aquinas, 2/80.2,
    3/5.2

Generosity
Pastor of Hermas, 5/92.2
St Ambrose, 4/94.1
St Augustine, 5/67.2, 5/74.3,
    5/92.1

St Gregory the Great, 1/26.2
St Ignatius of Antioch, 4/97.1
St John Chrysostom, 5/74.1
St John Paul II, 1/18.3, 5/8.3
St Teresa, 1/26.3, 5/74.3
St Thomas Aquinas, 5/74.2

Good Shepherd
St Ambrose, 2/4.3
St Augustine, 1/7.2
St Thomas of Villanueva, 1/7.2

Grace
St Augustine, 5/77.2, 6/12.2
St Bede, 4/99.2
St Irenaeus, 1/51.1
St John Chrysostom, 4/97.2
St Teresa, 6/12.2
St Thomas Aquinas, 2/17.3,
    4/2.2, 5/30.1

Heaven
St Augustine, 2/82.3
St Cyprian, 3/97.1
St Cyril of Jerusalem, 2/82.1
St John Chrysostom, 2/12.2
St John Paul II, 3/58.2
St Leo the Great, 2/86.2

Hell
St Teresa, 3/58.2, 5/73.2
St Thomas Aquinas, 5/90.1,
    5/97.2, 5/97.3

Holy Spirit
Leo XIII, 2/83.1
St Augustine, 2/95.3
St Cyril of Jerusalem, 2/95.3,
    2/96.2
St Francis de Sales, 2/96.2
St John Paul II, 5/45.1
St Paul VI, 2/87.1
St Thomas Aquinas, 2/90.3,
    3/5.3, 5/45.1

Hope
John Paul I, 5/93.3
St Ambrose, 5/66.3
St Augustine, 1/4.1, 2/74.1
St Bernard, 2/74.3
St John Paul II, 4/57.1
Human dignity
St John Paul II, 7/28.3
Humility
John Paul I, 5/47.3
Leo XIII, 1/27.1
St Ambrose, 5/77.1
St Augustine, 1/2.2, 1/27.2,
1/47.3, 5/21.1, 5/39.2,
5/57.2, 5/60.2
St Bede, 3/4.1
St Bernard, 3/45.2
St Cyril of Alexandria, 1/50.1
St Francis de Sales, 1/27.2,
4/84.1, 4/84.3
St Gregory the Great, 1/8.2
St Jean Vianney, 1/27.2
St John Chrysostom, 4/84.1
St John Paul II, 1/27.1, 5/74.2
St Thomas Aquinas, 1/27.2

Ignorance
St John XXIII, 2/32.1
St John Chrysostom, 3/18.2
Incarnation
St Augustine, 3/3.1
Instruments of God
Cassian, 2/20.2
John Paul I, 5/2.1, 5/65.2
Leo XIII, 5/77.1
St Augustine, 5/51.3, 5/54.2
St Gregory the Great, 3/98.2
St John Chrysostom, 2/14.1,
3/88.2, 4/55.3
St Pius X, 5/77.3

St Thomas Aquinas, 2/70.1,
5/12.3
St John Paul II, 5/43.2
Theophylact, 5/54.2
Interior Life
Bl. Alvaro, 4/30.1
St John Paul II, 6/4.3

Joy
St Basil, 4/67.3
St Bede, 2/12.2
St John Chrysostom, 4/26.1
St John Paul II, 1/30.2,
2/77.1, 3/15.3
St Leo the Great, 1/30.3
St Paul VI, 2/26.2, 2/48.3,
5/27.1
St Thomas Aquinas, 2/48.3,
2/94.1, 3/15.3, 7/47.2
St Thomas More, 1/39.2
Judgement
St J. H. Newman, 5/73.1
Justice
St Cyril of Jerusalem, 5/83.2
St John Chrysostom, 4/85.2
St John Paul II, 1/35.3, 2/75.1,
3/19.1, 4/12.2, 4/16.3, 4/77.3
St John XXIII, 4/77.1
St Paul VI, 4/12.3
St Thomas Aquinas, 2/75.1,
4/77.2, 5/17.3, 5/27.2,
5/55.2

Leisure
St Augustine, 4/29.1, 4/29.2
St Gregory Nazianzen, 4/29.1
St Paul VI, 5/17.1
St Teresa, 4/29.2
Lent
St John Paul II, 2/1.1, 2/8.2

Little things
 St Augustine, **1**/16.2
 St Bernard, **5**/39.2
 St John Chrysostom, **2**/22.3
 St Francis de Sales, **4**/57.2

Love
 St Augustine, **3**/52.2
 St Gregory of Nyssa, **2**/93.2
 St John Chrysostom, **4**/71.2
 St John of the Cross, **2**/14.3,
  4/1.2
 St John Paul II, **4**/1.2, **5**/8.2,
  5/64.2, **5**/64.3, **5**/88.1
 St Teresa, **2**/14.3, **5**/55.2
 St Thomas Aquinas, **4**/97.2

Love of God
 Clement of Alexandria, **5**/3.1
 John Paul I, **2**/24.3, **5**/53.3,
  5/65.1
 St Alphonsus Liguori, **4**/66.1
 St Ambrose, **5**/28.2
 St Augustine, **2**/49.2, **4**/1.3,
  4/92.3, **5**/65.2
 St Bernard, **3**/99.1
 St Catherine of Siena, **3**/50.2
 St Francis de Sales, **5**/77.2
 St John Chrysostom, **2**/24.1,
  5/39.2
 St John of the Cross, **2**/69.2,
  3/104.2, **4**/95.2
 St John Paul II, **3**/104.3,
  4/95.1, **5**/5.1, **5**/5.3, **5**/38.2,
  5/66.2, **5**/75.3
 St Teresa, **2**/4.1, **2**/69.1,
  2/69.2, **5**/14.1, **5**/57.3,
  5/92.3, **5**/95.3
 St Thomas Aquinas, **4**/66.2,
  5/65.2

Lukewarmness
 St Augustine, **5**/3.3

St Gregory the Great, **1**/12.2,
  5/55.1
 St John Chrysostom, **4**/19.3,
  4/54.3
 St John of the Cross, **4**/19.2,
  5/76.2
 St Pius X, **3**/102.3
 St Teresa, **4**/19.2
 St Thomas Aquinas, **5**/30.1

Marxism
 St Paul VI, **2**/33.3

Marriage
 John Paul I, **5**/29.2
 St Francis de Sales, **4**/62.1
 St John Chrysostom, **4**/62.2
 St John Paul II, **4**/62.2, **5**/29.1

Mass
 Pius XII, **5**/52.2, **5**/92.2
 St Augustine, **2**/36.3
 St Ephraim, **4**/26.2
 St Gregory the Great, **2**/66.2
 St Jean Vianney, **2**/30.2,
  4/7.1, **4**/7.3
 St John Chrysostom, **4**/26.2
 St John Paul II, **2**/30.2, **2**/30.3
 St Paul VI, **2**/30.2

Materialism
 Bl. Alvaro, **4**/82.2
 John Paul I, **5**/46.3
 St Augustine, **5**/58.2
 St Gregory the Great, **5**/58.2
 St John Paul II, **4**/82.2,
  5/25.1, **7**/2.1
 St John XXIII, **2**/58.2
 St Paul VI, **5**/49.1

Mercy
 Clement of Alexandria, **5**/3.1
 St Augustine, **5**/15.2, **5**/93.2
 St Bernard, **5**/56.2

St Francis de Sales, **5**/93.2

St John Paul II, **4**/85.1, **5**/1.3, **5**/3.2, **5**/5.1, **5**/5.2, **5**/81.2

St Therese of Lisieux, **5**/3.3

St Thomas Aquinas, **3**/42.1, **5**/5.1, **5**/17.3, **5**/41.2, **5**/70.2, **5**/81.2

Morning Offering

St Bernard, **2**/79.1

Cassian, **2**/79.2

Mortification

St Augustine, **4**/8.1

St Francis de Sales, **2**/1.1

St Jean Vianney, **5**/26.1

St John Chrysostom, **2**/15.2, **4**/8.2

St John of the Cross, **2**/2.1, **2**/19.2

St Leo the Great, **2**/19.1

St Paul VI, **2**/15.2, **2**/19.1

St Peter of Alcantara, **3**/101.2

St Teresa, **2**/19.2

Obedience

Cassian, **2**/20.2

St Augustine, **1**/49.1

St Gregory the Great, **1**/5.2, **1**/49.2, **5**/19.3

St John Chrysostom, **1**/5.3, **1**/45.1

St Teresa, **1**/49.3, **5**/19.1, **5**/19.3

St Thomas Aquinas, **4**/88.2, **5**/19.2

St John Paul II, **4**/94.3, **7**/12.2

Optimism

St Teresa, **4**/49.1

St Thomas Aquinas, **4**/49.2

Our Lady

Benedict XV, **3**/105.1, **7**/13.2

Bl. Alvaro, **3**/28.2

Leo XIII, **2**/25.3, **3**/45.3, **5**/18.1, **7**/26.3, **7**/34.1

Origen, **3**/105.3

Pius IX, **1**/25.1, **7**/17.2

Pius XII, **2**/95.1, **7**/3.1, **7**/14.2, **7**/17.2

St Alphonsus Liguori, **1**/21.3, **3**/9.1, **4**/99.2, **5**/81.3, **7**/9.2, **7**/9.3, **7**/41.3, **7**/49.3

St Amadeus of Lausanne, **7**/14.1

St Ambrose, **1**/50.3

St Andrew of Crete, **7**/22.1

St Augustine, **1**/23.1, **1**/47.3

St Bernard, **1**/18.3, **1**/38.3, **1**/40.3, **2**/9.3, **2**/74.3, **2**/79.1, **3**/42.2, **3**/98.3, **5**/48.2, **5**/92.3, **6**/1.1, **6**/1.2, **6**/15.2, **6**/16.1, **6**/31.2, **7**/11.3, **7**/15.3, **7**/43.3

St Bonaventure, **7**/22.1

St Catherine of Siena, **6**/28.3

St Cyril of Alexandria, **1**/38.1, **7**/11.2

St Ephraim, **7**/17.1

St Francis de Sales, **5**/63.2

St Germanus of Constantinople, **5**/18.2

St Ildephonsus of Toledo, **7**/15.2

St J. H. Newman, **7**/43.2

St Jean Vianney, **2**/30.2, **5**/63.1

St John Damascene, **2**/46.3, **7**/6.1, **7**/14.2

St John Paul II, **1**/22.3, **1**/31.3, **1**/38.2, **2**/47.3, **2**/56.3, **2**/84.3, **2**/95.1, **3**/9.2, **3**/38.3, **3**/42.1, **4**/90.2, **4**/90.3, **4**/94.3, **4**/99.1, **4**/99.3, **5**/14.2, **5**/18.1, **5**/36.1, **6**/10.1, **6**/10.3, **6**/28.2, **6**/31.1,

6/51.3, 7/3.2, 7/3.3, 7/6.3,
7/9.1, 7/11.1, 7/15.2, 7/24.3
St Paul VI, 1/38.3, 2/48.3,
2/84.1, 2/84.3, 2/95.1,
2/95.3, 3/40.3, 2/105.3, 7/3.2
St Peter Damian, 4/90.1, 7/22.3
St Teresa, 6/31.3, 7/3.2
St Thomas Aquinas, 1/41.1,
4/90.1, 4/99.3, 5/18.1, 7/43.2
St Vincent Ferrer, 7/3.2

Passion
St Alphonsus Liguori, 2/37.1
St Augustine, 2/39.2, 2/45.1
St John Chrysostom, 2/37.1
St John Paul II, 5/22.2
St Leo the Great, 2/37.1
St Thomas Aquinas, 2/37.1

Patience
St Augustine, 5/94.1
St Francis de Sales, 5/94.2
St Gregory Nazianzen, 5/54.3
St John Chrysostom, 2/28.1,
2/28.3
St John of the Cross, 5/5.1
St Thomas Aquinas, 5/94.2

Peace
St Augustine, 2/77.2, 2/94.1,
3/98.3
St Gregory Nazianzen, 2/56.2
St Irenaeus, 2/56.2
St John Chrysostom, 1/3.2
St John of the Cross, 4/25.1
St John Paul II, 1/3.1, 1/3.3
St Paul VI, 2/33.1, 4/12.3

Penance
St Ambrose, 3/90.3
St Cyril of Jerusalem, 5/75.2
St Gregory the Great, 3/90.1
St John Chrysostom, 3/90.2

St John Paul II, 3/85.2, 5/1.3,
5/41.1
St Paul VI, 2/3.1

Perseverance
Cassian, 2/39.1
St Augustine, 5/4.3, 5/81.1,
5/86.3
St Gregory the Great, 7/4.1
St John Chrysostom, 4/80.2
St John Paul II, 5/57.1, 5/86.2
St Teresa, 2/92.2, 5/57.3
St Thomas Aquinas, 2/92.2

Poverty
St Augustine, 5/24.3, 7/31.2
St Gregory the Great, 2/16.2,
2/16.3
St John Chrysostom, 4/48.2
St Leo the Great, 2/1.2

Prayer
St Alphonsus Liguori, 2/12.3,
2/81.3, 5/48.1, 5/57.2, 7/9.1
St Augustine, 2/9.3, 4/39.2,
4/64.1, 4/64.2, 5/48.1,
5/48.3, 5/56.2, 5/81.1, 5/95.2
St Bernard, 5/48.1
St Cyprian, 3/94.1
St Gregory the Great, 3/40.3
St Jean Vianney, 2/9.1,
3/40.1, 7/35.1
St John Chrysostom, 2/68.2,
4/64.3
St John of the Cross, 3/51.1
St John Paul II, 1/29.2, 3/93.1,
4/39.1, 39.3, 4/91.1, 4/91.3,
4/95.2, 5/33.1, 5/57.1, 7/32.1
St Paul VI, 5/14.3
St Peter of Alcantara, 3/51.2,
5/57.3
St Teresa, 1/29.2, 1/29.3, 2/9.3,
2/15.1, 2/27.1, 2/27.3, 3/51.2,

3/94.1, 4/95.2, 5/14.1, 5/34.1,
5/57.1, 5/57.3, 6/18.2, 7/35.1
St Thomas Aquinas, 3/40.2,
4/64.2, 4/80.3

Presence of God
St Alphonsus Liguori, 5/61.1
St Augustine, 2/76.1, 2/76.2,
4/30.1
St Basil, 5/72.2
St Gregory the Great, 2/76.2
St John of the Cross, 2/76.2
St John Paul II, 2/61.2, 5/83.1

Pride
Cassian, 2/14.1, 5/63.3
St Ambrose, 5/54.1
St John Chrysostom, 2/25.2,
2/63.1, 2/63.3, 5/33.3
St Gregory the Great, 2/63.2
St Thomas Aquinas, 5/55.1

Priesthood
Bl. Alvaro, 1/51.3, 5/11.2
St Ambrose, 7/10.3
St Catherine of Siena, 4/20.3
St Ephraim, 5/71.1
St J. H. Newman, 6/9,3
St John Paul II, 1/7.2, 4/20.1,
5/57.1, 6/9.3, 7/10.1, 7/10.2

Providence, divine
Cassian, 5/33.2
St Augustine, 5/60.2
St Bernard, 3/96.3
St Jerome, 3/97.2
St John Paul II, 3/96.1
St Thomas Aquinas, 3/96.2

Prudence
St Augustine, 4/17.1
St John Paul II, 4/17.1, 4/17.2
St Teresa, 5/93.2

Purgatory
St Catherine of Genoa, 7/39.1

St John Paul II, 7/39.1
St Teresa, 7/39.1

Purity
St Ambrose, 5/90.1
St John Paul II, 3/8.1, 5/75.3

Reading of the Gospel
St Augustine, 2/73.1, 2/73.3,
4/86.3, 5/96.3
St Cyprian, 5/96.3
St Jerome, 7/8.3
St John Chrysostom, 5/96.1
St John Paul II, 4/86.2

Responsibility
St Augustine, 5/9.3
St Gregory the Great, 2/63.2,
5/68.2
St Ignatius of Antioch, 5/79.2
St Thomas Aquinas, 5/51.2

Roman Pontiff
St Ambrose, 6/7.2
St Augustine, 6/19.1, 6/19.3
St Catherine of Siena, 6/7.2
St Cyprian, 6/19.1
St John Paul II, 6/7.3
St Leo the Great, 6/7.2, 6/19.2

Rosary
Pius XI, 5/36.2, 7/32.3
Pius XII, 2/81.1
St John Paul II, 2/81.2,
5/36.2, 5/36.3
St John XXIII, 2/81.1, 7/33.1
St Paul VI, 2/81.1, 2/81.2,
5/18.3, 5/36.2

Sacraments
St Augustine, 2/46.1
St John Chrysostom, 4/36.1
St Pius X, 4/46.3

Saints, devotion to
St Catherine of Siena, **6**/32.1
St Jerome, **3**/72.2
St John Paul II, **3**/72.2, **6**/2
St John the Baptist
St Augustine, **1**/8.1
St John Chrysostom, **6**/55.3
St Joseph
Leo XIII, **4**/15.2, **6**/20.1, **6**/26.3
St Ambrose, **1**/22.1
St Augustine, **1**/22.2
St Bernard, **4**/15.3
St Bernardine of Siena,
1/40.3, **6**/20.3, **6**/25.3
St Francis de Sales, **6**/25.2
St John Chrysostom, **6**/24.1
St John Paul II, **5**/64.3, **5**/84.3,
6/20.2, **6**/26.3, **6**/27.3
St John XXIII, **6**/26.3
St Teresa, **1**/45.2, **4**/15.2,
6/26.1, **6**/26.3
St Thomas More
St Thomas More, **6**/54.3
Sanctity
Cassian, **5**/32.3
St John Paul II, **3**/7.3, **4**/4.3,
5/58.3, **6**/21.3, **7**/38.1
Search for God
St Augustine, **5**/16.3, **5**/37.2,
7/4.2
St Bernard, **5**/50.3
St Ignatius of Antioch, **5**/32.3
St John of the Cross, **2**/10.2
St John Paul II, **5**/66.1
Self-giving
St Augustine, **5**/3.3
St Gregory the Great, **5**/92.1
St John Paul II, **1**/26.1, **5**/90.3
Service
St Augustine, **5**/3.3

St John Chrysostom, **2**/24.1
St John Paul II, **2**/15.3, **5**/47.3
Simplicity
St Jerome, **1**/24.3
St John Chrysostom, **1**/24.3
Sin
Origen, **5**/93.1
St Augustine, **2**/17.3, **2**/21.3,
5/31.1, **5**/45.2, **5**/93.1
St Bede, **5**/31.1
St Francis de Sales, **2**/17.3
St Gregory the Great, **5**/9.1
St Jean Vianney, **2**/17.1, **3**/44.2
St John Chrysostom, **4**/85.2
St John of the Cross, **4**/2.2,
5/45.3
St John Paul II, **2**/17.1, **2**/17.3,
2/18.2, **2**/29.2, **3**/56.3, **4**/2.2,
4/34.1, **4**/34.2, **5**/3.2, **5**/41.1,
5/45.1, **5**/45.2, **5**/70.1, **5**/71.2
St Paul VI, **1**/51.1
Sincerity
St Augustine, **7**/18.2, **7**/18.3
St Francis de Sales, **2**/23.3
St John Chrysostom, **2**/23.1
St Thomas Aquinas, **5**/44.2
Society
Bl. Alvaro, **4**/12.2
Pius XI, **3**/37.1
St John Chrysostom, **3**/52.1
St Paul VI, **1**/35.1
Spiritual childhood
Cassian, **5**/34.1
St Alphonsus Liguori, **5**/57.2
St Ambrose, **4**/63.3
Spiritual direction
St John Climacus, **1**/7.3
St John of the Cross, **4**/76.1,
5/85.2
St Teresa, **5**/85.2

St Thomas Aquinas, 5/19.3
St Vincent Ferrer, 4/92.3

Spiritual reading
St Augustine, 3/18.2
St Basil, 3/43.2, 3/43.3
St Jerome, 7/36.3
St John Chrysostom, 7/8.2
St John Eudes, 7/8.3
St Peter of Alcantara, 7/8.3

Suffering
St Augustine, 5/69.2
St Bede, 7/20.2
St Francis de Sales, 2/31.2
St John Chrysostom, 2/64.3,
   5/31.1
St John Paul II, 2/31.3,
   5/15.1, 5/15.2, 5/22.2,
   5/69.1, 6/17.3, 6/22.1
St Teresa, 5/69.3
St Thomas More, 2/38.3

Supernatural outlook
Pius XII, 3/55.2
St Augustine, 5/34.1, 5/80.1
St Bede, 4/69.2
St Gregory the Great, 4/80.2
St John Chrysostom, 4/82.1
St John Paul II, 5/58.3, 5/97.1
St John XXIII, 5/89.3
St Paul VI, 5/83.3
St Teresa, 5/76.3
St Theophilus, 3/55.2

Temperance
St John Paul II, 4/35
St Peter Alcantara, 4/35.1

Temptations
St Athanasius, 4/3.1
St Basil, 5/9.2
St Thomas Aquinas, 5/42.2,
   6/3.3

Time
St Augustine, 4/65.3
St Paul VI, 5/17.1

Trust in God
Tertullian, 5/42.2
St Augustine, 2/4.3, 5/67.2,
   5/93.1
St Cyprian, 5/35.2
St Francis de Sales, 5/43.3
St Teresa, 5/60.3, 5/65.1
St Thomas Aquinas, 5/33.2
St Thomas More, 5/61.3

Truth
St Augustine, 4/18.3
St John Chrysostom, 4/28.2
St Thomas Aquinas, 5/44.2

Understanding
St Augustine, 2/21.2
St Gregory the Great, 2/72.2
St Jerome, 2/72.1, 4/27.3
St John Paul II, 7/18.2
St Teresa, 2/87.2

Unity
Aristides, 2/56.3
Cassian, 3/72.2
Pius XI, 5/87.3, 5/91.2
St Augustine, 2/56.3, 2/78.3,
   4/92.1
St Cyprian, 4/13.3
St Irenaeus, 2/56.1, 2/56.2
St John Chrysostom, 2/56.1,
   3/50.7
St John Paul II, 2/56.1,
   2/56.2, 3/57.1, 5/32.2,
   5/68.2, 6/18.1
St Paul VI, 2/56.2, 6/5.2
St Thomas Aquinas, 2/56.2

Virtues
  Bl. Alvaro, **2**/22.2, **4**/33.1
  Pius XI, **4**/33.1
  St Augustine, **3**/19.3, **3**/100.1
  St Francis de Sales, **3**/6.2
  St Gregory the Great, **4**/25.2
  St Jerome, **3**/86.3
  St John Chrysostom, **3**/52.1
  St Teresa, **3**/54.3, **3**/100.1
  St Thomas Aquinas, **3**/6.2
**Visit to the Blessed
  Sacrament**
  Pius XII, **2**/51.2
  St Alphonsus Liguori, **2**/51.3,
    4/56.3
  St John Chrysostom, **2**/51.3
  St Paul VI, **4**/56.3
  St Teresa, **2**/51.3
Vocation
  Bl. Alvaro, **2**/32.1,
  John Paul I, **1**/45.1
  Pius XI, **4**/22.2
  St Bernard, **4**/22.1
  St Bernardine of Siena,
    6/20.3

St Gregory the Great, **3**/88.2
St John Chrysostom, **7**/25.1
St John Paul II, **4**/22.3,
  5/38.2, **5**/43.1, **5**/90.2,
  7/29.2, **7**/45.1
St Thomas Aquinas, **6**/20.2,
  7/45.2
Will of God
  St John Paul II, **5**/43.1
  St Augustine, **5**/35.1
  St Teresa, **2**/57.2, **5**/35.3
Worldly Respect
  St Bede, **5**/44.2
  St Jean Vianney, **2**/62.1
  St Thomas Aquinas, **5**/30.1
Work
  Bl. Alvaro, **4**/30.3
  Didache, **4**/78.1
  St John Chrysostom, **1**/43.1,
    3/41.2
  St John Paul II, **1**/46.2, **3**/11.2,
    5/13.2, **5**/32.2, **5**/84.3
  St John XXIII, **3**/11.2

SUBJECT INDEX

Abandonment
and responsibility, 3/96.2,
7/46.2
confidence in God's Will,
3/61.1, 3/96.1, 5/35, 5/53.1,
5/58.1
healthy concern for *today*,
3/61.3
omnia in bonum, 3/96.3,
5/58.3, 5/60.2
unnecessary worries, 3/61.2,
5/17.3, 5/82.3

Advent
expectation of second
coming, 1/20.1
joy of, 1/2.1
meaning of, 1/1.3
period of hope, 1/21.1
period of joy, 1/15.1
preparation for Christmas,
1/1.1

Affability, 3/6.1, 3/6.2, 3/6.3

Angels, 7/27, 7/28, 7/29, 7/30

Anger, can be just and
virtuous, 1/11.3

Anointing of the Sick,
2/31.3, 3/31

Apostolate
a duty, 2/53.1, 2/85.1, 3/21.3,
3/69.1, 4/40.3, 5/10.2,
5/25.1, 5/51.3, 5/87.3,
6/30.3, 7/2.3
ad fidem, 1/44.3, 4/21.1
and difficulties, 1/9.2, 1/41.3,
2/32.3, 2/53.2, 2/62.2,
3/89.2, 5/52.1, 6/52.3,
6/57.3, 6/58.2
and doctrine, 4/18.1, 5/46.3
and example, 2/32.2, 4/44.3,
5/13.1, 5/51.2, 5/76.3, 6/58.1
and faith, 3/5.1, 7/34.3
and God's help, 1/9.2, 2/59.2,
5/26.1, 5/52, 6/34.3
and humility, 1/8.2, 5/57.2
and joy, 1/15.3, 3/68.3,
3/69.1, 5/25.3, 5/27.2,
5/55.1, 5/55.3, 7/4.3
and meekness, 1/11.3
and optimism, 2/53.3, 3/21.2
and patience, 2/52.2, 2/52.3,
3/21.2, 5/94.3
and prayer, 3/3.1, 3/88.2,
5/57.1, 7/46.3
and prudence, 3/5.2
and proselytism, 2/62.2,
5/10.2, 7/46.2
and worldly respect, 2/62.3,
3/89.3, 4/44, 5/30.1, 5/44.2,
5/62, 5/72.3
basis of, 1/9.1, 3/3.3, 3/35.2,
3/68.1, 5/10.2
being instruments, 3/21.1,

3/36.3, 5/51.3, 5/52
constancy in, 1/12.2, 2/85.2,
    4/69.2, 5/20.2, 5/50.2, 5/68.3,
    5/94.3, 6/2.3, 7/55.3
fruits of, 2/85.2, 3/21.3,
    5/52.2, 5/68.3, 5/91.3
how to do it, 2/52.3, 2/59.3,
needs formation, 2/54.3
of friendship, 1/8.3, 1/9.2,
    2/53.3, 5/25.2, 7/42.2
of public opinion, 4/45.2,
    4/45.3, 5/44, 6/32.2, 7/2.2
part of the Christian vocation,
    1/8.1, 2/53.1, 2/86.3, 3/69.2,
    5/72.2
role of women, 2/85.3, 5/8,
    7/36.1
universal meaning of, 1/44.3,
    5/37.3, 5/43.1, 6/58.3,
    7/25.3
upright intention, 2/62.3
virtues required, 3/36.1,
    3/36.2, 3/36.3, 4/33.3,
    5/20.1, 6/11.2
witnesses to Christ, 1/6.2,
    1/8.3, 3/35.2, 4/66.3, 5/66.3,
    5/87.3, 6/53, 7/2
Ascetical Struggle
beginning again, 1/12.2,
    1/12.3, 1/24.3, 2/28.2,
    4/14.3, 5/9.3, 5/50.2, 5/60.2,
    5/70.2, 6/30.2, 7/20.2
constancy, 2/28.1, 4/14.1,
    5/42.3, 5/48.1, 5/70.2, 5/94
develop a spirit of, 1/13.3,
    1/19.1, 1/43.3, 5/34.2, 5/43.2
expect defeats, 1/12.3, 4/14.2,
    5/93.3
fortitude in the face of
    weaknesses, 1/12.1, 1/45.3,

4/11.2, 5/42.2, 5/61.2,
    5/70.2, 5/93
until the last moments,
    1/12.1, 5/97.3
Aspirations, 1/29.3, 1/40.2,
    1/40.3, 2/35.3
remembering to say, 2/35.2
Atonement, 6/35.3, 49.3, 6/50.2

Baptism
effects of, 1/51.2, 5/43, 5/59,
    5/71.2
gratitude for having received
    it, 1/51.1
incorporation into the
    Church, 1/51.3, 4/13.2
institution of, 1/51.1
of children, 1/51.3
Beatitudes, 3/25.1, 3/25.2
Blessed Trinity, 2/76.1, 6/3.1,
    6/39, 6/40

Calumny, 3/19.1, 3/19.2,
    3/19.3
Celibacy
see Chastity, Virginity
Charity
and forgiveness, 2/21.1,
    2/21.2, 2/21.3, 5/1.1
and judgements, 2/72.1, 5/41.3
effectiveness of, 2/72.3,
    4/10.1, 5/20.3, 5/68.2, 5/94.3
its essence, 3/27.1, 3/27.2,
    5/23.1, 5/31.3, 5/52.1,
    5/79.3, 6/50.3
ordered, 1/25.3, 3/81.2, 4/21.3
sins of omission, 4/21.2
understanding, 2/72.1, 2/72.2,
    3/52.1, 3/52.2, 3/81.3,
    5/11.2, 5/6.1, 5/15.3, 5/67.3,

5/93.2

Chastity

and little things, 1/16.2, 5/90.3

clean of heart shall see God,
1/16.3, 3/8.1, 3/48.1, 5/16.1,
5/53.2, 5/75.3, 5/90

fruits of purity, 1/23.2,
5/63.3, 5/75.3, 5/90

guard of the heart, 1/16.2,
5/90.3

purity of heart, 1/16.1, 1/19.3,
1/23.1, 4/62.3, 5/90

ways of living purity well,
1/23.3, 3/8.2, 3/8.3, 5/90.3

Christians

early, 2/70.1, 5/52.3, 5/62.3,
5/68.3, 5/71.1, 5/74.2,
5/79.1, 5/84.1, 5/86.2

exemplary, 2/29.1, 2/70.2,
3/74, 3/102

Christmas

a call to interior purification,
1/16.1

humility and simplicity in
knowing Christ, 1/30.2

joy at, 1/30.3

receiving Christ, 1/30.1

the *Chair of Bethlehem*,
1/30.2

Church

characteristics of, 3/10.1,
3/57.3, 4/37.1, 5/5.2, 6/8

indefectibility, 2/60.1, 4/37.2,
4/37.3

its institution, 3/47.1, 6/4.1

love for, 2/59.2, 3/10.3,
4/13.1, 4/13.3, 7/16.3

mission of, 4/16.1, 4/16.2,
5/1.3, 5/28.1, 5/31.2, 5/41.1,
5/47.2, 5/48.2, 5/75.3,

5/87.1

prayer for, 3/47.2, 6/4.2,
7/27.3

Civic Duties, 4/58.1, 5/21,
5/51.2, 5/67, 5/74

Commandments of God

first, 3/76.1, 3/76.2, 3/76.3,
5/55.2, 5/65.1

fourth, 3/38.1, 3/38.2, 3/38.3

ninth, 3/86.1, 3/86.2, 3/86.3

second, 5/34

Communion

confession, a preparation for,
1/2.3, 5/7.3

dispositions for, 1/2.1, 1/2.2,
5/7.3

effects of, 2/65.3, 3/29.3,
4/46.2, 4/47.3, 4/56, 4/65.3,
5/40.3, 6/46.3

preparation for, 1/2.3, 4/46.3,
5/7.2, 5/7.3, 5/95.2

spiritual communions, 3/29.1,
3/29.2

Viaticum, 4/56.1

see Eucharist

Communion of the Saints

and optimism, 4/49.3

and penance, 2/10.2

entry into, 1/51.2, 2/66.2

gaining merit for others,
1/10.3, 2/66.1, 5/5/33.3,
5/68

indulgences, 2/66.3, 5/71.3

Compassion, 4/10.2, 4/27.3,
5/7.1, 5/15.1, 5/31, 5/33.1,
5/58.1, 5/62.1, 5/88.1

Concupiscence, 1/1.2, 5/58.2

Confession

a good for the whole church,
1/10.3

and contrition, 1/37.2, 1/47.3,
2/41.2, 2/41.3, 3/90.2, 4/9.2,
5/5.3

and peace, 1/3.1, 5/27.2

and the Good Shepherd, 1/7.2

apostolate of, 1/9.1, 2/34.2,
5/5.3

frequent, 1/10.2, 1/16.2,
3/7.3, 4/9.3, 5/5.3, 5/27.2

fruits of, 2/4.2, 2/8.3, 2/18.3,
5/1.3, 5/27.2

institution of, 4/60.1, 5/3.2,
5/93.2

need for and importance of,
1/10.1, 5/7.3, 5/53.2

penance, 2/34.3, 5/5.3

personal, auricular and
complete, 1/10.1

preparation for, 1/9.3, 2/8.2,
2/8.3, 3/7.2, 4/9.3

preparation for Communion,
1/1.2, 5/7.3

respect, gratitude and
veneration for, 1/9.3,
4/60.2, 5/39.2

the power of forgiving, 1/9.3,
2/8.2, 2/34.1, 4/60.3, 5/.1,
5/41.2

Confidence in God
and divine filiation, 1/36.2,
2/60.3, 4/5.2, 4/5.3, 5/9.3,
5/33.2, 5/81, 7/7.1

its never too late, 1/36.2,
4/55.3, 5/60, 5/93

Consumerism, 1/6.2, 5/25.1,
5/46.3, 5/49.1, 5/55.2, 5/58.2,
7/31.3

Contrition, 4/9.2, 5/5.3, 5/9.1,
5/16.2, 5/28.2, 5/60.2

Conversion, 1/18.3, 2/1.1,

5/9.3, 5/15.3, 5/54.3, 5/70.2,
7/20.1

Culture, 7/2.1

Death, 3/63.1, 3/63.2, 3/63.3,
5/71, 5/75, 5/80, 5/97.1,
5/97.3, 6/25.1

Dedication, 4/3.1, 4/3.3, 5/9.2,
5/12.1, 5/86, 7/41.2

Detachment
examples, 2/16.2, 3/28.3,
3/64.2, 5/24.2, 5/24.3

its need, 1/28.1, 2/16.1,
3/17.1, 4/19.2, 4/48.3,
5/24.1

our practice, 2/16.3, 3/17.2,
3/17.3, 3/65.2, 4/6.2, 5/21.3,
5/38.3, 5/49.2

Devil, 2/6.1, 2/6.2, 2/6.3,
5/42.1, 5/42.2

Difficulties
and faith, 4/50.2, 5/61.1,
5/85.1, 7/21.3

current forms of, 1/32.2,
5/42.1

Christian reaction to, 1/32.2,
1/36.1, 1/41.3, 4/25.2,
5/56.1, 5/59.2, 5/60.2,
5/61.2, 5/69.2, 5/82.3, 5/93,
7/12.3, 7/16.2

develop hope, 1/32.3, 4/5.3,
4/25.3, 5/85.1, 7/5.2

suffered for Christ, 1/32.1,
1/32.3, 4/25.1, 4/96.2,
5/31.3, 7/12.1, 7/23.2

Dignity, human, 3/11.1,
3/11.2, 3/11.3, 5/3.2, 5/75,
5/76, 7/22.2, 7/28.2

Dispositions, interior
humility, 2/20.1, 2/20.2

need for, 1/18.1, 5/16.1, 5/53.2

Divine filiation
and fraternity, 1/39.2, 4/98.3, 5/33.1, 5/79.3
and petition, 4/39.2, 4/39.3, 5/60.3
consequences of, 1/39.2, 3/2.2, 4/24.2, 4/24.3, 4/63.2, 4/98.2, 5/33.2, 5/46.3, 5/59.3, 5/60.2, 5/72, 5/75.3
everything is for the good, 1/36.3, 3/96.3, 5/22.1, 5/58.3, 5/65.1
foundation for peace and joy, 1/3.3, 1/39.3, 5/27.2, 5/33.1, 5/59.2
God is our Father, 1/24.3, 1/36.3, 3/2.1, 3/56, 4/24.1, 4/39.1, 4/58, 4/98.1, 5/3.2, 5/33.2, 5/59, 5/60.1, 5/64
gratitude for, 1/39.1
truly sons, 1/39.1, 3/62.2, 5/33.1, 5/47.1, 5/59.1

Docility
a virtue, 1/24.3, 1/43.3, 7/5.1
and spiritual guidance, 2/20.3, 5/45.3

Doctrine
and piety, 6/14
giving it, 4/28.2, 4/28.3, 5/46.3, 7/16.1
need for, 7/13.1

Ecumenism, 6/4, 6/5, 6/6, 6/7, 6/8
Education, 7/6.3
Eucharist
Adoro te devote, 2/65.1, 3/4.1, 3/4.2, 5/61.1, 5/95.2, 5/95.3

3/4.3, 4/43.3, 4/97.2
and adoration, 1/44.1, 5/40.3, 5/61, 5/89.3
and faith, 6/45
institution, of, 2/44.2, 4/26.1, 4/26.2
pledge of Heaven, 4/65.1, 4/65.2, 5/40.3, 6/48
real presence, 4/43, 5/7.3, 5/16.3, 6/41, 6/42, 6/43, 6/44, 6/46
true food, 4/46, 4/47, 4/65.1, 5/40.2, 5/61
see Communion

Examination of Conscience
a means against evil inclinations, 1/19.2, 5/41.3
a meeting with God, 1/14.2
and hope, 4/57.2
and self-knowledge, 1/14.1, 5/54.2, 5/73.3
contrition and resolutions, 1/14.3
fruits of, 1/14.1, 5/73.3
how to do it, 1/14.3
particular, 2/67.1, 2/67.2, 2/67.3, 4/19.3, 5/23.3
Example, 3/34, 3/74.1, 4/4.3, 4/10.1, 4/40.2, 4/58.2, 5/1.2, 5/13.2, 55/6.3, 5/62.2, 5/68.3, 5/76.3

Faith
and apostolate, 1/9.2
and charity, 6/52.3
and Christ, 1/43.3, 2/20.1, 3/16.1, 3/67.1, 4/50.1, 4/50.2, 4/55.2, 4/55.3, 5/38.3, 5/56.2, 5/64.2, 6/54, 7/1.1, 7/37.2

and optimism, 4/49.2

docility in spiritual guidance,
1/43.1, 1/43.3, 5/45.3

firmness in, 1/43.1, 3/73.2,
4/54.1, 5/4.3, 5/30.2, 5/48,
5/85.1, 6/52.1, 7/1.3

giving it to others, 1/14.3,
6/6.3, 6/13.3, 6/52.2

need for it, 1/6.1, 5/30.3

of Our Lady, 1/6.3, 3/43.3,
3/55.3, 4/54.3, 5/51.3,
5/64.2

operative, 2/54.2, 2/60.3,
2/62.1, 3/12.3, 3/67.1,
4/54.3, 5/48.3, 5/60.2

ways to conserve and
increase it, 1/6.1, 1/6.2,
1/18.2, 3/55.1, 4/31.1,
4/54.2, 5/4.2, 6/6.1, 6/13

Faithfulness

a virtue, 3/104.1, 3/104.2,
5/86, 7/14.3

in little things, 2/50.2,
3/104.3, 5/91.3

Family

domestic church, 1/31.3,
3/95.1, 5/29.3, 5/55.3,
7/19.1

mission of parents, 1/31.2,
3/95.2, 7/6.2, 7/19.1, 7/28.2,
7/54.2

of Jesus, 4/32, 7/54.1

prayer in the, 3/95.3, 7/6.3,
7/19.2, 7/19.3

Family, Holy

example for all families,
1/31.3, 7/6.1, 7/54.1

love in the, 1/22.2, 1/27.3,
5/64.3

meeting with Simeon, 1/41.1

Redemption rooted here,
1/31.1

simplicity and naturalness,
1/42.2

Fear, 1/36.1, 2/93, 3/99, 5/82.2

Feasts, 2/61.1, 2/61.2, 2/61.3,
3/71.1

and Sundays, 3/71.2, 3/71.3

Formation, doctrinal

and interior life, 3/13.3,
3/18.3

in the truths of the faith,
3/13.1, 3/18.1

need to receive and to give it,
3/13.2, 3/18.2

Fortitude

gift of, 2/92.1

in daily life, 1/45.3, 3/32.2,
3/32.3, 3/97.3, 5/94.2

in difficult moments, 2/64.2,
7/21.1

virtue of, 3/32.1, 3/97.3,
4/44.2, 5/94.1

Fraternal correction, 1/7.2,
3/24.1, 3/24.2, 3/24.3

Freedom, 1/35.1

Friendship

and apostolate, 2/80.3,
4/41.3

qualities of a true friendship,
2/80.2, 5/6.2, 5/78.2

true friendship, 2/80.1, 6/11.1

with God, 4/41, 4/55, 5/4.2,
5/61.3, 5/88.1, 7/7.2, 7/7.3

Generosity

prize for it, 1/26.3

towards God, 3/46.1, 4/67.1,
4/98.1, 5/38.3, 5/55.2,
5/67.2, 5/72.3, 5/74, 5/92

with others, **1**/26.2, **5**/8.3,
5/66.2, **5**/67

God's Love for men
gratuitous, **3**/62.1, **5**/3.2,
5/65.2
infinite and eternal, **2**/24.1,
2/24.2, **3**/62.1, **4**/66.1, **5**/1,
5/74.3
personal and individual,
3/62.3, **5**/3.1, **5**/38.2, **5**/66.2,
5/70.2, **5**/88
returning his love, **2**/57.1,
3/62.2, **3**/62.3, **4**/66.2, **5**/9.3,
5/37.2, **5**/39.3, **5**/65.2, **5**/87.3
unconditional reply expected,
2/24.3, **5**/51.1

Goods of the Earth
supernatural end, **4**/68.1,
5/21, **5**/24, **5**/38.2, **5**/38.3,
5/49, **5**/55.2

Good Shepherd
and spiritual guidance, **1**/7.3,
1/43.2
in the Church, **1**/7.2, **2**/68.1
Jesus Christ is, **1**/1, **2**/68.1,
5/66.3, **5**/70
role of every Christian, **1**/7.2
virtues of, **1**/7.2, **5**/63.3

Gospel
reading of, **1**/48.2, **2**/73.1,
5/96, **7**/36.3
teaching is current, **1**/48.3,
5/96.2

Grace
corresponding to it, **2**/40.2,
4/19.3, **5**/9.3, **5**/51.1, **6**/2.1,
7/41.2
its effects and fruits, **3**/23.2,
3/23.3, **3**/84.1, **3**/91.1, **5**/77,
7/40.3

its nature, **3**/23.2, **3**/84.2,
3/91.2, **5**/30.1

Guardian Angels
help us, **2**/7.2, **3**/77.2, **3**/77.1,
5/42.3, **5**/73.3, **5**/77.3,
5/84.3
love and devotion for, **2**/7.1,
2/7.3, **3**/77.2, **3**/77.3

Heaven, **2**/82.1, **2**/82.2, **2**/82.3,
5/21.1, **5**/73.2, **5**/83.3, **5**/90,
5/97
hope of, **2**/12.2, **2**/82.1,
3/58.3, **4**/48.2, **5**/37.1,
5/80.1, **5**/97.1, **7**/12.2,
7/14.2, **7**/15.3, **7**/52.1
and the Eucharist, **4**/65

Holy days of Obligation,
4/29.3

Holy Spirit
and Mary, **2**/95.2, **2**/95.3,
7/44.1
and supernatural virtues,
2/83.1
devotion to, **2**/76.3
fruits, **2**/94, **5**/23.2, **5**/45,
5/52.1
gifts,
counsel, **2**/90
fear, **2**/93
fortitude, **2**/92
knowledge, **2**/88
piety, **2**/91
understanding, **2**/87
wisdom, **2**/89

Hope
and discouragement, **1**/21.1,
2/4.3, **2**/74.2, **3**/79.2, **5**/23.1,
7/1.2
and heaven, **2**/12.2, **5**/37.1,

5/80.1, 5/97.1, 7/15.3
and Our Lady, 1/21.1, 2/74.3,
    5/36.3, 5/73.3, 6/31.2,
    7/14.2
confidence in Christ, 1/23.3,
    1/21.3, 2/74.1, 5/49.3,
    5/53.3, 5/66.3, 5/83.3, 6/12
in apostolate, 2/4.3
its object, 1/21.2, 3/79.1,
    4/57.1, 5/93.3

Humility
and prayer, 1/29.3, 4/51.1,
    5/4.1, 5/57.2
and pride, 2/25.1, 2/25.2,
    3/45.2, 3/50.1, 4/51.2
and simplicity, 1/42.1, 1/47.3,
    5/63.2
founded on charity, 1/27.2,
    2/25.3, 5/63.3, 5/74.2
fruits of, 1/27.2, 3/50.1,
    5/21.1, 5/47.3, 5/77.1,
    5/93.3, 6/55.3
is truth, 1/27.1, 5/39.2, 5/63.2
needed for the apostolate,
    1/8.2, 5/77.3
ways to achieve it, 1/27.3,
    2/14.3, 2/25.3, 3/45.3,
    3/50.3, 4/51.3, 5/9.2

Illness, 2/31.1, 2/31.2, 5/69.3,
    5/94.2

Jesus Christ
and Our Lady, 1/17.2, 5/18.3,
    7/49.1
and the Cross, 1/20.1, 2/30.1,
    4/36.1, 4/53.1, 5/2.3, 5/19.3,
    5/22, 5/28.3, 5/69, 5/70.1,
    7/12.2
divinity, 4/52.1, 6/28.1

growth of, 1/50.1
hidden life, 1/46.1, 1/46.2,
    1/50.1, 4/45.1, 5/84.2
high priest, 6/38
humanity, 1/17.3, 1/50.1,
    4/52.2, 5/16.2, 5/28.3,
    5/31.2, 5/78.1, 5/84.3, 5/88,
    6/28, 6/47.3, 6/49, 7/7.2,
    7/35.2
humility, 1/30.2, 5/47.2,
    5/52.2, 5/63.1
Kingship, 2/42.3, 5/34.2,
    5/34.3, 5/83.2, 5/87, 5/91
merits of, 4/4.2
Name of, 1/40.1, 1/40.2,
    5/34.1
Only-Begotten Son, 1/17.1,
    5/59.1
our knowledge of, 1/17.3,
    1/48.2, 5/53.3, 5/96
our Model, 1/17.3, 1/49.3,
    4/52.3, 5/2.2, 5/15.2, 5/31.2,
    5/47.1, 5/66.2, 5/78.1,
    7/38.3
our support, 1/36.1, 3/73.1,
    5/56.1, 5/61.1, 5/69.3,
    5/70.1
our Teacher, 1/48.1, 5/2.1
search for, 2/12.3, 2/49.3,
    5/16.3, 5/32.2, 5/37.2,
    5/38.3, 5/56.2, 5/66.1,
    5/83.1, 5/85.1

Joseph, Saint
and work, 6/33
devotion to, 4/15.2, 6/20,
    6/21, 6/22, 6/23, 6/24, 6/25,
    6/26, 6/27
exemplar of virtues, 1/45.2,
    4/15.3, 5/63.3, 6/21
his dealings with Jesus and

Mary, **1**/22.2, **1**/22.3,
1/31.1, **4**/15.2, **5**/64.3,
5/84.3, **6**/22
his intercession, **1**/45.2
his mission, **1**/22.1, **4**/15.1
his obedience and fortitude,
1/6.3, **1**/45.1
honour and veneration, **1**/22.3
invoking his name, **1**/40.3
ite ad, **4**/15.3
patron of the Church, **4**/15.2,
4/15.3

Joy
and apostolate, **3**/15.3, **5**/25.3,
5/55, **5**/76.3, **5**/78.3
and divine filiation, **1**/15.2,
3/15.1, **5**/27.2, **5**/33.1,
5/59.2
and generosity, **2**/26.3, **4**/67,
5/27.2, **5**/38.3, **5**/55.2,
5/67.2, **5**/74.3
and sadness, **2**/48.2, **3**/15.2,
4/67.3, **5**/55.1, **7**/47.3
and suffering **2**/26.1, **2**/26.2,
3/15.2, **4**/96.1, **7**/23.3
being close to Jesus, **1**/15.1,
3/15.1, **3**/25.3, **4**/96.1, **7**/4.2,
7/47.1
in the family, **3**/15.3
its foundation, **1**/15.2, **3**/15.1,
5/5/27
spreading it, **2**/48.3, **5**/55.3

Judgement
particular, **1**/20.3, **5**/73.2
preparation for, **1**/20.3, **5**/73
universal, **1**/20.2, **5**/73.3, **5**/83

Justice
and charity, **1**/35.3
and mercy, **1**/35.3, **5**/17.3
and the individual, **2**/33.1,
2/33.2
consequences of, **1**/35.2,
2/75.1
its aim, **2**/75.3

Laity
role of, **7**/10.2
Leisure
and tiredness, **3**/33.1, **3**/33.3
learning to sanctify it, **3**/33.2,
4/29, **5**/17.1
Little things
and ascetical struggle, **1**/12.1,
1/19.2, **1**/50.2, **3**/78.1,
3/78.2, **3**/78.3, **4**/38, **4**/57.3,
5/39.2, **5**/50.2, **7**/20.3
Love
seeing God in ordinary
things, **1**/33.3, **5**/32.2,
5/50.2
Love of God
above all things, **4**/1, **5**/35.3,
5/38.1, **5**/49.1, **5**/55.2,
5/74.2, **7**/37.3
and the danger of
lukewarmness, **1**/13.1,
5/30.1, **5**/50.3
far-sighted, **1**/33.3
in daily incidents, **2**/24.3,
4/58
leading to abandonment,
2/57.3, **5**/55.2, **5**/60.3,
5/77.2
with deeds, **2**/57.2, **4**/66.2,
5/51.2, **5**/65.2, **5**/72.3,
5/73.1, **5**/82.2, **5**/84, **7**/4.1
Loyalty, **3**/87.1, **3**/87.2, **3**/87.3,
5/21.1, **5**/44.2, **5**/79.3, **5**/86
Lukewarmness
causes of, **1**/13.2, **1**/15.1,

5/28.2, 5/50.3
consequences of, 1/13.1,
   1/47.2, 3/83.1, 5/3.3, 5/16.2,
   5/30.1, 5/55.1, 5/76.2
remedy for, 1/13.3, 1/47.3,
   3/83.2

Magisterium
God speaks through it, 1/48.3
Magnanimity, 3/54.1, 3/54.2,
   3/54.3, 5/1.2, 5/46.2, 5/64.2
Marriage
   3/59.1, 3/59.2, 3/59.3, 5/29,
   5/90
dignity of, 4/62.1, 5/64.2,
   5/90
see Family life
Mass
attendance at, 4/36.2, 4/36.3
centre of interior life, 4/26.3,
   5/52.3
its value, 2/30.2, 2/30.3,
   3/49.1, 4/7.1, 5/52.2
fruits of, 3/103, 4/7.2, 4/7.3
our offering, 1/44.2, 3/49.3,
   4/61.2, 5/92.2
Materialism, 7/2.1
Maturity, 1/50.3, 1/51.3
Meekness
and peace, 1/11.1
dealings with others, 1/11.1,
   5/1.1
fruits of, 1/11.3
is foundation, 1/11.2
Jesus, model of, 1/11.1, 5/1,
   5/41.3
need for it, 1/11.3
Mercy
and justice, 1/35.3, 3/82.2,
   5/17.3

fruits of, 3/82.3
works of, 1/4.3, 4/16.3,
   4/27.3, 5/15
Mercy, divine
an example, 1/4.1, 3/82.1,
   5/5.1, 5/66.3
turn to it, 1/4.1, 5/3, 5/17.3,
   5/39.1, 5/45.2, 5/81, 5/93
with men, 1/4.2, 4/27.1,
   4/27.2, 5/1.3, 5/3, 5/41.2,
   5/56.2, 5/70.2, 5/81.1
Merit
of good works, 4/97
Morning Offering, 2/79
Mortification
and purity, 1/16.3
and the Cross, 2/2.1, 2/2.2,
   2/15.2, 2/43.2, 4/53.3,
   5/75.3
fasting, 2/3.1
interior, 1/19.2, 1/19.3,
   1/44.2, 2/3.2, 2/55.1, 5/26.1
of imagination, 2/55.2, 2/55.3
small sacrifices, 2/2.3, 2/3.3,
   4/8, 5/26, 5/28.3
Obedience
and docility, 1/24.3
and faith, 1/12.3, 1/45.1
and freedom, 1/49.3, 5/19.2
and God's Will, 1/5.2
and humility, 1/5.2
because of love, 1/49.3,
   5/11.2, 5/19.1
fruits of, 1/49.2
model of, 1/49.1, 5/11.3,
   5/19.3
Optimism, 4/49, 5/61.3, 5/78.3
Our Lady
and confession, 7/51.1

and faithfulness, **7**/14.3
and God's Will, **1**/25.3,
   4/99.1, **6**/29.2, **7**/45.3
and joy, **7**/47
and St John, **1**/33.2
and the Mass, **3**/105, **6**/48.3
and the Old Testament, **7**/5.1
and the Trinity, **6**/1.2
birth of, **7**/22.1
co-redemptrix, **1**/41.2,
   3/105.2, **5**/18, **7**/24.2
devotion, **1**/33.2, **1**/40.3,
   1/38.3, **2**/84.2, **7**/3.1, **7**/9.1,
   7/11, **7**/34.1, **7**/53.3
full of grace, **4**/99.2, **4**/99.3
generosity, **1**/26.1, **7**/41.1
her gifts, **7**/44.2, **7**/44.3
her help, **1**/38.2, **3**/9.1, **5**/36.1,
   5/48.2, **5**/81.3, **6**/16, **7**/3.2,
   7/34.2, **7**/49.3, **7**/52.3
her vocation, **1**/25.1, **5**/14.1,
   6/29, **7**/6.1, **7**/41.3, **7**/45.3
Immaculate Heart of, **6**/35.3,
   6/51
humility, **1**/27.1, **5**/14.2, **5**/63,
   6/27.3
invoke her name, **1**/40.3,
   3/9.1, **3**/42, **5**/81.3, **5**/92.3,
   7/5.3
mediatrix, **7**/9.2, **7**/9.3, **7**/11.3
Mother of God, **1**/17.2,
   1/38.1, **5**/18.3, **5**/81.3, **6**/1,
   7/11.2, **7**/26.3
our guide, **7**/43.2
our Mother, **1**/38.2, **2**/84.1,
   5/36.3, **5**/63.2, **6**/1.3, **7**/3.3,
   7/11.2, **7**/14.1, **7**/15, **7**/49.2
Queen, **7**/17
pilgrimages, **2**/84.3, **6**/31.1,
   6/35

rosary, **2**/38.3, **2**/79.3, **2**/81.1,
   2/81.2, **2**/81.3, **5**/18.3,
   5/27.3, **5**/36.2, **5**/36.3,
   7/13.2, **7**/13.3, **7**/32.3,
   7/33.1, **7**/48.3
service, **1**/26.1
to Jesus through Mary,
   6/37.2, **7**/52.1

Parables of the Gospel
banquet, **5**/37
good Samaritan, **4**/21, **5**/31
grain of wheat, **5**/34.2
leaven in dough, **4**/40
lost sheep, **4**/59. **5**/70.2
mustard seed, **5**/34.2
pearl of great value, **4**/42
Pharisee and tax-collector,
   5/57.2
prodigal son, **5**/3, **5**/41.1
shrewd steward, **5**/12
sowing seed, **4**/19, **5**/9
talents, **5**/51, **5**/82, **5**/87
two sons sent out, **5**/19
unjust judge, **5**/48, **5**/81.1
vineyard, **5**/10.2, **5**/28.1, **5**/54
virgins, **5**/73
wheat and cockle, **4**/28
working in vineyard, **4**/69,
   5/10, **5**/94.3
Patience, **2**/28.2, **2**/28.3,
   5/11.1, **5**/9.3, **5**/54, **5**/94
   see Meekness
Peace
and Christ, **1**/3.1, **2**/77.1
causes, lack of, **1**/3.1, **4**/12.2,
   5/14.3
foundation of, **1**/3.3, **1**/35.3,
   5/59.3
fruits of, **1**/3.2

gift of God, 1/3.1, 2/77.2,
    4/12.1
source of, 1/3.2, 4/12.3

Penance
and Fridays, 3/85.2
characteristics of, 3/85.3,
    5/1.3, 5/5.3, 5/26.2, 5/41,
    5/75.2

Persecution
    see Difficulties

Perseverance, 2/39.1, 2/40.3,
    5/4.3, 5/43.3, 5/57, 5/81,
    5/86, 7/4.1

Piety, 2/91
Way of the Cross, 2/3.2
    see Our Lady, rosary

Pope, 2/68.2, 2/68.3, 5/64.1,
    6/7, 6/19.3, 6/32.2, 7/16.3

Poverty
and sobriety, 1/28.3
evangelical poverty, 1/28.2
Jesus' example, 1/28.1
ways of practising it, 1/28.3,
    4/68.2, 5/24, 7/31.1, 7/31.2,
    7/50.3

Prayer
and humility, 1/29.3
and St Joseph, 1/29.3, 3/93.3,
    5/64.3, 5/84.3
and thanksgiving, 7/32
dealings with Jesus, 1/29.2,
    3/51.1, 5/56.2, 7/35.2,
    7/48.1
fruits of, 4/95.1, 5/33.3,
    5/57.3, 5/71.1
how to pray, 1/29.3, 2/27.2,
    2/27.3, 2/55.3, 3/40.1, 3/55.3,
    3/93.2, 4/64.2, 5/4.2, 5/33,
    5/40.1, 5/48, 5/96, 7/48.2
mental prayer, 7/34.3

need for it, 1/29.2, 2/38.2,
    3/93.1, 5/9.2, 5/14, 5/48.3,
    5/81, 7/9.1, 7/35.1
of petition, 2/9.1, 2/9.2, 2/9.3,
    3/9.3, 3/40.3, 4/5.1, 4/39.2,
    4/39.3, 4/64.1, 4/64.3,
    7/32.3
vocal prayers, 3/94.1, 3/94.2,
    3/94.3, 4/95.3, 5/94, 5/34.1,
    5/95

Presence of God, 2/12.3,
    2/76.2, 5/57.3, 5/61.1, 5/72.2,
    5/83.1

Priesthood, 2/44.2
identity and mission, 4/20.1,
    4/20.2. 5/48.2, 5/57.1,
    5/71.1, 6/9, 6/38, 7/10.1
love for, 7/10.3
prayer for, 4/20.3, 7/10.2

Prudence
essence of, 4/17.1, 5/93.2
false, 4/17.3
seeking advice, 4/17.2

Purgatory, 7/39.1

Purification
interior mortification, 1/19.3,
    5/26

Purity
    see Chastity

Recollection, interior
union with God, 4/19.1, 5/14
Our Lady's example, 1/29.1,
    5/14

Rectitude of intention, 2/63,
    5/11.1, 5/57.1, 5/67, 5/72,
    5/74.3

Redemption, 2/29.2, 2/36.1,
    2/36.2, 2/36.3, 5/52.1, 5/56.3,
    5/69.1, 5/75, 5/80.2

Resurrection
  of the body, 3/75.2, 3/75.3,
    5/75, 5/90.1, 5/97.2

Sacraments, 4/13.2, 4/36.1
Saints
  as intercessors, 3/72.1, 7/50.1
  cult to, 3/72.2
  veneration of relics, 3/72.3
Sanctity
  consequences of, 1/35.2,
    4/4.1, 5/68.1, 5/87.1
  developing talents, 4/68.2,
    4/68.3, 5/12.2, 5/51.2, 5/82,
    5/84
  in ordinary life, 1/46.1,
    2/11.2, 2/57.1, 2/69, 3/16.2,
    3/16.3, 3/92.2, 4/6.3, 4/40.1,
    4/45.3, 5/10.3, 5/32, 5/57.3,
    5/72, 6/9.2, 7/38.1, 7/55.2
  principal enemies of, 1/1.2,
    5/50.2
  universal call to, 3/92.1, 5/10.2,
    5/37.3, 5/43.1, 6/9.1, 7/38.2
Serenity, 3/98
Service, spirit of
  2/14.1, 2/14.3, 3/66.3, 5/3.3,
    5/67, 5/87.2, 6/37.1
Simplicity
  and humility, 1/42.1
  and spiritual childhood,
    1/24.3, 1/42.2
  fruits of, 1/42.3
  in dealings with God, 1/42.2,
    5/57.2, 7/18.3
  opposite of, 1/42.3
  rectitude of intention, 1/42.2,
    4/17.1
Sin
  consequences of, 2/10.1,

2/17.1, 2/18.1, 2/41.1,
  3/80.2, 4/2, 4/34.2, 5/28.2,
  5/31.1, 5/41.1, 5/45, 5/69.1,
  5/71.2, 5/85.1
forgiveness of, 3/44.2, 5/41.2,
  5/70.3
reality of, 1/47.2, 3/26.2,
  4/23.1, 4/34.1, 5/3.2, 5/45.3,
  5/93.1
sorrow for, 4/23.2, 4/23.3,
  5/9.1, 5/28.2
  see Confession
Sin, venial
  deliberate, 2/17.3, 3/26.3,
    4/34.3
  does damage, 1/10.2
Sincerity, 2/23, 3/60, 4/18.2,
  5/44, 7/18.2
Society
  and human solidarity, 3/37.2,
    4/58.3, 5/46.1, 5/68
  obligations to, 3/37.3, 3/53.3,
    4/58.1, 5/39.3, 5/44.3,
    5/46.1, 5/51.2
  service to, 3/53, 4/58.3, 5/67,
    5/74
Spiritual childhood
  and divine filiation, 1/24.2,
    4/63.2, 5/34, 5/59, 5/64
  and humility, 1/27.2, 3/100.1,
    4/63.3, 5/57.2
  consequences of, 1/42.2,
    5/33.2, 5/46.3, 5/59.3,
    5/60.2, 5/72, 5/75.3
  nature, 1/24.1, 5/64
  need for, 1/7.3
  virtues associated with it,
    1/24.3, 3/60.2, 3/100.2
Spiritual guidance
  and joy, 1/15.3

need for, **1**/7.3, **1**/43.2,
   4/31.3, **5**/19.3, **5**/43.1, **5**/85
Spiritual reading, **7**/8
 advice for, **7**/8.3
Suffering
 and consolation, **1**/34.3
 and divine filiation, **1**/24.2,
   5/59.2, **5**/60.2
 cross of each day, **1**/34.2,
   4/53.1, **7**/23.2, **7**/23.3
 fruits of, **2**/26.2, **2**/64.1,
   4/53.2, **7**/5.1
 helping others through,
   1/34.3, **5**/15, **5**/22.3, **5**/31.3,
   5/60.3
 in the world, **1**/34.1, **5**/22.2,
   5/69.1
 Our Lady's example, **1**/41.1,
   1/41.3, **5**/69.3, **6**/17, **7**/24.3
 redeeming and purifying
   value, **1**/34.2, **5**/69, **5**/94
Supernatural life
 and apostolate, **2**/78.3
 and ascetical struggle, **1**/1.3,
   3/9.2, **3**/22, **5**/60.2
 and human maturity, **1**/50.3
 practice of virtues, **1**/50.1,
   5/84, **5**/87.3
Supernatural outlook
 and God's calling, **1**/18.2,
   5/87
 examining situations with,
   1/18.2, **5**/12.3, **5**/17.1,
   5/32.2, **5**/53.1, **5**/58.3,
   5/82.3, **5**/84

Temperance, **3**/101, **4**/35
Temptations
 4/3.3, **4**/11.1, **4**/11.3, **5**/9.2,
   5/42, **5**/69.2, **5**/90.3

Thanksgiving, acts of
 1/37.2, **1**/51.1, **2**/71.1, **2**/71.3,
   5/101.1, **5**/39, **5**/60.2, **5**/78,
   5/95
 after Communion, **2**/71.3,
   3/29.3, **5**/95.2, **5**/95.3
 human virtue of gratitude,
   2/71.2, **4**/61.1, **4**/61.3, **5**/39,
   5/60.2, **5**/78.2
Time, good use of
 acts of contrition, **1**/37.2
 acts of thanksgiving, **1**/37.2,
   5/95
 Christian value, **1**/37.3, **5**/8.2,
   5/17.1
 our life is short, **1**/37.1,
   4/48.2, **4**/48.3, **5**/54.2,
   5/82.3, **5**/84.1
Trust, **4**/5.2
Truth, **2**/23.2, **2**/23.3
 love for, **4**/18.1, **4**/31.2, **5**/44
 speaking, **4**/18.3, **5**/44

Unity, **2**/56, **5**/32.2, **5**/68.1,
   5/87.3, **5**/91.2, **6**/4.3, **6**/5, **6**/7
Unity of life, **2**/29, **3**/74.2, **4**/16.3,
   5/122.2, **5**/13.3, **5**/32, **5**/46.2,
   5/72, **5**/79, **5**/84, **5**/87, **6**/54.3

Vigilance
 against evil inclinations,
   1/19.2, **5**/42.3, **5**/76.2
 Come Lord Jesus, **1**/19.1,
   5/83.1
 in waiting for Christ, **1**/19.1,
   5/49.2, **5**/73.2, **5**/80, **5**/97.3
 the means, **1**/19.2, **5**/43.3
Virginity
 apostolic celibacy,
   matrimony and, **1**/23.1,

4/62.2, **5**/63.3, **5**/64.2, **5**/90
free choice, **1**/23.1
of Our Lady, **1**/23.1, **5**/64.2
Virtues, **1**/50.3, **2**/22.1, **2**/22.3,
3/6.3, **4**/3.3, **5**/78, **5**/79.3

**Visit to the Blessed
Sacrament,** **2**/51.2, **2**/51.3,
4/43.3, **4**/56.3, **5**/61.1, **5**/88.1
Vocation
and apostolate, **7**/25.3, **7**/29.3
and freedom, **4**/22.1, **5**/37.1
and joy, **7**/25.2
and parents, **4**/22.3
grace for, **6**/36.2, **7**/45.2
of each person, **1**/8.1, **1**/33.1,
1/51.3, **5**/37.3, **6**/36.3
of Our Lady, **1**/25.1, **7**/41.3
of St Andrew, **7**/42.1
of St Bartholomew, **7**/18.1
of St John, **1**/33.1, **5**/23.1
of St John the Baptist, **1**/8.1,
5/13.1, **6**/55
of St Matthew, **7**/25.1
prayer to St Joseph, **6**/25.3
responding to it, **1**/25.2,
3/14.3, **4**/22.2, **4**/22.3,
4/42.3, **5**/38.2, **5**/43, **5**/51.1,
7/42.3
signs of, **1**/18.2, **1**/18.3
special calling, **1**/25.2, **3**/14.1,
4/22.1, **4**/42.2, **5**/43.1,
5/90.2, **6**/34.1, **6**/36.1,
6/56.1, **6**/57, **7**/37.1

Will of God
above earthly plans, **1**/47.3,
5/10.1
and peace of soul, **1**/5.3
and sanctity, **1**/5.1, **5**/35
embracing it, **1**/5.1, **1**/5.3,
1/18.3, **2**/15.1, **3**/20.3,
3/70.3, **5**/35, **5**/94.2, **7**/45.3
its manifestation, **1**/5.1,
3/20.2
Work
and prayer, **4**/30.3, **5**/84.3
in God's presence, **4**/30,
5/84.2, **7**/22.3
its dignity, **1**/46.3, **5**/84,
6/33.1
of Jesus, **1**/46.1, **1**/46.2, **3**/1.1,
3/30.2, **3**/41.1, **5**/84.1,
5/88.2
sanctification of, **1**/46.2,
1/46.3, **3**/1, **3**/30, **3**/39,
3/41, **5**/13.2, **5**/17.2, **5**/32.2,
5/51.2, **5**/84, **6**/33, **7**/36.1
Works of mercy
see Mercy
World
justice in the, **1**/35.1, **5**/60.3
re-evangelisation of, **2**/58.2,
2/58.3 , **5**/12.2, **5**/20, **5**/25,
5/87, **6**/18
Worship, divine, **3**/46.2,
3/46.3, **5**/65.3, **5**/89, **5**/92.2

to matters which preoccupy us. Prayer locates the soul in an environment of serenity and of peace, which then is transmitted to others. The joy it produces is a foretaste of happiness in Heaven.

No one on this earth has known how to treat Jesus better than his Mother, Mary, who spent long hours looking at him, speaking with him, handling him with simplicity and veneration. If we turn to Our Mother in Heaven, we will learn quite quickly to speak with Jesus confidently, to follow him closely, very united to his Cross.

schedule for the normal day. In the prayer we will always be on our guard against distractions. To a large extent this means mortifying the memory and the imagination, keeping distant whatever may impede our attentiveness to God. We have to avoid having our *senses awake and the soul asleep.*[22]

If we fight earnestly against distractions, the Lord will make it easy for us to take up again the threads of our dialogue with him. Our Guardian Angel too, has, among other things, the task of interceding on our behalf. What is important is that we do not want to be distracted, and certainly that we have no intention of being willingly distracted during our time of prayer. Involuntary distractions, which come about in spite of ourselves, and which we try to reject as soon as we are aware of them, do not lessen the merit or the benefit of the prayer. A father or mother does not get annoyed if the baby keeps uttering meaningless noises because it does not as yet know how to speak. God knows our weaknesses and is patient, but we have to ask him: *grant us the spirit of prayer.*[23]

It pleases Our Lord when we resolve to improve our mental prayer each day of our lives – even on those occasions when things require more effort, are difficult, or when we feel arid. For *prayer is not a question of what you say or feel, but of Love. And you love when you try to say something to the Lord, even though you might not actually say anything.*[24] If this is our approach, our life will continually be enriched and strengthened. Prayer is a powerful lamp which throws light on our problems, which enables us to get to know people better and thus to help them on their path to Christ, and to assign the proper place

---

[22] cf St J. Escrivá, *The Way*, 368
[23] *Divine Office, Lauds – Monday of Fourth Week of Lent*
[24] St J. Escrivá, *Furrow*, 464